THE
DIALOGUES OF PLATO

THE
DIALOGUES OF PLATO

TRANSLATED INTO ENGLISH
WITH ANALYSES AND INTRODUCTIONS

BY

B. JOWETT, M.A.

SOMETIME MASTER OF BALLIOL COLLEGE
REGIUS PROFESSOR OF GREEK IN THE UNIVERSITY OF OXFORD
AND DOCTOR IN THEOLOGY OF THE UNIVERSITY OF LEYDEN

IN FOUR VOLUMES
VOLUME III

FOURTH EDITION
Revised by order of
the Jowett Copyright Trustees

OXFORD
AT THE CLARENDON PRESS
1953

Oxford University Press, Amen House, London E.C. 4

GLASGOW NEW YORK TORONTO MELBOURNE WELLINGTON
BOMBAY CALCUTTA MADRAS KARACHI CAPE TOWN IBADAN

Geoffrey Cumberlege, Publisher to the University

FIRST EDITION   1871
SECOND EDITION   1875
THIRD EDITION   1892
REPRINTED 1924, 1930
FOURTH EDITION   1953

PRINTED IN GREAT BRITAIN

CONTENTS

ABBREVIATIONS

THE following abbreviations have been used in the notes added to this edition:

A.J.P.   — *American Journal of Philology.*

C.R.   — *Classical Review.*

C.P.   — *Classical Philology.*

P.M.W. — A. E. Taylor, *Plato, the Man and His Work,* 3rd edition, 1929.

P.T.K. — F. M. Cornford, *Plato's Theory of Knowledge,* 1935.

CRATYLUS

INTRODUCTION

THE *Cratylus* has always been a source of perplexity to the student of
Plato. While in fancy and humour, and perfection of style and
metaphysical originality, this dialogue may be ranked with the
best of the Platonic writings, there has been an uncertainty about the
motive of the piece, which interpreters have hitherto not succeeded in
dispelling. We need not suppose that Plato used words in order to
conceal his thoughts, or that he would have been unintelligible to an
educated contemporary. In the *Phaedrus* and *Euthydemus* we also find a
difficulty in determining the precise aim of the author. Plato wrote
satires in the form of dialogues, and his meaning, like that of other
satirical writers, has often slept in the ear of posterity. Two causes may
be assigned for this obscurity: first, the subtlety and allusiveness of this
species of composition; second, the difficulty of reproducing a state of
life and literature which has passed away. A satire is unmeaning unless
we can place ourselves back among the persons and thoughts of the
age in which it was written. Had the treatise of Antisthenes upon
words, or the speculations of Cratylus or some other Heracleitean of
the fourth century B.C. on the nature of language, been preserved to
us; or if we had lived at the time, and been 'rich enough to attend the
fifty-drachma course of Prodicus', we should have understood Plato
better, and many points which are now attributed to the extravagance
of Socrates' humour would have been found, like the allusions of
Aristophanes in the *Clouds*, to have gone home to the sophists and
grammarians of the day.

For the age was very busy with philological speculation; and many
questions were beginning to be asked about language which were
parallel to other questions about justice, virtue, knowledge, and were
illustrated in a similar manner by the analogy of the arts. Was there a
correctness in words, and were they given by nature or convention?
In the presocratic philosophy mankind had been striving to attain an
expression of their ideas; and now they were beginning to ask themselves whether the expression might not be distinguished from the
idea? They were also seeking to distinguish the parts of speech and to
inquire into the relation of subject and predicate. Grammar and logic
were moving about somewhere in the depths of the human soul, but
they were not yet awakened into consciousness and had not found

names for themselves, or terms by which they might be expressed. Of these beginnings of the study of language we know little, and there necessarily arises an obscurity when the surroundings of such a work as the *Cratylus* are taken away. Moreover, in this, as in most of the dialogues of Plato, allowance has to be made for the character of Socrates. For the theory of language can only be propounded by him in a manner which is consistent with his own profession of ignorance. Hence his ridicule of the new school of etymology is interspersed with many declarations, 'that he knows nothing', 'that he has learned from Euthyphro', and the like. Even the truest things which he says are depreciated by himself. He professes to be guessing, but the guesses of Plato are better than all the other theories of the ancients respecting language put together.

The dialogue hardly derives any light from Plato's other writings, and still less from scholiasts and Neoplatonist writers. Socrates must be interpreted from himself, and on first reading we certainly have a difficulty in understanding his drift, or his relation to the two other interlocutors in the dialogue. Does he agree with Cratylus or with Hermogenes, and is he serious in those fanciful etymologies, extending over more than half the dialogue, which he seems so greatly to relish? Or is he serious in part only; and can we separate his jest from his earnest?—'Sunt bona, sunt quaedam mediocria, sunt mala plura.' Most of them are ridiculously bad, and yet among them are found, as if by accident, principles of philology which are unsurpassed in any ancient writer, and even in advance of any philologer of the last century. May we suppose that Plato, like Lucian, has been amusing his fancy by writing a comedy in the form of a prose dialogue? And what is the final result of the inquiry? Is Plato an upholder of the conventional theory of language, which he acknowledges to be imperfect? or does he mean to imply that a perfect language can only be based on his own theory of ideas? Or if this latter explanation is refuted by his silence, then in what relation does his account of language stand to the rest of his philosophy? Or may we be so bold as to deny the connexion between them? [For the allusion to the Ideas at the end of the dialogue (439 c) is merely intended to show that we must not put words in the place of things or realities, which is a thesis strongly insisted on by Plato in many other passages.] . . . These are some of the first thoughts which arise in the mind of the reader of the *Cratylus*. And the consideration of them may form a convenient introduction to the general subject of the dialogue.

We must not expect all the parts of a dialogue of Plato to tend equally to some clearly defined end. His idea of literary art is not the absolute proportion of the whole, such as we appear to find in a Greek temple or statue; nor should his works be tried by any such standard. They have often the beauty of poetry, but they have also the freedom of conversation. 'Words are more plastic than wax' (*Rep.* 588 d), and may be moulded into any form. He wanders on from one topic to another, careless of the unity of his work, not fearing any 'judge, or spectator, who may recall him to the point' (*Theaet.* 173 c), 'whither the argument blows we follow' (*Rep.* 394 d). To have determined beforehand, as in a modern didactic treatise, the nature and limits of the subject would have been fatal to the spirit of inquiry or discovery, which is the soul of the dialogue. . . . These remarks are applicable to nearly all the works of Plato, but to the *Cratylus* and *Phaedrus* more than any others. See *Phaedrus*, Introduction, *sub init.*

There is another aspect under which some of the dialogues of Plato may be more truly viewed: they are dramatic sketches of an argument. We have found that in the *Lysis, Charmides, Laches, Protagoras, Meno*, we arrived at no conclusion—the different sides of the argument were personified in the different speakers; but the victory was not distinctly attributed to any of them, nor the truth wholly the property of any. And in the *Cratylus* we have no reason to assume that Socrates is either wholly right or wholly wrong, or that Plato, though he evidently inclines to him, had any other aim than that of personifying, in the characters of Hermogenes, Socrates, and Cratylus, the three theories of language which are respectively maintained by them.

The two subordinate persons of the dialogue, Hermogenes and Cratylus, are at the opposite poles of the argument. But after a while the disciple of the sophist and the follower of Heracleitus are found to be not so far removed from one another as at first sight appeared; and both show an inclination to accept the third view which Socrates interposes between them. First, Hermogenes, the poor brother of the rich Callias, expounds the doctrine that names are conventional; like the names of slaves, they may be given and altered at pleasure. This is one of those principles which, whether applied to society or language, explains everything and nothing. For in all things there is an element of convention; but the admission of this does not help us to understand the rational ground or basis in human nature on which the convention proceeds. Socrates first of all intimates to Hermogenes that his view of language is only a part of a sophistical whole, and ultimately tends to abolish the distinction between truth and falsehood. Hermogenes is very ready to throw aside the sophistical tenet, and listens with a sort of half admiration, half belief, to the speculations of Socrates.

Cratylus is of opinion that a name is either a true name or not a name at all. He is unable to conceive of degrees of imitation; a word is either the perfect expression of a thing, or a mere inarticulate sound (a fallacy which is still prevalent among the theorizers about the origin of language). He is at once a philosopher and a sophist; for while wanting to rest language on an immutable basis, he would deny the possibility of falsehood. He is inclined to derive all truth from language, and in language he sees reflected the philosophy of Heracleitus. His views are not like those of Hermogenes, hastily taken up, but are said to be the result of mature consideration, although he is described as still a young man. With a tenacity characteristic of the Heracleitean philosophers, he clings to the doctrine of the flux. (Cf. *Theaet.* 180a.) Of the real Cratylus we know nothing, except that he is recorded by Aristotle to have been the friend or teacher of Plato; nor have we any proof that he resembled the likeness of him in Plato any more than the Critias of Plato is like the real Critias, or the Euthyphro in this dialogue like the other Euthyphro, the diviner, in the dialogue which is called after him.

Between these two extremes, which have both of them a sophistical character, the view of Socrates is introduced, which is in a manner the union of the two. Language is conventional and also natural, and the true conventional-natural is the rational. It is a work not of chance, but of art; the dialectician is the artificer of words, and the legislator gives authority to them. They are the expressions or imitations in sound of things. In a sense, Cratylus is right in saying that things have by nature names (390e); for nature is not opposed either to art or to law. But vocal imitation, like any other copy, may be imperfectly executed; and in this way an element of chance or convention enters in. There is much which is accidental or exceptional in language. Some words have had their original meaning so obscured that they require to be helped out by convention. But still the true name is that which has a natural meaning. Thus nature, art, chance, all combine in the formation of language. And the three views respectively propounded by Hermogenes, Socrates, Cratylus, may be described as the conventional, the artificial or rational, and the natural. The view of Socrates is the meeting-point of the other two, just as conceptualism is the meeting-point of nominalism and realism.

We can hardly say that Plato was aware of the truth, that 'languages are not made, but grow'. But still, when he says that 'the legislator made language with the dialectician standing on his right hand', we need not infer from this that he conceived words, like coins, to be issued from the mint of the State. The creator of laws and of social life is naturally regarded as the creator of language, according to

Hellenic notions, and the philosopher is his natural adviser. We are
not to suppose that the legislator is performing any extraordinary
function; he is merely the Eponymus of the State, who prescribes rules
for the dialectician and for all other artists. According to a truly
Platonic mode of approaching the subject, language, like virtue in the
Republic, is examined by the analogy of the arts. Words are works of
art which may be equally made in different materials, and are well
made when they have a meaning. Of the process which he thus
describes, Plato had probably no very definite notion. But he means to
express generally that language is the product of intelligence, and that
languages belong to States and not to individuals.

A better conception of language could not have been formed in
Plato's age than that which he attributes to Socrates. Yet many
persons have thought that the mind of Plato is more truly seen in the
vague realism of Cratylus. This misconception has probably arisen
from two causes: first, the desire to bring Plato's theory of language
into accordance with the received doctrine of the Platonic Ideas;
secondly, the impression created by Socrates himself, that he is not in
earnest, and is only indulging the fancy of the hour.

1. We shall have occasion to show more at length, in the Introduction to future dialogues, that the so-called Platonic Ideas are only a
semi-mythical form, in which he attempts to realize abstractions, and
that they are replaced in his later writings by a rational theory of
psychology. (See Introductions to the *Meno* and the *Sophist*.) And in
the *Cratylus* he gives a general account of the nature and origin of
language, in which Adam Smith, Rousseau, and other writers of the
last century would have substantially agreed. At the end of the dialogue he speaks, as in the *Symposium* and *Republic*, of absolute beauty
and good; but he never supposed that they were capable of being
embodied in words. Of the names of the ideas he would have said, as
he says of the names of the Gods, that we know nothing. Even the
realism of Cratylus is not based upon the ideas of Plato, but upon the
flux of Heracleitus. Here, as in the *Sophist* and *Politicus*, Plato expressly
draws attention to the want of agreement in words and things. Hence
we are led to infer, that the view of Socrates is not the less Plato's own,
because not based upon the ideas; second, that Plato's theory of
language is not inconsistent with the rest of his philosophy.

2. We do not deny that Socrates is partly in jest and partly in
earnest. He is discoursing in a high-flown vein, which may be compared to the 'dithyrambics of the *Phaedrus*'. They are mysteries of
which he is speaking, and he professes a kind of ludicrous fear of his
imaginary wisdom. When he is arguing out of Homer, about the names

of Hector's son, or when he describes himself as inspired or maddened by Euthyphro, with whom he has been sitting from the early dawn (cf. Phaedrus and Lysias; *Phaedr.*) and expresses his intention of yielding to the illusion today, and tomorrow he will go to a priest and be purified, we easily see that his words are not to be taken seriously. In this part of the dialogue his dread of committing impiety, the pretended derivation of his wisdom from another, the extravagance of some of his etymologies, and, in general, the manner in which the fun, fast and furious, *vires acquirit eundo*, remind us strongly of the *Phaedrus*. The jest is a long one, extending over more than half the dialogue. But then, we remember that the *Euthydemus* is a still longer jest, in which the irony is preserved to the very end. There he is parodying the ingenious follies of early logic; in the *Cratylus* he is ridiculing the fancies of a new school of sophists and grammarians. The fallacies of the *Euthydemus* are still retained at the end of our logic books; and the etymologies of the *Cratylus* have also found their way into later writers. Some of these are not much worse than the conjectures of Hemsterhuis and other critics of the last century; but this does not prove that they are serious. For Plato is in advance of his age in his conception of language as much as he is in his conception of mythology. (Cf. *Phaedrus sub init.*)

When the fervour of his etymological enthusiasm has abated, Socrates ends, as he has begun, with a rational explanation of language. Still he preserves his 'know nothing' disguise, and himself declares his first notions about names to be reckless and ridiculous. Having explained compound words by resolving them into their original elements, he now proceeds to analyse simple words into the letters of which they are composed. The Socrates who 'knows nothing', here passes into the teacher, the dialectician, the arranger of species. There is nothing in this part of the dialogue which is either weak or extravagant. Plato is a supporter of the Onomatopoetic theory of language; that is to say, he supposes words to be formed by the imitation of ideas in sounds; he also recognizes the effect of time, the influence of foreign languages, the desire of euphony, to be formative principles; and he admits a certain element of chance. But he gives no intimation in all this that he is preparing the way for the construction of an ideal language, or that he has any Eleatic speculation to oppose to the Heracleiteanism of Cratylus.

The theory of language which is propounded in the *Cratylus* is in accordance with the later phase of the philosophy of Plato, and would have been regarded by him as in the main true. The dialogue is also a satire on the philological fancies of the day. Socrates in pursuit of his vocation as a detector of false knowledge, lights by accident on the truth. He is guessing, he is dreaming; he has heard, as he says in the *Phaedrus*, from another: no one is more surprised than himself at his own discoveries. And yet some of his best remarks, as for example his view of the derivation of Greek words from other languages, or of the permutations of letters, or again, his observation that in speaking of the gods we are only speaking of our names of them, occur among these flights of humour.

We can imagine a character having a profound insight into the nature of men and things, and yet hardly dwelling upon them seriously; blending inextricably sense and nonsense; sometimes enveloping in a blaze of jests the most serious matters, and then again allowing the truth to peer through; enjoying the flow of his own humour, and puzzling mankind by an ironical exaggeration of their absurdities. Such were Aristophanes and Rabelais; such, in a different style, were Sterne, Jean Paul, Hamann—writers who sometimes become unintelligible through the extravagance of their fancies. Such is the character which Plato intends to depict in some of his dialogues as the Silenus Socrates; and through this medium we have to receive our theory of language.

There remains a difficulty which seems to demand a more exact answer: In what relation does the satirical or etymological portion of the dialogue stand to the serious? Granting all that can be said about the provoking irony of Socrates, about the parody of Euthyphro, or Prodicus, or Antisthenes, how does the long catalogue of etymologies furnish any answer to the question of Hermogenes, which is evidently the main thesis of the dialogue: What is the truth, or correctness, or principle of names?

After illustrating the nature of correctness by the analogy of the arts, and then, as in the *Republic*, ironically appealing to the authority of the Homeric poems, Socrates shows that the truth or correctness of names can only be ascertained by an appeal to etymology. The truth of names is to be found in the analysis of their elements. But why does he admit etymologies which are absurd, based on Heracleitean fancies, fourfold interpretations of words, impossible unions and separations of syllables and letters?

1. The answer to this difficulty has been already anticipated in part: Socrates is not a dogmatic teacher, and therefore he puts on this wild and fanciful disguise, in order that the truth may be permitted to appear. 2. As Benfey remarks, an erroneous example may illustrate a principle of language as well as a true one. 3. Many of these etymologies, as, for example, that of δίκαιον, are indicated, by the manner in which Socrates speaks of them, to have been current in his

own age. 4. The philosophy of language had not made such progress as would have justified Plato in propounding real derivations. Like his master Socrates, he saw through the hollowness of the incipient sciences of the day, and tries to move in a circle apart from them, laying down the conditions under which they are to be pursued, but, as in the *Timaeus*, cautious and tentative, when he is speaking of actual phenomena. To have made etymologies seriously, would have seemed to him like the interpretation of the myths in the *Phaedrus*, the task 'of a not very fortunate individual, who had a great deal of time on his hands'. (See p. 6.) The irony of Socrates places him above and beyond the errors of his contemporaries.

The *Cratylus* is full of humour and satirical touches: the inspiration which comes from Euthyphro, and his prancing steeds, the light admixture of quotations from Homer, and the spurious dialectic which is applied to them; the jest about the fifty-drachma course of Prodicus, which is declared on the best authority, viz. his own, to be a complete education in grammar and rhetoric; the double explanation of the name Hermogenes, either as 'not being in luck', or 'being no speaker'; the dearly bought wisdom of Callias, the Lacedaemonian whose name was 'Rush', and, above all, the pleasure which Socrates expresses in his own dangerous discoveries, which 'tomorrow he will purge away', are truly humorous. While delivering a lecture on the philosophy of language, Socrates is also satirizing the endless fertility of the human mind in spinning arguments out of nothing, and employing the most trifling and fanciful analogies in support of a theory. Etymology in ancient as in modern times was a favourite recreation; and Socrates makes merry at the expense of the etymologists. The simplicity of Hermogenes, who is ready to believe anything that he is told, heightens the effect. (See especially 392 e; 395 a; 397 d.) Socrates in his genial and ironical mood hits right and left at his adversaries: Οὐρανὸς is so called ἀπὸ τοῦ ὁρᾶν τὰ ἄνω, which, as some philosophers say, is the way to have a pure mind; the sophists are by a fanciful explanation converted into heroes; 'the givers of names were like some philosophers who fancy that the earth goes round because their heads are always going round.' There is a great deal of 'mischief' lurking in the following: 'I found myself in greater perplexity about justice than I was before I began to learn'; 'The ρ in κάτοπτρον must be the addition of some one who cares nothing about truth, but thinks only of putting the mouth into shape'; 'Tales and falsehoods have generally to do with the Tragic and goatish life, and tragedy is the place of them.' Several philosophers and sophists are mentioned by name: first, Protagoras and Euthydemus are assailed; then the interpreters of Homer, οἱ παλαιοὶ Ὁμηρικοί (cf. Arist. *Met.* xiii. 6. 7), and the Orphic poets are alluded to by the way; then he discovers a hive of wisdom in the philosophy of Heracleitus;—the doctrine of the flux is contained in the word οὐσία (= ὠσία the pushing principle), an anticipation of Anaxagoras is found in ψυχή and σελήνη. Again, he ridicules the arbitrary methods of pulling out and putting in letters which were in vogue among the philologers of his time; or slightly scoffs at contemporary religious beliefs. Lastly, he is impatient of hearing from the half-converted Cratylus the doctrine that falsehood can neither be spoken, nor uttered, nor addressed; a piece of sophistry attributed to Gorgias, which reappears in the *Sophist* (261 c). And he proceeds to demolish, with no less delight than he had set up, the Heracleitean theory of language.

In the latter part of the dialogue Socrates becomes more serious, though he does not lay aside but rather aggravates his banter of the Heracleiteans, whom here, as in the *Theaetetus*, he delights to ridicule. What was the origin of this enmity we can hardly determine: was it due to the natural dislike which may be supposed to exist between the 'patrons of the flux' and the 'friends of Ideas' (*Soph.* 248 a)? or is it to be attributed to the indignation which Plato felt at having wasted his time upon 'Cratylus and the doctrines of Heracleitus' in the days of his youth? Socrates, touching on some of the characteristic difficulties of early Greek philosophy, endeavours to show Cratylus that imitation may be partial or imperfect, that a knowledge of things is higher than a knowledge of names, and that there can be no knowledge if all things are in a state of transition. But Cratylus, who does not easily apprehend the argument from common sense, remains unconvinced, and on the whole inclines to his former opinion. Some profound philosophical remarks are scattered up and down, admitting of an application not only to language but to knowledge generally; such as the assertion that 'consistency is no test of truth' (436 d ff.): or again, 'If we are over-precise about words, truth will say "too late" to us as to the belated traveller in Ægina' (433 e).

The place of the dialogue in the series cannot be determined with certainty. The style and subject, and the treatment of the character of Socrates, have a close resemblance to the earlier dialogues, especially to the *Phaedrus* and *Euthydemus*. The manner in which the Ideas are spoken of at the end of the dialogue also indicates a comparatively early date. The imaginative element is still in full vigour; the Socrates of the *Cratylus* is the Socrates of the *Apology* and *Symposium*, not yet Platonized; and he describes, as in the *Theaetetus*, the philosophy of Heracleitus by 'unsavoury' similes—he cannot believe that the world is like 'a leaky vessel', or 'a man who has a running at the nose'; he attributes the flux of the world to the swimming in some folks' heads. On the other hand, the relation of thought to language is omitted here, but is treated of in the *Sophist*. These grounds are not sufficient to enable us to arrive at a precise conclusion. But we shall not be far wrong in placing the *Cratylus* about the middle, or at any rate in the first half, of the series.[1]

ANALYSIS

383 Cratylus, the Heracleitean philosopher, and Hermogenes, the brother of Callias, have been arguing about names; the former maintaining that they are natural, the latter that they are conventional. Cratylus affirms that his own is a true name, but will not allow that the name of Hermogenes is equally true. Hermo-
384 genes asks Socrates to explain to him what Cratylus means; or, far rather, he would like to know, what Socrates himself thinks about the truth or correctness of names? Socrates replies, that hard is knowledge, and the nature of names is a considerable part of knowledge: he has never been to hear the fifty-drachma course of Prodicus; and having only attended the single-drachma course, he is not competent to give an opinion on such matters. When Cratylus denies that Hermogenes is a true name, he supposes him to mean that he is not a true son of Hermes, because he

---

[1] [This is probably still the prevailing view. But *Cratylus* is so closely linked to *Theaetetus* that they can hardly be separated by a long interval, and *Theaetetus* is now by general consent assigned to the period 369–368 B.C. (probably ten to fifteen years after the composition of the *Republic*), partly on grounds of style and partly on account of the reference in its Prologue to a battle at Corinth. Should not *Cratylus* be likewise ranked later?

Those who insist strongly upon the stylistic criterion maintain that the *Cratylus* is earlier than the *Phaedo* and *Republic* and belongs to approximately the same stage as *Meno*. (H. von Arnim, *Die sprachliche Forschung als Grundlage der Chronologie der platonischen Dialoge u. des Kratylos*, Vienna, 1929.) M. Warburg in his *Zwei Fragen zum Kratylos* (Berlin, 1929) gives an important criticism of the stylistic evidence and emphasizes the connexion between *Theaetetus* and *Cratylus*. Others have corroborated his argument, but it has not won general assent. He seems to have spoilt his presentation of the case by weak arguments and was wrong to regard the etymological part of the dialogue as satirical. He did not observe that the view of dialectical method, and of the Ideas, presupposed in *Cratylus*, is that which is characteristic of the later dialogues. It might be said also that the account of the function of language, which is attributed to Socrates in this dialogue, is not merely consistent with the analysis of judgement offered in the *Sophist* (263 foll.) but an indispensable complement thereto. On these grounds *Cratylus* is here ranked later than the *Republic*.]

is never in luck. But he would like to have an open council and to hear both sides.

Hermogenes is of opinion that there is no principle in names; they may be changed, as we change the names of slaves, whenever we please, and the altered name is as good as the original one.

You mean to say, for instance, rejoins Socrates, that if I agree 385 to call a man a horse, then a man will be rightly called a horse by me, and a man by the rest of the world? But, surely, there is in words a true and a false, as there are true and false propositions. If a whole proposition be true or false, then the parts of a proposition may be true or false, and the least parts as well as the greatest; and the least parts are names, and therefore names may be true or false. Would Hermogenes maintain that anybody may give a name to anything, and as many names as he pleases; and would all these names be always true at the time of giving them? Hermogenes replies that this is the only way in which he can conceive that names are correct; and he appeals to the practice of different nations, and of the different Hellenic tribes, in confirmation of his view. Socrates asks, whether the things differ as the words which represent them differ: Are we to maintain with 386 Protagoras, that what appears is? Hermogenes has always been puzzled about this, but acknowledges, when he is pressed by Socrates, that there are a few very good men in the world, and a great many very bad; and the very good are the wise, and the very bad are the foolish; and this is not mere appearance but reality. Nor is he disposed to say with Euthydemus, that all things equally and always belong to all men; in that case, again, there would be no distinction between bad and good men. But then, the only remaining possibility is, that all things have their several distinct natures, and are independent of our notions about them. And not only things, but actions, have distinct natures, and are done by different processes. There is a natural way of 387 cutting or burning, and a natural instrument with which men cut or burn, and any other way will fail;—this is true of all actions. And speaking is a kind of action, and naming is a kind of speaking, and we must name according to a natural process, and with a proper instrument. We cut with a knife, we pierce with an awl, we weave with a shuttle, we name with a name. And as a shuttle 388 separates the warp from the woof, so a name distinguishes the nature of things. The weaver will use the shuttle well,—that is, like a weaver; and the teacher will use the name well,—that is, like a teacher. The shuttle will be made by the carpenter; the awl by the smith or skilled person. But who makes a name? Does not the law give names, and does not the teacher receive 389 them from the legislator? He is the skilled person who makes them, and of all skilled workmen he is the rarest. But how does the carpenter make or repair the shuttle, and to what will he look? Will he not look at the ideal which he has in his mind? And as the different kinds of work differ, so ought the instruments which perform them to differ. The several kinds of shuttles ought to answer in material and form to the several kinds of webs. And 390 the legislator ought to know the different materials and forms of which names are made in Hellas and other countries. But who is to be the judge of the proper form? The judge of shuttles is the weaver who uses them; the judge of lyres is the player of the lyre; the judge of ships is the pilot. And will not the judge who is able to direct the legislator in his work of naming, be he who knows how to use the names—he who can ask and answer questions—in short, the dialectician? The pilot directs the carpenter how to make the rudder, and the dialectician directs the legislator how he is to impose names; for to express the ideal forms of things in syllables and letters is not the easy task, Hermogenes, which you imagine.

391 'I should be more readily persuaded, if you would show me this natural correctness of names.'

Indeed I cannot; but I see that you have advanced; for you now admit that there is a correctness of names, and that not every one can give a name. But what is the nature of this correctness or truth, you must learn from the sophists, of whom your brother Callias has bought his reputation for wisdom rather dearly; and since they require to be paid, you, having no money, had better learn from him at second-hand. 'Well, but I have just given up Protagoras, and I should be inconsistent in going to learn of him.' Then if you reject him you may learn of the poets, and in particular of Homer, who distinguishes the names given by Gods and men to the same things, as in the verse about the river God who 392 fought with Hephaestus, 'whom the Gods call Xanthus, and men call Scamander'; or in the lines in which he mentions the bird which the Gods call 'Chalcis', and men 'Cymindis'; or the hill which men call 'Batieia', and the Gods 'Myrinna's Tomb'. Here is an important lesson; for the Gods must of course be right in their use of names. And this is not the only truth about philology which may be learnt from Homer. Does he not say that Hector's son had two names—

Hector called him Scamandrius, but the others Astyanax?

Now, if the men called him Astyanax, is it not probable that the other name was conferred by the women? And which are more likely to be right—the wiser or the less wise, the men or the women? Homer evidently agreed with the men : and of the name given by them he offers an explanation;—the boy was called Astyanax ('king of the city'), because his father saved the city. The names Astyanax and Hector, moreover, are really the same, —the one means a king, and the other is 'a holder or possessor'. 393 For as the lion's whelp may be called a lion, or the horse's foal a foal, so the son of a king may be called a king. But if the horse had produced a calf, then that would be called a calf. Whether the syllables of a name are the same or not makes no difference, provided the meaning is retained. For example; the names of letters, whether vowels or consonants, do not correspond to their sounds, with the exception of ϵ, v, o, ω. The name Beta has three letters added to the sound—and yet this does not alter the sense of the word, or prevent the whole name having the value which the legislator intended. And the same may be said of a 394 king and the son of a king, who like other animals resemble each other in the course of nature; the words by which they are signified may be disguised, and yet amid differences of sound the etymologist may recognize the same notion, just as the physician recognizes the power of the same drugs under different disguises of colour and smell. Hector and Astyanax have only one letter alike, but they have the same meaning; and Agis (leader) is altogether different in sound from Polemarchus (chief in war), or Eupolemus (good warrior); but the two words present the same idea of leader or general, like the words Iatrocles and Acesimbrotus, which equally denote a physician. The son succeeds the father as the foal succeeds the horse; but when, out of the course of nature, a prodigy occurs, and the offspring no longer resembles

395 the parent, then the names no longer agree. This may be illus-
     trated by the case of Agamemnon and his son Orestes, of whom
     the former has a name significant of his patience at the siege of
     Troy; while the name of the latter indicates his savage, man-of-
     the-mountain nature. Atreus again, for his murder of Chrysippus,
     and his cruelty to Thyestes, is rightly named Atreus, which, to
     the eye of the etymologist, is ἀτηρός (destructive), ἀτειρής (stub-
     born), ἄτρεστος (fearless); and Pelops is ὁ τὰ πέλας ὁρῶν (he who
     sees what is near only), because in his eagerness to win Hippo-
     damia, he was unconscious of the remoter consequences which the
     murder of Myrtilus would entail upon his race. The name Tan-
     talus, if slightly changed, offers two etymologies; either ἀπὸ τῆς
     τοῦ λίθου ταλαντείας, or ἀπὸ τοῦ ταλάντατον εἶναι, signifying at
     once the hanging of the stone over his head in the world below,
396 and the misery which he brought upon his country. And the
     name of his father, Zeus, Διός, Ζηνός, has an excellent meaning,
     though hard to be understood, because really a phrase which is
     divided into two parts (Ζεύς, Διός). For he, being the lord and
     king of all, is the author of our being, and in him all live: this is
     implied in the double form, Διός, Ζηνός, which being put together
     and interpreted is δι' ὃν ζῇ πάντα. There may, at first sight, appear
     to be some irreverence in calling him the son of Cronos, who is a
     proverb for stupidity; but the meaning is that Zeus himself is the
     son of a mighty intellect; Κρόνος, quasi κόρος, not in the sense of a
     youth, but quasi τὸ καθαρὸν καὶ ἀκήρατον τοῦ νοῦ—the pure and
     garnished mind, which in turn is begotten of Uranus, who is so
     called ἀπὸ τοῦ ὁρᾶν τὰ ἄνω, from looking upwards; which, as
     philosophers say, is the way to have a pure mind. The earlier
     portion of Hesiod's genealogy has escaped my memory, or I
     would try more conclusions of the same sort. 'You talk like an
     oracle.' I caught the infection from Euthyphro, who gave me a
     long lecture which began at dawn, and has not only entered into
     my ears, but filled my soul, and my intention is to yield to the
397 inspiration today; and tomorrow I will be exorcised by some
     priest or sophist. 'Go on; I am anxious to hear the rest.' Now that
     we have a general notion, how shall we proceed? What names
     will afford the most crucial test of natural fitness? Those of
     heroes and ordinary men are often deceptive, because they are
     patronymics or expressions of a wish; let us try gods and demi-

gods. Gods are so called, ἀπὸ τοῦ θεῖν, from the verb 'to run'; because the sun, moon, and stars run about the heaven; and they being the original gods of the Hellenes, as they still are of the Barbarians, their name is given to all gods. The demons are the golden race of Hesiod, and by golden he means not literally golden, but good; and they are called demons, quasi δαήμονες, which in old Attic was used for δαίμονες—good men are well said 398 to become δαίμονες when they die, because they are knowing. Ἥρως is the same word as ἔρως: 'the sons of God saw the daughters of men that they were fair'; or perhaps they were a species of sophists or rhetoricians, and so called ἀπὸ τοῦ ἐρωτᾶν, or εἴρειν, from their habit of spinning questions; for εἴρειν is equivalent to λέγειν. I get all this from Euthyphro; and now a new and ingenious idea comes into my mind, and, if I am not careful, I shall be wiser than I ought to be by tomorrow's dawn. My idea is, that we may put in and pull out letters at pleasure and alter the accents (as, for example, Διὶ φίλος may be turned into Δίφιλος), and we may make words into sentences and sentences 399 into words. The name ἄνθρωπος is a case in point, for a letter has been omitted and the accent changed; the original meaning being ὁ ἀναθρῶν ἃ ὄπωπεν—he who looks up at what he sees. Ψυχή may be thought to be the reviving, or refreshing, or animating principle—ἡ ἀναψύχουσα τὸ σῶμα; but I am afraid that Euthyphro and his disciples will scorn this derivation, and I must find another: shall we identify the soul with the 'ordering mind' of Anaxagoras, and say that ψυχή, quasi φυσέχη = ἡ φύσιν ἔχει or ὀχεῖ?—this might easily be refined into ψυχή. 'That is a more 400 artistic etymology.'

After ψυχή follows σῶμα; this, by a slight permutation, may be either = (1) the 'grave' of the soul, or (2) may mean 'that by which the soul signifies (σημαίνει) her wishes'. But more probably, the word is Orphic, and simply denotes that the body is the place of ward in which the soul suffers the penalty of sin,—ἐν ᾧ σώζεται. 'I should like to hear some more explanations of the names of the gods, like that excellent one of Zeus.' The truest names of the gods are those which they give themselves; but these are unknown to us. Less true are those by which we propitiate them, as men say in prayers, 'May he graciously receive any name by which I call him.' And to avoid offence, I should like to let them

401 know beforehand that we are not presuming to inquire about them, but only about the names which they usually bear. Let us begin with Hestia. What did he mean who gave the name Hestia? 'That is a very difficult question.' O, my dear Hermogenes, I believe that there was a power of philosophy and talk among the first inventors of names, both in our own and in other languages; for even in foreign words a principle is discernible. Hestia is the same with ἐσσία, which is an old form of οὐσία, and means the first principle of things: this agrees with the fact that to Hestia the first sacrifices are offered. There is also another reading—ὠσία, which implies that 'pushing' (ὠθοῦν) is the first principle of all

402 things. And here I seem to discover a delicate allusion to the flux of Heracleitus—that antediluvian philosopher who cannot walk twice in the same stream; and this flux of his may accomplish yet greater marvels. For the names Cronos and Rhea cannot have been accidental; the giver of them must have known something about the doctrine of Heracleitus. Moreover, there is a remarkable coincidence in the words of Hesiod, when he speaks of Oceanus, 'the origin of gods'; and in the verse of Orpheus, in which he describes Oceanus espousing his sister Tethys. Tethys is nothing more than the name of a spring—τὸ διαττώμενον καὶ ἠθούμενον. Poseidon is ποσίδεσμος, the chain of the feet, because you cannot walk on the sea—the ε is inserted by way of ornament; or perhaps the name may have been originally πολλείδων, meaning,

403 that the god knew many things (πολλὰ εἰδώς): he may also be the shaker, ἀπὸ τοῦ σείειν,—in this case, π and δ have been added. Pluto is connected with πλοῦτος, because wealth comes out of the earth; or the word may be a euphemism for Hades, which is usually derived ἀπὸ τοῦ ἀειδοῦς, because the god is concerned with the invisible. But the name Hades was really given him from his knowing (εἰδέναι) all good things. Men in general are foolishly afraid of him, and talk with horror of the world below from which no one may return. The reason why his subjects never wish to come back, even if they could, is that the god enchains them by the strongest of spells, namely, by the desire of virtue, which they hope to obtain by constant association with him. He is the perfect and accomplished Sophist and the great benefactor of the other world; for he has much more than he wants there, and hence he

404 is called Pluto or the rich. He will have nothing to do with the

souls of men while in the body, because he cannot work his will with them so long as they are confused and entangled by fleshly lusts. Demeter is the mother and giver of food—ἡ διδοῦσα μήτηρ τῆς ἐδωδῆς. Hera is ἐρατή τις, or perhaps the legislator may have been thinking of the weather, and has merely transposed the letters of the word ἀήρ. Pherephatta, that word of awe, is φερεπάφα, which is only an euphonious contraction of ἡ τοῦ φερομένου ἐφαπτομένη,—all things are in motion, and she in her wisdom moves with them, and the wise god Hades consorts with her—there is nothing very terrible in this, any more than in her other appellation Persephone, which is also significant of her wisdom (σοφή). Apollo is another name, which is supposed to have some dreadful meaning, but is susceptible of at least four perfectly innocent explanations. First, he is the purifier or purger or 405 absolver (ἀπολούων); secondly, he is the true diviner, Ἅπλους, as he is called in the Thessalian dialect (derived from ἁπλοῦς, sincere); thirdly, he is the archer (ἀεὶ βάλλων), always shooting; or again, supposing α to mean ἅμα or ὅμου, Apollo becomes equivalent to ἅμα πολῶν, which points to both his musical and his heavenly attributes; for there is a 'moving together' alike in music and in the harmony of the spheres. The second λ is inserted in order to avoid the ill-omened sound of destruction. The Muses are so called—ἀπὸ τοῦ μῶσθαι. The gentle Leto or Letho is named from 406 her willingness (ἐθελήμων), or because she is ready to forgive and forget (λήθη). Artemis is so called from her healthy well-balanced nature, διὰ τὸ ἀρτεμές, or as ἀρετῆς ἵστωρ; or as a lover of virginity, ἄροτον μισήσασα. One of these explanations is probably true—perhaps all of them. Dionysus is ὁ διδοὺς τὸν οἶνον, and οἶνος is quasi οἰόνους because wine makes those think (οἴεσθαι) that they have a mind (νοῦς) who have none. The established derivation of Ἀφροδίτη διὰ τὴν τοῦ ἀφροῦ γένεσιν may be accepted on the authority of Hesiod. Again, there is the name of Pallas, or Athene, which we, who are Athenians, must not forget. Pallas is derived from armed dances—ἀπὸ τοῦ πάλλειν τὰ ὅπλα. For Athene we 407 must turn to the allegorical interpreters of Homer, who make the name equivalent to θεονόη, or possibly the word was originally ἠθονόη and signified moral intelligence (ἐν ἤθει νόησις). Hephaestus, again, is the lord of light—ὁ τοῦ φάεος ἵστωρ. This is a good notion; and, to prevent any other getting into our heads, let us go on to Ares. He is the manly one (ἄρρην), or the unchangeable one (ἄρρατος). Enough of the Gods; for, by the Gods, I am afraid of them; but if you suggest other words, you will see how the horses of Euthyphro prance. 'Only one more god; tell me about my godfather Hermes.' He is ἑρμηνεύς, the messenger or cheater or thief or bargainer; or ὁ εἴρειν μώμενος, that is, εἰρέμης or ἔρμης

408 —the speaker or contriver of speeches. 'Well said Cratylus, then, that I am no son of Hermes.' Pan, as the son of Hermes, is speech or the brother of speech, and is called Pan because speech indicates everything—ὁ πᾶν μηνύων. He has two forms, a true and a false; and is in the upper part smooth, and in the lower part shaggy. He is the goat of Tragedy, in which there are plenty of falsehoods.

'Will you go on to the elements—sun, moon, stars, earth, aether, air, fire, water, seasons, years?' Very good: and which

409 shall I take first? Let us begin with ἥλιος, or the sun. The Doric form ἅλιος helps us to see that he is so called because at his rising he gathers (ἁλίζει) men together, or because he rolls about (εἱλεῖ) the earth, or because he variegates (αἰολεῖ = ποικίλλει) the earth. Selene is an anticipation of Anaxagoras, being a contraction of σελαενονεοάεια, the light (σέλας) which is ever old and new, and which, as Anaxagoras says, is borrowed from the sun; the name was harmonized into σελαναία, a form which is still in use. 'That is a true dithyrambic name.' Μείς is so called ἀπὸ τοῦ μειοῦσθαι, from suffering diminution, and ἄστρον is from ἀστραπή (lightning), which is an improvement of ἀναστρωπή, that which turns the eyes inside out. 'How do you explain πῦρ and ὕδωρ?' I suspect that

410 πῦρ, which, like ὕδωρ and κύων, is found in Phrygian, is a foreign word; for the Hellenes have borrowed much from the barbarians, and I always resort to this theory of a foreign origin when I am at a loss. Ἀήρ may be explained, ὅτι αἴρει τὰ ἀπὸ τῆς γῆς; or, ὅτι ἀεὶ ῥεῖ; or, ὅτι πνεῦμα ἐξ αὐτοῦ γίνεται (compare the poetic word ἀῆται). So αἰθήρ quasi ἀειθεὴρ ὅτι ἀεὶ θεῖ περὶ τὸν ἀέρα: γῆ, γαῖα quasi γεννήτειρα (compare the Homeric form γεγάασι); ὥρα, or, according to the old Attic form, ὅρα, is derived ἀπὸ τοῦ ὁρίζειν, because it divides the year; ἐνιαυτός and ἔτος are the same thought—ὁ ἐν ἑαυτῷ ἐτάζων, cut into two parts, ἐν ἑαυτῷ and ἐτάζων, like δι' ὃν ζῇ into Διός and Ζηνός.

'You make surprising progress.' You may soon have still more cause to admire my wisdom. 'I should like very much to hear your account of the virtues. What principle of correctness is 411 there in those charming words wisdom, understanding, justice, and the rest?' To explain all that will be a serious business; still, as I have put on the lion's skin, appearances must be maintained. My opinion is that primitive men were like some modern philosophers who, by always going round in their search after the nature of things, become dizzy; and this phenomenon, which was really in themselves, they imagined to take place in the external world. You have no doubt remarked that the doctrine of the universal flux, or generation of things, is indicated in names. 'No, I never did.' Φρόνησις is only φορᾶς καὶ ῥοῦ νόησις, or perhaps φορᾶς ὄνησις, and in any case is connected with φέρεσθαι; γνώμη is γονῆς σκέψις καὶ νώμησις; νόησις is νέου or γιγνομένου ἔσις; the word νέος implies that creation is always going on—the original form was νεόεσις; σωφροσύνη is σωτηρία φρονήσεως; ἐπιστήμη is ἡ 412 ἑπομένη τοῖς πράγμασιν—the faculty which keeps close, neither anticipating nor lagging behind; σύνεσις is equivalent to συνιέναι, συμπορεύεσθαι τὴν ψυχήν, and is a kind of conclusion—συλλο-γισμός τις, akin therefore in idea to ἐπιστήμη; σοφία is very diffi-cult, and has a foreign look—the meaning is, touching the motion or stream of things, and may be illustrated by the poetical ἐσύθη and the Lacedaemonian proper name Σοῦς, or Rush; ἀγαθόν is τὸ ἀγαστὸν ἐν τῇ ταχυτῆτι,—for all things are in motion, and some are swifter than others; δικαιοσύνη is clearly ἡ τοῦ δικαίου σύνεσις. The word δίκαιον is more troublesome, and appears to mean the subtle penetrating power which, as the lovers of motion say, preserves all things, and is the cause of all things, quasi διαϊόν going through—the letter κ being inserted for the sake of euphony. This is a great mystery which has been confided to me; but when 413 I ask for an explanation I am thought obtrusive, and another derivation is proposed to me. Justice is said to be ὁ καίων, or the sun; and when I joyfully repeat this beautiful notion I am answered, 'What, is there no justice when the sun is down?' And when I entreat my questioner to tell me his own opinion he replies that justice is fire in the abstract, or heat in the abstract; which is not very intelligible. Others laugh at such notions and say with Anaxagoras that justice is the ordering mind. 'I think that some one must have told you this.' And not the rest? Let me proceed, then, in the hope of proving to you my originality.

414 Ἀνδρεία is quasi ἀνρεία quasi ἡ ἄνω ῥοή, the stream which flows upwards, and is opposed to injustice, which clearly hinders the principle of penetration; ἄρρην and ἀνήρ have a similar derivation; γυνή is the same as γονή; θῆλυ is derived ἀπὸ τῆς θηλῆς, because the teat makes things flourish (τεθηλέναι), and the word θάλλειν itself implies increase of youth, which is swift and sudden ever (θεῖν and ἄλλεσθαι). I am getting over the ground fast, but much has still to be explained. There is τέχνη, for instance. This, by an aphaeresis of τ and an epenthesis of ο in two places, may be identified with ἐχονόη, and signifies 'that which has mind'.

'You swallow letters.' Yes; but you must remember that all language is in process of change; letters are taken in and put out for the sake of euphony, and time is also a great alterer of words. For example, what business has the letter ρ in the word κάτοπτρον, or the letter σ in the word σφίγξ? The additions are often such that it is impossible to make out the original word; and yet if you may put in and pull out as you like, any name is equally good for any object. The fact is that great dictators of literature like yourself should observe the rules of moderation. 'I will do my best.' But do not be too much of a precisian, or

415 you will paralyse me. If you will let me add μηχανή, ἀπὸ τοῦ μήκους, which means πολύ, and ἄνειν, I shall be at the summit of my powers, from which elevation I will examine the two words κακία and ἀρετή. The first is easily explained in accordance with what has preceded; for all things being in a flux, κακία is τὸ κακῶς ἰόν. This derivation is illustrated by the word δειλία, which ought to have come after ἀνδρεία, and may be regarded as ὁ λίαν δεσμὸς τῆς ψυχῆς, just as ἀπορία signifies an impediment to motion (from α, not, and πορεύεσθαι, to go), and ἀρετή is εὐπορία, which is the opposite of this—the ever-flowing (ἀεὶ ῥέουσα or ἀειρειτή), or the eligible, quasi αἱρετή. You will think that I am inventing, but

416 I say that if κακία is right then ἀρετή is also right. But what is κακόν? That is a very obscure word, to which I can only apply my old notion and declare that κακόν is a foreign word. Next, let us proceed to καλόν, αἰσχρόν. The latter is doubtless contracted from ἀεισχοροῦν, quasi ἀεὶ ἴσχον ῥοῦν. The inventor of words being a patron of the flux, was a great enemy to stagnation. Καλόν is τὸ καλοῦν τὰ πράγματα—this is mind (νοῦς or διάνοια); which is

also the principle of beauty; and which, doing the works of beauty, is therefore rightly called the beautiful. The meaning of συμφέρον 417 is explained by previous examples—like ἐπιστήμη signifying that the soul moves in harmony with the world (σύμφορα, συμφέροντα). Κέρδος is τὸ πᾶσι κεραννύμενον—that which mingles with all things; λυσιτελοῦν is equivalent to τὸ τῆς φορᾶς λύον τὸ τέλος, and is not to be taken in the vulgar sense of gainful but rather in that of swift, being the principle which makes motion immortal and unceasing; ὠφέλιμον is ἀπὸ τοῦ ὀφέλλειν—that which gives increase: this word, which is Homeric, is of foreign origin. Βλαβερόν is τὸ βλάπτον, or βουλόμενον ἅπτειν, τὸν ῥοῦν—that which injures or seeks to bind the stream. The proper word would be βουλαπτεροῦν, but this is too much of a mouthful—like a prelude on the flute in honour of Athene. The word ζημιῶδες is difficult; 418 great changes, as I was saying, have been made in words, and even a small change will alter their meaning very much. The word δέον is one of these disguised words. You know that according to the old pronunciation, which is especially affected by the women, who are great conservatives, ι and δ were used where we should now use η and ζ: for example, what we now call ἡμέρα was formerly called ἱμέρα; and this shows the meaning of the word to have been 'the desired one coming after night', and not, as is often supposed, 'that which makes things gentle' (ἥμερα). So, again, ζυγόν is δυογόν, quasi δέσις δυεῖν εἰς ἀγωγήν—the binding of two together for the purpose of drawing. Δέον, as ordinarily 419 written, has an evil sense, signifying the chain (δεσμός) or hindrance of motion; but in its ancient form διόν is expressive of good, quasi διόν, that which penetrates or goes through all. Ζημιώδης is really δημιώδης, and means that which binds motion (δοῦντι τὸ ἰόν); ἡδονή is ἡ πρὸς τὴν ὄνησιν τείνουσα πρᾶξις—the δ is an insertion; λύπη is derived ἀπὸ τῆς διαλύσεως τοῦ σώματος; ἀνία is from α and ἰέναι, to go; ἀληδών is a foreign word, and is so called ἀπὸ τοῦ ἀλγεινοῦ; ὀδυνή is ἀπὸ τῆς ἐνδύσεως τῆς λύπης; ἀχθηδών is in its very sound a burden; χαρά expresses the flow of soul; τέρψις is ἀπὸ τοῦ τερπνοῦ, and τερπνόν is properly ἕρπνον, because the sensation of pleasure is likened to a breath (πνοή) which creeps (ἕρπει) through the soul; εὐφροσύνη is named from φέρεσθαι, because the soul moves in harmony with nature; ἐπιθυμία is ἡ ἐπὶ τὸν θυμὸν ἰοῦσα δύναμις; θυμός is ἀπὸ τῆς θύσεως τῆς

420 ψυχῆς; ἵμερος—ὅτι ἱέμενος ῥεῖ ἡ ψυχή; πόθος, the desire which is
in another place, ἄλλοθί που; ἔρως was anciently ἔσρος, and so
called because it flows into (ἐσρεῖ) the soul from without; δόξα is
ἡ δίωξις τοῦ εἰδέναι, or expresses the shooting from a bow (τόξον).
The latter etymology is confirmed by the words βούλεσθαι, βουλή,
ἀβουλία, which all have to do with shooting (βολή); and similarly
οἴησις is nothing but the movement (οἶσις) of the soul towards
essence. Ἑκούσιον is τὸ εἶκον—the yielding—ἀνάγκη is ἡ ἂν' ἄγκη
ἰοῦσα, the passage through ravines which impede motion: ἀλήθεια
421 is θεία ἄλη, divine motion. Ψεῦδος is the opposite of this, implying
the principle of constraint and forced repose, which is expressed
under the figure of sleep, τὸ εὗδον; the ψ is an addition. Ὄνομα,
a name, affirms the real existence of that which is sought after—
ὂν οὗ μάσμα ἔστιν. Ὄν and οὐσία are only ἰόν with an ι broken off;
and οὐκ ὄν is οὐκ ἰόν. 'And what are ἰόν, ῥέον, δοῦν?' One way of
explaining them has been already suggested—they may be of
foreign origin; and possibly this is the true answer. But mere
antiquity may often prevent our recognizing words, after all the
complications which they have undergone; and we must remember that however far we carry back our analysis some ultimate
elements or roots will remain which can be no farther analysed.
For example, the word ἀγαθός was supposed by us to be a com-
422 pound of ἀγαστός and θοός, and probably θοός may be farther
resolvable. But if we take a word of which no further resolution
seems attainable, we may fairly conclude that we have reached
one of these original elements, and the truth of such a word must
be tested by some new method. Will you help me in the search?

All names, whether primary or secondary, are intended to show
the nature of things; and the secondary, as I conceive, derive
their significance from the primary. But then, how do the primary
names indicate anything? And let me ask another question—If
we had no faculty of speech, how should we communicate with
one another? Should we not use signs, like the deaf and dumb?
423 The elevation of our hands would mean lightness—heaviness
would be expressed by letting them drop. The running of any
animal would be described by a similar movement of our own
frames. The body can only express anything by imitation; and
the tongue or mouth can imitate as well as the rest of the body.
But this imitation of the tongue or voice is not yet a name, because

people may imitate sheep or goats without naming them. What, then, is a name? In the first place, a name is not a musical, or, secondly, a pictorial imitation, but an imitation of that kind which expresses the nature of a thing; and is the invention not of 424 a musician or of a painter but of a namer.

And now, I think that we may consider the names about which you were asking. The way to analyse them will be by going back to the letters or primary elements of which they are composed. First, we separate the alphabet into classes of letters, distinguishing the consonants, mutes, vowels, and semivowels; and when we have learnt them singly, we shall learn to know them in their various combinations of two or more letters; just as the painter knows how to use either a single colour or a combination of colours. And like the painter, we may apply letters to the expres- 425 sion of objects, and form them into syllables; and these again into words, until the picture or figure—that is, language—is completed. Not that I am literally speaking of ourselves, but I mean to say that this was the way in which the ancients framed language. And this leads me to consider whether the primary as well as the secondary elements are rightly given. I may remark, as I was saying about the Gods, that we can only attain to conjecture of them. But still we insist that ours is the true and only method of discovery; otherwise we must have recourse, like the tragic poets, to a *Deus ex machina*, and say that God gave the first names, and therefore they are right; or that the barbarians are older than we are, and that we learnt of them; or that antiquity has cast a veil over the truth. Yet all these are not reasons; they 426 are only ingenious excuses for having no reasons.

I will freely impart to you my own notions, though they are somewhat crude:—The letter ρ appears to me to be the general instrument which the legislator has employed to express all motion or κίνησις. (I ought to explain that κίνησις is just ἴεσις (going), for the letter η was unknown to the ancients; and the root, κίειν, is a foreign form of ἰέναι: of κίνησις or εἶσις, the opposite is στάσις.) This use of ρ is evident in the words tremble, break, crush, crumble, and the like; the imposer of names perceived that the tongue is most agitated in the pronunciation of this letter, just as he used ι to express the subtle power which 427 penetrates through all things. The letters φ, ψ, σ, ζ, which require a great deal of wind, are employed in the imitation of such notions as shivering, seething, shaking, and in general of what is windy. The letters δ and τ convey the idea of binding and rest in a place: the λ denotes smoothness, as in the words slip, sleek, sleep, and the like. But when the slipping tongue is detained by the heavier sound of γ, then arises the notion of a glutinous, clammy nature; ν is sounded from within, and has a notion of inwardness; α is the expression of size; η of length; ο of roundness, and therefore there is plenty of ο in the word γόγγυλον. That is my view, Hermogenes, of the correctness of names; and I should like to hear what Cratylus would say. 'But, Socrates, as I was telling you, Cratylus mystifies me; I should like to ask him, in your presence, what he means by the fitness of names.' To this appeal, Cratylus replies 'that he cannot explain so important a subject all in a moment.'

428 'No, but you may "add little to little", as Hesiod says.' Socrates here interposes his own request, that Cratylus will give some account of his theory. Hermogenes and himself are mere sciolists, but Cratylus has reflected on these matters, and has had teachers. Cratylus replies in the words of Achilles: ' "Illustrious Ajax, you have spoken in all things much to my mind", whether Euthyphro or some Muse inhabiting your own breast was the inspirer.' Socrates replies that he is afraid of being self-deceived, and therefore he must 'look fore and aft', as Homer remarks. Does not Cratylus agree with him that names teach us the nature of things? 'Yes.' And naming is an art, and the artists are legis-

429 lators, and like artists in general some of them are better and some of them are worse than others, and give better or worse laws, and make better or worse names. Cratylus cannot admit that one name is better than another; they are either true names, or they are not names at all; and when he is asked about the name of Hermogenes, who is acknowledged to have no luck in him, he affirms this to be the name of somebody else. Socrates supposes him to mean that falsehood is impossible, to which his own answer would be that there has never been a lack of liars. Cratylus presses him with the old sophistical argument that falsehood is saying that which is not, and therefore saying nothing; you cannot utter the word which is not. Socrates complains that this argument is too subtle for an old man to understand: suppose a person addressing Cratylus were to say, Hail, Athenian

Stranger, Hermogenes! would these words be true or false? 'I 430 should say that they would be mere unmeaning sounds, like the hammering of a brass pot.' But you would acknowledge that names, as well as pictures, are imitations, and also that pictures may give a right or wrong representation of a man or woman—why may not names then equally give a representation true and right or false and wrong? Cratylus admits that pictures may give a true or false representation, but denies that names can. Socrates argues that he may go up to a man and say 'this is your picture', and again, he may go and say to him 'this is your name'—in the 431 one case appealing to his sense of sight, and in the other to his sense of hearing; may he not? 'Yes.' Then you will admit that there is a right or a wrong assignment of names, and if of names, then of verbs and nouns; and if of verbs and nouns, then of the sentences which are made up of them; and comparing nouns to pictures, you may give them all the appropriate sounds, or only some of them. And as he who gives all the colours makes a good picture and he who gives only some of them a bad or imperfect one, but still a picture; so he who gives all the sounds makes a good name and he who gives only some of them a bad or imperfect one, but a name still. The artist of names, that is, the legislator, may be a good or he may be a bad artist. 'Yes, Socrates, but the cases are not parallel; for if you subtract or mis- 432 place a letter, the name ceases to be a name.' Socrates admits that the number 10, if a unit is subtracted, would cease to be 10, but denies that names are of this purely quantitative nature. Suppose that there are two objects—Cratylus and the image of Cratylus; and let us imagine that some god makes them perfectly alike, both in their outward form and in their inner nature and qualities: then there will be two Cratyluses, and not merely Cratylus and the image of Cratylus. But an image in fact always falls short in some degree of the original, and if images are not exact counterparts, why should names be? If they were, they would be the doubles of their originals, and indistinguishable from them; and how ridiculous would this be! Cratylus admits the truth of Socrates' remark. But then Socrates rejoins, he should have the courage to acknowledge that letters may be wrongly 433 inserted in a noun, or a noun in a sentence; and yet the noun or the sentence may retain a meaning. Better to admit this, that we

may not be punished like the traveller in Egina who goes about
at night, and that Truth herself may not say to us, 'Too late'.
And, errors excepted, we may still affirm that a name to be
correct must have proper letters, which bear a resemblance to the
434 thing signified. I must remind you of what Hermogenes and I
were saying about the letter ρ, which was held to be expressive of
motion and hardness, as λ is of smoothness; and this you will
admit to be their natural meaning. But then, why do the Eretrians
call that σκληρότηρ which we call σκληρότης? We can understand
one another, although the letter ρ is not equivalent to the letter *s*:
why is this? You reply, because the two letters are sufficiently
alike for the purpose of expressing motion. Well, then, there is
the letter λ; what business has this in a word meaning hardness?
'Why, Socrates, I retort upon you, that we put in and pull out
letters at pleasure.' And the explanation of this is custom or
435 agreement: we have made a convention that the ρ shall mean *s*
and a convention may indicate by the unlike as well as by the
like. How could there be names for all the numbers unless you
allow that convention is used? Imitation is a poor thing, and has
to be supplemented by convention, which is another poor thing;
although I agree with you in thinking that the most perfect form
of language is found only where there is a perfect correspondence
of sound and meaning. But let me ask you what is the use and
force of names? 'The use of names, Socrates, is to inform, and
he who knows names knows things.' Do you mean that the
436 discovery of names is the same as the discovery of things? 'Yes.'
But do you not see that there is a degree of deception about
names? He who first gave names, gave them according to his
conception, and that may have been erroneous. 'But then why,
Socrates, is language so consistent? all words have the same laws.'
Mere consistency is no test of truth. In geometrical problems, for
example, there may be a flaw at the beginning, and yet the
conclusion may follow consistently. And therefore a wise man
will take especial care of first principles. But are words really
consistent? are there not as many terms of praise which signify
437 rest as which signify motion? There is ἐπιστήμη, which is connected with στάσις, as μνήμη is with μένω. Βέβαιον, again, is the
expression of station and position; ἱστορία is clearly descriptive
of the stopping (ἱστάναι) of the stream; πιστόν indicates the

cessation of motion; and there are many words having a bad
sense, which are connected with ideas of motion, such as συμφορά, ἁμαρτία, &c.: ἀμαθία, again, might be explained, as ἡ ἅμα
θεῷ ἰόντος πορεία, and ἀκολασία as ἡ ἀκολουθία τοῖς πράγμασιν.
Thus the bad names are framed on the same principle as the
good, and other examples might be given, which would favour a
theory of rest rather than of motion. 'Yes; but the greater number
of words express motion.' Are we to count them, Cratylus; and is
correctness of names to be determined by the voice of a majority?

Here is another point: we were saying that the legislator gives 438
names, and therefore we must suppose that he knows the things
which he names; but how can he have learnt things from names
before there were any names? 'I believe, Socrates, that some
power more than human first gave things their names, and that
these were necessarily true names.' Then how came the giver of
names to contradict himself, and to make some names expressive
of rest, and others of motion? 'I do not suppose that he did make
them both.' Then which did he make—those which are expressive
of rest, or those which are expressive of motion? ... But if some
names are true and others false, we can only decide between
them, not by counting words, but by appealing to things. And
if so, we must allow that things may be known without names; 439
for names, as we have several times admitted, are the images of
things; and the higher knowledge is of things, and is not to be
derived from names; and though I do not doubt that the inventors of language gave names, under the idea that all things
are in a state of motion and flux, I believe that they were mistaken; and that having fallen into a whirlpool themselves, they
are trying to drag us after them. For is there not a true beauty and
a true good, which is always beautiful and always good? Can the
thing beauty be vanishing away from us while the words are yet
in our mouths? And they could not be known by any one if they 440
are always passing away—for if they are always passing away, the
observer has no opportunity of observing their state. Whether the
doctrine of the flux or of the eternal nature be the truer is hard
to determine. But no man of sense will put himself, or the education of his mind, in the power of names: he will not condemn
himself to be an unreal thing, nor will he believe that everything
is in a flux like the water in a leaky vessel, or that the world is a

man who has a running at the nose. This doctrine may be true, Cratylus, but is also very likely to be untrue; and therefore I would have you reflect while you are young, and find out the truth, and when you know come and tell me. 'I have thought, Socrates, and after a good deal of thinking I incline to Heracleitus.' Then another day, my friend, you shall give me a lesson. 'Very good, Socrates, and I hope that you will continue to study these things yourself.'

INTRODUCTION

We may now (I) consider how far Plato in the *Cratylus* has discovered the true principles of language, and then (II) proceed to compare modern speculations respecting the origin and nature of language with the anticipations of his genius.

I. (1) Plato is aware that language is not the work of chance; nor does he deny that there is a natural fitness in names. He only insists that this natural fitness shall be intelligibly explained. But he has no idea that language is a natural organism. He would have heard with surprise that languages are the common work of whole nations in a primitive or semi-barbarous age. How, he would probably have argued, could men devoid of art have contrived a structure of such complexity? No answer could have been given to this question, either in ancient or in modern times, until the nature of primitive antiquity had been thoroughly studied, and the instincts of man had been shown to exist in greater force when his state approaches more nearly to that of children or animals. The philosophers of the last century, after their manner, would have vainly endeavoured to trace the process by which proper names were converted into common, and would have shown how the last effort of abstraction invented prepositions and auxiliaries. The theologian would have proved that language must have had a divine origin, because in childhood, while the organs are pliable, the intelligence is wanting, and when the intelligence is able to frame conceptions, the organs are no longer able to express them. Or, as others have said: Man is man because he has the gift of speech; and he could not have invented that which he is. But this would have been an 'argument too subtle' for Socrates (429 d), who rejects the theological account of the origin of language 'as an excuse for not giving a reason', which he compares to the introduction of the *Deus ex machina* by the tragic poets when they have to solve a difficulty; thus anticipating many modern controversies in which the primary agency of the Divine Being is confused with the secondary cause; and God is assumed to have worked a miracle in order to fill up a lacuna in human knowledge. (Cf. *Timaeus*, 46d, e.)

Neither is Plato wrong in supposing that an element of design and art enters into language. The creative power abating is supplemented by a mechanical process. 'Languages are not made but grow', but they are made as well as grow; bursting into life like a plant or a flower, they are also capable of being trained and improved and engrafted upon one another. The change in them is effected in earlier ages by musical and euphonic improvements, at a later stage by the influence of grammar and logic, and by the poetical and literary use of words. They develop rapidly in childhood, and when they are full grown and set they may still put forth intellectual powers, like the mind in the body, or rather we may say that the nobler use of language only begins when the framework is complete. The savage or primitive man, in whom the natural instinct is strongest, is also the greatest improver of the forms of language. He is the poet or maker of words, as in civilized ages the dialectician is the definer or distinguisher of them. The latter calls the second world of abstract terms into existence, as the former has created the picture sounds which represent natural objects or processes. Poetry and philosophy—these two are the two great formative principles of language, when they have passed their first stage, of which, as of the first invention of the arts in general, we only entertain conjecture. And mythology is a link between them, connecting the visible and invisible, until at length the sensuous exterior falls away, and the severance of the inner and outer world, of the idea and the object of sense, becomes complete. At a later period logic and grammar, sister arts, preserve and enlarge the decaying instinct of language by rule and method, which they gather from analysis and observation.

(2) There is no trace in any of Plato's writings that he was acquainted with any language but Greek. Yet he has conceived very truly the relation of Greek to foreign languages, which he is led to consider because he finds that many Greek words are incapable of explanation. Allowing a good deal for accident, and also for the fancies of the *conditores linguae Graecae*, there is an element of which he is unable to give an account. These unintelligible words he supposes to be of foreign origin, and to have been derived from a time when the Greeks were either barbarians, or in close relation to the barbarians. Socrates is aware that this principle is liable to great abuse and, like the *Deus ex machina*, explains nothing. Hence he excuses himself for the employment of such a device, and remarks that in foreign words there is still

a principle of correctness, which applies equally both to Greeks and barbarians.

(3) But the greater number of primary words do not admit of derivation from foreign languages; they must be resolved into the letters out of which they are composed, and therefore the letters must have a meaning. The framers of language were aware of this; they observed that α was adapted to express size; η length; ο roundness; ν inwardness; ρ rush or roar; λ liquidity; γλ the detention of the liquid or slippery element; δ and τ binding; φ, ψ, σ, ξ, wind and cold, and so on. Plato's analysis of the letters of the alphabet shows a wonderful insight into the nature of language. He does not expressly distinguish between mere imitation and the symbolical use of sound to express thought, but he recognizes in the examples which he gives both modes of imitation. Gesture is the mode which a deaf and dumb person would take of indicating his meaning. And language is the gesture of the tongue; in the use of the letter ρ to express a rushing or roaring, or of ο to express roundness, there is a direct imitation; while in the use of the letter α to express size, or of η to express length, the imitation is symbolical. The use of analogous or similar sounds in order to express similar or analogous ideas seems to have escaped him.

In passing from the gesture of the body to the movement of the tongue Plato makes a great step in the physiology of language. He was probably the first who said that 'language is imitative sound', which is the greatest and deepest truth of philology, although he is not aware of the laws of euphony and association by which imitation must be regulated. He was probably also the first who made a distinction between simple and compound words, a truth second only in importance to that which has just been mentioned. His great insight in one direction curiously contrasts with his blindness in another; for he appears to be wholly unaware (cf. his derivation of ἀγαθός from ἀγαστός and θοός) of the difference between the root and termination. But we must recollect that he was necessarily more ignorant than any schoolboy of Greek grammar, and had no table of the inflexions of verbs and nouns before his eyes, which might have suggested to him the distinction.

(4) Plato distinctly affirms that language is not truth, or *philosophie une langue bien faite*. At first, Socrates has delighted himself with discovering the flux of Heracleitus in language. But he is covertly satirizing the pretence of that or any other age to find philosophy in words; and he afterwards corrects any erroneous inference which might be gathered from his experiment. For he finds as many, or almost as many, words expressive of rest as he had previously found expressive

of motion. And even if this had been otherwise, who would learn of words when he might learn of things? There is a great controversy and high argument between Heracleiteans and Eleatics, but no man of sense would commit his soul in such inquiries to the imposers of names. . . . In this and other passages Plato shows that he is as completely emancipated from the influence of 'Idols of the tribe' as Bacon himself.

The lesson which may be gathered from words is not metaphysical or moral, but historical. They teach us the affinity of races, they tell us something about the association of ideas, they occasionally preserve the memory of a disused custom; but we cannot safely argue from them about right and wrong, matter and mind, freedom and necessity, or the other problems of moral and metaphysical philosophy. For the use of words on such subjects may often be metaphorical, accidental, derived from other languages, and may have no relation to the contemporary state of thought and feeling. Nor in any case is the invention of them the result of philosophical reflection; they have been commonly transferred from matter to mind, and their meaning is the very reverse of their etymology. Because there is or is not a name for a thing, we cannot argue that the thing has or has not an actual existence; or that the antitheses, parallels, conjugates, correlatives of language have anything corresponding to them in nature. There are too many words as well as too few; and they generalize the objects or ideas which they represent. The greatest lesson which the philosophical analysis of language teaches us is that we should be above language, making words our servants, and not allowing them to be our masters.

Plato does not add the further observation that the etymological meaning of words is in process of being lost. If at first framed on a principle of intelligibility, they would gradually cease to be intelligible, like those of a foreign language. He is willing to admit that they are subject to many changes, and put on many disguises. He acknowledges that the 'poor creature' imitation is supplemented by another 'poor creature'—convention. But he does not see that 'habit and repute', and their relation to other words, are always exercising an influence over them. Words appear to be isolated, but they are really the parts of an organism which is always being reproduced. They are refined by civilization, harmonized by poetry, emphasized by literature, technically applied in philosophy and art; they are used as symbols on the border-ground of human knowledge; they receive a fresh impress from individual genius, and come with a new force and association to every lively-minded person. They are fixed by the simultaneous utterance of millions, and yet are always imperceptibly changing; not the inventors of language, but writing and speaking, and particularly great writers, or works which pass into the hearts of nations, Homer, Shakespeare, Dante, the German or English Bible, Kant, and Hegel, are the makers of them in later ages. They carry with them the faded recollection of their own past history; the use of a word in a striking and familiar passage gives a complexion to its use everywhere else, and the new use of an old and familiar phrase has also a peculiar power over us. But these and other subtleties of language escaped the observation of Plato. He is not aware that the languages of the world are organic structures, and that every word in them is related to every other; nor does he conceive of language as the joint work of the speaker and the hearer, requiring in man a faculty not only of expressing his thoughts but of understanding those of others.

On the other hand, he cannot be justly charged with a desire to frame language on artificial principles. Philosophers have sometimes dreamed of a technical or scientific language, in words which should have fixed meanings and stand in the same relation to one another as the substances which they denote. But there is no more trace of this in Plato than there is of a language corresponding to the Ideas; nor, indeed, could the want of such a language be felt until the sciences were far more developed. Those who would extend the use of technical phraseology beyond the limits of science or of custom seem to forget that freedom and suggestiveness and the play of association are essential characteristics of language. The great master has shown how he regarded pedantic distinctions of words or attempts to confine their meaning in the satire on Prodicus in the *Protagoras*.

(5) In addition to these anticipations of the general principles of philology we may note also a few curious observations on words and sounds. 'The Eretrians say σκληρότης for σκληρότηρ'; 'the Thessalians call Apollo Ἅπλους'; 'the Phrygians have the words πῦρ, ὕδωρ, κύνες slightly changed'; 'there is an old Homeric word ἐμήσατο, meaning "he contrived"'; 'our forefathers, and especially the women, who are most conservative of the ancient language, loved the letters ι and δ, but now ι is changed into η and ε, and δ into ζ; this is supposed to increase the grandeur of the sound'. Plato was very willing to use inductive arguments, so far as they were within his reach; but he would also have assigned a large influence to chance. Nor indeed is induction applicable to philology in the same degree as to most of the physical sciences. For after we have pushed our researches to the farthest point, in language as in all the other creations of the human mind there will always remain an element of exception or accident or free will, which cannot be eliminated.

The question 'whether falsehood is impossible', which Socrates characteristically sets aside as too subtle for an old man (429 d; cf. *Euthyd.* 284), could only have arisen in an age of imperfect consciousness, which had not yet learned to distinguish words from things. Socrates replies in effect that words have an independent existence; thus anticipating the solution of the medieval controversy of Nominalism and Realism. He is aware, too, that languages exist in various degrees of perfection (435), and that the analysis of them can only be carried to a certain point (422). 'If we could always, or almost always, use likenesses, which are the appropriate expressions, that would be the most perfect state of language' (439 d). These words suggest a question of deeper interest than the origin of language; viz. what is the ideal of language, how far by any correction of their usages existing languages might become clearer and more expressive than they are, more poetical, and also more logical; or whether they are now finally fixed and have received their last impress from time and authority.

On the whole, the *Cratylus* seems to contain deeper truths about language than any other ancient writing. But feeling the uncertain ground upon which he is walking, and partly in order to preserve the character of Socrates, Plato envelops the whole subject in a robe of fancy, and allows his principles to drop out as if by accident.

II. What is the result of recent speculations about the origin and nature of language? Like other modern metaphysical inquiries, they end at last in a statement of facts. But, in order to state or understand the facts, a metaphysical insight seems to be required. There are more things in language than the human mind easily conceives. And many fallacies have to be dispelled, as well as observations made. The true spirit of philosophy or metaphysics can alone charm away metaphysical illusions, which are always reappearing, formerly in the fancies of Neoplatonist writers, now in the disguise of experience and common sense. An analogy, a figure of speech, an intelligible theory, a superficial observation of the individual, have often been mistaken for a true account of the origin of language.

Speaking is one of the simplest natural operations, and also the most complex. Nothing would seem to be easier or more trivial than a few words uttered by a child in any language. Yet into the formation of those words have entered causes which the human mind is not capable of calculating. They are a drop or two of the great stream or ocean of speech which has been flowing in all ages. They have been transmitted from one language to another; like the child himself, they go back to the beginnings of the human race. How they originated, who can tell?

Nevertheless we can imagine a stage of human society in which the circle of men's minds was narrower and their sympathies and instincts stronger; in which their organs of speech were more flexible, and the sense of hearing finer and more discerning; in which they lived more in company, and after the manner of children were more given to express their feelings; in which 'they moved all together', like a herd of wild animals, 'when they moved at all'. Among them, as in every society, a particular person would be more sensitive and intelligent than the rest. Suddenly, on some occasion of interest (at the approach of a wild beast, shall we say?), he first, they following him, utter a cry which resounds through the forest. The cry is almost or quite involuntary, and may be an imitation of the roar of the animal. Thus far we have not speech, but only the inarticulate expression of feeling or emotion in no respect differing from the cries of animals; for they, too, call to one another and are answered. But now suppose that someone at a distance not only hears the sound, but apprehends the meaning: or we may imagine that the cry is repeated to a member of the society who had been absent; the others act the scene over again when he returns home in the evening. And so the cry becomes a word. The hearer in turn gives back the word to the speaker, who is now aware that he has acquired a new power. Many thousand times he exercises this power; like a child learning to talk, he repeats the same cry again, and again he is answered; he tries experiments with a like result, and the speaker and the hearer rejoice together in their newly discovered faculty. At first there would be few such cries, and little danger of mistaking or confusing them. For the mind of primitive man had a narrow range of perceptions and feelings; his senses were microscopic; twenty or thirty sounds or gestures would be enough for him, nor would he have any difficulty in finding them. Naturally he broke out into speech—like the young infant he laughed and babbled; but not until there were hearers as well as speakers did language begin. Not the interjection or the vocal imitation of the object, but the interjection or the vocal imitation of the object understood, is the first rudiment of human speech.

After a while the word gathers associations, and has an independent existence. The imitation of the lion's roar calls up the fears and hopes of the chase, which are excited by his appearance. In the moment of hearing the sound, without any appreciable interval, these and other latent experiences wake up in the mind of the hearer. Not only does he receive an impression, but he brings previous knowledge to bear upon that impression. Necessarily the pictorial image becomes less vivid, while the association of the nature and habits of the animal is more distinctly perceived. The picture passes into a symbol, for there would be too many of them and they would crowd the mind; the vocal imitation, too, is always in process of being lost and being renewed, just as the picture is brought back again in the description of the poet. Words now can be used more freely because there are more of them. What was once an involuntary expression becomes voluntary. Not only can men utter a cry or call, but they can communicate and converse; they can not only use words, but they can even play with them. The word is separated both from the object and from the mind; and slowly nations and individuals attain to a fuller consciousness of themselves.

Parallel with this mental process the articulation of sounds is gradually becoming perfected. The finer sense detects the differences of them and begins, first to agglomerate, then to distinguish them. Times, persons, places, relations of all kinds, are expressed by modifications of them. The earliest parts of speech, as we may call them by anticipation, like the first utterances of children, probably partook of the nature of interjections and nouns; then came verbs; at length the whole sentence appeared, and rhythm and metre followed. Each stage in the progress of language was accompanied by some corresponding stage in the mind and civilization of man. In time, when the family became a nation, the wild growth of dialects passed into a language. Then arose poetry and literature. We can hardly realize to ourselves how much with each improvement of language the powers of the human mind were enlarged; how the inner world took the place of the outer; how the pictorial or symbolical or analogical word was refined into a notion; how language, fair and large and free, was at last complete.

So we may imagine the speech of man to have begun as with the cries of animals, or the stammering lips of children, and to have attained by degrees the perfection of Homer and Plato. Yet we are far from saying that this or any other theory of language is proved by facts. It is not difficult to form an hypothesis which by a series of imaginary transitions will bridge over the chasm which separates man from the animals. Differences of kind may often be thus resolved into differences of degree. But we must not assume that we have in this way discovered the true account of them. Through what struggles the harmonious use of the organs of speech was acquired; to what extent the conditions of human life were different; how far the genius of individuals may have contributed to the discovery of this as of the other arts, we cannot say: Only we seem to see that language is as much the creation of the ear as of the tongue, and the expression of a movement stirring the hearts not of one man only but of many, 'as the trees of the wood are stirred by the wind'. The theory is consistent or not inconsistent with our own mental experience and throws some degree of light upon a dark corner of the human mind.

In the later analysis of language, we trace the opposite and contrasted elements of the individual and nation, of the past and present, of the inward and outward, of the subject and object, of the notional and relational, of the root or unchanging part of the word and the changing inflexion, if such a distinction be admitted, of the vowel and the consonant, of quantity and accent, of speech and writing, of poetry and prose. We observe also the reciprocal influence of sounds and conceptions on each other, like the connexion of body and mind; and further remark that although the names of objects were originally proper names, as the grammarian or logician might call them, yet at a later stage they become universal notions, which combine into particulars and individuals, and are taken out of the first rude agglomeration of sounds that they may be replaced in a higher and more logical order. We see that in the simplest sentences are contained grammar and logic—the parts of speech, the Eleatic philosophy, and the Kantian categories. So complex is language, and so expressive not only of the meanest wants of man, but of his highest thoughts; so various are the aspects in which it is regarded by us. Then again, when we follow the history of languages, we observe that they are always slowly moving, half dead, half alive, half solid, half fluid; the breath of a moment, yet like the air, continuous in all ages and countries—like the glacier, too, containing within them a trickling stream which deposits debris of the rocks over which it passes. There were happy moments, as we may conjecture, in the lives of nations, at which they came to the birth—as in the golden age of literature the man and the time seem to conspire; the eloquence of the bard or chief, as in later times the creations of the great writer who is the expression of his age, became impressed on the minds of their countrymen, perhaps in the hour of some crisis of national development—a migration, a conquest, or the like. The picture of the word which was beginning to be lost is now revived; the sound again echoes to the sense; men find themselves capable not only of expressing more feelings, and describing more objects, but of expressing and describing them better. The world before the flood, that is to say the world of ten, twenty, a hundred thousand years ago, has passed away and left no sign. But the best conception that we can form of it, though imperfect and uncertain, is gained from the analogy of causes still in action, some powerful and sudden, others working slowly in the course of infinite

ages. Something too may be allowed to 'the persistency of the strongest', to 'the survival of the fittest', in this as in the other realms of
nature.

These are some of the reflections which the modern philosophy of
language suggests to us about the powers of the human mind and the
forces and influences by which the efforts of men to utter articulate
sounds were inspired. Yet in making these and similar generalizations
we may note also dangers to which we are exposed. (1) There is the
confusion of ideas with facts—of mere possibilities and generalities
and modes of conception with actual and definite knowledge. The
words 'evolution', 'birth', 'law', 'development', 'instinct', 'implicit',
'explicit', and the like have a false clearness or comprehensiveness
which adds nothing to our knowledge. The metaphor of a flower or a
tree, or some other work of nature or art, is often in like manner only a
pleasing picture. (2) There is the fallacy of resolving the languages
which we know into their parts, and then imagining that we can
discover the nature of language by reconstructing them. (3) There is
the danger of identifying language not with thoughts but with ideas.
(4) There is the error of supposing that the analysis of grammar and
logic has always existed, or that their distinctions were familiar to
Socrates and Plato. (5) There is the fallacy of exaggerating, and also
of diminishing the interval which separates articulate from inarticulate
language—the cries of animals from the speech of man—the instinct
of animals from the reason of man. (6) There is the danger which besets
all inquiries into the early history of man—of interpreting the past by
the present, and of substituting the definite and intelligible for the
true but dim outline which is the horizon of human knowledge.

The greatest light is thrown upon the nature of language by analogy.
We have the analogy of the cries of animals, of the songs of birds ('man,
like the nightingale, is a singing bird, but is ever binding up thoughts
with musical notes'), of music, of children learning to speak, of
barbarous nations in which the linguistic instinct is still undecayed,
of ourselves learning to think and speak a new language, of the deaf
and dumb who have words without sounds, of the various disorders
of speech; and we have the after-growth of mythology, which, like
language, is an unconscious creation of the human mind. We can
observe the social and collective instincts of animals; and may remark
how, when domesticated, they have the power of understanding but
not of speaking while, on the other hand, some birds which are comparatively devoid of intelligence make a nearer approach to articulate
speech. We may note how in the animals there is a want of that
sympathy with one another which appears to be the soul of language.

We can compare the use of speech with other mental and bodily operations; for speech, too, is a kind of gesture, and in the child or savage accompanied with gesture. We may observe that the child learns to speak, as he learns to walk or to eat, by a natural impulse; yet in either case not without a power of imitation which is also natural to him—he is taught to read, but he breaks forth spontaneously in speech. We can trace the impulse to bind together the world in ideas beginning in the first efforts to speak and culminating in philosophy. But there remains an element which cannot be explained, or even adequately described. We can understand how man creates or constructs consciously and by design; and see, if we do not understand, how nature, by a law, calls into being an organized structure. But the intermediate organism which stands between man and nature, which is the work of mind yet unconscious, and in which mind and matter seem to meet, and mind unperceived to herself is really limited by all other minds, is neither understood nor seen by us, and is with reluctance admitted to be a fact.

Language is an aspect of man, of nature, and of nations, the transfiguration of the world in thought, the meeting-point of the physical and mental sciences, and also the mirror in which they are reflected, present at every moment to the individual, and yet having a sort of eternal or universal nature. When we analyse our own mental processes, we find words everywhere in every degree of clearness and consistency, fading away in dreams and more like pictures, rapidly succeeding one another in our waking thoughts, attaining a greater distinctness and consecutiveness in speech, and a greater still in writing, taking the place of one another when we try to become emancipated from their influence. For in all processes of the mind which are conscious we are talking to ourselves; the attempt to think without words is a mere illusion—they are always reappearing when we fix our thoughts. And speech is not a separate faculty, but the expression of all our faculties, to which all our other powers of expression, signs, looks, gestures, lend their aid, of which the instrument is not the tongue only, but more than half the human frame.

The minds of men are sometimes carried on to think of their lives and of their actions as links in a chain of causes and effects going back to the beginning of time. A few have seemed to lose the sense of their own individuality in the universal cause or nature. In like manner we might think of the words which we daily use as derived from the first speech of man, and of all the languages in the world as the expressions or varieties of a single force or life of language of which the thoughts of men are the accident. Such a conception enables us to grasp the power

and wonder of languages, and is very natural to the scientific philo-
logist. For he, like the metaphysician, believes in the reality of that
which absorbs his own mind. Nor do we deny the enormous influence
which language has exercised over thought. Fixed words, like fixed
ideas, have often governed the world. But in such representations we
attribute to language too much the nature of a cause, and too little of
an effect—too much of an absolute, too little of a relative character—
too much of an ideal, too little of a matter-of-fact existence.

Or again, we may frame a single abstract notion of language of
which all existent languages may be supposed to be the perversion.
But we must not conceive that this logical figment had ever a real
existence, or is anything more than an effort of the mind to give unity
to infinitely various phenomena. There is no abstract language *in
rerum natura*, any more than there is an abstract tree, but only languages
in various stages of growth, maturity, and decay. Nor do other logical
or even grammatical distinctions exactly correspond to the facts of
language; for they, too, are attempts to give unity and regularity to a
subject which is partly irregular.

We find, however, that there are distinctions of another kind by
which this vast field of language admits of being mapped out. There is
the distinction between biliteral and triliteral roots, and the various
inflexions which accompany them; between the mere mechanical
cohesion of sounds or words, and the 'chemical' combination of them
into a new word; there is the distinction between languages which
have had a free and full development of their organisms, and languages
which have been stunted in their growth—lamed in their hands or
feet, and never able to acquire afterwards the powers in which they
are deficient; there is the distinction between synthetical languages
like Greek and Latin, which have retained their inflexions, and
analytical languages like English or French, which have lost them.
Innumerable as are the languages and dialects of mankind, there are
comparatively few classes to which they can be referred.

Another road through this chaos is provided by the physiology of
speech. The organs of language are the same in all mankind, and are
only capable of uttering a certain number of sounds. Every man has
tongue, teeth, lips, palate, throat, mouth, which he may close or open
and adapt in various ways; making first, vowels and consonants; and
secondly, other classes of letters. The elements of all speech, like the
elements of the musical scale, are few and simple, though admitting
of infinite gradations and combinations. Whatever slight differences
exist in the use or formation of these organs, owing to climate or the
sense of euphony or other causes, they are as nothing compared with

their agreement. Here, then, is a real basis of unity in the study of philology, unlike that imaginary abstract unity of which we were just now speaking.

Whether we regard language from the psychological, or historical, or physiological point of view, the materials of our knowledge are inexhaustible. The comparisons of children learning to speak, of barbarous nations, of musical notes, of the cries of animals, of the song of birds, increase our insight into the nature of human speech. Many observations which would otherwise have escaped us are suggested by them. But they do not explain why in man and in man only the speaker met with a response from the hearer, and the half articulate sound gradually developed into Sanskrit and Greek. They hardly enable us to approach any nearer the secret of the origin of language, which, like some of the other great secrets of nature—the origin of birth and death, or of animal life—remains inviolable. That problem is indissolubly bound up with the origin of man; and if we ever know more of the one, we may expect to know more of the other.[1]

[1] Cf. W. Humboldt, *Ueber die Verschiedenheit des menschlichen Sprachbaues*; M. Müller, *Lectures on the Science of Language*; Steinthal, *Einleitung in die Psychologie und Sprachwissenschaft.*

CRATYLUS

Persons of the Dialogue

SOCRATES, HERMOGENES, CRATYLUS

Hermogenes. SUPPOSE that we make Socrates a party to the 383 argument?

Cratylus. If you please.

Her. I should explain to you, Socrates, that our friend Cratylus has been arguing about names; he says that they are natural and not conventional; not a portion of the human voice which men agree to use; but that there is a truth or correctness in them, which is the same by nature for all, both Hellenes and b barbarians. Whereupon I ask him whether his own name is truly Cratylus or not, and he answers, 'Yes.' And Socrates—is that a true name? 'Yes.' Then every man's name, as I tell him, is that which he is called. To this he replies—'If all the world were to call you Hermogenes, that would not be your name.' And when I am anxious to have a further explanation he is ironical and mysterious, and seems to imply that he has a notion 384 of his own about the matter if he would only tell, and could entirely convince me if he chose to be intelligible. Tell me, Socrates, what this oracle means; or rather tell me, if you will be so good, what is your own view of the truth or correctness of names, which I would far sooner hear.

Socrates. Son of Hipponicus, there is an ancient saying that 'hard is the knowledge of the good'. And the knowledge of b names is a great part of knowledge. If I had not been poor, I might have heard the fifty-drachma course of the great Prodicus, which is a complete education in grammar and language— these are his own words—and then I should have been at once able to answer your question about the correctness of names. But, indeed, I have only heard the single-drachma course, and therefore I do not know the truth about such matters; I will, c however, gladly assist you and Cratylus in the investigation of them. When he declares that your name is not really Hermogenes, I suspect that he is only making fun of you; he means to say that you are no true son of Hermes, because you are always looking for a fortune and never in luck. But, as I was saying, it is difficult to obtain certain knowledge of such things and therefore we had better inquire which view is better, yours or that of Cratylus, each of us contributing what he can.

Her. I have often talked over this matter, both with Cratylus and others, and cannot convince myself that there is any prin-

d ciple of correctness in names other than convention and agreement; any name which you give, in my opinion, is the right one, and if you change that and give another, the new name is as correct as the old—we frequently change the names of our slaves, and the newly imposed name is as good as the old: for there is no name given to anything by nature; all is convention and habit of the users; such is my view. But if I am mistaken I shall be happy to hear and learn of Cratylus, or of anyone else.

385 *Soc.* I dare say that you may be right, Hermogenes: let us see—your meaning is, that the name of each thing is only that which anybody agrees to call it?

Her. That is my notion.

Soc. Whether the giver of the name be an individual or a city?

Her. Yes.

Soc. Well, now, let me take an instance; suppose that I call a man a horse or a horse a man, you mean to say that a man will be rightly called a horse by me individually, and rightly called a man by the rest of the world; and a horse again would be rightly called a man by me and a horse by the world—that is your meaning?

b *Her.* He would, according to my view,

Soc. But how about truth, then? you would acknowledge that there is sense in speaking of true and false statement?

Her. Certainly.

Soc. And so there are true and false propositions?

Her. To be sure.

Soc. And a true proposition shows that which is as it is, and a false proposition as it is not?

Her. Yes.

Soc. Then it is possible for our speech to represent things which are, or which are not?

Her. Certainly.

Soc. Consider the true proposition—is it true as a whole only c while the parts are not true?

Her. No; the parts are true as well as the whole.

Soc. Would you say the large parts and not the smaller ones, or every part?

Her. I should say that every part is true.

Soc. Is a proposition resolvable into any part smaller than a name?

Her. No; that is the smallest.

Soc. Then the name is a part of the true proposition?

Her. Yes.

Soc. Yes, and a true part, as you say.

Her. Yes.

Soc. And is not the part of a falsehood also a falsehood?

Her. Yes.

Soc. Then, if propositions may be true and false, names may be true and false?

Her. So we must infer.

Soc. And the name of anything is that which anyone affirms d to be the name?

Her. Yes.

Soc. And will there be so many names of each thing as everybody says that there are? and will they be true names at the time of uttering them?

Her. Yes, Socrates, I can conceive no correctness of names other than this; you give one name, and I another; and in different cities and countries there are different names for the e same things; Hellenes differ from barbarians in their use of names, and the several Hellenic tribes from one another.

Soc. But would you say, Hermogenes, that the things differ as the names differ? and are they relative to individuals, as 386 Protagoras tells us? For he says that man is the measure of all things, and that things are to me as they appear to me, and that they are to you as they appear to you. Do you agree with him, or would you say that things have a permanent essence of their own?

Her. There have been times, Socrates, when I have been driven in my perplexity to take refuge with Protagoras; not that I altogether agree with him.

Soc. What! have you ever been driven to admit that there
b was no such thing as a bad man?

Her. No, indeed; I have often had reason to think that
there are very bad men, and a good many of them.

Soc. Well, and have you ever found any very good ones?

Her. Not many.

Soc. Still you have found them?

Her. Yes.

Soc. And would you hold that the very good were the very
wise, and the very evil very foolish? Would that be your view?

Her. It would.

c   *Soc.* But if Protagoras is right, and the truth is that things
are as they appear to anyone, how can some of us be wise and
some of us foolish?

Her. Impossible.

Soc. And if, on the other hand, wisdom and folly are really
distinguishable you will allow, I think, that the assertion of
Protagoras can hardly be correct. For if what appears to each
man is true to him, one man cannot in reality be wiser than
another.

d   *Her.* He cannot.

Soc. Nor will you be disposed, I presume, to say with Euthydemus, that all things equally belong to all men at the same
moment and always; for neither on his view can there be some
good and others bad, if virtue and vice are always equally to be
attributed to all.

Her. There cannot.

Soc. But if neither is right, and things are not relative to
individuals, and all things do not equally belong to all at the
same moment and always, they must be supposed to have their
e own proper and permanent essence: they are not in relation to
us, or influenced by us, fluctuating according to our fancy, but
they are independent, and maintain to their own essence the
relation prescribed by nature.

Her. I think, Socrates, that you have said the truth.

Soc. Does what I am saying apply only to the things themselves, or equally to the actions which proceed from them? Are
not actions also a class of being?

Her. Yes, the actions are real as well as the things.

Soc. Then the actions also are done according to their proper 387
nature, and not according to our opinion of them? When, for
example, we set out to cut something, can we do so in any way
we please, and with any chance instrument? I think rather that
if we cut with the proper instrument only, and according to the
natural process of cutting, then we shall be successful in our
cutting and perform this action rightly; but if we go against
nature we shall fail and achieve nothing. And again in burning, not every way is the right way; but the right way is
the natural way, and the right instrument the natural instrument.

Her. Yes, I think that is true.

Soc. And this holds good of all actions?

Her. Yes.

Soc. What of speaking? Is not that one of our actions?

Her. True.

Soc. And will a man speak correctly who speaks as he pleases?
Will not the successful speaker rather be he who speaks in the c
natural way of speaking, and as things ought to be spoken, and
with the natural instrument? Any other mode of speaking will
result in error and failure.

Her. I quite agree with you.

Soc. And is not naming a part of speaking? for in giving names
men speak.[1]

Her. That is true.

Soc. And if it is agreed that speaking is a sort of action and
has a relation to things, is not naming also a sort of action?

Her. True.

Soc. And we saw that actions were not relative to ourselves, d
but had a special nature of their own?

Her. Precisely.

Soc. Then the argument would lead us to infer that names
ought to be given according to a natural process, and with a
proper instrument, and not at our pleasure: in this and no other
way shall we name with success.

Her. I agree.

Soc. Now we have said that that which has to be cut has to be
cut with something?

[1] [Or: 'for the process of speech is one of assigning names'.]

Her. Yes.

c   *Soc.* And that which has to be woven or pierced has to be woven or pierced with something?

Her. Certainly.

Soc. And presumably that which has to be named has to be named with something?

Her. True.

Soc. What is that with which we pierce?

Her. An awl.

388   *Soc.* And with which we weave?

Her. A shuttle.

Soc. And with which we name?

Her. A name.

Soc. Very good: then a name is an instrument?

Her. Certainly.

Soc. Suppose that I ask, 'What sort of instrument is a shuttle?' And you answer, 'A weaving instrument.'

Her. Well.

b   *Soc.* And I ask again, 'What do we do when we weave?'— The answer is, that we separate or disengage the warp from the woof.

Her. Very true.

Soc. And may not a similar description be given of an awl, and of instruments in general?

Her. To be sure.

Soc. And now suppose that I ask a similar question about names: will you answer me? Regarding the name as an instrument, what do we do when we name?

Her. I cannot say.

Soc. Do we not give information to one another, and distinguish things according to their natures?

Her. Certainly we do.

c   *Soc.* Then a name is an instrument of teaching and of distinguishing natures, as the shuttle is of distinguishing the threads of the web.

Her. Yes.

Soc. And the shuttle is the instrument of the weaver?

Her. Assuredly.

Soc. Then the weaver will use the shuttle well—and well

means like a weaver? and the teacher will use the name well—
and well means like a teacher?

Her. Yes.

Soc. And when the weaver uses the shuttle, whose work will
he be using well?

Her. That of the carpenter.

Soc. And is every man a carpenter, or the skilled only?

Her. Only the skilled.

Soc. And when the piercer uses the awl, whose work will he d
be using well?

Her. That of the smith.

Soc. And is every man a smith, or only the skilled?

Her. The skilled only.

Soc. Good. And when the teacher uses the name, whose
work will he be using?

Her. There again I am puzzled.

Soc. Cannot you at least say who gives us the names which
we use?

Her. Indeed I cannot.

Soc. Does not the law seem to you to give us them?

Her. Yes, I suppose so.

Soc. Then the teacher, when he uses a name, uses the work e
of the legislator?

Her. I agree.

Soc. And is every man a legislator, or the skilled only?

Her. The skilled only.

Soc. Then, Hermogenes, not every man is able to give a name
but only a maker of names; and this seems to be the legislator, 389
who of all skilled artisans in the world is the rarest.

Her. True.

Soc. And how does the legislator make names? and to what
does he look? Consider this in the light of the previous instances:
to what does the carpenter look in making the shuttle? Does he
not look to the way in which the shuttle must, in the nature of
things, operate?

Her. Certainly.

Soc. And suppose the shuttle to be broken in making, will b
he make another, looking to the broken one? or will he look to
the form according to which he made the other?

Her. To the latter, I should imagine.

Soc. Might not that be justly called the true or ideal shuttle?

Her. I think so.

Soc. And whatever shuttles are wanted, for the manufacture of garments, thin or thick, of flaxen, woollen, or other material, all these must, indeed, have the form of the shuttle; but the

c maker must also produce in each one that form which is naturally most suitable to its special work.

Her. Yes.

Soc. And the same holds of other instruments: when a man has discovered the instrument which is naturally adapted to each work, he must express this natural form, and not others which he fancies, in the material, whatever it may be, which he employs; for example, he ought to know how to put into iron the forms of awls adapted by nature to their several uses?

Her. Certainly.

Soc. And how to put into wood forms of shuttles adapted by nature to their uses?

Her. True.

d *Soc.* For the several forms of shuttles naturally answer to the several kinds of webs; and this is true of instruments in general.

Her. Yes.

Soc. Then, as to names: ought not our legislator also to know how to put the true natural name of each thing into sounds and syllables, and to make and give all names with a view to the ideal name, if he is to be a namer in any true sense? And we must not misinterpret the fact that different legislators will not

e use the same syllables. For neither does every smith, although he may be making the same instrument for the same purpose, make them all of the same iron. The form must be the same, but the material may vary, and still the instrument may be equally

390 good of whatever iron made, whether in Hellas or in a foreign country;—there is no difference.

Her. Very true.

Soc. And the legislator, whether he be Hellene or barbarian, is not therefore to be deemed by you a worse legislator, provided he expresses the form of the name proper to each subject in whatever syllables; this or that country makes no matter.

Her. Quite true.

Soc. But who then is to determine whether the proper form b
is given to the shuttle, whatever sort of wood may be used? the
carpenter who makes, or the weaver who is to use them?

Her. I should say, he who is to use them, Socrates.

Soc. And who uses the work of the lyre-maker? Will not he be
the man who best knows how to direct the work while it is being
done, and who will know also whether the finished work has
been well done or not?

Her. Certainly.

Soc. And who is he?

Her. The player of the lyre.

Soc. And who will direct the shipwright?

Her. The pilot.   c

Soc. And who will be best able to direct the legislator in his
work, and is competent to judge whether the work is well done,
in this or any other country? Will not the user be the man?

Her. Yes.

Soc. Must not this be he who knows how to ask questions?

Her. Yes.

Soc. And how to answer them?

Her. Yes.

Soc. And him who knows how to ask and answer you would
call a dialectician?

Her. Yes; that would be his name.

Soc. Then the work of the carpenter is to make a rudder, and d
the pilot has to direct him, if the rudder is to be well made.

Her. True.

Soc. And the work of the legislator is to give names, and the
dialectician must be his director if the names are to be rightly
given?

Her. That is true.

Soc. Then, Hermogenes, I should say that this giving of names
can be no such light matter as you fancy, or the work of light or
chance persons; and Cratylus is right in saying that things have
names by nature, and that not every man is an artificer of e
names, but he only who looks to the name which each thing by
nature has, and is able to express this name in letters and
syllables.

Her. I cannot see how to answer your arguments, Socrates;

391 but I find a difficulty in changing my opinion all in a moment, and I think that I should be more readily persuaded, if you would show me what this is which you term the natural fitness of names.

Soc. My good Hermogenes, I have none to show. Was I not telling you just now (but you have forgotten), that I knew nothing, and proposing to share the inquiry with you? But now that you and I have talked over the matter, a step has been gained; for we have discovered that names have by nature a
b truth, and that not every man knows how to give a thing a name.

Her. Very good.

Soc. After this, then, we should proceed to inquire (supposing that you desire to know it) what is this truth or correctness of names.

Her. Certainly, I desire to know.

Soc. Then reflect.

Her. How shall I reflect?

Soc. The true way is to have the assistance of those who know, and you must pay them well both in money and in thanks; these
c are the sophists, of whom your brother, Callias, has—rather dearly—bought the reputation of wisdom. But you have not yet come into your inheritance, and therefore you had better go to him, and beg and entreat him to tell you what he has learnt from Protagoras about the fitness of names.

Her. But how inconsistent should I be, if, whilst repudiating Protagoras and his truth,[1] I were to attach any value to what he and his book affirm!

d *Soc.* Then if you despise him, you must learn of Homer and the poets.

Her. And where does Homer say anything about names, and what does he say?

Soc. He often speaks of them; notably and nobly in the places where he distinguishes the different names which Gods and men give to the same things. Does he not in these passages make a profound and surprising statement about the correctness of
e names? For the Gods must clearly be supposed to call things by their right and natural names; do you not think so?

---

[1] 'Truth' was the title of the book of Protagoras; cf. *Theaet.* 161 e.

Her. Why, of course they call them rightly, if they call them at all. But to what are you referring?

Soc. Do you not know what he says about the river in Troy which fought a single combat with Hephaestus?

'Whom', as he says, 'the Gods call Xanthus, and men call Scamander.'

Her. I remember.

Soc. Well, and about this river—to know that he ought to be 392 called Xanthus and not Scamander—is not that a solemn lesson? Or about the bird which, as he says,

'The Gods call Chalcis, and men Cymindis':

to be taught how much more correct the name Chalcis is than the name Cymindis,—do you deem that a light matter? Or about Batieia and Myrina?[1] And there are many other observations of the same kind in Homer and other poets. Now, I think b that this is beyond the understanding of you and me; but the names of Scamandrius and Astyanax, which he affirms to have been the names of Hector's son, are more within the range of human faculties, as I am disposed to think; and what the poet means by correctness may be more readily apprehended in that instance: you will remember, I dare say, the lines to which I refer.[2]

Her. I do.

Soc. Let me ask you, then, which did Homer think the more correct of the names given to Hector's son—Astyanax or Scamandrius?

Her. I do not know. c

Soc. How would you answer, if you were asked whether the wise or the unwise are more likely to give correct names?

Her. I should say the wise, of course.

Soc. And are the men or the women of a city, taken as a class, the wiser?

Her. I should say, the men.

Soc. And Homer, as you know, says that the Trojan men called him Astyanax (king of the city); but if the men called d

---

[1] Cf. *Il.* ii. 813, 814: 'The hill which men call Batieia and the immortals the tomb of the sportive Myrina.'
[2] *Il.* vi. 402.

him Astyanax, the other name of Scamandrius could only have been given to him by the women.

Her. That may be inferred.

Soc. And must not Homer have imagined the Trojans to be wiser than their wives?

Her. To be sure.

Soc. Then he must have thought Astyanax to be a more correct name for the boy than Scamandrius?

Her. Apparently.

Soc. And what is the reason of this? Let us consider: does he not himself suggest a very good reason, when he says,

e   'For he alone defended their city and long walls'?

This appears to be a good reason for calling the son of the saviour king of the city which, according to Homer's account, his father was saving.

Her. I see.

Soc. Why, Hermogenes, I do not as yet see myself; and do you?

Her. No, indeed; not I.

393   *Soc.* But tell me, friend, did not Homer himself also give Hector his name?

Her. What of that?

Soc. The name appears to me to be very nearly the same as the name of Astyanax—both are Hellenic; and a king (ἄναξ) and a holder (ἕκτωρ) have nearly the same meaning, and are both descriptive of a king; for a man is, I presume, the holder of that of which he is king; he evidently rules, and owns, and

b holds it. But, perhaps, you may think that I am talking nonsense; and indeed perhaps I delude myself when I imagine that I have found some indication of the opinion of Homer about the correctness of names.

Her. I assure you that I think otherwise, and I believe you to be on the right track.

Soc. There is reason, I think, in calling the lion's whelp a lion, and the foal of a horse a horse; I am speaking only of the ordinary course of nature, when an animal produces after his kind,

c and not of extraordinary births;—if contrary to nature a horse have a calf, then I should not call that a foal but a calf; nor do I call any inhuman birth, of human parents, by the name man.

And the same may be said of trees and other things. Do you agree with me?

Her. Yes, I agree.

Soc. Thank you; you must watch me and see that I do not lead you astray. For on the same principle the son of a king is to be called a king. And whether the syllables of the name are d the same or not the same, makes no difference, provided the meaning is retained; nor does the addition or subtraction of a letter make any difference so long as the essence of the thing remains in possession of the name and appears in it.

Her. What do you mean?

Soc. A very simple matter. I may illustrate my meaning by the names of letters, which you know are not the same as the letters themselves with the exception of the four, ϵ, v, o, ω; for the rest, whether vowels or consonants, we compose names by the addition of other letters; but so long as we introduce and e explain the value of the letter, such names, which clearly indicate the thing, are correct ones. Take, for example, the letter *beta*—the addition of η, τ, a, gives no offence, and does not prevent the whole name from having the value which the legislator intended—so well did he know how to give the letters names.

Her. I believe you are right.

Soc. And may not the same be said of a king? a king will 394 often be the son of a king, the good son or the noble son of a good or noble sire; and similarly the offspring of every kind, in the regular course of nature, is like the parent, and must therefore have the same name. Yet the syllables may be disguised until they appear different to the ignorant person, and he may not recognize them, although they are the same, just as any one of us would not recognize the same drugs under different disguises of colour and smell, although to the physician, who regards the power of them, they are the same, and he is not put b out by the addition; and in like manner the etymologist considers the force of each name and is not put out by the addition or transposition or subtraction of a letter or two, or indeed when the same meaning is expressed in wholly different letters. As was just now said, the names of Hector and Astyanax have only one letter alike, which is the τ, and yet they have the same meaning. And how little in common with the letters of their c names has Archepolis (ruler of the city)—and yet the meaning is the same. And there are many other names which just mean 'king'. Again, there are several names for a general, as, for example, Agis (leader) and Polemarchus (chief in war) and Eupolemus (good warrior); and others which denote a physician, as Iatrocles (famous healer) and Acesimbrotus (curer of mortals); and there are many others which might be cited, differing in their syllables and letters, but having the same meaning. Would you not say so?

d   *Her.* Yes.

Soc. The same names, then, ought to be assigned to those who follow their parents in the course of nature?

Her. Yes.

Soc. And what of those who follow out of the course of nature, and are prodigies? for example, when a good and religious man has an irreligious son, he ought to bear the name not of his father, but of the class to which he belongs, just as in the case which was before supposed of a horse foaling a calf.

Her. Quite true.

Soc. Then the irreligious son of a religious father should
e receive the proper class name?

Her. Certainly.

Soc. He should not be called Theophilus (beloved of God) or Mnesitheus (mindful of God), or any of these names: if names are correctly given, his should have an opposite meaning.

Her. Certainly, Socrates.

Soc. Again, Hermogenes, there is Orestes (the man of the mountains) who appears to be rightly called; whether chance gave the name, or perhaps some poet who meant to express the brutality and fierceness and mountain wildness of his hero's nature.

395 *Her.* That is very likely, Socrates.

Soc. And his father's name is also according to nature.

Her. Apparently.

Soc. Yes, for as his name, so also is his nature; Agamemnon (admirable for remaining) is one who is patient and persevering in the accomplishment of his resolves, and by his virtue crowns them; and his continuance at Troy with all the vast army is a
b proof of that admirable endurance in him which is signified by

the name Agamemnon.[1] I also think that Atreus is rightly
called; for his murder of Chrysippus and his exceeding cruelty
to Thyestes are damaging and destructive to his reputation—the
name is a little altered and disguised so as not to be intelligible
to everyone, but to the etymologist there is no difficulty in
seeing the meaning, for whether you think of him as ἀτειρής the   c
stubborn, or as ἄτρεστος the fearless, or as ἀτηρός the destructive
one, the name is perfectly correct in every point of view. And I
think that Pelops is also named appropriately; for, as the name
implies, he is rightly called Pelops who sees what is near only
(ὁ τὰ πέλας ὁρῶν).

Her. How so?

Soc. Because, according to the tradition, he had no forethought or foresight of all the evil which the murder of Myrtilus
would entail upon his whole race in remote ages; he saw only   d
what was at hand and immediate,—or in other words, πέλας
(near), in his eagerness to win Hippodamia by all means for his
bride. Everyone would agree that the name of Tantalus is
rightly given and in accordance with nature, if the traditions
about him are true.

Her. And what are the traditions?

Soc. Many terrible misfortunes are said to have happened to
him in his life—last of all, came the utter ruin of his country;
and after his death he had the stone suspended (ταλαντεία) over   e
his head in the world below—all this agrees wonderfully well
with his name. You might imagine that some person who wanted
to call him ταλάντατος (the most weighed down by misfortune),
disguised the name by altering it into Tantalus; and into this
form by some accident of tradition, it has actually been trans-
muted. The name of Zeus, who is his alleged father, has also an
excellent meaning, although hard to be understood, because   396
really like a sentence, which is divided into two parts, for some
call him Zena (Ζῆνα), and use the one half, and others who
use the other half call him Dia (Δία); the two together signify
the nature of the God, and the business of a name, as we were
saying, is to express the nature. For there is none who is more
the author of life to us and to all, than the lord and king of all.
Wherefore we are right in calling him Zena and Dia, which are

[1] Ἀγαμέμνων = ἀγαστὸς μένων.

b one name, although divided, meaning the God through whom all creatures always have life (δι' ὃν ζῆν ἀεὶ πᾶσι τοῖς ζῴοισιν ὑπάρχει). There is an irreverence, at first sight, in calling him son of Cronos (who is a proverb for stupidity), and we might rather expect Zeus to be the child of a mighty intellect. Which is the fact; for this is the meaning of his father's name: Κρόνος quasi Κόρος (κορέω, to sweep), not in the sense of a youth, but signifying τὸ καθαρὸν καὶ ἀκήρατον τοῦ νοῦ, the pure and garnished mind (sc. ἀπὸ τοῦ κορεῖν). He, as we are informed by tradition,

c was begotten of Uranus, rightly so called (ἀπὸ τοῦ ὁρᾶν τὰ ἄνω) from looking upwards; which, as astronomers tell us, is the way to have a pure mind, and the name Uranus is therefore correct. If I could remember the genealogy of Hesiod, I would have gone on and tried more conclusions of the same sort on the remoter ancestors of the gods,—then I might have seen whether this wisdom, which has come to me all in an instant, I know not

d whence, will or will not hold good to the end.

Her. You seem to me, Socrates, to be quite like a prophet newly inspired, and to be uttering oracles.

Soc. Yes, Hermogenes, and I believe that I caught the inspiration from the great Euthyphro of the Prospaltian deme, who gave me a long lecture which commenced at dawn: he talked and I listened, and his wisdom and enchanting ravishment has not only filled my ears but taken possession of my soul.

e I think that this will be the right course—today I shall let his superhuman power work and finish the investigation of names; but tomorrow, if you are so disposed, we will conjure him away, and make a purgation of him, if we can only find some priest or

397 sophist[1] who is skilled in purifications of this sort.

Her. With all my heart; for I am very curious to hear the rest of the inquiry about names.

Soc. Then let us proceed; and where would you have us begin, now that we have got a sort of outline of the inquiry? Are there any names which witness of themselves that they are not given arbitrarily, but have a natural fitness? The names of

b heroes and of men in general are apt to be deceptive because they are often called after ancestors with whose names, as we

---

[1] [At *Sophist* 231 b, the sophist is defined as one who by questioning can purge the mind of a vain conceit of knowledge.]

were saying, they may have no business; or they are the expression of a wish like Eutychides (the son of good fortune), or
Sosias (the Saviour), or Theophilus (the beloved of God), and
others. But I think that we had better leave such instances as
these, for there will be more chance of finding correctness in
the names of things which are eternal and immutable;—there
ought to have been most care taken about them when they
were named, and perhaps there may be some such names c
which were given by some more than human power.

Her. I think so, Socrates.

Soc. Ought we not to begin with the consideration of the
gods, and show for what reason they are rightly so named?

Her. Yes, that will be well.

Soc. My notion would be something of this sort:—I suspect
that the sun, moon, earth, stars, and heaven, which are still the
gods of many barbarians, were the only gods known to the d
aboriginal Hellenes. Seeing that they were always moving and
running, from their running nature they were called gods or
runners (θεούς, θέοντας); and when men became acquainted
with the other gods, they proceeded to apply the same name to
them all. Do you think that likely?

Her. I think it very likely indeed.

Soc. What shall follow the gods?

Her. Must not demons and heroes and men[1] come next?   e

Soc. And what do you imagine can be the meaning of this
word 'demon'? Tell me if my view is right.

Her. Let me hear.

Soc. You know how Hesiod uses the word?

Her. I do not.

Soc. Do you not remember that he speaks of a golden race of
men who came first?

Her. Yes, so much I do know.

Soc. He says of them—

> 'But now that fate has closed over this race
> They are named holy demons beneath the earth,
> Beneficent, averters of ills, guardians of mortal men.'[2]

---

[1] [Reading δῆλον δὴ ὅτι δαίμονάς τε καὶ ἥρωας καὶ ἀνθρώπους. 'Demons' in Greek
usage are beings intermediary between God and man.]

[2] Hesiod, *Works and Days*, 120 ff.

398   *Her.* What is the inference?

  Soc. What is the inference! Why, I suppose that he means by the golden men, not men literally made of gold, but good and noble; and I am convinced of this, because he further says that we are the iron race.

  Her. That is true.

  Soc. And do you not suppose that good men of our own day
b would by him be said to be of golden race?

  Her. Very likely.

  Soc. And are not the good wise?

  Her. Yes, they are wise.

  Soc. And therefore I have the most entire conviction that he called them demons, because they were δαήμονες (knowing or wise), and in our older Attic dialect the word itself occurs. Now he and other poets say truly, that when a good man dies he has honour and a mighty portion among the dead, and becomes a
c demon; which is a name given to him signifying wisdom. And I say too, that every man who happens to be a good man is more than human (δαιμόνιον) both in life and death, and is rightly called a demon.

  Her. Then I rather think that I am of one mind with you; but what is the meaning of the word 'hero'? (ἥρως, in the old writing ἔρως.)

  Soc. I think that there is no difficulty in explaining, for the name is not much altered, and signifies that they were born of love.

  Her. What do you mean?

  Soc. Do you not know that the heroes are demigods?

  Her. What then?

d   *Soc.* All of them sprang either from the love of a god for a mortal woman, or of a mortal man for a goddess; think of the word in the old Attic, and you will see better that the name heros is only a slight alteration of Eros, from whom the heroes sprang: either this is the meaning, or, if not this, then they must have been skilful as rhetoricians and dialecticians, and able to put the question (ἐρωτᾶν), for εἴρειν is equivalent to λέγειν.[1] And therefore, as I was saying, in the Attic dialect the heroes
e turn out to be rhetoricians and questioners. All this is easy

[1] [Cf. 408 a.]

enough; the noble breed of heroes are a kind of sophists and rhetors. But can you tell me why men are called ἄνθρωποι?—that is more difficult.

Her. No, indeed I cannot; and I would not try even if I could, because I think that you are the more likely to succeed.

Soc. That is to say, you trust to the inspiration of Euthyphro. 399

Her. Of course.

Soc. Your faith is not vain; for at this very moment a new and ingenious thought strikes me, and, if I am not careful, before tomorrow's dawn I shall be wiser than I ought to be. Now, attend to me; and first, remember that we often put in and pull out letters in words, and give names as we please and change the accents. Take, for example, the word Διὶ φίλος; in b order to convert this from a phrase into a noun, we omit one of the iotas and sound the middle syllable grave instead of acute; as, on the other hand, letters are sometimes inserted in words instead of being omitted, and the acute takes the place of the grave.

Her. That is true.

Soc. The name ἄνθρωπος, which was once a phrase, and is now a noun, appears to be a case just of this sort, for one letter, which is the α, has been omitted, and the acute on the last syllable has been changed to a grave.

Her. What do you mean?

Soc. I mean to say that the word 'man' implies that other c animals never examine, or consider, or look up at (ἀναθρεῖ) what they see, but that man not only sees (ὄπωπε) but considers and looks up at that which he sees, and hence he alone of all animals is rightly called ἄνθρωπος, meaning ἀναθρῶν ἃ ὄπωπεν.

Her. May I ask you to examine another word about which I am curious?

Soc. Certainly.

Her. I will take that which appears to me to follow next in d order. Within a man, as you know, we distinguish soul and body.

Soc. Of course.

Her. Let us endeavour to analyse them like the previous words.

Soc. You want me first of all to examine the natural fitness of the word ψυχή (soul) and then of the word σῶμα (body)?

Her. Yes.

Soc. If I am to say what occurs to me at the moment, I should imagine that those who first used the name ψυχή meant to express that the soul when in the body is the source of life,
e and gives the power of breath and revival (ἀναψῦχον), and when this reviving power fails then the body perishes and dies, and this, if I am not mistaken, they called psyche. But please stay a moment; I fancy that I can discover something which will be
400 more acceptable to the disciples of Euthyphro, for I am afraid that they will scorn this explanation, and think it banal. What do you say to another?

Her. Let me hear.

Soc. What is that which holds and carries and gives life and motion to the entire nature of the body? What else but the soul?

Her. Just that.

Soc. And do you not believe with Anaxagoras, that mind or soul is the ordering and containing principle of all things?

Her. Yes; I do.

b *Soc.* Then you may well call that power φυσέχη which carries and holds nature (ἡ φύσιν ὀχεῖ καὶ ἔχει), and this may be refined away into ψυχή.

Her. Certainly; and this derivation is, I think, more scientific than the other.

Soc. It is so; although the name in its original form was assuredly a quaint one.

Her. But what shall we say of the next word?

Soc. You mean σῶμα (the body).

Her. Yes.

Soc. That may be variously interpreted; and yet more variously if a little permutation is allowed. For some say that
c the body is the grave (σῆμα) of the soul which may be thought to be buried in our present life; or again the index of the soul, because the soul gives indications to (σημαίνει) the body.[1] But it seems to me most probable that the Orphic poets were the inventors of the name, and they were under the impression that the soul is suffering the punishment for certain sins, and that the body is an enclosure or prison in which the soul is incarcerated, kept safe (σῶμα, σώζηται), as the name σῶμα implies,

[1] [Or: 'gives indications with the body'.]

until the penalty is paid; according to this view, not even a letter of the word need be changed.

Her. I think, Socrates, that we have said enough of this class d of words. But have we any more explanations of the names of the gods, like that which you were giving of Zeus? I should like to know whether any similar principle of correctness is to be applied to them.

Soc. Yes, indeed, Hermogenes; and there is one excellent principle which, as men of sense, we must acknowledge,—that of the gods we know nothing, either of their natures or of the names which they give themselves; but we are sure that the names by which they call themselves, whatever they may be, are true. And this is the best of all principles; and the next best e is to say, as is customary in prayers, that we will call them by any sort or kind of names or patronymics in which they rejoice, because we do not know of any other. That custom is, in my 401 opinion, a good one. Let us, then, if you please, in the first place announce to them that we are not inquiring about them; we do not presume that we are able to do so; but we are inquiring about the meaning of men in giving them these names,—in this there can be small blame.

Her. I think, Socrates, that you are quite right, and I should like to do as you say.

Soc. Shall we begin, then, with Hestia, according to custom? b

Her. Yes, that will be very proper.

Soc. What may we suppose him to have meant who gave the name Hestia?

Her. That is another and certainly a most difficult question.

Soc. My dear Hermogenes, the first imposers of names must surely have been no ordinary men, but ambitious inquirers and talkers.

Her. Well, and what of them?

Soc. It is to such men that I should attribute the imposition of names. Even in foreign names, if you analyse them, a meaning c is still discernible. For example, that which we term οὐσία is by some called ἐσσία, and by others again ὠσία. Now that the essence of things should be called ἑστία, which is akin to the first of these (ἐσσία = ἑστία), is rational enough. And there is reason in the Athenians calling that ἑστία which participates in

οὐσία. For in ancient times we too seem to have said ἐσσία for
d οὐσία, and this you may note to have been the idea of those
who appointed that sacrifices should be first offered to ἑστία,
which was natural enough if they meant that ἑστία was the
essence of all things. Those again who say ὠσία seem to be
inclined to the opinion of Heracleitus, that all things flow and
nothing stands; with them the pushing principle (ὠθοῦν) is the
cause and ruling power of all things, and is therefore rightly
called ὠσία. Enough of this, which is all that we who know
e nothing can affirm. Next in order after Hestia we ought to
consider Rhea and Cronos, although the name of Cronos has
been already discussed. But I dare say that I am talking great
nonsense.

Her. Why, Socrates?

Soc. My good friend, I have discovered a hive of wisdom.

Her. Of what nature?

402 *Soc.* Well, absurd in the description, and yet, I think, quite
plausible.

Her. How plausible?

Soc. I fancy to myself Heracleitus repeating wise traditions
of antiquity as old as the days of Cronos and Rhea, and of
which Homer also spoke.

Her. How do you mean?

Soc. Heracleitus is supposed to say that all things are in
motion and nothing at rest; he compares them to the stream of
a river, and says that you cannot go into the same water twice.

Her. That is true.

b *Soc.* Well, then, how can we avoid inferring that he who
gave the names of Cronos and Rhea to the ancestors of the gods,
agreed pretty much in the doctrine of Heracleitus? Is the giving
of the names of streams to both of them purely accidental?
Compare the line in which Homer, and, as I believe, Hesiod also,
tells of

'Ocean, the origin of gods, and mother Tethys.'[1]

And again, Orpheus says, that

'The fair river of Ocean was the first to marry, and he espoused his
sister Tethys, who was his mother's daughter.'[2]

[1] *Il.* xiv. 201, 302: the line is not found in the extant works of Hesiod.
[2] [Cf. *Theaet.* 180 d.]

You see that this is a remarkable coincidence, and all in the c direction of Heracleitus.

Her. I think that there is something in what you say, Socrates; but I do not understand the meaning of the name Tethys.

Soc. Well, that is almost self-explained, being only the name of a spring, a little disguised; for the expressions strained and filtered (διαττώμενον, ἠθούμενον) are meant to describe a spring, d and the name Tethys is made up of these two words.

Her. The idea is ingenious, Socrates.

Soc. To be sure. But what comes next?—of Zeus we have spoken.

Her. Yes.

Soc. Then let us next take his two brothers, Poseidon and Pluto, whether the latter is called by that or by his other name.

Her. By all means.

Soc. Poseidon is ποσίδεσμος, the chain of the feet; the original e inventor of the name had been stopped by the watery element in his walks, and not allowed to go on, and therefore he called the ruler of this element Poseidon; the ε was probably inserted as an ornament. Yet, perhaps, not so; but the name may have been originally written with a double λ and not with a σ, 403 meaning that the god knew many things (πολλὰ εἰδώς). And perhaps also he being the shaker of the earth, has been named from shaking (σείειν), and then π and δ have been added. Pluto gives wealth (πλοῦτος), and his name means the giver of wealth, which comes out of the earth beneath. People in general appear to imagine that the term Hades is connected with the invisible (ἀειδές); and since they fear this name, they call the god Pluto instead.

Her. And what is your own opinion, Socrates? b

Soc. I consider that men make various mistakes about the power of this deity, and fear him without good reason. For example, they are afraid because, when a man is dead, he will be for ever in that place [Hades]; and they are afraid because the soul denuded of the body passes to him.[1] But my belief is that all is quite consistent, and that the office and name of the god really correspond.

Her. Why, how is that?

---

[1] Cf. *Rep.* 3. 386, 387.

c   *Soc.* I will tell you my own opinion; but first, I should like
to ask you which chain does any animal feel to be the stronger?
and which confines him more to the same spot,—desire or
necessity?

Her. Desire, Socrates, is stronger far.

Soc. And do you not think that many a one would escape
from Hades, if he did not bind those who depart to him by the
strongest of chains?

Her. Assuredly they would.

Soc. And if by the greatest of chains, then by some desire,
as I should certainly infer, and not by necessity?

Her. So it appears.

Soc. Desire, however, is of many kinds?

Her. Yes.

d   *Soc.* And therefore by the greatest desire, if the chain is to be
the greatest?

Her. Yes.

Soc. And is any desire stronger than the thought that you
will be made better by associating with another?

Her. Certainly not.

Soc. And is not that the reason, Hermogenes, why no one,
who has been to him, is willing to come back to us? Even the
Sirens, like all the rest of the world, have been laid under his
e   spells. Such a charm, as I imagine, is the God able to infuse
into his words. And, according to this view, he is the perfect
and accomplished sophist, and the great benefactor of the
inhabitants of the other world; and even to us who are upon
earth he sends from below exceeding blessings. For he has
much more than he wants down there; wherefore he is called
Pluto (or the rich). Note also, that he will have nothing to do
with men while they are in the body, but only when the soul is
404   liberated from the desires and evils of the body. Do you not
think that this marks him as a philosopher, who is well aware
that in their liberated state he can bind them with the desire of
virtue, but while they are flustered and maddened by the body,
not even his father Cronos himself would suffice to keep them
with him in his own far-famed chains.

Her. There is a deal of truth in what you say.

b   *Soc.* Yes, Hermogenes, and the legislator called him Hades, not from the unseen,—far otherwise, but from his knowledge (εἰδέναι) of all noble things.

Her. Very good; and what do we say of Demeter, and Hera, and Apollo, and Athene, and Hephaestus, and Ares, and the other deities?

Soc. Demeter's name seems to mean ἡ διδοῦσα μήτηρ, who gives food like a mother; Hera is the lovely one (ἐρατή)—for Zeus, according to tradition, loved and married her; possibly c also the name may have been given when the legislator was thinking of the heavens, and may be only a disguise of the air (ἀήρ), putting the end in the place of the beginning. You will recognize the truth of this if you repeat the letters of Hera several times over. People dread the name of Pherephatta as they dread the name of Apollo,—and with as little reason; the fear, if I am not mistaken, only arises from their ignorance of the nature of names. But they go changing the name into Phersephone, and they are terrified at this; whereas the new name means only that the goddess is wise (σοφή); for seeing d that all things in the world are in motion (φερομένων), that principle which embraces and touches and is able to follow them, is wisdom. And therefore the goddess may be truly called Pherepaphe (Φερεπάφα), or some name like it, because she touches that which is in motion (τοῦ φερομένου ἐφαπτομένη), herein showing her wisdom, (perhaps this is why Hades, who is himself wise, has chosen her for his companion); but they alter her name into Pherephatta nowadays, because the present generation care for euphony more than truth. There is the other name, Apollo, which, as I was saying, is generally supposed to e have some terrible signification. Have you remarked this fact?

Her. To be sure I have, and what you say is true.

Soc. But the name, in my opinion, is really most expressive of the power of the God.

Her. How so?

Soc. I will endeavour to explain, for I do not believe that any single name could have been better adapted to express the 405 attributes of the God, embracing and in a manner signifying all four of them,—music, and prophecy, and medicine, and archery.

Her. That must be a strange name, and I should like to hear the explanation.

Soc. Say rather an harmonious name, as beseems the God of Harmony. In the first place, the purgations and purifications which doctors and diviners use, and their fumigations with
b drugs magical or medicinal, as well as their washings and lustral sprinklings, have all one and the same object, which is to make a man pure both in body and soul.

Her. Very true.

Soc. And is not Apollo the purifier, and the washer, and the absolver from all impurities?

Her. Very true.

Soc. Then in reference to his ablutions and absolutions, as
c being the physician who orders them, he may be rightly called Ἀπολούων (purifier); or in respect of his powers of divination, and his truth and sincerity, which is the same as truth, he may be most fitly called Ἁπλῶς, from ἁπλοῦς (sincere), as in the Thessalian dialect, for all the Thessalians call him Ἅπλους; also he is ἀεὶ βάλλων (always shooting), because he is a master archer who never misses; or again, the name may refer to his musical attributes, and then, as in ἀκόλουθος, and ἄκοιτις, and in many other words the ἀ is supposed to mean 'together', so the meaning of the name Apollo will be 'moving together', whether in the poles of heaven as they are called, or in the harmony of song,
d which is termed concord, because all these move at once (ἅμα πολεῖ) with a certain harmony, as we hear from those who are expert in music and astronomy. And he is the god who presides over that harmony, and makes all things move together, both among gods and among men. And as in the words ἀκόλουθος and ἄκοιτις the ἀ is substituted for ὁμο, so the name Ἀπόλλων is
e equivalent to ὁμοπολῶν; only the second λ is added in order to avoid the ill-omened sound of destruction (ἀπολῶν). Now the suspicion of this destructive power still haunts the minds of some who do not consider the true value of the name, which,
406 as I was saying just now, has reference to all the powers of the god, who is the single one, the ever-darting, the purifier, the mover together (ἁπλοῦς, ἀεὶ βάλλων, ἀπολούων, ὁμοπολῶν). The name of the Muses and of music would seem to be derived from their making philosophical inquiries (μῶσθαι); and Leto is called by this name, because she is such a gentle goddess, and so willing (ἐθελήμων) to grant our requests; or her name may be

Letho, as she is often called by strangers—they seem to imply by it her amiability, and her smooth and easy-going way of b behaving (λεῖον ἦθος). Artemis is named from her healthy (ἀρτεμής), well-ordered nature, and because of her love of virginity, perhaps because she is a proficient in virtue (ἀρετή), and perhaps also as hating intercourse of the sexes (τὸν ἄροτον μισήσασα). He who gave the goddess her name may have had any or all of these reasons.

Her. What is the meaning of Dionysus and Aphrodite?

Soc. Son of Hipponicus, you ask a solemn question; there is a serious and also a facetious explanation of both these names; the serious explanation is not to be had from me, but there is c no objection to your hearing the facetious one; for the Gods too love a joke. Διόνυσος is simply διδοὺς οἶνον (giver of wine), Διδοίνυσος, as he might be called in fun,—and οἶνος is properly οἰόνους, because wine makes those who drink, think (οἴεσθαι) that they have a mind (νοῦν) when they have none. The derivation of Aphrodite, born of the foam (ἀφρός), may be fairly d accepted on the authority of Hesiod.

Her. Still there remains Athene, whom you, Socrates, as an Athenian, will surely not forget; there are also Hephaestus and Ares.

Soc. I am not likely to forget them.

Her. No, indeed.

Soc. There is no difficulty in explaining the other appellation of Athene.

Her. What other appellation?

Soc. We call her Pallas.

Her. To be sure.

Soc. And we cannot be wrong in supposing that this is derived from armed dances. For the elevation of oneself or e anything else above the earth, or by the use of the hands, we call shaking (πάλλειν), or dancing; and the same words have a 407 reflexive use.

Her. That is quite true.

Soc. Then that is the explanation of the name Pallas?

Her. Yes; but what do you say of the other name?

Soc. Athene?

Her. Yes.

Soc. That is a graver matter, and there, my friend, the modern interpreters of Homer may, I think, assist in explaining the view
b of the ancients. For most of these in their explanations of the poet, assert that he meant by Athene 'mind' (νοῦς) and 'intelligence' (διάνοια), and the maker of names appears to have had a similar notion about her; and indeed calls her by a still higher title, 'divine intelligence' (θεοῦ νόησις), as though he would say: This is she who has the mind of God (θεονόα);—using α as a dialectical variety for η, and taking away ι and σ.[1] Perhaps, however, the name θεονόη may mean 'she who knows divine things' (θεῖα νοοῦσα) better than others. Nor shall we be far wrong in supposing that the author of it wished to identify this goddess with moral intelligence (ἐν ἤθει νόησιν), and therefore
c gave her the name ἠθονόη; which, however, either he or his successors have altered into what they thought a nicer form, and called her Athene.

Her. But what do you say of Hephaestus?

Soc. Speak you of the princely lord of light (φάεος ἵστορα)?

Her. Surely.

Soc. Ἥφαιστος is Φαῖστος, and has added the η by attraction; that is obvious to anybody.

Her. That is very probable, until some more probable notion gets into your head.

Soc. To prevent that, you had better ask what is the derivation of Ares.

Her. What is Ares?

d *Soc.* Ares may be called, if you will, from his manhood (ἄρρεν) and manliness, or if you please, from his hard and unchangeable nature, which is the meaning of ἄρρατος: the latter is a derivation in every way appropriate to the god of war.

Her. Very true.

Soc. And now, by the Gods, let us have no more of the Gods, for I am afraid to discourse about them; ask about anything but them, and thou shalt see how the steeds of Euthyphro can prance.

e *Her.* Only one more god! I should like to know about

---

[1] There seems to be some error in the manuscripts. The meaning is that the word θεονόα = θεουνόα is a curtailed form of θεοῦ νόησις, but the omitted letters do not agree.

Hermes, of whom I am said not to be a true son. Let us make him out, and then I shall know whether there is any meaning in what Cratylus says.

Soc. I should imagine that the name Hermes has to do with speech, and signifies that he is the interpreter (ἑρμηνεύς), or 408 messenger, or thief, or liar, or bargainer; all that sort of thing has a great deal to do with language; as I was telling you,[1] the word εἴρειν is expressive of the use of speech, and there is an often-recurring Homeric word ἐμήσατο, which means 'he contrived'—out of these two words, εἴρειν and μήσασθαι, the legislator formed the name of the god who invented language and speech;[2] and we may imagine him dictating to us the use of this name: 'O my friends,' says he to us, 'seeing that he is the b contriver of tales or speeches, you may rightly call him Εἰρέμης.' And this has been improved by us, as we think, into Hermes. Iris also appears to have been called from the verb 'to tell' (εἴρειν), because she was a messenger.[3]

Her. Then I am very sure that Cratylus was quite right in saying that I was no true son of Hermes (Ἑρμογένης), for I am not a good hand at speeches.

Soc. There is also reason, my friend, in Pan being the double-formed son of Hermes.

Her. How do you make that out? c

Soc. You are aware that speech signifies all things (πᾶν), and is always turning them round and round, and has two forms, true and false?

Her. Certainly.

Soc. Is not the truth that is in him the smooth or sacred form which dwells above among the Gods, whereas falsehood dwells among men below, and is rough like the goat of tragedy; for tales and falsehoods have generally to do with the tragic or goatish life, and tragedy is the place of them?

Her. Very true.

Soc. Then surely Pan, who is the declarer of all things (πᾶν) and the perpetual mover (ἀεὶ πολῶν) of all things, is rightly d called αἰπόλος (goatherd), he being the two-formed son of Hermes, smooth in his upper part, and rough and goatlike in

---

[1] [398 d.]   [2] Omitting τὸ δὲ λέγειν δή ἐστιν εἴρειν.
[3] [Cf. *Theaet.* 155 d.]

his lower regions. And, as the son of Hermes, he is speech or the brother of speech, and that brother should be like brother is no marvel. But, as I was saying, my dear Hermogenes, let us get away from the gods.

Her. From these sort of gods, by all means, Socrates. But why should we not discuss another kind of gods—the sun, e moon, stars, earth, aether, air, fire, water, the seasons, and the year?

Soc. You impose a great many tasks upon me. Still, I will not refuse, if it will please you.

Her. Indeed it will.

Soc. How would you have me begin? Shall I take first of all him whom you mentioned first—the sun?

Her. Very good.

Soc. The origin of the sun will probably be clearer in the 409 Doric form, for the Dorians call him ἅλιος, and this name may perhaps be given to him because when he rises he gathers (ἁλίζοι) men together or perhaps because he is always rolling in his course (ἀεὶ εἱλεῖν ἰών) about the earth; or from αἰολεῖν, of which the meaning is the same as ποικίλλειν (to variegate), because he variegates the productions of the earth.

Her. But what is σελήνη (the moon)?

Soc. That name is rather unfortunate for Anaxagoras.

Her. How so?

b *Soc.* The word seems to forestall his recent discovery, that the moon receives her light from the sun.

Her. Why do you say so?

Soc. The two words σέλας (brightness) and φῶς (light) have much the same meaning?

Her. Yes.

Soc. This light about the moon is always new (νέον) and always old (ἔνον), if the disciples of Anaxagoras say truly. For the sun in his revolution always adds new light, and there is the old light of the previous month.

Her. Very true.

Soc. The moon is not infrequently called σελαναία.

Her. True.

Soc. And as she has a light which is always old and always c new (ἔνον νέον ἀεί), she may very properly have the name σελαενονεοάεια; and this when hammered into shape becomes σελαναία.

Her. A real dithyrambic sort of name that, Socrates. But what do you say of the month and the stars?

Soc. Μείς (month) is called from μειοῦσθαι (to lessen), because suffering diminution; the name of ἄστρα (stars) seems to be derived from ἀστραπή (blinding light), which is an improvement on ἀναστρωπή, signifying the upsetting of the eyes (ἀναστρέφειν ὦπα).

Her. What do you say of πῦρ (fire) and ὕδωρ (water)?

Soc. I am at a loss how to explain πῦρ; either the muse of d Euthyphro has deserted me, or there is some very great difficulty in the word. Please, however, to note the contrivance which I adopt whenever I am in a difficulty of this sort.

Her. What is it?

Soc. I will tell you; but I should like to know first whether you can tell me what is the meaning of the word πῦρ.

Her. Indeed I cannot.

Soc. Shall I tell you what I suspect to be the true explanation of this and several other words?—My belief is that they are of foreign origin. For the Hellenes, especially those who were under e the dominion of the barbarians, often borrowed from them.

Her. What is the inference?

Soc. Anyone who seeks to demonstrate the fitness of these names according to the Hellenic language, and not according to the language from which the words are derived, is rather likely to be at fault.

Her. Yes, certainly.

Soc. Well then, consider whether this πῦρ is not foreign; for 410 the word is not easily brought into relation with the Hellenic tongue, and the Phrygians may be observed to have the same word slightly changed, just as they have ὕδωρ (water) and κύνες (dogs), and many other words.

Her. That is true.

Soc. Any violent interpretations of the words should be avoided; for something to say about them may easily be found.[1] And thus I get rid of πῦρ and ὕδωρ. Ἀήρ (air), Hermogenes, may b be explained as the element which raises (αἴρει) things from the

---

[1] [Or: 'for by such a course they might be easily explained'.]

earth, or as ever flowing (ἀεὶ ῥεῖ), or because the flux of the air
is wind, and the poets call the winds 'air-blasts', (ἀῆται); he
who uses the term may mean, so to speak, air-flux (ἀητόρρουν),
in the sense of wind-flux (πνευματόρρουν); and because this
moving wind may be expressed by either term he employs the
word air (ἀήρ = ἀήτης ῥέω). Αἰθήρ (aether) I should interpret as
ἀειθεήρ; this may be correctly said, because this element is
always running in a flux about the air (ἀεὶ θεῖ περὶ τὸν ἀέρα ῥέων).
The meaning of the word γῆ (earth) comes out better when in
c the form of γαῖα, for the earth may be truly called 'mother'
(γαῖα, γεννήτειρα), as in the language of Homer [Od. ix. 118;
xiii. 160] γεγάασι means γεγεννῆσθαι. So far, so good. What
shall we take next?

Her. There are ὧραι (the seasons), Socrates, and the two
names of the year, ἐνιαυτός and ἔτος.

Soc. The ὧραι should be spelt in the old Attic way, if you
desire to know the probable truth about them; they are rightly
called the ὅραι because they divide (ὁρίζουσιν) the summers
and winters and winds and the fruits of the earth. The words
d ἐνιαυτός and ἔτος appear to be the same,—'that which brings
to light the plants and growths of the earth in their turn, and
passes them in review within itself (ἐν ἑαυτῷ ἐξετάζει)': this is
broken up into two words, ἐνιαυτός from ἐν ἑαυτῷ, and ἔτος
from ἐτάζει, just as the name of Ζεύς was divided, as we noticed
before, into Ζῆνα and Δία; and the whole proposition means that
this power of reviewing from within is one, but has two names,
two words ἔτος and ἐνιαυτός being thus formed out of a single
proposition.

e *Her.* Indeed, Socrates, you make surprising progress.

Soc. You think, perhaps, that these are daring flights of
wisdom.

Her. I do.

Soc. And you may soon be more inclined to say so.

411 *Her.* I should like very much to know, in the next place, how
you would explain the names given to the virtues. What principle
of correctness is there in those charming words—wisdom, understanding, justice, and the rest of them?

Soc. That is a tremendous class of names which you are dis-
interring; still, as I have put on the lion's skin, I must not be

faint of heart; and I suppose that I must consider the meaning of wisdom (φρόνησις) and understanding (σύνεσις), and judgement (γνώμη), and knowledge (ἐπιστήμη), and all those other charming b words, as you call them?

Her. Surely, we must not leave off until we find out their meaning.

Soc. By the dog of Egypt I believe that the notion which came into my head just now[1] was not ill founded; that is, that the primeval givers of names were undoubtedly like too many of our modern philosophers, who, in their search after the nature of things, are always getting dizzy from constantly going round and round, and then they imagine that the world is going round and round and moving in all directions; and this appearance, which c arises out of their own internal condition, they suppose to be a reality of nature; they think that there is nothing stable or permanent, but only flux and motion, and that the world is always full of every sort of motion and change. The consideration of the names which I mentioned has led me into making this reflection.

Her. How is that, Socrates?

Soc. Perhaps you did not observe that in the names which have just been cited, the motion or flux or generation of things is most surely indicated.

Her. No, indeed, I was hardly aware of it.

Soc. Take the first of those which you mentioned; clearly that d is a name indicative of motion.

Her. What was the name?

Soc. Φρόνησις (wisdom), which may signify φορᾶς καὶ ῥοῦ νόησις (perception of motion and flux), or perhaps φορᾶς ὄνησις (the blessing of motion), but is at any rate connected with φέρεσθαι (motion); γνώμη (judgement), again, certainly implies the ponderation or consideration (νώμησις) of generation (γονή), for to ponder is the same as to consider; or, if you would rather, here is νόησις, the very word just now mentioned, which is νέου ἕσις (the desire of the new); the word νέος implies that the world is always in process of creation. The giver of the name wanted to e express this longing of the soul, for the original name was νόεεσις, and not νόησις; but η took the place of a double ε. The word σωφροσύνη is the salvation (σωτηρία) of that wisdom (φρόνησις)

[1] [401 d.]

412 which we were just now considering. Ἐπιστήμη (knowledge) is akin to this, and indicates that the soul which is good for anything follows (ἔπεται) the motion of things, neither anticipating them nor falling behind them; wherefore the word should rather be read as ἐπεϊστήμη, inserting ε. Σύνεσις (understanding) may be regarded in like manner as a kind of inference; the word is derived from συνιέναι (to go along with), and, like ἐπίστασθαι (to

b know), implies the progression of the soul in company with the nature of things. Σοφία (wisdom) is more obscure, and appears not to be of native growth; the meaning is, touching the motion or stream of things. You must remember that the poets, when they speak of the commencement of any rapid motion, often use the word ἐσύθη (he rushed); and there was a famous Lacedaemonian who was named Σοῦς (Rush), for by this word the Lacedaemonians signify rapid motion, and the touching (ἐπαφή) of motion is expressed by σοφία, for all things are supposed to be in motion.

c Good (ἀγαθόν) is the name which is intended as a title of the admirable (ἀγαστῷ) in all nature; for, although all things move, still there are degrees of motion; some are swifter, some slower; but there are some things which are admirable for their swiftness, and this admirable part of nature is called ἀγαθόν.

Δικαιοσύνη (justice) is clearly δικαίου σύνεσις (understanding of the just); but the actual word δίκαιον is more difficult: men are only agreed to a certain extent about the word justice, and then

d they begin to disagree. For those who suppose all things to be in motion conceive the greater part of nature to be a mere receptacle; and they say that there is a penetrating power which passes through all this, and is the instrument of creation in all, and is the subtlest and swiftest element; for if it were not the subtlest, and a power which none can keep out, and also the swiftest, passing by other things as if they were standing still, it could not penetrate through the moving universe. And this element, which

e superintends all things because it can pierce (διαϊόν) all, is rightly called δίκαιον; the letter κ is only added for the sake of euphony. Thus far, as I was saying, there is agreement among

413 many about the meaning of 'justice'; but I, Hermogenes, have been so persistent in my inquiry that I have learnt the whole truth as a secret, namely, that this justice of which I am speaking is also the cause: for a cause is that through which anything

comes into existence; and someone comes and whispers[1] in my
ear that justice is rightly so called because partaking of the nature
of the cause. But when I begin, after hearing what they have said,
to interrogate them gently: 'Well, my excellent friend, on your
assumption, what is it that is just?', they think that I ask tiresome
questions, and am leaping over the barriers, and have been
already sufficiently answered, and now, in their endeavour to b
satisfy me, they give various and discordant accounts. For one of
them says that justice is the sun, and that he only is the piercing
(διαϊόντα) and burning (κάοντα) element which is the guardian
of nature. And when I joyfully repeat this beautiful notion to
another, he answers with the satirical remark, 'What, is there no
justice in the world when the sun is down?' And when I earnestly
beg my questioner to tell me his own honest opinion about the c
same point, he says, 'Fire'; but this is not very intelligible.
Another says, 'No, not mere fire, but the element of heat in fire'.
Another man professes to laugh at them all, and says that justice
must, according to the doctrine of Anaxagoras, be mind, for
mind, as he says, has absolute power, and mixes with nothing,
and orders all things, and passes through all things. At last, my
friend, I find myself in far greater perplexity about the nature of
justice than I was before I began to learn. But still I am of
opinion that the name, which has led me into this digression, was d
given to justice for the reasons which I have mentioned.

Her. I think, Socrates, that you are not improvising now; you
must have heard this from someone else.

Soc. And not the rest?

Her. Hardly.

Soc. Well, then, let me go on in the hope of making you
believe in the originality of the rest. What remains after justice?
I do not think that we have as yet discussed courage (ἀνδρεία),—
injustice (ἀδικία), which is obviously nothing more than a hin- e
drance to the penetrating principle (διαϊόντος), need not be
considered. Well, then, the name of ἀνδρεία seems to imply a
battle;—this battle is in the world of existence, and according
to the doctrine of flux is only the counterflux (ἐναντία ῥοή): if
you extract the δ from ἀνδρεία, the name at once signifies the

[1] [Or, reading Δία for ἰδίᾳ, with Hermann: 'And someone has said that Zeus
is rightly named for this reason.']

thing, and you may clearly understand that ἀνδρεία is not the stream opposed to every stream, but only to that which is contrary to justice, for otherwise courage would not have been praised. The words ἄρρην (male) and ἀνήρ (man) also contain a similar allusion to the same principle of the upward flux (τῇ ἄνω ῥοῇ). Γυνή (woman) I suspect to be the same word as γονή (birth): θῆλυ (female) appears to be partly derived from θηλή (the teat), because the teat is like rain, and makes things flourish (τεθηλέναι).

Her. That is surely probable.

Soc. Yes; and the very word θάλλειν (to flourish) seems to figure the growth of youth, which is swift and sudden ever. And this is expressed by the legislator in the name, which is a compound of θεῖν (running), and ἄλλεσθαι (leaping). Pray observe how I gallop away when I get on smooth ground. There are a good many names generally thought to be of importance, which have still to be explained.

Her. True.

Soc. There is the meaning of the word τέχνη (art), for example.

Her. Very true.

Soc. That may be identified with ἐχονόη, and expresses the possession of mind: you have only to take away the τ and insert two o's, one between the χ and ν, and another between the ν and η.

Her. Your hunger for letters increases, Socrates.[1]

Soc. Yes, my dear friend; but then you know that the original names have been long ago buried and disguised by people sticking on and stripping off letters for the sake of euphony, and twisting and bedizening them in all sorts of ways: and time too may have had a share in the change. Take, for example, the word κάτοπτρον; why is the letter ρ inserted? This must surely be the addition of someone who cares nothing about the truth, but thinks only of putting the mouth into shape. And the additions are often such that at last no human being can possibly make out the original meaning of the word. Another example is the word σφίγξ, σφιγγός, which ought properly to be φίγξ, φιγγός, and there are other examples.

Her. That is quite true, Socrates.

Soc. And yet, if you are permitted to put in and pull out any

---

[1] [Cf. 455 c.]

letters which you please, names will be too easily made, and any name may be adapted to any object.

Her. True.   e

Soc. Yes, that is true. And therefore a wise dictator, like yourself, should observe the laws of moderation and probability.

Her. Such is my desire.

Soc. And mine, too, Hermogenes. But do not be too much of a precisian, or 'you will unnerve me of my strength'.[1] When you 415 have allowed me to add μηχανή (contrivance) to τέχνη (art) I shall be at the top of my bent, for I conceive μηχανή to be a sign of great accomplishment—ἄνειν; for μῆκος has the meaning of greatness, and these two, μῆκος and ἄνειν, make up the word μηχανή. But, as I was saying, being now at the top of my bent, I should like to consider the meaning of the two words ἀρετή (virtue) and κακία (vice); ἀρετή I do not as yet understand, but b κακία is transparent, and agrees with the principles which preceded, for all things being in a flux (ἰόντων), κακία is κακῶς ἰόν (going badly); and this evil motion when existing in the soul has the general name of κακία, or vice, specially appropriated to it. The meaning of κακῶς ἰέναι may be further illustrated by the use of δειλία (cowardice), which ought to have come after ἀνδρεία, c but was forgotten, and, as I fear, is not the only word which has been passed over. Δειλία signifies that the soul is bound with a strong chain (δεσμός), for λίαν means strength, and therefore δειλία expresses the greatest and strongest bond of the soul; and ἀπορία (difficulty) is an evil of the same nature (from a not, and πορεύεσθαι to go), like anything else which is an impediment to walking and movement. Then the word κακία appears to mean κακῶς ἰέναι, or going badly, or limping and halting; of which the consequence is, that the soul becomes filled with vice. And if κακία is the name of this sort of thing, ἀρετή will be the opposite of it, signifying in the first place ease of motion, then that the d stream of the good soul is unimpeded, and has therefore the attribute of ever flowing without let or hindrance, and is therefore called ἀρετή, or, more correctly, ἀειρειτή (ever-flowing), and may perhaps have had another form, αἱρετή (eligible), indicating that nothing is more eligible than virtue, and this has been hammered into ἀρετή. I daresay that you will deem this to be another

[1] *Il.* vi. 265.

invention of mine, but I think that if the previous word κακία was right, then ἀρετή is also right.

416   *Her.* But what is the meaning of κακόν, which has played so great a part in your previous discourse?

Soc. That is a very singular word about which I can hardly form an opinion, and therefore I must have recourse to my ingenious device.

Her. What device?

Soc. The device of a foreign origin, which I shall give to this word also.

Her. Very likely you are right; but suppose that we leave these words, and endeavour to see the rationale of καλόν and αἰσχρόν.

Soc. The meaning of αἰσχρόν is evident, being only ἀεὶ ἴσχον
b ῥοῆς (always preventing from flowing), and this is in accordance with our former derivations. For the name-giver was, I think, always a harsh critic of anything which tends to stagnation, and hence he gave the name ἀεισχοροῦν to that which hindered the flux (ἀεὶ ἴσχον ῥοῦν), and this is now beaten together into αἰσχρόν.

Her. But what do you say of καλόν?

Soc. That is more obscure; yet it speaks for itself; it has merely been altered by composition and lengthening of the o.

Her. What do you mean?

Soc. This name appears to denote mind.

Her. How so?

c   *Soc.* Let me ask you what is the cause why anything has a name; is not the principle which imposes the name the cause?

Her. Certainly.

Soc. And must not this be the mind of Gods, or of men, or of both?

Her. Yes.

Soc. And that which called (καλέσαν) and calls (καλοῦν) things by their names, is, once again, the mind?

Her. So it seems.

Soc. And are not the works of intelligence and mind worthy of praise, and are not other works worthy of blame?

Her. Certainly.

d   *Soc.* Physic does the work of a physician, and carpentering does the works of a carpenter?

Her. Exactly.

Soc. And the principle of beauty does the works of beauty?[1]

Her. Of course.

Soc. And that principle we affirm to be mind?

Her. Very true.

Soc. Then wisdom is rightly called beauty because she does the works which we recognize and speak of as the beautiful?

Her. That is evident.

Soc. What more names remain to us?　　　　　　　　　　　　e

Her. There are the words which are connected with ἀγαθόν and καλόν, such as συμφέρον and λυσιτελοῦν, ὠφέλιμον, κερδαλέον, 417 and their opposites.

Soc. The meaning of συμφέρον (expedient) I think that you may discover for yourself by the light of the previous examples,—for it is a sister word to ἐπιστήμη, meaning just the motion (φορά) of the soul accompanying the world, and things which are done upon this principle are probably called σύμφορα or συμφέροντα, because they are carried round with the world. Again, κερδαλέον (gainful) is called from κέρδος (gain), but you must alter the δ　b into ν if you want to get at the meaning; for this word also signifies good, but in another way; he who gave the name intended to express the power of admixture (κεραννύμενον) and universal penetration in the good; in forming the word, however, he inserted a δ instead of a ν, and so made κέρδος.

Her. Well, but what is λυσιτελοῦν (profitable)?

Soc. I suppose, Hermogenes, that the legislator did not use this word, as retailers do, to describe that which repays the cost (λύει τὰ τέλη); he regarded the profitable (λυσιτελοῦν) as that which, c being the swiftest thing in existence, allows of no stay in things and no pause or end of motion, but always, if there begins to be any end, lets things go again (λύει), and makes motion immortal and unceasing: and from this point of view, as appears to me, the good was happily denominated λυσιτελοῦν—being that which looses (λύον) the end (τέλος) of motion. Ὠφέλιμον (the advantageous) is derived from ὀφέλλειν, meaning that which creates[2] and increases; this latter is a common Homeric word, and has a foreign character.

---

[1] [Burnet's emendation of καλόν in 416 d 4 to καλοῦν does not improve the argument; but there is some play on the words καλόν (beautiful) and καλοῦν (calling).]

[2] [Text uncertain: perhaps 'increases and fattens'.]

d   *Her.* And what do you say of their opposites?

Soc. Of such as are mere negatives I hardly think that I need speak.

Her. Which are they?

Soc. The words ἀξύμφορον (inexpedient), ἀνωφελές (unprofitable), ἀλυσιτελές (unadvantageous), ἀκερδές (ungainful).

Her. True.

Soc. I would rather take the words βλαβερόν (harmful), ζημιῶδες (hurtful).

Her. Good.

Soc. The word βλαβερόν is that which is said to hinder or
e   harm (βλάπτειν) the stream (ῥοῦν); βλάπτον is βουλόμενον ἅπτειν (seeking to hold or bind); for ἅπτειν is the same as δεῖν, and δεῖν is always a term of censure; βουλόμενον ἅπτειν ῥοῦν (wanting to bind the stream) would properly be βουλαπτεροῦν, and this, as I imagine, is improved into βλαβερόν.

Her. You bring out curious results, Socrates, in the derivation of names; and when I hear the word βουλαπτεροῦν I cannot help imagining that you are making your mouth into a flute, and
418 puffing away at some prelude to Athene.

Soc. That is the fault of the makers of the name, Hermogenes; not mine.

Her. Very true; but what is the derivation of ζημιῶδες?

Soc. What is the meaning of ζημιῶδες?—let me remark, Hermogenes, how right I was in saying that great changes are made in the meaning of words by putting in and pulling out letters; even a very slight permutation will sometimes give an
b   entirely opposite sense; I may instance the word δέον, which occurs to me at the moment, and reminds me of what I was going to say to you, that the fine fashionable language of modern times has twisted and disguised and entirely altered the original meaning both of δέον, and also of ζημιῶδες, which in the old language is clearly indicated.

Her. What do you mean?

Soc. I will try to explain. You are aware that our forefathers loved the sounds ι and δ, especially the women, who are most
c   conservative of the ancient language, but now they change ι into η or ε, and δ into ζ; this is supposed to increase the grandeur of the sound.

Her. How do you mean?

Soc. For example, in very ancient times they called the day either ἱμέρα or ἑμέρα, which is called by us ἡμέρα.

Her. That is true.

Soc. Do you observe that only the ancient form shows the intention of the giver of the name? of which the reason is, that men long for (ἱμείρουσι) and love the light which comes after the d darkness, and is therefore called ἱμέρα, from ἵμερος, desire.

Her. Clearly.

Soc. But now the name is so travestied that you cannot tell the meaning, although there are some who imagine the day to be called ἡμέρα because it makes things gentle (ἥμερα).[1]

Her. Such is my view.

Soc. And do you know that the ancients said δυογόν and not ζυγόν?

Her. They did so.

Soc. And ζυγόν (yoke) has no meaning,—it ought to be δυογόν, which word expresses the binding of two together (δυεῖν ἀγωγή) e for the purpose of drawing;—this has been changed into ζυγόν, and there are many other examples of similar changes.

Her. There are.

Soc. Proceeding in the same train of thought I may remark that the word δέον (obligation) has a meaning which is the opposite of all the other appellations of good; for δέον is here a species of good, and is, nevertheless, the chain (δεσμός) or hinderer of motion, and therefore own brother of βλαβερόν.

Her. Indeed, Socrates, it appears so.

Soc. Not if you restore the ancient form, which is more likely to be the correct one, and read διόν instead of δέον; if you convert 419 the ε into an ι after the old fashion, this word will then agree with other words meaning good; for δίον, not δέον, then signifies the good, and is a term of praise; and the author of names has not contradicted himself, but in all these various appellations, δέον (obligatory), ὠφέλιμον (advantageous), λυσιτελοῦν (profitable), κερδαλέον (gainful), ἀγαθόν (good), συμφέρον (expedient), εὔπορον (plenteous), the same conception is implied of the ordering or all-pervading principle which is praised, and the restraining and

---

[1] [As at *Tim.* 45 b, where ἡμέρα, day, is derived from φῶς ἥμερον, gentle light.]

b binding principle which is censured. And this is further illustrated
by the word ζημιώδης (hurtful), which if the ζ is only changed
into δ as in the ancient language, becomes δημιώδης; and this
name, as you will perceive, is given to that which binds motion
(δοῦντι ἰόν).

Her. What do you say of ἡδονή (pleasure), λύπη (pain), ἐπιθυμία (desire), and the like, Socrates?

Soc. I do not think, Hermogenes, that there is any great difficulty about them—ἡδονή looks like a name for the action which
tends to advantage (ὄνησις); and the original form may be supposed to have been ἠονή, but this has been altered by the insertion
c of the δ. Λύπη appears to be derived from the relaxation (λύειν)
which the body feels when in sorrow; ἀνία (trouble) is the
hindrance of motion (ἀ and ἰέναι); ἀλγηδών (distress), if I am
not mistaken, is a foreign word, which is derived from ἀλγεινός
(grievous); ὀδύνη (grief) is called from the putting on (ἔνδυσις)
sorrow; in ἀχθηδών (vexation) 'the word too labours', as anyone
may see; χαρά (joy) is the very expression of the fluency and
diffusion of the soul (χέω); τέρψις (delight) is so called from the
d pleasure creeping (ἕρπον) through the soul, which may be likened
to a breath (πνοή) and is properly ἑρπνοῦν, but has been altered
by time into τερπνόν; εὐφροσύνη (cheerfulness) and ἐπιθυμία explain themselves; the former, which ought to be εὐφεροσύνη and
has been changed into εὐφροσύνη, is named, as everyone may see,
from the soul moving (φέρεσθαι) in harmony with nature; ἐπιθυμία is really ἡ ἐπὶ τὸν θυμὸν ἰοῦσα δύναμις, the power which enters
e into the soul; θυμός (passion) is probably called from the rushing
(θύσεως) and boiling of the soul; ἵμερος (desire) denotes the
stream (ῥοῦς) which most draws the soul διὰ τὴν ἕσιν τῆς ῥοῆς—
because flowing with desire (ἱέμενος ῥεῖ), and expresses a longing
420 after things and violent attraction of the soul to them, and is
termed ἵμερος from possessing this power; πόθος (longing) is
expressive of the desire of that which is not present but absent,
and in another place (που); this is the reason why the name πόθος
is applied to things absent, as ἵμερος is to things present; ἔρως
(love) is so called because flowing in (ἐσρῶν) from without; the
stream is not inherent in those affected, but is an influence intro-
b duced through the eyes, and from flowing in was called ἔσρος
(influx) in the old time when they used o for ω, and is called

ἔρως, now that ω is substituted for o. But why do you not give me
another word?

Her. What do you think of δόξα (opinion), and that class of
words?

Soc. Δόξα is either derived from δίωξις (pursuit), and expresses
the march of the soul in the pursuit of knowledge, or from the
shooting of a bow (τόξον); the latter is more likely, and is confirmed by οἴησις (thinking), which is only οἶσις[1] (moving), and c
implies the movement of the soul to the essential nature of each
thing—just as βουλή (counsel) has to do with shooting (βολή); and
βούλεσθαι (to wish) combines the notion of aiming and deliberat-
ing—all these words seem to follow δόξα, and all involve the idea
of shooting, just as ἀβουλία, absence of counsel, on the other hand,
is a mishap, or missing, or mistaking of the mark, or aim, or
proposal, or object.

Her. You are quickening your pace now, Socrates.   d

Soc. Why yes, I am in the last lap of the race; but I have still
to deal with ἀνάγκη (necessity), which ought to come next,
and ἑκούσιον (the voluntary). Ἑκούσιον is certainly the yielding
(εἶκον) and unresisting—the notion implied is yielding and not
opposing, yielding, as I was just now saying, to that motion
which is in accordance with our will; but the necessary and
resistant being contrary to our will, implies error and ignorance;
the idea is taken from walking through a ravine which is impassable, and rugged, and overgrown, and impedes motion—   e
and this is the derivation of the word ἀναγκαῖον (necessary) ἀν᾽
ἄγκη ἰόν, going through a ravine. But while my strength lasts let
us persevere, and I hope that you will persevere with your
questions.

Her. Well, then, let me ask about the greatest and noblest, 421
such as ἀλήθεια (truth) and ψεῦδος (falsehood) and ὄν (being), not
forgetting to inquire why the word ὄνομα (name), which is the
theme of our discussion, has this name of ὄνομα.

Soc. You know the word μαίεσθαι (to seek)?

Her. Yes;—meaning the same as ζητεῖν (to inquire).

Soc. The word ὄνομα seems to be a compressed sentence,
signifying that the object for which there is a search, is a name;

[1] [This word should perhaps be accented ὄισις, 'shooting, as at a target', with
reference to the metaphor of the bow which has just been used.]

as is still more obvious in ὀνομαστόν (notable), which states in so many words that real existence is that for which there is a seeking

b (ὃν οὗ μάσμα); ἀλήθεια is also an agglomeration of θεία ἄλη (divine wandering), implying the divine motion of existence; ψεῦδος (falsehood) is the opposite of motion; here is another ill name given by the legislator to stagnation and forced inaction, which he compares to sleep (εὕδειν); but the original meaning of the word is disguised by the addition of ψ; ὄν and οὐσία are ἰόν with an ἰ broken off; this agrees with the true principle, for being (ὄν) is also moving (ἰόν), and the same may be said of not being, which

c is likewise called not going (οὐκίον or οὐκὶ ὄν = οὐκ ἰόν).

Her. You have hammered away manfully, Socrates, at these names; but suppose that someone were to say to you, What of such words as ἰόν and ῥέον and δοῦν?—show me their fitness.

Soc. You mean to say, how should I answer him?

Her. Yes.

Soc. One way of giving the appearance of an answer has been already suggested.

Her. What way?

Soc. To say that names which we do not understand are of

d foreign origin; and something of this kind may be true of many of them. In other cases the original forms of words may have been lost in the lapse of ages; names have been so twisted in all manner of ways, that we need not be surprised if the old language when compared with that now in use would appear to us to be a barbarous tongue.

Her. Very likely.

Soc. Yes, very likely. But still the inquiry demands our earnest attention and we must not flinch. For we should remember, that if a person goes on analysing names into words, and inquiring also

e into the elements out of which the words are formed, and keeps on always repeating this process, he who has to answer him must at last give up the inquiry in despair.

Her. Very true.

422   *Soc.* And at what point ought he to lose heart and give up the inquiry? Must he not stop when he comes to the names which are the elements of all other names and sentences? for these cannot fairly be supposed to be made up of other names. The word ἀγαθόν (good), for example, is, as we were saying, a com-

pound of ἀγαστός (admirable) and θοός (swift). And we should perhaps declare that θοός is made up of other elements, and these again of others. But if, in the end, we obtain something which is b incapable of further resolution, then we shall be right in saying that we have at last reached a primary element, which we are no longer obliged to resolve into other names.

Her. I believe you to be in the right.

Soc. And suppose the names about which you are now asking should turn out to be primary elements, must not their correctness be tested according to some new method?

Her. Very likely.

Soc. Quite so, Hermogenes; all that has preceded seems to converge upon this point. If this impression is correct, as I think c it is, then I shall again say to you, come and help me, that I may not fall into some absurdity in stating the principle of primary names.

Her. Let me hear, and I will do my best to assist you.

Soc. I think that you will acknowledge with me, that one principle is applicable to all names, from the simplest to the most complex—when they are regarded simply as names, there is no difference in them.

Her. I will.

Soc. But now in the explanation which we have just completed, d names were judged correct according to their power to show what each thing is like.

Her. Of course.

Soc. And that this is characteristic of the primary quite as much as of the secondary names, is implied in their being names.

Her. Surely.

Soc. But the secondary, as I conceive, derive their significance from the primary.

Her. So it seems.

Soc. Very good; but then how do the primary names which are not founded upon others show the natures of things, as far as they can be shown; which they must do, if they are to be real e names? And here I will ask you a question: Suppose that we had no voice or tongue, and wanted to indicate objects to one another, should we not, like the deaf and dumb, make signs with the hands and head and the rest of the body?

Her. There would be no choice, Socrates.

423   *Soc.* We should imitate the nature of the thing; the elevation of our hands to heaven would mean lightness and upwardness; heaviness and downwardness would be expressed by letting them drop to the ground; if we were describing the running of a horse, or any other animal, we should make our bodies and their gestures as like as we could to them.

Her. Yes, we should have been obliged to do as you say.

Soc. We should have had to take this course, I suppose, in
b order to indicate anything with the body; it must imitate the thing to which it would refer.

Her. Very true.

Soc. And so when we want to express something with the voice, or tongue, or mouth, the expression will be achieved by imitation, through one of these organs, of that which we want to express?

Her. It must be so, I think.

Soc. Then a name is, it seems, a vocal imitation of any object; and a man is said to *name* any object when he imitates it with the voice.

Her. I think so.

c   *Soc.* Nay, my friend, I am disposed to think that we have not reached the truth as yet.

Her. Why not?

Soc. Because if we have we shall be obliged to admit that the people who imitate sheep, or cocks, or other animals, name that which they imitate.

Her. Quite true.

Soc. Then could I have been right in what I was saying?

Her. In my opinion, no. But I wish that you would tell me, Socrates, what sort of an imitation is a name?

Soc. In the first place, I should reply, not a musical imitation,
d although that is also vocal; nor, again, an imitation of what music imitates; these, in my judgement, would not be naming. Let me put the matter as follows: All objects have sound and figure, and many have colour?

Her. Certainly.

Soc. But the art of naming appears not to be concerned with imitations of this kind; the arts which have to do with them are music and drawing?

Her. True.

Soc. Again, is there not in our opinion an essence of each thing, e just as there is a colour, or sound? Firstly, is there not an essence of colour and sound themselves as well as of anything else?

Her. I should think so.

Soc. Well, and if anyone could express that essence of each thing in letters and syllables, would he not express the real nature of each thing?

Her. Quite so.   424

Soc. The musician and the painter were the two names which you gave to the two other imitators. What will this imitator be called?

Her. I imagine, Socrates, that he must be the namer, or name-giver, of whom we are in search.

Soc. If this is true, then I think that we are in a condition to consider the names ῥοή (stream), ἰέναι (to go), σχέσις (retention), about which you were asking; and we may see whether the namer has grasped the nature of them in letters and syllables in b such a manner as to give a faithful rendering of the essence or not.

Her. Very good.

Soc. But are these the only primary names, or are there others?

Her. There must be others.

Soc. So I should expect. But from what kind of analysis does the imitator begin? Since it is assumed that he has to imitate the essence by syllables and letters, would it not be correct for him first to separate the letters, just as those who are propounding a c theory of rhythm first distinguish the values of elementary, and then of compound sounds, and when they have done so, but not before, they proceed to the consideration of rhythms?

Her. Yes.

Soc. Must we not begin in the same way with letters? first separating the vowels, and then classifying the consonants and mutes,[1] according to the received terminology of the learned; also the semivowels, which are neither vowels, nor yet mutes; and distinguishing into classes the vowels themselves. And having perfected this classification, we must turn our attention to all d those existing things[2] which are to receive names, and see whether,

---

[1] Letters which are neither vowels nor semivowels.
[2] [Retaining τὰ ὄντα in the text.]

as in the case of letters, there are any classes to which they may be all referred;[1] and hence we shall see their natures, and see, too, whether they have in them classes as there are in the letters; and when we have well considered all this, we must understand how to apply them to what they resemble—whether one letter is used to denote one thing, or whether there is to be an admixture of several of them; just as, in painting, the painter who wants to depict anything sometimes uses purple only, or any other colour, e and sometimes mixes up several colours, as his method is when he has to paint flesh colour or anything of that kind—he uses his colours as his figures appear to require them; and so, too, we shall apply letters to the expression of objects, either single letters when required, or several letters; and so we shall form syllables, as they are called, and from a compound of syllables make nouns 425 and verbs; and thus, at last, from the combinations of nouns and verbs arrive at language, large and fair and whole; and as the painter made a figure, even so shall we make speech by the art of the namer or the rhetorician, or however it should be termed. Not that I am literally speaking of ourselves, but I was carried away—meaning to say that this was the way in which (not we but) the ancients formed language, and what they put together we must take to pieces in like manner, if we are to attain a scientific view of the whole subject; and we must see whether the b primary, and also whether the secondary elements are rightly given or not, for if they are not, the composition of them, my dear Hermogenes, will be a sorry piece of work, and in the wrong direction.

Her. That, Socrates, I can quite believe.

Soc. Well, but do you suppose that you will be able to analyse them in this way? for I am certain that I should not.

Her. Much less am I likely to be able.

Soc. Shall we leave them, then? or shall we seek to discover, if we can, something about them, according to the measure of our c ability, saying by way of preface, as I said before of the Gods, that of the truth about them we know nothing, and do but entertain human notions of them. And in this present inquiry, let us say to ourselves, before we proceed, that the higher method is the one which we or others who would analyse language to any good

[1] Cf. *Phaedrus*, 271.

purpose[1] must follow; but under the circumstances, as men say, we must do as well as we can. What do you think?

Her. I very much approve.

Soc. That objects should be imitated in letters and syllables, d and so find expression, may appear ridiculous, Hermogenes, but it cannot be avoided—there is no better principle to which we can look for the truth of first names. Deprived of this, we must have recourse to divine help, like the tragic poets, who in any perplexity have their gods waiting in the air; and must get out of our difficulty in like fashion, by saying that 'the Gods gave the first names, and therefore they are right'. Will this be the best con- e trivance—or should it be said that we have derived them from some barbarous people, and that the barbarians are older than we are? or that antiquity has cast a veil over them, which is the same sort of excuse as the last? No! all these are not reasons but 426 only ingenious excuses for failure to explain in what respect the primary names have been properly imposed. And yet any sort of ignorance of these names involves an ignorance of secondary words; for one would be reduced to explaining these from elements of which he knows nothing. Clearly then the professor of the science of language should be able to give a very lucid explanation of first names, or let him be assured he will only talk b nonsense about the rest. Do you not suppose this to be true?

Her. Certainly, Socrates.

Soc. My first notions of original names are truly wild and ridiculous, though I have no objection to imparting them to you if you desire, and I hope that you will communicate to me in return anything better which you may have.

Her. Fear not; I will do my best.

Soc. In the first place, the letter ρ appears to me to be the general c instrument expressing all motion (κίνησις). But I have not yet explained the meaning of this latter word, which is just ἴεσις[2] (going); for the letter η was not in use among the ancients, who only employed ε; and the root is κίειν, which is a foreign form, the same as ἰέναι. And the old word κίνησις will be correctly given

---

[1] [Retaining χρηστόν at 425 c 4, in place of the emendation χρῆν, which is adopted by Burnet.]

[2] [A better reading than ἔσις, which is adopted here and at c 7 in the Oxford Greek text.]

as ἴεσις in corresponding modern letters. Assuming this foreign
root κίειν, and allowing for the change of the η and the insertion
d of the ν, we have κίνησις, which should have been κιείνησις or
εἶσις; and στᾶσις[1] is the negative of ἰέναι (or εἶσις), and has been
improved into στάσις. Now the letter ρ, as I was saying, appeared
to the imposer of names an excellent instrument for the expression
of motion; and he frequently uses the letter for this purpose: for
example, in the actual words ρεῖν and ροή he represents motion
by ρ; also in the words τρόμος (trembling), τραχύς (rugged); and
e again, in words such as κρούειν (strike), θραύειν (crush), ἐρείκειν
(bruise), θρύπτειν (break), κερματίζειν (crumble), ῥυμβεῖν (whirl):
of all these sorts of movements he generally finds an expression in
the letter R, because, as I imagine, he had observed that the
tongue was most agitated and least at rest in the pronunciation
of this letter, which he therefore used in order to express motion,
just as by the letter ι he expresses the subtle elements which pass
through all things. This is why he uses the letter ι as imitative of
427 motion, ἰέναι, ἴεσθαι. And there is another class of letters, φ, ψ, σ
and ζ, of which the pronunciation is accompanied by great
expenditure of breath; these are used in the imitation of such
notions as ψυχρόν (shivering), ζέον (seething), σείεσθαι (to be
shaken), σεισμός (shock), and are always introduced by the giver
of names when he wants to imitate what is φυσῶδες (windy). He
b seems to have thought that the closing and pressure of the tongue
in the utterance of δ and τ was expressive of binding and rest in a
place: he further observed the liquid movement of λ, in the
pronunciation of which the tongue slips, and in this he found the
expression of smoothness, as in λεῖος (level), and in the word
ὀλισθάνειν (to slip) itself, λιπαρόν (sleek), in the word κολλῶδες
(gluey), and the like: the heavier sound of γ detained the slipping
tongue, and the union of the two gave the notion of a glutinous
clammy nature, as in γλίσχρος, γλυκύς, γλοιῶδες. The ν he ob-
c served to be sounded from within, and therefore to have a notion
of inwardness; hence he introduced the sound in ἔνδον and ἐντός:
α he assigned to the expression of size, and η of length, because
they are great letters: ο was the sign of roundness, and therefore
there is plenty of ο mixed up in the word γογγύλον (round). And,
in general, by this kind of adaptation, sometimes of letters, and

[1 The word should probably be so accented in 426 d 1.]

sometimes of whole syllables, the legislator seems to have created signs and names for every existing thing; and from these he proceeded to design compounds in order to perfect his imitation. That is my view, Hermogenes, of the truth of names; but I d should like to hear what Cratylus has more to say.

Her. But, Socrates, as I was telling you before, Cratylus has often greatly mystified me; he says that there is a fitness of names, but he never explains what is this fitness, so that I cannot tell whether his obscurity whenever this subject is raised is intended or not. Tell me now, Cratylus, here in the presence of Socrates, e do you agree in what Socrates has been saying about names, or have you something better of your own? and if you have, tell me what your view is, and then you will either learn of Socrates, or Socrates and I will learn of you.

Crat. Well, but surely, Hermogenes, you do not suppose that you can learn, or I explain, any subject of importance all in a moment; at any rate, not such a subject as language, which is, perhaps, the very greatest of all.

Her. No, indeed; but, as Hesiod says, and I agree with him, 428 'to add little to little' is worth while. And, therefore, if you think that you can add anything at all, however small, to our knowledge, do not flinch, but oblige Socrates, and me too, who certainly have a claim upon you.

Soc. I am by no means positive, Cratylus, in the view which Hermogenes and myself have worked out; and therefore do not hesitate to say what you think, which if it be better than my own view I shall gladly accept. And I should not be at all surprised to b find that you have found some better notion. For you have evidently reflected on these matters and have had teachers, and if you have really a better theory of the truth of names, you may count me in the number of your disciples.

Crat. You are right, Socrates, in saying that I have made a study of these matters, and I might possibly convert you into a disciple. But I fear that the opposite is more probable, and I c already find myself moved to say to you what Achilles in the 'Prayers' says to Ajax,—

Illustrious Ajax, son of Telamon, lord of the people,
You appear to have spoken in all things much to my mind.

And you, Socrates, appear to me to be an oracle, and to give answers much to my mind, whether you are inspired by Euthyphro, or whether some Muse may have long been an inhabitant of your breast, unconsciously to yourself.

d *Soc.* Excellent Cratylus, I have long been wondering at my own wisdom, finding it beyond belief. And I think that I ought to stop and ask myself, What am I saying? for there is nothing worse than self-deception—when the deceiver is always at home and always with you—it is quite terrible, and therefore I ought often to retrace my steps and endeavour to 'look fore and aft', in the words of the aforesaid Homer. And now let me see; where

e are we? Have we not been saying that the correct name indicates the nature of the thing:—has this proposition been sufficiently proven?

Crat. Yes, Socrates, it has in my opinion been well established.

Soc. Names, then, are given in order to instruct?

Crat. Certainly.

Soc. And naming is an art, and has artificers?

Crat. Yes.

Soc. And who are they?

429 *Crat.* The legislators, as you declared at first.

Soc. And does this art grow up among men like other arts? Let me explain what I mean: of painters, some are better and some worse?

Crat. Yes.

Soc. The better painters execute their works, I mean their figures, better, and the worse execute them worse; and of builders also, the better sort build fairer houses, and the worse build them worse.

Crat. True.

b *Soc.* And among legislators likewise, there are some who do their work better and some worse?

Crat. No; there I do not agree with you.

Soc. Then you do not think that some laws are better and others worse?

Crat. No, indeed.

Soc. Nor is one name, I suppose, in your opinion, more properly imposed than another?

Crat. Certainly not.

Soc. Then all names are rightly imposed?

Crat. Yes, if they are names at all.

Soc. Well, what do you say to the name of our friend Hermo- c
genes, which was mentioned before:—assuming that he has
nothing of the nature of Hermes in him, shall we say that this is
a wrong name, or not his name at all?

Crat. I should reply that Hermogenes is not his name at all,
but only appears to be his, and is really the name of somebody
else, who has the nature which corresponds to it.

Soc. Must we not add that one who calls him Hermogenes,
does not speak falsely? For there may well be a doubt whether
you can call him Hermogenes, if he is not.

Crat. What do you mean?

Soc. Does your statement amount to this, that it is altogether d
impossible to speak falsely? For there are many who say this, my
dear Cratylus, and there have been many in the past.

Crat. Why, Socrates, how can a man say that which is not?—
say something and yet say nothing? For is not falsehood saying
the thing which is not?

Soc. Your argument, friend, is too subtle for a man of my age.
But I should like to know whether you are one of those philosophers who think that falsehood may be spoken but not said? e

Crat. Neither spoken nor said.

Soc. Nor uttered nor addressed? For example: If a person,
saluting you in a foreign country, were to take your hand and
say: 'Hail, Athenian stranger, Hermogenes, son of Smicrion'—
these words, whether spoken, said, uttered, or addressed, would
have no application to you but only to our friend Hermogenes, or
perhaps to nobody at all?

Crat. In my opinion, Socrates, the speaker would only be
talking nonsense.

Soc. Well, but that will be quite enough for me, if you will 430
tell me whether the nonsense would be true or false, or partly
true and partly false; for even that would be enough.

Crat. I should say that he would be putting himself in motion
to no purpose; and that his words would be an unmeaning sound
like the noise of hammering at a brazen pot.

Soc. But let us see, Cratylus, whether we cannot find a meeting-
point, for you would admit that the name is not the same with the
thing named?

Crat. I should.

b　*Soc.* And would you further acknowledge that the name is an imitation of the thing?

Crat. Certainly.

Soc. And you would say that pictures are also imitations of things, but in another way?

Crat. Yes.

Soc. I believe you may be right, but I do not rightly understand you. Please to say, then, whether both sorts of imitation (I mean both pictures or words) are not equally attributable and applicable to the things of which they are the imitation.

c　*Crat.* They are.

Soc. First look at the matter thus: one might attribute the likeness of the man to the man, and of the woman to the woman; and so on?

Crat. Certainly.

Soc. And conversely one might attribute the likeness of the man to the woman, and of the woman to the man?

Crat. Very true.

Soc. And are both modes of assigning them right, or only the first?

Crat. Only the first.

Soc. That is to say, the mode of assignment which attributes to each that which belongs to them and is like them?

Crat. That is my view.

d　*Soc.* Now then, as I am desirous that we being friends should have a good understanding about the argument, let me state my view to you: the first mode of assignment, whether applied to figures or to names, I call right, and when applied to names only, true as well as right; and the other mode, whereby that which is unlike is given or assigned, I call wrong, and in the case of names, false as well as wrong.

Crat. I suggest that may be true, Socrates, in the case of pictures; they may be wrongly assigned; but not in the case of
e　names—they must necessarily be always right.

Soc. Why, what is the difference? May I not go to a man and say to him, 'This is your picture', showing him his own likeness, or perhaps the likeness of a woman; and when I say 'show', I mean bring before the sense of sight.

Crat. Certainly.

Soc. And may I not go to him again, and say, 'This is your name'?—for the name, like the picture, is an imitation. May I 431 not say to him—'This is your name'? and may I not then bring to his sense of hearing the imitation of himself, when I say, 'This is a man'; or of a female of the human species, when I say, 'This is a woman', as the case may be? Is not all that possible—does it not sometimes happen?

Crat. I would fain agree with you, Socrates; and therefore I say, Granted.

Soc. For that I am grateful, my friend, if the fact is true; it is hardly necessary to persist in the dispute at present. But if I can assign names as well as pictures to objects, the right assignment of b them we may call truth, and the wrong assignment of them falsehood. Now if there be such a wrong assignment of names, there may also be a wrong or inappropriate assignment of verbs; and if of names and verbs then of the sentences, which are made up of them. What do you say, Cratylus? c

Crat. I agree; and think that what you say is very true.

Soc. And further, primitive nouns may be compared to pictures, and in pictures you may either render all the appropriate colours and figures, or you may not render them all—some may be wanting; or there may be too many or too much of them— may there not?

Crat. Very true.

Soc. And he who renders all gives a perfect picture and image; and he who takes away or adds also produces a picture or image, but not a good one.

Crat. Yes. d

Soc. In like manner, he who by syllables and letters imitates the substance of things, if he renders all that is appropriate will produce a good image, or in other words a name; but if he subtracts or perhaps adds a little, he will make an image but not a good one; whence I infer that some names are well and others ill made.

Crat. Perhaps.

Soc. Perhaps then the artist of names may be sometimes good, e or he may be bad?

Crat. Yes.

Soc. And this artist of names is called the legislator?

Crat. Yes.

Soc. Then like other artists the legislator may be good or he may be bad; it must surely be so if our former admissions hold good?

Crat. Very true, Socrates; but the case of language, you see, is different; for when by the help of grammar we assign the letters 432 α or β, or any other letters to a certain name, then, if we add, or subtract, or misplace a letter, the name which is written is not only written wrongly, but not written at all; and in any of these cases at once becomes other than a name.[1]

Soc. But I doubt whether your inference is altogether correct, Cratylus.

Crat. How so?

Soc. I believe that what you say may be true about these things which, if they are to be at all, must be composed of a certain number; for example, the number ten at once becomes other than ten if a unit be added or subtracted, and so of any other number:

b but this does not apply to that which is qualitative or to anything which is represented under an image. I should say rather that the image, if expressing in every point the entire reality, would no longer be an image. Let us suppose the existence of two objects: one of them shall be Cratylus, and the other the image of Cratylus; and we will suppose, further, that some God makes not only a representation such as a painter would make of your outward form and colour, but also creates an inward organization like yours, having the same warmth and softness; and into

c this infuses motion, and soul, and mind, such as you have, and in a word copies all your qualities, and places them by you in another form; would you say that this was Cratylus and the image of Cratylus, or that there were two Cratyluses?

Crat. I should say that there were two Cratyluses.

Soc. Then you see, my friend, that we must find some different principle of truth in images, and in the other cases mentioned;[2] and not insist that an image is no longer an image when some-

d thing is added or subtracted. Do you not perceive that images are very far from having qualities which are the exact counterpart of the realities which they represent?

---

[1] [Or: 'at once becomes another name'.]

[2] [i.e. those in which a definite number of components is essential.]

Crat. Yes, I see.

Soc. But then how ridiculous would be the effect of names on the things named, if they were always made like them in every way! Surely we should then have two of everything, and no one would be able to determine which were the names and which were the realities.

Crat. Quite true.

Soc. Then fear not, but have the courage to admit that one name may be correctly and another incorrectly given; and do e not insist that the name shall include all the letters, so that it will be exactly the same with the thing; but allow the occasional substitution of a wrong letter, and if of a letter also of a noun in a sentence, and if of a noun in a sentence also of a sentence which is not appropriate to the matter, and acknowledge that the thing may be named, and described, so long as the general character of the thing which you are describing is retained; and this, as you will remember, was remarked by Hermogenes and myself in the particular instance of the names of the letters. 433

Crat. Yes, I remember.

Soc. Good; and when the general character is preserved, even if some of the proper letters are wanting, still the thing is signified; —well, if all the letters are given; not well, when only a few of them are given. I think that we had better admit this, lest we be punished like travellers in Ægina who wander about the street late at night: and be likewise told by truth herself that we have b arrived too late; or if not, you must find out some new notion of correctness of names, and no longer maintain that a name is the expression of a thing in letters or syllables; for if you say both, you will be inconsistent with yourself.

Crat. I quite acknowledge, Socrates, what you say to be very reasonable.

Soc. Then as we are agreed thus far, let us ask ourselves whether a name rightly imposed ought not to have the proper letters.

Crat. Yes.

Soc. And the proper letters are those which are like the things? c

Crat. Yes.

Soc. Enough then of names which are rightly given. And in names which are incorrectly given, the greater part may be supposed to be made up of proper and similar letters, or there would be no likeness; but there will be likewise a part which is improper and spoils the beauty and formation of the word: you would admit that?

Crat. There would be no use, Socrates, in my quarrelling with you, since I cannot be satisfied that a name which is incorrectly given is a name at all.

d   *Soc.* Do you admit a name to be the representation of a thing?

Crat. Yes, I do.

Soc. But do you not allow that some nouns are primitive, and some derived and compound?

Crat. Yes, I do.

Soc. Then if primitive or first nouns are meant to be representations of things, can you think of any better way of framing them than to assimilate them as closely as possible to those objects e   which they are to represent? or do you prefer the notion of Hermogenes and of many others, who say that names are conventional, and have a meaning to those who have agreed about them, and who have previous knowledge of the things intended by them, and that it is convention which makes a name right; and whether you abide by our present convention, or make a new and opposite one, according to which you call small great and great small—that, they would say, makes no difference, if you are only agreed. Which of these two notions do you prefer?

434   *Crat.* Representation by likeness, Socrates, is infinitely better than representation by any chance sign.

Soc. Very good: but if the name is to be like the thing, the letters out of which the first names are composed must also have a natural resemblance to things. Returning to the image of the picture, I would ask, How could any one ever compose a picture which would be like anything at all, if there were not pigments b   in nature which resembled the things imitated by portraiture, and out of which the picture is composed?

Crat. Impossible.

Soc. No more could names ever resemble any actually existing thing, unless the elements of which they are compounded bore, from the first, some degree of resemblance to the objects of which the names are the imitation: And the original elements are letters?

Crat. Yes.

Soc. Let me now invite you to consider what Hermogenes and I were saying about sounds. Do you agree with me that the letter ρ is expressive of rapidity, motion, and hardness? Were we right or wrong in saying so?

Crat. I should say that you were right.

Soc. And that λ was expressive of smoothness, and softness, and the like?

Crat. There again you were right.

Soc. And yet, as you are aware, that which is called by us σκληρότης, is by the Eretrians called σκληρότηρ.

Crat. Very true.

Soc. But are the letters ρ and σ similar to the same thing; and is there the same significance to them in the termination ρ, which there is to us in σ, or is there no significance to one of us?

Crat. Nay, surely there is a significance to both of us.

Soc. In as far as ρ and σ are like, or in as far as they are unlike?

Crat. In as far as they are like.

Soc. Are they altogether alike?

Crat. Yes; for the purpose of expressing motion.

Soc. And what do you say of the insertion of the λ? for that is expressive not of hardness but of softness.

Crat. Why, perhaps the letter λ is wrongly inserted, Socrates, and should be altered into ρ, as you were saying to Hermogenes, and in my opinion rightly, when you spoke of adding and subtracting letters upon occasion.

Soc. Good. But still the word is intelligible to both of us; when I say σκληρός (hard), you know what I mean.

Crat. Yes, my dear friend, and the explanation of that is custom.

Soc. And what is custom but convention? When I utter *this* sound, I have *that* thing in mind, and you know that I have it in mind; is not this what you mean by 'custom'?

Crat. Yes.

Soc. And if when I speak you know my meaning, there is an indication given by me to you?

Crat. Yes.

Soc. This indication of my meaning may proceed from unlike as well as from like, for example, in the λ of σκληρότης. But if this is true, then you have made a convention with yourself, and the correctness of a name turns out to be convention, since letters which are unlike are indicative equally with those which are like, if they are sanctioned by custom and convention. And even sup-

b posing that you distinguish custom from convention ever so much, still you must say that the signification of words is given by custom and not by likeness, for custom may indicate by the unlike as well as by the like. But as we are agreed thus far, Cratylus (for I shall assume that your silence gives consent), then custom and convention must be supposed to contribute to the indication of our thoughts; for suppose we take the instance of number, how can you ever imagine, my good friend, that you will find names resembling every individual number, unless you allow that which

c you term convention and agreement to have authority in deter- mining the correctness of names? I quite agree with you that words should as far as possible resemble things; but I fear that this dragging in of resemblance, as Hermogenes says,[1] is a kind of hunger, which has to be supplemented by the mechanical aid of convention with a view to correctness; for I believe that if we could always, or almost always, use expressions which are similar, and therefore appropriate, this would be the most perfect state

d of language; as the opposite is the most imperfect. But let me ask you, what is the force of names, and what is the use of them?

Crat. The use of names, Socrates, as I should imagine, is to inform: the simple truth is, that he who knows names knows also the things which are expressed by them.

Soc. I suppose you mean to say, Cratylus, that as the name is, so also is the thing; and that he who knows the one will also know

e the other, because they are similars, and all similars fall under the same art or science; and therefore you would say that he who knows names will also know things.

Crat. That is precisely what I mean.

Soc. But let us consider what is the nature of this information about things which, according to you, is given us by names. Is it the best sort of information? or is there any other? What do you say?

436   *Crat.* I believe that to be both the only and the best sort of information about them; there can be no other.

---

[1] *Vide supra,* 414 c.

Soc. But do you believe that it is by the same process that things are discovered, and that he who discovers the names discovers also the things; or is this only the method of learning, and is there some other method of inquiry and discovery?

Crat. I certainly believe that the methods of inquiry and discovery are of the same nature as instruction.

Soc. Well, but do you not see, Cratylus, that he who follows names in the search after things, and analyses their meaning, is b
in great danger of being deceived?

Crat. How so?

Soc. Why clearly he who first gave names gave them according to his conception of the things which they signified—did he not?

Crat. True.

Soc. And if his conception was erroneous, and he gave names according to his conception, in what position shall we who are his followers find ourselves? Shall we not be deceived by him?

Crat. But, Socrates, perhaps no such case arises, because it is necessary that one who imposes names should have *knowledge*; or c
else, as I have long maintained, his names would not be names at all? And you have a clear proof that he has not missed the truth, and the proof is—that he is perfectly consistent. Did you not yourself[1] make the remark that all the words which you utter have a common character and purpose?

Soc. But that, friend Cratylus, is no answer. For if he did begin in error, he may have forced the remainder into agreement with the original error and with himself; there would be nothing d
strange in this, any more than in geometrical diagrams, which have often a slight and invisible flaw in the first part of the process, and are consistently mistaken in the long deductions which follow.[2] And this is the reason why every man should expend his chief thought and attention on the consideration of his first principles:—are they or are they not rightly laid down? and when he has duly sifted them, it is time to consider the consistency of the rest. Even so, I should be astonished to find that names are e
really consistent. And here let us revert to our former discussion: Were we not saying that our vocabulary indicates the essence of things on the assumption that all things are in motion and

---

[1] [411 c.]
[2] [Or: 'and lead consistently to errors of great magnitude'.]

progress and flux? Do you not conceive that to be the meaning
of them?

Crat. Yes; that is assuredly their meaning, and the true
meaning.

437 *Soc.* Let us revert to ἐπιστήμη (knowledge), and observe how
ambiguous this word is, seeming rather to signify stopping the
soul at things than going round with them; and therefore we
should leave the beginning as at present, and not reject the ε (cf.
412 a), but make an insertion of an ι instead of an ε (not πιστήμη,
but ἐπιστήμη). Take another example: βέβαιον (sure) is clearly
the expression of station and position, and not of motion. Again,
b the word ἱστορία (inquiry) bears upon the face of it the stopping
(ἱστάναι) of the stream; and the word πιστόν (faithful) certainly
indicates cessation of motion; then, again, μνήμη (memory), as
any one may see, expresses rest in the soul, and not motion. Moreover, words such as ἁμαρτία and συμφορά, which have a bad
sense, viewed in the light of their etymologies will be the same
as σύνεσις and ἐπιστήμη and other words which have a good sense
(cf. ὁμαρτεῖν, συνιέναι, ἕπεσθαι, συμφέρεσθαι) ; and much the same
may be said of ἀμαθία and ἀκολασία, for ἀμαθία may be explained
c as ἡ ἅμα θεῷ ἰόντος πορεία, and ἀκολασία as ἡ ἀκολουθία τοῖς
πράγμασιν. Thus the names which in these instances we find to
have the worst sense, will turn out to be framed on the same
principle as those which have the best. And anyone I believe
who would take the trouble might find many other examples in
which the giver of names indicates, not that things are in motion
or progress, but that they are at rest; which is the opposite of
motion.

d   *Crat.* Yes, Socrates, but observe; the greater number express
motion.

Soc. What of that, Cratylus? Are we to count them like votes?
and is correctness of names the voice of the majority? Are we to
say of whichever sort there are most, those are the true ones?

Crat. No; that is not reasonable.

Soc. Certainly not. [¹But let us have done with this question and
proceed to another, about which I should like to know whether

---

¹ [The passage bracketed is omitted in the best Greek manuscripts. Burnet,
who omitted it from the Oxford text, later regarded this as a mistake: see *Vindiciae
Platonicae* II in *C.Q.* xiv (1920), p. 136.]

you think with me. Were we not lately acknowledging that the e first givers of names in states, both Hellenic and barbarous, were the legislators, and that the art which gave names was the art of the legislator?

Crat. Quite true.

Soc. Tell me, then, did the first legislators, who were the givers of the first names, know or not know the things which they named?

Crat. They must have known, Socrates.

Soc. Why, yes, friend Cratylus, they could hardly have been 438 ignorant.

Crat. I should say not.]

Soc. Let us return to the point from which we digressed. You were saying, if you remember, that he who gave names must have known the things which he named; are you still of that opinion?

Crat. I am.

Soc. And would you say that the giver of the first names had also a knowledge of the things which he named?

Crat. I should.

Soc. But how could he have learned or discovered things from names if the primitive names were not yet given? For, if we are b correct in our view, the only way of learning and discovering things, is either to discover names for ourselves or to learn them from others.

Crat. I think that there is a good deal in what you say, Socrates.

Soc. But if things are only to be known through names, how can we suppose that the givers of names had knowledge, or were legislators, before there were names at all, and therefore before they could have known them?

Crat. I believe, Socrates, the true account of the matter to be, c that a power more than human gave things their first names, and that the names which are thus given are necessarily their true names.

Soc. Then how came the giver of the names, if he was an in-spired being or God, to contradict himself? For were we not saying just now that he made some names expressive of rest and others of motion? Were we mistaken?

Crat. But I suppose one of the two not to be names at all.

Soc. And which, then, did he make, my good friend; those which are expressive of rest, or those which are expressive of motion? This is a point which, as I said before, cannot be determined by counting them.

d   *Crat.* No indeed, Socrates, that would be unfair.

Soc. But if this is a battle of names, some of them asserting that they are like the truth, others contending that *they* are, how or by what criterion are we to decide between them? For there are no other names to which appeal can be made, but obviously recourse must be had to another standard which, without employing names, will make clear which of the two are right; and this must be a standard which shows the truth of things.

e   *Crat.* I agree.

Soc. But if that is true, Cratylus, then I suppose that things may be known without names?

Crat. Apparently.

Soc. But by what other device would you expect to know them? What other way can there be of knowing them, except the true and natural way, through their affinities, when they are akin to each other, and through themselves? For that which is other and different from them must signify something other and different from them.

Crat. What you are saying is, I think, true.

439   *Soc.* One moment! have we not several times acknowledged that names rightly given are the likenesses and images of the things which they name?

Crat. Yes.

Soc. Let us suppose that to any extent you please you can learn things through the medium of names, and suppose also that you can learn them from the things themselves—which is likely to be the nobler and clearer way; to learn of the image, whether the image and the truth of which the image is the expression have

b been rightly conceived, or to learn of the truth whether the truth and the image of it have been duly executed?

Crat. I should say that to learn of the truth must be the best way.

Soc. How real existence is to be studied or discovered is, I suspect, beyond you and me. We must rest content with the admission that the knowledge of things is not to be derived from names.

No; they must rather be studied and investigated in their connexion with one another.

Crat. Clearly, Socrates.

Soc. There is another point. I should not like us to be imposed upon by the appearance of such a multitude of names, all tending c in the same direction. I myself do not deny that the givers of names did really give them under the idea that all things were in motion and flux; which was their sincere but, I think, mistaken opinion. And having fallen into a kind of whirlpool themselves, they are carried round, and want to drag us in after them. There is a matter, master Cratylus, about which I often dream, and should like to ask your opinion: Tell me, whether there is or is not some permanent nature of goodness, beauty, and several d other things.

Crat. Certainly, Socrates, I think so.

Soc. Then let us make the true beauty the object of our inquiry: not asking whether a face is fair, or anything of that sort, for all such things appear to be in a flux; but let us ask whether the true beauty does not always retain its essential quality.

Crat. Certainly.

Soc. And if it is continually escaping from our grasp, how can e we properly apply to it the predicates *that* or *of such a kind*? Must it not rather become different, and retire, and no longer be 'thus', while the word is in our mouths?

Crat. Undoubtedly.

Soc. Then how can that be a real thing which is never in the same state? for if a thing remains for a moment in the same state, during that time at least it undergoes no change; whilst if it remains ever the same and in the same state, it is not a subject of motion or change at all, since it does not vary from its original form.

Crat. It is not.

Soc. Nor yet can the variable be known by anyone; for at the 440 moment that the observer approaches, it will become other and of another nature, so that you cannot get any further in knowing its nature or state, for no knowledge, I assume, can know that which is known to have no state.

Crat. True.

Soc. Nor can we reasonably say, Cratylus, that there is any knowing at all, if everything is in a state of transition and there is nothing abiding. For if this power of knowing does *not* vary and lose its identity, then knowing may continue always to abide and

b exist. But if the very nature of knowing is liable to change, then it will be transformed into something other than knowing, and knowing will thereby cease to exist; and if the transition is always going on, there will always be no knowing, and, according to this view, there will be no one to know and nothing to be known. But if that which knows and that which is known exists ever, and the beautiful exists and the good exists, and every other thing also exists, then I do not think that they can resemble a process or flux, as we were just now supposing. Whether there is this eternal

c nature in things, or whether the truth is what Heracleitus and his followers and many others say, is a question hard to determine; and no man of sense will like to put himself or the education of his mind in the power of names: neither will he so far trust names or the givers of names as to be confident in any knowledge which condemns himself and other existences to an unhealthy state of unreality; he will not believe that all things leak like a pot, or that the whole external world is afflicted with rheum and

d catarrh. This may be true, Cratylus, but is also very likely to be untrue; and therefore I would not have you be too easily persuaded of it. Reflect well and like a man, and do not easily accept such a doctrine; for you are young and of an age to learn. And when you have found the truth, come and share it with me.

Crat. I will do as you say, though I can assure you, Socrates, that I have been considering the matter already, and the result

e of a great deal of trouble and consideration is that I incline to Heracleitus.

Soc. Then, another day, my friend, when you come back, you shall give me a lesson; but at present, go into the country, as you are intending, and Hermogenes shall set you on your way.

Crat. Very good, Socrates; I hope, however, that you will continue to think about these things yourself.

PHAEDRUS[1]

INTRODUCTION

THE *Phaedrus* is closely connected with the *Symposium*, and may be regarded either as introducing or following it. The two dialogues together contain the whole philosophy of Plato on the nature of love, which in the *Republic* and in the later writings of Plato is only introduced playfully or as a figure of speech. But in the *Phaedrus* and *Symposium* love and philosophy join hands, and one is an aspect of the other. The spiritual and emotional part is elevated into the ideal, to which in the *Symposium* mankind are described as looking forward, and which in the *Phaedrus*, as well as in the *Phaedo*, they are seeking to recover from a former state of existence. Whether the subject of the dialogue is love or rhetoric, or the union of the two, or the relation of

[1] [Jowett, who elsewhere assumes that the *Phaedrus* is an early work, argues below, pp. 129–30, in favour of a later date. Campbell recognized that several features of Plato's later style are conspicuous in the *Phaedrus*, but held that 'the most casual reader cannot fail to see that in the *Phaedrus* these are but decorations of a sort of carnival dress that is worn for the occasion only' (*Republic*, ii. 49). Accordingly, though he does not rank the *Phaedrus* among the first dialogues, he assumes that it preceded the *Republic*. He nowhere deals with its philosophical content.

Modern opinion is unanimous in holding, for various reasons, that the dialogue should follow the *Republic*, though doubtful as to its exact place. (*a*) Later stylistic research yields a more definite result than that of Campbell. (*b*) *Phaedrus* is evidently later than *Symposium*, when these two dialogues are compared in their treatment of the same topics. (*c*) The account of reincarnation in the two myths in *Republic*, Book X, and *Phaedrus* 248–9 is closely similar; but many details in the latter would be barely intelligible without the former. (*d*) The view of the Soul as self-motion brings the *Phaedrus* into the same sphere of doctrine as the *Timaeus* and *Laws*. (*e*) We find in *Phaedrus* 265–6 the same view of dialectical method as in the *Sophist* and *Statesman*.

What is singular in this dialogue is the blend of earlier and later features, and the exuberance and gaiety to which Campbell refers in the words quoted above. It must have been written at a time when Plato contemplated the introduction of rhetorical training into the Academy, and had to defend his aims in reply to some challenge from Isocrates, the pupil of Gorgias. The *Menexenus* and *Euthydemus* must be viewed in the same light. But the stages of this controversy, which may have extended over many years, are obscure. The *Phaedrus* is placed in this edition immediately after the *Cratylus*, but it might well be maintained that it should come rather with *Philebus* and *Timaeus*. See L. Robin, *La théorie platonicienne de l'Amour* (1908), and the same scholar's commentary on the *Phaedrus* in the *Collection Guillaume Budé* (1933); J. Stenzel, *Plato's Method of Dialectic*, chap. ix (1931); Jaeger, *Paideia*, vol. 2 (1944); and A. E. Taylor, *P.M.W.*, chap. 12.]

philosophy to love and to art in general, and to the human soul, will be hereafter considered. And perhaps we may arrive at some conclusion such as the following—that the dialogue is not strictly confined to a single subject, but passes from one to another with the natural freedom of conversation.

ANALYSIS

227 Phaedrus has been spending the morning with Lysias, the celebrated rhetorician, and is going to refresh himself by taking a walk outside the wall, when he is met by Socrates, who professes that he will not leave him until he has delivered up the speech
228 with which Lysias has regaled him, and which he is carrying about in his mind, or more probably in a book hidden under his cloak, and is intending to study as he walks. The imputation is not denied, and the two agree to direct their steps out of the public way along the stream of the Ilissus towards a plane-tree which is seen in the distance. There, lying down amidst pleasant sounds
229 and scents, they will read the speech of Lysias. The country is a novelty to Socrates, who never goes out of the town; and hence he is full of admiration for the beauties of nature, which he seems to be drinking in for the first time.

As they are on their way, Phaedrus asks the opinion of Socrates respecting the local tradition of Boreas and Oreithyia. Socrates, after a satirical allusion to the 'rationalizers' of his day, replies that he has no time for these 'nice' interpretations of mythology, and he pities anyone who has. When you once begin there is no end of them, and they spring from an uncritical philosophy after all. 'The proper study of mankind is man'; and he is a far more
230 complex and wonderful being than the serpent Typho. Socrates as yet does not know himself; and why should he care to know about unearthly monsters? Engaged in such conversation, they arrive at the plane-tree; when they have found a convenient resting-place, Phaedrus pulls out the speech and reads:—

The speech consists of a foolish paradox which is to the effect
231 that the non-lover ought to be accepted rather than the lover—because he is more rational, more agreeable, more enduring, less suspicious, less hurtful, less boastful, less engrossing, and because there are more of them, and for a great many other reasons which are equally unmeaning. Phaedrus is captivated with the beauty of

the periods, and wants to make Socrates say that nothing was or ever could be written better. Socrates does not think much of the 235 matter, but then he has only attended to the form, and in that he has detected several repetitions and other marks of haste. He cannot agree with Phaedrus in the extreme value which he sets upon this performance, because he is afraid of doing injustice to Anacreon and Sappho and other great writers, and is almost inclined to think that he himself, or rather some power residing within him, could make a speech better than that of Lysias on the same theme, and also different from his, if he may be allowed 236 the use of a few commonplaces which all speakers must equally employ.

Phaedrus is delighted at the prospect of having another speech, and promises that he will set up a golden statue of Socrates at Delphi, if he keeps his word. Some raillery ensues, and at length Socrates, conquered by the threat that he shall never again hear a speech of Lysias unless he fulfils his promise, veils his face and 237 begins.

First, invoking the Muses and assuming ironically the person of the non-lover (who is a lover all the same), he will inquire into the nature and power of love. For this is a necessary preliminary to the other question—How is the non-lover to be distinguished from the lover? In all of us there are two principles—a better and a worse—reason and desire, which are generally at war with one another; and the victory of the rational is called temperance, and the victory of the irrational intemperance or excess. The latter takes many forms and has many bad names—gluttony, 238 drunkenness, and the like. But of all the irrational desires or excesses the greatest is that which is led away by desires of a kindred nature to the enjoyment of personal beauty. And this is the master power of love.

Here Socrates fancies that he detects in himself an unusual flow of eloquence—this newly found gift he can only attribute to the inspiration of the place, which appears to be dedicated to the nymphs. Starting again from the philosophical basis which has 239 been laid down, he proceeds to show how many advantages the non-lover has over the lover. The one encourages softness and effeminacy and exclusiveness; he cannot endure any superiority in his beloved; he will train him in luxury, he will keep him out

240 of society, he will deprive him of parents, friends, money, knowledge, and of every other good, that he may have him all to himself. Then again his ways are not ways of pleasantness; he is
mighty disagreeable; 'crabbed age and youth cannot live together'. At every hour of the night and day he is intruding upon
him; there is the same face, now devoid of youthful charm—and
he is always repeating, in season or out of season, the praises or
dispraises of his beloved, which are bad enough when he is sober,
241 and published all over the world when he is drunk. At length his
love ceases; he is converted into an enemy, and the spectacle may
be seen of the lover running away from the beloved, who pursues
him with vain reproaches, and demands his reward which the
other refuses to pay. Too late the beloved learns, after all his
pains and disagreeables, that 'As wolves love lambs so lovers love
their loves.' (Cf. *Char.* 155 d.) Here is the end; the 'other' or
'non-lover' part of the speech had better be understood, for if in
the censure of the lover Socrates has broken out in verse, what
242 will he not do in his praise of the non-lover? He has said his say
and is preparing to go away.

   Phaedrus begs him to remain, at any rate until the heat of noon
has passed; he would like to have a little more conversation
before they go. Socrates, who has risen, recognizes the oracular
243 sign which forbids him to depart until he has done penance. His
conscience has been awakened, and like Stesichorus when he had
reviled the lovely Helen he will sing a palinode for having blas-
phemed the majesty of love. His palinode takes the form of a myth.

244   Socrates begins his tale with a glorification of madness, which
he divides into four kinds: first, there is the art of divination or
prophecy—this, in a vein similar to that pervading the *Cratylus*
and *Io*, he connects with madness by an etymological explanation
(μαντική, μανική)—compare οἰονοιστική, οἰωνιστική, ''tis all one
reckoning, save the phrase is a little variations'; secondly, there
245 is the art of purification by mysteries; thirdly, poetry or the
inspiration of the Muses (cf. *Ion,* 533 ff.), without which no man
can enter their temple. All this shows that madness is one of
heaven's blessings, and may sometimes be a great deal better
than sense. There is also a fourth kind of madness—that of love—
which cannot be explained without inquiring into the nature of
the soul.

All soul is immortal, for she is the source of all motion both in herself and in others. Her form may be described in a figure as 246 a composite nature made up of a charioteer and a pair of winged steeds. The steeds of the gods are immortal, but ours are one mortal and the other immortal. The immortal soul soars upwards into the heavens, but the mortal drops her plumes and settles upon the earth.

Now the use of the wing is to rise and carry the downward element into the upper world—there to behold beauty, wisdom, goodness, and the other things of God by which the soul is nourished. On a certain day Zeus the lord of heaven goes forth in a 247 winged chariot; and an array of gods and demi-gods, and of human souls in their train, follows him. There are glorious and blessed sights in the interior of heaven, and he who will may freely behold them. The greatest vision of all is seen at the feast of the gods, when they ascend the heights of the empyrean—all but Hestia, who is left at home to keep house. The chariots of the gods glide readily upwards and stand upon the outside; the revolution of the spheres carries them round, and they have a vision of the world beyond. But the others labour in vain; for the mortal steed, if he has not been properly trained, keeps them down and sinks them towards the earth. Of the world which is beyond the heavens, who can tell? There is an essence formless, colourless, intangible, perceived by the mind only, dwelling in the region of true knowledge. The divine mind in her revolution enjoys this fair prospect, and beholds justice, temperance, and knowledge in their everlasting essence. When fulfilled with the sight of them she returns home, and the charioteer puts up the horses in their stable, and gives 248 them ambrosia to eat and nectar to drink. This is the life of the gods; the human soul tries to reach the same heights, but hardly succeeds; and sometimes the head of the charioteer rises above, and sometimes sinks below, the fair vision, and he is at last obliged, after much contention, to turn away and leave the plain of truth. But if the soul has followed in the train of her god and once beheld truth she is preserved from harm, and is carried round in the next revolution of the spheres; and if always following, and always seeing the truth, is then for ever unharmed. If, however, she drops her wings and falls to the earth, then she takes the form of man, and the soul which has seen most of the truth passes into a philosopher or lover; that which has seen truth in the second degree, into a king or warrior; the third, into a householder or money-maker; the fourth, into a gymnast; the fifth, into a prophet or mystic; the sixth, into a poet or imitator; the seventh, into a husbandman or craftsman; the eighth, into a sophist or demagogue; the ninth, into a tyrant. All these are states of probation, wherein he who lives righteously is improved, and he who lives unrighteously deteriorates. After death comes the judgement; the bad depart to houses of correction under the earth, the good to places of joy in heaven. When a thousand years have elapsed the souls meet together and choose the lives which they will lead for another period of existence. The soul which three times in succession has chosen the life of a philosopher or of a lover who is not without philosophy receives her wings at the close of the third millennium; the remainder have to complete a cycle of ten thousand years before their wings are restored to

249 them. Each time there is full liberty of choice. The soul of a man may descend into a beast, and return again into the form of man. But the form of man will only be taken by the soul which has once seen truth and acquired some conception of the universal:— this is the recollection of the knowledge which she attained when in the company of the Gods. And men in general recall only with difficulty the things of another world, but the mind of the philosopher has a better remembrance of them. For when he beholds the visible beauty of earth his enraptured soul passes in thought

250 to those glorious sights of justice and wisdom and temperance and truth which she once gazed upon in heaven. Then she celebrated holy mysteries and beheld blessed apparitions shining in pure light, herself pure, and not as yet entombed in the body. And still, like a bird eager to quit its cage, she flutters and looks upwards, and is therefore deemed mad. Such a recollection of past days she receives through sight, the keenest of our senses, because beauty, alone of the ideas, has any representation on earth: wisdom is invisible to mortal eyes. But the corrupted nature, blindly excited by this vision of beauty, rushes on to enjoy, and

251 would fain wallow like a brute beast in sensual pleasures. Whereas the true mystic, who has seen the many sights of bliss, when he beholds a god-like form or face is amazed with delight, and if he were not afraid of being thought mad he would fall

down and worship. Then the stiffened wing begins to relax and grow again; desire which has been imprisoned pours over the soul of the lover; the germ of the wing unfolds, and stings, and pangs of birth, like the cutting of teeth, are everywhere felt. (Cf. *Symp.* 206 ff.) Father and mother, and goods and laws and 252 proprieties are nothing to him; his beloved is his physician, who can alone cure his pain. An apocryphal sacred writer says that the power which thus works in him is by mortals called love, but the immortals call him dove, or the winged one, in order to represent the force of his wings—such at any rate is his nature. Now the characters of lovers depend upon the god whom they followed in the other world; and they choose their loves in this world accordingly. The followers of Ares are fierce and violent; those 253 of Zeus seek out some philosophical and imperial nature; the attendants of Hera find a royal love; and in like manner the followers of every god seek a love who is like their god; and to him they communicate the nature which they have received from their god. The manner in which they take their love is as follows:—

I told you about the charioteer and his two steeds, the one a noble animal who is guided by word and admonition only, the other an ill-looking villain who will hardly yield to blow or spur. Together all three, who are a figure of the soul, approach the vision of love. And now a fierce conflict begins. The ill-condi- 254 tioned steed rushes on to enjoy, but the charioteer, who beholds the beloved with awe, falls back in adoration, and forces both the steeds on their haunches; again the evil steed rushes forwards and pulls shamelessly. The conflict grows more and more severe; and at last the charioteer, throwing himself backwards, forces the bit out of the clenched teeth of the brute, and pulling harder than ever at the reins, covers his tongue and jaws with blood, and forces him to rest his legs and haunches with pain upon the ground. When this has happened several times, the villain is tamed and humbled, and from that time forward the soul of the lover follows the beloved in modesty and holy fear. And now their 255 bliss is consummated; the same image of love dwells in the breast of either; and if they have self-control, they pass their lives in the greatest happiness which is attainable by man—they continue masters of themselves, and conquer in one of the three heavenly

256 victories. But if they choose the lower life of ambition they may still have a happy destiny, though inferior, because they have not the approval of the whole soul. At last they leave the body and proceed on their pilgrim's progress, and those who have once begun can never go back. When the time comes they receive their wings and fly away, and the lovers have the same wings.

Socrates concludes:—

257 These are the blessings of love, and thus have I made my recantation in finer language than before: I did so in order to please Phaedrus. If I said what was wrong at first, please to attribute my error to Lysias, who ought to study philosophy instead of rhetoric, and then he will not mislead his disciple Phaedrus.

Phaedrus is afraid that he will lose conceit of Lysias, and that Lysias will be out of conceit with himself, and leave off making speeches, for the politicians have been deriding him. Socrates is of opinion that there is small danger of this; the politicians are 258 themselves the great rhetoricians of the age, who desire to attain immortality by the authorship of laws. And therefore there is nothing with which they can reproach Lysias in being a writer; but there may be disgrace in being a bad one.

And what is good or bad writing or speaking? While the sun is hot in the sky above us, let us ask that question: since by rational conversation man lives, and not by the indulgence of 259 bodily pleasures. And the grasshoppers who are chirruping around may carry our words to the Muses, who are their patronesses; for the grasshoppers were human beings themselves in a world before the Muses, and when the Muses came they died of hunger for the love of song. And they carry to them in heaven the report of those 260 who honour them on earth.

The first rule of good speaking is to know and speak the truth; 261 as a Spartan proverb says, 'true art is truth'; whereas rhetoric is an art of enchantment, which makes things appear good and evil, like and unlike, as the speaker pleases. Its use is not confined, as people commonly suppose, to arguments in the law courts and speeches in the assembly; it is rather a part of the art of disputation, under which are included both the rules of Gorgias and the eristic of Zeno. But it is not wholly devoid of truth. Superior knowledge enables us to deceive another by the help of resemblances, and to escape from such a deception when employed against ourselves. We see therefore that even in rhetoric an element of truth is required. For if we do not know the truth, 262 we can neither make the gradual departures from truth by which men are most easily deceived, nor guard ourselves against deception.

Socrates then proposes that they shall use the two speeches as 263 illustrations of the art of rhetoric; first distinguishing between the debatable and undisputed class of subjects. In the debatable class there ought to be a definition of all disputed matters. But 264 there was no such definition in the speech of Lysias; nor is there any order or connexion in his words any more than in a nursery rhyme. With this he compares the regular divisions of the other 265 speech, which was his own (and yet not his own, for the local deities must have inspired him). Although only a playful composition, it will be found to embody two principles: first, that of synthesis or the comprehension of parts in a whole; secondly, 266 analysis, or the resolution of the whole into parts. These are the processes of division and generalization which are so dear to the dialectician, that king of men. They are effected by dialectic, and not by rhetoric, of which the remains are but scanty after order and arrangement have been subtracted. There is nothing left but a heap of 'ologies' and other technical terms invented by Polus, Theodorus, Evenus, Tisias, Gorgias, and others, who have 267 rules for everything, and who teach how to be short or long at pleasure. Prodicus showed his good sense when he said that there was a better thing than either to be short or long, which was to be of convenient length.

Still, notwithstanding the absurdities of Polus and others, 268 rhetoric has great power in public assemblies. This power, however, is not given by any technical rules, but is the gift of genius. The real art is always being confused by rhetoricians with the preliminaries of the art. The perfection of oratory is like the 269 perfection of anything else; natural power must be aided by art. But the art is not that which is taught in the schools of rhetoric; it is nearer akin to philosophy. Pericles, for instance, who was the most accomplished of all speakers, derived his eloquence not from 270 rhetoric but from the philosophy of nature which he learnt of Anaxagoras. True rhetoric is like medicine, and the rhetorician

271 has to consider the natures of men's souls as the physician considers the natures of their bodies. Such and such persons are to be
affected in this way, such and such others in that; and he must
272 know the times and the seasons for saying this or that. This is not
an easy task, and this, if there be such an art, is the art of rhetoric.

I know that there are some professors of the art who maintain
273 probability to be stronger than truth. But we maintain that
probability is engendered by likeness of the truth which can only
be attained by the knowledge of it, and that the aim of the good
274 man should not be to please or persuade his fellow servants, but
to please his good masters who are the gods. Rhetoric has a fair
beginning in this.

Enough of the art of speaking; let us now proceed to consider
the true use of writing. There is an old Egyptian tale of Theuth,
the inventor of writing, showing his invention to the god Thamus,
275 who told him that he would only spoil men's memories and take
away their understandings. From this tale, of which young
Athens will probably make fun, may be gathered the lesson that
writing is inferior to speech. For it is like a picture, which can
give no answer to a question, and has only a deceitful likeness of
a living creature. It has no power of adaptation, but uses the
same words for all. It is not a legitimate son of knowledge, but a
276 bastard, and when an attack is made upon this bastard neither
parent nor anyone else is there to defend it. The husbandman
will not seriously incline to sow his seed in such a hot-bed or
277 garden of Adonis; he will rather sow in the natural soil of the
human soul which has depth of earth; and he will anticipate the
inner growth of the mind, by writing only, if at all, as a remedy
against old age. The natural process will be far nobler, and will
bring forth fruit in the minds of others as well as in his own.

The conclusion of the whole matter is just this,—that until a
man knows the truth, and the manner of adapting the truth to the
278 natures of other men, he cannot be a good orator; also, that the
living is better than the written word, and that the principles of
justice and truth when delivered by word of mouth are the legitimate offspring of a man's own bosom, and their lawful descendants take up their abode in others. Such an orator as he is who
is possessed of them, you and I would fain become. And to all
composers in the world, poets, orators, legislators, we hereby

announce that if their compositions are based upon these principles, then they are not only poets, orators, legislators, but
philosophers. All others are mere flatterers and putters together
of words. This is the message which Phaedrus undertakes to carry
to Lysias from the local deities, and Socrates himself will carry a 279
similar message to his favourite Isocrates, whose future distinction
as a great rhetorician he prophesies. The heat of the day has
passed, and after offering up a prayer to Pan and the nymphs,
Socrates and Phaedrus depart.

INTRODUCTION

There are two principal controversies which have been raised about
the *Phaedrus*; the first relates to the subject, the second to the date of
the Dialogue.

There seems to be a notion that the work of a great artist like Plato
cannot fail in unity, and that the unity of a dialogue requires a single
subject. But the conception of unity really applies in very different
degrees and ways to different kinds of art; to a statue, for example, far
more than to any kind of literary composition, and to some species of
literature far more than to others. Nor does the dialogue appear to
be a style of composition in which the requirement of unity is most
stringent; nor should the idea of unity derived from one sort of art be
hastily transferred to another. The double titles of several of the
Platonic dialogues are a further proof that the severer rule was not
observed by Plato. The *Republic* is divided between the search after
justice and the construction of the ideal state; the *Parmenides* between
the criticism of the Platonic Ideas and of the Eleatic One or being; the
Gorgias between the art of speaking and the nature of the good; the
Sophist between the detection of the sophist and the correlation of
ideas. The *Theaetetus*, the *Politicus*, and the *Philebus* have also digressions which are but remotely connected with the main subject.

Thus the comparison of Plato's other writings, as well as the reason
of the thing, lead us to the conclusion that we must not expect to find
one idea pervading a whole work, but one, two, or more, as the
invention of the writer may suggest, or his fancy wander. If each
dialogue were confined to the development of a single idea, this would
appear on the face of the dialogue, nor could any controversy be raised
as to whether the *Phaedrus* treated of love or rhetoric. But the truth is
that Plato subjects himself to no rule of this sort. Like every great
artist he gives unity of form to the different and apparently distracting
topics which he brings together. He works freely and is not to be

supposed to have arranged every part of the dialogue before he begins to write. He fastens or weaves together the frame of his discourse loosely and imperfectly, and which is the warp and which is the woof cannot always be determined.

The subjects of the *Phaedrus* (exclusive of the short introductory passage about mythology which is suggested by the local tradition) are first the false or conventional art of rhetoric; secondly, love or the inspiration of beauty and knowledge, which is described as madness; thirdly, dialectic or the art of composition and division; fourthly, the true rhetoric, which is based upon dialectic, and is neither the art of persuasion nor knowledge of the truth alone, but the art of persuasion founded on knowledge of truth and knowledge of character; fifthly, the superiority of the spoken over the written word. The continuous thread which appears and reappears throughout is rhetoric; this is the ground into which the rest of the Dialogue is worked, in parts embroidered with fine words which are not in Socrates' manner, as he says, 'in order to please Phaedrus'. The speech of Lysias which has thrown Phaedrus into an ecstasy is adduced as an example of the false rhetoric; the first speech of Socrates, though an improvement, partakes of the same character; his second speech, which is full of that higher element said to have been learned of Anaxagoras by Pericles, and which in the midst of poetry does not forget order, is an illustration of the higher or true rhetoric. This higher rhetoric is based upon dialectic, and dialectic is a sort of inspiration akin to love (cf. *Symp.* 210 ff.); in these two aspects of philosophy the technicalities of rhetoric are absorbed. And so the example becomes also the deeper theme of discourse. The true knowledge of things in heaven and earth is based upon enthusiasm or love of the ideas going before us and ever present to us in this world and in another; and the true order of speech or writing proceeds accordingly. Love, again, has three degrees: first, of interested love corresponding to the conventionalities of rhetoric; secondly, of disinterested or mad love, fixed on objects of sense, and answering, perhaps, to poetry; thirdly, of disinterested love directed towards the unseen, answering to dialectic or the science of the ideas. Lastly, the art of rhetoric in the lower sense is found to rest on a knowledge of the natures and characters of men, which Socrates at the commencement of the Dialogue has described as his own peculiar study.

Thus amid discord a harmony begins to appear; there are many links of connexion which are not visible at first sight. At the same time the *Phaedrus*, although one of the most beautiful of the Platonic dialogues, is also more irregular than any other. For insight into the world, for sustained irony, for depth of thought, there is no dialogue superior, or perhaps equal to it. Nevertheless the form of the work has tended to obscure some of Plato's higher aims.

The first speech is composed 'in that balanced style in which the wise love to talk' (*Symp.* 185 c). The characteristics of rhetoric are insipidity, mannerism, and monotonous parallelism of clauses. There is more rhythm than reason; the creative power of imagination is wanting.

> 'Tis Greece, but living Greece no more.

Plato has seized by anticipation the spirit which hung over Greek literature for a thousand years afterwards. Yet doubtless there were some who, like Phaedrus, felt a delight in the harmonious cadence and the pedantic reasoning of the rhetoricians newly imported from Sicily, which had ceased to be awakened in them by really great works, such as the odes of Anacreon or Sappho or the orations of Pericles. That the first speech was really written by Lysias is improbable. Like the poem of Solon, or the story of Thamus and Theuth, or the funeral oration of Aspasia (if genuine), or the pretence of Socrates in the *Cratylus* that his knowledge of philology is derived from Euthyphro, the invention is really due to the imagination of Plato, and may be compared to the parodies of the sophists in the *Protagoras.* Numerous fictions of this sort occur in the dialogues, and the gravity of Plato has sometimes imposed upon his commentators. The introduction of a considerable writing of another would seem not to be in keeping with a great work of art, and has no parallel elsewhere.

In the second speech Socrates is exhibited as beating the rhetoricians at their own weapons; he 'an unpractised man and they masters of the art'. True to his character, he must, however, profess that the speech which he makes is not his own, for he knows nothing of himself. (Cf. *Symp.* 201 d.) Regarded as a rhetorical exercise, the superiority of his speech seems to consist chiefly in a better arrangement of the topics; he begins with a definition of love, and he gives weight to his words by going back to general maxims; a lesser merit is the greater liveliness of Socrates, which hurries him into verse and relieves the monotony of the style.

But Plato had doubtless a higher purpose than to exhibit Socrates as the rival or superior of the Athenian rhetoricians. Even in the speech of Lysias there is a germ of truth, and this is further developed in the parallel oration of Socrates. First, passionate love is overthrown by the sophistical or interested, and then both yield to that higher view of love which is afterwards revealed to us. The extreme of commonplace is contrasted with the most ideal and imaginative of speculations.

Socrates, half in jest and to satisfy his own wild humour, takes the disguise of Lysias, but he is also in profound earnest and in a deeper vein of irony than usual. Having improvised his own speech, which is based upon the model of the preceding, he condemns them both. Yet the condemnation is not to be taken seriously, for he is evidently trying to express an aspect of the truth. To understand him, we must make abstraction of morality and of the Greek manner of regarding the relation of the sexes. In this, as in his other discussions about love, what Plato says of the loves of men must be transferred to the loves of women before we can attach any serious meaning to his words. Had he lived in our times he would have made the transposition himself. But seeing in his own age the impossibility of woman being the intellectual helpmate or friend of man (except in the rare instances of a Diotima or an Aspasia), seeing that, even as to personal beauty, her place was taken by young mankind instead of womankind, he tries to work out the problem of love without regard to the distinctions of nature. And full of the evils which he recognized as flowing from the spurious form of love, he proceeds with a deep meaning, though partly in joke, to show that the 'non-lover's' love is better than the 'lover's'.

Both speeches are strongly condemned by Socrates as sinful and blasphemous towards the god Love, and as worthy only of some haunt of sailors to which good manners were unknown. The meaning of this and other wild language to the same effect, which is introduced by way of contrast to the formality of the two speeches (Socrates has a sense of relief when he has escaped from the trammels of rhetoric), seems to be that the two speeches proceed upon the supposition that love is and ought to be interested, and that no such thing as a real or disinterested passion, which would be at the same time lasting, could be conceived. 'But did I call this "love"? O God, forgive my blasphemy. This is not love. Rather it is the love of the world. But there is another kingdom of love, a kingdom not of this world, divine, eternal. And this other love I will now show you in a mystery.'

Then follows the famous myth, which is a sort of parable, and like other parables ought not to receive too minute an interpretation. In all such allegories there is a great deal which is merely ornamental, and the interpreter has to separate the important from the unimportant. Socrates himself has given the right clue when, in using his own discourse afterwards as the text for his examination of rhetoric, he characterizes it as a 'partly true and tolerably credible mythus', in which amid poetical figures, order and arrangement were not forgotten.

The soul is described in magnificent language as the self-moved and the source of motion in all other things. This is the philosophical theme or proem of the whole. But ideas must be given through something, and under the pretext that to realize the true nature of the soul would be not only tedious but impossible, we at once pass on to describe the souls of gods as well as men under the figure of two winged steeds and a charioteer. No connexion is traced between the soul as the great motive power and the triple soul which is thus imaged. There is no difficulty in seeing that the charioteer represents the reason, or that the black horse is the symbol of the sensual or concupiscent element of human nature. The white horse also represents rational impulse, but the description in 253, 'a lover of honour and modesty and temperance, and a follower of true glory', though similar, does not at once recall the 'spirit' ($\theta\nu\mu\acute{o}s$) of the *Republic*. The two steeds really correspond in a figure more nearly to the appetitive and moral or semi-rational soul of Aristotle. And thus, for the first time perhaps in the history of philosophy, we have represented to us the threefold division of psychology. The image of the charioteer and the steeds has been compared with a similar image which occurs in the verses of Parmenides; but it is important to remark that the horses of Parmenides have no allegorical meaning, and that the poet is only describing his own approach in a chariot to the regions of light and the house of the goddess of truth.

The triple soul has had a previous existence, in which following in the train of some god, from whom she derived her character, she beheld partially and imperfectly the vision of absolute truth. All her after existence, passed in many forms of men and animals, is spent in regaining this. The stages of the conflict are many and various; and she is sorely let and hindered by the animal desires of the inferior or concupiscent steed. Again and again she beholds the flashing beauty of the beloved. But before that vision can be finally enjoyed the animal desires must be subjected.

The moral or spiritual element in man is represented by the immortal steed which, like $\theta\nu\mu\acute{o}s$ in the *Republic*, always sides with the reason. Both are dragged out of their course by the furious impulses of desire. In the end something is conceded to the desires, after they have been finally humbled and overpowered. And yet the way of philosophy, or perfect love of the unseen, is total abstinence from bodily delights. 'But all men cannot receive this saying': in the lower life of ambition they may be taken off their guard and stoop to folly unawares, and then, although they do not attain to the highest bliss, yet if they have once conquered they may be happy enough.

The language of the *Meno* and the *Phaedo* as well as of the *Phaedrus* seems to show that at one time of his life Plato was quite serious in maintaining a former state of existence. His mission was to realize the abstract; in that, all good and truth, all the hopes of this and another life seemed to centre. To him abstractions, as we call them, were another kind of knowledge—an inner and unseen world, which seemed to exist far more truly than the fleeting objects of sense which were without him. When we are once able to imagine the intense power which abstract ideas exercised over the mind of Plato, we see that there was no more difficulty to him in realizing the eternal existence of them, and of the human minds which were associated with them, in the past and future than in the present. The difficulty was not how they could exist, but how they could fail to exist. In the attempt to regain this 'saving' knowledge of the Ideas, the sense was found to be as great an enemy as the desires; and hence two things which to us seem quite distinct are inextricably blended in the representation of Plato.

Thus far we may believe that Plato was serious in his conception of the soul as a motive power, in his reminiscence of a former state of being, in his elevation of the reason over sense and passion, and perhaps in his doctrine of transmigration. Was he equally serious in the rest? For example, are we to attribute his tripartite division of the soul to the gods? Or is this merely assigned to them by way of parallelism with men? The latter is the more probable; for the horses of the gods are both white, i.e. their every impulse is in harmony with reason; their dualism, on the other hand, only carries out the figure of the chariot. Is he serious, again, in regarding love as 'a madness'? That seems to arise out of the antithesis to the former conception of love. At the same time he appears to intimate here, as in the *Ion*, *Apology*, *Meno*, and elsewhere, that there is a faculty in man, whether to be termed in modern language genius, or inspiration, or imagination, or idealism, or communion with God, which cannot be reduced to rule and measure. Perhaps, too, he is ironically repeating the common language of mankind about philosophy, and is turning their jest into a sort of earnest. (Cf. *Phaedo*, 61 b; *Symp.* 218 b.) Or is he serious in holding that each soul bears the character of a god? He may have had no other account to give of the differences of human characters to which he afterwards refers. Or, again, in his absurd derivation of μαντική and οἰωνιστική and ἵμερος (cf. *Cratylus*)? It is characteristic of the irony of Socrates to mix up sense and nonsense in such a way that no exact line can be drawn between them. And allegory helps to increase this sort of confusion.

As is often the case in the parables and prophecies of Scripture, the meaning is allowed to break through the figure, and the details are not always consistent. When the charioteers and their steeds stand upon the dome of heaven they behold the intangible invisible essences which are not objects of sight. This is because the force of language can no farther go. Nor can we dwell much on the circumstance that at the completion of ten thousand years all are to return to the place from whence they came; because he represents their return as dependent on their own good conduct in the successive stages of existence. Nor again can we attribute anything to the accidental inference which would also follow, that even a tyrant may live righteously in the condition of life to which fate has called him ('he aiblins might, I dinna ken'). But to suppose this would be at variance with Plato himself and with Greek notions generally. He is much more serious in distinguishing men from animals by their recognition of the universal which they have known in a former state, and in denying that this gift of reason can ever be obliterated or lost. In the language of some modern theologians he might be said to maintain the 'final persever-ance' of those who have entered on their pilgrim's progress. Other intimations of a 'metaphysic' or 'theology' of the future may also be discerned in him: (1) The moderate predestinarianism which here, as in the *Republic*, acknowledges the element of chance in human life, and yet asserts the freedom and responsibility of man; (2) The recog-nition of a moral as well as an intellectual principle in man under the image of an immortal steed; (3) The notion that the divine nature exists by the contemplation of ideas of virtue and justice—or, in other words, the assertion of the essentially moral nature of God; (4) Again, there is the hint that human life is a life of aspiration only, and that the true ideal is not to be found in art; (5) There occurs the first trace of the distinction between necessary and contingent matter; (6) The conception of the soul itself as the motive power and reason of the universe.

The conception of the philosopher, or the philosopher and lover in one, as a sort of madman, may be compared with the *Republic* and *Theaetetus*, in both of which the philosopher is regarded as a stranger and monster upon the earth. The whole myth, like the other myths of Plato, describes in a figure things which are beyond the range of human faculties, or inaccessible to the knowledge of the age. That philosophy should be represented as the inspiration of love is a con-ception that has already become familiar to us in the *Symposium*, and is the expression partly of Plato's enthusiasm for the idea, and is also an indication of the real power exercised by the passion of friendship over the mind of the Greek. The master in the art of love knew that there was a mystery in these feelings and their associations, and especially in the contrast of the sensible and permanent which is afforded by them; and he sought to explain this, as he explained universal ideas, by a reference to a former state of existence. The capriciousness of love is also derived by him from an attachment to some god in a former world. The singular remark that the beloved is more affected than the lover at the final consummation of their love, seems likewise to hint at a psychological truth.

It is difficult to exhaust the meanings of a work like the *Phaedrus*, which indicates so much more than it expresses; and is full of inconsistencies and ambiguities which were not perceived by Plato himself. For example, when he is speaking of the soul does he mean the human or the divine soul? and are they both equally self-moving and constructed on the same threefold principle? We should certainly be disposed to reply that the self-motive is to be attributed to God only; and on the other hand that the appetitive and passionate elements have no place in His nature. So we should infer from the reason of the thing, but there is no indication in Plato's own writings that this was his meaning. Or, again, when he explains the different characters of men by referring them back to the nature of the God whom they served in a former state of existence, we are inclined to ask whether he is serious: Is he not rather using a mythological figure, here as elsewhere, to draw a veil over things which are beyond the limits of mortal knowledge? Once more, in speaking of beauty is he really thinking of some external form such as might have been expressed in the works of Phidias or Praxiteles; and not rather of an imaginary beauty, of a sort which extinguishes rather than stimulates vulgar love (254 e),— a heavenly beauty like that which flashed from time to time before the eyes of Dante or Bunyan? Surely the latter. But it would be idle to reconcile all the details of the passage: it is a picture, not a system, and a picture which is for the greater part an allegory, and an allegory which allows the meaning to come through. The image of the charioteer and his steeds is placed side by side with the absolute forms of justice, temperance, and the like, which are abstract ideas only, and which are seen with the eye of the soul in her heavenly journey. The first impression of such a passage, in which no attempt is made to separate the substance from the form, is far truer than an elaborate philosophical analysis.

It is too often forgotten that the whole of the second discourse of Socrates is only an allegory, or figure of speech. For this reason, it is unnecessary to inquire whether the love of which Plato speaks is the love of men or of women. It is really a general idea which includes both, and in which the sensual element, though not wholly eradicated, is reduced to order and measure. We must not attribute a meaning to every fanciful detail. Nor is there any need to call up revolting associations, which as a matter of good taste should be banished, and which were far enough away from the mind of Plato. These and similar passages should be interpreted by the *Laws*, book viii. 836. Nor is there anything in the *Symposium*, 219, or in the *Charmides*, 155 d, in reality inconsistent with the sterner rule which Plato lays down in the *Laws*. At the same time it is not to be denied that love and philosophy are described by Socrates in figures of speech which would not be used in Christian times; or that nameless vices were prevalent at Athens and in other Greek cities; or that friendships between men were a more sacred tie, and had a more important social and educational influence than among ourselves. (See note on *Symposium*, sub fin.)

In the *Phaedrus*, as well as in the *Symposium*, there are two kinds of love, a lower and a higher, the one answering to the natural wants of the animal, the other rising above them and contemplating with religious awe the forms of justice, temperance, holiness, yet finding them also 'too dazzling bright for mortal eye', and shrinking from them in amazement. The opposition between these two kinds of love may be compared to the opposition between the flesh and the spirit in the Epistles of St. Paul. It would be unmeaning to suppose that Plato, in describing the spiritual combat, in which the rational soul is finally victor and master of both the steeds, condescends to allow any indulgence of unnatural lusts.

Two other thoughts about love are suggested by this passage. First of all, love is represented here, as in the *Symposium*, as one of the great powers of nature, which takes many forms and two principal ones, having a predominant influence over the lives of men. And these two, though opposed, are not absolutely separated the one from the other. Plato, with his great knowledge of human nature, was well aware how easily one is transformed into the other, or how soon the noble but fleeting aspiration may return into the nature of the animal, while the lower instinct which is latent always remains. The intermediate sentimentalism, which has exercised so great an influence on the literature of modern Europe, had no place in the classical times of Hellas; the higher love, of which Plato speaks, is the subject, not of poetry or fiction, but of philosophy.

Secondly, there seems to be indicated a natural yearning of the human mind that the great ideas of justice, temperance, wisdom, should be expressed in some form of visible beauty, like the absolute purity and goodness which Christian art has sought to realize in the person of the Madonna. But although human nature has often attempted to represent outwardly what can be only 'spiritually discerned', men feel that in pictures and images, whether painted or carved, or described in words only, we have not the substance but the shadow of the truth which is in heaven. There is no reason to suppose that in the fairest works of Greek art, Plato ever conceived himself to behold an image, however faint, of ideal truths. 'Not in that way was wisdom seen' (250 d.)

We may now pass on to the second part of the Dialogue, which is a criticism on the first. Rhetoric is assailed on various grounds: first, as desiring to persuade, without a knowledge of the truth; and secondly as ignoring the distinction between certain and probable matter. The three speeches are then passed in review: the first of them has no definition of the nature of love, and no order in the topics (being in these respects far inferior to the second); while the third of them is found (though a fancy of the hour) to be framed upon real dialectical principles. But dialectic is not rhetoric; nothing on that subject is to be found in the endless treatises of rhetoric, however prolific in hard names. When Plato has sufficiently put them to the test of ridicule he touches, as with the point of a needle, the real error, which is the confusion of preliminary knowledge with creative power. No attainments will provide the speaker with genius; and the sort of attainments which can alone be of any value are the higher philosophy and the power of psychological analysis, which is given by dialectic, but not by the rules of the rhetoricians.

In this latter portion of the Dialogue there are many texts which may help us to speak and to think. The names dialectic and rhetoric are passing out of use; we hardly examine seriously into their nature and limits, and probably the arts both of speaking and of conversation have been unduly neglected by us. But the mind of Socrates pierces through the differences of times and countries into the essential nature of man; and his words apply equally to the modern world and to the Athenians of old. Would he not have asked of us, or rather is he not asking of us, Whether we have ceased to prefer appearances to reality? Let us take a survey of the professions to which he refers and try them by his standard. Is not all literature passing into criticism, just as Athenian literature in the age of Plato was degenerating into sophistry and rhetoric? We can discourse and write about poems and paintings, but we seem to have lost the gift of creating them. Can we wonder that few of them 'come sweetly from nature', while ten thousand reviewers (μάλα μυρίοι) are engaged in dissecting them? Young men, like

Phaedrus, are enamoured of their own literary clique and have but a feeble sympathy with the master-minds of former ages. They recognize 'a *poetical* necessity in the writings of their favourite author, even when he boldly wrote off just what came in his head'. They are beginning to think that Art is enough, just at the time when Art is about to disappear from the world. And would not a great painter, such as Michael Angelo, or a great poet, such as Shakespeare, returning to earth, 'courteously rebuke' us—would he not say that we are putting 'in the place of Art the preliminaries of Art', confusing Art the expression of mind and truth with Art the composition of colours and forms; and perhaps he might more severely chastise some of us for trying to invent 'a new shudder' instead of bringing to the birth living and healthy creations? These he would regard as the signs of an age wanting in original power.

Turning from literature and the arts to law and politics, again we fall under the lash of Socrates. For do we not often make 'the worse appear the better cause'; and do not 'both parties sometimes agree to tell lies'? Is not pleasing 'an art of speaking unconnected with the truth'? There is another text of Socrates which must not be forgotten in relation to this subject. In the endless maze of English law is there any 'dividing the whole into parts or reuniting the parts into a whole' —any semblance of an organized being 'having hands and feet and other members'? Instead of a system there is the Chaos of Anaxagoras (ὁμοῦ πάντα χρήματα) and no Mind or Order. Then again in the noble art of politics, who thinks of first principles and of true ideas? We avowedly follow not the truth but the will of the many (cf. *Rep.* 493). Is not legislation too a sort of literary effort, and might not statesmanship be described as the 'art of enchanting' the house? While there are some politicians who have no knowledge of the truth, but only of what is likely to be approved by 'the many who sit in judgement', there are others who can give no form to their ideal, neither having learned 'the art of persuasion', nor having any insight into the 'characters of men'. Once more, has not medical science become a professional routine, which many 'practise without being able to say who were their instructors'—the application of a few drugs taken from a book instead of a life-long study of the natures and constitutions of human beings? Do we see as clearly as Hippocrates 'that the nature of the body can only be understood as a whole'? (270 c; cf. *Charm.* 156 e). And are not they held to be the wisest physicians who have the greatest distrust of their art? What would Socrates think of our newspapers, of our theology? Perhaps he would be afraid to speak of them;—the one *vox populi*, the other *vox Dei*, he might hesitate to attack them; or he might trace a fanciful connexion between them, and ask doubtfully, whether they are not equally inspired? He would remark that we are always searching for a belief and deploring our unbelief, seeming to prefer popular opinions unverified and contradictory to unpopular truths which are assured to us by the most certain proofs: that our preachers are in the habit of praising God 'without regard to truth and falsehood, attributing to Him every species of greatness and glory, saying that He is all this and the cause of all that, in order that we may exhibit Him as the fairest and best of all' (*Symp.* 198), without any consideration of His real nature and character or of the laws by which He governs the world—seeking for a 'private judgement' and not for the truth or 'God's judgement'. What would he say of the Church, which we praise in like manner, 'meaning ourselves' (258 a), without regard to history or experience? Might he not ask, whether we 'care more for the truth of religion, or for the speaker and the country from which the truth comes'? or, whether the 'select wise' are not 'the many' after all? (*Symp.* 194 c.) So we may fill up the sketch of Socrates, lest, as Phaedrus says, the argument should be too 'abstract and barren of illustrations'. (Cf. *Symp.*, *Apol.*, *Euthyphro.*)

He next proceeds with enthusiasm to define the royal art of dialectic as the power of dividing a whole into parts, and of uniting the parts in a whole, and which may also be regarded (cf. *Soph.*) as the process of the mind talking with herself. The latter view has probably led Plato to the paradox that speech is superior to writing, in which he may seem also to be doing an injustice to himself. For the two cannot be fairly compared in the manner which Plato suggests. The contrast of the living and dead word, and the example of Socrates, which he has represented in the form of the dialogue, seem to have misled him. For speech and writing have really different functions; the one is more transitory, more diffuse, more elastic and capable of adaptation to moods and times; the other is more permanent, more concentrated, and is uttered not to this or that person or audience, but to all the world. In the *Politicus* (294 ff.) the paradox is carried farther; the mind or will of the king is preferred to the written law; he is supposed to be the Law personified, the ideal made Life.

Yet in both these statements there is also contained a truth; they may be compared with one another, and also with the other famous paradox, that 'knowledge cannot be taught'. Socrates means to say, that what is truly written is written in the soul, just as what is truly taught grows up in the soul from within and is not forced upon it from without. When planted in a congenial soil the little seed becomes a tree, and 'the birds of the air build their nests in the branches'. There is an echo of this in the prayer at the end of the Dialogue, 'Give me beauty in the inward soul, and may the inward and outward man be at one'. We may further compare the words of St. Paul, 'Written not on tables of stone, but on fleshly tables of the heart'; and again, 'Ye are my epistles known and read of all men'. There may be a use in writing as a preservative against the forgetfulness of old age, but to live is higher far, to be ourselves the book, or the epistle, the truth embodied in a person, the Word made flesh. Something like this we may believe to have passed before Plato's mind when he affirmed that speech was superior to writing. So in other ages, weary of literature and criticism, of making many books, of writing articles in reviews, some have desired to live more closely in communion with their fellow men, to speak heart to heart, to speak and act only, and not to write, following the example of Socrates and of Christ. . . .

Some other touches of inimitable grace and art and of the deepest wisdom may be also noted; such as the prayer or 'collect' which has just been cited, 'Give me beauty', &c.; or 'the great name which belongs to God alone' (278); or 'the saying of wiser men than our-selves that a man of sense should try to please not his fellow-servants, but his good and noble masters' (274), like St. Paul again; or the description of the 'heavenly originals' at p. 250. . . .

The chief criteria for determining the date of the dialogue are (1) the ages of Lysias and Isocrates; (2) the character of the work.

Lysias was born in the year 458; Isocrates in the year 436, about seven years before the birth of Plato. The first of the two great rhetoricians is described as in the zenith of his fame; the second is still young and full of promise. Now it is argued that this must have been written in the youth of Isocrates, when the promise was not yet ful-filled. And thus we should have to assign the dialogue to a year not later than 406, when Isocrates was thirty and Plato twenty-three years of age, and while Socrates himself was still alive.

Those who argue in this way seem not to reflect how easily Plato can 'invent Egyptians or anything else', and how careless he is of historical truth or probability. Who would suspect that the wise Critias,[1] the virtuous Charmides, had ended their lives among the thirty tyrants? Who would imagine that Lysias, who is here assailed by Socrates, is the son of his old friend Cephalus? or that Isocrates himself is the enemy of Plato and his school? No arguments can be drawn from the appropriateness or inappropriateness of the characters of Plato. (Else, perhaps, it might be further argued that, judging from

[1 See below, p. 788, note.]

their extant remains, insipid rhetoric is far more characteristic of
Isocrates than of Lysias.) But Plato makes use of names which have
often hardly any connexion with the historical characters to whom
they belong. In this instance the comparative favour shown to
Isocrates may possibly be accounted for by the circumstance of his
belonging to the aristocratical, as Lysias to the democratical party.

Few persons will be inclined to suppose, in the superficial manner
of some ancient critics, that a dialogue which treats of love must
necessarily have been written in youth. As little weight can be
attached to the argument that Plato must have visited Egypt before
he wrote the story of Theuth and Thamus. For there is no real proof
that he ever went to Egypt; and even if he did, he might have known
or invented Egyptian traditions before he went there. The late date of
the *Phaedrus* will have to be established by other arguments than these:
the maturity of the thought, the perfection of the style, the insight, the
relation to the other Platonic dialogues, seem to contradict the notion
that it could have been the work of a youth of twenty or twenty-three
years of age. The cosmological notion of the mind as the *primum
mobile*, and the admission of impulse into the immortal nature, also
afford grounds for assigning a later date. (Cf. *Tim.*, *Soph.*, *Laws*.)
Add to this that the picture of Socrates, though in some lesser particulars,—e.g. his going without sandals, his habit of remaining within
the walls, his emphatic declaration that his study is human nature,—
an exact resemblance, is in the main the Platonic and not the real
Socrates. Can we suppose 'the young man to have told such lies' about
his master while he was still alive? Moreover, when two dialogues are
so closely connected as the *Phaedrus* and *Symposium*, there is great
improbability in supposing that one of them was written at least
twenty years after the other. The conclusion seems to be, that the
dialogue was written at some comparatively late but unknown period
of Plato's life, after he had deserted the purely Socratic point of view,
but before he had entered on the more abstract speculations of the
Sophist or the *Philebus*. Taking into account the divisions of the soul,
the doctrine of transmigration, the contemplative nature of the philosophic life, and the character of the style, we shall not be far wrong in
placing the *Phaedrus* in the neighbourhood of the *Republic*; remarking
only that allowance must be made for the poetical element in the
Phaedrus, which, while falling short of the *Republic* in definite philosophic results, seems to have glimpses of a truth beyond.

Two short passages, which are unconnected with the main subject
of the dialogue, may seem to merit a more particular notice: (1) the
locus classicus about mythology; (2) the tale of the grasshoppers.

The first passage is remarkable as showing that Plato was entirely free from what may be termed the Euhemerism of his age. For there were Euhemerists in Hellas long before Euhemerus. Early philosophers, like Anaxagoras and Metrodorus, had found in Homer and mythology hidden meanings. Plato, with a truer instinct, rejects these attractive interpretations; he regards the inventor of them as 'unfortunate'; and they draw a man off from the knowledge of himself. There is a latent criticism, and also a poetical sense in Plato, which enable him to discard them, and yet in another way to make use of poetry and mythology as a vehicle of thought and feeling. What would he have said of the discovery of Christian doctrines in these old Greek legends? While acknowledging that such interpretations are 'very nice', would he not have remarked that they are found in all sacred literatures? They cannot be tested by any criterion of truth, or used to establish any truth; they add nothing to the sum of human knowledge; they are— what we please, and if employed as 'peacemakers' between the new and old are liable to serious misconstruction, as he elsewhere remarks (*Rep.* 378 e). And therefore he would have 'bid Farewell to them; the study of them would take up too much of his time; and he has not as yet learned the true nature of religion'. The 'sophistical' interest of Phaedrus, the little touch about the two versions of the story, the ironical manner in which these explanations are set aside—'the common opinion about them is enough for me'—the allusion to the serpent Typho may be noted in passing; also the general agreement between the tone of this speech and the remark of Socrates which follows afterwards, 'I am a diviner, but a poor one'.

The tale of the grasshoppers is naturally suggested by the surrounding scene. They are also the representatives of the Athenians as children of the soil. Under the image of the lively chirruping grasshoppers who inform the Muses in heaven about those who honour them on earth, Plato intends to represent an Athenian audience (τεττίγεσσιν ἐοικότες). The story is introduced, apparently, to mark a change of subject, and also, like several other allusions which occur in the course of the dialogue, in order to preserve the scene in the recollection of the reader.

No one can duly appreciate the dialogues of Plato, especially the *Phaedrus*, *Symposium*, and portions of the *Republic*, who has not a sympathy with mysticism. To the uninitiated, as he would himself have acknowledged, they will appear to be the dreams of a poet who is disguised as a philosopher. There is a twofold difficulty in apprehending this aspect of the Platonic writings. First, we do not immediately realize that under the marble exterior of Greek literature was concealed a soul thrilling with spiritual emotion. Secondly, the forms or figures which the Platonic philosophy assumes are not like the images of the prophet Isaiah, or of the Apocalypse, familiar to us in the days of our youth. By mysticism we mean, not the extravagance of an erring fancy, but the concentration of reason in feeling, the enthusiastic love of the good, the true, the one, the sense of the infinity of knowledge and of the marvel of the human faculties. When feeding upon such thoughts the 'wing of the soul' is renewed and gains strength; she is raised above 'the manikins of earth' and their opinions, waiting in wonder to know, and working with reverence to find out, what God in this or in another life may reveal to her.

PHAEDRUS

Persons of the Dialogue

SOCRATES, PHAEDRUS

SCENE: Under a plane-tree, by the banks of the Ilissus

Socrates. My dear Phaedrus, whence come you, and whither are you going?

Phaedrus. I have come from the house of Lysias the son of Cephalus, and I am going to take a walk outside the wall, for I have been sitting with him the whole morning; and following the advice of our common friend Acumenus I take my walk along the road rather than around the race-tracks; he says it is less tiring.

Soc. There he is right. Lysias then, I suppose, was in the town? b

Phaedr. Yes, he was staying with Epicrates, here at the house of Morychus; that house which is near the temple of Olympian Zeus.

Soc. And how did he entertain you? Can I be wrong in supposing that Lysias gave you a feast of discourse?

Phaedr. You shall hear, if you can spare time to accompany me.

Soc. Do you doubt that I should deem the conversation of you and Lysias 'a thing of higher import', as I may say in the words of Pindar, 'than any business'?

Phaedr. Will you go on? c

Soc. And will you go on with the narration?

Phaedr. My tale, Socrates, is one of your sort, for love was the theme which occupied us—love after a fashion: Lysias has been writing about a fair youth who was being tempted, but not by a lover; and this was the point: he ingeniously proved that the non-lover should be accepted rather than the lover.

Soc. O that is noble of him! I wish that he would say the poor man rather than the rich, and the old man rather than the young one;—then he would meet the case of me and of many a man; d his words would be quite refreshing, and he would be a public benefactor. For my part, I do so long to hear his speech, that if you walk all the way to Megara, and when you have reached the wall come back, as Herodicus recommends, without going in, I will keep you company.

Phaedr. What do you mean, my good Socrates? How can you
228 imagine that my unpractised memory can do justice to an
elaborate work, which the greatest rhetorician of the age spent a
long time in composing. Indeed, I cannot; I would prefer such
a talent to a large sum of money.

Soc. I believe that I know Phaedrus about as well as I know
myself, and I am very sure that the speech of Lysias was repeated
to him, not once only, but again and again;—he insisted on
hearing it many times over and Lysias was very willing to gratify
b him; at last, when nothing else would do, he got hold of the book,
and looked at what he most wanted to see,—this occupied him
during the whole morning;—and then when he was tired with
sitting, he went out to take a walk, not until, by the dog, as I
believe, he had simply learned by heart the entire discourse,
unless it was unusually long, and he started on a walk outside the
wall that he might practise his lesson. There he saw a certain lover
of discourse who had a similar weakness;—he saw and rejoiced;
now thought he, 'I shall have a partner in my revels'. And he
c invited him to lead on. But when the lover of discourse begged
that he would repeat the tale, he gave himself airs and said, 'No
I cannot', as if he were not longing to do so; although, if the
hearer had refused, he would sooner or later have been compelled by him to listen whether he would or no. Therefore,
Phaedrus, bid him do at once what he will soon do whether
bidden or not.

Phaedr. I see that you will by no means let me off until I speak
in some fashion or other; and, in truth, my best plan is to speak
as I best can.

Soc. You judge my intention correctly.

d *Phaedr.* I will do as I say; but believe me, Socrates, I did not
learn the very words—O no; nevertheless I have a general notion
of what he said, and will give you a summary of the points in
which the lover differed from the non-lover. Let me begin at the
beginning.

Soc. Yes, my sweet one; but you must first of all show what
you have in your left hand under your cloak, for that roll, as I
suspect, is the actual discourse. Now, much as I love you, I would
not have you suppose that I am going to have your memory
e exercised at my expense, if you have Lysias himself here.

Phaedr. Enough; I see that I have no hope of practising my art upon you. But if I am to read, where would you please to sit? 229

Soc. Let us turn aside and go by the Ilissus; we will sit down at some quiet spot.

Phaedr. I am fortunate in not having my sandals, and as you never have any, I think that we may go along the brook and cool our feet in the water; this will be the easiest way, and at midday and in the summer is far from being unpleasant.

Soc. Lead on, and look out for a place in which we can sit down.

Phaedr. Do you see that tallest plane-tree in the distance?

Soc. Yes.

Phaedr. There are shade and gentle breezes, and grass on which b we may either sit or lie down.

Soc. Move forward.

Phaedr. I should like to know, Socrates, whether the place is not somewhere here at which Boreas is said to have carried off Orithyia from the banks of the Ilissus?

Soc. Such is the tradition.

Phaedr. And is this the exact spot? The little stream is delightfully clear and bright; I can fancy that there might be maidens playing near.

Soc. I believe that the spot is not exactly here, but about a c quarter of a mile lower down, where you cross to the shrine of Agra,[1] and there is, I think, some sort of an altar of Boreas at the place.

Phaedr. I have never noticed it; but I beseech you to tell me, Socrates, do you believe this tale?

Soc. The wise are doubtful, and I should not be singular if, like them, I too doubted. I might have a rational explanation that Orithyia was playing with Pharmacia, when a northern gust carried her over the neighbouring rocks; and this being the manner of her death, she was said to have been carried away by Boreas. There is a discrepancy, however, about the locality; according to another version of the story she was taken from the d Areopagus, and not from this place. Now I quite acknowledge that these allegories are very nice, but he is not to be envied who

[1] [A temple of Demeter situated in the Athenian deme of Agra. There is no reference, as was once supposed, to Artemis Agrotera or Agraia.]

has to invent them; much labour and ingenuity will be required of him; and when he has once begun, he must go on and rehabilitate Hippocentaurs and chimeras dire. Gorgons and winged e steeds flow in apace, and numberless other inconceivable and portentous natures. And if he is sceptical about them, and would fain reduce them one after another to the rules of probability, this sort of crude philosophy will take up a great deal of time. Now I have no leisure for such inquiries; shall I tell you why? I 230 must first know myself, as the Delphian inscription says; to be curious about that which is not my concern, while I am still in ignorance of my own self, would be ridiculous. And therefore I bid farewell to all this; the common opinion is enough for me. For, as I was saying, I want to know not about this, but about myself: am I a monster more complicated and swollen with passion than Typho, or a creature of a gentler and simpler sort, possessing, by divine grace, a nature devoid of pride. But meanwhile let me ask you, friend: have we not reached the plane-tree to which you were conducting us?

b   *Phaedr.* Yes, this is the tree.

Soc. By Hera, a fair resting-place, full of summer sounds and scents. Here is this lofty and spreading plane-tree, and the agnus castus high and clustering, in the fullest blossom and the greatest fragrance; and the stream which flows beneath the plane-tree is deliciously cold to the feet. Judging from the ornaments and images, this must be a spot sacred to Achelous and the Nymphs. c How delightful is the breeze:—so very sweet; and there is a sound in the air shrill and summerlike which makes answer to the chorus of the cicadae. But the greatest charm of all is the grass, like a pillow gently sloping to the head. My dear Phaedrus, you have been an admirable guide.

Phaedr. What an incomprehensible being you are, Socrates: when you are in the country, as you say, you really are like some d stranger who is led about by a guide. Do you ever cross the border? I rather think that you never venture even outside the gates.

Soc. I must ask your forgiveness, my good friend. I am a lover of knowledge, and the men who dwell in the city are my teachers, and not the trees or the country. Though I do indeed believe that you have found a spell with which to draw me out of the city into the country, like a hungry animal before whom a bough or a bunch of fruit is waved. For only hold up before me in like manner a book, and you may lead me all round Attica, and over e the wide world. And now having arrived, I intend to lie down, and do you choose any posture in which you can read best. Begin.

Phaedr. Listen. 'You know how matters stand with me; and how, as I conceive, this affair may be arranged for the advantage 231 of both of us. And I maintain that I ought not to fail in my suit, because I am not your lover: for lovers repent of the kindnesses which they have shown when their passion ceases, but to the non-lovers who are free and not under any compulsion, no time of repentance ever comes; for they confer their benefits according to the measure of their ability, in the way which is most conducive to their own interest. Then again, lovers consider how by reason of their love they have neglected their own concerns and ren-dered service to others: and when to these benefits conferred they add on the troubles which they have endured, they think that b they have long ago made to the beloved a very ample return. But the non-lover has no such tormenting recollections; he has never neglected his affairs or quarrelled with his relations; he has no troubles to add up or excuses to invent; and being well rid of all these evils, why should he not freely do what, as he supposes, will gratify the beloved? If you say that the lover is more to be esteemed, because his love is thought to be greater; for he is c willing to say and do what is hateful to other men, in order to please his beloved;—that, if true, is only a proof that he will prefer any future love to his present, and will injure his old love at the pleasure of the new. And how, in a matter of such infinite importance, can a man be right in trusting himself to one who is afflicted with a malady which no experienced person would d attempt to cure, for the patient himself admits that he is not in his right mind, and acknowledges that he is wrong in his mind, but says that he is unable to control himself? And if he came to his right mind, would he ever imagine that the desires were good which he conceived when in his wrong mind? Once more, there are many more non-lovers than lovers; and if you choose the best of the lovers, you will not have many to choose from; but if you choose the most congenial of the non-lovers, the choice will be larger, and you will be far more likely to find among them a e person who is worthy of your friendship. If public opinion be

your dread, and you would avoid discovery and reproach, in all
232 probability the lover, who is always thinking that other men are
as emulous of him as he is of them, will boast to some one of his
successes, and make a show of them openly in the pride of his
heart;—he wants others to know that his labour has not been
lost; but the non-lover is more his own master, and is desirous of
solid good, and not of the opinion of mankind. Again, the lover
may be generally noted or seen following the beloved (this is his
regular occupation), and whenever they are observed to exchange
two words they are supposed to meet about some affair of love
b either past or in contemplation; but when non-lovers meet, no
one asks the reason why, because people know that talking to
another is natural, whether friendship or mere pleasure be the
motive. Once more, if you fear the fickleness of friendship, consider that in any other case a quarrel might be a mutual calamity; but now, when you have given up what is most precious to
c you, you will be the greater loser, and therefore, you will have
more reason in being afraid of the lover, for his vexations are
many, and he is always fancying that every one is leagued against
him. Wherefore also he debars his beloved from the society of
others; he will not have you intimate with the wealthy, lest they
should outbid him by their wealth, or with men of education, lest
they should vanquish him by their understanding; and he is
d equally afraid of anybody's influence who has any other advantage over himself. If he can persuade you to make yourself hateful
to them, you are left without a friend in the world; or if, out of a
regard to your own interest, you have more sense than to comply
with his desire, you will have to quarrel with him. But those who are
non-lovers, and whose success in love is the reward of their merit,
will not be jealous of the companions of their beloved, and will
rather hate those who refuse to be his associates, thinking that
their favourite is slighted by the latter and benefited by the former;
e so that the affair is, in this case, likely to bring him much more
love than hatred. Many lovers too have loved the person of a
youth before they knew his character or obtained experience of
his circumstances; so that they can not be sure whether, when
their passion has passed away, they will continue to be his friends;
233 whereas, in the case of non-lovers who were always friends, the
friendship is not lessened by the favours granted; but the recollec-

tion of these remains with them, and is an earnest of good things
to come. Further, I say that you are likely to be more improved
by me than by a lover. For they praise your words and actions in
a wrong way; partly, because they are afraid of offending you,
and also, their judgement is weakened by passion. Such are the b
feats which love exhibits; he makes things painful to the disappointed which give no pain to others; he compels the successful
lover to praise what ought not to give him pleasure, and therefore
the beloved is to be pitied rather than envied. But if you listen to
me, in the first place, I, in my intercourse with you, shall not
merely regard present enjoyment, but also future advantage,
being not mastered by love, but my own master; nor for small c
causes taking violent dislikes, but even when the cause is great,
slowly laying up little wrath—unintentional offences I shall forgive, and intentional ones I shall try to prevent; for these are the
marks of a friendship which will last. Do you think that a lover
only can be a firm friend? reflect:—if this were true, we should
set small value on sons, or fathers, or mothers; nor should we d
ever have loyal friends, for our love of them arises not from
passion, but from other associations. Further, if we ought to
shower favours on those who are the most eager suitors,—on that
principle, we ought always to do good, not to the most virtuous,
but to the most needy; for they are the persons who will be most
relieved, and will therefore be the most grateful; and when you
make a feast you should invite not your friend, but the beggar e
and the empty soul; for they will love you, and attend you, and
come about your doors, and will be the best pleased, and the
most grateful, and will invoke many a blessing on your head. Yet
surely you ought not to be granting favours to those who besiege
you with prayer, but to those who are best able to reward you;
nor to the lover only, but to those who are worthy of love; nor to
those who will enjoy the bloom of your youth, but to those who 234
will share their possessions with you as you grow older; nor to
those who, having succeeded, will glory in their success to others,
but to those who will be modest and tell no tales; nor to those
who care about you for a moment only, but to those who will
continue your friends through life; nor to those who, when their
passion is over, will pick a quarrel with you, but rather to those
who, when the charm of youth has left you, will show their own

b virtue. Remember what I have said; and consider yet this further point: friends admonish the lover under the idea that his way of life is bad, but no one of his kindred ever yet censured the non-lover, or thought that he was ill advised about his own interests.

'Perhaps you will ask me whether I propose that you should indulge every non-lover. To which I reply that not even the lover would advise you to be so disposed towards all lovers, for the c indiscriminate favour is less esteemed by the rational recipient, and less easily hidden by him who would escape the censure of the world. Now love ought to be for the advantage of both parties, and for the injury of neither.

'I believe that I have said enough; but if there is anything more which you desire or which in your opinion needs to be supplied, ask and I will answer.'

Now, Socrates, what do you think? Is not the discourse excellent, more especially in the matter of the language?

d *Soc.* Yes, quite admirable; the effect on me was ravishing. And this I owe to you, Phaedrus, for I observed you while reading to be in an ecstasy, and thinking that you are more experienced in these matters than I am, I followed your example, and, like you, my divine darling, I became inspired with a phrenzy.

Phaedr. Indeed, you are pleased to be merry.

Soc. Do you mean that I am not in earnest?

e *Phaedr.* Now don't talk in that way, Socrates, but let me have your real opinion; I adjure you, by Zeus, the god of friendship, to tell me whether you think that any Hellene could have said more or spoken better on the same subject.

Soc. Well, but are you and I expected to praise the sentiments of the author, or only the clearness, and roundness, and finish, and tournure of the language? As to the first I willingly submit
235 to your better judgement, for I am not worthy to form an opinion, having only attended to the rhetorical manner; and I was doubting whether this could have been defended even by Lysias himself; I thought, though I speak under correction, that he repeated himself two or three times, either from want of fluency in speaking at length on a single topic, or from want of interest in such a subject; and also, he appeared to me ostentatiously to exult in showing how well he could say the same thing in two different ways.

Phaedr. Nonsense, Socrates; what you call repetition was the b
especial merit of the speech; for he omitted no topic of which the
subject rightly allowed, and I do not think that anyone could
have spoken better or more exhaustively.

Soc. There I cannot go along with you. Ancient sages, men
and women, who have spoken and written of these things, would
rise up in judgement against me, if out of complaisance I assented
to you.

Phaedr. Who are they, and where did you hear anything better c
than this?

Soc. I am sure that I must have heard; but at this moment I
do not remember from whom; perhaps from Sappho the fair, or
Anacreon the wise; or, possibly, from a prose writer. What
ground have I for saying so? Why, because I perceive that my
bosom is full, and that I could make another speech as good as
that of Lysias, and different. Now I am certain that this is not an
invention of my own, who am well aware that I know nothing,
and therefore I can only infer that I have been filled through the d
ears, like a pitcher, from the waters of another, though I have
actually forgotten in my stupidity how this occurred, and who
was my informant.

Phaedr. That is grand:—but never mind how you heard the
discourse or from whom; let that be a mystery not to be divulged
even at my earnest desire. Only, as you say, promise[1] to make
another and better oration, equal in length and entirely new, on
the same subject; and I, like the nine Archons, will promise to
set up a golden image at Delphi, not only of myself, but of you
and as large as life.
                                                              e
Soc. You are a dear friend, of golden disposition indeed, if you
suppose me to mean that Lysias has altogether missed the mark,
and that I can make a speech from which all his arguments are
to be excluded. The worst of authors will say something which is
to the point. Who, for example, could speak on this thesis of yours
without praising the discretion of the non-lover and blaming the 236
indiscretion of the lover? These are the commonplaces of the
subject which must come in (for what else is there to be said?)
and must be allowed and excused; the only merit is in the arrangement of them, for there can be none in the invention; but

[1] Reading ὑπόσχες εἰπεῖν.

when you leave the commonplaces, then there may be some originality.

Phaedr. I admit that there is reason in what you say, and I too will be reasonable, and will allow you to start with the premiss

b that the lover is more disordered in his wits than the non-lover; if in what remains you make a longer and better speech than Lysias, and use other arguments, then I say again, that a statue you shall have of beaten gold, and take your place by the colossal offerings of the Cypselids at Olympia.

Soc. How profoundly in earnest is the lover, because to tease him I lay a finger upon his love! And so, Phaedrus, you really imagine that I am going to improve upon the ingenuity of Lysias?

Phaedr. There I have you as you had me, and you must just

c speak 'as you best can'. Do not let us exchange *tu quoque* as in a farce, or compel me to say to you as you said to me, 'I know Socrates as well as I know myself, and he was wanting to speak, but he gave himself airs.' Rather I would have you consider that from this place we stir not until you have unbosomed yourself of the speech; for here are we all alone, and I am stronger, remember,

d and younger than you:—Wherefore perpend, and do not compel me to use violence.

Soc. But, my sweet Phaedrus, how ridiculous it would be of me to compete with Lysias in an extempore speech! He is a master in his art and I am an untaught man.

Phaedr. You see how matters stand; and therefore let there be no more pretences; for, indeed, I know the word that is irresistible.

Soc. Then don't say it.

Phaedr. Yes, but I will; and my word shall be an oath. 'I say, or rather swear'—but what god will be the witness of my oath?—

e 'By this plane-tree I swear, that unless you repeat the discourse here in the face of this very plane-tree, I will never again either recite or report to you any speech by any author.'

Soc. Villain! I am conquered; the poor lover of discourse has no more to say.

Phaedr. Then why are you still at your tricks?

Soc. I am not going to play tricks now that you have taken the oath, for I cannot allow myself to be starved.

Phaedr. Proceed.

237   *Soc.* Shall I tell you what I will do?

Phaedr. What?

Soc. I will veil my face and gallop through the discourse as fast as I can, for if I see you I shall feel ashamed and not know what to say.

Phaedr. Only go on and you may do anything else which you please.

Soc. Come, O ye Muses, whether you have received your name Ligeiai [clear-toned] from the character of your strains, or because the Ligurians are a musical race, help, O help me in the tale which my good friend here desires me to rehearse, in order that his friend whom he always deemed wise may seem to him to be wiser now than ever.   b

Once upon a time there was a fair boy, or, more properly speaking, a youth; he was very fair and had a great many lovers; and there was one special cunning one, who had persuaded the youth that he did not love him, but he really loved him more than any; and one day when he was paying his addresses to him, he used this very argument—that he ought to accept the non-lover rather than the lover; his words were as follows:—

'All good counsel begins in the same way; a man should know what he is advising about, or his counsel will all come to nought.   c But most people are not aware of their ignorance of a thing's essential nature, and, not having come to an understanding at first because they think that they know, they end, as might be expected, in contradicting one another and themselves. Now you and I must not be guilty of this fundamental error which we condemn in others; but as our question is whether the lover or non-lover is to be preferred, let us first of all agree in defining the nature and power of love, and then, keeping our eyes upon the   d definition and to this appealing, let us further inquire whether love brings advantage or disadvantage.

'Every one sees that love is a desire, and we know that even non-lovers desire the beautiful. Now in what way is the lover to be distinguished from the non-lover? Let us note that in every one of us there are two guiding and ruling principles which lead us whither they will; one is the natural desire of pleasure, the other is an acquired opinion which aspires after the best; and these two are sometimes in harmony and then again at war, and   e sometimes the one, sometimes the other conquers. When opinion

by the help of reason leads us to the best, and proves superior,
238 its government is called temperance; but when desire, which is
devoid of reason, rules in us and drags us to pleasure, that power
of misrule is called excess (*hubris*). Now excess has many names,
being composed of many members, and many forms, and any of
these forms when very marked gives its own name to the possessor,
a name neither honourable nor creditable. The desire of eating,
for example, which gets the better of the higher reason and the
b other desires, is called gluttony, and he who has it is called a
glutton; the tyrannical desire of drink, which inclines the possessor of the desire to drink, has a name which is only too obvious,
and there can be as little doubt by what name any other appetite
of the same family would be called;—it will be the name of that
which happens to be dominant. And now I think that you will
perceive the drift of my discourse; but as every spoken word is in
a manner plainer than the unspoken, I had better say further
that the irrational desire which overcomes the tendency of opin-
c ion towards right, and is led away to the enjoyment of beauty,
and especially of personal beauty, by the desires which are her
own kindred—that supreme desire, I say, which by leading
conquers and by the force of passion is reinforced, from this very
force, receiving a name, is called love (ἐρρωμένως ἔρως).'

And now, dear Phaedrus, I shall pause for an instant to ask
whether you do not think me, as I appear to myself, inspired?

Phaedr. Yes, Socrates, you seem to have a very unusual flow of
words.

Soc. Listen to me, then, in silence; for surely the place is holy;
d so that you must not wonder, if, as I proceed, I appear to be in a
divine fury, for already I am getting into dithyrambics.

Phaedr. Nothing can be truer.

Soc. The responsibility rests with you. But hear what follows,
and perhaps the fit may be averted; all is in their hands above.
I will go on talking to my youth. Listen:—

Thus, my friend, we have declared and defined the nature of
the subject. Keeping the definition in view, let us now inquire
e what advantage or disadvantage is likely to ensue from the lover
or the non-lover to him who accepts their advances.

He who is the victim of his passions and the slave of pleasure
will of course desire to make his beloved as agreeable to himself

as possible. Now to him who has a mind diseased anything is agreeable which is not opposed to him; but that which is equal or superior is hateful; and therefore the lover will not brook any superiority or equality on the part of his beloved; he is always 239 employed in reducing him to inferiority. And the ignorant is the inferior of the wise, the coward of the brave, the slow of speech of the speaker, the dull of the clever. Such, or even graver than these, are the mental defects in which a lover will necessarily delight when they are implanted by nature; and which otherwise he must contrive to implant, if he would not be deprived of his fleeting joy. But then he cannot help being jealous, and will debar his beloved from the advantages of society which would b most tend to make a man of him, doing him great harm; and especially harmful is it to withdraw him from that society which would have given him wisdom. That is to say, in his excessive fear lest he should come to be despised in his eyes he will be compelled to banish from him divine philosophy; and there is no greater injury which he can inflict upon him than this. He will contrive that his beloved shall be wholly ignorant, and in everything shall look to him; he is to be the delight of the lover's heart, and a curse to himself. Verily, a lover is a profitable guardian and c associate for him in all that relates to his mind.

Let us next see how his master, whose law of life is pleasure and not good, will keep and train the body of his servant. Will he not choose a beloved who is delicate rather than sturdy and strong? One brought up in shady bowers and not in the bright sun, a stranger to manly exercises and the sweat of toil, accustomed only to a soft and luxurious diet, instead of the hues of health having the colours of paint and ornament, and the rest of a piece?—such d a life as any one can imagine and which I need not detail at length. But I may sum up all that I have to say in a word, and pass on. Such a person in war, or in any of the great crises of life, will be the anxiety of his friends and also of his lover, and certainly not the terror of his enemies.

Leaving this obvious point, let us tell what advantage or disadvantage the beloved will receive from the guardianship and e society of his lover in the matter of his property; this is the next point to be considered. The lover will be the first to see what, indeed, will be sufficiently evident to all men, that he desires

above all things to deprive his beloved of those dearest and most
240 kindly disposed to him, and of his dearest and holiest possessions;
father, mother, kindred, friends,—he would be glad to see him
deprived of all who he thinks may be hinderers or reprovers of
their most sweet converse; he will even cast a jealous eye upon
his gold and silver or other property, because these make him a
less easy prey, and when caught less manageable; hence a lover
is of necessity displeased at his possession of them and rejoices at
their loss; and he would like him to be wifeless, childless, home-
less, as well; and the longer the better, for what he desires is to
prolong his selfish fruition for as long as possible.

There are some sort of animals, such as flatterers, who are
b dangerous and mischievous enough, and yet nature has mingled
a temporary pleasure and grace in their composition. You may
say that a courtesan is hurtful, and disapprove of many such
creatures and practices, and yet for the time they are very pleasant.
But the lover is not only hurtful to his love; he is also an extremely
disagreeable companion. The old proverb says that 'birds of a
c feather flock together'; I suppose that equality of years inclines
them to the same pleasures, and similarity begets friendship; yet
you may have more than enough even of this. Constraint, also, is
said to be grievous to all men at all times. But the relation between
the lover and his beloved, apart from their unlikeness, is as
constrained as possible. For he is old and his love is young, and
neither day nor night will he leave him if he can help; necessity
d and the sting of desire drive him on, and allure him with the
pleasure which he receives from seeing, hearing, touching, perceiving him in every way. And therefore he is delighted to fasten
upon him and to minister to him. But what pleasure or consola-
tion can the beloved be receiving all this time? Must he not feel
the extremity of disgust when he looks at a face from which
youthful charm has faded, as indeed it has from the whole
e person of the lover? If the mention of such things is disagreeable,
much worse is it to be forced into daily contact with them; for he
is jealously watched and guarded against everything and everybody, and has to hear misplaced and exaggerated praises of himself,
and censures equally inappropriate, which are intolerable when
the man is sober, and, when he is drunk, become disgusting, as
well as intolerable, in their wearisome and unrestrained frankness.

And not only while his love continues is he mischievous and unpleasant, but when his love ceases he becomes a perfidious enemy of him on whom he showered his oaths and prayers and 241 promises, and yet could hardly prevail upon him to tolerate the tedium of his company even from motives of interest. The hour of payment arrives, and now he is the servant of another master; instead of love and infatuation, wisdom and temperance are his bosom's lords; but the beloved has not discovered the change which has taken place in him, when he asks for a return and recalls to his recollection former sayings and doings; he believes himself to be speaking to the same person, and the other, not b having the courage to confess the truth, and not knowing how to fulfil the oaths and promises which he made when under the dominion of folly, and having now grown wise and temperate, does not want to do as he did or to be as he was before. And so he runs away and is constrained to be a defaulter; the oyster-shell[1] has fallen with the other side uppermost—he changes pursuit into flight, while the other is compelled to follow him with passion and imprecation, not knowing that he ought never from the first to have accepted a demented lover instead of a sensible non- c lover; and that in making such a choice he was giving himself up to a faithless, morose, envious, disagreeable being, hurtful to his estate, hurtful to his bodily health, and still more hurtful to the cultivation of his mind, than which there neither is nor ever will be anything more honoured in the eyes both of gods and men. Consider this, fair youth, and know that in the friendship of the lover there is no real kindness; he has an appetite and wants to feed upon you:

> As wolves love lambs so lovers love their loves.   d

But I told you so, I am speaking in verse, and therefore I had better make an end; enough.

Phaedr. I thought that you were only half-way and were going to make a similar speech about all the advantages of accepting the non-lover. Why do you not proceed?

Soc. Does not your simplicity observe that I have got out of e dithyrambics into heroics, when only uttering a censure on the

---

[1] In allusion to a game in which two parties fled or pursued according as an oyster-shell which was thrown into the air fell with the dark or light side uppermost.

lover? And if I am to add the praises of the non-lover what will become of me? Do you not perceive that my wits are plainly overpowered by the Nymphs to whom you have mischievously exposed me? And therefore I will only add that the non-lover has all the advantages in which the lover is accused of being deficient. And now I will say no more; there has been enough of 242 both of them. Leaving the tale to its fate, I will cross the river and make the best of my way home, lest a worse thing be inflicted upon me by you.

Phaedr. Not yet, Socrates; not until the heat of the day has passed; do you not see that the hour is almost noon? there is the midday sun standing still, as people say, in the meridian. Let us rather stay and talk over what has been said, and then return in the cool.

Soc. Your love of discourse, Phaedrus, is superhuman, simply marvellous, and I do not believe that there is any one of your b contemporaries who has either made or in one way or another has compelled others to make an equal number of speeches. I would except Simmias the Theban, but all the rest are far behind you. And now I do verily believe that you have been the cause of another, which I have to pronounce.

Phaedr. That is good news. But what do you mean?

Soc. I mean to say that as I was about to cross the stream the usual sign was given to me,—that sign which always forbids, but c never bids, me to do anything which I am going to do; and I thought that I heard a voice saying in my ear that I had been guilty of impiety, and that I must not go away until I had made an atonement. Now I am a diviner, though not a very good one, but I have enough religion for my own use, as you might say of a bad speller—his spelling is good enough for him; and I now clearly perceive my error. O my friend, how prophetic is the human soul! Some time ago, while I was still speaking, I had a d sort of misgiving, and, like Ibycus, 'I was troubled; I feared that I might be buying honour from men at the price of sinning against the gods.' Now I recognize my error.

Phaedr. What error?

Soc. That was a dreadful speech which you brought with you, and you made me utter one as bad.

Phaedr. How so?

Soc. It was foolish, I say,—to a certain extent, impious; can anything be more dreadful?

Phaedr. Nothing, if the speech was really such as you describe.

Soc. Well, and is not Eros the son of Aphrodite, and a god?

Phaedr. So men say.

Soc. But that was not acknowledged by Lysias in his speech, nor by you in that other speech which you by a charm drew from e my lips. For if love be, as he surely is, a divinity, he cannot be evil. Yet this was the error of both the speeches. There was also a simplicity about them which was refreshing; having no truth or 243 honesty in them, nevertheless they pretended to be something, hoping to succeed in deceiving the manikins of earth and gain celebrity among them. Wherefore I must have a purgation. And I bethink me of an ancient purgation of mythological error which was devised, not by Homer, for he never had the wit to discover why he was blind, but by Stesichorus, who was a philosopher and knew the reason why; and therefore, when he lost his eyes, for that was the penalty which was inflicted upon him for reviling the lovely Helen, he at once purged himself. And the purgation was a recantation, which began thus,—

False is that word of mine—the truth is that thou didst not embark in well-benched ships, nor ever go to the citadel of Troy; b

and when he had completed his poem, which is called 'the recantation', immediately his sight returned to him. Now I will be wiser than either Stesichorus or Homer, in that I am going to make my recantation for reviling love before I suffer; and this I will attempt, not as before, veiled and ashamed, but with forehead bold and bare.

Phaedr. Nothing could be more agreeable to me than to hear you say so.

Soc. Only think, my good Phaedrus, what an utter want of c delicacy was shown in the two discourses; I mean, in my own and in that which you recited out of the book. Would not any one who was himself of a noble and gentle nature, and who loved or ever had loved a nature like his own, when we tell of the petty causes of lovers' jealousies, and of their exceeding animosities, and of the injuries which they do to their beloved, have imagined that our ideas of love were taken from some haunt of sailors to

which good manners were unknown—he would certainly never
d have admitted the justice of our censure?

Phaedr. I dare say not, Socrates.

Soc. Therefore, because I blush at the thought of this person,
and also because I am afraid of Love himself, I desire to wash the
brine out of my ears with water from the spring; and I would
counsel Lysias not to delay, but to write another discourse, which
shall prove that *ceteris paribus* the lover ought to be accepted rather
than the non-lover.

Phaedr. Be assured that he shall. You shall speak the praises of
the lover, and Lysias shall be compelled by me to write another
e discourse on the same theme.

Soc. You will be true to your nature in that, and therefore I
believe you.

Phaedr. Speak, and fear not.

Soc. But where is the fair youth whom I was addressing before,
and who ought to listen now; lest, if he hear me not, he should
accept a non-lover before he knows what he is doing?

Phaedr. He is close at hand, and always at your service.

Soc. Know then, fair youth, that the former discourse was the
244 word of Phaedrus, the son of Pythocles, of the deme Myrrhina.
And this which I am about to utter is the recantation of Stesichorus
the son of Euphemus, who comes from the town of Himera, and
is to the following effect: 'False was that word of mine' that the
beloved ought to accept the non-lover when he might have the
lover, because the one is sane, and the other mad. It might be so if
madness were simply an evil; but there is also a madness which
is a divine gift, and the source of the chiefest blessings granted
to men. For prophecy is a madness, and the prophetess at Delphi
b and the priestesses at Dodona when out of their senses have conferred great benefits on Hellas, both in public and private life, but
when in their senses few or none. And I might also tell you how
the Sibyl and other inspired persons have given to many an one
many an intimation of the future which has saved them from
falling. But it would be tedious to speak of what every one knows.

There will be more reason in appealing to the ancient inventors of names,[1] who would never have connected prophecy
c (μαντική), which foretells the future and is the noblest of arts,

[1] Cf. *Crat.* 388 foll.

with madness (μανική), or called them both by the same name, if they had deemed madness to be a disgrace or dishonour;—they must have thought that there was an inspired madness which was a noble thing; for the two words, μαντική and μανική, are really the same, and the letter τ is only a modern and tasteless insertion. And this is confirmed by the name which was given by them to the rational investigation of futurity, whether made by the help of birds or other signs—this, for as much as it is an art which supplies from the reasoning faculty mind (νοῦς) and information (ἰστορία) to human thought (οἴησις), they originally termed οἰονοιστική, but the word has been lately altered and made sonorous by the modern introduction of the letter Omega (οἰονοι-στική and οἰωνιστική), and in proportion as prophecy (μαντική) is more perfect and august than augury, both in name and fact, in the same proportion, as the ancients testify, is madness superior to a sane mind (σωφροσύνη), for the one is only of human, but the other of divine, origin. Again, where plagues and mightiest woes have bred in certain families, owing to some ancient blood-guiltiness, there madness, inspiring and taking possession of those whom destiny has appointed,[1] has found deliverance, having recourse to prayers and religious rites. And learning thence the use of purifications and mysteries, it has sheltered from evil, future as well as present, the man who has some part in this gift, and has afforded a release from his present calamity to one who is truly possessed, and duly out of his mind. The third kind is the madness of those who are possessed by the Muses; which taking hold of a delicate and virgin soul, and there inspiring frenzy, awakens lyrical and all other numbers; with these adorning the myriad actions of ancient heroes for the instruction of posterity. But he who, having no touch of the Muses' madness in his soul, comes to the door and thinks that he will get into the temple by the help of art—he, I say, and his poetry are not admitted; the sane man disappears and is nowhere when he enters into rivalry with the madman.

I might tell of many other noble deeds which have sprung from inspired madness. And therefore, let not the mere thought of this

d

e

245

b

[1 The comma in line d 7 should come after οἷς ἔδει. In the same line, it seems necessary to insert ἦν after γενῶν, with Hermann; and in line e 7 ἑαυτῆς should be retained in the text.]

frighten us, and let us not be scared and confused by an argument which says that the temperate friend is to be chosen rather than the inspired, but let him further show that love is not sent by the gods for any good to lover or beloved; if he can do so we will allow him to carry off the palm. And we, on our part, must prove in answer to him that the madness of love is the greatest of heaven's

c blessings, and the proof shall be one which the wise will receive, and the witling disbelieve. But first of all, let us view the affections and actions of the soul divine and human, and try to ascertain the truth about them. The beginning of our proof is as follows:—

[1]The soul through all her being is immortal, for that which is ever in motion[2] is immortal; but that which moves another and is moved by another, in ceasing to move ceases also to live. Only the self-moving, since it cannot depart from itself, never ceases to move, and is the fountain and beginning of motion to all that moves besides. Now, the beginning is unbegotten, for that which

d is begotten must have a beginning; but this itself cannot be begotten of anything, for if it were dependent upon something, then the begotten would not come from a *beginning*.[3] But since it is unbegotten, it must also be indestructible. For surely if a beginning were destroyed, then it could neither come into being itself from any source, nor serve as the beginning of other things, if it be true that all things must have a beginning. Thus it is proved that the self-moving is the beginning of motion; and this can neither be destroyed nor begotten, else the whole heavens and all

e creation[4] would collapse and stand still, and, lacking all power of motion, never again have birth. But whereas the self-moving is proved to be immortal, he who affirms that this is the very meaning and essence of the soul will not be put to confusion. For every body which is moved from without is soul-less, but that which is self-moved from within is animate, and our usage makes it plain

246 what is the nature of the soul. But if this be true, that the soul is identical with the self-moving, it must follow of necessity that the soul is unbegotten and immortal. Enough of her immortality: let us pass to the description of her form.

---

[1] Translated by Cic. *Tus. Quaest.* I. 24.

[2] [Or, reading αὐτοκίνητον with Oxyrhynchus papyrus 1016 (third century A.D.), 'that which moves itself'. For a defence of this reading, see Robin's Introduction to this dialogue, p. lxxvii.]   [3] [Reading ἐξ ἀρχῆς with the manuscripts.]

[4] [According to another reading, 'and the whole earth'.]

To show her true nature would be a theme of large and more than mortal discourse, but an image of it may be given in a briefer discourse within the scope of man; in this way, then, let us speak. Let the soul be compared to a pair of winged horses and charioteer joined in natural union. Now the horses and the charioteers of the gods are all of them noble and of noble descent, but those of other races are mixed. First, you must know that the b human charioteer drives a pair; and next, that one of his horses is noble and of noble breed, and the other is ignoble and of ignoble breed; so that the management of the human chariot cannot but be a difficult and anxious task. I will endeavour to explain to you in what way the mortal differs from the immortal creature. The soul in her totality has the care of inanimate being everywhere, and traverses the whole heaven in divers forms appearing;—when perfect and fully winged she soars upward, c and orders the whole world; whereas the imperfect soul, losing her wings and drooping in her flight at last settles on the solid ground—there, finding a home, she receives an earthly frame which appears to be self-moved, but is really moved by her power; and this composition of soul and body is called a living and mortal creature. For immortal no such union can be reasonably believed to be; although fancy, not having seen nor surely known the nature of God, may imagine an immortal creature having both a body and also a soul which are united throughout d all time. Let that, however, be as God wills, and be spoken of acceptably to him. And now let us ask the reason why the soul loses her wings!

The wing is the corporeal element which is most akin to the divine, and which by nature tends to soar aloft and carry that which gravitates downwards into the upper region, which is the habitation of the gods. The divine is beauty, wisdom, goodness, e and the like; and by these the wing of the soul is nourished, and grows apace; but when fed upon evil and foulness and the opposite of good, wastes and falls away. Zeus, the mighty lord, holding the reins of a winged chariot, leads the way in heaven, ordering all and taking care of all; and there follows him the array of gods and demi-gods, marshalled in eleven bands; Hestia 247 alone abides at home in the house of heaven; of the rest they who are reckoned among the princely twelve march in their appointed order. They see many blessed sights in the inner heaven, and there are many ways to and fro, along which the blessed gods are passing, every one doing his own work; he may follow who will and can, for jealousy has no place in the celestial choir. But when

b they go to banquet and festival, then they move up the steep to the top of the vault of heaven. The chariots of the gods in even poise, obeying the rein, glide rapidly; but the others labour, for the vicious steed goes heavily, weighing down the charioteer to the earth when his steed has not been thoroughly trained:—and this is the hour of agony and extremest conflict for the soul. For the immortals, when they are at the end of their course, go forth and stand upon the outside of heaven; its revolution carries

c them round, and they behold the things beyond. But of the heaven which is above the heavens, what earthly poet ever did or ever will sing worthily? It is such as I will describe; for I must dare to speak the truth, when truth is my theme. There abides the very being with which true knowledge is concerned; the colourless, formless, intangible essence, visible only to mind, the

d pilot of the soul. The divine intelligence, being nurtured upon mind and pure knowledge, and the intelligence of every soul which is capable of receiving the food proper to it, rejoices at beholding reality once more, after so long a time, and gazing upon truth, is replenished and made glad, until the revolution of the world brings her round again to the same place. In the revolution she beholds justice, and temperance, and knowledge absolute, not that to which becoming belongs, nor that which is found, in varying forms, in one or other of those regions

e which we men call *real*, but real knowledge really present where true being is. And beholding the other true existences in like manner, and feasting upon them, she passes down into the interior of the heavens and returns home; and there the charioteer putting up his horses at the stall, gives them ambrosia to eat and nectar to drink.

248 Such is the life of the gods; but of other souls, that which follows God best and is likest to him lifts the head of the charioteer into the outer world, and is carried round in the revolution, troubled indeed by the steeds, and with difficulty beholding true being; while another only rises and falls, and sees, and again fails to see by reason of the unruliness of the steeds. The rest of the

souls are also longing after the upper world and they all follow,
but not being strong enough they are carried round below the
surface, plunging, treading on one another, each striving to be b
first; and there is confusion and perspiration and the extremity of
effort; and many of them are lamed or have their wings broken
through the ill driving of the charioteers; and all of them after a
fruitless toil, not having attained to the mysteries of true being,
go away, and feed upon opinion [or appearance]. The reason
why the souls exhibit this exceeding eagerness to behold the
Plain of Truth is that pasturage is found there, which is suited
to the highest part of the soul; and the wing on which the soul c
soars is nourished with this. And there is a law of Destiny, that the
soul which attains any vision of truth in company with a god
is preserved from harm until the next period, and if attaining
always is always unharmed. But when she is unable to follow,
and fails to behold the truth, and through some ill-hap sinks
beneath the double load of forgetfulness and vice, and her wings
fall from her and she drops to the ground, then the law ordains
that this soul shall at her first birth pass, not into any other d
animal, but only into man; and the soul which has seen most of
truth shall be placed in the seed from which a philosopher, or
artist, or some musical and loving nature will spring; that which
has seen truth in the second degree shall be some righteous king
or warrior chief; the soul which is of the third class shall be a
politician, or economist, or trader; the fourth shall be a lover of
gymnastic toils, or a physician; the fifth shall lead the life of a
prophet or hierophant; to the sixth the character of a poet or e
some other imitative artist will be assigned; to the seventh the
life of an artisan or husbandman; to the eighth that of a sophist
or demagogue; to the ninth that of a tyrant;—all these are states
of probation, in which he who does righteously improves, and he
who does unrighteously deteriorates, his lot.

Ten thousand years must elapse before the soul of each one
can return to the place from whence she came, for she cannot
grow her wings in less, save only the soul of a philosopher, 249
guileless and true, or of a lover, who has been guided by
philosophy. And these when the third period comes round, if
they have chosen this life three times in succession, have wings
given them, and go away at the end of three thousand years. But

the others[1] receive judgement when they have completed their first life, and after the judgement they go, some of them to the houses of correction which are under the earth, and are punished; others to some place in heaven whither they are lightly borne by justice, and there they live in a manner worthy of the life which
b they led here when in the form of men. And in the thousandth year, both arrive at a place where they must draw lots and choose their second life, and they may take any which they please. And now the soul of a man may pass into the life of a beast, or that which has once been a man return again from the beast into human form. But the soul which has never seen the truth will not pass into the human form. For a man must have intelligence by what is called the Idea, a unity gathered[2] together by reason from
c the many particulars of sense. This is the recollection of those things which our soul once saw while following God—when regardless of that which we now call being she raised her head up towards the true being. And therefore the mind of the philosopher alone has wings; and this is just, for he is always, according to the measure of his abilities, clinging in recollection to those things in which God abides, and in beholding which He is what He is. And he who employs aright these memories is ever being initiated into perfect mysteries and alone becomes truly perfect. But, as he
d forgets earthly interests and is rapt in the divine, the vulgar deem him mad, and rebuke him; they do not see that he is inspired.

Thus far I have been speaking of the fourth and last kind of madness, which is imputed to him who, when he sees the beauty of earth, is transported with the recollection of the true beauty; he would like to fly away, but he cannot; he is like a bird fluttering and looking upward and careless of the world below; and he is therefore thought to be mad. And I have shown this of all
e inspirations to be the noblest and highest and the offspring of the highest to him who has or shares in it, and that he who loves the beautiful is called a lover because he partakes of it. For, as has been already said, every soul of man has in the way of nature beheld true being; this was the condition of her passing into the
250 form of man. But all souls do not easily recall the things of the

---

[1] The philosopher alone is not subject to judgement (κρίσις), for he has never lost the vision of truth.
[2] [Plato proposes here an etymology of the word ξυνιέναι, understand.]

other world; they may have seen them for a short time only, or they may have been unfortunate in their earthly lot, and, having had their hearts turned to unrighteousness through some corrupting influence, they may have lost the memory of the holy things which once they saw. Few only retain an adequate remembrance of them; and they, when they behold here any image of that other world, are rapt in amazement; but they are ignorant of what this rapture means, because they do not clearly perceive. For there is no radiance in our earthly copies of justice or temperance or those other things which are precious to souls: they are seen through a glass dimly; and there are few who, going to the images, behold in them the realities, and these only with difficulty. But beauty could be seen, brightly shining, by all who were with that happy band,—we philosophers following in the train of Zeus, others in company with other gods; at which time we beheld the beatific vision and were initiated into a mystery which may be truly called most blessed, celebrated by us in our state of innocence, before we had any experience of evils to come, when we were admitted to the sight of apparitions innocent and simple and calm and happy, which we beheld shining in pure light, pure ourselves and not yet enshrined in that living tomb which we carry about, now that we are imprisoned in the body, like an oyster in his shell. Let me linger over the memory of scenes which have passed away.

But of beauty, I repeat that we saw her there shining in company with the celestial forms; and coming to earth we find her here too, shining in clearness through the clearest aperture of sense. For sight is the most piercing of our bodily senses; though not by that is wisdom seen; her loveliness would have been transporting if there had been a visible image of her, and the other ideas, if they had visible counterparts, would be equally lovely. But this is the privilege of beauty, that being the loveliest she is also the most palpable to sight. Now he who is not newly initiated or who has become corrupted, does not easily rise out of this world to the sight of true beauty in the other, when he contemplates her earthly namesake, and instead of being awed at the sight of her, he is given over to pleasure, and like a brutish beast he rushes on to enjoy and beget; he consorts with wantonness, and is not afraid or ashamed of pursuing pleasure in violation of nature. But he whose initiation is recent, and who has been the spectator of many glories in the other world, is amazed when he sees anyone having a godlike face or form, which is the expression of divine beauty; and at first a shudder runs through him, and again the old awe steals over him; then looking upon the face of his beloved as of a god he reverences him, and if he were not afraid of being thought a downright madman, he would sacrifice to his beloved as to the image of a god; then while he gazes on him there is a sort of reaction, and the shudder

b passes into an unusual heat and perspiration; for, as he receives the effluence of beauty through the eyes, the wing moistens and he warms. And as he warms, the parts out of which the wing grew, and which had been hitherto closed and rigid, and had prevented the wing from shooting forth, are melted, and as nourishment streams upon him, the lower end of the wing begins to swell and grow from the root upwards; and the growth extends under the whole soul—for once the whole was winged. During this process the whole soul is all in a state of ebullition and

c effervescence,—which may be compared to the irritation and uneasiness in the gums at the time of cutting teeth,—bubbles up, and has a feeling of uneasiness and tickling; but when in like manner the soul is beginning to grow wings, the beauty of the beloved meets her eye and she receives the sensible warm motion of particles which flow towards her, therefore called emotion (ἵμερος), and is refreshed and warmed by them, and then she

d ceases from her pain with joy. But when she is parted from her beloved and her moisture fails, then the orifices of the passage out of which the wing shoots dry up and close, and intercept the germ of the wing; which, being shut up with the emotion, throbbing as with the pulsations of an artery, pricks the aperture which is nearest, until at length the entire soul is pierced and maddened and pained, and at the recollection of beauty is again delighted. And from both of them together the soul is oppressed at the strangeness of her condition, and is in a great strait and

e excitement, and in her madness can neither sleep by night nor abide in her place by day. And wherever she thinks that she will behold the beautiful one, thither in her desire she runs. And when she has seen him, and bathed herself in the waters of beauty, her constraint is loosened, and she is refreshed, and has no more

pangs and pains; and this is the sweetest of all pleasures at the
time, and is the reason why the soul of the lover will never 252
forsake his beautiful one, whom he esteems above all; he has
forgotten mother and brethren and companions, and he thinks
nothing of the neglect and loss of his property; the rules and
proprieties of life, on which he formerly prided himself, he now
despises, and is ready to sleep like a servant, wherever he is
allowed, as near as he can to his desired one, who is the object of
his worship, and the physician who can alone assuage the great- b
ness of his pain. And this state, my dear imaginary youth to
whom I am talking, is by men called love, and among the gods
has a name at which you, in your simplicity, may be inclined to
mock; there are two lines in the apocryphal writings of Homer
in which the name occurs. One of them is rather outrageous, and
not altogether metrical. They are as follows:—

> Mortals call him fluttering love,
> But the immortals call him winged one,
> Because the growing of wings[1] is a necessity to him.

You may believe this, but not unless you like. At any rate the c
plight of lovers and its cause are such as I have described.

Now the lover who is taken to be the attendant of Zeus is better
able to bear the winged god, and can endure a heavier burden;
but the attendants and companions of Ares, who made the
circuit in his company, when under the influence of love, if they
fancy that they have been at all wronged, are ready to kill and
put an end to themselves and their beloved. And he who followed
in the train of any other god, while he is unspoiled and the im- d
pression lasts, honours and imitates him, as far as he is able; and
after the manner of his god he behaves in his intercourse with
his beloved and with the rest of the world during the first period
of his earthly existence. Every one chooses his love from the
ranks of beauty according to his character, and this he makes his
god, and fashions and adorns as a sort of image which he is to
fall down and worship. The followers of Zeus desire that their e
beloved should have a soul like him; and therefore they seek out
someone of a philosopical and imperial nature, and when they
have found him and loved him, they do all they can to confirm

---

[1] Or, reading πτερόφοιτον, 'the movement of wings'.

such a nature in him, and if they have no experience of such a disposition hitherto, they learn of anyone who can teach them, and themselves follow in the same way. And they have the less

253 difficulty in finding the nature of their own god in themselves, because they have been compelled to gaze intensely on him; their recollection clings to him, and they become possessed of him, and receive from him their character and disposition, so far as man can participate in God. The qualities of their god they attribute to the beloved, wherefore they love him all the more, and if, like the Bacchic Nymphs, they draw inspiration from Zeus, they pour out their own fountain upon him, wanting to make him as like as possible to their own god. But those who

b were the followers of Hera seek a royal love, and when they have found him they do just the same with him; and in like manner the followers of Apollo, and of every other god walking in the ways of their god, seek a love who is to be made like him whom they serve, and when they have found him, they themselves imitate their god, and persuade their love to do the same, and educate him into the manner and nature of the god as far as they each can; for no feelings of envy or jealousy are entertained by them towards their beloved, but they do their utmost to create in

c him the greatest likeness of themselves and of the god whom they honour. Thus fair and blissful to the beloved is the desire of the inspired lover, and the initiation of which I speak into the mysteries of true love, if he be captured by the lover and their purpose is effected. Now the beloved is taken captive in the following manner:—

At the beginning of this tale, I divided each soul into three parts—two having the form of horses and the third being like a

d charioteer; the division may remain. I have said that one horse was good, the other bad, but I have not yet explained in what the goodness or badness of either consists, and to that I will now proceed. The right-hand horse is upright and cleanly made; he has a lofty neck and an aquiline nose; his colour is white, and his eyes dark; he is one who loves honour with modesty and temperance, and the follower of true opinion; he needs no touch of the whip, but is guided by word and admonition only. The other is

e a crooked, lumbering animal, put together anyhow; he has a short, thick neck; he is flat-faced and of a dark colour, with grey

eyes and blood-red complexion;[1] the mate of insolence and pride, shag-eared and deaf, hardly yielding to whip and spur. Now when the charioteer beholds the vision of love, and has his whole soul warmed through sense, and is full of the prickings and ticklings of desire, the obedient steed, then as always under the govern-   254
ment of shame, refrains from leaping on the beloved; but the other, heedless of the pricks and of the blows of the whip, plunges and runs away, giving all manner of trouble to his companion and the charioteer, whom he forces to approach the beloved and to remember the joys of love. They at first indignantly oppose him and will not be urged on to do terrible and unlawful deeds; b
but at last, when he persists in plaguing them, they yield and agree to do as he bids them. And now they are at the spot and behold the flashing beauty of the beloved; which when the charioteer sees, his memory is carried to the true beauty, whom he beholds in company with Modesty like an image placed upon a holy pedestal. He sees her, but he is afraid and falls backwards in adoration, and by his fall is compelled to pull back the reins c
with such violence as to bring both the steeds on their haunches, the one willing and unresisting, the unruly one very unwilling; and when they have gone back a little, the one is overcome with shame and wonder, and his whole soul is bathed in perspiration; the other, when the pain is over which the bridle and the fall had given him, having with difficulty taken breath, is full of wrath and reproaches, which he heaps upon the charioteer and his fellow steed, for want of courage and manhood, declaring that they have been false to their agreement and guilty of desertion. Again they d
refuse, and again he urges them on, and will scarce yield to their prayer that he would wait until another time. When the appointed hour comes, they make as if they had forgotten, and he reminds them, fighting and neighing and dragging them on, until at length he, on the same thoughts intent, forces them to draw near again. And when they are near he stoops his head and puts up his tail, and takes the bit in his teeth and pulls shamelessly. Then the charioteer is worse off than ever; he falls back like a e
racer at the barrier, and with a still more violent wrench drags the bit out of the teeth of the wild steed and covers his abusive tongue and jaws with blood, and forces his legs and haunches to

---

[1] Or with grey and blood-shot eyes.

the ground and punishes him sorely. And when this has happened several times and the villain has ceased from his wanton way, he is tamed and humbled, and follows the will of the charioteer, and when he sees the beautiful one he is ready to die of fear. And from that time forward the soul of the lover follows the beloved in modesty and holy fear.

255 And so the beloved who, like a god, has received every true and loyal service from his lover, not in pretence but in reality, being also himself of a nature friendly to his admirer,[1] if in former days he has blushed to own his passion and turned away his lover, because his youthful companions or others slanderously told him that he would be disgraced, now as years advance, at the ap-
b pointed age and time, is led to receive him into communion. For fate which has ordained that there shall be no friendship among the evil has also ordained that there shall ever be friendship among the good. And the beloved when he has received him into communion and intimacy, is quite amazed at the good will of the lover; he recognizes that the inspired friend is worth all other friends or kinsmen; they have nothing of friendship in them worthy to be compared with his. And when this feeling continues and he is nearer to him and embraces him, in gymnastic exercises
c and at other times of meeting, then the fountain of that stream, which Zeus when he was in love with Ganymede named Desire, overflows upon the lover, and some enters into his soul, and some when he is filled flows out again; and as a breeze or an echo rebounds from the smooth rocks and returns whence it came, so does the stream of beauty, passing through the eyes which are the windows of the soul, come back to the beautiful one; there
d arriving and quickening the passages of the wings, watering them and inclining them to grow, and filling the soul of the beloved also with love. And thus he loves, but he knows not what; he does not understand and cannot explain his own state; he appears to have caught the infection of blindness from another; the lover is his mirror in whom he is beholding himself, but he is not aware of this. When he is with the lover, both cease from their pain, but when he is away then he longs as he is longed for, and has love's
e image, love for love [Anteros] lodging in his breast, which he calls and believes to be not love but friendship only, and his

---

[1] Omitting εἰς ταὐτὸν ἄγει τὴν φιλίαν.

desire is as the desire of the other, but weaker; he wants to see him, touch him, kiss, embrace him, and probably not long afterwards his desire is accomplished. When they meet, the wanton steed of the lover has a word to say to the charioteer; he would like to have a little pleasure in return for many pains, but 256 the wanton steed of the beloved says not a word, for he is bursting with passion which he understands not;—he throws his arms round the lover and embraces him as his dearest friend; and, when they are side by side, he is not in a state in which he can refuse the lover anything, if he ask him; although his fellow steed and the charioteer oppose him with the arguments of shame and reason. After this their happiness depends upon their self-control; if the better elements of the mind which lead to order and philosophy prevail, then they pass their life here in happiness b and harmony—masters of themselves and orderly—enslaving the vicious and emancipating the virtuous elements of the soul; and when the end comes, they are light and winged for flight, having conquered in one of the three heavenly or truly Olympian victories; nor can human discipline or divine inspiration confer any greater blessing on man than this. If, on the other hand, they leave philosophy and lead the lower life of ambition, then prob- c ably, after wine or in some other careless hour, the two wanton animals take the two souls when off their guard and bring them together, and they accomplish that desire of their hearts which to the many is bliss; and this having once enjoyed they continue to enjoy, yet rarely, because they have not the approval of the whole soul. They too are dear, but not so dear as the others; and it is for each other that they live, throughout the time of their love and d afterwards. They consider that they have given and taken from each other the most sacred pledges, and they may not break them and fall into enmity. At last they pass out of the body, unwinged, but eager to soar, and thus obtain no mean reward of love and madness. For those who have once begun the heavenward pilgrimage may not go down again to darkness and the journey beneath the earth, but they live in light always; happy com- panions in their pilgrimage, and when the time comes at which they receive their wings they have the same plumage because of e their love.

Thus great are the heavenly blessings which the friendship of a

lover will confer upon you, my youth. Whereas the attachment
of the non-lover, which is alloyed with a worldly prudence and
has worldly and niggardly ways of doling out benefits, will breed
in your soul those vulgar qualities which the populace applaud,
257 will send you bowling round the earth during a period of nine
thousand years, and leave you a fool in the world below.

And thus, dear Eros, I have made and paid my recantation,
as well and as fairly as I could; more especially in the matter of
the poetical figures which I was compelled to use, because
Phaedrus would have them.[1] And now forgive the past and
accept the present, and be gracious and merciful to me, and do
not in thine anger deprive me of sight, or take from me the art of
love which thou hast given me, but grant that I may be yet more
b esteemed in the eyes of the fair. And if Phaedrus or I myself said
anything rude in our first speeches, blame Lysias, who is the
father of the brat, and let us have no more of his progeny; bid
him study philosophy, like his brother Polemarchus; and then
his lover Phaedrus will no longer halt between two opinions, but
will dedicate himself wholly to love and to philosophical discourses.

Phaedr. I join in the prayer, Socrates, and say with you, if this
c be for my good, may your words come to pass. But I have long
been amazed at this second oration, which you have made so
much finer than the first. And I begin to be afraid that I shall lose
conceit of Lysias, and that he will appear tame in comparison,
even if he be willing to put another as fine and as long as yours
into the field, which I doubt. For quite lately one of your politicians was abusing him on this very account; and called him a
'speech-writer' again and again. So that a feeling of pride may
probably induce him to give up writing speeches.

Soc. What a very amusing notion! But I think, my young man,
d that you are much mistaken in your friend if you imagine that he
is frightened at a little noise; and, possibly, you think that his
assailant meant his remark as a reproach?

Phaedr. I thought, Socrates, that he did. And you are doubtless
aware that the greatest and most influential statesmen are
ashamed of writing speeches and leaving other written compositions, lest they should be called sophists by posterity.

[1] See 234 c.

Soc. You seem to be unconscious, Phaedrus, that the 'sweet elbow'[1] of the proverb is really the long arm of the Nile. And you appear to be equally unaware of the fact that this sweet elbow of theirs is also a long arm. For there is nothing of which our great politicians are so fond as of writing speeches and bequeathing books to posterity. You may see how ardent is their love of praise, for whenever they write something, they head the writing with the names of their local admirers.

Phaedr. What do you mean? I do not understand.

Soc. Why, do you not know that when a politician writes, he begins with the names of his approvers?

Phaedr. How so?

Soc. Why, he begins in this manner: 'Be it enacted by the senate, the people, or both, on the motion of a certain person', which is our author's solemn and laudatory way of describing himself. Only after this preamble does he proceed, displaying his own wisdom to his admirers in what is often a long and tedious composition. Now what is that sort of thing but a regular piece of authorship?

Phaedr. True.

Soc. And if the piece is finally approved, then the author leaves the theatre in high delight; but if it is rejected and he is done out of his speech-writing, and declared to be a poor composer, then he and his party are in mourning.

Phaedr. Very true.

Soc. So far are they from despising, or rather so highly do they value, the practice of writing.

Phaedr. No doubt.

Soc. And when the king or orator has the power, as Lycurgus or Solon or Darius had, of attaining an immortality of authorship in a state, is he not thought by posterity when they see his compositions, and does he not think himself while he is yet alive, to be an equal of the gods?

Phaedr. Very true.

Soc. Then do you think that any one of this class, however ill disposed, would reproach Lysias simply with being an author?

---

[1] A proverb, like 'the grapes are sour', applied to pleasures which cannot be had, meaning sweet things which, like the elbow, are out of the reach of the mouth. The promised pleasure turns out to be a long and tedious affair.

Phaedr. Not upon your view; for according to you he would be casting a slur upon his own favourite pursuit.

d　　*Soc.* Any one may see that there is no disgrace in the mere fact of writing.

Phaedr. Certainly not.

Soc. The disgrace, I assume, begins when a man speaks or writes not well, but badly.

Phaedr. Clearly.

Soc. And what is well and what is badly—need we ask Lysias, or any other poet or orator, who ever wrote or will write either a political or any other work, in metre or out of metre, poet or prose writer, to teach us this?

e　　*Phaedr.* Need we? For what should a man live if not for the pleasures of discourse? Surely not for the sake of those pleasures, which have previous pain as a condition of them, as almost all bodily pleasures have, and therefore are rightly called slavish.

Soc. There is time enough. And I believe that the grasshoppers 259 chirruping after their manner in the heat of the sun over our heads are talking to one another and looking down at us. What would they say if they saw that we, like the many, are not conversing, but slumbering at mid-day, lulled by their voices, too indolent to think? Would they not have a right to laugh at us? They might imagine that we were slaves, who, coming to rest at a place of resort of theirs, like sheep lie asleep at noon around the well. But if they see us discoursing, and like Odysseus sailing past them, deaf to their siren voices, they may perhaps, out of respect, b give us of the gifts which they receive from the gods that they may impart them to men.

Phaedr. What gifts do you mean? I never heard of any.

Soc. A lover of music like yourself ought surely to have heard the story of the grasshoppers, who are said to have been human beings in an age before the Muses. And when the Muses came and song appeared they were ravished with delight; and singing c always, never thought of eating and drinking, until at last in their forgetfulness they died. And now they live again in the grasshoppers, who, as a special gift from the Muses, require no nourishment, but from the hour of their birth are always singing, and never eating or drinking; and when they die they go and inform the Muses in heaven which of us honours one or other of them. They win the love of Terpsichore for the dancers by their report of them; of Erato for the lovers, and of the other Muses for d those who do them honour, according to the several ways of honouring them;—and to Calliope the eldest Muse and Urania who is next to her, they make a report of those who honour music of their kind, and spend their time in philosophy; for these are the Muses who are chiefly concerned with the heavens and with reasoning, divine as well as human, and they have the sweetest utterance. For many reasons, then, we ought always to talk and not to sleep at mid-day.

Phaedr. Let us talk.

Soc. Shall we discuss the rules of writing and speech as we were e proposing?

Phaedr. Very good.

Soc. Before there can be any question of excellence in speech, must not the mind of the speaker be furnished with knowledge of the truth of the matter about which he is going to speak?

Phaedr. And yet, Socrates, I have heard that he who would be an orator has no need to study true justice, but only that which is 260 likely to be approved by the many who sit in judgement; nor the truly good or honourable, but only opinion about them, since it is from opinion, and not from the truth, that persuasion comes.

Soc. 'The words of the wise are not to be set aside'; for there is probably something in them; and therefore the meaning of this saying is not hastily to be dismissed.

Phaedr. Very true.

Soc. Let us put the matter thus:—Suppose that I wished to b persuade you to buy a horse and go to the wars. Neither of us knew what a horse was like, but I happened to know this much, that Phaedrus believed a horse to be of tame animals the one which has the longest ears.

Phaedr. That would be ridiculous.

Soc. No, not yet. Suppose, further, that in sober earnest I, having persuaded you of this, went and composed a speech in honour of the ass, calling it the horse, and saying that this animal is quite invaluable to possess for domestic use and military service, and that you may sit on his back and fight, and that he will carry baggage, besides being useful in other ways. c

Phaedr. How ridiculous!

Soc. Ridiculous! Yes; but is not even a ridiculous friend better than a cunning enemy?

Phaedr. Certainly.

Soc. And when the orator instead of putting an ass in the place of a horse, puts good for evil, being himself as ignorant of their true nature as the city on which he imposes is ignorant; and, having studied the notions of the multitude, falsely persuades them not about 'the shadow of an ass', which he confounds with a horse, but about good which he confounds with evil, and induces them to do it,—what will be the harvest which rhetoric d will be likely to gather after the sowing of that seed?

Phaedr. The reverse of good.

Soc. But perhaps rhetoric has been too roughly abused by us, and she might answer: What amazing nonsense you are talking! As if I insisted that ignorance of the truth is indispensable to one who is learning to speak! Whatever my advice may be worth, I should have told him to arrive at the truth first, and then take me. At the same time I boldly assert that mere knowledge of the truth, without my help, will not give you the art of persuasion.

e *Phaedr.* There is reason in the lady's defence of herself.

Soc. Quite true; if only the other arguments which remain to be brought up bear her witness that she is an art at all. But I seem to hear them arraying themselves on the opposite side, declaring that she speaks falsely, and that rhetoric is a mere routine and trick, not an art. Lo! a Spartan appears, and says that there neither is nor ever will be a real art of speaking which is divorced from the truth.

261 *Phaedr.* These witnesses must be called, Socrates? Bring them out that we may examine them.

Soc. Come out, fair children, and convince Phaedrus, who is the father of similar beauties, that he will never be able to speak soundly on any subject unless he have a sound philosophy. And let Phaedrus answer you.

Phaedr. Put the question.

Soc. Is not rhetoric, taken generally, a universal art of enchanting the mind by arguments; which is practised not only in courts and public assemblies, but in private houses also, having b to do with all matters, great as well as small; and which, if correctly exercised, is equally to be esteemed whether the subject be serious or trivial—that is what you have heard?

Phaedr. Nay, not that at all; I should say rather that the art is said to be primarily displayed in speaking and writing in lawsuits, and in speaking in public assemblies—I have not heard it more widely extended.

Soc. Then I suppose that you have only heard of the rhetoric of Nestor and Odysseus, which they composed in their leisure hours when at Troy, and never of the rhetoric of Palamedes?

Phaedr. No more than of Nestor and Odysseus, unless Gorgias is c your Nestor, and Thrasymachus or Theodorus your Odysseus.

Soc. Perhaps that is my meaning. But let us leave them. And do you tell me, instead, what are plaintiff and defendant doing in a law-court—are they not contending?

Phaedr. Exactly so.

Soc. About the just and unjust—that is the matter in dispute?

Phaedr. Yes.

Soc. And a professor of the art will make the same thing appear to the same persons to be at one time just, at another time, if he d is so inclined, to be unjust?

Phaedr. Exactly.

Soc. Likewise when he speaks in the assembly, he will make the same things seem good to the city at one time, and at another time the reverse of good?

Phaedr. That is true.

Soc. Have we not heard of the Eleatic Palamedes [Zeno], that his art in speaking is such that he can make the same things appear to his hearers like and unlike, one and many, at rest and in motion?

Phaedr. Very true.

Soc. The art of disputation, then, is not confined to the courts and the assembly, but is one and the same in every use of lan- e guage; this is the art, if there be such an art, by which one will be able to find a likeness of everything to which a likeness can be found, and to draw into the light of day the likenesses and disguises which are used by others?

Phaedr. How do you mean?

Soc. I think the truth will appear if we ask this question: When will there be more chance of deception—when the difference is large or small?

262 *Phaedr.* When the difference is small.

Soc. And you will be less likely to be discovered in passing by degrees into the other extreme than when you go all at once?

Phaedr. Of course.

Soc. He, then, who would deceive others, and not be deceived, must exactly know the real likenesses and differences of things?

Phaedr. He must.

Soc. But if he is ignorant of the true nature of any subject, how can he detect the greater or less degree of likeness in other things to that of which by the hypothesis he is ignorant?

b *Phaedr.* He cannot.

Soc. Now when men are deceived and their notions are at variance with realities, it is clear that the error slips in through resemblances?

Phaedr. Yes, that is the way.

Soc. Then unless our orator has understood the real nature of everything, he will not be a skilled artist in making the gradual departure from truth into the opposite of truth which is effected by the help of resemblances, or in avoiding this when he is on the defensive.

Phaedr. He will not.

c *Soc.* And so the 'art of rhetoric' displayed by a man who being ignorant of the truth has pursued appearances will be of a ridiculous sort, and not an art at all?

Phaedr. That may be expected.

Soc. Shall I propose that we look for examples of art and want of art, according to our notion of them, in the speech of Lysias which you have in your hand, and in my own speech?

Phaedr. Nothing could be better; and indeed I think that our previous argument has been too abstract and wanting in illustrations.

Soc. Yes; and the two speeches happen to afford a very good d example of the way in which the speaker who knows the truth may, without any serious purpose, steal away the hearts of his hearers. This piece of good fortune I attribute to the local deities; and, perhaps, the prophets of the Muses who are singing over our heads may have imparted their inspiration to me. For I do not imagine that I have any rhetorical art of my own.

Phaedr. Granted; if you will only please to get on.

Soc. Suppose that you read me the first words of Lysias' speech.

Phaedr. 'You know how matters stand with me, and how, as I e conceive, this affair may be arranged for the advantage of both of us; and I maintain that I ought not to fail in my suit, because I am not your lover. For lovers repent——'

Soc. Enough:—Now, shall I point out the error and want of art in those words?

Phaedr. Yes.

Soc. This at least is plain to everyone, that about some such 263 things we are agreed, whereas about other things we differ in our notions.

Phaedr. I think that I understand you; but will you explain yourself?

Soc. When anyone speaks of iron and silver, is not the same thing present in the minds of all?

Phaedr. Certainly.

Soc. But when anyone speaks of justice and goodness we part company and are at odds with one another and with ourselves?

Phaedr. Precisely.

Soc. Then in some things we agree, but not in others? b

Phaedr. That is true.

Soc. In which are we more likely to be deceived, and in which has rhetoric the greater power?

Phaedr. Clearly, in the uncertain class.

Soc. Then the would-be exponent of the art of rhetoric ought, before all else, to make a regular division, and discover a characteristic mark of each class, I mean the things concerning which the mass of men will necessarily diverge, and those concerning which they will not?

Phaedr. He who made such a distinction would have an excel- c lent principle.

Soc. Yes; and in the next place he must have a keen eye for the observation of particulars, and not make a mistake in referring to one of those two classes the subject on which he intends to speak.

Phaedr. Certainly.

Soc. Now to which class does love belong—to the debatable or to the undisputed class?

Phaedr. To the debatable, clearly; for if not, do you think that it would have been open to you to say as you did, that love is an evil both to the lover and the beloved, and then later that it is the greatest possible good?

d   *Soc.* Capital. But will you tell me whether I defined love at the beginning of my speech? for, having been in an ecstasy, I cannot well remember.

Phaedr. Yes, indeed; that you did, and no mistake.

Soc. Then I perceive that the Nymphs of Achelous and Pan the son of Hermes, who inspired me, were far better rhetoricians than Lysias the son of Cephalus. Alas! how inferior to them he is! But perhaps I am mistaken; and Lysias at the commencement of his lover's speech did insist on our supposing love to be something or other which he fancied him to be, and, with reference to this e   notion, fashioned and framed the remainder of his discourse. Suppose we read his beginning over again:

Phaedr. If you please; but you will not find what you want.

Soc. Read, that I may have his exact words.

Phaedr. 'You know how matters stand with me, and how, as I conceive, this affair may be arranged for the advantage of both 264   of us; and I maintain I ought not to fail in my suit because I am not your lover, for lovers repent of the kindnesses which they have shown, when their passion ceases.'

Soc. Here he appears to have done just the reverse of what he ought; for he has begun at the end, and is swimming on his back through the flood to the place of starting. His address to the fair youth begins where the lover would have ended. Am I not right, sweet Phaedrus?

b   *Phaedr.* Yes, indeed, Socrates; he does begin at the end.

Soc. Then as to the other topics—are they not thrown down anyhow? Is there any principle in them? Why should the next topic follow next in order, or any other topic? I cannot help fancying in my ignorance that he wrote off boldly just what came into his head, but I dare say that you would recognize a rhetorical necessity in the succession of the several parts of the composition?

Phaedr. You have too good an opinion of me if you think that I c   have any such insight into his principles of composition.

Soc. At any rate, you will allow that every discourse ought to be a living creature, having a body of its own and a head and feet; there should be a middle, beginning, and end, adapted to one another and to the whole?

Phaedr. Certainly.

Soc. Can this be said of the discourse of your friend? See whether you can find any more connexion in his words than in the epitaph which is said by some to have been inscribed on the grave of Midas the Phrygian.

Phaedr. What is there remarkable in the epitaph? d

Soc. It is as follows:—

I am a maiden of bronze and lie on the tomb of Midas;
So long as water flows and tall trees grow,
So long here on this spot by his sad tomb abiding,
I shall declare to passers-by that Midas sleeps below.

Now in this rhyme whether a line comes first or comes last, as e
you will perceive, makes no difference.

Phaedr. You are making fun of that oration of ours.

Soc. Well, I will say no more about your friend's speech lest I should give offence to you; although I think that it might furnish many other examples of what a man ought rather to avoid. But I will proceed to the other speeches, which, as I think, are also suggestive to students of rhetoric.

Phaedr. In what way? 265

Soc. The two speeches, as you may remember, were unlike; the one argued that the lover and the other that the non-lover ought to be accepted.

Phaedr. And right manfully.

Soc. You should rather say 'madly'; and madness was the argument of them, for, as I said, 'love is a madness'.

Phaedr. Yes.

Soc. And of madness there were two kinds; one produced by human infirmity, the other was a divine release of the soul from the yoke of custom and convention.

Phaedr. True. b

Soc. The divine madness was subdivided into four kinds, prophetic, initiatory, poetic, erotic, having four gods presiding over them; the first was the inspiration of Apollo, the second that of Dionysus, the third that of the Muses, the fourth that of Aphrodite and Eros. In the description of the last kind of madness, which was also said to be the best, we spoke of the affection of

love in a figure, into which we introduced a tolerably credible and possibly true though partly erring myth, which was also a
c hymn in honour of Love, who is your lord and also mine, Phaedrus, and the guardian of fair children, and to him we sang the hymn in measured and solemn strain.

Phaedr. I know that I had great pleasure in listening to you.

Soc. Let us take this instance and note how the transition was made from blame to praise.

Phaedr. What do you mean?

Soc. I mean to say that the composition was mostly playful. Yet in these chance fancies of the hour were involved two principles, of the power of which we should be grateful for a description
d in technical terms, if that were possible.

Phaedr. What are they?

Soc. First, the survey of scattered particulars, leading to their comprehension in one idea; as in our definition of love, which whether true or false certainly gave clearness and consistency to the discourse, the speaker should define his several notions and so make his meaning clear.

Phaedr. What is the other principle, Socrates?

e *Soc.* The second principle is that of division into species according to the natural formation, where the joint is, not breaking any part as a bad carver might. Just as our two discourses alike assumed, first of all, a single form of unreason; and then, as the body which from being one becomes double and may be divided
266 into a left side and right side, each having parts right and left of the same name—after this manner the speaker in our first speech proceeded to divide the parts of the left side and did not desist until he found in them an evil or left-handed love which he justly reviled; whereas the other discourse leading us to the madness which lay on the right side, found another love, also having the same name, but divine, which the speaker held up before us and
b applauded and affirmed to be the author of the greatest benefits.

Phaedr. Most true.

Soc. I am myself a great lover of these processes of division and generalization; they help me to speak and to think. And if I find any man who is able to see 'a One and Many' in nature,[1] him I follow, and 'walk in his footsteps as if he were a god'. And those

[1] [Or, reading πεφυκόθ᾽, 'any man who is by nature able to see . . .'.]

who have this art, I have hitherto been in the habit of calling dialecticians; but God knows whether the name is right or c not. But now I should like to know what name you and Lysias would have me give them, and whether this may not be that famous art of rhetoric which Thrasymachus and others teach and practise? Skilful speakers they are, and impart their skill to any who are willing to bring tribute to them, as to kings.

Phaedr. Yes, they are royal men; but they have no skill in those operations which you call, and rightly, in my opinion, dialectical:—Still we are in the dark about rhetoric.

Soc. What do you mean? Can anything of value be brought d under rules of art, save by these processes? At any rate, it is not to be despised by you and me, and we ought to try to say what is this remaining part of rhetoric.

Phaedr. There is a great deal surely to be found in books of rhetoric?

Soc. Yes; thank you for reminding me:—There is the exordium, showing how the speech should begin, if I remember rightly; that is what you mean—the niceties of the art?

Phaedr. Yes.   e

Soc. Then follows the statement of facts, and upon that witnesses; thirdly, proofs; fourthly, probabilities are to come; the great Byzantian word-maker also speaks, if I am not mistaken, of confirmation and further confirmation.

Phaedr. You mean the excellent Theodorus.

Soc. Yes; and he tells how refutation or further refutation is to 267 be managed, whether in accusation or defence. I ought also to bring forward the illustrious Parian, Evenus, who first invented insinuations and indirect praises; and also indirect censures, which, according to some, the ingenious man put into verse to help the memory. But shall I 'to dumb forgetfulness consign' Tisias and Gorgias, who are not ignorant that probability is superior to truth, and who, by force of eloquence, make the little appear great and the great little, disguise the new in old fashions b and the old in new fashions, and have discovered a method of speaking on every subject either concisely or at infinite length. I remember Prodicus laughing when I told him of this; he said that he had himself discovered the true rule of art, that a speech should be neither long nor short, but of a convenient length.

Phaedr. Well done, Prodicus!

Soc. And I can not pass over Hippias, for I imagine that this colleague from Elis would vote with him.

Phaedr. Yes.

Soc. And there is also Polus, who has treasuries of diplasiology,
c and gnomology, and eikonology, and who teaches in them the names of which Licymnius made him a present; they were to give a polish.

Phaedr. Had not Protagoras something of the same sort?

Soc. Yes, rules of correct diction and many other fine precepts; for the 'sorrows of a poor old man', or any other pathetic case, no one is better than the Chalcedonian giant;[1] he can put a whole
d company of people into a passion and out of one again by his mighty magic, and is first-rate at inventing or disposing of any sort of calumny on any grounds or none. All of them agree in asserting that a speech should end in a recapitulation, though they do not all agree to use the same word.

Phaedr. You mean that there should be a summing up of the arguments in order to remind the hearers of them?

Soc. I have now said all that I have to say of the art of rhetoric: have you anything to add?

Phaedr. Not much; nothing very important.

268   *Soc.* Leave the unimportant and let us bring the devices we have mentioned into the light of day, and ask: To what extent, and when, have they the force of art?

Phaedr. They have a very great power in public meetings.

Soc. So they have. But I should like to know whether you have the same feeling as I have about the rhetoricians? To me there seem to be a great many holes in their web.

Phaedr. Give an example.

Soc. I will. Suppose a person to come to your friend Eryximachus, or to his father Acumenus, and to say to him: 'I know how to apply drugs which shall have either a heating or a cooling
b effect, and I can give a vomit and also a purge, and all that sort of thing; and knowing all this, as I do, I claim to be a physician and to make physicians by imparting this knowledge to others',— what do you suppose that they would say?

Phaedr. They would be sure to ask him whether he also knew

[1] [Thrasymachus.]

'to whom' he ought to give each kind of treatment, and 'when', and 'how much'.

Soc. And suppose that he were to reply: 'No; I know nothing of all that; I expect the person who has learnt what I have to c teach to be able to do these things for himself'?

Phaedr. They would say in reply that he is a madman or a pedant who fancies that he is a physician because he has read something in a book, or has stumbled on a prescription or two, although he has no real understanding of the art of medicine.

Soc. And suppose a person were to come to Sophocles or Euripides and say that he knows how to make a very long speech about a small matter,[1] and a short speech about a great matter, and also a sorrowful speech, or a terrible or threatening speech, or any other kind of speech, and in teaching this fancies that he is d teaching the art of tragedy——

Phaedr. They too would surely laugh at him if he fancies that tragedy is anything but the arranging of these elements in a manner which will be suitable to one another and to the whole.

Soc. But I do not suppose that they would be rude or abusive to him: would they not treat him as a musician would a man who thinks that he is a harmonist because he knows how to pitch the highest and lowest note; happening to meet such an one he would not say to him savagely, 'Fool, you are mad!' But like a e musician, in a gentle and harmonious tone of voice, he would answer: 'My good friend, he who would be a harmonist must certainly know this, and yet one who has not got beyond your stage of knowledge may understand nothing of harmony, for you only know the necessary preliminaries of harmony and not harmony itself.'

Phaedr. Very rightly.

Soc. And will not Sophocles say to the display of the would-be 269 tragedian, that this is not tragedy but the preliminaries of tragedy, and will not Acumenus say the same of medicine to the would-be physician?

Phaedr. Quite true.

Soc. And if Adrastus the mellifluous or Pericles heard of these wonderful arts, brachylogies and eikonologies and all the hard names which we have been endeavouring to draw into the light

[1] [Cf. 267 b.]

b of day, what would they say? Instead of losing temper and applying uncomplimentary epithets, as you and I have been doing, to the authors of such an imaginary art, their superior wisdom would rather censure us, as well as them. 'Have a little patience, Phaedrus and Socrates', they would say; 'you should not be in such a passion with those who from some want of dia-lectical skill are unable to define the nature of rhetoric, and consequently suppose that they have found the art when they c have studied only the necessary preliminaries, and in teaching these to others, fancy that the whole art of rhetoric has been taught by them; but as to using these types of speech in a persuasive manner, or making the composition a whole,—this they regard as an easy thing which their disciples ought to be able to supply for themselves.'

Phaedr. I quite admit, Socrates, that the art of rhetoric which these men teach and of which they write is such as you describe— there I agree with you. But I still want to know where and how d the true art of rhetoric and persuasion is to be acquired.

Soc. The perfection which is required of the finished orator is, or rather must be, like the perfection of anything else, partly given by nature, but may also be assisted by art. If you have the natural power and add to it knowledge and practice, you will be a distinguished speaker; if you fall short in either of these, you will be to that extent defective. But the art, as far as there is an art, of rhetoric does not lie in the direction of Lysias or Thrasymachus.

Phaedr. In what direction, then?

e   *Soc.* I conceive Pericles to have been the most accomplished of rhetoricians.

Phaedr. What of that?

Soc. All the great arts require discussion and high speculation 270 about the truths of nature; hence come loftiness of thought and completeness of execution. And this, as I conceive, was the quality which, in addition to his natural gifts, Pericles acquired from his intercourse with Anaxagoras whom he happened to know. He was thus imbued with the higher philosophy, and attained the knowledge of Mind and the negative of Mind,[1] which were favourite themes of Anaxagoras, and thence applied what suited his purpose to the art of speaking.

[1] [Reading ἀνοίας.]

Phaedr. Explain.

Soc. The procedure of rhetoric is like that of medicine.   b

Phaedr. How so?

Soc. Why, because medicine has to define the nature of the body and rhetoric of the soul—if we would proceed, not empirically but scientifically, in the one case to impart health and strength by giving medicine and food, in the other to implant the conviction or virtue which you desire, by the right application of words and training.

Phaedr. There, Socrates, I suspect that you are right.

Soc. And do you think that you can know the nature of c the soul intelligently without knowing the nature of the universe?

Phaedr. If Hippocrates the Asclepiad is to be trusted, even the nature of the body cannot be understood without that sort of inquiry.[1]

Soc. Yes, friend, and he was right:—still, we ought not to be content with the name of Hippocrates, but to examine and see whether reason gives any support to his statement.

Phaedr. I agree.

Soc. Then consider what true reasoning as well as Hippocrates says about nature. In examining the nature of anything, ought we not to consider first whether that of which we desire to have, d and to impart to others, expert knowledge, is a simple or multiform thing, and if simple, then to inquire what power it has of acting or being acted upon in relation to other things, and if multiform, then to number the forms; and see first in the case of one of them, and then in the case of all of them, what is that power of acting or being acted upon which makes each and all of them to be what they are?

Phaedr. You may very likely be right, Socrates.

Soc. The method which proceeds without analysis is like the groping of a blind man. Yet, surely, he who is an artist ought not e to admit of a comparison with the blind or deaf. The rhetorician, whose teaching of eloquence is scientific, will particularly set

---

[1] [A. Diès in *Autour de Platon*, vol. i, pp. 31–37, compares this with the existing Hippocratic writings. The thought is not the same as at *Char.* 156 c, where it was said simply that an ailment of the eyes or head cannot be cured without reference to the whole *body*.]

forth the nature of that being to which he addresses his speeches;
and this I conceive to be the soul.

Phaedr. Certainly.

271   *Soc.* His whole effort is directed to the soul; for in that he seeks
to produce conviction.

Phaedr. Yes.

Soc. Then clearly, Thrasymachus or anyone else who teaches
rhetoric in earnest as an art, will first give an exact description of
the nature of the soul; which will enable us to see whether she
be single and same, or, like the body, multiform. That is what we
should call showing the nature of the soul.

Phaedr. Exactly.

Soc. He will explain, secondly, the mode in which she acts or
is acted upon.

Phaedr. True.

b   *Soc.* Thirdly, having classified both speeches and the minds of
men, and their kinds and affections, he will proceed to survey all
the causes, and, adapting one thing to another, show what kind
of soul is persuaded, or not persuaded, by what particular form
of argument, from what causal necessity.

Phaedr. Ideally, it seems, that is how he should proceed.

Soc. Yes, that is the true and only way in which any subject
can be set forth or treated by rules of art, whether in speaking or

c writing. But our authors of handbooks of speaking, at whose feet
you have sat, craftily conceal the nature of the soul which they
know quite well. Nor, until they adopt our method of speaking
and writing, can we admit that they write by rules of art?

Phaedr. What is our method?

Soc. I cannot give you the exact details; but I am prepared to
tell you generally, as far as is in my power, how a man ought to
proceed according to rules of art.

Phaedr. Let me hear.

Soc. Since the power of speech is a guidance of the soul, he who

d proposes to become an orator must know what forms [or parts]
the soul has. They are so many—they are of such-and-such a
character—whence there arise men of such-and-such kinds. When
this analysis has been finished, he must in turn enumerate the
kinds of speech and state the character of each. Now such-and-
such persons are easily persuaded to *this* action by *this* kind of

speech for *this* reason; such other persons are hard to persuade
for *that* reason.

After he has obtained a sufficient intellectual grasp of these
points, a man must, if he is to derive any practical benefit from
his theoretical training, rapidly apprehend by perception the e
various forms when he beholds them in the environment of
life and action. At last, when he can be relied upon both to judge
what sort of man can be persuaded by what means, and also to
assess the character of the individual whom he meets, and declare
to himself: 'This is the man, this is the character, whom I 272
formerly heard discussed'—the man being now present in the
flesh—'and in order to persuade him to *this* course, I ought to
use *these* arguments in *this* way'; when he is proficient in all this
(not forgetting judgement of the right *time* for beginning
to speak and pausing, and of good or ill occasions for the
use of pithy sayings, pathetic appeals, sensational effects, and all
the other modes of speech which he has learned), then, but not till
then, can it be said that the art has been finished and perfected;
but if a man fails in any of these points, whether as speaker, b
teacher, or writer, and yet claims to speak by rules of art, one will
be entitled to disbelieve him.—Well, our author will say, do you,
Phaedrus and Socrates, accept this account of the art of rhetoric;
or, failing this, will you allow it to be described as an art?

Phaedr. I doubt whether any alternative is possible, Socrates,
but the task sounds an immense one.

Soc. Very true; and therefore let us consider all our arguments
in every light, and see whether we cannot find a shorter and
easier road; there is no use in taking a long, rough, roundabout c
way if there be a shorter and easier one. And I wish that you
would try to remember whether you have heard from Lysias
or any one else anything which might be of service to us.

Phaedr. If trying would avail, then I might; but at the moment
I can think of nothing.

Soc. Suppose I tell you something which I have heard from
some students of the subject.

Phaedr. Certainly.

Soc. May not 'the wolf', as the proverb says, 'claim a hearing'?

Phaedr. Do you say what can be said for him.   d

Soc. Well then, they say that there is no use in putting a solemn

face on these matters, or in going round and round, until you
arrive at first principles; for, as I said at first, when the question
is of justice and good, or is a question in which men are concerned
who are just and good, either by nature or habit, he who would
be a skilful rhetorician has no need of truth—for that in courts of
law men literally care nothing about truth, but only about con-
e viction: and this is based on probability, to which he who would
be a skilful orator should therefore give his whole attention. And
they say also that there are cases in which the actual facts, if they
are improbable, ought to be withheld, and only the probabilities
should be told either in accusation or defence, and that always in
speaking, the orator should keep probability in view, and say
273 good-bye to the truth. And the observance of this principle
throughout a speech is said to furnish the whole art.

Phaedr. That is what the professors of rhetoric do actually say,
Socrates. I have not forgotten that we have quite briefly touched
upon this matter[1] already; with them the point is all-important.

Soc. I dare say that you are thoroughly at home in the views
of Tisias. Now we have one more thing to ask him. Does he not
b define probability to be that which the many think?

Phaedr. Certainly, he does.

Soc. I believe that he has a clever and ingenious case of this
sort:—He supposes a feeble and valiant man to have assaulted a
strong and cowardly one, and to have robbed him of his coat or of
something or other; he is brought into court, and then Tisias says
that both parties should tell lies: the coward should say that he
was assaulted by more men than one; the other should prove that
c they were alone, and should argue thus: 'How could a weak man
like me have assaulted a strong man like him?' The complainant
will not like to confess his own cowardice, and will therefore
invent some other lie which his adversary will thus gain an
opportunity of refuting. And there are other devices of the same
kind which have a place in the system. Am I not right, Phaedrus?

Phaedr. Certainly.

Soc. Bless me, what a wonderfully mysterious art is this which
Tisias or some other gentleman, in whatever name or country
he rejoices, has discovered. Shall we say a word to him or not?
d   *Phaedr.* What shall we say to him?

[1] Cf. 259 e.

Soc. Let us tell him that, before he appeared, you and I were saying that the probability of which he speaks was engendered in the minds of the many by the likeness of the truth, and we had just been affirming that he who knew the truth would always know best how to discover the resemblances of the truth. If he has anything else to say about the art of speaking we should like to hear him; but if not, we are satisfied with the view recently expressed, that unless a man estimates the various characters of his hearers and is able to divide all things into classes and to comprehend e every one under single ideas, he will never be a skilful rhetorician even within the limits of human power. And this skill he will not attain without a great deal of trouble, which a good man ought to undergo, not for the sake of speaking and acting before men, but in order that he may be able to say what is acceptable to God and always to act acceptably to Him as far as in him lies; for there is a saying of wiser men than ourselves, that a man of sense should not try to please his fellow servants (at least this should not be his first object) but his good and noble masters; and therefore, 274 Tisias, if the way is long and circuitous, marvel not at this, for, where the end is great, there we may take the longer road, but not for lesser ends such as yours. However, our argument says that even these are best secured as the consequence of higher aims.

Phaedr. I think, Socrates, that this is admirable, if only practicable.

Soc. But provided one's aim is honourable, so is any ill success b which may ensue.

Phaedr. True.

Soc. Enough appears to have been said by us of a true and false art of speaking.

Phaedr. Certainly.

Soc. But there is something yet to be said of propriety and impropriety of writing.

Phaedr. Yes.

Soc. Do you know how you can speak or act about rhetoric in a manner which will be acceptable to God?

Phaedr. No, indeed. Do you?

Soc. I have heard a tradition of the ancients, whether true or c not they only know; although if we had found the truth ourselves, do you think that we should care much about the opinions of men?

Phaedr. Your question needs no answer; but simply tell me what you say that you have heard.

Soc. At the Egyptian city of Naucratis there was a famous old god whose name was Theuth; the bird which is called the Ibis is sacred to him, and he was the inventor of many arts, such as arithmetic and calculation and geometry and astronomy as well d as draughts and dice, but his great discovery was the use of letters. Now in those days [the god] Thamus was the king of the whole country of Egypt; and he dwelt in that great city of Upper Egypt which the Hellenes call Egyptian Thebes, and the god himself is called by them Ammon. To him came Theuth and showed his inventions, desiring that the other Egyptians might be allowed to have the benefit of them; he enumerated them, and Thamus inquired about their several uses, and praised some of them and censured others, as he approved or disapproved of e them. It would take a long time to repeat all that Thamus said to Theuth in praise or blame of the various arts. But when they came to letters, Theuth said: O king, here is a study which will make the Egyptians wiser and give them better memories; it is a specific both for the memory and for the wit. Thamus replied: O most ingenious Theuth, the parent or inventor of an art is not always the best judge of the utility or inutility of his own inventions to 275 the users of them. And in this instance, you who are the father of letters, from a paternal love of your own children have been led to attribute to them a quality which they cannot have; for this discovery of yours will create forgetfulness in the learners' souls, because they will not use their memories; they will trust to the external written characters and not remember of themselves. And so the specific which you have discovered is an aid not to memory, but to reminiscence. As for wisdom, it is the reputation, not the reality, that you have to offer to those who learn from you; they will have heard many things and yet received no teaching; they will appear to be omniscient and will generally b know nothing; they will be tiresome company, having acquired not wisdom, but the show of wisdom.

Phaedr. Yes, Socrates, you can easily invent tales of Egypt, or of any other country.

Soc. There was a tradition in the temple of Dodona that oaks first gave prophetic utterances. The men of old, far simpler than you sophisticated young men, deemed that if they heard the truth even from 'oak or rock', it was enough; whereas you seem to consider not whether a thing is or is not true, but who the c speaker is and from what country the tale comes.

Phaedr. I acknowledge the justice of your rebuke; and I think that the Theban is right in his view about letters.

Soc. He would be a very simple person, and quite a stranger to the oracles of Thamus or Ammon, who should suppose that he had left his 'Art' in writings or who should accept such an inheritance in the hope that the written word would give anything intelligible or certain; or who deemed that writing could be any more than a reminder to one who already knows d the subject.

Phaedr. That is most true.

Soc. I cannot help feeling, Phaedrus, that writing has one grave fault in common with painting; for the creations of the painter have the attitude of life, and yet if you ask them a question they preserve a solemn silence. And the same may be said of books. You would imagine that they had intelligence, but if you require any explanation of something that has been said, they preserve one unvarying meaning. And when they have been once written down they are tumbled about anywhere, all alike, e among those who understand them and among strangers, and do not know to whom they should or should not reply: and, if they are maltreated or abused, they have no parent to protect them; for the book cannot protect or defend itself.

Phaedr. That again is most true.

Soc. Is there not another kind of word or speech far better than 276 this, and having far greater power—a son of the same family, but lawfully begotten?

Phaedr. Whom do you mean, and what is his origin?

Soc. I mean an intelligent word graven in the soul of the learner, which can defend itself, and knows with whom to speak and with whom to be silent.

Phaedr. You mean the living word of knowledge which has a soul, and of which the written word is properly no more than an image?

b   *Soc.* Yes, of course that is what I mean. And now may I be allowed to ask you a question?: Would a husbandman, who is a man of sense, take seeds which he values and which he wishes to bear fruit, and in sober seriousness plant them during the heat of summer, in some garden of Adonis, that he may rejoice when he sees them in eight days appearing in beauty? At least he would do so, if at all, only for the sake of amusement and for show. But when he is in earnest he employs his art of husbandry and sows in fitting soil, and is satisfied if in eight months the seeds which he has sown arrive at perfection?

c   *Phaedr.* Yes, Socrates, that will be his way when he is in earnest; he might act otherwise for the reasons which you give.

Soc. And can we suppose that he who knows the just and good and honourable has less understanding than the husbandman about his own seeds?

Phaedr. Certainly not.

Soc. Then he will not seriously incline to 'write' his thoughts 'in water' with pen and ink, sowing words which can neither speak for themselves nor teach the truth adequately to others?

Phaedr. No, that is not likely.

d   *Soc.* No, that is not likely—in the garden of letters he will sow and plant, but only for the sake of recreation and amusement; he will write them down as memorials to be treasured against the forgetfulness of old age, by himself, or by any other man who is treading the same path. He will rejoice in beholding their tender growth; and while others are refreshing their souls with banqueting and the like, this will be the pastime in which his days are spent.

e   *Phaedr.* A pastime, Socrates, as noble as the other is ignoble, the pastime of a man who can be amused by serious talk, and can discourse merrily about justice and the like.

Soc. True, Phaedrus. But nobler far is the serious pursuit of the dialectician, who, finding a congenial soul, by the help of science sows and plants therein words which are able to defend them-
277 selves and him who planted them, and are not unfruitful, but have in them a seed which others brought up in different soils render immortal, making the possessors of it happy to the utmost extent of human happiness.

Phaedr. Far nobler, certainly.

Soc. And now at last, Phaedrus, having agreed upon this, we may decide the original question.

Phaedr. What question was that?

Soc. I mean those problems, in trying to solve which we have made our way hither; we wished to examine the censure passed on Lysias for his professional speech-writing [257 b], and to dis- b tinguish the speech composed with art from that which is composed without art. And I think that we have now pretty well distinguished the artistic from its opposite.

Phaedr. Yes, I thought so, but I wish that you would repeat what was said.

Soc. Until a man knows the truth of the several particulars of which he is writing or speaking, and is able to define them as they are, and having defined them again to divide them until they can be no longer divided; and until in like manner he is able to discern the nature of the soul, and discover the different modes of dis- c course which are adapted to different natures, and to arrange and dispose them in such a way that the simple form of speech may be addressed to the simpler nature, and the complex form, with many variations of key, to the more complex nature—until he has accomplished all this, he will be unable to handle arguments according to rules of art, as far as their nature allows them to be subjected to art, either for the purpose of teaching or persuading;—such is the view which is implied in the whole preceding argument.

Phaedr. Yes, that was our view, certainly.

Soc. Secondly, as to the censure which was passed on the d speaking or writing of discourses, and when they might be rightly or wrongly censured—did not our previous argument show—?

Phaedr. Show what?

Soc. That whether Lysias or any other writer that ever was or will be, whether private man or statesman, proposes laws and so becomes the author of a political treatise, fancying that there is any great certainty and clearness in his performance, the fact of his so writing is only a disgrace to him, whatever men may say. For not to know the nature of justice and injustice, and good and evil, and not to be able to distinguish the dream from the reality, cannot in truth be otherwise than disgraceful to him, even though e he have the applause of the whole world.

Phaedr. Certainly.

Soc. But he who thinks that in the written word, whatever its subject, there is necessarily much which is not serious, and that no discourse worthy of study has ever yet been written in poetry or prose, and that spoken ones are no better if, like the recitations of rhapsodes, they are delivered for the sake of persuasion, 278 and not with any view to criticism or instruction; and who thinks that even the best of writings are but a memorandum for those who know, and that only in principles of justice and goodness and nobility taught and communicated orally for the sake of instruction and graven in the soul, which is the true way of writing, is there clearness and perfection and seriousness, and that such principles should be deemed a man's own and his legitimate offspring;—being, in the first place, the word which he finds in his b own bosom; secondly, the brethren and descendants and relations of his idea which have been duly implanted by him in the souls of others;—and who cares for them and no others—this is the right sort of man; and you and I, Phaedrus, would pray that we may become like him.

Phaedr. That is most assuredly my desire and prayer.

Soc. And now the play is played out; and of rhetoric enough. Go and tell Lysias that to the fountain and school of the Nymphs we went down, and were bidden by them to convey a message c to him and to other composers of speeches—to Homer and other writers of poems, whether set to music or not; and to Solon and others who have composed writings in the form of political discourses which they would term laws—to all of them we are to say that if their compositions are based on knowledge of the truth, and they can defend or prove them, when they are put to the test, by spoken arguments, which leave their writings poor in comparison of them, then they are to be called, not only poets, orators, legislators, but are worthy of a higher name, befitting the serious d pursuit of their life.

Phaedr. What name would you assign to them?

Soc. Wise, I may not call them; for that is a great name which belongs to God alone,—lovers of wisdom or philosophers is their modest and befitting title.

Phaedr. Very suitable.

Soc. And he who cannot rise above his own compilations and

compositions, which he has been long patching and piecing, e
adding some and taking away some, may be justly called poet or
speech-maker or law-maker.

Phaedr. Certainly.

Soc. Now go and tell this to your companion.

Phaedr. But there is also a friend of yours who ought not to be
forgotten.

Soc. Who is he?

Phaedr. Isocrates the fair:—What message will you send to
him, and how shall we describe him?

Soc. Isocrates is still young, Phaedrus; but I am willing to 279
hazard a prophecy concerning him.

Phaedr. What would you prophesy?

Soc. I think that he has a genius which soars above the orations
of Lysias, and that his character is cast in a finer mould. It would
not in fact surprise me if, as he grows older, he comes to excel
all former rhetoricians in the kind of speech he now attempts,
making them seem mere children; nor would it surprise me if he
finds this insufficient, but is urged by some more divine impulse
to things higher still. For he has an element of philosophy in his
nature. This is the message of the gods dwelling in this place, and b
which I will myself deliver to my beloved Isocrates; and do you
give the other to Lysias, who is yours.

Phaedr. I will; and now as the heat is abated let us depart.

Soc. Should we not offer up a prayer first of all to the local
deities?

Phaedr. By all means.

Soc. Beloved Pan, and all ye other gods who haunt this place,
give me beauty in the inward soul; and may the outward and
inward man be at one. May I reckon the wise to be the wealthy, c
and may I have such a quantity of gold as a temperate man and
he only can bear and carry.—Anything more? The prayer, I
think, is enough for me.

Phaedr. Ask the same for me, for friends should have all things
in common.

Soc. Let us go.

THEAETETUS

INTRODUCTION AND ANALYSIS

Some dialogues of Plato are of so various a character that their relation to the other dialogues cannot be determined with any degree of certainty. The *Theaetetus*, like the *Parmenides*, has points of similarity both with his earlier and his later writings. The perfection of style, the humour, the dramatic interest, the complexity of structure, the fertility of illustration, the shifting of the points of view are characteristic of his best period of authorship. The vain search, the negative conclusion, the figure of the midwives, the constant profession of ignorance on the part of Socrates also bear the stamp of the early dialogues, in which the original Socrates is not yet Platonized. Had we no other indications, we should be disposed to range the *Theaetetus* with the *Apology* and the *Phaedrus*, and perhaps even with the *Protagoras* and the *Laches*.

But when we pass from the style to an examination of the subject, we trace a connexion with the later rather than with the earlier dialogues. In the first place there is the connexion, indicated by Plato himself at the end of the dialogue, with the *Sophist*, to which in many respects the *Theaetetus* is so little akin. (1) The same persons reappear, including the younger Socrates, whose name is just mentioned in the *Theaetetus* (147 c); (2) the theory of rest, which at p. 133 d Socrates has declined to consider, is resumed by the Eleatic Stranger; (3) there is a similar allusion in both dialogues to the meeting of Parmenides and Socrates (*Theaet.* 183 e, *Soph.* 217); and (4) the inquiry into not-being in the *Sophist* supplements the question of false opinion which is raised in the *Theaetetus*. (Compare also *Theaet.* 168 a, 210 and *Soph.* 230 b; *Theaet.* 174 d, e and *Soph.* 227 a; *Theaet.* 188 e and *Soph.* 237 d; *Theaet.* 179 a and *Soph.* 233 b; *Theaet.* 172 d and *Soph.* 253 c, for parallel turns of thought.) Secondly, the later date of the dialogue is confirmed by the absence of the doctrine of recollection and of any doctrine of ideas except that which derives them from generalization and from reflection of the mind upon itself. The general character of the *Theaetetus* is dialectical, and there are traces of the same Megarian influences which appear in the *Parmenides*, and which later writers, in their matter of fact way, have explained by the residence of Plato at Megara. Socrates disclaims the character of a professional eristic (164 c), and also, with a sort of ironical admiration, expresses his inability to attain the Megarian precision in the use of terms (197 a).

Yet he too employs a similar sophistical skill in overturning every conceivable theory of knowledge.

The direct indications of a date amount to no more than this: the conversation is said to have taken place when Theaetetus was a youth, and shortly before the death of Socrates. At the time of his own death he is supposed to be a full-grown man. Allowing nine or ten years for the interval between youth and manhood, the dialogue could not have been written earlier than 390, when Plato was about thirty-nine years of age. No more definite date is indicated by the engagement in which Theaetetus is said to have fallen or to have been wounded, and which may have taken place any time during the Corinthian war, between the years 390–387. The later date which has been suggested, 369, when the Athenians and Lacedaemonians disputed the Isthmus with Epaminondas, would make the age of Theaetetus at his death forty-five or forty-six. This a little impairs the beauty of Socrates' remark, that 'he would be a great man if he lived'.[1]

We cannot exclude the possibility which has been already noticed in reference to other works of Plato, that the *Theaetetus* may not have been all written continuously; or the probability that the *Sophist* and *Politicus*, which differ greatly in style, were only appended after a long interval of time. The allusion to Parmenides at 183, compared with *Sophist* 217, would probably imply that the dialogue which is called by his name was already in existence; unless, indeed, we suppose the passage in which the allusion occurs to have been inserted afterwards. Again, the *Theaetetus* may be connected with the *Gorgias*, either dialogue from different points of view containing an analysis of the real and apparent (Schleiermacher); and both may be brought into relation with the *Apology* as illustrating the personal life of Socrates. The *Philebus*, too, may with equal reason be placed either after or before what, in the language of Thrasyllus, may be called the Second Platonic Trilogy. Both the *Parmenides* and the *Sophist*, and still more the *Theaetetus*, have points of affinity with the *Cratylus*, in which the principles of rest and motion are again contrasted, and the sophistical or Protagorean theory of language is opposed to that which is attributed to the disciple of Heracleitus, not to speak of lesser resemblances

[1] [The date 368–367 is today generally accepted. See A. E. Taylor, *P.M.W.*, chap. xiii. The dialogue would thus have been written shortly before Plato, who was now sixty years old, left Athens on his second visit to Sicily. The *Parmenides* is probably earlier than the *Theaetetus*, being written (as far as 137 c) in the reported style which is now dismissed with some impatience (*Theaet*. 143). It is not clear why, as is said above, the assumption of this date should 'impair the beauty of Socrates' remark', since Theaetetus lived to realize the expectation which Socrates had formed of him.]

in thought and language. The *Parmenides*, again, has been thought by some to hold an intermediate position between the *Theaetetus* and the *Sophist*; upon this view, *Soph.* 250 ff. may be regarded as the answer to the problems about One and Being which have been raised in the *Parmenides*. Any of these arrangements may suggest new views to the student of Plato; none of them can lay claim to an exclusive probability in its favour.

The *Theaetetus* is one of the narrated dialogues of Plato, and is the only one which is supposed to have been written down. In a short introductory scene, Euclides and Terpsion are described as meeting before the door of Euclides' house in Megara. This may have been a spot familiar to Plato (for Megara was within a walk of Athens), but no importance can be attached to the accidental introduction of the founder of the Megarian philosophy. The real intention of the preface is to create an interest about the person of Theaetetus, who has just been carried up from the army at Corinth in a dying state. The expectation of his death recalls the promise of his youth, and especially the famous conversation which Socrates had with him when he was quite young, a few days before his own trial and death, as we are once more reminded at the end of the dialogue. Yet we may observe that Plato has himself forgotten this, when he represents Euclides as from time to time coming to Athens and correcting the copy from Socrates' own mouth. The narrative, having introduced Theaetetus, and having guaranteed the authenticity of the dialogue (cf. *Symposium, Phaedo, Parmenides*), is then dropped. No further use is made of the device. As Plato himself remarks, who in this as in some other minute points is imitated by Cicero (*De Amicitia*, c. 1), the interlocutory words are omitted.

Theaetetus, the hero of the battle of Corinth and of the dialogue, is a disciple of Theodorus, the great geometrician, whose science is thus indicated to be the propaedeutic to philosophy. An interest has been already excited about him by his approaching death, and now he is introduced to us anew by the praises of his master Theodorus. He is a youthful Socrates, and exhibits the same contrast of the fair soul and the ungainly face and frame, the Silenus mask and the god within, which are described in the *Symposium*. The picture which Theodorus gives of his courage and patience and intelligence and modesty is verified in the course of the dialogue. His courage is shown by his behaviour in the battle, and his other qualities shine forth as the argument proceeds. Socrates takes an evident delight in 'the wise Theaetetus', who has more in him than 'many bearded men'; he is quite inspired by his answers. At first the youth is lost in wonder, and is almost too modest to speak (151 e), but, encouraged by Socrates, he rises to the occasion, and grows full of interest and enthusiasm about the great question. Like a youth (162 d), he has not finally made up his mind, and is very ready to follow the lead of Socrates, and to enter into each successive phase of the discussion which turns up. His great dialectical talent is shown in his power of drawing distinctions (163 e), and of foreseeing the consequences of his own answers (154 d). The inquiry about the nature of knowledge is not new to him; long ago he has felt the 'pang of philosophy', and has experienced the youthful intoxication which is depicted in the *Philebus* (p. 15). But he has hitherto been unable to make the transition from mathematics to metaphysics. He can form a general conception of square and oblong numbers (p. 148), but he is unable to attain a similar expression of knowledge in the abstract. Yet at length (p. 185) he begins to recognize that there are universal conceptions of being, likeness, sameness, number, which the mind contemplates in herself, and with the help of Socrates is conducted from a theory of sense to a theory of ideas.

There is no reason to doubt that Theaetetus was a real person, whose name survived in the next generation.[1] But neither can any

---

[1] [The notice in Proclus is based on the history of Mathematics by Eudemus and need not be viewed with distrust.

'Eudemus named him along with Archytas and Leodamas as one of the three prominent geometers of the fourth century. From notices in the Scholia to Euclid's *Elements* and elsewhere, we gather that he was one of the first mathematicians to begin the systematic study of the types of 'quadratic surd' worked out to its completion in Euclid's Tenth Book, and he is still more often referred to as the geometer who completed the theory of the regular solids, by adding to the three known to the Pythagoreans (tetrahedron, cube, dodecahedron), the remaining two (octahedron, icosahedron).' Taylor, *P.M.W.*, chap. xiii.

The younger Socrates, who is introduced here as a companion of Theaetetus, and who later takes over the respondent's part (*Statesman*, 257), likewise became in later life an exponent of the mathematical philosophy of the Academy. Aristotle in *Metaph.*, Book *Z*, reproduces and criticizes an argument whereby he endeavoured to prove that the ultimate Forms are Numbers. And on several occasions, speaking of the famous Socrates, he terms him Socrates *the elder*. This would suggest that Socrates was still alive when Aristotle lectured. If, as Plato implies, he was a boy in 399 B.C., he must have been some twenty years older than Aristotle. Socrates is again mentioned in the eleventh *Epistle*, which, if genuine (as it seems to be), was written between 361 and 357 B.C. Plato writes to Leodamas of Thasos, another eminent mathematician, giving reasons why neither he nor Socrates can in present circumstances come to Thasos.

Since the dialogues *Sophist* and *Statesman* had in all probability been published before this date, this may provide the answer to an old question, viz. whether persons still living are ever introduced as characters in the dialogues of Plato. (See Pasquali, *Le Lettere di Platone*, pp. 259–66; and the article *Sokrates* in Pauly–Wissowa, *Realenzyklopädie*.)]

importance be attached to the notices of him in Suidas and Proclus, which are probably based on the mention of him in Plato. According to a confused statement in Suidas, who mentions him twice over, first, as a pupil of Socrates, and then of Plato, he is said to have written the first work on the Five Solids. But no early authority cites the work, the invention of which may have been easily suggested by the division of roots, which Plato attributes to him, and the allusion to the backward state of solid geometry in the *Republic* (vii. 528 b). At any rate, there is no occasion to recall him to life after the battle of Corinth, in order that we may allow time for the completion of such a work (Müller). We may also remark that such a supposition entirely destroys the pathetic interest of the introduction.

Theodorus, the geometrician, had once been the friend and disciple of Protagoras, but he is very reluctant to leave his retirement and defend his old master. He is too old to learn Socrates' game of question and answer, and prefers the digressions to the main argument, because he finds them easier to follow. The mathematician, as Socrates says in the *Republic*, is not capable of giving a reason in the same manner as the dialectician (vii. 531 d, e), and Theodorus could not therefore have been appropriately introduced as the chief respondent. But he may be fairly appealed to, when the honour of his master is at stake. He is the 'guardian of his orphans', although this is a responsibility which he wishes to throw upon Callias, the friend and patron of all sophists, declaring that he himself had early 'run away' from philosophy, and was absorbed in mathematics. His extreme dislike for the Heraclitean fanatics, which may be compared with the dislike of Theaetetus (155 e) for the materialists, and his ready acceptance of the noble words of Socrates (175, 176), are noticeable traits of character.

The Socrates of the *Theaetetus* is the same as the Socrates of the earlier dialogues. He is the invincible disputant, now advanced in years, of the *Protagoras* and *Symposium*; he is still pursuing his divine mission, his 'Herculean labours', of which he has described the origin in the *Apology*; and he still hears the voice of his oracle, bidding him receive or not receive the truant souls. There he is supposed to have a mission to convict men of self-conceit; in the *Theaetetus* he has assigned to him by God the functions of a man-midwife, who delivers men of their thoughts, and under this character he is present throughout the dialogue. He is the true prophet who has an insight into the natures of men, and can divine their future (142 c); and he knows that sympathy is the secret power which unlocks their thoughts. The hit at Aristides, the son of Lysimachus, who was specially committed to his charge in the *Laches*, may be remarked by the way. The attempt to discover the definition of knowledge is in accordance with the character of Socrates as he is described in the *Memorabilia*, asking What is justice? What is temperance? and the like. But there is no reason to suppose that he would have analysed the nature of perception, or traced the connexion of Protagoras and Heracleitus, or have raised the difficulty respecting false opinion. The humorous illustrations, as well as the serious thoughts, run through the dialogue. The snubnosedness of Theaetetus, a characteristic which he shares with Socrates, and the man-midwifery of Socrates, are not forgotten in the closing words. At the end of the dialogue, as in the *Euthyphro*, he is expecting to meet Meletus at the porch of the king Archon; but with the same indifference to the result which is everywhere displayed by him, he proposes that they shall reassemble on the following day at the same spot. The day comes, and in the *Sophist* the three friends again meet, but no further allusion is made to the trial, and the principal share in the argument is assigned, not to Socrates, but to an Eleatic Stranger; the youthful Theaetetus also plays a different and less independent part. And there is no allusion in the Introduction to the second and third dialogues, which are afterwards appended. There seems, therefore, reason to think that there is a real change, both in the characters and in the design.

The dialogue is an inquiry into the nature of knowledge, which is interrupted by two digressions. The first is the digression about the midwives, which is also a leading thought or continuous image, like the wave in the *Republic*, appearing and reappearing at intervals. Again and again we are reminded that the successive conceptions of knowledge are extracted from Theaetetus, who in his turn truly declares that Socrates has got a great deal more out of him than ever was in him. Socrates is never weary of working out the image in humorous details,—discerning the symptoms of labour, carrying the child round the hearth, fearing that Theaetetus will bite him, comparing his conceptions to wind-eggs, asserting an hereditary right to the occupation. There is also a serious side to the image, which is an apt similitude of the Socratic theory of education (cf. *Rep.* vii. 518 d, *Sophist* 230), and accords with the ironical spirit in which the wisest of men delights to speaks of himself.

The other digression is the famous contrast of the lawyer and philosopher. This is a sort of landing-place or break in the middle of the dialogue. At the commencement of a great discussion, the reflection naturally arises, How happy are they who, like the philosopher, have time for such discussions (cf. *Rep.* v. 450)! There is no reason for the introduction of such a digression; nor is a reason always needed, any more than for the introduction of an episode in a poem, or of a topic in conversation. That which is given by Socrates is quite sufficient, viz. that the philosopher may talk and write as he pleases. But though not very closely connected, neither is the digression out of keeping with the rest of the dialogue. The philosopher naturally desires to pour forth the thoughts which are always present to him, and to discourse of the higher life. The idea of knowledge, although hard to be defined, is realized in the life of philosophy. And the contrast is the favourite antithesis between the world, in the various characters of sophist, lawyer, statesman, speaker, and the philosopher,—between opinion and knowledge,—between the conventional and the true.

The greater part of the dialogue is devoted to setting up and throwing down definitions of science and knowledge. Proceeding from the lower to the higher by three stages, in which perception, opinion, reasoning are successively examined, we first get rid of the confusion of the idea of knowledge and specific kinds of knowledge,—a confusion which has been already noticed in the *Lysis*, *Laches*, *Meno*, and other dialogues. In the infancy of logic, a form of thought has to be invented before the content can be filled up. We cannot define knowledge until the nature of definition has been ascertained. Having succeeded in making his meaning plain, Socrates proceeds to analyse (1) the first definition which Theaetetus proposes: 'Knowledge is sensible perception'. This is speedily identified with the Protagorean saying, 'Man is the measure of all things'; and of this again the foundation is discovered in the perpetual flux of Heracleitus. The relativeness of sensation is then developed at length, and for a moment the definition appears to be accepted. But soon the Protagorean thesis is pronounced to be suicidal; for the adversaries of Protagoras are as good a measure as he is, and they deny his doctrine. He is then supposed to reply that the perception may be true at any given instant. But the reply is in the end shown to be inconsistent with the Heraclitean foundation, on which the doctrine has been affirmed to rest. For if the Heraclitean flux is extended to every sort of change in every instant of time, how can any thought or word be detained even for an instant? Sensible perception, like everything else, is tumbling to pieces. Nor can Protagoras himself maintain that one man is as good as another in his knowledge of the future; and 'the expedient', if not 'the just and true', belongs to the sphere of the future.

And so we must ask again, What is knowledge? The comparison of sensations with one another implies a principle which is above sensation, and which resides in the mind itself. We are thus led to look for knowledge in a higher sphere, and accordingly Theaetetus, when again interrogated, replies (2) that 'knowledge is true opinion'. But how is false opinion possible? The Megarian or Eristic spirit within us revives the question, which has been already asked and indirectly answered in the *Meno*: 'How can a man be ignorant of that which he knows?' No answer is given to this not unanswerable question. The comparison of the mind to a block of wax, or to a decoy of birds, is found wanting.

But are we not inverting the natural order in looking for opinion before we have found knowledge? And knowledge is not true opinion; for the Athenian dicasts have true opinion but not knowledge. What then is knowledge? We answer (3), 'True opinion, with definition or explanation'. But all the different ways in which this statement may be understood are set aside, like the definitions of courage in the *Laches*, or of friendship in the *Lysis*, or of temperance in the *Charmides*. At length we arrive at the conclusion, in which nothing is concluded.

There are two special difficulties which beset the student of the *Theaetetus*: (1) he is uncertain how far he can trust Plato's account of the theory of Protagoras; and he is also uncertain (2) how far, and in what parts of the dialogue, Plato is expressing his own opinion. The dramatic character of the work renders the answer to both these questions difficult.[1]

1. In reply to the first, we have only probabilities to offer. Three main points have to be decided: (*a*) Would Protagoras have identified his own thesis, 'Man is the measure of all things', with the other, 'All knowledge is sensible perception'? (*b*) Would he have based the relativity of knowledge on the Heraclitean flux? (*c*) Would he have asserted the absoluteness of sensation at each instant? Of the work of Protagoras on 'Truth' we know nothing, with the exception of the two famous fragments, which are cited in this dialogue, 'Man is the measure of all things', and, 'Whether there are gods or not, I cannot tell'. Nor have we any other trustworthy evidence of the tenets of Protagoras, or of the sense in which his words are used. For later writers, including Aristotle in his *Metaphysics*, have mixed up the Protagoras of Plato, as they have the Socrates of Plato, with the real person.

Returning then to the *Theaetetus*, as the only possible source from which an answer to these questions can be obtained, we may remark that Plato had 'The Truth' of Protagoras before him, and frequently refers to the book. He seems to say expressly that in this work the doctrine of the Heraclitean flux was not to be found (p. 152); 'he told

[1] [These questions are dealt with by F. M. Cornford in *Plato's Theory of Knowledge*, and by G. B. Kerferd in an essay on 'Plato's account of the relativism of Protagoras', *Durham University Journal*, xlii (1949).]

the real truth' (not in the book, which is so entitled, but) 'privately to his disciples',—words which imply that the connexion between the doctrines of Protagoras and Heracleitus was not generally recognized in Greece, but was really discovered or invented by Plato. On the other hand, the doctrine that 'Man is the measure of all things', is expressly identified by Socrates with the other statement, that 'What appears to each man *is* to him'; and a reference is made to the books in which the statement occurs;—this, Theaetetus, who has 'often read the books', is supposed to acknowledge (152 a: so *Cratylus* 385 e). And Protagoras, in the speech attributed to him, never says that he has been misunderstood: at p. 166 c he rather seems to imply that the absoluteness of sensation at each instant was to be found in his words (cf. 158 e). He is only indignant at the *reductio ad absurdum* devised by Socrates for his *homo mensura*, which Theodorus also considers to be 'really too bad'.

The question may be raised, how far Plato in the *Theaetetus* could have misrepresented Protagoras without violating the laws of dramatic probability. Could he have pretended to cite from a well-known writing what was not to be found there? But such a shadowy inquiry is not worth pursuing farther. We need only remember that in the criticism which follows of the thesis of Protagoras, we are criticizing the Protagoras of Plato, and not attempting to draw a precise line between his real sentiments and those which Plato has attributed to him.

2. The other difficulty is a more subtle, and also a more important, one, because bearing on the general character of the Platonic dialogues. On a first reading of them, we are apt to imagine that the truth is only spoken by Socrates, who is never guilty of a fallacy himself, and is the great detector of the errors and fallacies of others. But this natural presumption is disturbed by the discovery that the sophists are some-times in the right and Socrates in the wrong. Like the hero of a novel, he is not to be supposed always to represent the sentiments of the author. There are few modern readers who do not side with Prota-goras, rather than with Socrates, in the dialogue which is called by his name. The *Cratylus* presents a similar difficulty: in his etymologies, as in the number of the State, we cannot tell how far Socrates is serious; for the Socratic irony will not allow him to distinguish between his real and his assumed wisdom. No one is the superior of the invincible Socrates in argument (except in the first part of the *Parmenides*, where he is introduced as a youth); but he is by no means supposed to be in possession of the whole truth. Arguments are often put into his mouth (cf. Introduction to the *Gorgias*) which must have seemed quite as

untenable to Plato as to a modern writer. In this dialogue a great part of the answer of Protagoras is just and sound; remarks are made by him on verbal criticism, and on the importance of understanding an opponent's meaning, which are conceived in the true spirit of philosophy. And the distinction which he is supposed to draw between Eristic and Dialectic (167, 168) is really a criticism of Plato on himself and his own criticism of Protagoras.

The difficulty seems to arise from not attending to the dramatic character of the writings of Plato. There are two, or more, sides to questions; and these are parted among the different speakers. Sometimes one view or aspect of a question is made to predominate over the rest, as in the *Gorgias* or *Sophist*; but in other dialogues truth is divided, as in the *Laches* and *Protagoras*, and the interest of the piece consists in the contrast of opinions. The confusion caused by the irony of Socrates, who, if he is true to his character, cannot say anything of his own knowledge, is increased by the circumstance that in the *Theaetetus* and some other dialogues he is occasionally playing both parts himself, and even charging his own arguments with unfairness. In the *Theaetetus* he is designedly held back from arriving at a conclusion. For we cannot suppose that Plato conceived a definition of knowledge to be impossible. But this is his manner of approaching and surrounding a question. The lights which he throws on his subject are indirect, but they are not the less real for that. He has no intention of proving a thesis by a cut-and-dried argument; nor does he imagine that a great philosophical problem can be tied up within the limits of a definition. If he has analysed a proposition or notion, even with the severity of an impossible logic, if half-truths have been compared by him with other half-truths, if he has cleared up or advanced popular ideas, or illustrated a new method, his aim has been sufficiently accomplished.

The writings of Plato belong to an age in which the power of analysis had outrun the means of knowledge; and through a spurious use of dialectic, the distinctions which had been already 'won from the void and formless infinite' seemed to be rapidly returning to their original chaos. The two great speculative philosophies, which a century earlier had so deeply impressed the mind of Hellas, were now degenerating into Eristic. The contemporaries of Plato and Socrates were vainly trying to find new combinations of them, or to transfer them from the object to the subject. The Megarians, in their first attempts to attain a severer logic, were making knowledge impossible (cf. *Theaet.* 202). They were asserting 'the one good under many names', and, like the Cynics, seem to have denied predication, while the Cynics themselves were depriving virtue of all which made virtue desirable in the eyes of Socrates and Plato. And besides these, we find mention in the later writings of Plato, especially in the *Theaetetus, Sophist,* and *Laws,* of certain impenetrable godless persons, who will not believe what they 'cannot hold in their hands'; and cannot be approached in argument, because they cannot argue (*Theaet.* 155 e; *Soph.* 246 a). No school of Greek philosophers exactly answers to these persons, in whom Plato may perhaps have blended some features of the Atomists with the vulgar materialistic tendencies of mankind in general (cf. Introduction to the *Sophist*).

And not only was there a conflict of opinions, but the stage which the mind had reached presented other difficulties hardly intelligible to us who live in a different cycle of human thought. All times of mental progress are times of confusion; we only see, or rather seem to see, things clearly when they have been long fixed and defined. In the age of Plato, the limits of the world of imagination and of pure abstraction, of the old world and the new, were not yet fixed. The Greeks in the fourth century before Christ had no words for 'subject' and 'object', and no distinct conception of them; yet they were always hovering about the question involved in them. The analysis of sense and the analysis of thought were equally difficult to them; and hopelessly confused by the attempt to solve them, not through an appeal to facts, but by the help of general theories respecting the nature of the universe.

Plato, in his *Theaetetus,* gathers up the sceptical tendencies of his age, and compares them. But he does not seek to reconstruct out of them a theory of knowledge. The time at which such a theory could be framed had not yet arrived. For there was no measure of experience with which the ideas swarming in men's minds could be compared; the meaning of the word 'science' could scarcely be explained to them, except from the mathematical sciences, which alone offered the type of universality and certainty. Philosophy was becoming more and more vacant and abstract, and not only the Platonic Ideas and the Eleatic Being, but all abstractions seemed to be at variance with sense and at war with one another.

The want of the Greek mind in the fourth century before Christ was not another theory of rest or motion, or Being or atoms, but rather a philosophy which could free the mind from the power of abstractions and alternatives, and show how far rest and how far motion, how far the universal principle of Being and the multitudinous principle of atoms, entered into the composition of the world; which could distinguish between the true and false analogy, and allow the negative as well as the positive a place in human thought. To such a philosophy Plato, in the *Theaetetus*, offers many contributions. He has followed philosophy into the region of mythology, and pointed out the similarities of opposing phases of thought. He has also shown that extreme abstractions are self-destructive, and, indeed, hardly distinguishable from one another. But his intention is not to unravel the whole subject of knowledge, if this had been possible; and several times in the course of the dialogue he rejects explanations of knowledge which have germs of truth in them; as, for example, 'the resolution of the compound into the simple'; or 'right opinion with a mark of difference'.

————

ANALYSIS

142 Terpsion, who has come to Megara from the country, is described as having looked in vain for Euclides in the Agora; the latter explains that he has been down to the harbour, and on his way thither had met Theaetetus, who was being carried up from the army to Athens. He was scarcely alive, for he had been badly wounded at the battle of Corinth, and had taken the dysentery which prevailed in the camp. The mention of his condition suggests the reflection, 'What a loss he will be!' 'Yes, indeed,' replies Euclides; 'only just now I was hearing of his noble conduct in the battle.' 'That I should expect; but why did he not remain at Megara?' 'I wanted him to remain, but he would not; so I went with him as far as Erineum; and as I parted from him, I remembered that Socrates had seen him when he was a youth, and had a remarkable conversation with him, not long before his own death; and he then prophesied of him that he would be a great man if he lived.' 'How true that has been; how like all that

143 Socrates said! And could you repeat the conversation?' 'Not from memory; but I took notes when I returned home, which I afterwards filled up at leisure, and got Socrates to correct them from time to time, when I came to Athens.' . . . Terpsion had long intended to ask for a sight of this writing, of which he had already heard. They are both tired, and agree to rest and have the conversation read to them by a servant. . . . 'Here is the roll, Terpsion; I need only observe that I have omitted, for the sake of convenience, the interlocutory words, "said I", "said he"; and that Theaetetus, and Theodorus, the geometrician of Cyrene, are the persons with whom Socrates is conversing.'

Socrates begins by asking Theodorus whether, in his visit to Athens, he has found any Athenian youth likely to attain distinction in science. 'Yes, Socrates, there is one very remarkable youth, with whom I have become acquainted. He is no beauty, and therefore you need not imagine that I am in love with him; and, to say the truth, he is very like you, for he has a snub nose, and projecting eyes, although these features are not so marked in him as in you. He combines the most various qualities, quickness, 144 patience, courage; and he is gentle as well as wise, always silently flowing on, like a river of oil. Look! he is the middle one of those who are entering the palaestra.'

Socrates, who does not know his name, recognizes him as the son of Euphronius, who was himself a good man and a rich. He is informed by Theodorus that the youth is named Theaetetus, but the property of his father has disappeared in the hands of trustees; this does not, however, prevent him from adding liberality to his other virtues. At the desire of Socrates he invites Theaetetus to sit by them.

'Yes,' says Socrates, 'that I may see in you, Theaetetus, the image of my ugly self, as Theodorus declares. Not that his remark is of any importance; for though he is a philosopher, he is not a painter, and therefore he is no judge of our faces; but, as 145 he is a man of science, he may be a judge of our intellects. And if he were to praise the mental endowments of either of us, in that case the hearer of the eulogy ought to examine into what he says, and the subject should not refuse to be examined.' Theaetetus consents, and is caught in a trap (cf. the similar trap which is laid for Theodorus, at 166, 168 d). 'Then, Theaetetus, you will have to be examined, for Theodorus has been praising you in a style of which I never heard the like.' 'He was only jesting.' 'Nay, that is not his way; and I cannot allow you, on that pretence, to retract the assent which you have already given, or I shall make Theodorus repeat your praises, and swear to them.' Theaetetus, in reply, professes that he is willing to be examined, and Socrates begins by asking him what he learns of Theodorus. He is himself anxious to learn anything of anybody; and now he has a little question to which he wants Theaetetus or Theodorus (or whichever of the company would not be 'donkey' to the rest) to find an answer. Without further preface, but at the same time

146 apologizing for his eagerness, he asks, 'What is knowledge?'
Theodorus is too old to answer questions, and begs him to interrogate Theaetetus, who has the advantage of youth.

Theaetetus replies that knowledge is what he learns of Theodorus, i.e. geometry and arithmetic; and that there are other
kinds of knowledge—shoemaking, carpentering, and the like.
But Socrates rejoins, that this answer contains too much and also
too little. For although Theaetetus has enumerated several kinds
147 of knowledge, he has not explained the common nature of them;
as if he had been asked, 'What is clay?' and instead of saying,
'Clay is moistened earth', he had answered, 'There is one clay
of image-makers, another of potters, another of oven-makers.'
Theaetetus at once divines that Socrates means him to extend to
all kinds of knowledge the same process of generalization which
he has already learned to apply to arithmetic. For he has discovered a division of numbers into square numbers, 4, 9, 16, &c.,
which are composed of equal factors, and represent figures which
148 have equal sides, and oblong numbers, 3, 5, 6, 7, &c., which are
composed of unequal factors, and represent figures which have
unequal sides. But he has never succeeded in attaining a similar
conception of knowledge, though he has often tried; and, when
this and similar questions were brought to him from Socrates, has
been sorely distressed by them. Socrates explains to him that he
149 is in labour. For men as well as women have pangs of labour; and
both at times require the assistance of midwives. And he, Socrates,
is a midwife, although this is a secret; he has inherited the art
from his mother bold and bluff, and he ushers into light, not
children, but the thoughts of men. Like the midwives, who are
'past bearing children', he too can have no offspring—the god
will not allow him to bring anything into the world of his own.
He also reminds Theaetetus that the midwives are or ought to be
the only matchmakers (this is the preparation for a biting jest,
151 b); for those who reap the fruit are most likely to know on
150 what soil the plants will grow. But respectable midwives avoid
this department of practice—they do not want to be called
procuresses. There are some other differences between the two
sorts of pregnancy. For women do not bring into the world at
one time real children and at another time idols which are with
difficulty distinguished from them. 'At first,' says Socrates in his

character of the man-midwife, 'my patients are barren and stolid, but after a while they "round apace", if the gods are propitious to them; and this is due not to me but to themselves; I and the god only assist in bringing their ideas to the birth. Many of them have left me too soon, and the result has been that they have produced abortions; or when I have delivered them of children they have lost them by an ill bringing up, and have ended by seeing themselves, as others see them, to be great fools. Aristides, the son of Lysimachus, is one of these, and there have been others. The truants often return to me and beg to be 151 taken back; and then, if my familiar allows me, which is not always the case, I receive them, and they begin to grow again. There come to me also those who have nothing in them, and have no need of my art; and I am their matchmaker (see above), and marry them to Prodicus or some other inspired sage who is likely to suit them. I tell you this long story because I suspect that you are in labour. Come then to me, who am a midwife, and the son of a midwife, and I will deliver you. And do not bite me, as the women do, if I abstract your first-born; for I am acting out of good will towards you; the god who is within me is the friend of man, though he will not allow me to dissemble the truth. Once more then, Theaetetus, I repeat my old question—"What is knowledge?" Take courage, and by the help of God you will discover an answer.' 'My answer is, that knowledge is perception.' 'That is the theory of Protagoras, who has another way of 152 expressing the same thing when he says, "Man is the measure of all things." He was a very wise man, and we should try to understand him. In order to illustrate his meaning let me suppose that there is the same wind blowing in our faces, and one of us may be hot and the other cold. How is this? Protagoras will reply that the wind is hot to him who is cold, cold to him who is hot. And "is" means "appears", and when you say "appears to him", that means "he feels". Thus feeling, appearance, perception, coincide with being. I suspect, however, that this was only a "façon de parler", by which he imposed on the common herd like you and me; he told "the truth" [in allusion to the title of his book, which was called "The Truth"] in secret to his disciples. For he was really a votary of that famous philosophy in which all things are said to be relative; nothing is great or small, or heavy or light, or one, but all is in motion and mixture and transition and flux and generation, not "being", as we ignorantly affirm, but "becoming". This has been the doctrine, not of Protagoras only, but of all philosophers, with the single exception of Parmenides; Empedocles, Heracleitus, and others, and all the poets, with Epicharmus, the king of Comedy, and Homer, the king of Tragedy, at their head, have said the same; the latter has these words—

Ocean, whence the gods sprang, and mother Tethys.

153 And many arguments are used to show that motion is the source of life, and rest of death: fire and warmth are produced by friction, and living creatures owe their origin to a similar cause; the bodily frame is preserved by exercise and destroyed by indolence; and if the sun ceased to move, "chaos would come again". Now apply this doctrine of "All is motion" to the senses, and first of all to the sense of sight. The colour of white, or any other colour, is neither in the eyes nor out of them, but ever in 154 motion between the object and the eye, and varying in the case of every percipient. All is relative, and, as the followers of Protagoras remark, endless contradictions arise when we deny this; e.g. here are six dice; they are more than four and less than twelve; "more and also less", would you not say?' 'Yes.' 'But Protagoras will retort: "Can anything be more or less without addition or subtraction?" '

'I should say "No" if I were not afraid of contradicting my former answer.'

'And if you say "Yes", the tongue will escape conviction but not the mind, as Euripides would say?' 'True.' 'The thoroughbred sophists, who know all that can be known, would have a sparring match over this, but you and I, who have no professional 155 pride, want only to discover whether our ideas are clear and consistent. And we cannot be wrong in saying, first, that nothing can be greater or less while remaining equal; secondly, that there can be no becoming greater or less without addition or subtraction; thirdly, that what is and was not, cannot be without having become. But then how is this reconcilable with the case of the dice, and with similar examples?—that is the question.' 'I am often perplexed and amazed, Socrates, by these difficulties.'

'That is because you are a philosopher, for philosophy begins in wonder, and Iris is the child of Thaumas. Do you know the original principle on which the doctrine of Protagoras is based?' 'No.' 'Then I will tell you; but we must not let the uninitiated hear, and by the uninitiated I mean the obstinate people who believe in nothing which they cannot hold in their hands. The 156 brethren whose mysteries I am about to unfold to you are far more ingenious. They maintain that all is motion; and that motion has two forms, action and passion, out of which endless phenomena are created, also in two forms—sense and the object of sense—which come to the birth together. There are two kinds of motions, a slow and a fast; the motions of the agent and the patient are slower, because they move and create in and about themselves, but the things which are born of them have a swifter motion, and pass rapidly from place to place. The eye and the appropriate object come together, and give birth to whiteness and the sensation of whiteness; the eye is filled with seeing, and becomes not sight but a seeing eye, and the object is filled with whiteness, and becomes not whiteness but white; and no other compound of either with another would have produced the same effect. All sensation is to be resolved into a similar combination 157 of an agent and patient. Of either, taken separately, no idea can be formed; and the agent may become a patient, and the patient an agent. Hence there arises a general reflection that nothing is, but all things become; no name can detain or fix them. Are not these speculations charming, Theaetetus, and very good for a person in your interesting situation? I am offering you specimens of other men's wisdom, because I have no wisdom of my own, and I want to deliver you of something; and presently we will see whether you have brought forth wind or not. Tell me, then, what do you think of the notion that "All things are becoming"?'

'When I hear your arguments, I am marvellously ready to assent.'

'But I ought not to conceal from you that there is a serious objection which may be urged against this doctrine of Protagoras. For there are states, such as madness and dreaming, in which 158 perception is false; and half our life is spent in dreaming; and who can say that at this instant we are not dreaming? Even the fancies of madmen are real at the time. But if knowledge is perception, how can we distinguish between the true and the false in such cases? Having stated the objection, I will now state the answer. Protagoras would deny the continuity of phenomena; 159 he would say that what is different is entirely different, and whether active or passive has a different power. There are infinite agents and patients in the world, and these produce in every combination of them a different perception. Take myself as an instance:—Socrates may be ill or he may be well,—and remember that Socrates, with all his accidents, is spoken of. The wine which I drink when I am well is pleasant to me, but the same wine is unpleasant to me when I am ill. And there is nothing else 160 from which I can receive the same impression, nor can another receive the same impression from the wine. Neither can I and the object of sense become separately what we become together. For the one in becoming is relative to the other, but they have no other relation; and the combination of them is absolute at each moment. [In modern language, the act of sensation is really indivisible, though capable of a mental analysis into subject and object.] My sensation alone is true, and true to me only. And therefore, as Protagoras says, "To myself I am the judge of what is and what is not." Thus the flux of Homer and Heracleitus, the great Protagorean saying that "Man is the measure of all things", the doctrine of Theaetetus that "Knowledge is perception", have all the same meaning. And this is thy new-born child, which by 161 my art I have brought to light; and you must not be angry if instead of rearing your infant we expose him.'

'Theaetetus will not be angry,' says Theodorus; 'he is very good-natured. But I should like to know, Socrates, whether you mean to say that all this is untrue?'

'First reminding you that I am not the bag which contains the arguments, but that I extract them from Theaetetus, shall I tell you what amazes me in your friend Protagoras?'

'What may that be?'

'I like his doctrine that what appears is; but I wonder that he did not begin his great work on Truth with a declaration that a pig, or a dog-faced baboon, or any other monster which has sensation, is a measure of all things; then, while we were reverencing him as a god, he might have produced a magnificent effect by expounding to us that he was no wiser than a tadpole. For if sensations are always true, and one man's discernment is as good as another's, and every man is his own judge, and everything that he judges is right and true, then what need of Protagoras to be our instructor at a high figure; and why should we be less knowing than he is, or have to go to him, if every man is the measure of all things? My own art of midwifery, and all dialectic, is an enormous folly, if Protagoras' "Truth" be indeed truth, and the philosopher is not merely amusing himself by giving oracles out of his book.'

Theodorus thinks that Socrates is unjust to his master, Protagoras; but he is too old and stiff to try a fall with him, and therefore refers him to Theaetetus, who is already driven out of his former opinion by the arguments of Socrates. 162

Socrates then takes up the defence of Protagoras, who is supposed to reply in his own person—'Good people, you sit and declaim about the gods, of whose existence or non-existence I have nothing to say, or you discourse about man being reduced to the level of the brutes; but what proof have you of your statements? And yet surely you and Theodorus had better reflect whether probability is a safe guide. Theodorus would be a bad geometrician if he had nothing better to offer.' . . . Theaetetus is affected by the appeal to geometry, and Socrates is induced by him to put the question in a new form. He proceeds as follows:—'Should we say that we know what we see and hear,—e.g. the sound of words or the sight of letters in a foreign tongue?' 163

'We should say that the figures of the letters, and the pitch of the voice in uttering them, were known to us, but not the meaning of them.'

'Excellent; I want you to grow, and therefore I will leave that answer and ask another question: Is not seeing perceiving?' 'Very true.' 'And he who sees knows?' 'Yes.' 'And he who remembers, remembers that which he sees and knows?' 'Very true.' 'But if he closes his eyes, does he not remember?' 'He does.' 164 'Then he may remember and not see; and if seeing is knowing, he may remember and not know. Is not this a *reductio ad absurdum* of the hypothesis that knowledge is sensible perception? Yet perhaps we are crowing too soon; and if Protagoras, "the father of the myth", had been alive, the result might have been very

different. But he is dead, and Theodorus, whom he left guardian
of his "orphan", has not been very zealous in defending him.'

165   Theodorus objects that Callias is the true guardian, but he
hopes that Socrates will come to the rescue. Socrates prefaces his
defence by resuming the attack. He asks whether a man can
know and not know at the same time? 'Impossible.' Quite possible, if you maintain that seeing is knowing. The confident
adversary, suiting the action to the word, shuts one of your eyes;
and now, says he, you see and do not see, but do you know and
not know? And a fresh opponent darts from his ambush, and
transfers to knowledge the terms which are commonly applied to
sight. He asks whether you can know near and not at a distance;
whether you can have a sharp and also a dull knowledge. While
you are wondering at his incomparable wisdom, he gets you into
his power, and you will not escape until you have come to an
understanding with him about the money which is to be paid for
your release.

But Protagoras has not yet made his defence; and already he
166   may be heard contemptuously replying that he is not responsible
for the admissions which were made by a boy, who could not
foresee the coming move, and therefore had answered in a manner
which enabled Socrates to raise a laugh against himself. 'But I
cannot be fairly charged', he will say, 'with an answer which I
should not have given; for I never maintained that the memory
of a feeling is the same as a feeling, or denied that a man might
know and not know the same thing at the same time. Or, if you
will have extreme precision, I say that man in different relations
is many or rather infinite in number. And I challenge you, either
to show that his perceptions are not individual, or that if they are,
what appears to him is not what is. As to your pigs and baboons,
you are yourself a pig, and you make my writings a sport of other
swine. But I still affirm that man is the measure of all things,
although I admit that one man may be a thousand times better
than another, in proportion as he has better impressions. Neither
do I deny the existence of wisdom or of the wise man. But I maintain that wisdom is a practical remedial power of turning evil into
good, the bitterness of disease into the sweetness of health, and
does not consist in any greater truth or superior knowledge. For
the impressions of the sick are as true as the impressions of the

healthy; and the sick are as wise as the healthy. Nor can any man 167
be cured of a false opinion, for there is no such thing; but he may
be cured of the evil habit which generates in him an evil opinion.
This is effected in the body by the drugs of the physician, and in
the soul by the words of the Sophist; and the new state or opinion
is not truer, but only better than the old. And philosophers are
not tadpoles, but physicians and husbandmen, who till the soil
and infuse health into animals and plants, and make the good
take the place of the evil, both in individuals and States. Wise and
good rhetoricians make the good to appear just in States (for that
is just which appears just to a State), and in return, they deserve
to be well paid. And you, Socrates, whether you please or not,
must continue to be a measure. This is my defence, and I must
request you to meet me fairly. We are professing to reason, and
not merely to dispute; and there is a great difference between
reasoning and disputation. For the disputer is always seeking to
trip up his opponent; and this is a mode of argument which
disgusts men with philosophy as they grow older. But the reasoner
is trying to understand him and to point out his errors to him,
whether arising from his own or from his companions' fault; he 168
does not argue from the customary use of names, which the
vulgar pervert in all manner of ways. If you are gentle to an
adversary he will follow and love you; and if defeated he will lay
the blame on himself, and seek to escape from his own prejudices
into philosophy. I would recommend you, Socrates, to adopt this
humaner method, and to avoid captious and verbal criticisms.'

Such, Theodorus, is the very slight help which I am able to
afford to your friend; had he been alive, he would have helped
himself in far better style.

'You have made a most valorous defence.'

Yes; but did you observe that Protagoras bade me be serious,
and complained of our getting up a laugh against him with the
aid of a boy? He meant to intimate that you must take the place
of Theaetetus, who may be wiser than many bearded men, but
not wiser than you, Theodorus.

'The rule of the Spartan Palaestra is, Strip or depart; but you 169
are like the giant Antaeus, and will not let me depart unless I try
a fall with you.'

Yes, that is the nature of my complaint. And many a Hercules,

many a Theseus mighty in deeds and words has broken my head;
but I am always at this rough game. Please, then, to favour me.
'On the condition of not exceeding a single fall, I consent.'

170   Socrates now resumes the argument. As he is very desirous of
doing justice to Protagoras, he insists on citing his own words,—
'What appears to each man *is* to him.' And how, asks Socrates,
are these words reconcilable with the fact that all mankind are
agreed in thinking themselves wiser than others in some respects,
and inferior to them in others? In the hour of danger they are
ready to fall down and worship anyone who is their superior in
wisdom as if he were a god. And the world is full of men who are
asking to be taught and willing to be ruled, and of other men who
are willing to rule and teach them. All which implies that men do
judge of one another's impressions, and think some wise and others
foolish. How will Protagoras answer this argument? For he cannot say that no one deems another ignorant or mistaken. If you
form a judgement, thousands and tens of thousands are ready to
maintain the opposite. The multitude may not and do not assent
to Protagoras' own thesis that 'Man is the measure of all things';
171   and then who is to decide? Upon his own showing must not his
'truth' depend on the number of suffrages, and be more or less
true in proportion as he has more or fewer of them? And he
must acknowledge further, that they speak truly who deny him
to speak truly, which is a famous jest. And if he admits that they
speak truly who deny him to speak truly, he must admit that he
himself does not speak truly. But his opponents will refuse to
admit this of themselves, and he must allow that they are right
in their refusal. The conclusion is, that all mankind, including
Protagoras himself, will deny that he speaks truly; and his truth
will be true neither to himself nor to anybody else.

Theodorus is inclined to think that this is going too far. Socrates
ironically replies that he is not going beyond the truth. But if the
old Protagoras could only pop his head out of the world below, he
would doubtless give them both a sound castigation and be off to
the shades in an instant. Seeing that he is not within call, we must
examine the question for ourselves. It is clear that there are great
differences in the understandings of men. Admitting, with Protagoras, that immediate sensations of hot, cold, and the like, are
to each one such as they appear, yet this hypothesis cannot be

extended to judgements or opinions. And even if we were to 172
admit further,—and this is the view of some who are not thorough-
going followers of Protagoras,—that right and wrong, holy and
unholy, are to each state or individual such as they appear, still
Protagoras will not venture to maintain that every man is equally
the measure of expediency, or that that which seems to a city
expedient, really is so. But this begins a new question. 'Well,
Socrates, we have plenty of leisure.' Yes, we have, and, after the
manner of philosophers, we are digressing; I have often observed
how ridiculous this habit of theirs makes them when they appear
in court. 'What do you mean?' I mean to say that a philosopher
is a gentleman, but a lawyer is a servant. The one can have his
talk out, and wander at will from one subject to another, as the
fancy takes him; like ourselves, he may be long or short, as he
pleases. But the lawyer is always in a hurry; there is the clepsydra
limiting his time, and the brief limiting his topics, and his
adversary is standing over him and exacting his rights. He is a
servant disputing about a fellow servant before his master, who
holds the cause in his hands; the track never changes, and often 173
the race is for his life. Such experiences render him keen and
shrewd; he learns the arts of flattery, and is perfect in the practice
of crooked ways; dangers have come upon him too soon, when
the tenderness of youth was unable to meet them with truth and
honesty, and he has resorted to counter-acts of dishonesty and
falsehood, and become warped and distorted; without any health
or freedom or sincerity in him he has grown up to manhood, and
is or esteems himself to be a master of cunning. Such are the
lawyers; will you have the companion picture of philosophers?
or will this be too much of a digression?

'Nay, Socrates, the argument is our servant, and not our
master. Who is the judge or where is the spectator, having a
right to control us?'

I will describe the leaders, then; for the inferior sort are not
worth the trouble. The lords of philosophy have not learned the
way to the dicastery or ecclesia; they neither see nor hear the
laws and votes of the state, written or recited; societies, whether
political or festive, clubs, and singing maidens do not enter even
into their dreams. And the scandals of persons or their ancestors,
male and female, they know no more than they can tell the

number of pints in the ocean. Neither are they conscious of their own ignorance; for they do not practise singularity in order to gain reputation, but the truth is, that the outer form of them only is residing in the city; the inner man, as Pindar says, is going on a voyage of discovery, measuring as with line and rule the things 174 which are under and in the earth, interrogating the whole of nature, only not condescending to notice what is near them.

'What do you mean, Socrates?'

I will illustrate my meaning by the jest of the witty maid-servant, who saw Thales tumbling into a well, and said of him, that he was so eager to know what was going on in heaven, that he could not see what was before his feet. This is applicable to all philosophers. The philosopher is unacquainted with the world; he hardly knows whether his neighbour is a man or an animal. For he is always searching into the essence of man, and inquiring what such a nature ought to do or suffer different from any other. Hence, on every occasion in private life and public, as I was saying, when he appears in a law-court or anywhere, he is the joke, not only of maid-servants, but of the general herd, falling into wells and every sort of disaster; he looks such an awkward, inexperienced creature, unable to say anything personal, when he is abused, in answer to his adversaries (for he knows no evil of anyone); and when he hears the praises of others, he cannot help laughing from the bottom of his soul at their pretensions; and this also gives him a ridiculous appearance. A king or tyrant appears to him to be a kind of swine-herd or cow-herd, milking away at an animal who is much more troublesome and dangerous than cows or sheep; like the cow-herd, he has no time to be educated, and the pen in which he keeps his flock in the moun-tains is surrounded by a wall. When he hears of large landed properties of ten thousand acres or more, he thinks of the whole 175 earth; or if he is told of the antiquity of a family, he remembers that every one has had myriads of progenitors, rich and poor, Greeks and barbarians, kings and slaves. And he who boasts of his descent from Amphitryon in the twenty-fifth generation, may, if he pleases, add as many more, and double that again, and our philosopher only laughs at his inability to do a larger sum. Such is the man at whom the vulgar scoff; he seems to them as if he could not mind his feet. 'That is very true, Socrates.' But when he tries to draw the quick-witted lawyer out of his pleas and rejoinders to the contemplation of absolute justice or injustice in their own nature, or from the popular praises of wealthy kings to the view of happiness and misery in themselves, or to the reasons why a man should seek after the one and avoid the other, then the situation is reversed; the little wretch turns giddy, and is ready to fall over the precipice; his utterance becomes thick, and he makes himself ridiculous, not to servant-maids, but to every man of liberal education. Such are the two pictures: the one of the philosopher and gentleman, who may be excused for not having learned how to make a bed, or cook up flatteries; the other, a serviceable knave, who hardly knows how to wear his cloak,—still less can he awaken harmonious thoughts or hymn virtue's praises. 176

'If the world, Socrates, were as ready to receive your words as I am, there would be greater peace and less evil among mankind.'

Evil, Theodorus, must ever remain in this world to be the antagonist of good, out of the way of the gods in heaven. Wherefore also we should fly away from ourselves to them; and to fly to them is to become like them; and to become like them is to become holy, just, and true. But many live in the old wives' fable of appearances; they think that you should follow virtue in order that you may seem to be good. And yet the truth is, that God is righteous; and of men, he is most like him who is most righteous. To know this is wisdom; and in comparison of this the wisdom of the arts or the seeming wisdom of politicians is mean and common. The unrighteous man is apt to pride himself on his cunning; when others call him rogue, he says to himself: 'They only mean that I am one who deserves to live, and not a mere burden of the earth.' But he should reflect that his ignorance makes his condition worse than if he knew. For the penalty of injustice is not death or stripes, but the fatal necessity of becoming more and more unjust. Two patterns of life are set before him; the one blessed and divine, the other godless and wretched; and he is growing more and more like the one and unlike the other. 177 He does not see that if he continues in his cunning, the place of innocence will not receive him after death. And yet if such a man has the courage to hear the argument out, he often becomes dissatisfied with himself, and has no more strength in him than a child.—But we have digressed enough.

'For my part, Socrates, I like the digressions better than the argument, because I understand them better.'

To return. When we left off, the Protagoreans and Heracliteans were maintaining that the ordinances of the State were just, while 178 they lasted. But no one would maintain that the laws of the State were always good or expedient, although this may be the intention of them. For the expedient has to do with the future, about which we are liable to mistake. Now, would Protagoras maintain that man is the measure not only of the present and past, but of the future; and that there is no difference in the judgements of men about the future? Would an untrained man, for example, be as likely to know when he is going to have a fever as the physician who attended him? And if they differ in opinion, which of them is likely to be right; or are they both right? Is not a vine-grower a better judge of a vintage which is not yet gathered, or a cook of a dinner which is in preparation, or Protagoras of the 179 probable effect of a speech than an ordinary person? The last example speaks *ad hominem*. For Protagoras would never have amassed a fortune if every man could judge of the future for himself. He is, therefore, compelled to admit that he is a measure; but I, who know nothing, am not equally convinced that I am. This is one way of refuting him; and he is refuted also by the authority which he attributes to the opinions of others, who deny his opinions. I am not equally sure that we can disprove the truth of immediate states of feeling. But this leads us to the doctrine of the universal flux, about which a battle-royal is always going on in the cities of Ionia. 'Yes; the Ephesians are downright mad about the flux; they cannot stop to argue with you, but are in perpetual motion, obedient to their text-books. Their restlessness 180 is beyond expression, and if you ask any of them a question, they will not answer, but dart at you some unintelligible saying, and another and another, making no way either with themselves or with others; for nothing is fixed in them or their ideas,—they are at war with fixed principles.' I suppose, Theodorus, that you have never seen them in time of peace, when they discourse at leisure to their disciples? 'Disciples! they have none; they are a set of uneducated fanatics, and each of them says of the others that they have no knowledge. We must trust to ourselves, and not to them for the solution of the problem.' Well, the doctrine is old, being derived from the poets, who speak in a figure of Oceanus and Tethys; the truth was once concealed, but is now revealed by the superior wisdom of a later generation, and made intelligible to the cobbler, who, on hearing that all is in motion, and not some things only, as he ignorantly fancied, may be expected to fall down and worship his teachers. And the opposite doctrine must not be forgotten :—

Alone being remains unmoved which is the name for all,

as Parmenides affirms. Thus we are in the midst of the fray; both parties are dragging us to their side; and we are not certain which 181 of them are in the right; and if neither, then we shall be in a ridiculous position, having to set up our own opinion against ancient and famous men.

Let us first approach the river-gods, or patrons of the flux.

When they speak of motion, must they not include two kinds of motion, change of place and change of nature?—And all things must be supposed to have both kinds of motion; for if not, the same things would be at rest and in motion, which is contrary to 182 their theory. And did we not say, that all sensations arise thus: they move about between the agent and patient together with a perception, and the patient ceases to be a perceiving power and becomes a percipient, and the agent a quale instead of a quality; but neither has any absolute existence? But now we make the further discovery, that neither white or whiteness, nor any sense or sensation, can be predicated of anything, for they are in a perpetual flux. And therefore we must modify the doctrine of Theaetetus and Protagoras, by asserting further that knowledge is and is not sensation; and of everything we must say equally, 183 that this is and is not, or becomes or becomes not. And still the word 'this' is not quite correct, for language fails in the attempt to express their meaning.

At the close of the discussion, Theodorus claims to be released from the argument, according to his agreement. But Theaetetus insists that they shall proceed to consider the doctrine of rest. This is declined by Socrates, who has too much reverence for the 184 great Parmenides lightly to attack him. [We shall find that he returns to the doctrine of rest in the *Sophist*; but at present he does not wish to be diverted from his main purpose, which is to deliver Theaetetus of his conception of knowledge.] He proceeds to interrogate him further. When he says that 'knowledge is perception', with what does he perceive? The first answer is, that he perceives sights with the eye, and sounds with the ear. This leads Socrates to make the reflection that nice distinctions of words are sometimes pedantic, but sometimes necessary; and he proposes in this case to substitute the word 'through' for 'with'. For the senses are not like the Trojan warriors in the horse, but

185 have a common centre of perception, in which they all meet. This common principle is able to compare them with one another, and must therefore be distinct from them (cf. *Rep*. vii. 523, 524). And as there are facts of sense which are perceived through the organs of the body, there are also mathematical and other abstractions, such as sameness and difference, likeness, and un-

186 likeness, which the soul perceives by herself. Being is the most universal of these abstractions. The good and the beautiful are abstractions of another kind, which exist in relation and which above all others the mind perceives in herself, comparing within her past, present, and future. For example; we know a thing to be hard or soft by the touch, of which the perception is given at birth to men and animals. But the essence of hardness or softness, or the fact that this hardness is, and is the opposite of softness, is slowly learned by reflection and experience. Mere perception does not reach being, and therefore fails of truth; and therefore has no share in knowledge. But if so, knowledge is not perception.

187 What then is knowledge? The mind, when occupied by herself with being, is said to have opinion—shall we say that 'Knowledge is true opinion'? But still an old difficulty recurs; we ask ourselves, 'How is false opinion possible?' This difficulty may be stated as follows:—

188 Either we know or do not know a thing (for the intermediate processes of learning and forgetting need not at present be considered); and in thinking or having an opinion, we must either know or not know that which we think, and we cannot know and be ignorant at the same time; we cannot confuse one thing which we do not know, with another thing which we do not know; nor can we think that which we do not know to be that which we

know, or that which we know to be that which we do not know.
And what other case is conceivable, upon the supposition that
we either know or do not know all things? Let us try another
answer in the sphere of being: 'When a man thinks, and thinks
that which is not.' But would this hold in any parallel case?
Can a man see and see nothing? or hear and hear nothing? or 189
touch and touch nothing? Must he not see, hear, or touch some
one existing thing? For if he thinks about nothing he does not
think, and not thinking he cannot think falsely. And so the path
of being is closed against us, as well as the path of knowledge.
But may there not be 'heterodoxy', or transference of opinion;—
I mean, may not one thing be supposed to be another? Theaetetus is confident that this must be 'the true falsehood', when
a man puts good for evil or evil for good. Socrates will not discourage him by attacking the paradoxical expression 'true falsehood', but passes on. The new notion involves a process of
thinking about two things, either together or alternately. And
thinking is the conversing of the mind with herself, which is 190
carried on in question and answer, until she no longer doubts,
but determines and forms an opinion. And false opinion consists
in saying to yourself, that one thing is another. But did you ever
say to yourself, that good is evil, or evil good? Even in sleep, did
you ever imagine that odd was even? Or did any man in his
senses ever fancy that an ox was a horse, or that two are one?
So that we can never think one thing to be another; for you must
not meet me with the verbal quibble that one—ἕτερον—is other
—ἕτερον [both 'one' and 'other' in Greek are called 'other'—
ἕτερον]. He who has both the two things in his mind, cannot misplace them; and he who has only one of them in his mind, cannot
misplace them—on either supposition transplacement is inconceivable.

But perhaps there may still be a sense in which we can think 191
that which we do not know to be that which we know: e.g.
Theaetetus may know Socrates, but at a distance he may mistake
another person for him. This process may be conceived by the
help of an image. Let us suppose that every man has in his mind
a block of wax of various qualities, the gift of Memory, the mother
of the Muses; and on this he receives the seal or stamp of those
sensations and perceptions which he wishes to remember. That

which he succeeds in stamping is remembered and known by
him as long as the impression lasts; but that, of which the impression is rubbed out or imperfectly made, is forgotten, and not
192 known. No one can think one thing to be another, when he has
the memorial or seal of both of these in his soul, and a sensible
impression of neither; or when he knows one and does not know
the other, and has no memorial or seal of the other; or when he
knows neither; or when he perceives both, or one and not the
other, or neither; or when he perceives and knows both, and
identifies what he perceives with what he knows (this is still more
impossible); or when he does not know one, and does not know
and does not perceive the other; or does not perceive one, and
does not know and does not perceive the other; or has no perception or knowledge of either—all these cases must be excluded.
But he may err when he confuses what he knows or perceives, or
what he perceives and does not know, with what he knows, or
what he knows and perceives with what he knows and perceives.

Theaetetus is unable to follow these distinctions; which Socrates
proceeds to illustrate by examples, first of all remarking, that
knowledge may exist without perception, and perception without
193 knowledge. I may know Theodorus and Theaetetus and not see
them; I may see them, and not know them. 'That I understand.'
But I could not mistake one for the other if I knew you both, and
had no perception of either; or if I knew one only, and perceived
neither; or if I knew and perceived neither, or in any other of the
excluded cases. The only possibility of error is: 1st, when knowing
you and Theodorus, and having the impression of both of you on
the waxen block, I, seeing you both imperfectly and at a distance,
194 put the foot in the wrong shoe—that is to say, put the seal or
stamp on the wrong object: or 2ndly, when knowing both of you
I only see one; or when, seeing and knowing you both, I fail to
identify the impression and the object. But there could be no
error when perception and knowledge correspond.

The waxen block in the heart of a man's soul, as I may say in
the words of Homer, who played upon the words κῆρ and κηρός,
may be smooth and deep, and large enough, and then the signs
are clearly marked and lasting, and do not get confused. But in
the 'hairy heart', as the all-wise poet sings, when the wax is
muddy or hard or moist, there is a corresponding confusion and

want of retentiveness; in the muddy and impure there is indistinct- 195
ness, and still more in the hard, for there the impressions have no
depth of wax, and in the moist they are too soon effaced. Yet
greater is the indistinctness when they are all jolted together in a
little soul, which is narrow and has no room. These are the sort
of natures which have false opinion; from stupidity they see and
hear and think amiss; and this is falsehood and ignorance. Error,
then, is a confusion of thought and sense.

Theaetetus is delighted with this explanation. But Socrates has 196
no sooner found the new solution than he sinks into a fit of
despondency. For an objection occurs to him:—May there not
be errors where there is no confusion of mind and sense? e.g. in
numbers. No one can confuse the man whom he has in his 197
thoughts with the horse which he has in his thoughts, but he may
err in the addition of five and seven. And observe that these are
purely mental conceptions. Thus we are involved once more in
the dilemma of saying, either that there is no such thing as false
opinion, or that a man knows what he does not know.

We are at our wit's end, and may therefore be excused for
making a bold diversion. All this time we have been repeating
the words 'know', 'understand', yet we do not know what
knowledge is. 'Why, Socrates, how can you argue at all without
using them?' Nay, but the true hero of dialectic would have
forbidden me to use them until I had explained them. And I must
explain them now. The verb 'to know' has two senses, to have
and to possess knowledge, and I distinguish 'having' from 'possessing'. A man may possess a garment which he does not wear;
or he may have wild birds in an aviary; these in one sense he
possesses, and in another he has none of them. Let this aviary
be an image of the mind, as the waxen block was; when we
are young, the aviary is empty; after a time the birds are put
in; for under this figure we may describe different forms of
knowledge;—there are some of them in groups, and some single,
which are flying about everywhere; and let us suppose a hunt 198
after the science of odd and even, or some other science. The
possession of the birds is clearly not the same as the having them
in the hand. And the original chase of them is not the same as
taking them in the hand when they are already caged.

This distinction between use and possession saves us from the 199 absurdity of supposing that we do not know what we know, because we may know in one sense, i.e. possess, what we do not know in another, i.e. use. But have we not escaped one difficulty only to encounter a greater? For how can the exchange of two kinds of knowledge ever become false opinion? As well might we suppose that ignorance could make a man know, or that blindness could make him see. Theaetetus suggests that in the aviary there may be flying about mock birds, or forms of ignorance, and we put forth our hands and grasp ignorance, when we are intend-

200 ing to grasp knowledge. But how can he who knows the forms of knowledge and the forms of ignorance imagine one to be the other? Is there some other form of knowledge which distinguishes them? and another, and another? Thus we go round and round in a circle and make no progress.

All this confusion arises out of our attempt to explain false opinion without having explained knowledge. What then is knowledge? Theaetetus repeats that knowledge is true opinion.

201 But this seems to be refuted by the instance of orators and judges. For surely the orator cannot convey a true knowledge of crimes at which the judges were not present; he can only persuade them, and the judge may form a true opinion and truly judge. But if true opinion were knowledge they could not have judged without knowledge.

Once more. Theaetetus offers a definition which he has heard: Knowledge is true opinion accompanied by definition or explanation. Socrates has had a similar dream, and has further heard

202 that the first elements are names only, and that definition or explanation begins when they are combined; the letters are

203 unknown, the syllables or combinations are known. But this new hypothesis when tested by the letters of the alphabet is found to break down. The first syllable of Socrates' name is SO. But what is SO? Two letters, S and O, a sibilant and a vowel, of which no further explanation can be given. And how can anyone be ignorant of either of them, and yet know both of them? There is, however, another alternative:—We may suppose that the syllable has a separate form or idea distinct from the letters or parts. The all of the parts may not be the whole. Theaetetus is

204 very much inclined to adopt this suggestion, but when interrogated by Socrates he is unable to draw any distinction between

the whole and all the parts. And if the syllables have no parts, 205
then they are those original elements of which there is no explanation. But how can the syllable be known if the letter remains
unknown? In learning to read as children, we are first taught the 206
letters and then the syllables. And in music, the notes, which are
the letters, have a much more distinct meaning to us than the
combination of them.

Once more, then, we must ask the meaning of the statement,
that 'Knowledge is right opinion, accompanied by explanation or
definition.' Explanation may mean, (1) the reflection or expression of a man's thoughts—but every man who is not deaf and
dumb is able to express his thoughts—or (2) the enumeration of
the elements of which anything is composed. A man may have a 207
true opinion about a wagon, but then, and then only, has he
knowledge of a wagon when he is able to enumerate the hundred
planks of Hesiod. Or he may know the syllables of the name
Theaetetus, but not the letters; yet not until he knows both can
he be said to have knowledge as well as opinion. But on the other
hand he may know the syllable 'The' in the name Theaetetus,
yet he may be mistaken about the same syllable in the name 208
Theodorus, and in learning to read we often make such mistakes.
And even if he could write out all the letters and syllables of your
name in order, still he would only have right opinion. Yet there
may be a third meaning of the definition, besides the image or
expression of the mind, and the enumeration of the elements,
viz. (3) perception of difference.

For example, I may see a man who has eyes, nose, and mouth; 209
—that will not distinguish him from any other man. Or he may
have a snub-nose and prominent eyes;—that will not distinguish
him from myself and you and others who are like me. But when
I see a certain kind of snub-nosedness, then I recognize Theaetetus. And having this sign of difference, I have knowledge. But
have I knowledge or opinion of this difference? If I have only
opinion I have not knowledge; if I have knowledge we assume
a disputed term; for knowledge will have to be defined as right 210
opinion with knowledge of difference.

And so, Theaetetus, knowledge is neither perception nor true
opinion, nor yet definition accompanying true opinion. And I
have shown that the children of your brain are not worth rearing.

Are you still in labour, or have you brought all you have to say about knowledge to the birth? If you have any more thoughts, you will be the better for having got rid of these; or if you have none, you will be the better for not fancying that you know what you do not know. Observe the limits of my art, which, like my mother's, is an art of midwifery; I do not pretend to compare with the good and wise of this and other ages.

And now I go to meet Meletus at the porch of the King Archon; but tomorrow I shall hope to see you again, Theodorus, at this place.

INTRODUCTION

I. The saying of Theaetetus, that 'Knowledge is sensible perception', may be assumed to be a current philosophical opinion of the age. 'The ancients', as Aristotle (*De Anim.* iii. 3) says, citing a verse of Empedocles, 'affirmed knowledge to be the same as perception.' We may now examine these words, first, with reference to their place in the history of philosophy, and secondly, in relation to modern speculations.

(*a*) In the age of Socrates the mind was passing from the object to the subject. The same impulse which a century before had led men to form conceptions of the world, now led them to frame general notions of the human faculties and feelings, such as memory, opinion, and the like. The simplest of these is sensation, or sensible perception, by which Plato seems to mean the generalized notion of feelings and impressions of sense, without determining whether they are conscious or not.

The theory that 'Knowledge is sensible perception' is the antithesis of that which derives knowledge from the mind (*Theaet.* 185), or which assumes the existence of ideas independent of the mind (*Parm.* 134). Yet from their extreme abstraction these theories do not represent the opposite poles of thought in the same way that the corresponding differences would in modern philosophy. The most ideal and the most sensational have a tendency to pass into one another; Heracleitus, like his great successor Hegel, has both aspects. The Eleatic isolation of Being and the Megarian or Cynic isolation of individuals are placed in the same class by Plato (*Soph.* 251 c, d); and the same principle which is the symbol of motion to one mind is the symbol of rest to another. The Atomists, who are sometimes regarded as the Materialists of Plato, denied the reality of sensation. And in the ancient as well as the modern world there were reactions from theory to experience, from ideas to sense. This is a point of view from which the philosophy of sensation presented great attraction to the ancient thinker. Amid the conflict of ideas and the variety of opinions, the impression of sense remained certain and uniform. Hardness, softness, cold, heat, &c. are not absolutely the same to different persons (cf. 171 d), but the art of measuring could at any rate reduce them all to definite natures (*Rep.* x, 602 d). Thus the doctrine that knowledge is perception supplies or seems to supply a firm standing ground. Like the other notions of the earlier Greek philosophy, it was held in a very simple way, without much basis of reasoning, and without suggesting the questions which naturally arise in our own minds on the same subject.

(β) The fixedness of impressions of sense furnishes a link of connexion between ancient and modern philosophy. The modern thinker often repeats the parallel axiom, 'All knowledge is experience.' He means to say that the outward and not the inward is both the original source and the final criterion of truth, because the outward can be observed and analysed; the inward is only known by external results, and is dimly perceived by each man for himself. In what does this differ from the saying of Theaetetus? Chiefly in this—that the modern term 'experience', while implying a point of departure in sense and a return to sense, also includes all the processes of reasoning and imagination which have intervened. The necessary connexion between them by no means affords a measure of the relative degree of importance which is to be ascribed to either element. For the inductive portion of any science may be small, as in mathematics or ethics, compared with that which the mind has attained by reasoning and reflection on a very few facts.

II. The saying that 'All knowledge is sensation' is identified by Plato with the Protagorean thesis that 'Man is the measure of all things.' The interpretation which Protagoras himself is supposed to give of these latter words is: 'Things are to me as they appear to me, and to you as they appear to you.' But there remains still an ambiguity both in the text and in the explanation, which has to be cleared up. Did Protagoras merely mean to assert the relativity of knowledge to the human mind? or did he mean to deny that there is an objective standard of truth?

These two questions have not been always clearly distinguished; the relativity of knowledge has been sometimes confounded with uncertainty. The untutored mind is apt to suppose that objects exist independently of the human faculties, because they really exist independently of the faculties of any individual. In the same way, knowledge appears to be a body of truths stored up in books, which when

once ascertained are independent of the discoverer. Further consideration shows us that these truths are not really independent of the mind;
there is an adaptation of one to the other, of the eye to the object of
sense, of the mind to the conception. There would be no world, if
there neither were nor ever had been anyone to perceive the world. A
slight effort of reflection enables us to understand this; but no effort of
reflection will enable us to pass beyond the limits of our own faculties,
or to imagine the relation or adaptation of objects to the mind to be
different from that of which we have experience. There are certain
laws of language and logic to which we are compelled to conform, and
to which our ideas naturally adapt themselves; and we can no more
get rid of them than we can cease to be ourselves. The absolute and
infinite, whether explained as self-existence, or as the totality of
human thought, or as the Divine nature, if known to us at all, cannot
escape from the category of relation.

But because knowledge is subjective or relative to the mind, we are
not to suppose that we are therefore deprived of any of the tests or
criteria of truth. One man still remains wiser than another, a more
accurate observer and relater of facts, a truer measure of the proportions of knowledge. The nature of testimony is not altered, nor the
verification of causes by prescribed methods less certain. Again, the
truth must often come to a man through others, according to
the measure of his capacity and education. But neither does this affect
the testimony, whether written or oral, which he knows by experience
to be trustworthy. He cannot escape from the laws of his own mind; and
he cannot escape from the further accident of being dependent for his
knowledge on others. But still this is no reason why he should always
be in doubt; of many personal, of many historical and scientific facts
he may be absolutely assured. And having such a mass of acknowledged
truth in the mathematical and physical, not to speak of the moral
sciences, the moderns have certainly no reason to acquiesce in the
statement that truth is appearance only, or that there is no difference
between appearance and truth.

The relativity of knowledge is a truism to us, but was a great
psychological discovery in the fifth century before Christ. Of this
discovery, the first distinct assertion is contained in the thesis of
Protagoras. Probably he had no intention either of denying or affirming an objective standard of truth. He did not consider whether man
in the higher or man in the lower sense was a 'measure of all things'.
Like other great thinkers, he was absorbed with one idea, and that
idea was the absoluteness of perception. Like Socrates, he seemed to
see that philosophy must be brought back from 'nature' to 'truth',

from the world to man. But he did not stop to analyse whether he meant 'man' in the concrete or man in the abstract, any man or some men, *quod semper quod ubique* or individual private judgement. Such an analysis lay beyond his sphere of thought; the age before Socrates had not arrived at these distinctions. Like the Cynics, again, he discarded knowledge in any higher sense than perception. For 'truer' or 'wiser' he substituted the word 'better', and is not unwilling to admit that both states and individuals are capable of practical improvement. But this improvement does not arise from intellectual enlightenment, nor yet from the exertion of the will, but from a change of circumstances and impressions; and he who can effect this change in himself or others may be deemed a philosopher. In the mode of effecting it, while agreeing with Socrates and the Cynics in the importance which he attaches to practical life, he is at variance with both of them. To suppose that practice can be divorced from speculation, or that we may do good without caring about truth, is by no means singular, either in philosophy or life. The singularity of this, as of some other (so-called) sophistical doctrines, is the frankness with which they are avowed, instead of being veiled, as in modern times, under ambiguous and convenient phrases.

Plato appears to treat Protagoras much as he himself is treated by Aristotle; that is to say, he does not attempt to understand him from his own point of view. But he entangles him in the meshes of a more advanced logic. To which Protagoras is supposed to reply by Megarian quibbles, which destroy logic, 'Not only man, but each man, and each man at each moment.' In the arguments about sight and memory there is a palpable unfairness which is worthy of the great 'brainless brothers', Euthydemus and Dionysodorus, and may be compared with the ἐγκεκαλυμμένος ('obvelatus') of Eubulides. For he who sees with one eye only cannot be truly said both to see and not to see; nor is memory, which is liable to forget, the immediate knowledge to which Protagoras applies the term. Theodorus justly charges Socrates with going beyond the truth; and Protagoras has equally right on his side when he protests against Socrates arguing from the common use of words, which 'the vulgar pervert in all manner of ways'.

III. The theory of Protagoras is connected by Aristotle as well as Plato with the flux of Heracleitus. But Aristotle is only following Plato, and Plato, as we have already seen, did not mean to imply that such a connexion was admitted by Protagoras himself. His metaphysical genius saw or seemed to see a common tendency in them, just as the modern historian of ancient philosophy might perceive a parallelism between two thinkers of which they were probably unconscious themselves. We must remember throughout that Plato is not speaking of Heracleitus, but of the Heracliteans, who succeeded him; nor of the great original ideas of the master, but of the Eristic into which they had degenerated a hundred years later. There is nothing in the fragments of Heracleitus which at all justifies Plato's account of him. His philosophy may be resolved into two elements—first, change, secondly, law or measure pervading the change: these he saw everywhere, and often expressed in strange mythological symbols. But he has no analysis of sensible perception such as Plato attributes to him; nor is there any reason to suppose that he pushed his philosophy into that absolute negation in which Heracliteanism was sunk in the age of Plato. He never said that 'change means every sort of change'; and he expressly distinguished between 'the general and particular understanding'. Like a poet, he surveyed the elements of mythology, nature, thought, which lay before him, and sometimes by the light of genius he saw or seemed to see a mysterious principle working behind them. But as has been the case with other great philosophers, and with Plato and Aristotle themselves, what was really permanent and original could not be understood by the next generation, while a perverted logic carried out his chance expressions with an illogical consistency. His simple and noble thoughts, like those of the great Eleatic, soon degenerated into a mere strife of words. And when thus reduced to mere words, they seem to have exercised a far wider influence in the cities of Ionia (where the people 'were mad about them') than in the lifetime of Heracleitus—a phenomenon which, though at first sight singular, is not without a parallel in the history of philosophy and theology.

It is this perverted form of the Heraclitean philosophy which is supposed to effect the final overthrow of Protagorean sensationalism. For if all things are changing at every moment, in all sorts of ways, then there is nothing fixed or defined at all, and therefore no sensible perception, nor any true word by which that or anything else can be described. Of course Protagoras would not have admitted the justice of this argument any more than Heracleitus would have acknowledged the 'uneducated fanatics' who appealed to his writings. He might have said, 'The excellent Socrates has first confused me with Heracleitus, and Heracleitus with his Ephesian successors, and has then disproved the existence both of knowledge and sensation. But I am not responsible for what I never said, nor will I admit that my common-sense account of knowledge can be overthrown by unintelligible Heraclitean paradoxes.'

IV. Still at the bottom of the arguments there remains a truth, that knowledge is something more than sensible perception;—this alone would not distinguish man from a tadpole. The absoluteness of sensations at each moment destroys the very consciousness of sensations (cf. *Phileb.* 21 d), or the power of comparing them. The senses are not mere holes in a 'Trojan horse', but the organs of a presiding nature, in which they meet. A great advance has been made in psychology when the senses are recognized as organs of sense, and we are admitted to see or feel 'through them' and not 'by them', a distinction of words which, as Socrates observes, is by no means pedantic. A still further step has been made when the most abstract notions, such as being and not-being, sameness and difference, unity and plurality, are acknowledged to be the creations of the mind herself, working upon the feelings or impressions of sense. In this manner Plato describes the process of acquiring them, in the words (186 d) 'Knowledge consists not in the feelings or affections (παθήμασι), but in the process of reasoning about them (συλλογισμῷ).' Here, as in the *Parmenides* (132 a), he means something not really different from generalization. As in the *Sophist*, he is laying the foundation of a rational psychology, which is to supersede the Platonic reminiscence of Ideas as well as the Eleatic Being and the individualism of Megarians and Cynics.

V. Having rejected the doctrine that 'Knowledge is perception', we now proceed to look for a definition of knowledge in the sphere of opinion. But here we are met by a singular difficulty: How is false opinion possible? For we must either know or not know that which is presented to the mind or to sense. We of course should answer at once: 'No; the alternative is not necessary, for there may be degrees of knowledge; and we may know and have forgotten, or we may be learning, or we may have a general but not a particular knowledge, or we may know but not be able to explain'; and many other ways may be imagined in which we know and do not know at the same time. But these answers belong to a later stage of metaphysical discussion; whereas the difficulty in question naturally arises owing to the childhood of the human mind, like the parallel difficulty respecting Not-being. Men had only recently arrived at the notion of opinion; they could not at once define the true and pass beyond into the false. The very word δόξα was full of ambiguity, being sometimes, as in the Eleatic philosophy, applied to the sensible world, and again used in the more ordinary sense of opinion. There is no connexion between sensible appearance and probability, and yet both of them met in the word δόξα, and could hardly be disengaged from one another in the mind of the Greek living in the fifth or fourth century B.C. To this was often added, as at the end of the fifth book of the *Republic*, the idea of relation, which is equally distinct from either of them; also a fourth notion, the conclusion of the dialectical process, the making up of the mind after she has been 'talking to herself' (*Theaet.* 190).

We are not then surprised that the sphere of opinion and of not-being should be a dusky, half-lighted place (*Rep.* v, p. 478), belonging neither to the old world of sense and imagination, nor to the new world of reflection and reason. Plato attempts to clear up this darkness. In his accustomed manner he passes from the lower to the higher, without omitting the intermediate stages. This appears to be the reason why he seeks for the definition of knowledge first in the sphere of opinion. Hereafter we shall find that something more than opinion is required.

False opinion is explained by Plato at first as a confusion of mind and sense, which arises when the impression on the mind does not correspond to the impression made on the senses. It is obvious that this explanation (supposing the distinction between impressions on the mind and impressions on the senses to be admitted) does not account for all forms of error; and Plato has excluded himself from the consideration of the greater number, by designedly omitting the inter-mediate processes of learning and forgetting; nor does he include fallacies in the use of language or erroneous inferences. But he is struck by one possibility of error, which is not covered by his theory, viz. errors in arithmetic. For in numbers and calculation there is no combination of thought and sense, and yet errors may often happen. Hence he is led to discard the explanation which might nevertheless have been supposed to hold good (for anything which he says to the contrary) as a rationale of error, in the case of facts derived from sense.

Another attempt is made to explain false opinion by assigning to error a sort of positive existence. But error or ignorance is essentially negative—a not-knowing; if we knew an error, we should be no longer in error. We may veil our difficulty under figures of speech, but these, although telling arguments with the multitude, can never be the real foundation of a system of psychology. Only they lead us to dwell upon mental phenomena which if expressed in an abstract form would not be realized by us at all. The figure of the mind receiving impressions is one of those images which have rooted themselves for ever in language. It may or may not be a 'gracious aid' to thought; but it cannot be got rid of. The other figure of the enclosure is also remarkable as affording the first hint of universal all-pervading ideas,—a notion further carried out in the *Sophist*. This is implied in the birds, some in flocks, some solitary, which fly about anywhere and everywhere. Plato discards both figures, as not really solving the question which to us appears so simple: 'How do we make mistakes?' The failure of the inquiry seems to show that we should return to knowledge, and begin with that; and we may afterwards proceed, with a better hope of success, to the examination of opinion.

But is true opinion really distinct from knowledge? The difference between these he seeks to establish by an argument, which to us appears singular and unsatisfactory. The existence of true opinion is proved by the rhetoric of the law courts, which cannot give knowledge, but may give true opinion. The rhetorician cannot put the judge or juror in possession of all the facts which prove an act of violence, but he may truly persuade them of the commission of such an act. Here the idea of true opinion seems to be a right conclusion from imperfect knowledge. But the correctness of such an opinion will be purely accidental; and is really the effect of one man, who has the means of knowing, persuading another who has not. Plato would have done better if he had said that true opinion was a contradiction in terms.

Assuming the distinction between knowledge and opinion, Theaetetus, in answer to Socrates, proceeds to define knowledge as true opinion, with definite or rational explanation. This Socrates identifies with another and different theory, of those who assert that knowledge first begins with a proposition.

The elements may be perceived by sense, but they are names, and cannot be defined. When we assign to them some predicate, they first begin to have a meaning (ὀνομάτων συμπλοκὴ λόγου οὐσία). This seems equivalent to saying that the individuals of sense become the subject of knowledge when they are regarded as they are in nature in relation to other individuals.

Yet we feel a difficulty in following this new hypothesis. For must not opinion be equally expressed in a proposition? The difference between true and false opinion is not the difference between the particular and the universal, but between the true universal and the false. Thought may be as much at fault as sight. When we place individuals under a class, or assign to them attributes, this is not knowledge, but a very rudimentary process of thought; the first generalization of all, without which language would be impossible. And has Plato kept altogether clear of a confusion, which the analogous word λόγος tends to create, of a proposition, and a definition? And is not the confusion increased by the use of the analogous term 'elements', or 'letters'? For there is no real resemblance between the relation of letters to a syllable, and of the terms to a proposition.

Plato, in the spirit of the Megarian philosophy, soon discovers a flaw in the explanation. For how can we know a compound of which the simple elements are unknown to us? Can two unknowns make a known? Can a whole be something different from the parts? The answer of experience is that they can; for we may know a compound, which we are unable to analyse into its elements; and all the parts, when united, may be more than all the parts separated: e.g. the number four, or any other number, is more than the units which are contained in it; any chemical compound is more than and different from the simple elements. But ancient philosophy in this, as in many other instances, proceeding by the path of mental analysis, was perplexed by doubts which warred against the plainest facts.

Three attempts to explain the new definition of knowledge still remain to be considered. They all of them turn on the explanation of λόγος. The first account of the meaning of the word is the reflection of thought in speech—a sort of nominalism: 'La science est une langue bien faite.' But anybody who is not dumb can say what he thinks; therefore mere speech cannot be knowledge. And yet we may observe that there is in this explanation an element of truth which is not recognized by Plato; viz. that truth and thought are inseparable from language, although mere expression in words is not truth. The second explanation of λόγος is the enumeration of the elementary parts of the complex whole. But this is only definition accompanied by right opinion, and does not yet attain to the certainty of knowledge. Plato does not mention the greater objection, which is that the enumeration of particulars is endless; such a definition would be based on no principle, and would not help us at all in gaining a common idea. The third is the best explanation,—the possession of a characteristic mark, which seems to answer to the logical definition by genus and difference. But this, again, is equally necessary for right opinion; and we have already determined, although not on very satisfactory grounds, that knowledge must be distinguished from opinion. A better distinction is drawn between them in the *Timaeus* (p. 51 e). They might be opposed as philosophy and rhetoric, and as conversant respectively with necessary and contingent matter. But no true idea of the nature of either of them, or of their relation to one another, could be framed until science obtained a content. The ancient philosophers in the age of Plato thought of science only as pure abstraction, and to this opinion stood in no relation.

Like Theaetetus, we have attained to no definite result. But an interesting phase of ancient philosophy has passed before us. And the negative result is not to be despised. For on certain subjects, and in certain states of knowledge, the work of negation or clearing the ground must go on, perhaps for a generation, before the new structure can begin to rise. Plato saw the necessity of combating the illogical logic of the Megarians and Eristics. For the completion of the edifice, he makes preparation in the *Theaetetus*, and crowns the work in the *Sophist*.

Many (1) fine expressions, and (2) remarks full of wisdom, (3) also germs of a metaphysic of the future, are scattered up and down in the dialogue. Such, for example, as (1) the comparison of Theaetetus' progress in learning to the 'noiseless flow of a river of oil'; the satirical touch, 'flavouring a sauce or fawning speech'; or the remarkable expression, 'full of impure dialectic'; or the lively images under which the argument is described,—'the flood of arguments pouring in', the fresh discussions 'bursting in like a band of revellers'. (2) As illustrations of the second head, may be cited the remark of Socrates, that 'distinctions of words, although sometimes pedantic, are also necessary'; or the fine touch in the character of the lawyer, that 'dangers came upon him when the tenderness of youth was unequal to them'; or the description of the manner in which the spirit is broken in a wicked man who listens to reproof until he becomes like a child; or the punishment of the wicked, which is not physical suffering, but the perpetual companionship of evil (cf. *Gorgias*); or the saying, often repeated by Aristotle and others, that 'philosophy begins in wonder, for Iris is the child of Thaumas'; or the superb contempt with which the philosopher takes down the pride of wealthy landed proprietors by comparison of the whole earth. (3) Important metaphysical ideas are: (*a*) the conception of thought as the mind talking to herself; (*b*) the notion of a common sense, developed further by Aristotle, and the explicit declaration, that the mind gains her conceptions of Being, sameness, number, and the like, from reflection on herself; (*c*) the excellent distinction of Theaetetus (which Socrates, speaking with emphasis, 'leaves to grow') between seeing the forms or hearing the sounds of words in a foreign language, and understanding the meaning of them; and (*d*) the distinction of Socrates himself between 'having' and 'possessing' knowledge, in which the answer to the whole discussion appears to be contained.

THEAETETUS

Persons of the Dialogue

SOCRATES, THEODORUS, THEAETETUS

Euclides and Terpsion meet in front of Euclides' house in Megara; they enter the
house, and the dialogue is read to them by a servant

Euclides. Have you only just arrived from the country, 142
Terpsion?

Terpsion. No, I came some time ago: and I have been in the
Agora looking for you, and wondering that I could not find you.

Euc. But I was not in the city.

Terp. Where then?

Euc. As I was going down to the harbour, I met Theaetetus—
he was being carried up to Athens from the army at Corinth.

Terp. Was he alive or dead?

Euc. He was scarcely alive, for he has been badly wounded; b
but he was suffering even more from the sickness which has
broken out in the army.

Terp. The dysentery, you mean?

Euc. Yes.

Terp. Alas! what a loss he will be!

Euc. Yes, Terpsion, he is a noble fellow; only today I heard
some people highly praising his behaviour in this very battle.

Terp. No wonder; I should rather be surprised at hearing
anything else of him. But why did he go on, instead of stopping c
at Megara?

Euc. He wanted to get home: although I entreated and advised
him to remain, he would not listen to me; so I set him on his way,
and turned back, and then I remembered what Socrates had said
of him, and thought how remarkably this, like all his predictions,
had been fulfilled. I believe that he had seen him a little before
his own death, when Theaetetus was a youth, and he had a
memorable conversation with him, which he repeated to me
when I came to Athens; he was full of admiration of his genius, d
and said that he would most certainly be a great man, if he
lived.

Terp. The prophecy has certainly been fulfilled; but what was the conversation? can you tell me?

143   *Euc.* No, indeed, not offhand; but I took notes of it as soon as I got home; these I filled up from memory, writing them out at leisure; and whenever I went to Athens, I asked Socrates about any point which I had forgotten, and on my return I made corrections; thus I have nearly the whole conversation written down.

Terp. I remember—you told me; and I have always been intending to ask you to show me the writing, but have put off doing so; and now, why should we not read it through?—having just come from the country, I should greatly like to rest.

b   *Euc.* I too shall be very glad of a rest, for I went with Theaetetus as far as Erineum. Let us go in, then, and, while we are reposing, the servant shall read to us.

Terp. Very good.

Euc. Here is the roll, Terpsion; I may observe that I have introduced Socrates, not as narrating to me, but as actually conversing with the persons whom he mentioned—these were, Theodorus the geometrician (of Cyrene), and Theaetetus. I have

c   omitted, for the sake of convenience, the interlocutory words 'I said', 'I remarked', which he used when he spoke of himself, and again, 'he agreed', or 'disagreed', in the answer, lest the repetition of them should be troublesome.

Terp. Quite right, Euclides.

Euc. And now, boy, you may take the roll and read.

Euclides' servant reads

d   *Socrates.* If I cared enough about the Cyrenians, Theodorus, I would ask you whether there are any rising geometricians or philosophers in that part of the world. But I am more interested in our own Athenian youth, and I would rather know who among them are likely to do well. I observe them as far as I can myself, and I inquire of any one whom they follow, and I see that a great many of them follow you, in which they are quite right, consider-

e   ing your eminence in geometry and in other ways. Tell me then, if you have met with any one who is at all remarkable.

Theodorus. Yes, Socrates, I have become acquainted with one very remarkable Athenian youth, whom I commend to you as well worthy of your attention. If he had been a beauty I should have been afraid to praise him, lest you should suppose that I was in love with him; but he is no beauty, and you must not be offended if I say that he is very like you; for he has a snub nose and projecting eyes, although these features are less marked in him than in you. Seeing, then, that he has no personal attractions, 144 I may freely say, that in all my acquaintance, which is very large, I never knew any one who was his equal in natural gifts: for he has a quickness of apprehension which is almost unrivalled, and he is exceedingly gentle, and also the most courageous of men; there is a union of qualities in him such as I have never seen in any other, and should scarcely have thought possible; for those who, like him, have quick and ready and retentive wits, have b generally also quick tempers; they are ships without ballast, and go darting about, and are mad rather than courageous; and the steadier sort, when they have to face study, prove stupid and cannot remember. Whereas he moves surely and smoothly and successfully in the path of knowledge and inquiry; and he is full of gentleness, flowing on silently like a river of oil; at his age, it is wonderful.

Soc. That is good news; whose son is he?

Theod. The name of his father I have forgotten, but the youth himself is the middle one of those who are approaching us; he c and his companions have been anointing themselves in the outer court, and now they seem to have finished, and are coming towards us. Look and see whether you know him.

Soc. I know the youth, but I do not know his name; he is the son of Euphronius the Sunian, who was himself an eminent man, and such another as his son is according to your account of him; I believe that he left a considerable fortune.

Theod. Theaetetus, Socrates, is his name; but I rather think d that the property disappeared in the hands of trustees; notwithstanding which he is wonderfully liberal.

Soc. He must be a fine fellow; tell him to come and sit by me.

Theod. I will. Come hither, Theaetetus, and sit by Socrates.

Soc. By all means, Theaetetus, in order that I may see the reflection of myself in your face, for Theodorus says that we are alike; and yet if each of us held in his hands a lyre, and he said e that they were tuned alike, should we at once take his word, or should we ask whether he who said so was or was not a musician?

Theaetetus. We should ask.

Soc. And if we found that he was, we should take his word; and if not, not?

Theaet. True.

Soc. And if this supposed likeness of our faces is a matter of any interest to us, we should inquire whether he who says that we are alike is a painter or not?

145 *Theaet.* Certainly we should.

Soc. And is Theodorus a painter?

Theaet. I never heard that he was.

Soc. Is he a geometrician?

Theaet. Of course he is, Socrates.

Soc. And is he an astronomer and calculator and musician, and in general an educated man?

Theaet. I think so.

Soc. If, then, he remarks on a similarity in our persons, either by way of praise or blame, there is no particular reason why we should attend to him.

Theaet. I should say not.

b *Soc.* But if he praises the virtue or wisdom which are the spiritual endowments of either of us, then he who hears the praises will naturally desire to examine him who is praised : and he again should be willing to exhibit himself.

Theaet. Very true, Socrates.

Soc. Then now is the time, my dear Theaetetus, for me to examine, and for you to exhibit; since although Theodorus has praised many a citizen and stranger in my hearing, never did I hear him praise any one as he has been praising you.

c *Theaet.* I am glad to hear it, Socrates; but what if he spoke only in jest?

Soc. Nay, Theodorus is not given to jesting; and I cannot allow you to retract your consent on any such pretence as that. If you do, he will have to swear to his words; and we are perfectly sure that no one will be found to impugn him. Do not be shy then, but stand to your word.

Theaet. I suppose I must, if you wish it.

Soc. In the first place, I should like to ask what you learn of Theodorus: something of geometry, perhaps?

Theaet. Yes.

Soc. And astronomy and harmony and calculation?   d

Theaet. I am making an effort, at least.

Soc. And so am I, my friend, hoping to learn of him, or of anybody who seems to understand these things. And I get on pretty well in general; but there is a little difficulty which I want you and the company to aid me in investigating. Will you answer me a question: 'Is not learning growing wiser about that which you learn?'

Theaet. Of course.

Soc. And it is by wisdom, I suppose, that the wise are wise?

Theaet. Yes.

Soc. And is that different in any way from knowledge?   e

Theaet. What?

Soc. Wisdom; are not men wise in that which they know?

Theaet. Certainly they are.

Soc. Then wisdom and knowledge are the same?

Theaet. Yes.

Soc. Herein lies the difficulty which I can never solve to my   146
satisfaction—What is knowledge? Can we answer that question? What say you? which of us will speak first? whoever misses shall sit down, as at a game of ball, and shall be donkey, as the boys say; he who lasts out his competitors in the game without missing, shall be our king, and shall have the right of putting to us any questions which he pleases. . . . Why is there no reply? I hope, Theodorus, that I am not betrayed into rudeness by my love of conversation? I only want to make us talk and be friendly and sociable.

Theod. The reverse of rudeness, Socrates: but I would rather   b
that you would ask one of the young fellows; for the truth is, that I am unused to your method of discussion, and I am too old to learn; the young will be more suitable, and they will improve more than I shall, for it is a true saying that youth is the age for improvement. And so having made a beginning with Theaetetus, I would advise you to go on with him and not let him off.

Soc. Do you hear, Theaetetus, what Theodorus says? You would not, I think, like to disobey him, nor is it right for a younger   c man to disobey such a command from a wise man. Take courage, then, and nobly say what you think that knowledge is.

Theaet. Well, Socrates, I will answer as you and he bid me; and if I make a mistake, you will doubtless correct me.

Soc. We will, if we can.

Theaet. Then, I think that the sciences which I learn from Theodorus—geometry, and those which you just now mentioned d —are knowledge; and I would include the art of the cobbler and other craftsmen; these, each and all of them, are just what is meant by knowledge.

Soc. Enough, my friend! the nobility and liberality of your nature make you give many and diverse things, when I am asking for one simple thing.

Theaet. What do you mean, Socrates?

Soc. Perhaps nothing. I will, however, say what I believe to be my meaning: When you speak of cobbling, you mean the knowledge of the making of shoes?

Theaet. Just so.

e　　*Soc.* And when you speak of carpentering, you mean knowledge of the making of wooden implements?

Theaet. I do.

Soc. In both cases, then, it is the *subject known* that you are defining.

Theaet. True.

Soc. But that, Theaetetus, was not the point of my question: we did not ask about the subjects of knowledge, nor yet the number of its forms, for we were not going to count them, but we wanted to know the nature of knowledge in the abstract. Am I not right?

Theaet. Perfectly right.

147　　*Soc.* Let me offer an illustration: Suppose that a person were to ask about some very trivial and obvious thing—for example, What is clay? and we were to reply, that there is a clay of potters, there is a clay of oven-makers, there is a clay of brick-makers; would not the answer be ridiculous?

Theaet. Yes, perhaps.

Soc. In the first place, there would be an absurdity in assuming that he who asked the question would understand from our answer the meaning of 'clay', merely because we added 'of the

image-makers', or of any other workers. How can a man under- b
stand the name of anything, when he does not know what the
thing is?

Theaet. He cannot.

Soc. Likewise, a man who does not know what 'knowledge'
stands for, cannot understand the phrase 'knowledge of shoemaking'?

Theaet. No, he cannot.

Soc. And therefore the same man will not understand the
name 'cobbling', or the name of any other art?

Theaet. No.

Soc. And when a man is asked what knowledge is, to give in
answer the name of some art is ridiculous; for his reply 'A c
knowledge of this or that' is no answer to the question that was
asked.

Theaet. True.

Soc. Moreover, he might answer shortly and simply, but he
makes an enormous circuit. For example, when asked about the
clay, he might have given the simple and perhaps trivial answer
that clay is moistened earth—what sort of clay is not to the
point.

Theaet. Yes, Socrates, there is no difficulty as you put the
question. You mean, if I am not mistaken, something like what
occurred to me and to my friend here, your namesake Socrates, d
in a recent discussion.

Soc. What was that, Theaetetus?

Theaet. Theodorus was writing out for us something about
roots, such as the sides of squares three or five feet in area,
showing that they are incommensurable by the unit:[1] he took the
other examples up to seventeen, but there for some reason he
stopped. Now as there are innumerable such roots, the notion
occurred to us of attempting to find some common description
which can be applied to them all.

Soc. And did you find any such thing?   e

Theaet. I think that we did; but I should like to have your
opinion.

[1] [For an explanation of the passage with reference to mathematical history,
see Heath, *Greek Mathematics*, i, p. 155. Δύναμις here means what we call a square
root, but in other passages in Plato, such as *Rep.* 587 d, it is a *square*.]

Soc. Let me hear.

Theaet. We divided all numbers into two classes: those which are made up of equal factors multiplying into one another, which we compared to square figures and called square or equilateral numbers;—that was one class.

Soc. Very good.

148 *Theaet.* The intermediate numbers, such as three and five, and every other number which is made up of unequal factors, either of a greater multiplied by a less, or of a less multiplied by a greater, and, when regarded as a figure, is contained in unequal sides;—all these we compared to oblong figures, and called them oblong numbers.

Soc. Capital; and what followed?

Theaet. The lines, or sides, which have for their squares the b equilateral plane numbers, were called by us lengths; and the lines whose squares are equal to the oblong numbers, were called powers or roots; the reason of this latter name being, that they are commensurable with the former not in linear measurement, but in the area of their squares. And a similar distinction was made among solids.

Soc. Excellent, my boys; I think that you fully justify the praises of Theodorus, and that he will not be found guilty of false witness.

Theaet. But I am unable, Socrates, to give you an answer about knowledge similar to this answer about the length and the power, which is what you appear to want; and therefore Theodorus is a deceiver after all.

Soc. Well, but if some one were to praise you for running, and c to say that he never met your equal among boys, and afterwards you are beaten in a race by a grown-up man, who was a great runner—would the praise be any the less true?

Theaet. Certainly not.

Soc. And is the discovery of the nature of knowledge so small a matter, as I just now said? Is it not one which would task the powers of men perfect in every way?

Theaet. Yes, indeed, of men who were the cream of perfection!

Soc. Well, then, be of good cheer; do not say that Theodorus d was mistaken about you, but do your best to ascertain the true nature of knowledge, as well as of other things.

Theaet. I am eager enough, Socrates, if that would bring to light the truth.

Soc. Come, then, you were on the right road just now; let your own answer about roots be your model, and as you comprehended them all in one class, try and bring the many sorts of knowledge under one definition.

Theaet. I can assure you, Socrates, that I have tried very often, e when the report of questions asked by you was brought to me; but I can neither persuade myself that I have a satisfactory answer to give, nor hear of any one who answers as you would have him; and yet I cannot help being troubled by the problem.

Soc. These are the pangs of labour, my dear Theaetetus; you have something within you which you are bringing to the birth.

Theaet. I do not know, Socrates; I only say what I feel.

Soc. And have you never heard, simpleton, that I am the son 149 of a midwife, brave and burly, whose name was Phaenarete?

Theaet. Yes, I have.

Soc. And that I myself practise midwifery?

Theaet. No, never.

Soc. Let me tell you that I do though, my friend: but you must not reveal the secret, as the world in general have not found me out; and therefore they only say of me, that I am the strangest of mortals and drive men to their wits' end. Did you ever hear that too? b

Theaet. Yes.

Soc. Shall I tell you the reason?

Theaet. By all means.

Soc. Bear in mind the whole business of the midwives, and then you will see my meaning better:—No woman, as you are probably aware, who is still able to conceive and bear, attends other women, but only those who are past bearing.

Theaet. Yes, I know.

Soc. It is said that Artemis was responsible for this, because, though she is the goddess of childbirth, she is not herself a mother. She could not, indeed, allow the barren to be midwives, because c human nature cannot know the mystery of an art without experience; but she assigned this office to those who are too old to bear, honouring their resemblance to herself.

Theaet. I dare say.

Soc. And I dare say too, or rather I am absolutely certain, that the midwives know better than others who is pregnant and who is not?

Theaet. Very true.

Soc. And by the use of potions and incantations they are able
d to arouse the pangs and to soothe them at will; they can make those bear who have a difficulty in bearing, and if they think fit they can smother the embryo[1] in the womb.

Theaet. They can.

Soc. Did you ever remark that they are also most cunning matchmakers, and have a thorough knowledge of what unions are likely to produce a brave brood?

Theaet. No, I cannot say that I knew it.

Soc. Then let me tell you that this is their greatest pride, more
e than cutting the umbilical cord. And if you reflect, you will see that the same art which cultivates and gathers in the fruits of the earth, will be most likely to know in what soils the several plants or seeds should be deposited.

Theaet. Yes, the same art.

Soc. And do you suppose that with women the arts of planting and of harvesting are different?

150 *Theaet.* I should think not.

Soc. Certainly not; but midwives are respectable women who have a character to lose, and they avoid this department of their profession, because they are afraid of being called procuresses, which is a name given to those who join together man and woman in an unlawful and unscientific way; and yet the true midwife is also the true and only matchmaker.

Theaet. Clearly.

Soc. Such are the midwives, whose task is a very important one, but not so important as mine; for women do not bring into the world at one time real children, and at another time counter-
b feits which are with difficulty distinguished from them; if they did, then the discernment of the true and false birth would be the crowning achievement of the art of midwifery—you would think so?

Theaet. Indeed I should.

Soc. Well, my art of midwifery is in most respects like theirs;

¹ [Retaining the MS. reading ἐὰν νέον ὂν δόξῃ ἀμβλίσκειν.]

but differs, in that I attend men and not women, and I look after
their souls when they are in labour, and not after their bodies:
and the triumph of my art is in thoroughly examining whether c
the thought which the mind of the young man brings forth is false
and lifeless, or fertile and true. And again I resemble the midwives in being barren of wisdom, and the reproach which is often
made against me, that I ask questions of others and have not the
wit to pronounce upon any subject myself, is very just—the
reason is, that the god compels me to be a midwife, but has not
allowed me to bring forth. I myself, then, am not particularly
wise, nor have I anything to show which is the invention or d
birth of my own soul. But of those who converse with me, some
at first appear utterly stupid; and all, as our acquaintance ripens,
if the god is gracious to them, make astonishing progress; and
this in the opinion of others as well as in their own. It is quite
clear that they never learned anything from me; the many fine
discoveries to which they give birth are of their own making.
But to me and the god they owe their delivery. And the proof of
my words is, that many of them, ignorantly taking all the credit
to themselves, and despising me, have gone away too soon, either e
of their own accord or under the influence of others; and have
not only lost the children of whom I had previously delivered
them by an ill bringing up, but have stifled whatever else they
had in them by evil communications, being fonder of lies and
shams than of the truth; and they have at last ended by seeing
themselves, as others see them, to be great fools. Aristeides, the
son of Lysimachus, is one of them, and there are many others. 151
The truants often return to me, and beg that I would consort
with them again—they are ready to go to me on their knees—
and then, if my divine sign allows, which is not always the case,
I receive them, and they begin to improve again. Dire are the
pangs which my art is able to arouse and to allay in those who
consort with me, just like the pangs of women in childbirth;
night and day they are full of perplexity and travail which is
even worse than that of the women. So much for them. And there b
are others, Theaetetus, who come to me apparently not in a state
of pregnancy; and as I know that they have no need of my art, I
coax them into marrying some one, and by the grace of God I can
generally tell who is likely to do them good. Many of them I have

given away to Prodicus, and many to other inspired sages. I tell
you this long story, friend Theaetetus, because I suspect, as
indeed you seem to think yourself, that you are in labour—great
with some conception. Come then to me, who am a midwife's
c son and myself a midwife, and do your best to answer the questions which I will ask you. And if I abstract and expose your first-
born, because I discover upon inspection that the conception
which you have formed is a vain shadow, do not quarrel with me
on that account, as the manner of women is when their first
children are taken from them. For I have actually known some
who were ready to bite me when I deprived them of a darling
folly; they did not perceive that I acted from goodwill, not know-
d ing that no god is the enemy of man—that was not within the
range of their ideas; neither am I their enemy in all this, but I
hold it an impiety to admit falsehood, or to stifle the truth. Once
more, then, Theaetetus, tell me from the beginning 'What is
knowledge?'—and do not say that you cannot answer; quit
yourself like a man, and if God is willing you will be able to
answer.

Theaet. At any rate, Socrates, after such an exhortation I
e should be ashamed of not trying to do my best. Now he who
knows anything perceives what he knows, and, as far as I can
see at present, knowledge is simply perception.

Soc. Bravely said, boy; that is the way in which you should
express your opinion. And now, let us examine together this
conception of yours, and see whether it is fertile or a mere wind-
egg:—You say that knowledge is perception?

Theaet. Yes.

Soc. Well, you have delivered yourself of a very important
152 doctrine about knowledge; it is indeed the opinion of Protagoras,
although he has another way of expressing the same view. Man,
he says, 'is the measure of all things, of the existence of things that
are, and of the non-existence of things that are not':—You have
read him?[1]

Theaet. O yes, again and again.

[1] [This translation implies that Protagoras' canon of truth applied only to
judgements about the existence of things. Probably the 'things' of which he spoke
included judgements of fact such as 'this is warm, sweet, &c.', and we ought to
translate: 'of things that are, that they are, and of those that are not, that they
are not.']

Soc. Does he not say [or mean] that things are to you such as they appear to you, and to me such as they appear to me, and that you and I are men?

Theaet. Yes, he says so.

Soc. A wise man is not likely to talk nonsense. Let us try to b understand him: the same wind is blowing, and yet one of us may be cold and the other not, or one may be slightly and the other very cold?

Theaet. Quite true.

Soc. Now at such a time is the wind, regarded not in relation to us but absolutely, cold or not; or are we to say, with Protagoras, that the wind is cold to him who is cold, and not to him who is not?

Theaet. I suppose the last.

Soc. And, moreover, it appears so to each of them?

Theaet. Yes.

Soc. And 'appears to him' means the same as 'he perceives'.

Theaet. True.

Soc. Then appearing and perceiving coincide in the case of hot c and cold, and in similar instances. For we must presume that they really are for each man such as he perceives them to be.

Theaet. Yes.

Soc. Then perception is always of existence, and being the same as knowledge is unerring?

Theaet. Apparently.

Soc. In the name of the Graces, what an almighty wise man Protagoras must have been! He spoke these things in a parable to the common herd, like you and me, but told the truth, 'his Truth',[1] in secret to his own disciples.

Theaet. What do you mean, Socrates? d

Soc. I will explain, and tell you of a high argument, which proclaims that nothing in the world is by itself *one*, or can rightly be called *this* or *of this kind*; but if anything is termed great, it will appear to be also small, if heavy, light, and so forth. There is no *one thing*, no *this*, and no *such*. It is from motion, and change, and admixture with each other, that there *come to be* all those things which we declare to *be*, speaking incorrectly, for there is no being at all, but only perpetual becoming. The whole e

[1] In allusion to a book of Protagoras, which bore this title.

succession of philosophers with the exception of Parmenides may be supposed to agree with you in this—Protagoras, Heracleitus, Empedocles, and the rest. So may all the great masters of either kind of poetry—Epicharmus, the prince of Comedy, and Homer of Tragedy; when the latter sings of

Ocean whence sprang the gods, and mother Tethys,

does he not mean that all things are the offspring of flux and motion?

Theaet. I think so.

153 *Soc.* And who could take up arms against such a great army having Homer for its general, and not appear ridiculous?[1]

Theaet. Who indeed, Socrates?

Soc. Yes, Theaetetus; for here are some other cogent proofs that motion is the source of what is called being and of becoming, and inactivity of not-being and of destruction. Firstly, fire and warmth, which are supposed to be the parent and guardian of all other things, are born of local movement and of friction, which are forms of movement in the wider sense. Are they not both the origin of fire?

b *Theaet.* They are.

Soc. And again the race of animals is generated in the same way?

Theaet. Certainly.

Soc. And is not the bodily habit spoiled by rest and idleness, but preserved for a long time by motion and exercise?

Theaet. True.

Soc. And what of the mental habit? Is it not by study and attention (which are motions) that the soul both acquires and retains learning, and generally improves? while through rest, which, in the soul, means stupidity or want of mental exercise,

c she remains ignorant and is liable to forget whatever she has learned?

Theaet. True.

Soc. Then motion is a good, and rest an evil, to the soul as well as to the body?

Theaet. It seems so.

Soc. Need I go on to mention that breathless calm, stillness and

[1] Cf. *Crat.* 401 e ff.

the like waste and impair, while wind and storm preserve; and as the palmary argument of all, I may adduce the golden chain in Homer, by which he means the sun, thereby indicating that so d long as the sun and the heavens go round in their orbits, all things human and divine are and are preserved, but if they were chained up and their motions ceased, then all things would be destroyed, and, as the saying is, turned upside down.

Theaet. I believe, Socrates, that you have truly explained his meaning.

Soc. Then let us apply his doctrine in this manner, my good friend, and first of all to vision; that which you call white colour is not in your eyes, and is not a distinct thing which exists out of them. And you must not assign any place to it: for if it had e position it would be, and be at rest, and would not be in process of becoming.

Theaet. Then what is colour?

Soc. Let us carry out the principle which has just been affirmed, that there is nothing which, *per se, is* and *is one*, and then we shall see that white, black, and every other colour, arises out of the eye meeting the appropriate motion, and that the colour to which we attribute 'being' is in each case neither the active 154 nor the passive element, but something which *comes to be* between them, and is peculiar to each percipient; for you would not affirm that the several colours appear to a dog or to any animal whatever as they appear to you?

Theaet. Far from it.

Soc. Or that anything appears the same to you as to another man? Are you so profoundly convinced of this? Rather would it not be true that it never appears exactly the same to you, because you are never exactly the same?

Theaet. The latter.

Soc. And if that with which I compare myself in size, or which b I apprehend by touch, *were* great or white or hot, it could not have become different by mere contact with another subject, while its own nature is in no way changed; nor again, if the comparing or apprehending subject *were* great or white or hot, could this have been made different by any approximation or affection of any other thing, while its own nature is not affected. The fact is that in our ordinary way of speaking we allow ourselves to be driven into most ridiculous and wonderful contradictions, as Protagoras and all who take his line of argument would remark.

Theaet. How? and of what sort do you mean?

c   *Soc.* A little instance will sufficiently explain my meaning: When six dice are compared with four, we say that they are 'more' and 'one and a half times' as many; when compared with twelve, that they are 'fewer' and 'half'; and no other way of speaking is tolerable.

Theaet. Very true.

Soc. Well, then, suppose that Protagoras or some one asks whether anything can become greater or more if not by increasing, how would you answer him, Theaetetus?

Theaet. I should say 'No', Socrates, if I were to speak my mind

d   in reference to this last question, but if I were thinking of my former answer, consistency would oblige me to say 'Yes'.

Soc. Capital! excellent! spoken like an oracle, my boy! And if you reply 'Yes', there will be a case for Euripides; for our tongue will be unconvinced, but not our mind.[1]

Theaet. Very true.

Soc. The thoroughbred Sophists, who know all that can be known about the mind, and argue only out of the superfluity of

e   their wits, would have had a regular sparring-match over this, and would have knocked their arguments together finely. But you and I, who have no professional aims, only desire to see what is the mutual relation of these principles,—whether they are consistent with each other or quite irreconcilable.

Theaet. Yes, that would certainly be my desire.

Soc. And mine too. But since this is our feeling, and there is plenty of time, why should we not calmly and patiently review

155   our own thoughts, and thoroughly examine and see what these appearances in us really are? If I am not mistaken, they will be described by us as follows:—first, that nothing can become greater or less, either in size or number, while remaining equal to itself—you would agree?

Theaet. Yes.

b   *Soc.* Secondly, that without addition or subtraction there is no increase or diminution of anything, but only equality.

---

[1] In allusion to the well-known line of Euripides, *Hippol.* 612:

ἡ γλῶσσ' ὀμώμοχ', ἡ δὲ φρὴν ἀνώμοτος.

Theaet. Quite true.

Soc. Thirdly, it is surely clear that what was not before cannot be afterwards, without becoming and having become.

Theaet. Yes, so it seems.

Soc. These three axioms, if I am not mistaken, are fighting with one another in our minds in the case of the dice, or, again, in such a case as this—if I were to say that I, who am of a certain height and taller than you, who are still young, may within a year, without gaining or losing in height, be not so tall—not that I should have lost, but that you would have increased. In such a case, I am afterwards what I once was not, and yet I have not c become; for I could not have become without becoming, neither could I have become less without losing somewhat of my height; and I could give you ten thousand examples of similar contradictions, if we admit them at all. I believe that you follow me, Theaetetus; for I suspect that you have heard these questions raised before now.

Theaet. Yes, Socrates, and I am amazed when I think of them; by the Gods I am! and I want to know what on earth they mean; and there are times when my head quite swims with the contemplation of them.

Soc. I see, my dear Theaetetus, that Theodorus had a true d insight into your nature when he said that you were a philosopher, for wonder is the feeling of a philosopher, and philosophy begins in wonder. He was not a bad genealogist who said that Iris [the messenger of heaven] is the child of Thaumas [wonder]. But do you begin to see what is the explanation of this perplexity on the hypothesis which we attribute to Protagoras?

Theaet. Not as yet.

Soc. Then you will be obliged to me if I help you to unearth the hidden 'truth' of a famous man or school.

Theaet. To be sure, I shall be very much obliged.   e

Soc. Take a look round, then, and see that none of the uninitiated are listening. Now by the uninitiated I mean the people who think that nothing *is* save what they can grasp in their hands, and who will not allow that action or generation or anything invisible can have real existence.

Theaet. Indeed, Socrates, they are themselves a very hard and metallic sort of men.

156   *Soc.* Yes, my boy, outer barbarians. Far more ingenious are
the brethren whose mysteries I am about to reveal to you. Their
first principle is, that all is motion, and upon this all the affections
of which we were just now speaking are supposed to depend: all
is movement, and nothing else exists; a movement which has
two forms, one active and the other passive, both in endless
number; and out of the union and friction of them there is
generated a progeny endless in number, having twin forms, an
b object of sense, and a sensation which always breaks forth together
with it and is born at the same moment. The senses are variously
named, seeing, hearing, smelling, and heat and cold; and then
there are the senses of pleasure, pain, desire, fear, and many more
which have names, as well as innumerable others which are
without them; each has its kindred sensible object,—each variety
c of seeing has a corresponding variety of colour, each kind of
hearing a corresponding kind of sound, and there are sensible
objects adapted to all the types of sensation. Do you see, Theaetetus, the bearings of this tale on the preceding argument?
    Theaet. Indeed I do not.
    Soc. Then attend, and I will try to finish the story. The purport
is that all these things are in motion, as I was saying, and that
this motion is of two kinds, a slower and a quicker; and the
slower elements have their motions in the same place and with
d reference to things near them, and so they beget; but what is
begotten is swifter, for it is carried to and fro, and its motion is
from place to place. Apply this to sense:—When the eye and the
appropriate object meet together and give birth to whiteness and
the sensation connatural with it, which could not have been given
by either of them going elsewhere, then, while the sight is flowing
from the eye, whiteness proceeds from the object which combines
in producing the colour; and so the eye is fulfilled with sight, and
really sees, and becomes, not sight, but a seeing eye; and the
e object which combined to form the colour is fulfilled with whiteness, and becomes not whiteness but a white thing, whether wood
or stone or whatever the object may be which happens to be
coloured white. And this is true of all sensible objects, hard,
warm, and the like, which are similarly to be regarded, as I was
157 saying before, not as having any absolute existence, but as
being all of them of whatever kind generated by motion in their

intercourse with one another; for of the agent and patient, as existing in separation, no trustworthy conception, as they say, can be formed, for the agent has no existence until united with the patient, and the patient has no existence until united with the agent; and that which by uniting with something becomes an agent, by meeting with some other thing is converted into a patient. And from all these considerations, as I said at first, there arises a general reflection, that there is no one self-existent thing, but everything is becoming and in relation; and being must be altogether abolished, although from habit and ignorance we are b compelled even in this discussion to retain the use of the term. But these wise men tell us that we are not to allow either the word 'something', or 'belonging to something', or 'to me', or 'this' or 'that', or any other name which would bring things to a stand; but, as nature directs, we must speak of them as becoming, being made, being destroyed, changing; he who attempts to fix them is easily refuted. And this should be the way of speaking, not only of particulars but of aggregates; such aggregates as are expressed in the word 'man', or 'stone', or any name of an animal c or of a class. O Theaetetus, are not these speculations sweet as honey? And do you not like the taste of them in the mouth?

Theaet. I do not know what to say, Socrates; for, indeed, I cannot make out whether you are giving your own opinion or only wanting to draw me out.

Soc. You forget, my friend, that I am ignorant, and claim none of these theories as my own; you are the person who is in labour, I am the barren midwife; and this is why I soothe you, and offer you one good thing after another, that you may taste them. And I hope that I may at last help to bring your own opinion into the light of day: when this has been accomplished, then we will d determine whether what you have brought forth is only a wind-egg or a living truth. Therefore, keep up your spirits, and answer like a man what you think.

Theaet. Ask me.

Soc. Then once more: Is it your opinion that there is no such thing as being good and beautiful and so forth, only a becoming?

Theaet. When I hear you discoursing in this style, I think that there is a great deal in what you say, and I am very ready to assent.

e *Soc.* Let us not leave the argument unfinished, then; for there still remains to be considered an objection which may be raised about dreams and diseases, in particular about madness, and the various illusions of hearing and sight, or of other senses. For you know that in all these cases the theory which has been stated

158 appears to be unmistakably refuted, since in dreams and illusions we certainly have false perceptions; and far from saying that everything is which appears to any man, we should rather say that nothing *is* which appears.

Theaet. Very true, Socrates.

Soc. But then, my boy, what argument is left for one who holds that knowledge is perception, or that the truth really is for every man such as it appears to him to be?

Theaet. I am afraid to say, Socrates, that I have nothing to answer, because you rebuked me just now for making this excuse;

b but I certainly cannot undertake to argue that madmen or dreamers do not think falsely, when they imagine, some of them that they are gods, and others that they can fly, and are flying in their sleep.

Soc. Do you see another question which can be raised about these phenomena, notably about dreaming and waking?

Theaet. What question?

Soc. A question which I think that you must often have heard persons ask:—How can you determine whether at this moment we are sleeping, and all our thoughts are a dream; or whether

c we are awake, and talking to one another in the waking state?

Theaet. Indeed, Socrates, I do not know how it could be determined, for in both cases the facts precisely correspond; and there is no difficulty in supposing that during all this discussion we have been talking to one another in a dream; and when in a dream[1] we seem to be narrating dreams, the resemblance of the . two states is quite astonishing.

Soc. You see, then, that a doubt about the reality of sense is

d easily raised, since there may even be a doubt whether we are awake or in a dream. And as our time is equally divided between sleeping and waking, in either sphere of existence the soul contends that the thoughts which are present to our minds at the time are true; and during one half of our lives we affirm the truth

---

[1] Or perhaps, reading ὕπαρ, 'in our waking state'.

of the one, and, during the other half, of the other, and are equally confident of both.

Theaet. Most true.

Soc. And may not the same be said of madness and other disorders? the difference is only that the times are not equal.

Theaet. Certainly.

Soc. And is truth or falsehood to be determined by duration of time?

Theaet. That would be in many ways ridiculous.   e

Soc. But can you certainly determine by any other means which of these opinions is true?

Theaet. I do not think that I can.

Soc. Listen, then, to the explanation of the same facts which might be given by the champions of appearance. They would ask, as I imagine—When one thing is entirely different from another, can it have any power in common with that other thing? and observe, Theaetetus, that the word 'other' means not 'partially', but 'wholly other'.

Theaet. Certainly, putting the question as you do, that which   159 is wholly other cannot either in its power or in any other way be the same.

Soc. And must therefore be admitted to be unlike?

Theaet. True.

Soc. If, then, anything happens to become like or unlike itself or another, while it becomes like we shall say it is becoming the same, while unlike, other?

Theaet. Certainly.

Soc. Were we not saying that there are agents many and infinite, and patients many and infinite?

Theaet. Yes.

Soc. And also that each of these, with a different partner, will produce offspring which are not the same, but different?

Theaet. Certainly.   b

Soc. Let us take you and me, or anything as an example:— There is Socrates in health, and Socrates sick—Are they like or unlike?

Theaet. You mean to compare Socrates in health as a whole, and Socrates in sickness as a whole?

Soc. Exactly; that is my meaning.

Theaet. I answer, they are unlike.

Soc. And if unlike, they are so far other?

Theaet. Certainly.

c   *Soc.* And would you not say the same of Socrates sleeping and waking, or in any of the states which we were mentioning?

Theaet. I should.

Soc. It follows that everything which is by nature active, will find a different patient in Socrates, according as he is well or ill.

Theaet. Of course.

Soc. And I who am the patient, and that which is the agent, will engender something different in each of the two cases?

Theaet. Certainly.

Soc. The wine which I drink when I am in health, appears sweet and pleasant to me?

Theaet. True.

Soc. For, according to our acknowledged view, the patient and

d   agent meet together and produce sweetness and a perception of sweetness, which are in simultaneous motion, and the perception which comes from the patient makes the tongue percipient, and the quality of sweetness which arises out of and is moving about the wine, makes the wine both to be and to appear sweet to the healthy tongue.

Theaet. Certainly; that has been already acknowledged.

Soc. But when I am sick,—firstly, the wine really acts upon another and a different person?

Theaet. Yes.

e   *Soc.* Once more, then, the combination of the draught of wine, and the Socrates who is sick, produces quite another result; which is the sensation of bitterness in the tongue, and the motion and creation of bitterness in and about the wine, which becomes not bitterness but something bitter; as I myself become not perception but percipient?

Theaet. True.

Soc. There is no other object of which I shall ever have the

160 same perception, for another object would give another perception, and would make the percipient other and different; nor can that object which affects me, meeting another subject, produce the same, or become similar, for that too will produce another result from another subject, and become different.

Theaet. True.

Soc. Neither can I by myself have this sensation, nor the object by itself this quality.

Theaet. Certainly not.

Soc. It is necessary both that I, if I am to become percipient, must be related to an object—there can be no such thing as perceiving and perceiving nothing; and that the object, whether b it become sweet, bitter, or of any other quality, must have relation to a percipient; nothing can become sweet which is sweet to no one.

Theaet. Certainly not.

Soc. Then the inference is, that we [the agent and patient] are or become in relation to one another; there is a law which binds us one to the other, but not to any other existence, nor each of us to himself; and therefore we can only be bound to one another; so that whether a person prefers to say that a thing is or that it becomes, he must say that it is or becomes to or of or in relation to something else; but he must not say or allow any one else to say that anything is or becomes absolutely:—such is the c conclusion of the view we have explained.

Theaet. Very true, Socrates.

Soc. Then, if that which acts upon me has relation to me and to no other, I and no other am the percipient of it?

Theaet. Of course.

Soc. Then my perception is true to me, being inseparable from my own 'being';[1] and, as Protagoras says, to myself I am judge of what is and what is not to me.

Theaet. I suppose so.

Soc. How then, since I never err, and since my mind never d trips in the conception of being or becoming, can I fail of knowing that which I perceive?

Theaet. You cannot.

Soc. Then you were quite right in affirming that knowledge is only perception; and the meaning turns out to be the same, whether with Homer and Heracleitus, and all that company, one says that all is motion and flux, or with the great sage Protagoras, that man is the measure of all things; or with Theaetetus, that, given these premises, perception is knowledge. Am I not right, e

[1] [i.e. my own real world, to which no other percipient has access.]

Theaetetus, and may we compare this to a new-born child, to which you, with my assistance, have given birth? What say you?

Theaet. I cannot but agree, Socrates.

Soc. Then this is the child, however he may turn out, which you and I have with difficulty brought into the world. And now that he is born, we must run round the hearth with him, and see 161 whether he is worth rearing, or is only a wind-egg and a sham. Is he to be reared in any case, and not exposed? or will you bear to see him examined, and not get into a passion if I take away your first-born?

Theod. Theaetetus will not be angry, for he is very good-natured. But tell me, Socrates, in heaven's name, what can be said in disproof of all this?

Soc. You, Theodorus, are a lover of theories, and now you innocently fancy that I am a bag full of them, and can easily pull one out which will overthrow its predecessor. But you do not see b that in reality none of these theories come from me; they all come from him who talks with me. I only know just enough to extract them from the wisdom of another, and to receive them in a spirit of fairness. And now I shall say nothing myself, but shall endeavour to elicit something from our young friend.

Theod. Do as you say, Socrates; you are quite right.

Soc. Shall I tell you, Theodorus, what amazes me in your acquaintance Protagoras.

c *Theod.* What is it?

Soc. I am charmed with his doctrine, that what appears is to each one, but I wonder that he did not begin his book on Truth with a declaration that a pig or a dog-faced baboon, or some other yet stranger monster which has sensation, is the measure of all things; then he might have shown a magnificent contempt for our opinion of him by informing us at the outset that while we were reverencing him like a God for his wisdom he was no more d intelligent than a tadpole, not to speak of his fellow-men. Would you not say so, Theodorus? If the judgement which each man forms through sensation is true for him, and no man can either discern another's feelings better than he, or have any superior right to determine whether his opinion is true or false, but each, as we have several times repeated, is to himself the sole judge, and everything that he judges is true and right,—why, my

friend, should Protagoras be preferred to the place of wisdom
and instruction, and deserve to be well paid, and we poor e
ignoramuses have to go to him, if each one is the measure of his
own wisdom? Must he not be flattering the public in all this? I
say nothing of the ridiculous predicament in which my own
midwifery and, I think, the whole art of dialectic is placed; for
the attempt to supervise or refute the notions or opinions of others
would be a tedious and enormous piece of folly, if to each man 162
his own are right; and this must be the case if Protagoras' Truth
is the real truth, and the philosopher is not merely amusing himself by giving oracles out of the shrine of his book.

Theod. He was a friend of mine, Socrates, as you were saying,
and therefore I cannot have him refuted by my lips, nor can
I oppose you when I agree with you; please, then, to take
Theaetetus again; he seemed to answer very nicely.

Soc. If you were to go into a Lacedaemonian palestra, Theo- b
dorus, would you have a right to look on at the naked wrestlers,
some of them making a poor figure, if you did not strip and give
them an opportunity of judging your own person?

Theod. Why not, Socrates, if they would allow me to remain
as a spectator, as I think you will, in consideration of my age and
stiffness; let some more supple youth try a fall with you, and do
not drag me into the gymnasium.

Soc. What is dear to you, Theodorus, is not displeasing to me,
as the proverb says, and therefore I will return to the sage c
Theaetetus: Tell me, Theaetetus, in reference to what I was
saying, are you not lost in wonder, like myself, when you find
that all of a sudden you are raised to the level of the wisest of
men, or indeed of the gods?—for you would assume the measure
of Protagoras to apply to the gods as well as men?

Theaet. Certainly I should, and I confess to you that I am lost
in wonder. While we were working out the meaning of the theory
that whatever appears to each man is true for him, I was quite d
satisfied, but now the face of things has changed.

Soc. Why, my dear boy, you are young, and therefore your
ear is quickly caught and your mind influenced by popular
arguments. Protagoras, or some one speaking on his behalf, will
doubtless say in reply,—Good people, young and old, you meet
and harangue, and bring in the gods, whose existence or non-

e existence I banish from writing and speech,[1] or you talk about the reason of man being degraded to the level of the brutes, which is a telling argument with the multitude, but not one word of proof or demonstration do you offer. All is probability with you, and yet surely you and Theodorus had better reflect whether you are

163 disposed to admit of probability and plausible comparisons in matters of such importance. He or any other mathematician who argued from probability in geometry, would not be worth an ace.

Theaet. But neither you nor we, Socrates, would be satisfied with such arguments.

Soc. Then you and Theodorus mean to say that we must look at the matter in some other way?

Theaet. Yes, in quite another way.

Soc. And the way will be to ask whether perception is or is not the same as knowledge; for this was the real point of our argument, and with a view to this we raised (did we not?) those many strange questions.

b *Theaet.* Certainly.

Soc. Shall we admit that we at once know whatever we perceive by sight or hearing? for example, shall we say that not having learned, we do not *hear* the language of foreigners when they speak to us? or shall we say that we hear and therefore know what they are saying? Or again, in looking at letters which we do not understand, shall we say that we do not *see* them? or shall we aver that, seeing them, we must know them?

Theaet. We shall say, Socrates, that we know what we actually see and hear of them—that is to say, we see, and hence know, the

c figure and colour of the letters, and we hear and know the elevation or depression of the sound; but we do not perceive by sight and hearing, and hence do not know, that which grammarians and interpreters teach about them.

Soc. Capital, Theaetetus; and about this there shall be no dispute, because I want you to grow; but look! there is another difficulty coming, and you must advise how we shall repulse it.

Theaet. What is it?

[1] [Referring to his famous statement: 'Concerning the gods, I cannot feel sure either that they are or that they are not, nor what they are like in figure; for there are many things that hinder knowledge, the obscurity of the subject and the shortness of human life.']

Soc. Some one will say, Can a man who has ever known any- d
thing, and still has and preserves a memory of that which he
knows, not know that which he remembers at the time when he
remembers? I have, I fear, a tedious way of putting a simple
question, which is only, whether a man who has learned, and
remembers, can fail to know?

Theaet. Impossible, Socrates; the supposition is monstrous.

Soc. Am I talking nonsense, then? Think: is not seeing perceiving, and is not sight perception?

Theaet. True.

Soc. And if our recent definition holds, every man knows that e
which he has seen?

Theaet. Yes.

Soc. And now, you would admit that there is such a thing as
memory?

Theaet. Yes.

Soc. Is this memory of something or of nothing?

Theaet. Of something, surely.

Soc. Of things learned and perceived, that is?

Theaet. Certainly.

Soc. Often a man remembers that which he has seen?

Theaet. True.

Soc. Even if he closes his eyes? Or would he then forget?

Theaet. Who, Socrates, would dare to say so?   164

Soc. But we must say so, if the previous argument is to be
maintained.

Theaet. What do you mean? I am not quite sure that I understand you, though I have a strong suspicion that you are right.

Soc. As thus: he who sees knows, as we say, that which he sees;
for perception and sight and knowledge are admitted to be the
same.

Theaet. Certainly.

Soc. But he who saw, and has knowledge of that which he saw,
remembers, when he closes his eyes, that which he no longer sees.

Theaet. Yes.

Soc. But seeing is knowing, and therefore not-seeing is not- b
knowing?

Theaet. True.

Soc. Then the inference is, that a man who has attained the knowledge of something, though he still remembers this, may *not* know it since he does not see it; and this has been affirmed by us to be a monstrous supposition.

Theaet. Most true.

Soc. Thus, then, the assertion that knowledge and perception are one, seems to involve an impossible consequence.

Theaet. Yes.

Soc. Then they must be distinguished?

Theaet. I suppose that they must.

c *Soc.* It seems that we must go back to our original question, What is knowledge?—But hold! Theaetetus, whatever are we proposing to do?

Theaet. About what?

Soc. Like a good-for-nothing cock, without having won the victory, we spring away from the argument and crow.

Theaet. How do you mean?

Soc. After the manner of disputers,[1] we were satisfied with mere verbal consistency, and were well pleased if in this way we could gain an advantage. Although professing not to be mere eristics,

d but philosophers, I suspect that we have unconsciously fallen into the error of that ingenious class of persons.

Theaet. I do not as yet understand you.

Soc. Then I will try to explain myself: just now we asked the question, whether a man who had learned and remembered could fail to know, and we showed that a person who had seen might remember when he had his eyes shut and could not see, and then he would at the same time remember and not know. But this was an impossibility. And so the Protagorean fable came to nought, and yours also, who maintained that knowledge is the

e same as perception.

Theaet. So it seems.

Soc. And yet, my friend, I rather suspect that if Protagoras, who was the father of the first of the two brats, had been alive, he would have had a great deal to say on their behalf. But he is dead, and we insult over his orphan child; and even the guardians whom he left, and of whom our friend Theodorus is one, are unwilling to give any help, and therefore I suppose that we must take up his cause ourselves and see justice done?

---

[1] *Lys.* 216 a; *Phaedo* 90 b, 101 e; *Rep.* v, 453 e ff.

Theod. Not I, Socrates, but rather Callias, the son of Hip- 165 ponicus, is his executor. For my part, I was too soon diverted from the abstractions of dialectic to geometry. Nevertheless, I shall be grateful to you if you assist him.

Soc. Very good, Theodorus; you shall see how I will come to the rescue. If a person does not attend to the meaning of terms as they are commonly used in argument, he may be involved even in greater paradoxes than these. Am I to explain this matter to you or to Theaetetus?

Theod. To both of us, and let the younger answer; he will incur less disgrace if he is discomfited. b

Soc. Then now let me ask the awful question, which is this:— Can the same man know and also not know that which he knows?

Theod. How shall we answer, Theaetetus?

Theaet. He cannot, I should say.

Soc. He can, if you maintain that seeing is knowing. When you are imprisoned in a well, as the saying is, and the self-assured adversary closes one of your eyes with his hand, and asks whether you can see his cloak with the eye which he has closed, how will c you answer the inevitable man?

Theaet. I should answer, 'Not with that eye but with the other'.

Soc. Then you see and do not see the same thing at the same time.

Theaet. Yes, in a certain sense.

Soc. None of that, he will reply; I do not ask or bid you answer in what sense you know, but only whether you know that which you do not know. You have been proved to see that which you do not see; and you have already admitted that seeing is knowing, and that not-seeing is not-knowing: I leave you to draw the inference.

Theaet. Yes; the inference is the contradictory of my assertion. d

Soc. Yes, my marvel, and there might have been yet worse things in store for you, if an opponent had gone on to ask whether you can have a sharp and also a dull knowledge, and whether you can know near, but not at a distance, or know the same thing with more or less intensity, and so on without end. Such are the questions which might have been fired at you by a light-armed mercenary, who argued for pay. He would have lain in wait for you, and when you took up the position that sense and knowledge are the same, he would have made an assault upon hearing, smelling, and the other senses; he would have pressed the

e attack, until, in your envy and admiration of his wisdom, you were taken captive; and once he had got you into his net, you would not have escaped until you had come to an understanding about the sum to be paid for your release. Well, you ask, and how will Protagoras reinforce his position? Shall I answer for him?

Theaet. By all means.

Soc. He will repeat all those things which we have been urging

166 on his behalf, and then he will close with us in disdain, and say :— The worthy Socrates asks a little boy, whether the same man could at once remember and not know the same thing; and when the boy, because he is frightened and unable to see what is coming, says No, he thinks, it appears, that he has held me up to ridicule. The truth is, O slatternly Socrates, that when you ask questions about any assertion of mine, and the person asked is found tripping, if he has answered as I should have answered,

b then I am refuted, but if he answers something else, then he is refuted and not I. For firstly do you really suppose that any one would admit the memory which a man has of an impression which has passed away to be similar to that which he experienced at the time? Assuredly not. Or would he hesitate to acknowledge that the same man may know and not know the same thing? Or, if he is afraid of making this admission, would he ever grant that one who is becoming unlike is the same as before he became unlike? Or rather would he admit that a man is one at all, and not many and infinite as the changes which take place in him? But must we speak by the card in order to guard

c against precise criticism of each other's words? No, my good sir, he will say, examine my view itself in a more generous spirit; and either show, if you can, that our sensations are not private to each individual, or, if you admit them to be so, prove that this does not involve the consequence that the appearance becomes, or, if you will have the word, *is*, to the individual only. As to your talk about pigs and baboons, you are yourself behaving like a pig, and you teach your hearers to make sport of my writings

d in the same ignorant manner; but this is not to your credit. For I declare that the truth is as I have written,—that while each of us is a measure of existence and of non-existence,[1] one man may be a thousand times better than another from the very fact that different things are and appear to him. And I am far from saying that wisdom and the wise man have no existence; but my definition of a wise man is, precisely, one who can take any of us to whom evil appears, and is, and by changing him make good appear and be to him instead. And once again I would beg you not to press my words in the letter, but to take the meaning of them as I will explain them. Remember what has been already said,— that to the sick man his food appears to be and is bitter, and to the man in health it is and appears the opposite. Now I cannot conceive that one of these men can be or ought to be made wiser than the other: nor can you call the sick man foolish because he has one impression, and say that the healthy man because he has another is wise. But it can be said that the one state requires to be changed into the other, the worse into the better. So also in education, an improvement has to be effected, and the sophist accomplishes by words the change which the physician works by the aid of drugs. Not that any one ever made another think truly, who previously thought falsely. For no one can think what is not, or think anything different from that which he feels; present feeling is always true. But when men of inferior mind have thoughts of a kindred nature, I conceive that a good mind has often caused them to have good thoughts; and these appearances which the inexperienced call true, I maintain to be only better, and not truer than others. And, O my dear Socrates, I do not call wise men tadpoles: far from it; I call them 'physicians' and 'husbandmen' where the human body and plants are concerned—for the husbandmen also take away the evil sensations of sickly plants, and infuse into them good and healthy sensations;[2] and the wise and good rhetoricians make the good instead of the evil to seem just to states; for whatever appears to each state to be just and fair, so long as it is regarded as such, is just and fair to it; and what the wise man does is to cause good to appear, and be real, for each of them instead of evil. And in like manner the sophist who is able to train his pupils in this spirit is a wise man, and deserves to be well paid by them. And so I say both that some men are wiser than others, and that no one thinks falsely,

e

167

b

c

d

---

[1] [See note on p. 246.]   [2] [Omitting τε καὶ ἀληθεῖς.]

and you, whether you will or not, must endure to be a measure.
On these foundations the argument stands firm, which you,
Socrates, may, if you please, overthrow by an argument proceeding from an opposite principle, or if you like you may put questions to me—a method to which no intelligent person will object,
e quite the reverse. But I must beg you to put fair questions: for
there is great inconsistency in saying that you have a zeal for
virtue, and yet giving a constant exhibition of injustice in argument. Injustice it is when one does not converse differently in
disputation and in serious discussion: the disputer may trip up his
opponent as often as he likes, and make fun; but the dialectician
will be in earnest, and only correct his interlocutor when necessary, telling him the errors into which he has fallen through his
own fault, or that of the company which he has previously kept.
168 If you do so, your companion will lay the blame of his own confusion and perplexity on himself, and not on you. He will follow
and love you, and will hate himself, and escape from himself into
philosophy, in order that he may become different and be quit
of his former self. But the other mode of arguing, which is practised by the many, will have just the opposite effect upon him;
b and as he grows older, instead of turning philosopher, he will
come to hate philosophy. I would recommend you, therefore, as
I said before, not to encourage yourself in this polemical and
controversial temper, but to find out, in a friendly and congenial
spirit, what we really mean when we say that all things are in
motion, and that to every individual and state what appears, is.
In this manner you will consider whether knowledge and sensation are the same or different, but you will not argue, as you were
c just now doing, from the customary use of names and words,
which the vulgar pervert in all sorts of ways, causing infinite
perplexity to one another. Such, Theodorus, is the very slight
help which I am able to offer to your old friend;[1] had he been
living, he would have helped himself in a far more gloriose style.

　　Theod. You are jesting, Socrates; indeed, your defence of him
has been most valorous.

　　Soc. Thank you, friend; and I hope that you observed Protagoras bidding us be serious, as the text, 'Man is the measure of all
things', was a solemn one; and he reproached us with making a

　　　　　　[1] Reading προσήρκεσα.

boy the medium of discourse, and said that the boy's timidity was d made to tell against his argument; he also declared that we made a joke of him.

Theod. How could I fail to observe all that, Socrates?

Soc. Well, and shall we do as he says?

Theod. By all means.

Soc. But if his wishes are to be regarded, you and I must take up the argument, and in all seriousness, and ask and answer one e another, for you see that the rest of us are nothing but boys. In no other way can we escape the imputation, that in our analysis of his thesis we are making fun with boys.

Theod. Well, but is not Theaetetus better able to follow a philosophical inquiry than a great many men who have long beards?

Soc. Yes, Theodorus, but not better than you; and therefore please not to imagine that I am to defend by every means in my power your departed friend, and you not at all. At any rate, my 169 good man, do not sheer off until we know whether you should be preferred as the measure of diagrams, or whether all men are judges equal to you, and sufficient for themselves, in astronomy and geometry, and the other branches of knowledge in which you are supposed to excel them.

Theod. He who is sitting by you, Socrates, will not easily avoid being drawn into an argument; and when I said just now that you would excuse me, and not, like the Lacedaemonians, compel me to strip and fight, I was talking nonsense—I should rather compare you to Sciron [who threw travellers from the rocks]; for b the Lacedaemonian rule is 'strip or depart', but you seem to go about your work more after the fashion of Antaeus: you will not allow any one who approaches you to depart until you have stripped him, and he has been compelled to try a fall with you in argument.

Soc. There, Theodorus, you have hit off precisely the nature of my complaint; but I am even more pugnacious than the giants of old, for I have met with no end of heroes; many a Heracles, many a Theseus, mighty in words, has broken my head; nevertheless I am always at this rough exercise, which inspires me like c a passion. Please, then, to try a fall with me, whereby you will do yourself good as well as me.

Theod. I consent; lead me whither you will, for I know that you are like destiny; no man can escape from any argument which you may weave for him. But I am not disposed to submit to your scrutiny farther than you suggest.

Soc. That will be enough; and now take particular care that d we do not again unwittingly expose ourselves to the reproach of talking childishly.

Theod. I will do my best to avoid that error.

Soc. In the first place, let us return to our old objection, and see whether we were right in blaming and taking offence at the argument on the ground that it made every man self-sufficient in wisdom; upon which Protagoras admitted that there was a better and worse, and that in respect of this, some who as he said were the wise excelled others.

Theod. Very true.

Soc. Had Protagoras been living and answered for himself, e instead of our answering for him, there would have been no need of our reviewing or reinforcing the argument. But as he is not here, and some one may accuse us of speaking without authority on his behalf, had we not better come to a clearer agreement about his meaning, for a great deal may be at stake?

Theod. True.

170 *Soc.* Then let us obtain, not through any third person, but from his own statement and in the fewest words possible, the basis of agreement.

Theod. In what way?

Soc. In this way:—His words are, 'What seems to a man, is to him.'

Theod. Yes, so he says.

Soc. And are not we, Protagoras, uttering the opinion of man, or rather of all mankind, when we say that every one thinks himself wiser than other men in some things, and their inferior in others? In the hour of danger, when they are in perils of war, or b of the sea, or of sickness, do they not look up to those in authority as if they were gods, and expect salvation from them, only because they excel them in knowledge? Is not the world full of men who are looking for master-craftsmen and teachers and rulers of men and of the animals? and of others who think that they are able to teach and able to rule? Now, in all this is implied that ignorance and wisdom exist among them, at least in their own opinion.

Theod. Certainly.

Soc. And wisdom is assumed by them to be true thought, and ignorance to be false opinion.

Theod. Exactly.   c

Soc. How then, Protagoras, would you have us treat the argument? Shall we say that the opinions of men are always true, or sometimes true and sometimes false? In either case, the result is the same, and their opinions are not always true, but sometimes true and sometimes false. For tell me, Theodorus, do you suppose that you yourself, or any other follower of Protagoras, would contend that no one deems another ignorant or mistaken in his opinion?

Theod. The thing is incredible, Socrates.

Soc. And yet that absurdity is necessarily involved in the thesis d which declares man to be the measure of all things.

Theod. How so?

Soc. Why, suppose that you determine in your own mind something to be true, and declare your opinion to me; let us assume, as he argues, that this is true to you. Now, if so, you must either say that the rest of us cannot be judges of this judgement of yours, or that we judge you always to have a true opinion. But are there not thousands upon thousands who, whenever you form a judgement, take up arms against you and are of an opposite judgement and opinion, deeming that you judge falsely?

Theod. Yes, indeed, Socrates, thousands and tens of thousands, e as Homer says, who give me a world of trouble.

Soc. Well, but are we to assert that what you think is true to you and false to the ten thousand others?

Theod. No other inference seems to be possible.

Soc. And how about Protagoras himself? If neither he nor the multitude thought, as indeed they do not think, that man is the measure of all things, must it not follow that the Truth of which 171 Protagoras wrote would be true to no one? But if he himself thought this, while the multitude does not agree with him, you must begin by allowing that in whatever proportion the many are more than one, in that proportion his truth is more untrue than true.

Theod. That would follow if the truth is supposed to vary with individual opinion.

Soc. Moreover, the best of the joke is, that he acknowledges the truth of their opinion who believe his own opinion to be false; for he admits that the opinions of all men are true.

Theod. Certainly.

b *Soc.* He should, then, allow that his own opinion is false, if he admits that the opinion of those who think him false is true?

Theod. Of course.

Soc. Whereas the other side do not admit that they speak falsely?

Theod. They do not.

Soc. And he, as may be inferred from his writings, agrees that this opinion is also true.

Theod. So it seems.

Soc. Then all mankind, beginning with Protagoras, will contend (or rather, I should say that he will *allow*, when he concedes
c that his adversary has a true opinion), Protagoras, I say, will himself allow that neither a dog nor any ordinary man is the measure of anything which he has not learned—am I not right?

Theod. Yes.

Soc. And the Truth of Protagoras being doubted by all, will be true neither to himself nor to any one else?

Theod. I think, Socrates, that we are running my old friend too hard.

Soc. But I do not know that we are going beyond the truth.
d Doubtless, as he is older, he may be expected to be wiser than we are. And if he could only just get his head out of the world below, he would have overthrown both of us again and again, me for talking nonsense and you for assenting to me, and have been off and underground in a trice. But as he is not within call, we must make the best use of our own faculties, such as they are, and speak out what appears to us to be true. And one thing which no one will deny is, that there are great differences in the understandings of men.

Theod. In that opinion I quite agree.

Soc. And is there not most likely to be firm ground in the dis-
e tinction which we were indicating on behalf of Protagoras, viz. that most sensations, such as hot, dry, sweet, and all others of that class, are only such as they appear; if, however, superiority of opinion is to be allowed at all, surely we must allow it in

respect of health or disease? for every woman, child, or living creature has not such a knowledge of what conduces to health as to enable them to cure themselves.

Theod. I quite agree.

Soc. Or again, in politics, while affirming that just and unjust, honourable and disgraceful, holy and unholy, are in reality to each state such as the state thinks and makes lawful, and that in determining these matters no individual or state is wiser than another, still the followers of Protagoras will not deny that in determining what is or is not *expedient* for the community one state is wiser and one counsellor better than another—they will scarcely venture to maintain, that what a city enacts in the belief that it is expedient will always be really expedient. But in the other case, I mean when they speak of justice and injustice, piety and impiety, they are confident that in nature these have no existence or essence of their own—the truth is that which is agreed on at the time of the agreement, and as long as the agreement lasts; and this is the philosophy of many who do not altogether go along with Protagoras. Here arises a new question, Theodorus, which threatens to be more serious than the last.

Theod. Well, Socrates, we have plenty of leisure.

Soc. That is true, and your remark recalls to my mind an observation which I have often made, that it is not surprising that those who have spent a long time upon any kind of philosophy are ridiculously at fault when they have to appear and speak in court.

Theod. What do you mean?

Soc. I mean to say, that those who have been trained in philosophy and liberal pursuits are as unlike those who from their youth upwards have been knocking about in the courts and such places, as a freeman is in breeding unlike a slave.

Theod. In what is the difference seen?

Soc. In the leisure spoken of by you, which a freeman can always command: he has his talk out in peace, and, like ourselves, he wanders at will from one subject to another, and from a second to a third,—if the fancy takes him, he begins again, as we are doing now, caring not whether his words are many or few; his only aim is to attain the truth. But the lawyer can never speak at leisure; there is the water of the clepsydra driving him e on, and not allowing him to expatiate at will: and there is his adversary standing over him, and frequently glancing at an outline of points from which he is not allowed to deviate. He is a servant, and is continually disputing about a fellow servant before his master, who is seated, and has the cause in his hands; the trial is never about some indifferent matter, but always concerns himself; and often the race is for his life. The

173 consequence has been, that he has become keen and shrewd; he has learned how to flatter his master in word and indulge him in deed; but his soul is small and unrighteous. His condition, which has been that of a slave from his youth upwards, has deprived him of growth and uprightness and independence; dangers and fears, which were too much for his truth and honesty, came upon him in early years, when the tenderness of youth was unequal to them, and he has been driven into crooked ways; from the first he has practised deception and retaliation, and has become

b stunted and warped. And so he has passed out of youth into manhood, having no soundness in him; and is now, as he thinks, a master in wisdom. Such are these men, Theodorus. Will you have the companion picture of the philosopher, who is of our brotherhood; or shall we return to the argument? Do not let us abuse the freedom of digression which we claim.

Theod. Nay, Socrates, not until we have finished what we are

c about; for you truly said that we belong to a brotherhood which is free, and are not the servants of the argument; but the argument is our servant, and must wait our leisure. Who is our judge? Or where is the spectator having any right to censure or control us, as he might the poets?

Soc. Then, as this is your wish, I will describe the leaders; for there is no use in talking about those who pursue philosophy in a meaner spirit. In the first place, our leaders have never, from

d their youth upwards, known their way to the Agora, or the dicastery, or the council, or any other political assembly; they neither see nor hear the laws or decrees, as they are called, of the state written or recited; the eagerness of political societies in the attainment of offices—clubs, and banquets, and revels in the company of flute-girls,—do not enter even into their dreams. Whether someone in the city is of good or base birth, what disgrace may have descended to any one from his ancestors, male or female, are matters of which the philosopher no more knows than he can tell, as they say, how many pints are contained in the ocean. Neither is he conscious of his ignorance. For he does not hold aloof in order that he may gain a reputation; but the truth e is, that the outer form of him only is in the city: his mind, regarding all these things with disdain as of slight or no worth, soars—to use the expression of Pindar—everywhere 'beneath the earth, and again beyond the sky', measuring the land, surveying the heavens, and exploring the whole nature of the world and of every thing in its entirety, but not condescending to 174 anything which is within reach.

Theod. What do you mean, Socrates?

Soc. I will illustrate my meaning, Theodorus, by the jest which the clever witty Thracian handmaid is said to have made about Thales, when he fell into a well as he was looking up at the stars. She said, that he was so eager to know what was going on in heaven, that he could not see what was before his feet. This is a jest which is equally applicable to all philosophers. For the b philosopher is wholly unacquainted with his next-door neighbour; he is ignorant, not only of what he is doing, but he hardly knows whether he is a man or an animal; he is searching into the essence of man, and busy in inquiring what it is proper to such a nature to do or suffer different from any other;—I think that you understand me, Theodorus?

Theod. I do, and what you say is true.

Soc. And thus, my friend, on every occasion, private as well as public, as I said at first, when he appears in a law-court, or in any c place in which he has to speak of things which are at his feet and before his eyes, he is the jest, not only of Thracian handmaids but of the general herd, tumbling into wells and every sort of disaster through his inexperience. His awkwardness is fearful, and gives the impression of imbecility. When he is reviled, he has nothing personal to say in answer to the civilities of his adversaries, for he knows no scandals of any one, and they do not interest him; and therefore he is laughed at for his sheepishness; and d when others are being praised or glorifying themselves, his un-affected laughter, which he makes no attempt to conceal, causes him to be considered a downright idiot. When he hears a tyrant or king eulogized, he fancies that he is listening to the praises of some keeper of cattle—a swineherd, or shepherd, or perhaps a cowherd, who is congratulated on the quantity of milk which he squeezes from them; and he remarks that the creature whom they tend, and out of whom they squeeze the wealth, is of a less tractable and more insidious nature. Then, again, he observes that the great man is of necessity as ill mannered and uneducated

e as any shepherd—for he has no leisure, and he is surrounded by a wall, which is his mountain-pen. Hearing of enormous landed proprietors of ten thousand acres and more, our philosopher deems this to be a trifle, because he has been accustomed to think of the whole earth; and when they sing the praises of family, and say that some one is a gentleman because he can show seven generations of wealthy ancestors, he thinks that their sentiments

175 only betray a dull and narrow vision in those who utter them, and who are not educated enough to look always at the whole, nor to consider that every man has had thousands and ten thousands of progenitors, and among them have been rich and poor, kings and slaves, Hellenes and barbarians, innumerable. And when people pride themselves on having a pedigree of twenty-five ancestors, which goes back to Heracles, the son of Amphitryon, he cannot understand their poverty of ideas. Why

b are they unable to calculate that Amphitryon had a twenty-fifth ancestor, who might have been anybody, and was such as fortune made him, and he had a fiftieth, and so on? He amuses himself with the notion that they cannot count, and thinks that a little arithmetic would have got rid of their senseless vanity. Now, in all these cases our philosopher is derided by the vulgar, partly because he is thought to despise them, and also because he is ignorant of what is before him, and always at a loss.

Theod. That is very true, Socrates.

Soc. But, O my friend, when he draws the other into upper air,

c and gets him out of his pleas and rejoinders into the contemplation of justice and injustice in their own nature and in their difference from one another and from all other things; or from the commonplaces about the happiness of a king or of a rich man to the consideration of government, and of human happiness and misery in general—what they are, and how a man is to attain the

d one and avoid the other—when that narrow, keen, little legal mind is called to account about all this, he gives the philosopher his revenge; for dizzied by the height at which he is hanging, whence he looks down into space, which is a strange experience to him, he being dismayed, and lost, and stammering broken words, is laughed at, not by Thracian handmaidens or any other uneducated persons, for they have no eye for the situation, but by every man who has not been brought up a slave. Such are the two characters, Theodorus: the one of the freeman, who has been e trained in liberty and leisure, whom you call the philosopher,— him we cannot blame because he appears simple and of no account when he has to perform some menial task, such as packing up bed-clothes, or flavouring a sauce or fawning speech; the other character is that of the man who is able to do all this kind of service smartly and neatly, but knows not how to wear 176 his cloak like a gentleman; still less with the music of discourse can he rightly hymn that life which is lived by immortals or men blessed of heaven.

Theod. If you could only persuade everybody, Socrates, as you do me, of the truth of your words, there would be more peace and fewer evils among men.

Soc. Evils, Theodorus, can never pass away; for there must always remain something which is antagonistic to good. Having no place among the gods in heaven, of necessity they hover around the mortal nature, and this earthly sphere. Wherefore we ought to fly away from earth to heaven as quickly as we can; and b to fly away means to become like God, as far as this is possible; and to become like him, means to become holy, just, and wise. But, O my friend, you cannot easily convince mankind that they should pursue virtue or avoid vice, not merely in order that a man may seem to be good, which is the reason given by the world, and in my judgement is only a repetition of an old wives' fable. Whereas, the truth is that God is never in any way unrighteous— he is perfect righteousness; and he of us who is the most righteous c is of all things most like him. Herein is seen the true cleverness of a man, and also his nothingness and want of manhood. For to know this is true wisdom and virtue, and ignorance of this is manifest folly and vice. All other kinds of what might seem wisdom or cleverness, such as the wisdom of politicians, or the wisdom of the arts, are coarse and vulgar. The unrighteous man, or the d sayer and doer of unholy things, had far better not be encouraged in the illusion that his roguery is clever; for men glory in their shame—they fancy that they hear others saying of them, 'These are not mere good-for-nothing persons, mere burdens of the earth, but such as men should be who mean to dwell safely in a state.' Let us tell them that they are all the more truly what they do not think they are because they do not know it; for they do not know the penalty of injustice, which above all things they ought to know—not stripes and death, as they suppose, which evil-doers

e often escape, but a penalty which cannot be escaped.

Theod. What is that?

Soc. There are two patterns eternally set before them; the one divine and most happy, the other godless and most wretched: but they do not see them, or perceive that in their utter folly and infatuation they are growing like the one and unlike the other, by

177 reason of their evil deeds; and the penalty is, that they lead a life answering to the pattern which they are growing like. And if we tell them, that unless they depart from their cunning, the place of innocence will not receive them after death; and that here on earth, they will live ever in the likeness of their own evil selves, and with evil friends—when they hear this they in their superior cunning will seem to be listening to the talk of idiots.

Theod. Very true, Socrates.

b *Soc.* Too true, my friend, as I well know; there is, however, one peculiarity in their case: when they begin to reason in private about their dislike of philosophy, if they have the courage to hear the argument out, and do not run away, they grow at last strangely discontented with themselves; their rhetoric fades away, and they become helpless as children. These however are digressions from which we must now desist, or they will overflow, and

c drown the original argument; to which, if you please, we will now return.

Theod. For my part, Socrates, I would rather have the digressions, for at my age I find them easier to follow; but if you wish, let us go back to the argument.

Soc. Had we not reached the point at which the partisans of the perpetual flux, who say that things are as they seem to each one, were confidently maintaining that, as elsewhere, so in the special instance of justice, the ordinances which the state commanded and thought just, were just to the state which imposed

them, while they were in force; but as to the good, no one had
any longer the hardihood to contend of any ordinances which the
state enacted because it thought them beneficial to itself, that d
these, while they were in force, were really beneficial;—he who
said so would be playing with the name 'good', and would
not touch the real question—it would be a mockery, would
it not?

Theod. Certainly it would.

Soc. He ought not to speak of the name, but contemplate the e
thing for which it stands.

Theod. Right.

Soc. Whatever be the term used, the good or expedient is the
aim of legislation, and as far as it can have an opinion, the state
imposes all laws with a view to the greatest expediency; can
legislation have any other aim?

Theod. Certainly not. 178

Soc. But is the aim attained always? do not mistakes often
happen?

Theod. Yes, I think that there are mistakes.

Soc. The possibility of error will be more distinctly recognized,
if we put the question in reference to the whole class under which
the expedient falls. That whole class has to do with the future,
and laws are passed under the idea that they will be useful in
after-time; which, in other words, is the future.

Theod. Very true. b

Soc. Suppose now, that we ask Protagoras, or one of his
disciples, a question:—O, Protagoras, we will say to him, Man
is, as you declare, the measure of all things—white, heavy, light,
and the whole class of such things; for he has the criterion of
them in himself, and when he thinks that things are such as he
experiences them to be, he thinks what is and is true to himself.
Is it not so?

Theod. Yes.

Soc. What now of future events, Protagoras? we shall say.
Has each man the criterion of these also within himself, so that c
they *will be* for him as he supposes that they will be? For example,
take the case of heat:—When an ordinary man thinks that he is
going to have a fever, and that this kind of heat is coming on, and
another person, who is a physician, thinks the contrary, whose

opinion about the future is likely to prove right? Or are they both right?—he will have both heat and fever in his own judgement, and neither in the physician's judgement?

Theod. That would be ridiculous.

Soc. And the vinegrower, if I am not mistaken, is a better judge
d of the sweetness or dryness of the vintage which is not yet gathered than the harp-player?

Theod. Certainly.

Soc. And in musical composition the musician will know better than the training master what the training master himself will hereafter think harmonious or the reverse?

Theod. Of course.

Soc. And the cook will be a better judge than the guest, who is not a cook, of the pleasure to be derived from the dinner which
e is in preparation; for of present or past pleasure we are not as yet arguing; the question is whether everyone is to himself the best judge of that which will seem to be and will be to him in the future?—nay, would not you, Protagoras, better guess which arguments in a court would convince any one of us than the ordinary man?

Theod. Certainly, Socrates, he used to profess in the strongest manner that he was the superior of all men in this respect.

179　*Soc.* To be sure, friend: who would have paid a large sum for the privilege of talking to him, if he had really[1] persuaded his visitors that neither a prophet nor any other man was better able to judge what will be and seem to be in the future than everyone could for himself?

Theod. Who indeed?

Soc. But now legislation and expediency are all concerned with the future; and everyone will admit that states, in passing laws, must often fail of their highest interests?

Theod. Quite true.

Soc. Then we may fairly argue against your master, that he
b must admit one man to be wiser than another, and that the wiser is a measure: but I, who know nothing, am not at all obliged to accept the honour which the advocate of Protagoras was just

---

[1] [Reading δή, with Campbell. Or, retaining μή and omitting αὐτῷ below: 'if he had *not* persuaded his visitors that no other man was better able to judge the future than he' (Protagoras).]

now forcing upon me, whether I would or not, of being a measure of anything.

Theod. That is the best refutation of him, Socrates; although he is also caught when he ascribes truth to the opinions of others, who give the lie direct to his own opinion.

Soc. There are many ways, Theodorus, in which the doctrine c that every opinion of every man is true may be refuted; but there is more difficulty in proving that states of feeling, which are present to a man, and out of which arise sensations and opinions in accordance with them, are sometimes not true. And very likely I have been talking nonsense about them; for they may be un-assailable, and those who say that there is clear evidence of them, and that they are matters of knowledge, may probably be right; in which case our friend Theaetetus was not so far from the mark when he identified perception and knowledge. And therefore let d us draw nearer, as the advocate of Protagoras desires, and give the truth of the universal flux a ring: is the theory sound or not? at any rate, no small war is raging about it, and there are combatants not a few.

Theod. No small war, indeed, for in Ionia the sect makes rapid strides; the disciples of Heracleitus are most energetic upholders of the doctrine.

Soc. Then we are the more bound, my dear Theodorus, to examine the question from the foundation as it is set forth by e themselves.

Theod. Certainly we are. About these speculations of Hera-cleitus, which, as you say, are as old as Homer, or even older still,[1] the Ephesians themselves, who profess to know them, are downright mad, and you cannot talk with them on the subject. For, in accordance with their text-books, they are always in motion; but as for dwelling upon an argument or a question, and quietly asking and answering in turn, they can no more do so than 180 they can fly; or rather, the determination of these fellows not to have a particle of rest in them is more than the utmost powers of negation can express. If you ask any of them a question, he will produce, as from a quiver, sayings brief and dark, and shoot them at you; and if you inquire the reason of what he has said, you will be hit by some other new-fangled word, and will make no

[1] [Cf. 152 e above and *Crat.* 402 b.]

way with any of them, nor they with one another; their great care is, not to allow of any settled principle either in their arguments or in their minds, conceiving, as I imagine, that any such b principle would be stationary; for they are at war with the stationary, and do what they can to drive it out everywhere.

Soc. I suppose, Theodorus, that you have only seen them when they were fighting, and have never stayed with them in time of peace, for they are no friends of yours; and their peace doctrines are only communicated by them at leisure, as I imagine, to those disciples of theirs whom they want to make like themselves.

Theod. Disciples! my good sir, they have none; men of their c sort are not one another's disciples, but they grow up at their own sweet will, and get their inspiration anywhere, each of them saying of his neighbour that he knows nothing. From these men, then, as I was going to remark, you will never get a reason, whether with their will or without their will; we must take the question out of their hands, and make the analysis ourselves, as if we were doing a geometrical problem.

Soc. Quite right too; but as touching the aforesaid problem, have we not heard from the ancients, who concealed their d wisdom from the many in poetical figures, that Oceanus and Tethys, the origin of all things, are streams, and that nothing is at rest? And now the moderns, in their superior wisdom, have declared the same openly, that the cobbler too may hear and learn of them, and no longer foolishly imagine that some things are at rest and others in motion—having learned that all is motion, he will duly honour his teachers. But I had almost forgotten the opposite doctrine, Theodorus,

e   Alone Being remains unmoved, which is the name for the all.[1]

This is the language of Parmenides, Melissus, and their followers, who stoutly maintain that all being is one and self-contained, and has no place in which to move. What shall we do, friend, with all these people; for, advancing step by step, we have imperceptibly 181 got between the combatants, and, unless we can protect our retreat, we shall pay the penalty of our rashness—like the players in the palaestra who are caught upon the line, and are dragged different ways by the two parties. Therefore I think that we had

---

[1] [Text doubtful. See Cornford, *P.T.K.*, p. 94, n. 1.]

better begin by considering those whom we first accosted, 'the river-gods', and, if we find any truth in them, we will help them to pull us over, and try to get away from the others. But if the partisans of 'the whole' appear to speak more truly, we will fly off from the party which would move the immovable, to them. And if we find that neither of them have anything reasonable to b say, we shall be in a ridiculous position, having so great a conceit of our own poor opinion and rejecting that of ancient and famous men. O Theodorus, do you think that there is any use in proceeding when the danger is so great?

Theod. Nay, Socrates, not to examine thoroughly what the two parties have to say would be quite intolerable.

Soc. Then examine we must, since you, who were so reluctant to begin, are so eager to proceed. The nature of motion appears to be the question with which we begin. What do they mean c when they say that all things are in motion? That is to say, do they assert that there is only one kind of motion, or, as I think, two? I should like to have your opinion upon this point in addition to my own, that I may err, if I must err, in your company; tell me, then, when a thing changes from one place to another, or goes round in the same place, is not that what is called motion?

Theod. Yes.

Soc. Here then we have one kind of motion. But when a thing, remaining on the same spot, grows old, or becomes black from being white, or hard from being soft, or undergoes any other d change, may not this be properly called motion of another kind?

Theod. I think it must be so called.

Soc. Of motion then there are these two kinds, 'change', and 'motion in place'.

Theod. You are right.

Soc. And now, having made this distinction, let us address ourselves to those who say that all is motion, and ask them whether all things according to them have the two kinds of motion, and are changed as well as move in place, or is one thing moved in e both ways, and another in one only?

Theod. Indeed, I do not know what to answer; but I think they would say that all things are moved in both ways.

Soc. Yes, comrade; for, if not, they would have to say that the same things are in motion and at rest, and there would be no more truth in saying that all things are in motion, than that all things are at rest.

Theod. To be sure.

Soc. And if they are to be in motion, and nothing is to be devoid of motion, all things must always have every sort of motion?

Theod. Most true.

Soc. Consider a further point: did we not understand them to explain the generation of heat, whiteness, or anything else, in some such manner as the following:—were they not saying that each of these is a movement which takes place at the time of perception between an agent and a patient, whereby the patient ceases to be a perceiving power and becomes[1] a percipient, and the agent a quale instead of a quality? I suspect that quality may appear a strange and uncouth term to you, and that you do not understand the general expression. Then I will take particular instances: I mean to say that the producing power or agent becomes neither heat nor whiteness, but hot and white, and the like of other things. For I must repeat what I said before, that neither this agent and patient, nor anything else in the world, can exist in isolation, but when they come together and generate sensations and their objects, the one becomes a thing of a certain quality, and the other a percipient. You remember?

Theod. Of course.

Soc. We may leave the details of their theory unexamined, but we must not forget to ask them the only question with which we are concerned: Are all things in motion and flux?

Theod. Yes, they will reply.

Soc. And they are moved in both those ways which we distinguished; that is to say, they move in place and are also changed?

Theod. Of course, if the motion is to be perfect.

Soc. If they only moved in place and were not changed, we should be able to say what is the nature of the things which are in motion and flux?

Theod. Exactly.

Soc. But now, since not even white continues to flow white, and whiteness itself is a flux or change which is passing into

---

[1] [Retaining the ἔτι bracketed in the Oxford text.]

another colour, and is never to be caught standing still, can the name of any colour be rightly used at all?

Theod. How is that possible, Socrates, either in the case of this or of any other quality—if while we are using the word the object is escaping in the flux?

Soc. And what would you say of perceptions, such as sight and hearing, or any other kind of perception? Is there any stopping in the act of seeing and hearing?

Theod. Certainly not, if all things are in motion.

Soc. Then we must not speak of seeing any more than of not-seeing, nor of any other perception more than of any non-perception, if all things partake of every kind of motion?

Theod. Certainly not.

Soc. Yet perception is knowledge: so at least Theaetetus and I were saying.

Theod. Very true.

Soc. Then when we were asked what is knowledge, we no more answered what is knowledge than what is not knowledge?

Theod. I suppose not.

Soc. Here, then, is a fine result: we corrected our first answer 183 in our eagerness to prove that nothing is at rest and so save that answer. But now it is clear that if nothing is at rest, every answer upon whatever subject is equally right: you may say that a thing is or is not thus; or, if you prefer, 'becomes' thus; and if we say 'becomes', we shall not then hamper them with words expressive of rest.

Theod. Quite true.

Soc. Yes, Theodorus, except in saying 'thus' and 'not thus'. But you ought not to use the word 'thus', for there is no motion in 'thus' or in 'not thus'. The maintainers of the doctrine have as b yet no words in which to express themselves, and must get a new language. I might suggest to them the phrase 'no how', which being perfectly indefinite might suit them best.[1]

Theod. Yes, that is a manner of speaking in which they will be quite at home.

Soc. And so, Theodorus, we have done with your friend without assenting to his doctrine, that every man is the measure

---

[1] [Reading οὐδ' ὅπως in b 4, and retaining δ' οὕτως in the next line.]

c of all things—a wise man only is a measure; neither can we allow that knowledge is perception, at least on the hypothesis of a perpetual flux; but perhaps our friend Theaetetus intends it in some other sense.

Theod. Very good, Socrates; and now that the argument about the doctrine of Protagoras has been completed, I am discharged from answering; for this was the agreement.

Theaet. Not, Theodorus, until you and Socrates have discussed
d the doctrine of those who say that all things are at rest, as you were proposing.

Theod. You, Theaetetus, who are a young rogue, must not instigate your elders to a breach of faith, but should prepare to answer Socrates in the remainder of the argument.

Theaet. Yes, if he wishes; but I would rather have heard about the doctrine of rest.

Theod. Invite Socrates to an argument—invite horsemen to the open plain; do but ask him, and he will answer.

Soc. Nevertheless, Theodorus, I am afraid that I shall not be
e able to comply with the request of Theaetetus.

Theod. Not comply! for what reason?

Soc. My reason is that I have a kind of reverence; not so much for Melissus and the others, who say that 'All is one and at rest', as for the great leader himself, Parmenides, venerable and awful, as in Homeric language he may be called;—him I should be ashamed to approach in a spirit unworthy of him. I met him when he was an old man, and I was a mere youth, and he appeared to
184 me to have a glorious depth of mind. And I am afraid that we may not understand his words, and may be still farther from understanding his meaning; above all I fear that the nature of knowledge, which is the main subject of our discussion, may be thrust out of sight by the unbidden guests who will come pouring in upon our feast of discourse, if we let them in—besides, the question which is now stirring is of immense extent, and will be treated unfairly if only considered by the way; or if treated adequately and at length, will put into the shade the other question of knowledge. Neither the one nor the other can be allowed; but I must try by my art of midwifery to deliver
b Theaetetus of his conceptions about knowledge.

Theaet. Very well; do so if you will.

Soc. Then now, Theaetetus, take another view of the subject: you answered that knowledge is perception?

Theaet. I did.

Soc. And if any one were to ask you: With what does a man see black and white colours? and with what does he hear high and low sounds?—you would say, if I am not mistaken, 'With the eyes and with the ears.'

Theaet. I should.

Soc. The free use of words and phrases, rather than minute c precision, is generally characteristic of a liberal education, and the opposite is pedantic; but sometimes precision is necessary, and I believe that the answer which you have just given is open to the charge of incorrectness; for which is more correct, to say that we see or hear with the eyes and with the ears, or through the eyes and through the ears.

Theaet. I should say 'through', Socrates, rather than 'with'.

Soc. Yes, my boy, for no one can suppose that in each of us, as d in a sort of Trojan horse, there are perched a number of unconnected senses, which do not all meet in some one nature, the soul or whatever we please to call it, of which they are the instruments, and with which through them we perceive objects of sense.

Theaet. I agree with you in that opinion.

Soc. The reason why I am thus precise is, because I want to know whether, when we perceive black and white through the e eyes, and again, other qualities through other organs, we do not perceive them with one and the same part of ourselves; and whether, if you were asked, you could refer all such perceptions to the body. Perhaps, however, I had better allow you to answer for yourself and not interfere. Tell me, then, are not the organs through which you perceive warm and hard and light and sweet, organs of the body?

Theaet. Of the body, certainly.

Soc. And you would admit that what you perceive through 185 one faculty you cannot perceive through another; the objects of hearing, for example, cannot be perceived through sight, or the objects of sight through hearing?

Theaet. Of course not.

Soc. If you have any thought about both of them, this common perception cannot come to you, either through the one or the other organ?

Theaet. It cannot.

Soc. How about sounds and colours: in the first place you may reflect that they both *exist*?

Theaet. Yes.

Soc. And that either of them is different from the other, and the same with itself?

b   *Theaet.* Certainly.

Soc. And that both are two and each of them one?

Theaet. Yes.

Soc. You can further observe whether they are like or unlike one another?

Theaet. I dare say.

Soc. But through what do you perceive all this about them? for neither through hearing nor yet through seeing can you apprehend that which they have in common. Let me give you an illustration of the point at issue:—If there were any meaning in asking whether sounds and colours are saline or not, you would

c be able to tell me what faculty would consider the question. It would not be sight or hearing, but some other.

Theaet. Certainly; the faculty of taste.

Soc. Very good; and now tell me what is the power which discerns, not only in sensible objects, but in all things, universal properties, such as those which are called being and not-being, and those others about which we were just asking—what organs will you assign for the perception of these by the appropriate power in us?

Theaet. You are thinking of being and not-being, likeness and unlikeness, sameness and difference, and also of unity and any other number which occurs in our judgement of objects. And

d evidently your question applies to odd and even numbers and other arithmetical conceptions—through what bodily organ the soul perceives them.

Soc. You follow me excellently, Theaetetus; that is precisely what I am asking.

Theaet. Indeed, Socrates, I cannot answer; my only notion is, that these, unlike objects of sense, have no separate organ, but

e that the mind, by a power of her own, contemplates such common properties in all things.

Soc. You are a beauty, Theaetetus, and not ugly, as Theodorus was saying; for he who utters the beautiful is himself beautiful and good. And besides being beautiful, you have done me a kindness in releasing me from a very long discussion, if you believe that the soul views some things by herself and others through the bodily organs. For that was my own opinion, and I wanted you to agree with me.

Theaet. Indeed, I do believe it.

Soc. And to which class would you refer being or essence; for 186 this, of all our notions, is the most universal?

Theaet. I should say, to that class which the soul aspires to know of herself.

Soc. And would you say this also of like and unlike, same and other?

Theaet. Yes.

Soc. And would you say the same of the noble and base, and of good and evil?

Theaet. These also I conceive to be among the chief instances of those relative terms whose nature the soul perceives by comparing in herself things past and present with the future. b

Soc. Hold! does she not perceive the hardness of that which is hard by the touch, and the softness of that which is soft equally by the touch?

Theaet. Yes.

Soc. But their *being,* I mean the fact that they are, and their opposition to one another, and the being (to repeat that term) of this opposition, the soul herself endeavours to decide for us by the review and comparison of them?

Theaet. Certainly.

Soc. The simple sensations which reach the soul through the body are given at birth to men and animals by nature, but their c reflections on the being and use of them are slowly and hardly gained, if they are ever gained, by education and long experience.

Theaet. Assuredly.

Soc. And can a man attain truth who fails of attaining being?

Theaet. Impossible.

Soc. And can he who misses the truth of anything, have a knowledge of that thing?

Theaet. He cannot. d

Soc. Then knowledge does not consist in impressions of sense, but in reasoning about them; in that only, and not in the mere impression, truth and being can be attained?

Theaet. Apparently.

Soc. And would you call the two processes by the same name, when there is so great a difference between them?

Theaet. That would certainly not be right.

Soc. And what name would you give to seeing, hearing, smelling, being cold and being hot?

e   *Theaet.* I should call all of them perceiving—what other name could be given to them?

Soc. Perception would be the collective name of them?

Theaet. Certainly.

Soc. Which, as we say, has no part in the attainment of truth, since it does not attain to being?

Theaet. Certainly not.

Soc. And therefore not in knowledge?

Theaet. No.

Soc. Then perception, Theaetetus, can never be the same as knowledge?

Theaet. Apparently not, Socrates; and knowledge has now been most distinctly proved to be different from perception.

187   *Soc.* But the original aim of our discussion was to find out rather what knowledge is than what it is not; at the same time we have made some progress, for we no longer seek for knowledge in perception at all, but in that other process, however called, in which the mind is alone and engaged with being.

Theaet. And that, Socrates, if I am not mistaken, is called thinking or opining.

b   *Soc.* You conceive truly. And now, my friend, please to begin again at this point; and having wiped out of your memory all that has preceded, see if you have arrived at any clearer view, and once more say what is knowledge.

Theaet. I cannot say, Socrates, that all opinion is knowledge, because there may be a false opinion; but I will venture to assert, that knowledge is true opinion: let this then be my reply; and if this is hereafter disproved, we must try to find another.

Soc. That is the way in which you ought to answer, Theaetetus,
c   and not in your former hesitating strain, for if we are bold we shall

gain one of two advantages; either we shall find what we seek, or we shall be less likely to think that we know what we do not know—in either case we shall be richly rewarded. And now, what are you saying?—Are there two sorts of opinion, one true and the other false; and do you define knowledge to be the true?

Theaet. Yes, according to my present view.

Soc. Is it still worth our while to resume[1] the discussion touching opinion?

Theaet. To what are you alluding?

Soc. There is a point which troubles me, as it has often done d before; my discussion with myself or with others has left me in great perplexity about the nature or origin of the mental experience to which I refer.

Theaet. Pray what is it?

Soc. How a man can form a false opinion. But I am even now in doubt whether we ought to leave this question or examine it by another method than we used a short time ago.

Theaet. Begin again, Socrates,—at least if you think that there is the slightest necessity for doing so. Were not you and Theodorus just now remarking very truly, that in discussions of this kind we may take our own time?

Soc. You are quite right, and perhaps there will be no harm e in retracing our steps and beginning again.[2] Better a little which is well done, than a great deal imperfectly.

Theaet. Certainly.

Soc. Well, and what is the difficulty? Do we not speak of false opinion, and say that one man holds a false and another a true opinion, as though there were some natural distinction between them?

Theaet. We certainly say so.

Soc. And we can at least say that all things, and each thing 188 severally, are either known or not known. I leave out of view the intermediate conceptions of learning and forgetting, because they have nothing to do with our present question.

Theaet. There can be no doubt, Socrates, if you exclude these, that there is no other alternative but knowing or not knowing a thing.

---

[1] [Probably a reference back to 172 a, b.]
[2] [Or: 'in going back and following this new trail'.]

Soc. That point being now determined, must we not say that he who has an opinion, must either know or not know that to which his opinion refers?

Theaet. He must.

b   *Soc.* Moreover, he who knows, cannot not know, and he who does not know, cannot know, one and the same thing?

Theaet. Of course.

Soc. What shall we say then? When a man has a false opinion does he think that which he knows to be some other thing which he knows, and knowing both, is he at the same time ignorant of both?

Theaet. That, Socrates, is impossible.

Soc. But perhaps he thinks of something which he does not know as some other thing which he does not know; for example, he knows neither Theaetetus nor Socrates, and yet he fancies that Theaetetus is Socrates, or Socrates Theaetetus?

c   *Theaet.* How can he?

Soc. But surely he cannot suppose something which he *knows* to be a thing which he does not know, or what he does not know to be what he knows?

Theaet. That would be monstrous.

Soc. How, then, is false opinion formed? For if all things are either known or unknown, there can be no opinion which is not comprehended under this alternative; and within it we can find no scope for false opinion.

Theaet. Most true.

Soc. Suppose that we remove the question out of the sphere of
d knowing or not knowing, into that of being and not-being.

Theaet. What do you mean?

Soc. May we not suspect the simple truth to be that he who thinks on any subject that which *is not*, will necessarily think what is false, whatever in other respects may be the state of his mind?

Theaet. That, again, is not unlikely, Socrates.

Soc. Then suppose some one to say to us, Theaetetus:—Is it possible for any man to think, as you now say, that which *is not*, either as a self-existent substance or as a predicate of something else? And suppose that we answer, 'Yes, he can, when in think-
e ing he thinks what is not true.'—That will be our answer?

Theaet. Yes.

Soc. But is there any parallel to this?

Theaet. What do you mean?

Soc. Can a man see something and yet see nothing?

Theaet. Impossible.

Soc. But if he sees any one thing, he sees something that exists. Do you suppose that what is one is ever to be found among non-existing things?

Theaet. I do not.

Soc. He then who sees some one thing, sees something which is?

Theaet. Apparently.

Soc. And he who hears anything, hears some one thing,—a thing which *is*? 189

Theaet. Yes.

Soc. And he who touches anything, touches something which is one and therefore is?

Theaet. That again is true.

Soc. And does not he who thinks, think some one thing?

Theaet. Certainly.

Soc. And does not he who thinks some one thing, think something which is?

Theaet. I agree.

Soc. Then he who thinks of that which is not, thinks of nothing?

Theaet. Apparently not.

Soc. And he who thinks of nothing, does not think at all?

Theaet. That seems clear.

Soc. Then no one can think that which is not, either as a self-existent substance or as a predicate of something else? b

Theaet. Apparently not.

Soc. Then to think falsely is different from thinking that which is not?

Theaet. It would seem so.

Soc. Then false opinion has no existence in us, either in this way, or in that which we took a short time before.

Theaet. Certainly not.

Soc. But may not the following be the description of what we express by this name?

Theaet. What?

Soc. May we not suppose that false opinion or thought is a sort c of heterodoxy; a person may make an exchange in his mind, and say that one real object is another real object. For thus he always thinks that which is, but he puts one thing in place of another, and missing the aim of his thoughts, he may be truly said to have false opinion.

Theaet. Now you appear to me to have spoken the exact truth: when a man puts the base in the place of the noble, or the noble in the place of the base, then he has truly false opinion.

Soc. I see, Theaetetus, that your fear has disappeared, and that you are beginning to despise me.

Theaet. What makes you say so?

Soc. You think, if I am not mistaken, that your 'truly false' is
d safe from censure, and that I shall never ask whether there can be a swift which is slow, or a heavy which is light, or any other self-contradictory thing, which works, not according to its own nature, but according to that of its opposite. But I will not insist upon this, for I do not wish needlessly to discourage you. And so you are satisfied that false opinion is heterodoxy, or the thought of something else?

Theaet. I am.

Soc. It is possible then upon your view for the mind to conceive of one thing as another?

Theaet. True.

e *Soc.* But must not the mind, or thinking power, which misplaces them, have a conception either of both objects or of one of them?

Theaet. Certainly; either together or in succession.

Soc. Very good. And do you mean by conceiving, the same which I mean?

Theaet. What is that?

Soc. I mean the conversation which the soul holds with herself in considering of anything. I speak of what I scarcely under-
190 stand; but the soul when thinking appears to me to be just talking—asking questions of herself and answering them, affirming and denying. And when she has arrived at a decision, either gradually or by a sudden impulse, and has at last agreed, and does not doubt, this is called her opinion. I say, then, that to form an opinion is to speak, and opinion is a word spoken,—I mean, to oneself and in silence, not aloud or to another: What think you?

Theaet. I agree.

Soc. Then when any one thinks of one thing as another, he is saying to himself that one thing is another?

Theaet. Yes. b

Soc. But do you ever remember saying to yourself that the noble is certainly base, or the unjust just; or, in a word, have you ever attempted to convince yourself that one thing is another? Nay, not even in sleep, did you ever venture to say to yourself that odd is undoubtedly even, or anything of the kind?

Theaet. Never.

Soc. And do you suppose that any other man, either in his c senses or out of them, ever seriously tried to persuade himself that an ox is a horse, or that two are one?

Theaet. Certainly not.

Soc. But if thinking is talking to oneself, no one speaking and thinking of two objects, and apprehending them both in his soul, will say and think that the one is the other of them, and I must add, that you too had better let the word 'other' alone [i.e. not insist that 'one' and 'other' are the same[1]]. I mean to say, that no one thinks the noble to be base, or anything of the kind. d

Theaet. I will pass the word 'other', Socrates; and I agree to what you say.

Soc. If a man has both of them in his thoughts, he cannot think that the one of them is the other?

Theaet. So it seems.

Soc. Neither, if he has one of them only in his mind and not the other, will he ever think that one is the other?

Theaet. True; for we should have to suppose that he apprehends that which is not in his thoughts at all.

Soc. Then no one who has either both or only one of the two objects in his mind can think that the one is the other. And e therefore, he who maintains that false opinion is heterodoxy is talking nonsense; for neither in this, any more than in the two previous ways, can false opinion exist in us.

Theaet. No.

Soc. But if, Theaetetus, this experience is not shown to be real, we shall be driven into many absurdities.

---

[1] Both words in Greek are called ἕτερον: cf. *Parmen.* 147 c; *Euthyd.* 301 a [and Socrates asks for a concession because he permitted Theaetetus to say 'truly false'].

Theaet. What are they?

Soc. I will not tell you until I have endeavoured to consider the matter from every point of view. For I should be ashamed of us if we were driven in our perplexity to admit the absurd consequences of which I speak. But if we find the solution, and get away from them, we may regard them only as the difficulties of others, and the ridicule will not attach to us. On the other hand, if we utterly fail, I suppose that we must be humble, and allow the argument to trample us under foot, as the sea-sick passenger is trampled upon by the sailor, and to do anything to us. Listen, then, while I tell you how I hope to find a way out of our difficulty.

Theaet. Let me hear.

Soc. I think that we were wrong in denying that a man could think what he knew to be what he did not know; and that there is a way in which such a deception is possible.

Theaet. You mean to say, as I suspected at the time when we made that denial, that I may know Socrates, and at a distance see someone who is unknown to me, and suppose him to be Socrates whom I know—then the deception will occur?

Soc. But has not that position been relinquished by us, because involving the absurdity that we should know and not know the things which we know?

Theaet. True.

Soc. Let us make the assertion in another form, which may or may not have a favourable issue; but as we are in a great strait, every argument should be turned over and tested. Tell me, then, whether I am right in saying that you may learn a thing which at one time you did not know?

Theaet. Certainly you may.

Soc. And another and another?

Theaet. Yes.

Soc. I would have you imagine, then, that there exists in the mind of man a block of wax, which is of different sizes in different men; harder, moister, and having more or less of purity in one than another, and in some of an intermediate quality.

Theaet. I see.

Soc. Let us say that this tablet is a gift of Memory, the mother of the Muses; and that when we wish to remember anything

which we have seen, or heard, or thought in our own minds, we
hold the wax to the perceptions and thoughts, and in that material
receive the impression of them as from the seal of a ring; and that
we remember and know what is imprinted as long as the image
lasts; but when the image is effaced, or cannot be taken, then we
forget and do not know.   e

Theaet. Very good.

Soc. Now, when a person has this knowledge, and is considering something which he sees or hears, may not false opinion arise
in the following manner?

Theaet. In what manner?

Soc. When he thinks what he knows, sometimes to be what he
knows, and sometimes to be what he does not know. We were
wrong before in denying the possibility of this.

Theaet. And how would you amend the former statement?

Soc. I should begin by making a list of the impossible cases 192
which must be excluded. (1) No one can think one thing to be
another when he does not perceive either of them, but has the
memorial or seal of both of them in his mind; nor can any
mistaking of one thing for another occur, when he only knows
one, and does not know, and has no impression of the other; nor
can he think that one thing which he does not know is another
thing which he does not know, or that what he does not know is
what he knows; nor (2) that one thing which he perceives is
another thing which he perceives, or that something which he
perceives is something which he does not perceive; or that something which he does not perceive is something else which he does b
not perceive; or that something which he does not perceive is
something which he perceives; nor again (3) can he think that
something which he knows and perceives, and of which he has
the impression coinciding with sense, is something else which he
knows and perceives, and of which he has the impression coinciding with sense;—this last case, if possible, is still more inconceivable than the others; nor (4) can he think that something
which he knows and perceives, and of which he has the memorial
in good order, is something else which he knows; nor if his mind
is thus furnished, can he think that a thing which he knows and
perceives is another thing which he perceives; or that a thing c
which he does not know and does not perceive, is the same as

another thing which he does not know and does not perceive;—nor again, can he suppose that a thing which he does not know and does not perceive is the same as another thing which he does not know; or that a thing which he does not know and does not perceive is another thing which he does not perceive:—All these utterly and absolutely exclude the possibility of false opinion. The only cases, if any, which remain, are the following.

Theaet. What are they? If you tell me, I may perhaps understand you better; but at present I am unable to follow you.

Soc. A person may think that some things which he knows, or which he perceives and does not know, are some other things which he knows and perceives; or that some things which he d knows and perceives, are other things which he knows and perceives.

Theaet. I understand you less than ever now.

Soc. Hear me once more, then:—I, knowing Theodorus, and remembering in my own mind what sort of person he is, and also what sort of person Theaetetus is, at one time see them, and at another time do not see them, and sometimes I touch them, and at another time not, or at one time I may hear them or perceive them in some other way, and at another time not perceive you, but still I remember you, and know you in my own mind.

e *Theaet.* Very true.

Soc. Then, first of all, I want you to understand that a man may or may not perceive sensibly that which he knows.

Theaet. True.

Soc. And that which he does not know will sometimes not be perceived by him and sometimes will be perceived and only perceived?

Theaet. That is also true.

193 *Soc.* See whether you can follow me better now: Socrates can recognize Theodorus and Theaetetus, but he sees neither of them, nor does he perceive them in any other way; he cannot then by any possibility imagine in his own mind that Theaetetus is Theodorus. Am I not right?

Theaet. You are quite right.

Soc. Then that was the first case of which I spoke.

Theaet. Yes.

Soc. The second case was, that I, knowing one of you and not knowing the other, and perceiving neither, can never think him whom I know to be him whom I do not know.

Theaet. True. b

Soc. In the third case, not knowing and not perceiving either of you, I cannot think that one of you whom I do not know is the other whom I do not know. I need not again go over the catalogue of excluded cases, in which I cannot form a false opinion about you and Theodorus, either when I know both or when I am in ignorance of both, or when I know one and not the other. And the same of perceiving: do you understand me?

Theaet. I do.

Soc. The only possibility of erroneous opinion is, when knowing you and Theodorus, and having on the waxen block the impression of both of you given as by a seal, but seeing you imperfectly c and at a distance, I am eager to assign the right impression of memory to the right visual impression, and to fit this into its own print, in order that recognition may take place; but if I fail and transpose them, putting the foot into the wrong shoe—that is to say, putting the vision of either of you on to the wrong impression, or if my mind, like the sight in a mirror, which is transferred d from right to left, err by reason of some similar affection, then 'heterodoxy' and false opinion ensues.

Theaet. Yes, Socrates, you have described the nature of opinion with wonderful exactness.

Soc. Or again, when I know both of you, and perceive as well as know one of you, but not the other, and my knowledge of him does not accord with perception—that was the case put by me just now which you did not understand.

Theaet. No, I did not.

Soc. I meant to say, that when a person knows and perceives one of you, and his knowledge coincides with his perception, he e will never think him to be some other person, whom he knows and perceives, and the knowledge of whom coincides with his perception—for that also was a case supposed.

Theaet. True.

Soc. But there was an omission of the further case, in which, as we now say, false opinion may arise, when knowing both, and 194 seeing, or having some other sensible perception of both, I fail in holding the seal over against the corresponding sensation; like a bad archer, I miss and fall wide of the mark—and this is called falsehood.

Theaet. Yes; it is rightly so called.

Soc. When, therefore, perception is present to one of the seals or impressions but not to the other, and the mind fits the seal of the absent perception on the one which is present, in any case of this sort the mind is deceived; in a word, if our view is sound, b there can be no error or deception about things which a man does not know and has never perceived, but only in things which are known and perceived; in these alone opinion turns and twists about, and becomes alternately true and false;—true when the seals and impressions of sense meet straight and opposite—false when they go awry and are crooked.

Theaet. And is not that, Socrates, nobly said?

Soc. Nobly! yes; but wait a little and hear the explanation, and then you will say so with more reason; for to think truly is noble and to be deceived is base.

Theaet. Undoubtedly.

Soc. And the origin of truth and error, men say, is as follows:— When the wax in the soul of any one is deep and abundant, and smooth and perfectly tempered, then the impressions which pass through the senses and sink into the heart of the soul, as Homer says in a parable, meaning to indicate the likeness of the soul to wax (κῆρ κηρός); these, I say, being pure and clear, and having a d sufficient depth of wax, are also lasting, and minds such as these easily learn and easily retain, and are not liable to confuse the imprints of sensations, but have true thoughts; for, having clear impressions well spaced out, they can quickly 'say what they are', —that is, distribute them into their proper places on the block. And such men are called wise. Do you agree?

Theaet. Entirely.

e *Soc.* But when the heart of anyone is shaggy—a quality which the all-wise poet commends—or muddy and of impure wax, or very soft, or very hard, then there is a corresponding defect in the mind; the soft are good at learning, but apt to forget, and the hard are the reverse; the shaggy and rugged and gritty, or those who have an admixture of earth or dung in their composition, 195 have the impressions indistinct, as also the hard, for there is no depth in them; and the soft too are indistinct, for their impressions are easily confused and effaced. Yet greater is the indistinctness when they are all jostled together in a little soul, which has no room. These are the natures which are prone to false opinion; for when they see or hear or think of anything, they are slow in assigning the right objects to the right impressions—in their stupidity they confuse them, and are apt to see and hear and think amiss—and such men are said to be deceived in their knowledge of objects, and ignorant.

Theaet. No man, Socrates, can say anything truer than that.   b

Soc. Then now we may admit the existence of false opinion in us?

Theaet. Certainly.

Soc. And of true opinion also?

Theaet. Yes.

Soc. We have at length satisfactorily proven that beyond a doubt there are these two sorts of opinion?

Theaet. Undoubtedly.

Soc. Alas, Theaetetus, what a tiresome creature is a man who is fond of talking!

Theaet. What makes you say so?

Soc. Because I am disheartened at my own stupidity and tire- c some garrulity; for what other term will describe the habit of a man who is always arguing on all sides of a question; whose dullness cannot be convinced, and who will never leave off?

Theaet. But what puts you out of heart?

Soc. I am not only out of heart, but in positive despair; for I do not know what to answer if anyone were to ask me:—O Socrates, have you indeed discovered that false opinion arises neither in the comparison of perceptions with one another nor yet in thought, but in the linking of thought with perception? d Yes, I shall say, with the complacence of one who thinks that he has made a noble discovery.

Theaet. I see no reason why we should be ashamed of our demonstration, Socrates.

Soc. He will say: You mean to argue that the man whom we only think of and do not see, cannot be confused with the horse which we do not see or touch, but only think of and do not perceive? That I believe to be my meaning, I shall reply.

Theaet. Quite right.

e   *Soc.* Well, then, he will say, according to that argument, the number eleven, which is only thought, can never be mistaken for twelve, which is only thought: How would you answer him?

Theaet. I should say that a mistake may very likely arise between the eleven or twelve which are seen or handled, but that no similar mistake can arise between the eleven and twelve which are in the mind.

Soc. Well, but do you think that no one ever put before his
196   own mind five and seven,—I do not mean five or seven men or other such objects, but five or seven in the abstract, which, as we say, are recorded on the waxen block, and in which false opinion is held to be impossible;—did no man ever ask himself how many these numbers make when added together, and answer that they are eleven, while another thinks that they are twelve, or would all agree in thinking and saying that they are twelve?

b   *Theaet.* Certainly not; many would think that they are eleven, and in the higher numbers the chance of error is greater still; for I assume you to be speaking of numbers in general.

Soc. Exactly; and I want you to consider whether this does not imply that the twelve in the waxen block are supposed to be eleven?

Theaet. Yes, that seems to be the case.

Soc. Then do we not come back to the old difficulty? For he who makes such a mistake does think one thing which he knows to be another thing which he knows; but this, as we said, was
c   impossible, and afforded an irresistible proof of the non-existence of false opinion, because otherwise the same person would inevitably know and not know the same thing at the same time.

Theaet. Most true.

Soc. Then false opinion cannot be explained as a confusion of thought and sense, for in that case we could not have been mistaken about pure conceptions of thought; and thus we are obliged to say, either that false opinion does not exist, or that a man may not know that which he knows;—which alternative do you prefer?

Theaet. It is hard to determine, Socrates.

d   *Soc.* And yet the argument will scarcely admit of both. But, as we are at our wits' end, suppose that we do a shameless thing?

Theaet. What is it?

Soc. Let us attempt to explain what it is like 'to know'.

Theaet. And why should that be shameless?

Soc. You seem not to be aware that the whole of our discussion from the very beginning has been a search after knowledge, of which we are assumed not to know the nature.

Theaet. Nay, but I am well aware.

Soc. And is it not shameless when we do not know what knowledge is, to be explaining the verb 'to know'? The truth is, Theaetetus, that we have long been infected with logical im- e purity. Thousands of times have we repeated the words 'we know', and 'do not know', and 'we have or have not science or knowledge', as if we could understand what we are saying to one another, even while we remain ignorant about knowledge; and at this moment we are using the words 'we understand', 'we are ignorant', as though we could still employ them when deprived of knowledge or science.

Theaet. But if you avoid these expressions, Socrates, how will you ever argue at all?

Soc. I could not, being the man I am. The case would be 197 different if I were a true hero of dialectic: and O that such an one were present! for he would have told us to avoid the use of these terms; at the same time he would not have spared in you and me the faults which I have noted. But, seeing that we are no great wits, shall I venture to say what knowing is? for I think that the attempt may be worth making.

Theaet. Then by all means venture, and no one shall find fault with you for using the forbidden terms.

Soc. You have heard the common explanation of the verb 'to know'?

Theaet. I think so, but I do not remember it at the moment.

Soc. They explain the word 'to know' as meaning 'to have b knowledge'.

Theaet. True.

Soc. I propose that we make a slight change, and say 'to possess' knowledge.

Theaet. How do the two expressions differ?

Soc. Perhaps there may be no difference; but still I should like you to hear my view, that you may help me to test it.

Theaet. I will, if I can.

Soc. I should distinguish 'having' from 'possessing': for example, a man may buy and keep under his control a garment which he does not wear; and then we should say, not that he has,[1] but that he possesses the garment.

Theaet. It would be the correct expression.

c　*Soc.* Well, may not a man 'possess' and yet not 'have' knowledge in the sense of which I am speaking? As you may suppose a man to have caught wild birds—doves or any other birds—and to be keeping them in an aviary which he has constructed at home; we might say of him in one sense, that he always has them because he possesses them, might we not?

Theaet. Yes.

Soc. And yet, in another sense, he has none of them; but they are in his power, and he has got them under his hand in an enclosure of his own, and can take and have them whenever he likes;—he can catch any which he likes, and let the bird go d again, and he may do so as often as he pleases.

Theaet. True.

Soc. Once more, then, as in what preceded we made a sort of waxen tablet in the mind, so let us now suppose that in the mind of each man there is an aviary of all sorts of birds—some flocking together apart from the rest, others in small groups, others solitary, flying anywhere and everywhere.

e　*Theaet.* Let us imagine such an aviary—and what is to follow?

Soc. We may suppose that the birds are kinds of knowledge, and that when we were children, this receptacle was empty; whenever a man has gotten and detained in the enclosure a kind of knowledge, he may be said to have learned or discovered the thing which is the subject of the knowledge: and this is to know.

Theaet. Granted.

198　*Soc.* And further, when any one wishes to catch any of these knowledges or sciences, and having taken, to hold it, and again to let them go, how will he express himself?—will he describe the 'catching' of them and the original 'possession' in the same words? I will make my meaning clearer by an example:—You admit that there is an art of arithmetic?

Theaet. To be sure.

Soc. Conceive this as an attempt to capture knowledge of every species of the odd and even.

---

[1] [Because ἔχειν, have, is used in Greek as a synonym of φορεῖν, wear.]

Theaet. I follow.

Soc. Having the use of the art, the arithmetician, if I am not mistaken, has the conceptions of number under his hand, and can b transmit them to another.

Theaet. Yes.

Soc. And when transmitting them he may be said to teach them, and when receiving to learn them, and when having them in possession in the aforesaid aviary he may be said to know them.

Theaet. Exactly.

Soc. Attend to what follows: must not the perfect arithmetician know all numbers, for he has the science of all numbers in his mind?

Theaet. True.

Soc. And he can reckon abstract numbers in his head, or c things about him which are numerable?

Theaet. Of course he can.

Soc. And to reckon is simply to consider how much such and such a number amounts to?

Theaet. Very true.

Soc. And so he appears to be searching into something which he knows, as if he did not know it, for we have already admitted that he knows all numbers;—you have heard these perplexing questions raised?

Theaet. I have.

Soc. May we not pursue the image of the doves, and say that d the chase after knowledge is of two kinds? one kind is prior to possession and for the sake of possession, and the other for the sake of taking and holding in the hands that which is possessed already. And thus, when a man has learned and known something long ago, he may resume and get hold of the knowledge which he has long possessed, but has not at hand in his mind.

Theaet. True.

Soc. That was my reason for asking how we ought to speak e when an arithmetician sets about numbering, or a grammarian about reading? Shall we say, that although he knows, he comes back to himself on such an occasion to learn what he already knows?

Theaet. It would be too absurd, Socrates.

Soc. Shall we say then that he is going to read or number what
199 he does not know, although we have admitted that he knows all
letters and all numbers?

Theaet. That, again, would be an absurdity.

Soc. Then shall we say that we care nothing about the mere
names—any one may twist and turn the words 'knowing' and
'learning' in any way which he likes; but that since we have
made a clear distinction between the possession of knowledge and
the having or using it, we do assert that a man cannot not possess
that which he possesses; and, therefore, in no case can a man not
know that which he knows, but he may get a false opinion about
b it; for he may have the knowledge, not of this particular thing,
but of some other;—when the various numbers and forms of
knowledge are flying about in the aviary, and wishing to capture
a certain sort of knowledge out of the general store, he may take
the wrong one by mistake. Thus it is that he may think eleven to
be twelve, getting hold, as it were, of the ring-dove which he had
in his mind, when he wanted the pigeon.

Theaet. A very rational explanation.

Soc. But when he catches the one which he wants, then he is
not deceived, and has an opinion of what is; and thus both false
c and true opinion may exist, and the difficulties which were
previously raised disappear. I dare say that you agree with me,
do you not?

Theaet. Yes.

Soc. And so we are rid of the difficulty of a man's not knowing
what he knows, for we are not driven to the inference that he does
not possess what he possesses, whether he be or be not deceived.
And yet I fear that a greater difficulty is looking in at the window.

Theaet. What is it?

Soc. How can the exchange of one knowledge for another ever
become false opinion?

Theaet. What do you mean?

d   *Soc.* In the first place, how can a man who has the knowledge
of anything be ignorant of that which he knows, not by reason of
ignorance, but by reason of his own knowledge? And, again, is it
not an extreme absurdity that he should suppose another thing
to be this, and this to be another thing;—that, having knowledge
present with him in his mind, he should still know nothing and

be ignorant of all things?—you might as well argue that ignorance may make a man know, and blindness make him see, as that knowledge can make him ignorant.

Theaet. Perhaps, Socrates, we may have been wrong in making e only forms of knowledge our birds: whereas there ought to have been forms of ignorance as well, flying about together in the mind, and then he who sought to take one of them might sometimes catch a form of knowledge, and sometimes a form of ignorance; and thus he would have a false opinion from ignorance, but a true one from knowledge, about the same thing.

Soc. I cannot help praising you, Theaetetus, and yet I must beg you to reconsider your words. Let us grant what you say— 200 then, according to you, he who takes ignorance will have a false opinion—am I right?

Theaet. Yes.

Soc. He will certainly not think that he has a false opinion?

Theaet. Of course not.

Soc. He will think that his opinion is true, and he will fancy that he knows the things about which he has been deceived?

Theaet. Certainly.

Soc. Then he will think that he has captured a knowledge and not an ignorance?

Theaet. Clearly.

Soc. And thus, after going a long way round, we are once more face to face with our original difficulty. The hero of dialectic b will retort upon us:—'O my excellent friends', he will say, laughing, 'if a man knows both the specimen of ignorance and also that of knowledge, can he think that one of them which he knows is the other which he knows? or, if he knows neither of them, can he think that the one which he knows not is another which he knows not? or, if he knows one and not the other, can he think the one which he knows to be the one which he does not know? or the one which he does not know to be the one which he knows? or will you proceed to tell me that there are other knowledges which know the types of knowledge and ignorance, and which the owner keeps in some other aviaries or graven on waxen blocks according to your foolish images, c and which he may be said to know while he possesses them, even though he have them not at hand in his mind? And thus, in a perpetual circle, you will be compelled to go round and round, and you will make no progress.' What are we to say in reply, Theaetetus?

Theaet. Indeed, Socrates, I do not know what we are to say.

Soc. Are not his reproaches just, and does not the argument
d truly show that we are wrong in seeking for false opinion until we know what knowledge is; that must be first ascertained; then, the nature of false opinion?

Theaet. I cannot but agree with you, Socrates, so far as we have yet gone.

Soc. Then, once more, what shall we say that knowledge is?—for we are not going to lose heart as yet.

Theaet. Certainly, I shall not lose heart, if you do not.

Soc. What definition will be most consistent with our former
e views?

Theaet. I cannot think of any but our old one, Socrates.

Soc. What was it?

Theaet. Knowledge was said by us to be true opinion; and true opinion is surely unerring, and the results which follow from it are all noble and good.

Soc. He who led the way into the river, Theaetetus, said
201 'The experiment will show'; and perhaps if we go forward in the search, we may stumble upon the thing which we are looking for; but if we stay where we are, nothing will come to light.

Theaet. Very true; let us go forward and try.

Soc. The trail soon comes to an end, for a whole profession is against us.

Theaet. How is that, and what profession do you mean?

Soc. The profession of the great wise ones who are called orators and lawyers; for these persuade men by their art and make them think whatever they like, but they do not teach them.
b Do you imagine that there are any teachers in the world so clever as to be able to impart the full truth about past acts of robbery or violence, to men who were not eye-witnesses, while a little water is flowing in the clepsydra?

Theaet. Certainly not, they can only persuade them.

Soc. And would you not say that persuading them is making them have an opinion?

Theaet. To be sure.

Soc. When, therefore, judges are justly persuaded about matters which you can know only by seeing them, and not in any other way, and when thus judging of them from report they attain a true opinion about them, they judge without knowledge, and yet are rightly persuaded, if they have c judged well.

Theaet. Certainly.

Soc. And yet, O my friend, if true opinion in law courts[1] and knowledge are the same, the perfect judge could not have judged rightly without knowledge; and therefore I must infer that they are not the same.

Theaet. There is a distinction, Socrates, which I have heard made by someone else, but I had forgotten it. He said that true opinion, combined with reason, was knowledge, but that d the opinion which had no reason was out of the sphere of knowledge; and that things of which there is no rational account are not knowable—such was the singular expression which he used—and that things which have a reason or explanation are knowable.

Soc. Excellent; but then, how did he distinguish between things which are and are not 'knowable'? I wish that you would repeat to me what he said, and then I shall know whether you and I have heard the same tale.

Theaet. I do not know whether I can recall it; but if another person would tell me, I think that I could follow him.

Soc. Let me give you, then, a dream in return for a dream:—Methought that I too had a dream, and I heard in my dream that e the primeval letters or elements out of which you and I and all other things are compounded, have no reason or explanation; you can only name each of them individually, but no predicate 202 can be either affirmed or denied of them, for in the one case existence, in the other non-existence is already implied, neither of which must be added, if you mean to speak of this or that thing by itself alone. It should not be called 'itself', or 'that', or 'each', or 'alone', or 'this', or the like; for these go about everywhere and are applied to all things, but are distinct from them; whereas if the first elements could be described, and had a

---

[1] Reading κατὰ δικαστήρια: an emendation suggested by Professor Campbell.

definition[1] of their own, they would be spoken of apart from all
b else. But none of these primeval elements can be defined; they
can only be named, for they have nothing but a name; whereas
the things which are compounded of them, as they themselves
are complex, are defined by a combination of names, for the
combination of names is the essence of a definition.[1] Thus, then,
the elements or letters are only objects of perception, and cannot
be defined or known; but the syllables or combinations of them
are known and expressed, and are apprehended by true opinion.
When, therefore, any one forms the true opinion of anything
without rational explanation, you may say that his mind is truly
c exercised, but has no knowledge; for he who cannot give and
receive a reason for a thing, has no knowledge of that thing; but
when he adds rational explanation, then, he is perfected in
knowledge and may be all that I have been denying of him. Was
that the form in which the dream appeared to you?

Theaet. Precisely.

Soc. And you allow and maintain that true opinion, combined
with definition or rational explanation, is knowledge?

Theaet. Exactly.

d *Soc.* Then may we assume, Theaetetus, that today, and in this
casual manner, we have found a truth which in former times
many wise men have grown old and have not found?

Theaet. At any rate, Socrates, I am satisfied with the present
statement.

Soc. Which is probably correct—for how can there be knowledge apart from definition and true opinion? And yet there is
one point in what has been said which does not quite satisfy me.

Theaet. What was it?

Soc. What might seem to be the most ingenious notion of all:—
That the elements or letters are unknown, but that the syllable is
e known.

Theaet. And was that wrong?

Soc. We shall soon know; for we have as hostages the instances
which the author of the argument himself used.

---

[1] [Λόγος, above translated 'reason or explanation'. 'Names' are not here distinguished from 'verbs', as at *Sophist.* 261 e foll. The definition of λόγος as a combination of names *and verbs* occurs in many other passages, e.g. *Crat.* 425 a, *Sophist.*
262 a–d. 'Definition' must, throughout this passage, be understood somewhat
more widely than English usage would suggest.]

Theaet. What hostages?

Soc. The letters of the alphabet and their syllables. He who gave this account reasoned, did he not, from these?

Theaet. Yes; he did.

Soc. Let us take them and put them to the test, or rather, test ourselves:—Was this the way in which we learned letters, and, first of all, is it true that syllables have a definition, but that letters have none?

Theaet. I think so.

Soc. I think so too; for, suppose that someone asks you to spell the first syllable of my name:—Theaetetus, he says, what is SO?

Theaet. I should reply S and O.

Soc. That is the definition which you would give of the syllable?

Theaet. I should.

Soc. I wish that you would give me a similar definition of the S. **b**

Theaet. But how can any one, Socrates, tell the elements of an element? I can only reply, that S is a consonant, a mere noise, as of the tongue hissing; B, and most other letters, again, are neither vowel-sounds nor noises. Thus letters may be most truly said to be undefined; for even the most distinct of them, which are the seven vowels, have a sound only, but no definition at all.

Soc. Then, I suppose, my friend, that we have been so far right in our idea about knowledge?

Theaet. Yes; I think that we have.

Soc. Well, but have we been right in maintaining that the **c** syllables can be known, but not the letters?

Theaet. I think so.

Soc. And do we mean by a syllable simply the two letters, or if there are more, all of them, or a single form which arises out of the combination of them?

Theaet. I should say that we mean all the letters.

Soc. Take the case of the two letters S and O, which form the first syllable of my own name; must not he who knows the syllable, know both of them?

Theaet. Certainly.

Soc. He knows, that is, the S and O?

Theaet. Yes.

Soc. But can he be ignorant of them singly and knowing neither, yet know both together?

Theaet. Such a supposition, Socrates, is monstrous and un-meaning.

Soc. But if he cannot know both without knowing each, then if he is ever to know the syllable, he must know the letters first; and thus this fine theory will have taken wings and departed.

e   *Theaet.* Yes, with wonderful celerity.

Soc. Yes, we are not keeping watch properly. Perhaps we ought to have maintained that a syllable is not the letters, but rather one single entity framed out of them, distinct from the letters, and having its own peculiar form.

Theaet. Very true; and a more likely notion than the other.

Soc. Take care; let us not be cowards and betray a great and imposing theory.

204   *Theaet.* No, indeed.

Soc. Let us assume then, as we now say, that the syllable is a simple form arising out of the several combinations of harmonious elements—of letters or of any other elements.

Theaet. Very good.

Soc. And it must have no parts.

Theaet. Why?

Soc. Because that which has parts must be a whole of all the parts. Or would you say that a whole also, although formed out of the parts, is a single notion different from all the parts?

Theaet. I should.

Soc. And would you say that all and the whole are the same, b or different?

Theaet. I am not certain; but, as you like me to answer at once, I shall hazard the reply that they are different.

Soc. I approve of your readiness, Theaetetus, but I must take time to think whether I equally approve of your answer.

Theaet. Yes; the answer is the point.

Soc. According to this new view, the whole is supposed to differ from all?

Theaet. Yes.

Soc. Well, but is there any difference between all [in the plural] and the all [in the singular]? Take the case of number:— When we say one, two, three, four, five, six; or when we say

twice three, or three times two, or four and two, or three c
and two and one, are we speaking of the same or of different
numbers?

Theaet. Of the same.

Soc. That is of six?

Theaet. Yes.

Soc. And in each form of expression we spoke of all[1] the six?

Theaet. True.

Soc. Again, in speaking of all [in the plural], do we not express
one whole thing?

Theaet. Of course.

Soc. And that is six?

Theaet. Yes.

Soc. Then, at least in the case of things measured by number, d
the meaning is the same whether we predicate all in the singular
or in the plural.

Theaet. So it appears.

Soc. Again, the number of the acre and the acre are the same;
are they not?

Theaet. Yes.

Soc. And the number of the stadium in like manner is the
stadium?

Theaet. Yes.

Soc. And the army is the number of the army; and in all
similar cases, the entire number of anything is the entire thing?

Theaet. True.

Soc. And the number of each is the parts of each? e

Theaet. Exactly.

Soc. Then as many things as have parts are made up of parts?

Theaet. Apparently.

Soc. But all the parts are admitted to be the all, if we are to
regard the entire number as the all?

Theaet. True.

Soc. Then the whole is not made up of parts, for it would be
the all, if consisting of all the parts?

Theaet. That is the inference.

Soc. But is a part a part of anything but the whole?

Theaet. Yes, of the all.

[¹ Reading πάντα τά.]

205 *Soc.* You make a valiant defence, Theaetetus. And yet is not the all that of which nothing is wanting?

Theaet. Certainly.

Soc. And is not a whole likewise that from which no factor of any sort is absent? but that from which anything is absent is neither a whole nor all;—if wanting in anything, both equally lose their entirety of nature.

Theaet. I now think that there is no difference between a whole and all.

Soc. But were we not saying that when a thing has parts, all the parts will be a whole and an all?

Theaet. Certainly.

Soc. Then, as I was saying before, must not the alternative be that either the syllable is not the letters, and then the letters are
b not parts of the syllable, or that the syllable will be the same with the letters, and will therefore be equally known with them?

Theaet. You are right.

Soc. And, in order to avoid this, we suppose it to be different from them?

Theaet. Yes.

Soc. But if letters are not parts of syllables, can you tell me of any other parts of syllables, which are not letters?

Theaet. No, indeed, Socrates; for if I admit the existence of parts in a syllable, it would be ridiculous in me to give up letters and seek for other parts.

c *Soc.* Quite true, Theaetetus, and therefore, according to our present view, a syllable must surely be some indivisible form?

Theaet. So it seems.

Soc. But do you remember, my friend, that only a little while ago we admitted and approved the statement, that of the first elements out of which all other things are compounded there could be no definition, because each of them when taken by itself is uncompounded; nor can one rightly attribute to them the words 'being' or 'this', because they are alien and inappropriate words, and for this reason the letters or elements were indefinable and unknown?

Theaet. I remember.

d *Soc.* And is not this also the reason why they are simple and indivisible? I can see no other.

Theaet. No other reason is apparent.

Soc. Then is not the syllable in the same case as the elements or letters, if it has no parts and is one form?

Theaet. To be sure.

Soc. If, then, a syllable is a whole, and has many parts or letters, the letters as well as the syllable must be intelligible and expressible, since all the parts are acknowledged to be the same as the whole.

Theaet. True.   c

Soc. But if it be one and indivisible, then the syllables and the letters are alike undefined and unknown, and for the same reason?

Theaet. I cannot deny that.

Soc. We cannot, therefore, agree in the opinion of him who says that the syllable can be known and expressed, but not the letters.

Theaet. Certainly not; if we may trust the argument.

Soc. Well, but will you not be equally inclined to disagree with 206 him, when you remember your own experience in learning to read?

Theaet. What experience?

Soc. Why, that in learning you were kept trying to distinguish the separate letters both by the eye and by the ear, in order that, when you heard them spoken or saw them written, you might not be confused by their position.

Theaet. Very true.

Soc. And is the education of the harp-player complete unless he can tell what string answers to a particular note; the notes, as b everyone would allow, are the elements or letters of music?

Theaet. Exactly.

Soc. Then, if we argue from the letters and syllables of which we have experience to other simples and compounds, we shall say that the letters or simple elements as a class are much more distinctly known than the syllables, and much more indispensable to a perfect knowledge of any subject; and if some one says that the syllable is known and the letter unknown, we shall consider that either intentionally or unintentionally he is talking nonsense?

Theaet. Exactly.

Soc. And there might be given other proofs of this belief, if I c am not mistaken. But do not let us in looking for them lose sight of the question before us, which is the meaning of the statement, that right opinion with rational definition or explanation is the most perfect form of knowledge.

Theaet. We must not.

Soc. Well, and what does the author of this statement mean by the term 'explanation'? I think that we have a choice of three meanings.

Theaet. What are they?

d *Soc.* In the first place, the meaning may be, manifesting one's thought by the voice with verbs and nouns, imaging an opinion in the stream which flows from the lips, as in a mirror or water. Does not this appear to you to be one kind of explanation?

Theaet. Certainly; he who so manifests his thought, is said to explain himself.

Soc. But then, every one who is not born deaf or dumb is able sooner or later to manifest what he thinks of anything; and if so, all those who have a right opinion about anything will also have e right explanation; nor will right opinion be anywhere found to exist apart from knowledge.

Theaet. True.

Soc. Let us not, therefore, hastily charge him who gave this account of knowledge with uttering an unmeaning word; for perhaps he did not intend to say this, but that when a person was asked what was the nature of anything, he should be able to 207 answer his questioner by giving the elements of the thing.

Theaet. As for example, Socrates . . .?

Soc. As, for example, when Hesiod says that a wagon is made up of a hundred planks. Now, neither you nor I could describe all of them individually; but if any one asked what is a wagon, we should be content to answer, that a wagon consists of wheels, axle, body, rims, yoke.

Theaet. Certainly.

Soc. And our opponent will probably laugh at us, just as he would if we professed to be grammarians and to give a grammatical account of the name of Theaetetus, and yet could only tell the syllables and not the letters of your name. We might hold b a true opinion and make a correct statement; but *knowledge,* he would claim, is not attained until, combined with true opinion, there is an enumeration of the elements out of which anything is composed, as, I think, has already been remarked.

Theaet. It has.

Soc. In the same way, he might claim that while we merely have true opinion about the wagon, a man who can describe its essence by an enumeration of the hundred planks, adds rational c explanation to true opinion, and instead of opinion has art and knowledge of the nature of a wagon, in that he attains to the whole through the elements.

Theaet. And do you not agree in that view, Socrates?

Soc. Tell me, my friend, whether the view is yours—whether you admit the resolution of all things into their elements to be a rational explanation of them, and the consideration of them in syllables or larger combinations of them to be irrational—so that we can inquire whether that view is right.   d

Theaet. Indeed I admit it.

Soc. Well, and do you conceive that a man has knowledge of any element who at one time affirms and at another time denies that element of something, or thinks that the same thing is composed of different elements at different times?

Theaet. Assuredly not.

Soc. And do you not remember that in your case and in that of others this often occurred at first in the process of learning to read?

Theaet. You mean that we often put different letters into the e same syllables, and gave the same letter sometimes to the proper syllable, sometimes to a wrong one.

Soc. Yes.

Theaet. To be sure; I perfectly remember, and I am very far from supposing that they who are in this condition have knowledge.

Soc. When a person at that stage of learning writes the name of Theaetetus, and thinks that he ought to write and does write *Th* and *e*; but, again, meaning to write the name of Theodorus, 208 thinks that he ought to write and does write *T* and *e*—can we suppose that he knows the first syllables of your two names?

Theaet. We have already admitted that such a one has not yet attained knowledge.

Soc. And in like manner he may enumerate without knowing them the second and third and fourth syllables of your name?

Theaet. He may.

Soc. And in that case, when he has written the syllables in order, since he can enumerate all the letters he will have written 'Theaetetus' with right opinion?

Theaet. Clearly.

b *Soc.* But although we admit that he has right opinion, he will still be without knowledge?

Theaet. Yes.

Soc. And yet he will have explanation, as well as right opinion, for he knew his way through the letters when he wrote; and this we admit to be explanation.

Theaet. True.

Soc. Then, my friend, there is such a thing as right opinion united with definition or explanation, which should still not be called knowledge.

Theaet. It would seem so.

Soc. And what we fancied to be a perfect definition of knowledge is a dream only. But perhaps we had better not say so as c yet, for were there not three senses of 'explanation', one of which must, as we said, be adopted by him who maintains knowledge to be true opinion combined with rational explanation? And very likely there may be found some one who will not prefer this but the third.

Theaet. Your reminder is just; there is still one sense remaining. The first was the image or expression of the mind in speech; the second, which has just been mentioned, is a way of reaching the whole by an enumeration of the elements. But what is the third?

Soc. That which would occur to many people:—ability to tell the mark or sign of difference which distinguishes the thing in question from all others.

Theaet. Can you give me any example of such a definition?

d *Soc.* As, for example, in the case of the sun, I think that you would be contented with the statement that the sun is the brightest of the heavenly bodies which revolve about the earth.

Theaet. Certainly.

Soc. Understand why:—the reason is, as we were just now saying, that if you get at the difference and distinguishing characteristic of each thing, then, as many persons affirm, you

will secure its explanation; but while you lay hold only of the
common and not of the characteristic quality, your explanation
will relate to all things to which this common quality belongs.

Theaet. I understand you, and it is in my judgement correct to e
call this definition [or explanation].

Soc. But he, who having right opinion about anything, can
find out the difference which distinguishes it from other things
will have come to *know* that of which before he had only an
opinion.

Theaet. Yes; that is what we are maintaining.

Soc. Nevertheless, Theaetetus, on a nearer view, I find myself
quite disappointed; the picture, which at a distance was not so
bad, has now become altogether unintelligible.

Theaet. What do you mean?

Soc. I will endeavour to explain: I will suppose myself to have 209
true opinion of you, and if to this I add your definition, then I
have knowledge, but if not, opinion only.

Theaet. Yes.

Soc. The definition was assumed to be the interpretation of
your difference.

Theaet. True.

Soc. But when I had only opinion, I had no conception of your
distinguishing characteristics.

Theaet. I suppose not.

Soc. Then I must have conceived of some general or common
nature which no more belonged to you than to another.   b

Theaet. True.

Soc. Tell me, now—How in that case could I have formed a
judgement of you any more than of any one else? Suppose that I
imagine Theaetetus to be a man who has nose, eyes, and mouth,
and every other member complete; how would that enable me
to distinguish Theaetetus from Theodorus, or from some outer
barbarian?

Theaet. How could it?

Soc. Or if I had further conceived of you, not only as having
nose and eyes, but as having a snub nose and prominent eyes, c
should I have any more notion of you than of myself and others
who resemble me?

Theaet. Certainly not.

Soc. Surely I can have no conception of Theaetetus until your snub-nosedness has left an impression on my mind different from the snub-nosedness of all others whom I have ever seen, and until your other peculiarities have a like distinctness; and so when I meet you tomorrow the right opinion will be re-called?

Theaet. Most true.

d *Soc.* Then right opinion also implies the perception of differences?

Theaet. Clearly.

Soc. What meaning, then, remains for the reason or explanation which we are told to add to right opinion? If the meaning is, that we should form an extra opinion of the way in which something differs from another thing, the proposal is ridiculous.

Theaet. How so?

Soc. We are bidden to acquire a right opinion of the differences which distinguish one thing from another, which is just what we already have, and so we go round and round;—the revolution

e of the scytal, or pestle, or any other rotatory machine, in the same circles, is as nothing compared with such a requirement; and we may be truly described as the blind directing the blind; for to add those things which we already have, in order that we may learn what we already think, is like a soul utterly benighted.

Theaet. Tell me; what were you going to say just now, when you asked the question?

Soc. If, my boy, the argument, in speaking of adding the definition, had used the word to 'know', and not merely 'have an opinion' of the difference, this which is the most promising of all the definitions of knowledge would have come to a pretty end, for to know is surely to acquire knowledge.

210 *Theaet.* True.

Soc. And so, when the question is asked, What is knowledge? this fair argument will answer 'Right opinion with knowledge',—knowledge, that is, of difference, for this, as the said argument maintains, is adding the definition.

Theaet. That seems to be true.

Soc. But how utterly foolish, when we are asking what is knowledge, that the reply should only be, right opinion with knowledge whether of difference or of anything else! And so, Theaetetus, knowledge is neither sensation nor true opinion, nor

yet definition and explanation accompanying and added to true b
opinion?

Theaet. I suppose not.

Soc. And are you still in labour and travail, my dear friend, or
have you brought all that you have to say about knowledge to
the birth?

Theaet. I am sure, Socrates, that you have elicited from me a
good deal more than ever was in me.

Soc. And does not my art show that you have brought forth
wind, and that the offspring of your brain are not worth bringing up?

Theaet. Very true.

Soc. But if, Theaetetus, you should ever conceive afresh, you
will be all the better for the present investigation, and if not, you c
will be soberer and humbler and gentler to other men, and will
be too modest to fancy that you know what you do not know.
These are the limits of my art; I can no further go, nor do I
know aught of the things which great and famous men know or
have known in this or former ages. The office of a midwife I, like
my mother, have received from God; she delivered women, and
I deliver men; but they must be young and noble and fair. d

And now I have to go to the porch of the King Archon, where
I am to meet Meletus and his indictment. Tomorrow morning,
Theodorus, I shall hope to see you again at this place.

SOPHIST

INTRODUCTION AND ANALYSIS

THE dramatic power of the dialogues of Plato appears to diminish as the metaphysical interest of them increases (cf. Introd. to the *Philebus*). There are no descriptions of time, place, or persons in the *Sophist* and *Statesman*, but we are plunged at once into philosophical discussions; the poetical charm has disappeared, and those who have no taste for abstruse metaphysics will greatly prefer the earlier dialogues to the later ones. Plato is conscious of the change, and in the *Statesman* (286 b) expressly accuses himself of a tediousness in the two dialogues, which he ascribes to his desire of developing the dialectical method. On the other hand, the kindred spirit of Hegel seemed to find in the *Sophist* the crown and summit of the Platonic philosophy— here is the place at which Plato most nearly approaches to the Hegelian identity of Being and Not-being. Nor will the great importance of the two dialogues be doubted by any one who forms a conception of the state of mind and opinion which they are intended to meet. The sophisms of the day were undermining philosophy; the denial of the existence of Not-being, and of the connexion of ideas, was making truth and falsehood equally impossible. It has been said that Plato would have written differently, if he had been acquainted with the *Organon* of Aristotle. But could the *Organon* of Aristotle ever have been written unless the *Sophist* and *Statesman* had preceded? The swarm of fallacies which arose in the infancy of mental science, and which was born and bred in the decay of the pre-Socratic philosophies, was not dispelled by Aristotle, but by Socrates and Plato. The *summa genera* of thought, the nature of the proposition, of definition, of generalization, of synthesis and analysis, of division and cross-division, are clearly described, and the processes of induction and deduction are constantly employed in the dialogues of Plato. The 'slippery' nature of comparison, the danger of putting words in the place of things, the fallacy of arguing *a dicto secundum*, and in a circle, are frequently indicated by him. To all these processes of truth and error, Aristotle, in the next generation, gave distinctness; he brought them together in a separate science. But he is not to be regarded as the original inventor of any of the great logical forms, with the exception of the syllogism.

There is little worthy of remark in the characters of the *Sophist*. The most noticeable point is the final retirement of Socrates from the field of argument, and the substitution for him of an Eleatic Stranger, who is described as a pupil of Parmenides and Zeno, and is supposed to have descended from a higher world in order to convict the Socratic circle of error. As in the *Timaeus*, Plato seems to intimate by the withdrawal of Socrates that he is passing beyond the limits of his teaching; and in the *Sophist* and *Statesman*, as well as in the *Parmenides*, he probably means to imply that he is making a closer approach to the schools of Elea and Megara. He had much in common with them, but he must first submit their ideas to criticism and revision. He had once thought as he says, speaking by the mouth of the Eleatic, that he understood their doctrine of Not-being; but now he does not even comprehend the nature of Being. The friends of Ideas (*Soph.* 248) are alluded to by him as distant acquaintances, whom he criticizes *ab extra*; we do not recognize at first sight that he is criticizing himself.[1] The character of

---

[1] [It is not surprising that an Eleatic Stranger should criticize the doctrine of Plato or speak of it as being maintained by Friends of Ideas: and from such a reference it would not necessarily follow that Plato is about to propound an important change in the doctrine he has hitherto maintained.

Zeller held that the Friends of Ideas are not Platonists, but members of the Megarian school who assume a plurality of immobile Forms similar to the Eleatic One. Moreover, he maintained that an important change of doctrine is announced in the *Sophist*; and that Plato now proposes to regard the Ideas as active personal beings, or as concepts contained in the minds of such beings; and lastly, that they do in fact take this shape in later dialogues such as the *Timaeus*.

Such a reform in the theory of Ideas was supposed to be indicated at more than one point in the *Sophist*. Firstly, the Eleatic Stranger requires the Friends of Ideas to make a concession, which apparently is to consist in an equation between being (οὐσία) and power, δύναμις (246 a foll.).

Secondly, it is maintained, 'the completely real' cannot be lifeless, but must possess a mind, which must inhere in a soul (248–9); and, later, that Nature is simply another name for divine craftsmanship (265 d).

Thirdly, an Idea of Movement is now introduced, and is ranked as one of the 'highest kinds'.

Fourthly, the *Sophist* is remarkable for the emergence of a new problem, the mutual relationship (κοινωνία) of the Ideas. This must be distinguished from two problems with which Plato had always been concerned, (*a*) the presence of one Idea in many particular things or actions, and (*b*) the participation of one thing or one action in several Ideas.

Though Jowett differs from Zeller in declaring the Friends of Ideas to be the Platonists, he seems otherwise to follow him in this exposition of the *Sophist*; and it is therefore of interest to record some later views. In his thesis *La définition de l'être et la nature des Idées dans le 'Sophiste' de Platon* (1909, 2nd ed. 1932) A. Diès showed, in opposition to the views just stated: *first*, that the Idea of Movement occurs in the *Sophist* simply as a link in the chain of demonstration which is to prove that Not-Being is otherness; some other Idea might equally well have served this purpose, and the Ideas of Movement and Rest are, in any case, declared to be less extensive than that of Being. *Secondly*, that Plato does not transform the Ideas into personal agents or propound, for his own future use, a new definition

the Eleatic Stranger is colourless; he is to a certain extent the reflection of his father and master, Parmenides, who is the protagonist in the

of Being (οὐσία) as power (δύναμις). It is the Friends of Ideas who are asked, by an *argumentum ad hominem*, to agree to this modification in *their* view of οὐσία. If Plato is not among this party there is no reason why *his* doctrine should be affected by such a concession; and in any case the movement or affection which the Friends of Ideas are persuaded to admit as consistent with οὐσία, is simply the *passive* 'power' of being an object of apprehension. Further, Plato cannot here intend to propound a new definition of Being, since the burden of the Eleatic Stranger's argument is that Being is indefinable and that its nature cannot be expressed in terms of other Ideas.

Thirdly, when it is maintained that 'the completely real' must be endowed with a Soul and a Mind, this expression τὸ παντελῶς ὄν does not denote the intelligible world or world of Ideas but rather the totality of the *sensible* world; the effect of this remark, therefore, is not to transform the Ideas into personal agents, but to represent the sensible world as animated by a world-soul.

Fourthly, while it is true that the *Sophist* is remarkable for its elaborate study of the interrelation of Ideas, this was not a new problem; it had, for instance, received careful treatment in the *Phaedo*. Plato evidently did not suppose either there or in the *Sophist* that in order to account for such inter-relation, the Ideas must no longer be viewed as self-subsistent entities but as mental concepts.

Jowett's view of the later phase of the doctrine of Ideas, which is similar to Zeller's, has been rendered untenable by these criticisms. On the other hand, his judgement seems to be sound when he assumes that it is Plato's own earlier doctrine which is here attributed to the Friends of Ideas. Among those who deny this, (*a*) Zeller, as has been said, supposes the Friends of Ideas to be the Megarians, (*b*) others suppose them to be members of the Academy who have misunderstood Plato's doctrine so seriously that he thinks it necessary to give them a warning, (*c*) others (Burnet and Taylor) see some reference to a little-known Pythagorean sect, (*d*) Diès is inclined to think that no specific persons are meant and that Plato has dramatized a prevailing tendency. It is, according to him, a tendency with which Plato does not agree. Whereas the Friends of Ideas are said to deny the reality of all movement and change, 'Plato never denied the reality of movement. Plato never distinguished οὐσία and γένεσις without establishing a genuine relationship between them' (*La définition de l'être*, pp. 61 and 129). In the same spirit, H. Cherniss (*Riddle of the Academy*, chap. iii, p. 79; *Aristotle's Criticism of Plato and the Academy*, i, p. 439) says that the Friends of Ideas admit neither physical movement nor an Idea of movement, whereas such an Idea is both implicitly and explicitly asserted in Plato's earlier writings. He is unable, however, to quote an 'explicit' reference earlier than *Parmen.* 129 d, e. Cherniss also points out that the Friends of Ideas are not criticized by the Stranger for separating the intelligible too sharply from the sensible, so that, even if they are misguided members of the Academy, their mistake did not consist in taking the 'apparent separation' of the Ideas too literally. Directly contrary to this is the view of F. M. Cornford that every feature of the doctrine now ascribed to the Friends of Ideas can be illustrated from the *Phaedo*.

The question at issue here may be partly a verbal one. But it is plainly implied in such a passage as *Republic*, v. 476 a, and the whole subsequent argument, that movement and change and plurality are a hallucination due to imperfect powers of apprehension. They would have no meaning for a mind which could intuit the Ideas, and, indeed, the philosopher can to some extent liberate himself even

dialogue which is called by his name. Theaetetus himself is not distinguished by the remarkable traits which are attributed to him in the preceding dialogue. He is no longer under the spell of Socrates, or subject to the operation of his midwifery, though the fiction of question and answer is still maintained, and the necessity of taking Theaetetus along with him is several times insisted upon by his partner in the discussion. There is a reminiscence of the old Theaetetus in his remark that he will not tire of the argument, and in his conviction, which the Eleatic thinks likely to be permanent, that the course of events is governed by the will of God. Throughout the two dialogues Socrates continues a silent auditor, in the *Statesman* just reminding us of his presence, at the commencement, by a characteristic jest about the statesman and the philosopher, and by an allusion to his namesake, with whom on that ground he claims relationship, as he had already claimed an affinity with Theaetetus, grounded on the likeness of his ugly face. But in neither dialogue, any more than in the *Timaeus*, does he offer any criticism on the views which are propounded by another.

The style, though wanting in dramatic power—in this respect resembling the *Philebus* and the *Laws*—is very clear and accurate, and has several touches of humour and satire. The language is less fanciful and imaginative than that of the earlier dialogues; and there is more of bitterness, as in the *Laws*, though traces of a similar temper may also be observed in the description of the 'great brute' in the *Republic*, and in the contrast of the lawyer and philosopher in the *Theaetetus*. The following are characteristic passages: 'The ancient philosophers, of whom we may say, without offence, that they went on their way rather regardless of whether we understood them or not'; the picture of the materialists, or earth-born giants, 'who grasped oaks and rocks in their hands', and who must be improved before they can be reasoned with; and the equally humorous delineation of the Friends of Ideas, who defend themselves from a fastness in the invisible world; or the comparison of the Sophist to a painter or maker (cf. *Rep.* x), and the hunt after him in the rich meadow-lands of youth and wealth; or, again, the light and graceful touch with which the older philosophies are painted ('Ionian and Sicilian muses'), the comparison of

now from the illusion. The supposition of a Form of Movement is certainly foreign to the earlier dialogues and would have made chaos of Plato's earlier ontology. It is assumed in the *Cratylus* that there are Forms of actions such as cutting; but this dialogue is in all probability later than the *Republic*. Thus on this point the view of Jowett and Cornford is preferable to that of Diès and Cherniss; and it seems most probable that in the *Sophist* Plato intends, among other things, to announce a change in his own doctrine; though, as has been said, Zeller and Jowett seem to have misunderstood the nature of this change.]

them to mythological tales, and the fear of the Eleatic that he will be counted a parricide if he ventures to lay hands on his father Parmenides; or, once more, the likening of the Eleatic Stranger to a god from heaven.—All these passages, notwithstanding the decline of the style, retain the impress of the great master of language. But the equably diffused grace is gone; instead of the endless variety of the early dialogues, traces of the rhythmical monotonous cadence of the *Laws* begin to appear; and already an approach is made to the technical language of Aristotle, in the frequent use of the words 'essence', 'power', 'generation', 'motion', 'rest', 'action', 'passion', and the like.

The *Sophist*, like the *Phaedrus*, has a double character, and unites two inquiries, which are only in a somewhat forced manner connected with each other. The first is the search after the Sophist, the second is the inquiry into the nature of Not-being, which occupies the middle part of the work. For 'Not-being' is the hole or division of the dialectical net in which the Sophist has hidden himself. He is the imaginary impersonation of false opinion. Yet he denies the possibility of false opinion; for falsehood is that which is not, and therefore has no existence. At length the difficulty is solved; the answer, in the language of the *Republic*, appears 'tumbling out at our feet'. Acknowledging that there is a communion of kinds with kinds, and not merely one Being or Good having different names, or several isolated ideas or classes incapable of communion, we discover 'Not-being' to be the other of 'Being'. Transferring this to language and thought, we have no difficulty in apprehending that a proposition may be false as well as true. The Sophist, drawn out of the shelter which Cynic and Megarian paradoxes have temporarily afforded him, is proved to be a dissembler and juggler with words.

The chief points of interest in the dialogue are: (I) the character attributed to the Sophist; (II) the dialectical method; (III) the nature of the puzzle about 'Not-being'; (IV) the battle of the philosophers; (V) the relation of the *Sophist* to other dialogues.

I. The Sophist in Plato is the master of the art of illusion; the charlatan, the foreigner, the prince of *esprits-faux*, the hireling who is not a teacher, and who, from whatever point of view he is regarded, is the opposite of the true teacher. He is the 'evil one', the ideal representative of all that Plato most disliked in the moral and intellectual tendencies of his own age; the adversary of the almost equally ideal Socrates. He seems to be always growing in the fancy of Plato, now boastful, now eristic, now clothing himself in rags of philosophy, now more akin to the rhetorician or lawyer, now haranguing, now questioning, until the final appearance in the *Politicus* of his departing shadow in the disguise of a statesman. We are not to suppose that Plato intended by such a description to depict Protagoras or Gorgias, or even Thrasymachus, who all turn out to be 'very good sort of people when we know them', and all of them part on good terms with Socrates. But he is speaking of a being as imaginary as the wise man of the Stoics, and whose character varies in different dialogues. Like mythology, Greek philosophy has a tendency to personify ideas. And the Sophist is not merely a teacher of rhetoric for a fee of one or fifty drachmae (*Crat.* 384 b), but an ideal of Plato's in which the falsehood of all mankind is reflected.

A milder tone is adopted towards the sophists in a well-known passage of the *Republic* (vi. 492), where they are described as the followers rather than the leaders of the rest of mankind. Plato ridicules the notion that any individuals can corrupt youth to a degree worth speaking of in comparison with the greater influence of public opinion. But there is no real inconsistency between this and other descriptions of the sophist which occur in the Platonic writings. For Plato is not justifying the sophists in the passage just quoted, but only representing their power to be contemptible; they are to be despised rather than feared, and are no worse than the rest of mankind. But a teacher or statesman may be justly condemned, who is on a level with mankind when he ought to be above them. There is another point of view in which this passage should also be considered. The great enemy of Plato is the world, not exactly in the theological sense, yet in one not wholly different—the world as the hater of truth and lover of appearance, occupied in the pursuit of gain and pleasure rather than of knowledge, banded together against the few good and wise men, and devoid of true education. This creature has many heads: rhetoricians, lawyers, statesmen, poets, sophists. But the Sophist is the Proteus who takes the likeness of all of them; all other deceivers have a piece of him in them. And sometimes he is represented as the corrupter of the world; and sometimes the world as the corrupter of him and of itself.

Of late years the sophists have found an enthusiastic defender in the distinguished historian of Greece. He appears to maintain (1) that the term 'sophist' is not the name of a particular class, and would have been applied indifferently to Socrates and Plato, as well as to Gorgias and Protagoras; (2) that the bad sense was imprinted on the word by the genius of Plato; (3) that the principal sophists were not the corrupters of youth (for the Athenian youth were no more corrupted in the age of Demosthenes than in the age of Pericles), but honourable and estimable persons, who supplied a training in literature which was generally wanted at the time. We will briefly consider how far these statements appear to be justified by facts: and, 1, about the meaning of the word there arises an interesting question:

Many words are used both in a general and a specific sense, and the two senses are not always clearly distinguished. Sometimes the generic meaning has been narrowed to the specific, while in other cases the specific meaning has been enlarged or altered. Examples of the former class are furnished by some ecclesiastical terms: Apostles, Prophets, Bishops, Elders, Catholics. Examples of the latter class may also be found in a similar field: Jesuits, Puritans, Methodists, and the like. Sometimes the meaning is both narrowed and enlarged; and a good or bad sense will subsist side by side with a neutral one. A curious effect is produced on the meaning of a word when the very term which is stigmatized by the world (e.g. Methodists) is adopted by the obnoxious or derided class; this tends to define the meaning. Or, again, the opposite result is produced, when the world refuses to allow some sect or body of men the possession of an honourable name which they have assumed, or applies it to them only in mockery or irony.

The term 'sophist' is one of those words of which the meaning has been both contracted and enlarged. Passages may be quoted from Herodotus and the tragedians, in which the word is used in a neutral sense for a contriver or deviser or inventor, without including any ethical idea of goodness or badness. Poets as well as philosophers were called sophists in the fifth century before Christ. In Plato himself the term is applied in the sense of a 'master in art', without any bad meaning attaching to it (*Symp.* 208 c; *Meno* 85 b). In the later Greek, again, 'sophist' and 'philosopher' became almost indistinguishable. There was no reproach conveyed by the word; the additional association, if any, was only that of rhetorician or teacher. Philosophy had become eclecticism and imitation: in the decline of Greek thought there was no original voice lifted up 'which reached to a thousand years because of the god'. Hence the two words, like the characters represented by them, tended to pass into one another. Yet even here some differences appeared; for the term 'sophist' would hardly have been applied to the greater names, such as Plotinus, and would have been more often used of a professor of philosophy in general than of a maintainer of particular tenets.

But the real question is, not whether the word 'sophist' has all these senses, but whether there is not also a specific bad sense in which the term is applied to certain contemporaries of Socrates. Would an Athenian, as Mr. Grote supposes, in the fifth century before Christ, have included Socrates and Plato, as well as Gorgias and Protagoras, under the specific class of sophists? To this question we must answer,

No: if ever the term is applied to Socrates and Plato, either the application is made by an enemy out of mere spite, or the sense in which it is used is neutral. Plato, Xenophon, Isocrates, Aristotle, all give a bad import to the word; and the sophists are regarded as a separate class in all of them. And in later Greek literature, the distinction is quite marked between the succession of philosophers from Thales to Aristotle, and the sophists of the age of Socrates, who appeared like meteors for a short time in different parts of Greece. For the purposes of comedy, Socrates may have been identified with the sophists, and he seems to complain of this in the *Apology*. But there is no reason to suppose that Socrates, differing by so many outward marks, would really have been confounded in the mind of Anytus, or Callicles, or of any intelligent Athenian, with the splendid foreigners who from time to time visited Athens, or appeared at the Olympic games. The man of genius, the great original thinker, the disinterested seeker after truth, the master of repartee whom no one ever defeated in an argument, was separated, even in the mind of the vulgar Athenian, by an 'interval which no geometry can express', from the balancer of sentences, the interpreter and reciter of the poets, the divider of the meanings of words, the teacher of rhetoric, the professor of morals and manners.

2. The use of the term 'sophist' in the dialogues of Plato also shows that the bad sense was not affixed by his genius, but already current. When Protagoras says, 'I confess that I am a sophist', he implies that the art which he professes has already a bad name; and the words of the young Hippocrates, when with a blush upon his face which is just seen by the light of dawn he admits that he is going to be made 'a sophist', would lose their point, unless the term had been discredited. There is nothing surprising in the sophists having an evil name; that, whether deserved or not, was a natural consequence of their vocation. That they were foreigners, that they made fortunes, that they taught novelties, that they excited the minds of youth, are quite sufficient reasons to account for the opprobrium which attached to them. The genius of Plato could not have stamped the word anew, or have imparted the associations which occur in contemporary writers, such as Xenophon and Isocrates. Changes in the meaning of words can only be made with great difficulty, and not unless they are supported by a strong current of popular feeling. There is nothing improbable in supposing that Plato may have extended and envenomed the meaning, or that he may have done the sophists the same kind of disservice with posterity which Pascal did to the Jesuits. But the bad sense of the word was not and could not have been invented by him, and is found in his earlier dialogues, e.g. the *Protagoras*, as well as in the later.

3. There is no ground for disbelieving that the principal sophists, Gorgias, Protagoras, Prodicus, Hippias, were good and honourable men. The notion that they were corrupters of the Athenian youth has no real foundation, and partly arises out of the use of the term 'sophist' in modern times. The truth is, that we know little about them; and the witness of Plato in their favour is probably not much more historical than his witness against them. Of that national decline of genius, unity, political force, which has been sometimes described as the corruption of youth, the sophists were one among many signs; —in these respects Athens may have degenerated; but, as Mr. Grote remarks, there is no reason to suspect any greater moral corruption in the age of Demosthenes than in the age of Pericles. The Athenian youth were not corrupted in this sense, and therefore the sophists could not have corrupted them. It is remarkable, and may be fairly set down to their credit, that Plato nowhere attributes to them that peculiar Greek sympathy with youth, which he ascribes to Parmenides, and which was evidently common in the Socratic circle. Plato delights to exhibit them in a ludicrous point of view, and to show them always rather at a disadvantage in the company of Socrates. But he has no quarrel with their characters, and does not deny that they are respectable men.

The Sophist, in the dialogue which is called after him, is exhibited in many different lights, and appears and reappears in a variety of forms. There is some want of the higher Platonic art in the Eleatic Stranger eliciting his true character by a laborious process of inquiry, when he had already admitted that he knew quite well the difference between the Sophist and the Philosopher, and had often heard the question discussed;—such an anticipation would hardly have occurred in the earlier dialogues. But Plato could not altogether give up his Socratic method, of which another trace may be thought to be discerned in his adoption of a common instance before he proceeds to the greater matter in hand. Yet the example is also chosen in order to damage the 'hooker of men' as much as possible; each step in the pedigree of the angler suggests some injurious reflection about the Sophist. They are both hunters after a living prey, nearly related to tyrants and thieves, and the Sophist is the cousin of the parasite and flatterer. The effect of this is heightened by the accidental manner in which the discovery is made, as the result of a scientific division. His descent in another branch affords the opportunity of more 'unsavoury comparisons'. For he is a retail trader, and his wares are either imported or home-made, like those of other retail traders; his art is thus deprived of the character of a liberal profession. But the most distinguishing characteristic of him is, that he is a disputant, and higgles over an argument. A feature of the Eristic here seems to blend with Plato's usual description of the sophists, who in the early dialogues, and in the *Republic*, are frequently depicted as endeavouring to save themselves from disputing with Socrates by making long orations. In this character he parts company from the vain and impertinent talker in private life, who is a loser of money, while he is a maker of it.

But there is another general division under which his art may be also supposed to fall, and that is purification; and from purification is descended education, and the new principle of education is to interrogate men after the manner of Socrates, and make them teach themselves. Here again we catch a glimpse rather of a Socratic or Eristic than of a Sophist in the ordinary sense of the term. And Plato does not on this ground reject the claim of the Sophist to be the true philosopher. One more feature of the Eristic rather than of the Sophist is the tendency of the troublesome animal to run away into the darkness of Not-being. Upon the whole, we detect in him a sort of hybrid or double nature, of which, except perhaps in the *Euthydemus* of Plato, we find no other trace in Greek philosophy; he combines the teacher of virtue with the Eristic; which in his omniscience, in his ignorance of himself, in his arts of deception, and in his lawyer-like habit of writing and speaking about all things, he is still the antithesis of Socrates and of the true teacher.

II. The question has been asked, whether the method of *abscissio infiniti*, by which the Sophist is taken, is a real and valuable logical process. Modern science feels that this, like other processes of formal logic, presents a very inadequate conception of the actual complex procedure of the mind by which scientific truth is detected and verified. Plato himself seems to be aware that mere division is an unsafe and uncertain weapon, first, in the *Statesman*, when he says that we should divide in the middle, for in that way we are more likely to attain species; secondly, in the parallel precept of the *Philebus*, that we should not pass from the most general notions to infinity, but include all the intervening middle principles, until, as he also says in the *Statesman*, we arrive at the *infima species*; thirdly, in the *Phaedrus*, when he says that the dialectician will carve the limbs of truth without mangling them; and once more in the *Statesman*, if we cannot bisect species, we must carve them as well as we can. No better image of nature or truth, as an organic whole, can be conceived than this. So far is Plato from supposing that mere division and subdivision of general notions will guide men into all truth.

Plato does not really mean to say that the Sophist or the Statesman can be caught in this way. But these divisions and subdivisions were favourite logical exercises of the age in which he lived; and while indulging his dialectical fancy, and making a contribution to logical method, he delights also to transfix the Eristic Sophist with weapons borrowed from his own armoury. As we have already seen, the division gives him the opportunity of making the most damaging reflections on the Sophist and all his kith and kin, and to exhibit him in the most discreditable light.

Nor need we seriously consider whether Plato was right in assuming that an animal so various could not be confined within the limits of a single definition. In the infancy of logic, men sought only to obtain a definition of an unknown or uncertain term; the after-reflection scarcely occurred to them that the word might have several senses, which shaded off into one another, and were not capable of being comprehended in a single notion. There is no trace of this reflection in Plato. But neither is there any reason to think, even if the reflection had occurred to him, that he would have been deterred from carrying on the war with weapons fair or unfair against the outlaw Sophist.

III. The puzzle about 'not-being' appears to us to be one of the most unreal difficulties of ancient philosophy. We cannot understand the attitude of mind which could imagine that falsehood had no existence, if reality was denied to not-being: How could such a question arise at all, much less become of serious importance? The answer to this, and to nearly all other difficulties of early Greek philosophy, is to be sought for in the history of ideas, and the answer is only unsatisfactory because our knowledge is defective. In the passage from the world of sense and imagination and common language to that of opinion and reflection the human mind was exposed to many dangers, and often

Found no end in wandering mazes lost.

On the other hand, the discovery of abstractions was the great source of all mental improvement in after ages. It was the pushing aside of the old, the revelation of the new. But each one of the company of abstractions, if we may speak in the metaphorical language of Plato, became in turn the tyrant of the mind, the dominant idea, which would allow no other to have a share in the throne. This is especially true of the Eleatic philosophy: while the absoluteness of being was asserted in every form of language, the sensible world and all the phenomena of experience were comprehended under not-being. Nor was any difficulty or perplexity thus created, so long as the mind, lost in the contemplation of being, asked no more questions, and never thought of applying the categories of being or not-being to mind or opinion or practical life.

But the negative as well as the positive idea had sunk deep into the intellect of man. The effect of the paradoxes of Zeno extended far beyond the Eleatic circle. And now an unforeseen consequence began to arise. If the Many were not, if all things were names of the One, and nothing could be predicated of any other thing, how could truth be distinguished from falsehood? The Eleatic philosopher would have replied that being is alone true. But mankind had got beyond his barren abstractions: they were beginning to analyse, to classify, to define, to ask what is the nature of knowledge, opinion, sensation. Still less could they be content with the description which Achilles gives in Homer of the man whom his soul hates—

$$\text{ὅς χ' ἕτερον μὲν κεύθῃ ἐνὶ φρεσίν, ἄλλο δὲ εἴπῃ.}$$

For their difficulty was not a practical but a metaphysical one; and their conception of falsehood was really impaired and weakened by a metaphysical illusion.

The strength of the illusion seems to lie in the alternative: If we once admit the existence of being and not-being, as two spheres which exclude each other, no being or reality can be ascribed to not-being, and therefore not to falsehood, which is the image or expression of not-being. Falsehood is wholly false; and to speak of true falsehood, as Theaetetus does (*Theaet.* 189 c), is a contradiction in terms. The fallacy to us is ridiculous and transparent,—no better than those which Plato satirizes in the *Euthydemus*. It is a confusion of falsehood and negation, from which Plato himself is not entirely free. Instead of saying, 'This is not in accordance with facts', 'This is proved by experience to be false', and from such examples forming a general notion of falsehood, the mind of the Greek thinker was lost in the mazes of the Eleatic philosophy. And the greater importance which Plato attributes to this fallacy, compared with others, is due to the influence which the Eleatic philosophy exerted over him. He sees clearly to a certain extent; but he has not yet attained a complete mastery over the ideas of his predecessors—they are still ends to him, and not mere instruments of thought. They are too rough-hewn to be harmonized in a single structure, and may be compared to rocks which project or overhang in some ancient city's walls. There are many such imperfect syncretisms or eclecticisms in the history of philosophy. A modern philosopher, though emancipated from scholastic notions of essence or substance, might still be seriously affected by the abstract idea of necessity; or though accustomed, like Bacon, to criticize abstract notions, might not extend his criticism to the syllogism.

The saying or thinking the thing that is not, would be the popular definition of falsehood or error. If we were met by the Sophist's objection, the reply would probably be an appeal to experience. Ten thousands, as Homer would say (μάλα μυρίοι), tell falsehoods and fall into errors. And this is Plato's reply, both in the *Cratylus* (429 d) and *Sophist*. 'Theaetetus is flying', is a sentence in form quite as grammatical as 'Theaetetus is sitting'; the difference between the two sentences is, that the one is true and the other false. But, before making this appeal to common sense, Plato propounds for our consideration a theory of the nature of the negative.

The theory is, that not-being is relation. Not-being is the other of being, and has as many kinds as there are differences in being. This doctrine is the simple converse of the famous proposition of Spinoza,— not 'Omnis determinatio est negatio', but 'Omnis negatio est determinatio';—not, All distinction is negation, but, All negation is distinction. Not-being is the unfolding or determining of being, and is a necessary element in all other things that are. We should be careful to observe, first, that Plato does not identify being with not-being; he has no idea of progression by antagonism, or of the Hegelian vibration of moments: he would not have said with Heracleitus, 'All things are and are not, and become and become not.' Secondly, he has lost sight altogether of the other sense of not-being, as the negative of being; although he again and again recognizes the validity of the law of contradiction. Thirdly, he seems to confuse falsehood with negation. Nor is he quite consistent in regarding not-being as one class of being, and yet as coextensive with being in general. Before analysing further the topics thus suggested, we will endeavour to trace the manner in which Plato arrived at his conception of not-being.

In all the later dialogues of Plato, the idea of mind or intelligence becomes more and more prominent. That idea which Anaxagoras employed inconsistently in the construction of the world, Plato, in the *Philebus*, the *Sophist*, and the *Laws*, extends to all things, attributing to Providence a care, infinitesimal as well as infinite, of all creation. The divine mind is the leading religious thought of the later works of Plato. The human mind is a sort of reflection of this, having ideas of Being, Sameness, and the like. At times they seem to be parted by a great gulf (*Parmenides*); at other times they have a common nature, and the light of a common intelligence.

But this ever-growing idea of mind is really irreconcilable with the abstract Pantheism of the Eleatics. To the passionate language of

Parmenides, Plato replies in a strain equally passionate:—What! has not being mind? and is not being capable of being known? and, if this is admitted, then capable of being affected or acted upon?—in motion, then, and yet not wholly incapable of rest. Already we have been compelled to attribute opposite determinations to being. And the answer to the difficulty about being may be equally the answer to the difficulty about not-being.

The answer is, that in these and all other determinations of any notion we are attributing to it 'not-being'. We went in search of not-being and seemed to lose being, and now in the hunt after being we recover both. Not-being is a kind of being, and in a sense co-extensive with being. And there are as many divisions of not-being as of being. To every positive idea—'just', 'beautiful', and the like, there is a corresponding negative idea—'not-just', 'not-beautiful', and the like.

A doubt may be raised whether this account of the negative is really the true one. The common logicians would say that the 'not-just', 'not-beautiful', are not really classes at all, but are merged in one great class of the infinite or negative. The conception of Plato, in the days before logic, seems to be more correct than this. For the word 'not' does not altogether annihilate the positive meaning of the word 'just': at least, it does not prevent our looking for the 'not-just' in or about the same class in which we might expect to find the 'just'. 'Not-just is not-honourable' is neither a false nor an unmeaning proposition. The reason is that the negative proposition has really passed into an undefined positive. To say that 'not-just' has no more meaning than 'not-honourable'—that is to say, that the two cannot in any degree be distinguished, is clearly repugnant to the common use of language.

The ordinary logic is also jealous of the explanation of negation as relation, because seeming to take away the principle of contradiction. Plato, as far as we know, is the first philosopher who distinctly enunciated this principle; and though we need not suppose him to have been always consistent with himself, there is no real inconsistency between his explanation of the negative and the principle of contradiction. Neither the Platonic notion of the negative as the principle of difference, nor the Hegelian identity of being and not-being, at all touch the principle of contradiction. For what is asserted about being and not-being only relates to our most abstract notions, and in no way interferes with the principle of contradiction employed in the concrete. Because not-being is identified with difference, or being with not-being, this does not make the proposition 'Some have not eaten' any the less a contradiction of 'All have eaten'.

The explanation of the negative given by Plato in the *Sophist* is a true but partial one; for the word 'not', besides the meaning of 'other', may also imply 'opposition'. And difference or opposition may be either total or partial: the not-beautiful may be other than the beautiful, or in no relation to the beautiful, or a specific class in various degrees opposed to the beautiful. And the negative may be a negation of fact or of thought (οὐ and μή). Lastly, there are certain ideas, such as 'beginning', 'becoming', 'the finite', 'the abstract', in which the negative cannot be separated from the positive, and 'being' and 'not-being' are inextricably blended.

Plato restricts the conception of not-being to difference. Man is a rational animal, and *is not* as many other things as are not included under this definition. He is and is not, and is because he is not. Besides the positive class to which he belongs, there are endless negative classes to which he may be referred. This is certainly intelligible, but useless. To refer a subject to a negative class is unmeaning, unless the 'not' is a mere modification of the positive, as in the example of 'not honourable' and 'dishonourable'; or unless the class is characterized by the absence rather than the presence of a particular quality.

Nor is it easy to see how not-being any more than sameness or difference is one of the classes of being. They are aspects rather than classes of being. Not-being can only be included in being, as the denial of some particular class of being. If we attempt to pursue such airy phantoms at all, the Hegelian identity of being and not-being is a more apt and intelligible expression of the same mental phenomenon. For Plato has not distinguished between the being which is prior to not-being, and the being which is the negation of not-being (cf. *Parm.* 162 a, b).

But he is not thinking of this when he says that being comprehends not-being. Again, we should probably go back for the true explanation to the influence which the Eleatic philosophy exercised over him. Under 'not-being' the Eleatic had included all the realities of the sensible world. Led by this association and by the common use of language, which has been already noticed, we cannot be much surprised that Plato should have made classes of not-being. It is observable that he does not absolutely deny that there is an opposite of being. He is inclined to leave the question, merely remarking that the opposition, if admissible at all, is not expressed by the term 'not-being'.

On the whole, we must allow that the great service rendered by Plato to metaphysics in the *Sophist* is not his explanation of 'not-being' as difference. With this he certainly laid the ghost of 'not-being'; and we may attribute to him in a measure the credit of anticipating Spinoza and Hegel. But his conception is not clear or consistent; he does not recognize the different senses of the negative, and he confuses the different classes of not-being with the abstract notion. As the pre-Socratic philosopher failed to distinguish between the universal and the true, while he placed the particulars of sense under the false and apparent, so Plato appears to identify negation with falsehood, or is unable to distinguish them. The greatest service rendered by him to mental science is the recognition of the communion of classes, which, although based by him on his account of 'not-being', is independent of it. He clearly saw that the isolation of ideas or classes is the annihilation of reasoning. Thus, after wandering in many diverging paths, we return to common sense. And for this reason we may be inclined to do less than justice to Plato,—because the truth which he attains by a real effort of thought is to us a familiar and unconscious truism, which no one would any longer think either of doubting or examining.

IV. The later dialogues of Plato contain many references to contemporary philosophy. Both in the *Theaetetus* and in the *Sophist* he recognizes that he is in the midst of a fray; a huge irregular battle everywhere surrounds him (*Theaet.* 153 a). First, there are the two great philosophies going back into cosmogony and poetry: the philosophy of Heracleitus, supposed to have a poetical origin in Homer, and that of the Eleatics, which in a similar spirit he conceives to be even older than Xenophanes (cf. *Protag.* 316 e). Still older were theories of two and three principles, hot and cold, moist and dry, which were ever marrying and being given in marriage: in speaking of these, he is probably referring to Pherecydes and the early Ionians. In the philosophy of motion there were different accounts of the relation of plurality and unity, which were supposed to be joined and severed by love and hate, some maintaining that this process was perpetually going on (e.g. Heracleitus); others (e.g. Empedocles) that there was an alternation of them. Of the Pythagoreans or of Anaxagoras he makes no distinct mention. His chief opponents are, first, Eristics or Megarians; secondly, the Materialists.

The picture which he gives of both these latter schools is indistinct; and he appears reluctant to mention the names of their teachers. Nor can we easily determine how much is to be assigned to the Cynics, how much to the Megarians, or whether the 'repellent Materialists' (*Theaet.* 156 a) are Cynics or Atomists, or represent some unknown phase of opinion at Athens. To the Cynics and Antisthenes is commonly attributed, on the authority of Aristotle, the denial of predication, while the Megarians are said to have been Nominalists, asserting the One Good under many names to be the true Being of Zeno and the Eleatics, and, like Zeno, employing their negative dialectic in the refutation of opponents. But the later Megarians also denied predication; and this tenet, which is attributed to all of them by Simplicius, is certainly in accordance with their over-refining philosophy. The 'tyros young and old', of whom Plato speaks (*infra* 251 b), probably include both. At any rate, we shall be safer in accepting the general description of them which he has given, and in not attempting to draw a precise line between them.

Of these Eristics, whether Cynics or Megarians, several characteristics are found in Plato:

1. They pursue verbal oppositions; 2. they make reasoning impossible by their over-accuracy in the use of language; 3. they deny predication; 4. they go from unity to plurality, without passing through the intermediate stages; 5. they refuse to attribute motion or power to Being; 6. they are the enemies of sense;—whether they are the 'friends of ideas', who carry on the polemic against sense, is uncertain; probably under this remarkable expression Plato designates those who more nearly approached himself, and may be criticizing an earlier form of his own doctrines. We may observe (1) that he professes only to give us a few opinions out of many which were at that time current in Greece; (2) that he nowhere alludes to the ethical teaching of the Cynics—unless the argument in the *Protagoras*, that the virtues are one and not many, may be supposed to contain a reference to their views, as well as to those of Socrates; and unless they are the school alluded to in the *Philebus*, which is described as 'being very skilful in physics, and as maintaining pleasure to be the absence of pain'. That Antisthenes wrote a book called *Physicus* is hardly a sufficient reason for describing them as skilful in physics, which appear to have been very alien to the tendency of the Cynics.

The Idealism of the fourth century before Christ in Greece, as in other ages and countries, seems to have provoked a reaction towards Materialism. The maintainers of this doctrine are described in the *Theaetetus* as obstinate persons who will believe in nothing which they cannot hold in their hands, and in the *Sophist* (246 d) as incapable of argument. They are probably the same who are said in the Tenth Book of the *Laws* (888 e) to attribute the course of events to nature, art, and chance. Who they were, we have no means of determining except from Plato's description of them. His silence respecting the Atomists might lead us to suppose that here we have a trace of them. But the Atomists were not Materialists in the grosser sense of the term, nor were they incapable of reasoning; and Plato would hardly have described a great genius like Democritus in the disdainful terms which he uses of the Materialists. Upon the whole, we must infer that the persons here spoken of are unknown to us, like the many other writers and talkers at Athens and elsewhere, of whose endless activity of mind Aristotle in his *Metaphysics* has preserved an anonymous memorial.

V. The *Sophist* is the sequel of the *Theaetetus*, and is connected with the *Parmenides* by a direct allusion (cf. Introductions to *Theaetetus* and *Parmenides*). In the *Theaetetus* we sought to discover the nature of knowledge and false opinion. But the nature of false opinion seemed impenetrable; for we were unable to understand how there could be any reality in Not-being. In the *Sophist* the question is taken up again; the nature of Not-being is detected, and there is no longer any metaphysical impediment in the way of admitting the possibility of falsehood. To the *Parmenides*, the *Sophist* stands in a less defined and more remote relation. There human thought is in process of disorganization; no absurdity or inconsistency is too great to be elicited from the analysis of the simple ideas of Unity or Being. In the *Sophist* the same contradictions are pursued to a certain extent, but only with a view to their resolution. The aim of the dialogue is to show how the few elemental conceptions of the human mind admit of a natural connexion in thought and speech, which Megarian or other sophistry vainly attempts to deny.

ANALYSIS

True to the appointment of the previous day, Theodorus and Theaetetus meet Socrates at the same spot, bringing with them an Eleatic Stranger, whom Theodorus introduces as a true philosopher. Socrates, half in jest, half in earnest, declares that he must be a god in disguise, who, as Homer would say, has come to earth that he may visit the good and evil among men, and detect the foolishness of Athenian wisdom. At any rate he is a divine person, one of a class who are hardly recognized on earth; who appear in divers forms—now as statesmen, now as sophists, and are often deemed madmen. 'Philosopher, statesman, sophist', says Socrates, repeating the words—'I should like to ask our Eleatic friend what his countrymen think of them; do they regard them as one, or three?'

The Stranger has been already asked the same question by Theodorus and Theaetetus; and he at once replies that they are thought to be three; but to explain the difference fully would take time. He is pressed to give this fuller explanation, either in the form of a speech or of question and answer. He prefers the latter, and chooses as his respondent Theaetetus, whom he already knows, and who is recommended to him by Socrates.

We are agreed, he says, about the name Sophist, but we may not be equally agreed about his nature. Great subjects should be approached through familiar examples, and, considering that he is a creature not easily caught, I think that, before approaching him, we should try our hand upon some more obvious animal, who may be made the subject of logical experiment; shall we say an angler? 'Very good.'

219

In the first place, the angler is an artist; and there are two kinds of art,—productive art, which includes husbandry, manufactures, imitations; and acquisitive art, which includes learning, trading, fighting, hunting. The angler's is an acquisitive art, and acquisition may be effected either by exchange or by conquest; in the latter case, either by force or craft. Conquest by craft is called hunting, and of hunting there is one kind which pursues inanimate, and another which pursues animate objects; and animate objects may be either land animals or water animals, and water animals either fly over the water or live in the water. The hunting of the last is called fishing; and of fishing, one kind uses enclosures, catching the fish in nets and baskets, and another kind strikes them either with spears by night or with barbed spears or barbed hooks by day; the barbed spears are impelled from above, the barbed hooks are jerked into the head and lips of the fish, which are then drawn from below upwards. Thus, by a series of divisions, we have arrived at the definition of the angler's art.

220

221

And now by the help of this example we may proceed to bring to light the nature of the Sophist. Like the angler, he is an artist, and the resemblance does not end here. For they are both hunters, and hunters of animals; the one of water, and the other of land animals. But at this point they diverge, the one going to the sea and the rivers, and the other to the rivers of wealth and rich meadow-lands, in which generous youth abide. On land you may hunt tame animals, or you may hunt wild animals. And man is a tame animal, and he may be hunted either by force or persuasion;—either by the pirate, man-stealer, soldier, or by the

222

lawyer, orator, talker. The latter use persuasion, and persuasion is either private or public. Of the private practitioners of the art, some bring gifts to those whom they hunt: these are lovers. And
223 others take hire; and some of these flatter, and in return are fed; others profess to teach virtue and receive a round sum. And who are these last? Tell me who? Have we not unearthed the Sophist?

But he is a many-sided creature, and may still be traced in another line of descent. The acquisitive art had a branch of exchange as well as of hunting, and exchange is either giving or selling; and the seller is either a manufacturer or a merchant;
224 and the merchant either retails or exports; and the exporter may export either food for the body or food for the mind. And of this trading in food for the mind, one kind may be termed the art of display, and another the art of selling learning; and learning may be a learning of the arts or of virtue. The seller of the arts may be called an art-seller; the seller of virtue, a Sophist.

Again, there is a third line, in which a Sophist may be traced. For is he less a Sophist when, instead of exporting his wares to another country, he stays at home, and retails goods, which he not only buys of others, but manufactures himself?
225 Or he may be descended from the acquisitive art in the combative line, through the pugnacious, the controversial, the disputatious arts; and he will be found at last in the eristic section
226 of the latter, and in that division of it which disputes in private for gain about the general principles of right and wrong.

And still there is a track of him which has not yet been followed out by us. Do not our household servants talk of sifting, straining, winnowing? And they also speak of carding, spinning, and the like. All these are processes of division; and of division there are two kinds,—one in which like is divided from like, and another in which the good is separated from the bad. The latter of the
227 two is termed purification; and again, of purification, there are two sorts,—of animate bodies (which may be internal or external), and of inanimate. Medicine and gymnastic are the internal purifications of the animate, and bathing the external; and of the inanimate, fulling and cleaning and other humble processes, some of which have ludicrous names. Not that dialectic is a respecter of names or persons, or a despiser of humble occupations; nor does she think much of the greater or less benefits

conferred by them. For her aim is knowledge; she wants to know how the arts are related to one another, and would quite as soon learn the nature of hunting from the vermin-destroyer as from the general. And she only desires to have a general name, which shall distinguish purifications of the soul from purifications of the body.

Now purification is the taking away of evil; and there are two kinds of evil in the soul,—the one answering to disease in the 228 body, and the other to deformity. Disease is the discord or war of opposite principles in the soul; and deformity is the want of symmetry, or failure in the attainment of a mark or measure. The latter arises from ignorance, and no one is voluntarily ignorant; ignorance is only the aberration of the soul moving towards knowledge. And as medicine cures the diseases and gymnastic the deformity of the body, so correction cures the 229 injustice, and education (which differs among the Hellenes from mere instruction in the arts) cures the ignorance of the soul. Again, ignorance is twofold, simple ignorance, and ignorance having the conceit of knowledge. And education is also twofold: there is the old-fashioned moral training of our forefathers, which was very troublesome and not very successful; and another, of a 230 more subtle nature, which proceeds upon a notion that all ignorance is involuntary. The latter convicts a man out of his own mouth, by pointing out to him his inconsistencies and contradictions; and the consequence is that he quarrels with himself, instead of quarrelling with his neighbours, and is cured of prejudices and obstructions by a mode of treatment which is equally entertaining and effectual. The physician of the soul is aware that his patient will receive no nourishment unless he has been cleaned out; and the soul of the Great King himself, if he has not undergone this purification, is unclean and impure.

And who are the ministers of the purification? Sophists I may 231 not call them. Yet they bear about the same likeness to Sophists as the dog, who is the gentlest of animals, does to the wolf, who is the fiercest. Comparisons are slippery things; but for the present let us assume the resemblance of the two, which may probably be disallowed hereafter. And so, from division comes purification; and from this, mental purification; and from mental purification, instruction; and from instruction, education; and from

education, the nobly-descended art of Sophistry, which is engaged
in the detection of conceit. I do not however think that we have
yet found the Sophist, or that his will ultimately prove to be the
desired art of education; but neither do I think that he can long
escape me, for every way is blocked. Before we make the final
assault, let us take breath, and reckon up the many forms which
he has assumed: (1) he was the paid hunter of wealth and birth;
(2) he was the trader in the goods of the soul; (3) he was the
retailer of them; (4) he was the manufacturer of his own learned
wares; (5) he was the disputant; and (6) he was the purger away
of prejudices—although this latter point is admitted to be
doubtful.

232   Now, there must surely be something wrong in the professor of
any art having so many names and kinds of knowledge. Does not
the very number of them imply that the nature of his art is not
understood? And that we may not be involved in the misunderstanding, let us observe which of his characteristics is the most
prominent. Above all things he is a disputant. He will dispute
and teach others to dispute about things visible and invisible—
about man, about the gods, about politics, about law, about
233   wrestling, about all things. But can he know all things? 'He cannot'. How then can he dispute satisfactorily with any one who
knows? 'Impossible.' Then what is the trick of his art, and why
does he receive money from his admirers? 'Because he is believed
by them to know all things.' You mean to say that he seems to
have a knowledge of them? 'Yes.'

Suppose a person were to say, not that he would dispute about
all things, but that he would make all things, you and me, and all
other creatures, the earth and the heavens and the gods, and
234   would sell them all for a few pence—this would be a great jest;
but not greater than if he said that he knew all things, and could
teach them in a short time, and at a small cost. For all imitation
is a jest, and the most graceful form of jest. Now the painter is a
man who professes to make all things, and children, who see his
pictures at a distance, sometimes take them for realities: and the
Sophist pretends to know all things, and he, too, can deceive
young men, who are still at a distance from the truth, not through
their eyes, but through their ears, by the mummery of words, and
induce them to believe him. But as they grow older, and come

into contact with realities, they learn by experience the futility of
his pretensions. The Sophist, then, has not real knowledge; he 235
is only an imitator, or image-maker.

And now, having got him in a corner of the dialectical net, let
us divide and subdivide until we catch him. Of image-making
there are two kinds,—the art of making likenesses, and the art of
making appearances. The latter may be illustrated by sculpture 236
and painting, which often use illusions, and alter the proportions
of figures, in order to adapt their works to the eye. And the
Sophist also uses illusions, and his imitations are apparent and
not real. But how can any thing be an appearance only? Here
arises a difficulty which has always beset the subject of appear- 237
ances. For the argument is asserting the existence of not-being.
And this is what the great Parmenides was all his life denying in
prose and also in verse. 'You will never find,' he says, 'that not-
being is.' And the words prove themselves! Not-being cannot
be attributed to any being; for how can any being be wholly
abstracted from being? Again, in every predication there is an
attribution of singular or plural. But number is the most real of 238
all things, and cannot be attributed to not-being. Therefore not-
being cannot be predicated or expressed; for how can we say
'is', 'are not', without number?

And now arises the greatest difficulty of all. If not-being is 239
inconceivable, how can not-being be refuted? And am I not
contradicting myself at this moment, in speaking either in the
singular or the plural of that to which I deny both plurality and
unity? You, Theaetetus, have the might of youth, and I conjure
you to exert yourself, and, if you can, to find an expression for
not-being which does not imply being and number. 'But I cannot.' Then the Sophist must be left in his hole. We may call him
an image-maker if we please, but he will only say, 'And pray,
what is an image?' And we shall reply, 'A reflection in the water,
or in a mirror'; and he will say, 'Let us shut our eyes and open 240
our minds; what is the common notion of all images?' 'I should
answer, Such another, made in the likeness of the true.' Real or
not real? 'Not real; at least, not in a true sense.' And the real
'is', and the not-real 'is not'? 'Yes.' Then a likeness is really
unreal, and essentially not. Here is a pretty complication of being
and not-being, in which the many-headed Sophist has entangled

241 us. He will at once point out that he is compelling us to contradict ourselves, by affirming being of not-being. I think that we must cease to look for him in the class of imitators.

But ought we to give him up? 'I should say, certainly not.' Then I fear that I must lay hands on my father Parmenides; but do not call me a parricide; for there is no way out of the difficulty except to show that in some sense not-being is; and if this is not admitted, no one can speak of falsehood, or false opinion, or
242 imitation, without falling into a contradiction. You observe how unwilling I am to undertake the task; for I know that I am exposing myself to the charge of inconsistency in asserting the being of not-being. But if I am to make the attempt, I think that I had better begin at the beginning.

Lightly in the days of our youth, Parmenides and others told us tales about the origin of the universe: one spoke of three principles warring and at peace again, marrying and begetting children; another of two principles, hot and cold, dry and moist, which also formed relationships. There were the Eleatics in our part of the world, saying that all things are one; whose doctrine begins with Xenophanes, and is even older. Ionian, and, more recently, Sicilian muses speak of a one and many which are held together by enmity and friendship, ever parting, ever meeting.
243 Some of them do not insist on the perpetual strife, but adopt a gentler strain, and speak of alternation only. Whether they are right or not, who can say? But one thing we can say—that they went on their way without much caring whether we understood them or not. For tell me, Theaetetus, do you understand what they mean by their assertion of unity, or by their combinations and separations of two or more principles? I used to think, when I was young, that I knew all about not-being, and now I am in great difficulties even about being.

Let us proceed first to the examination of being. Turning to the dualist philosophers, we say to them: Is being a third element besides hot and cold? or do you identify one or both of the two
244 elements with being? At any rate, you can hardly avoid resolving them into one. Let us next interrogate the patrons of the one. To them we say: Are being and one two different names for the same thing? But how can there be two names when there is nothing but one? Or you may identify them; but then the name will be

either the name of nothing or of itself, i.e. of a name. **Again, the** notion of being is conceived of as a whole—in the words of Parmenides, 'like every way unto a rounded sphere'. And a 245 whole has parts; but that which has parts is not one, for unity has no parts. Is being, then, one, because the parts of being are one, or shall we say that being is not a whole? In the former case, one is made up of parts; and in the latter there is still plurality, viz. being, and a whole which is apart from being. And being, if not all things, lacks something of the nature of being, and becomes not-being. Nor can being ever have come into existence, for nothing comes into existence except as a whole; nor can being have number, for that which has number is a whole or sum of number. These are a few of the difficulties which are accumulating one upon another in the consideration of being.

We may proceed now to the less exact sort of philosophers. 246 Some of them drag down everything to earth, and carry on a war like that of the giants, grasping rocks and oaks in their hands. Their adversaries defend themselves warily from an invisible world, and reduce the substances of their opponents to the minutest fractions, until they are lost in generation and flux. The latter sort are civil people enough; but the materialists are rude and ignorant of dialectics; they must be taught how to argue before they can answer. Yet, for the sake of the argument, we may assume them to be better than they are, and able to give an account of themselves. They admit the existence of a mortal living creature, which is a body containing a soul, and to this they 247 would not refuse to attribute qualities—wisdom, folly, justice, and injustice. The soul, as they say, has a kind of body, but they do not like to assert of these qualities of the soul, either that they are corporeal, or that they have no existence; at this point they begin to make distinctions. 'Sons of earth,' we say to them, 'if both visible and invisible qualities exist, what is the common nature which is attributed to them by the term "being" or "existence"?' And, as they are incapable of answering this question, we may as well reply for them, that being is the power of doing or suffering. Then we turn to the friends of Ideas: to them 248 we say, 'You distinguish becoming from being?' 'Yes,' they will reply. 'And in becoming you participate through the bodily senses, and in being, by thought and the mind?' 'Yes.' And you

mean by the word 'participation' a power of doing or suffering?
To this they answer—I am acquainted with them, Theaetetus,
and know their ways better than you do—that being can neither
do nor suffer, though becoming may. And we rejoin: Does not
the soul know? And is not 'being' known? And are not 'knowing'
and 'being known' active and passive? That which is known is
249 affected by knowledge, and therefore is in motion. And, indeed,
how can we imagine that perfect being is a mere everlasting form,
devoid of motion and soul? for there can be no thought without
soul, nor can soul be devoid of motion. But neither can thought
or mind be devoid of some principle of rest or stability. And as
children say entreatingly, 'Give us both', so the philosopher must
include both the moveable and immoveable in his idea of being.
And yet, alas! he and we are in the same difficulty with which we
250 reproached the dualists; for motion and rest are contradictions—
how then can they both exist? Does he who affirms this mean to
say that motion is rest, or rest motion? 'No; he means to assert
the existence of some third thing, different from them both,
which neither rests nor moves.' But how can there be anything
which neither rests nor moves? Here is a second difficulty about
being, quite as great as that about not-being. And we may hope
251 that any light which is thrown upon the one may extend to the
other.

Leaving them for the present, let us inquire what we mean by
giving many names to the same thing, e.g. white, good, tall, to
man; out of which tyros old and young derive such a feast of
amusement. Their meagre minds refuse to predicate anything of
anything; they say that good is good, and man is man; and that
to affirm one of the other would be making the many one and the
one many. Let us place them in a class with our previous opponents, and interrogate both of them at once. Shall we assume (1)
that being and rest and motion, and all other things, are in-
252 communicable with one another? or (2) that they all have
indiscriminate communion? or (3) that there is communion of
some and not of others? And we will consider the first hypothesis
first of all.

(1) If we suppose the universal separation of kinds, all theories
alike are swept away; the patrons of a single principle of rest or
of motion, or of a plurality of immutable Ideas—all alike have the

ground cut from under them; and all creators of the universe by theories of composition and division, whether out of or into a finite or infinite number of elemental forms, in alternation or continuance, share the same fate. Most ridiculous is the discomfiture which attends the opponents of predication, who, like the ventriloquist Eurycles, have the voice that answers them in their own breast. For they cannot help using the words 'is', 'apart', 'from others', and the like; and their adversaries are thus saved the trouble of refuting them. But (2) if all things have communion with all things, motion will rest, and rest will move; here is a *reductio ad absurdum*. Two out of the three hypotheses are thus seen to be false. The third (3) remains, which affirms that only certain things communicate with certain other things. In the alphabet 253 and the scale there are some letters and notes which combine with others, and some which do not; and the laws according to which they combine or are separated are known to the grammarian and musician. And there is a science which teaches not only what notes and letters, but what classes admit of combination with one another, and what not. This is a noble science, on which we have stumbled unawares; in seeking after the Sophist we have found the philosopher. He is the master who discerns one whole or form pervading a scattered multitude, and many such wholes combined under a higher one, and many entirely apart—he is the true dialectician. Like the Sophist, he is hard to recognize, though for the opposite reasons; the Sophist runs 254 away into the obscurity of not-being, the philosopher is dark from excess of light. And now, leaving him, we will return to our pursuit of the Sophist.

Agreeing in the truth of the third hypothesis, that some things have communion and others not, and that some may have communion with all, let us examine the most important kinds which are capable of admixture; and in this way we may perhaps find out a sense in which not-being may be affirmed to have being. Now the highest kinds are being, rest, motion; and of these, rest and motion exclude each other, but both of them are included in being; and again, they are the same with themselves and the other of each other. What is the meaning of these words, 'same' and 'other'? Are there two more kinds to be added to the three others? For sameness cannot be either rest or motion, because 255 predicated both of rest and motion; nor yet being, because if being were attributed to both of them we should attribute sameness to both of them. Nor can other be identified with being; for then other, which is relative, would have the absoluteness of being. Therefore we must assume a fifth principle, which is universal, and runs through all things, for each thing is other than all other things. Thus there are five principles: (1) being, (2) motion, which is not (3) rest, and because participating both in the same and other, is and is not (4) the same with itself, and is and is not (5) other than the other. And motion is not being, but partakes of being, and therefore is and is not in the most

256 absolute sense. Thus we have discovered that not-being is the principle of the other which runs through all things, being not excepted. And 'being' is one thing, and 'not-being' includes and

257 is all other things. And not-being is not the opposite of being, but only the other. Knowledge has many branches, and the other or difference has as many, each of which is described by prefixing the word 'not' to some kind of knowledge. The not-beautiful is as real as the beautiful, the not-just as the just. And the essence of the not-beautiful is to be separated from and opposed to a certain

258 kind of existence which is termed beautiful. And this opposition and negation is the not-being of which we are in search, and is one kind of being. Thus, in spite of Parmenides, we have not only discovered the existence, but also the nature of not-being—that

259 nature we have found to be relation. In the communion of different kinds, being and other mutually interpenetrate; other is, but is other than being, and other than each and all of the remaining kinds, and therefore in an infinity of ways 'is not'. And the argument has shown that the pursuit of contradictions is childish and useless, and the very opposite of that higher spirit which criticizes the words of another according to the natural

260 meaning of them. Nothing can be more unphilosophical than the denial of all communion of kinds. And we are fortunate in having established such a communion for another reason, because in continuing the hunt after the Sophist we have to examine the nature of discourse, and there could be no discourse if there were no communion. For the Sophist, although he can no longer deny the existence of not-being, may still affirm that not-being cannot enter into discourse, and as he was arguing before that there

could be no such thing as falsehood, because there was no such
thing as not-being, he may continue to argue that there is no such
thing as the art of image-making and phantastic, because not-
being has no place in language. Hence arises the necessity of
examining speech, opinion, and imagination.

And first concerning speech; let us ask the same question 261
about words which we have already answered about the kinds
of being and the letters of the alphabet: To what extent do they
admit of combination? Some words have a meaning when combined, and others have no meaning. One class of words describes
action, another class agents: 'walks', 'runs', 'sleeps' are examples 262
of the first; 'stag', 'horse', 'lion' of the second. But no combination of words can be formed without a verb and a noun, e.g. 'A
man learns'; the simplest sentence is composed of two words, and
one of these must be a subject. For example, in the sentence,
'Theaetetus sits', which is not very long, 'Theaetetus' is the sub- 263
ject, and in the sentence 'Theaetetus flies', 'Theaetetus' is again
the subject. But the two sentences differ in quality, for the first
says of you that which is true, and the second says of you that
which is not true, or, in other words, attributes to you things
which are not as though they were. Here is false discourse in the
shortest form. And thus not only speech, but thought and opinion
and imagination are proved to be both true and false. For thought
is only the process of silent speech, and opinion is only the silent 264
assent or denial which follows this, and imagination is only the
expression of this in some form of sense. All of them are akin to
speech, and therefore, like speech, admit of true and false. And
we have discovered false opinion, which is an encouraging sign of
our probable success in the rest of the inquiry.

Then now let us return to our old division of likeness-making
and phantastic. When we were going to place the Sophist in one
of them, a doubt arose whether there could be such a thing as an
appearance, because there was no such thing as falsehood. At
length falsehood has been discovered by us to exist, and we have
acknowledged that the Sophist is to be found in the class of
imitators. All art was divided originally by us into two branches 265
—productive and acquisitive. And now we may divide both on a
different principle into the creations or imitations which are of
human, and those which are of divine, origin. For we must admit

that the world and ourselves and the animals did not come into existence by chance, or the spontaneous working of nature, but 266 by divine reason and knowledge. And there are not only divine creations but divine imitations, such as apparitions and shadows and reflections, which are equally the work of a divine mind. And there are human creations and human imitations too,— there is the actual house and the drawing of it. Nor must we forget that image-making may be an imitation of realities or an imitation of appearances, which last has been called by us 267 phantastic. And this phantastic may be again divided into imitation by the help of instruments and impersonations. And the latter may be either dissembling or unconscious, either with or without knowledge. A man cannot imitate you, Theaetetus, without knowing you, but he can imitate the form of justice or virtue if he have a sentiment or opinion about them. Not being well provided with names, the former I will venture to call the imitation of science, and the latter the imitation of opinion.

The latter is our present concern, for the Sophist has no claims to science or knowledge. Now the imitator, who has only opinion, 268 may be either the simple imitator, who thinks that he knows, or the dissembler, who is conscious that he does not know, but disguises his ignorance. And the last may be either a maker of long speeches, or of shorter speeches which compel the person conversing to contradict himself. The maker of longer speeches is the popular orator; the maker of the shorter is the Sophist, whose art may be traced as being the

|
contradictious
|
dissembling
|
without knowledge
|
human and not divine
|
juggling with words
|
phantastic or unreal
|
art of image-making.

INTRODUCTION

In commenting on the dialogue in which Plato most nearly approaches the great modern master of metaphysics there are several points which it will be useful to consider, such as the unity of opposites, the conception of the Ideas as causes, and the relation of the Platonic and Hegelian dialectic.

The unity of opposites was the crux of ancient thinkers in the age of Plato: How could one thing be or become another? That substances have attributes was implied in common language; that heat and cold, day and night, pass into one another was a matter of experience 'on a level with the cobbler's understanding' (*Theaet.* 180 d). But how could philosophy explain the connexion of ideas, how justify the passing of them into one another? The abstractions of one, other, being, not-being, rest, motion, individual, universal, which successive generations of philosophers had recently discovered, seemed to be beyond the reach of human thought, like stars shining in a distant heaven. They were the symbols of different schools of philosophy: but in what relation did they stand to one another and to the world of sense? It was hardly conceivable that one could be other, or the same different. Yet without some reconciliation of these elementary ideas thought was impossible. There was no distinction between truth and falsehood, between the Sophist and the philosopher. Everything could be predicated of everything, or nothing of anything. To these difficulties Plato finds what to us appears to be the answer of common sense—that Not-being is the relative or other of Being, the defining and distinguishing principle, and that some Ideas combine with others, but not all with all. It is remarkable however that he offers this obvious reply only as the result of a long and tedious inquiry; by a great effort he is able to look down as 'from a height' on the 'friends of the Ideas' (248 a) as well as on the pre-Socratic philosophies. Yet he is merely asserting principles which no one who could be made to understand them would deny.

The Platonic unity of differences or opposites is the beginning of the modern view that all knowledge is of relations; it also anticipates the doctrine of Spinoza that all determination is negation. Plato takes or gives so much of either of these theories as was necessary or possible in the age in which he lived. In the *Sophist*, as in the *Cratylus*, he is opposed to the Heraclitean flux and equally to the Megarian and Cynic denial of predication, because he regards both of them as making knowledge impossible. He does not assert that everything is and is not, or that the same thing can be affected in the same and in opposite ways at the same time and in respect of the same part of itself.

The law of contradiction is as clearly laid down by him in the *Republic* (iv. 436 ff.; v. 454 c, d) as by Aristotle in his *Organon*. Yet he is aware that in the negative there is also a positive element, and that oppositions may be only differences. And in the *Parmenides* he deduces the many from the one and Not-being from Being, and yet shows that the many are included in the one, and that Not-being returns to Being.

In several of the later dialogues Plato is occupied with the connexion of the sciences, which in the *Philebus* he divides into two classes of pure and applied, adding to them there as elsewhere (*Phaedr., Crat., Rep., States.*) a superintending science of dialectic. This is the origin of Aristotle's *Architectonic*, which seems, however, to have passed into an imaginary science of essence, and no longer to retain any relation to other branches of knowledge. Of such a science, whether described as 'philosophia prima', the science of οὐσία, logic, or metaphysics, philosophers have often dreamed. But even now the time has not arrived when the anticipation of Plato can be realized. Though many a thinker has framed a 'hierarchy of the sciences', no one has as yet found the higher science which arrays them in harmonious order, giving to the organic and inorganic, to the physical and moral, their respective limits, and showing how they all work together in the world and in man.

Plato arranges in order the stages of knowledge and of existence. They are the steps or grades by which he rises from sense and the shadows of sense to the idea of beauty and good. Mind is in motion as well as at rest (*Soph.* 249 b); and may be described as a dialectical progress which passes from one limit or determination of thought to another and back again to the first. This is the account of dialectic given by Plato in the sixth book of the *Republic* (511), which regarded under another aspect is the mysticism of the *Symposium* (*Symp.* 211). He does not deny the existence of objects of sense, but according to him they only receive their true meaning when they are incorporated in a principle which is above them (*Rep.* vi. 511 a, b). In modern language they might be said to come first in the order of experience, last in the order of nature and reason. They are assumed, as he is fond of repeating, upon the condition that they shall give an account of themselves and that the truth of their existence shall be hereafter proved. For philosophy must begin somewhere and may begin anywhere,—with outward objects, with statements of opinion, with abstract principles. But objects of sense must lead us onward to the ideas or universals which are contained in them; the statements of opinion must be verified; the abstract principles must be filled up and connected with one another. In Plato we find, as we might expect, the germs of many thoughts which have been further developed by the genius of Spinoza and Hegel. But there is a difficulty in separating the germ from the flower, or in drawing the line which divides ancient from modern philosophy. Many coincidences which occur in them are unconscious, seeming to show a natural tendency in the human mind towards certain ideas and forms of thought. And there are many speculations of Plato which would have passed away unheeded, and their meaning, like that of some hieroglyphic, would have remained undeciphered, unless two thousand years and more afterwards an interpreter had arisen of a kindred spirit and of the same intellectual family. For example, in the *Sophist* Plato begins with the abstract and goes on to the concrete, not in the lower sense of returning to outward objects, but to the Hegelian concrete or unity of abstractions. In the intervening period hardly any importance would have been attached to the question which is so full of meaning to Plato and Hegel.

They differ, however, in their manner of regarding the question. For Plato is answering a difficulty; he is seeking to justify the use of common language and of ordinary thought into which philosophy had introduced a principle of doubt and dissolution. Whereas Hegel tries to go beyond common thought, and to combine abstractions in a higher unity: the ordinary mechanism of language and logic is carried by him into another region in which all oppositions are absorbed and all contradictions affirmed, only that they may be done away with. But Plato, unlike Hegel, nowhere bases his system on the unity of opposites, although in the *Parmenides* he shows an Hegelian subtlety in the analysis of one and Being.

It is difficult within the compass of a few pages to give even a faint outline of the Hegelian dialectic. No philosophy which is worth understanding can be understood in a moment; common sense will not teach us metaphysics any more than mathematics. If all sciences demand of us protracted study and attention, the highest of all can hardly be matter of immediate intuition. Neither can we appreciate a great system without yielding a half assent to it—like flies we are caught in the spider's web; and we can only judge of it truly when we place ourselves at a distance from it. Of all philosophies Hegelianism is the most obscure: and the difficulty inherent in the subject is increased by the use of a technical language. The saying of Socrates respecting the writings of Heracleitus—'Noble is that which I understand, and that which I do not understand may be as noble; but the strength of a Delian diver is needed to swim through it'—expresses the feeling with which the reader rises from the perusal of Hegel. We may truly apply to him the words in which Plato describes the pre-Socratic philosophers: 'He went on his way rather regardless of whether we understood him or not'; or, as he is reported himself to have said of his own pupils: 'There is only one of you who understands me, and he does *not* understand me.'

Nevertheless the consideration of a few general aspects of the Hegelian philosophy may help to dispel some errors and to awaken an interest about it. (i) It is an ideal philosophy which, in popular phraseology, maintains not matter but mind to be the truth of things, and this not by a mere crude substitution of one word for another, but by showing either of them to be the complement of the other. Both are creations of thought, and the difference in kind which seems to divide them may also be regarded as a difference of degree. One is to the other as the real to the ideal, and both may be conceived together under the higher form of the notion. (ii) Under another aspect it views all the forms of sense and knowledge as stages of thought which have always existed implicitly and unconsciously, and to which the mind of the world, gradually disengaged from sense, has become awakened. The present has been the past. The succession in time of human ideas is also the eternal 'now'; it is historical and also a divine ideal. The history of philosophy stripped of personality and of the other accidents of time and place is gathered up into philosophy, and again philosophy clothed in circumstance expands into history. (iii) Whether regarded as present or past, under the form of time or of eternity, the spirit of dialectic is always moving onwards from one determination of thought to another, receiving each successive system of philosophy and subordinating it to that which follows—impelled by an irresistible necessity from one idea to another until the cycle of human thought and existence is complete. It follows from this that all previous philosophies which are worthy of the name are not mere opinions or speculations, but stages or moments of thought which have a necessary place in the world of mind. They are no longer the last word of philosophy, for another and another has succeeded them, but they still live and are mighty; in the language of the Greek poet, 'There is a great God in them, and he grows not old'. (iv) This vast ideal system is supposed to be based upon experience. At each step it professes to carry with it the 'witness of eyes and ears' and of common sense, as well as the internal evidence of its own consistency; it has a place for every science, and affirms that no philosophy of a narrower type is capable of comprehending all true facts.

The Hegelian dialectic may be also described as a movement from the simple to the complex. Beginning with the generalizations of sense, (1) passing through ideas of quality, quantity, measure, number, and the like, (2) ascending from presentations, that is pictorial forms of sense, to representations in which the picture vanishes and the essence is detached in thought from the outward form, (3) combining the I and the not-I, or the subject and object, the natural order of thought is at last found to include the leading ideas of the sciences and to arrange them in relation to one another. Abstractions grow together and again become concrete in a new and higher sense. They also admit of development from within in their own spheres. Everywhere there is a movement of attraction and repulsion going on—an attraction or repulsion of ideas of which the physical phenomenon described under a similar name is a figure. Freedom and necessity, mind and matter, the continuous and the discrete, cause and effect, are perpetually being severed from one another in thought, only to be perpetually reunited. The finite and infinite, the absolute and relative are not really opposed; the finite and the negation of the finite are alike lost in a higher or positive infinity, and the absolute is the sum or correlation of all relatives. When this reconciliation of opposites is finally completed in all its stages, the mind may come back again and review the things of sense, the opinions of philosophers, the strife of theology and politics, without being disturbed by them. Whatever is, if not the very best—and what is the best, who can tell?—is, at any rate, historical and rational, suitable to its own age, unsuitable to any other. Nor can any efforts of speculative thinkers or of soldiers and statesmen materially quicken the 'process of the suns'.

Hegel was quite sensible how great would be the difficulty of presenting philosophy to mankind under the form of opposites. Most of us live in the one-sided truth which the understanding offers to us, and if occasionally we come across difficulties like the time-honoured controversy of necessity and free-will, or the Eleatic puzzle of Achilles and the tortoise, we relegate some of them to the sphere of mystery, others to the book of riddles, and go on our way rejoicing. Most men (like Aristotle) have been accustomed to regard a contradiction in terms as the end of strife; to be told that contradiction is the life and mainspring of the intellectual world is indeed a paradox to them. Every abstraction is at first the enemy of every other, yet they are linked together, each with all, in the chain of Being. The struggle for existence is not confined to the animals, but appears in the kingdom of thought. The divisions which arise in thought between the physical and moral and between the moral and intellectual, and the like, are deepened and widened by the formal logic which elevates the defects of the human faculties into Laws of Thought; they become a part of the mind which makes them and is also made up of them. Such distinctions become so familiar to us that we regard the thing signified by them as absolutely fixed and defined. These are some of the illusions from which Hegel delivers us by placing us above ourselves, by teaching us to analyse the growth of 'what we are pleased to call our minds', by reverting to a time when our present distinctions of thought and language had no existence.

Of the great dislike and childish impatience of his system which would be aroused among his opponents, he was fully aware, and would often anticipate the jests which the rest of the world, 'in the superfluity of their wits', were likely to make upon him. Men are annoyed at what puzzles them; they think what they cannot easily understand to be full of danger. Many a sceptic has stood, as he supposed, firmly rooted in the categories of the understanding which Hegel resolves into their original nothingness. For, like Plato, he 'leaves no stone unturned' in the intellectual world. Nor can we deny that he is unnecessarily difficult, or that his own mind, like that of all metaphysicians, was too much under the dominion of his system and unable to see beyond; or that the study of philosophy, if made a serious business (cf. *Rep.* vii. 538), involves grave results to the mind and life of the student. For it may encumber him without enlightening his path; and it may weaken his natural faculties of thought and expression without increasing his philosophical power. The mind easily becomes entangled among abstractions, and loses hold of facts. The glass which is adapted to distant objects takes away the vision of what is near and present to us.

To Hegel, as to the ancient Greek thinkers, philosophy was a religion, a principle of life as well as of knowledge, like the Idea of good in the Sixth Book of the *Republic*, a cause as well as an effect, the source of growth as well as of light. In forms of thought which by most of us are regarded as mere categories, he saw or thought that he saw a gradual revelation of the Divine Being. He would have been said by his opponents to have confused God with the history of philosophy, and to have been incapable of distinguishing ideas from facts. And certainly we can scarcely understand how a deep thinker like Hegel could have hoped to revive or supplant the old traditional faith by an unintelligible abstraction: or how he could have imagined that philosophy consisted only or chiefly in the categories of logic. For abstractions, though combined by him in the notion, seem to be never really concrete; they are a metaphysical anatomy, not a living and thinking substance. Though we are reminded by him again and again that we are gathering up the world in ideas, we feel after all that we have not really spanned the gulf which separates φαινόμενα from ὄντα.

Having in view some of these difficulties, he seeks—and we may follow his example—to make the understanding of his system easier (*a*) by illustrations, and (*b*) by pointing out the coincidence of the speculative idea and the historical order of thought.

(*a*) If we ask how opposites can coexist, we are told that many different qualities inhere in a flower or a tree or in any other concrete object, and that any conception of space or matter or time involves the two contradictory attributes of divisibility and continuousness. We may ponder over the thought of number, reminding ourselves that every unit both implies and denies the existence of every other, and that the one is many—a sum of fractions, and the many one—a sum of units. We may be reminded that in nature there is a centripetal as well as a centrifugal force, a regulator as well as a spring, a law of attraction as well as of repulsion. The way to the West is the way also to the East; the north pole of the magnet cannot be divided from the south pole; two *minus* signs make a *plus* in Arithmetic and Algebra. Again, we may liken the successive layers of thought to the deposits of geological strata which were once fluid and are now solid, which were at one time uppermost in the series and are now hidden in the earth; or to the successive rinds or barks of trees which year by year pass inward; or to the ripple of water which appears and reappears in an ever-widening circle. Or our attention may be drawn to ideas which the moment we analyse them involve a contradiction, such as 'beginning' or 'becoming', or to the opposite poles, as they are sometimes termed, of necessity and freedom, of idea and fact. We may be told to observe that every negative is a positive, that differences of kind are resolvable into differences of degree, and that differences of degree may be heightened into differences of kind. We may remember the common remark that there is much to be said on both sides of a question. We may be recommended to look within and to explain how opposite ideas can coexist in our own minds; and we may be told to imagine the minds of all mankind as one mind in which the true ideas of all ages and countries inhere. In our conception of God in his relation to man or of any union of the divine and human nature, a contradiction appears to be unavoidable. Is not the reconciliation of mind and body a necessity, not only of speculation but of practical life? Reflections such as these will furnish the best preparation and give the right attitude of mind for understanding the Hegelian philosophy.

(*b*) Hegel's treatment of the early Greek thinkers affords the readiest illustration of his meaning in conceiving all philosophy under the form of opposites. The first abstraction is to him the beginning of thought. Hitherto there had only existed a tumultuous chaos of mythological fancy, but when Thales said 'All is water' a new era began to dawn upon the world. Man was seeking to grasp the universe under a single form which was at first simply a material element, the most equable and colourless and universal which could be found. But soon the human mind became dissatisfied with the emblem, and after ringing the changes on one element after another, demanded a more abstract and perfect conception, such as one or Being, which was absolutely at rest. But the positive had its negative, the conception of Being involved Not-being, the conception of one, many, the conception of a whole, parts. Then the pendulum swung to the other side, from rest to motion, from Xenophanes to Heracleitus. The opposition of Being and Not-being projected into space became the atoms and void of Leucippus and Democritus. Until the Atomists, the abstraction of the individual did not exist; in the philosophy of Anaxagoras the idea of mind, whether human or divine, was beginning to be realized. The pendulum gave another swing, from the individual to the universal, from the object to the subject. The Sophist first uttered the word 'Man is the measure of all things', which Socrates presented in a new form as the study of ethics. Once more we return from mind to the object of mind, which is knowledge, and out of knowledge the various degrees or kinds of knowledge more or less abstract were gradually developed. The threefold division of logic, physics, and ethics, foreshadowed in Plato, was finally established by Aristotle and the Stoics. Thus, according to Hegel, in the course of about two centuries, by a process of antagonism and negation, the leading thoughts of philosophy were evolved.

There is nothing like this progress of opposites in Plato, who in the *Symposium* denies the possibility of reconciliation until the opposition has passed away. In his own words, there is an absurdity in supposing that 'harmony is discord; for in reality harmony consists of notes of a higher and lower pitch which disagreed once, but are now reconciled by the art of music' (*Symp.* 187 a, b). He does indeed describe objects of sense as regarded by us sometimes from one point of view and sometimes from another. As he says at the end of the Fifth Book of the *Republic*, 'There is nothing light which is not heavy, or great which is not small', and he extends this relativity to the conceptions of just and good, as well as to great and small. In like manner he acknowledges that the same number may be more or less in relation to other numbers without any increase or diminution (*Theaet.* 155 a, b). But the perplexity only arises out of the confusion of the human faculties; the art of measuring shows us what is truly great and truly small. Though the just and good in particular instances may vary, the *idea* of good is eternal and unchangeable. And the *idea* of good is the source of knowledge and also of Being, in which all the stages of sense and knowledge are gathered up and from being hypotheses become realities.

SOPHIST

Persons of the Dialogue

THEODORUS.   THEAETETUS.   SOCRATES

An ELEATIC STRANGER, whom Theodorus and Theaetetus bring with them.
The younger SOCRATES, who is a silent auditor.[1]

Theodorus. Here we are, Socrates, true to our agreement of 216a
yesterday; and we bring with us a stranger who is a native of
Elea, and a disciple of Parmenides and Zeno, a true philosopher.

Socrates. Is he not rather a god, Theodorus, who comes to us
in the disguise of a stranger? For Homer says that all the gods
accompany such men as have any tinge of reverence and justice,
and that the god of hospitality, above all, takes note of men who b
disdain or observe the law. And may not your companion be one
of those higher powers, a cross-examining deity, who has come
to spy out our weakness in argument, and to cross-examine us?

Theod. Nay, Socrates, he is not one of the disputatious sort—
he is more reasonable. And, in my opinion, he is not a god at all;
but divine he certainly is, for this is a title which I should give to
all philosophers.   c

Soc. Capital, my friend! but I may add that you place him in
a class which is almost as hard to discern as are the gods. For the
true philosophers, and such as are not merely made up for the
occasion, appear in various forms unrecognized by the ignorance
of men, and they 'hover about cities', as Homer declares, looking
from above upon human life; and some think nothing of them,
and others can never think enough; and sometimes they appear
as statesmen, and sometimes as sophists; and then, again, to d
many they seem to be no better than madmen. I should like to
ask our Eleatic friend, if he would tell us, what is thought about 217
them in Italy, and to whom the terms are applied.

Theod. What terms?

Soc. Sophist, statesman, philosopher.

---

[1] [See the *Introduction* to the *Theaetetus*, p. 194, above.]

Theod. What is your difficulty about them, and what made you ask?

Soc. I want to know whether by his countrymen they are regarded as one or two; or do they, as the names are three, distinguish also three kinds, and assign one to each name?

Theod. I dare say that the Stranger will not object to discuss the question. What do you say, Stranger?

b *Stranger.* I am far from objecting, Theodorus, nor have I any difficulty in replying that by us they are regarded as three. But to define precisely the nature of each of them is by no means a slight or easy task.

Theod. You have happened to light, Socrates, almost on the very question which we were pressing upon our friend before we came hither, and he excused himself to us, as he does now to you; although he says that he has heard a thorough discussion, which he still remembers.

c *Soc.* Then do not, Stranger, deny us the first favour which we ask of you: I am sure that you will not, and therefore I shall only beg of you to say whether you like and are accustomed to make a long oration on a subject which you want to explain to another, or to proceed by the method of question and answer. I remember hearing a very noble discussion in which Parmenides employed the latter of the two methods, when I was a young man, and he was far advanced in years.[1]

d *Str.* I prefer to talk with another when he responds pleasantly, and is light in hand; if not, I would rather have my own say.

Soc. Any one of the present company will respond kindly to you, and you can choose whom you like of them; I should recommend you to take a young person—Theaetetus, for example—unless you have a preference for some one else.

Str. I feel ashamed, Socrates, being a new-comer into your society, instead of returning a short answer to each inquiry, to
e spin out a long soliloquy or address, and give a kind of display. For the true answer will certainly be a very long one, a great deal longer than might be expected from such a short and simple question. At the same time, I fear that I may seem rude and ungracious if I refuse your courteous request, especially after
218 what you have said. For I certainly cannot object to your

[1] Cf. *Parm.*, 137 foll.

proposal, that Theaetetus should respond, having already conversed with him myself, and being recommended by you to
take him.

Theaetetus. Do so, then, Stranger, and as Socrates has said, we
shall all be obliged to you.

Str. After that, Theaetetus, I think there is nothing more to be
said. Well then, I am to argue with you, and if you tire of the
argument, I beg you to blame your friends and not me.

Theaet. I do not at present expect that I shall tire, and if I do, b
I shall get my friend here, young Socrates, the namesake of the
elder Socrates, to help; he is about my own age, and my partner
at the gymnasium, and is accustomed to share most hard work
with me.

Str. Very good; you can decide about that for yourself as we
proceed. Meanwhile you and I will begin together and inquire
into the nature of the Sophist, first of the three: I should like you
to make out what he is and bring him to light in a discussion; for c
at present we are only agreed about the name, but of the thing to
which we both apply the name possibly you have one notion and
I another; whereas we ought always to come to an understanding
about the thing itself in terms of a definition, and not merely
about the name minus the definition. Now the tribe of Sophists
for which we propose now to go in search, is not the easiest of all
to catch or define; and the world has long ago agreed, that in
order to achieve success in some great exertion, it is best to practise d
in lesser and easier instances before we proceed to the greatest of
all. And as we suspect that the tribe of Sophists is troublesome
and hard to be caught, I should recommend that we practise
beforehand the method which is to be applied to them on some
simple and smaller thing, unless you can suggest an easier way.

Theaet. Indeed I cannot.

Str. Then suppose that we use this method upon some slight
example, and try to make it a pattern of the greater?

Theaet. Good. e

Str. What model can we take which is small and easy to
inspect and is yet as susceptible of definition as any larger thing?
Shall I say an angler? He is familiar to all of us, and not a very
interesting or important person.

Theaet. He is not.

219 *Str.* Yet I suspect that he will furnish us with the sort of definition and line of inquiry which we want.

Theaet. Very good.

Str. Let us begin by asking whether he is a man having art or not having art, but some other power.

Theaet. He is clearly a man of art.

Str. Next, the arts may be divided into two main kinds.

Theaet. What are they?

Str. Firstly, agriculture, and the tending of any sort of mortal creature, and the art of constructing or moulding those things b which we call implements; and also the art of imitation—all these may be appropriately called by a single name.

Theaet. What do you mean? And what is the name?

Str. He who brings into existence something that did not exist before is said to be a producer, and that which is brought into existence is said to be produced.

Theaet. True.

Str. And all the arts which were just now mentioned are characterized by this power of producing?

Theaet. They are.

Str. Then let us sum them up under the name of productive or creative art.

c *Theaet.* Very good.

Str. Secondly, there is the whole class of learning and cognition; as well as trade, fighting, hunting. And since none of these produces anything, but is only engaged in conquering by word or deed, or in preventing others from conquering, things which exist and have been already produced—in each and all of these branches there may be discerned an art which may be called acquisitive.

Theaet. Yes, that is the proper name.

d *Str.* Seeing, then, that all arts are either acquisitive or creative, in which class shall we place the art of the angler?

Theaet. Clearly in the acquisitive class.

Str. And the acquisitive may be subdivided into two parts: there is exchange, which is voluntary and is effected by gifts, hire, purchase; and the other part of acquisitive, which takes by force of word or deed, may be termed conquest?

Theaet. That is implied in what has been said.

Str. And may not conquest be again subdivided?

Theaet. How?

Str. Open force may be called fighting, and secret force may e have the general name of hunting?

Theaet. Yes.

Str. And then it would be absurd not to divide into two parts the art of hunting.

Theaet. How would you make the division?

Str. Into the hunting of living and of lifeless prey.

Theaet. Yes, if both kinds exist.

Str. Of course they exist; but the hunting after lifeless things 220 having no special name, except some sorts of diving, and other small matters, may well be omitted by us; the hunting after living things may be called animal hunting.

Theaet. Yes.

Str. And animal hunting may be truly said to have two divisions, land-animal hunting, which has many kinds and names, and water-animal hunting, or the hunting after animals who swim?

Theaet. True.

Str. And of swimming animals, one class lives on the wing and b the other in the water?

Theaet. Certainly.

Str. Fowling is the general term under which the hunting of all birds is included.

Theaet. True.

Str. The hunting of animals who live in the water has the general name of fishing.

Theaet. Yes.

Str. And this sort of hunting may be further divided also into two principal kinds?

Theaet. What are they?

Str. There is one kind which takes them where they are in nets, another which takes them by a blow.

Theaet. What do you mean, and how do you distinguish them?

Str. As to the first kind—all that surrounds and encloses any- c thing to prevent egress, may be rightly called an enclosure.

Theaet. Very true.

Str. For which reason twig baskets, casting-nets, nooses, creels, and the like may all be termed 'enclosures'?

Theaet. True.

Str. And therefore this first kind of capture may be called by us capture with enclosures, or something of that sort?

Theaet. Yes.

Str. The other kind, which is practised by a blow with hooks
d and three-pronged spears, when summed up under one name, may be called capture by striking, unless you, Theaetetus, can find some better name?

Theaet. Never mind the name—what you suggest will do very well.

Str. There is one mode of striking, which is done at night, and by the light of a fire, and is by the hunters themselves called firing, or spearing by firelight.

Theaet. True.

Str. And the fishing by day is called by the general name of barbing, because the spears, too, are barbed at the point.
e *Theaet.* Yes, that is the term.

Str. Of this barb-fishing, that which strikes the fish who is below from above is called spearing, because this is the way in which the three-pronged spears are mostly used.

Theaet. Yes, it is often called so.

Str. Then now there is only one kind remaining.

Theaet. What is that?

Str. When a hook is used, and the fish is not struck in any chance part of his body, as he is with the spear, but only about the head and mouth, and is then drawn out from below upwards
221 with reeds and rods:—What is the right name of that mode of fishing, Theaetetus?

Theaet. I suspect that we have now discovered the object of our search.

Str. Then now you and I have come to an understanding not only about the name of the angler's art, but about the
b definition of the thing itself. One half of all art was acquisitive— half of the acquisitive art was conquest or taking by force, half of this was hunting, and half of hunting was hunting animals, half of this was hunting water animals—of this again, the under half was fishing, half of fishing was striking; a part of striking was fishing with a barb, and one half of this again, being the kind
c which strikes with a hook and draws the fish from below upwards,

is the art which we have been seeking, and which from the nature of the operation is denoted angling or drawing up (ἀσπαλιευτική, ἀνασπᾶσθαι).

Theaet. The result has been quite satisfactorily brought out.

Str. And now, following this pattern, let us endeavour to find out what a Sophist is.

Theaet. By all means.

Str. The first question about the angler was, whether he was a skilled artist or unskilled?

Theaet. True.

Str. And shall we call our new friend unskilled, or a thorough d master of his craft?

Theaet. Certainly not unskilled, for his name, as, indeed, you imply, must surely express his nature.

Str. Then he must be supposed to have some art.

Theaet. What art?

Str. By heaven, they are cousins! it never occurred to us.

Theaet. Who are cousins?

Str. The angler and the Sophist.

Theaet. In what way are they related?

Str. They both appear to me to be hunters.

Theaet. How the Sophist? Of the other we have spoken.   e

Str. You remember our division of hunting, into hunting after swimming animals and land animals?

Theaet. Yes.

Str. And you remember that we subdivided the swimming and left the land animals, saying that there were many kinds of them?

Theaet. Certainly.   222

Str. Thus far, then, the Sophist and the angler, starting from the art of acquiring, take the same road?

Theaet. So it would appear.

Str. Their paths diverge when they reach the art of animal hunting; the one going to the sea-shore, and to the rivers, and to the lakes, and angling for the animals which are in them.

Theaet. Very true.

Str. While the other goes to land and water of another sort— rivers of wealth and broad meadow-lands of generous youth; and he also is intending to take the animals which are in them.

Theaet. What do you mean?   b

Str. Of hunting on land there are two principal divisions.

Theaet. What are they?

Str. One is the hunting of tame, and the other of wild animals.

Theaet. But are tame animals ever hunted?

Str. Yes, if you include man under tame animals. But if you like you may say that there are no tame animals, or that, if there are, man is not among them; or you may say that man is a tame animal but is not hunted—you shall decide which of these alternatives you prefer.

c   *Theaet.* I should say, Stranger, that man is a tame animal, and I admit that he is hunted.

Str. Then let us divide the hunting of tame animals into two parts.

Theaet. How shall we make the division?

Str. Let us define piracy, man-stealing, tyranny, the whole military art, by one name, as hunting with violence.

Theaet. Very good.

Str. But the art of the lawyer, of the popular orator, and the
d art of conversation may be called in one word the art of persuasion.

Theaet. True.

Str. And of persuasion, there may be said to be two kinds?

Theaet. What are they?

Str. One is private, and the other public.

Theaet. Yes; each of them forms a class.

Str. And again of private hunting, one sort receives hire, and the other brings gifts.

Theaet. I do not understand you.

Str. You seem never to have observed the manner in which lovers hunt.

Theaet. To what do you refer?

e   *Str.* I mean that they lavish gifts on those whom they hunt in addition to other inducements.

Theaet. Most true.

Str. Let us admit this, then, to be characteristic of the amatory art.

Theaet. Certainly.

Str. But that sort of hireling whose conversation is pleasing and who baits his hook only with pleasure and exacts nothing

but his maintenance in return, we should all, if I am not mis- 223
taken, describe as possessing flattery or an art of making things
pleasant.

Theaet. Certainly.

Str. And that sort, which professes to form acquaintances only
for the sake of virtue, and demands a reward in the shape of
money, may be fairly called by another name?

Theaet. To be sure.

Str. And what is the name? Will you tell me?

Theaet. It is obvious enough; for I believe that we have discovered the Sophist: which is, as I conceive, the proper name for
the class described.

Str. Then now, Theaetetus, his art may be traced as a branch b
of the appropriative,[1] acquisitive family—which hunts animals
—living—land—tame animals; which hunts man,—privately—
for hire—taking money in exchange—having the semblance of
education; and this is termed sophistry, and is a hunt after young
men of wealth and rank—such is the conclusion.

Theaet. Just so.

Str. Let us take another branch of his genealogy; for he is a c
professor of a great and many-sided art; and if we look back
at what has preceded we see that he presents another aspect,
besides that of which we are speaking.

Theaet. In what respect?

Str. There were two sorts of acquisitive art; the one concerned
with hunting, the other with exchange.

Theaet. There were.

Str. And of the art of exchange we may now distinguish two
forms, the one of giving, and the other of selling.

Theaet. Let us assume that.

Str. Next, we will suppose the art of selling to be divided into
two parts.

Theaet. How? d

Str. There is one part which is distinguished as the sale of a
man's own productions; another, which is the exchange of the
works of others.

---

[1] Omitting χειρωτικῆς and πεζοθηρίας. [Or, according to Burnet's text: 'as
a branch of the art of appropriation and conquest—which hunts animals—living—
land—human beings—by persuasion—privately—taking money, &c.'.]

Theaet. Certainly.

Str. And is not that part of exchange which takes place in the city, being about half of the whole, termed retailing?

Theaet. Yes.

Str. And that which exchanges the goods of one city for those of another by selling and buying is the exchange of the merchant?

Theaet. To be sure.

e   *Str.* And you are aware that this exchange of the merchant is of two kinds; it is partly concerned with food for the use of the body, and partly with the food of the soul which is bartered and received in exchange for money.

Theaet. What do you mean?

Str. You want to know what is the meaning of food for the soul; the other kind you surely understand.

Theaet. Yes.

Str. Take music in general, and painting and marionette play-
224 ing, and many other things, which are purchased in one city, and carried away and sold[1] in another—wares of the soul which are hawked about either for the sake of instruction or amusement;— may not he who takes them about and sells them be quite as truly called a merchant as he who sells meats and drinks?

Theaet. To be sure he may.

b   *Str.* And would you not call by the same name him who buys up knowledge and goes about from city to city exchanging his wares for money?

Theaet. Certainly I should.

Str. Of this merchandise of the soul, may not one part be fairly termed the art of display? And there is another part which, being a trade in learning, must be called by some name germane to the action, though it may sound as ridiculous as the last?

Theaet. Certainly.

Str. And this art—let us call it *mathematopoly*—has two divisions
c which must be separately named, one being the sale of the knowledge of virtue, and the other of the sale of other kinds of knowledge.

Theaet. Of course.

Str. The name of art-seller corresponds well enough to the latter; but you must try and tell me the name of the other.

---

[1] [Retaining the words καὶ πιπρασκομένην.]

Theaet. He must be the Sophist, whom we are seeking; no other name can possibly be right.

Str. No other; and so this trader in virtue again turns out to be our friend the Sophist, whose art may now be traced from the art of acquisition through exchange, trade, merchandise, to a merchandise of the soul which is concerned with speech [or d reasoning] and the knowledge of virtue.

Theaet. Quite true.

Str. And there may be a third reappearance of him;—for he may have settled down in a city, and may fabricate as well as buy these same wares, intending to live by selling them, and he would still be called a Sophist?

Theaet. Certainly.

Str. Then that part of the acquisitive art which exchanges, and e of exchange which either sells a man's own productions or retails those of others, as the case may be, and in either way sells the knowledge of virtue, you would again term sophistry?

Theaet. I must, if I am to keep pace with the argument.

Str. Let us consider once more whether there may not be yet another aspect of sophistry.

Theaet. What is it?

Str. In the acquisitive there was a subdivision of the combative 225 or fighting art.

Theaet. There was.

Str. It will be of assistance to divide it into two parts.

Theaet. What shall they be?

Str. There shall be one division of the competitive, and another of the pugnacious.

Theaet. Very good.

Str. That part of the pugnacious which is a contest of bodily strength may be properly called by some such name as violent.

Theaet. True.

Str. And when the war is one of words, it may be termed b controversy?

Theaet. Yes.

Str. And we can also distinguish two kinds of controversy?

Theaet. What are they?

Str. When long speeches are answered by long speeches, and there is public discussion about the just and unjust, that is forensic controversy.

Theaet. Yes.

Str. And there is a private sort of controversy, which is cut up into questions and answers, and this is commonly called disputation?

Theaet. Yes, that is the name.

Str. And of disputation, that sort which is only a discussion
c about contracts, and is carried on at random, and without rules of art, is recognized by the reasoning faculty to be a distinct class, but has hitherto had no distinctive name, and does not deserve to receive one from us.

Theaet. No; for the different sorts of it are too minute and heterogeneous.

Str. But that which proceeds by rules of art to dispute about justice and injustice in their own nature, and about things in general, we have been accustomed to call argumentation (Eristic)?

Theaet. Certainly.

d   *Str.* And of argumentation, one sort wastes money, and the other makes money.

Theaet. Very true.

Str. Suppose we try and give to each of these two classes a name.

Theaet. Let us do so.

Str. I should say that the habit which leads a man to neglect his own affairs for the pleasure of conversation, of which the style is far from being agreeable to the majority of his hearers, may be fairly termed loquacity: such is my opinion.

Theaet. That is the common name for it.

e   *Str.* But now who the other is, who makes money out of private disputation, it is your turn to say.

Theaet. There is only one true answer: he is the wonderful Sophist, of whom we are in pursuit, and who reappears again for the fourth time.

226   *Str.* Yes, and with a fresh pedigree, for he is the moneymaking species of the Eristic, disputatious, controversial, pugnacious, combative, acquisitive family, according to this latest turn of the argument.

Theaet. Certainly.

Str. How true was the observation that he was a many-sided animal, and not to be caught with one hand, as they say!

Theaet. Then you must catch him with two.

Str. Yes, we must, making every effort in our power. And b therefore let us try another track in our pursuit of him: You are aware that there are certain menial occupations which have names among servants?

Theaet. Yes, there are many such; which of them do you mean?

Str. I mean such as sifting, straining, winnowing, threshing.[1]

Theaet. Certainly.

Str. And besides these there are a great many more, such as carding, spinning, adjusting the warp and the woof; and thousands of similar expressions are used in the arts.

Theaet. Of what are they to be patterns, and what are we c going to do with them all?

Str. I think that in all of these there is implied a notion of division.

Theaet. Yes.

Str. Then if, as I was saying, there is one art which includes all of them, ought not that art to have one name?

Theaet. And what is the name of the art?

Str. The art of discerning or discriminating.

Theaet. Very good.

Str. Within this, again, can we perceive two forms? Consider.

Theaet. I should find it hard to obey so quickly.

Str. In all the previously named processes either like has been d separated from like or the better from the worse.

Theaet. That seems true enough, now that you have said it.

Str. I know no usual name for the first kind of separation; of the second, which throws away the worse and preserves the better, I do know one.

Theaet. What is it?

Str. Every discernment or discrimination of that kind, as I observe, is called a purification.

Theaet. Yes, that is the usual expression.

Str. And any one may see that purification is of two kinds. e

[1] Reading διακινεῖν, a conjecture of Professor Campbell's.

Theaet. Perhaps so, if he were allowed time to think; but I do not see at this moment.

Str. There are many purifications of bodies which may with propriety be comprehended under a single name.

Theaet. What are they, and what is their name?

227 *Str.* There is the purification of living bodies in their inward and in their outward parts, of which the former is duly effected by medicine and gymnastic, the latter by the not very dignified art of the bath-man; and there is the purification of inanimate substances—to this the arts of fulling and furbishing in general attend in a number of minute particulars, having a variety of names which are thought ridiculous.

Theaet. Very true.

Str. There can be no doubt that they are thought ridiculous, Theaetetus; but then the dialectical art never considers whether the benefit to be derived from the purge is greater or less than b that to be derived from the sponge, and has not more interest in the one than in the other; her endeavour is to know what is and is not kindred in all arts, with a view to the acquisition of intelligence; and having this in view, she honours them all alike, and when she makes comparisons, she counts one of them not a whit more ridiculous than another; nor does she esteem him who adduces as his example of hunting, the general's art, at all more decorous than another who cites that of the vermin-destroyer, but only as the greater pretender of the two. And as to your question concerning the name which was to comprehend all these arts of purification, whether of animate or inanimate bodies, the c art of dialectic is in no wise particular about fine words, if she may be only allowed to have a general name for all other purifications, binding them up together and separating them off from the purification of the soul or intellect. For this is the purification at which she wants to arrive, and this we should understand to be her aim.

Theaet. Yes, I understand; and I agree that there are two sorts of purification, and that one of them is concerned with the soul, and that there is another which is concerned with the body.

Str. Excellent; and now listen to what I am going to say, and d try to divide further the first of the two.

Theaet. Whatever line of division you suggest, I will endeavour to assist you.

Str. Do we admit that virtue is distinct from vice in the soul?

Theaet. Certainly.

Str. And purification, as we have seen, means leaving the good, and casting out any evil that may be found.

Theaet. True.

Str. Thus, in so far as we find some process by which evil is removed from the soul, this too may properly be called purification?

Theaet. Yes.

Str. And in the soul there are two kinds of evil.

Theaet. What are they?

Str. The one may be compared to disease in the body, the 228 other to deformity.

Theaet. I do not understand.

Str. Perhaps you have never reflected that disease and discord are the same.

Theaet. To this, again, I know not what I should reply.

Str. Do you not conceive discord to be a dissolution of kindred elements, originating in some disagreement?[1]

Theaet. Just that.

Str. And is deformity anything but the want of measure, which is always unsightly?

Theaet. Exactly.   b

Str. And do we not see that opinions are opposed to desires, anger to pleasures, reason to pains, and that all these elements are opposed to one another in inharmonious souls.

Theaet. Certainly.

Str. And yet they all have indissoluble ties with each other?

Theaet. Of course.

Str. Then we shall be right in calling vice a discord and disease of the soul?

Theaet. Most true.

Str. And when things having motion, and aiming at an c appointed mark, continually miss their aim and glance aside,

[1] [Or, following Galen's reading adopted in the Oxford text: 'a disagreement between kindred elements, originating in some perversion'.]

shall we say that this is the effect of symmetry among them, or of the want of symmetry?

Theaet. Clearly of the want of symmetry.

Str. But surely we know that no soul is voluntarily ignorant of anything?

Theaet. Certainly not.

Str. And what is ignorance but the aberration of a mind which d is bent on truth, and in which the process of understanding is perverted?

Theaet. True.

Str. Then we are to regard an unintelligent soul as deformed and devoid of symmetry?

Theaet. So it seems.

Str. Then there are, it appears, these two kinds of evil in the soul—the one which is generally called vice, and is obviously a disease of the soul. . . .

Theaet. Yes.

Str. And there is the other, which they call ignorance, and which, because existing only in the soul,[1] they will not allow to be vice.

e *Theaet.* I must certainly admit what I failed to grasp when it was first mentioned by you—that there are two kinds of vice in the soul, and that we ought to consider cowardice, intemperance, and injustice to be all alike forms of disease in the soul, and ignorance, of which there are all sorts of varieties, to be deformity.

Str. And in the case of the body are there not two arts which have to do with the two bodily states?

Theaet. What are they?

229 *Str.* There is gymnastic, which has to do with deformity, and medicine, which has to do with disease.

Theaet. So it appears.

Str. And where there is insolence and injustice and cowardice, is not the Justice which metes out punishment the art that is principally required?[2]

Theaet. That certainly appears to be the opinion of mankind.

Str. Again, of the various kinds of ignorance, may not instruction be rightly said to be the remedy?

---

[1] Or, 'although there is no other vice in the soul but this'.

[2] [Retaining here the MS. reading ἡ κολαστικὴ . . . δίκη.]

Theaet. True.

Str. And of the art of instruction, shall we say that there is one b or many kinds? At any rate there are two principal ones. Think.

Theaet. I will.

Str. I believe that I can see how we shall soonest arrive at the answer to this question.

Theaet. How?

Str. If we can discover a line which divides ignorance into two halves. For a division of ignorance into two parts will certainly imply that the art of instruction is also twofold, answering to the two divisions of ignorance.

Theaet. Well, and do you see what you are looking for?

Str. I do seem to myself to see one very large and bad sort of c ignorance which is quite separate, and may be weighed in the scale against all other sorts of ignorance put together.

Theaet. What is it?

Str. When a person supposes that he knows, and does not know; this appears to be the great source of all the errors of the intellect.

Theaet. True.

Str. And this, if I am not mistaken, is the kind of ignorance which specially earns the title of stupidity.

Theaet. True.

Str. What name, then, shall be given to the sort of instruction which gets rid of this?

Theaet. The instruction which you mean, Stranger, is, I d should imagine, not the teaching of handicraft arts, but what, thanks to us, has been termed education in this part of the world.

Str. Yes, Theaetetus, and by nearly all Hellenes. But we have still to consider whether education admits of any further division deserving a name.

Theaet. We have.

Str. I think that there is a point at which such a division is possible.

Theaet. Where?

Str. In theoretical teaching two roads may be followed, one e rougher and the other smoother.

Theaet. How are we to distinguish the two?

Str. There is the time-honoured mode which our fathers

commonly practised towards their sons, and which is still adopted
230 by many—either of roughly reproving their errors, or of gently
advising them; which varieties may be correctly included under
the general term of admonition.

Theaet. True.

Str. But whereas some appear to have arrived at the conclusion
that all ignorance is involuntary, and that no one who thinks
himself wise is willing to learn any of those things in which he is
conscious of his own cleverness, and that the admonitory sort of
education gives much trouble and does little good——

Theaet. There they are quite right.

b   *Str.* Accordingly, they set to work to eradicate the spirit of
conceit in another way.

Theaet. In what way?

Str. They cross-examine a man's words, when he thinks that
he is saying something and is really saying nothing, and easily
convict him of inconsistencies in his opinions; these they then
collect by the dialectical process, and placing them side by side,
show that they contradict one another about the same things, in
relation to the same things, and in the same respect. He, seeing
this, is angry with himself, and grows gentle towards others, and
c thus is entirely delivered from stubborn prejudices about himself,
in a way which is most amusing to the hearer, and produces the
most lasting good effect on the person who is the subject of the
operation. For as the physician considers that the body will
receive no benefit from taking food until the internal obstacles
have been removed, so the purifier of the soul is conscious that
his patient will receive no benefit from the application of know-
d ledge until he is refuted, and from refutation learns modesty; he
must be purged of his prejudices first and made to think that he
knows only what he knows, and no more.

Theaet. That is certainly the best and wisest state of mind.

Str. For all these reasons, Theaetetus, we must admit that
refutation is the greatest and chiefest of purifications, and he who
has not been refuted, though he be the Great King himself, is in
e an awful state of impurity; he is uninstructed and deformed in
those things in which he who would be truly blessed ought to be
fairest and purest.

Theaet. Very true.

Str. And who are the ministers of this art? I am afraid to say
the Sophists.

Theaet. Why?

Str. Lest we should assign to them too high a prerogative.

Theaet. Yet the Sophist has a certain likeness to our minister
of purification.

Str. Yes, the same sort of likeness which a wolf, who is the
fiercest of animals, has to a dog, who is the gentlest. But he who
would not be found tripping, ought to be very careful in this
matter of comparisons, for they are most slippery things. Nevertheless, let us assume that the Sophists are the men. I say this
provisionally, for I think that the boundary in dispute will prove
to be an important one, should it ever be resolutely defended.   b

Theaet. Likely enough.

Str. Let us grant, then, that from the discerning art comes
purification, and from purification let there be separated off a
part which is concerned with the soul; of this mental purification
instruction is a portion, and of instruction education; and of
education, the refutation of vain conceit must, according to the
argument which has now appeared in view, be called by you and
me sophistry of the highest lineage.

Theaet. Very well; and yet, considering the number of forms
in which he has presented himself, I begin to doubt how I can c
with any truth or confidence describe the real nature of the
Sophist.

Str. You naturally feel perplexed; and yet I think that he
must be still more perplexed in his attempt to escape us, for as
the proverb says, when every way is blocked, there is no escape;[1]
now, then, is the time of all others to set upon him.

Theaet. True.

Str. First let us stand a moment and recover breath, and while
we are resting, we may reckon up in how many forms he has d
appeared. In the first place, he was discovered to be a paid
hunter after wealth and youth.

Theaet. Yes.

Str. In the second place, he was a merchant in the goods of
the soul.

Theaet. Certainly.

[1] [Or, 'it is not easy to escape every hold' (in wrestling).]

Str. In the third place, he has turned out to be a retailer of the same sort of wares.

Theaet. Yes; and in the fourth place, he himself manufactured the learned wares which he sold.

Str. Quite right; I will try and remember the fifth myself.
e He belonged to the fighting class, and was further distinguished as a hero of debate, who professed the eristic art.

Theaet. True.

Str. The sixth point was doubtful, and yet we at last allowed his claim to be a purger of souls, who cleared away notions obstructive to knowledge.

Theaet. Very true.

232 *Str.* Do you not consider that when a man appears to have knowledge of many subjects, but is called by the name of a single art, it is a sign that something is wrong; and anyone who is deceived, and applies many names where one is required, is evidently not able to perceive the common principle to which all these studies tend?

Theaet. I should imagine this to be the case.

b *Str.* Then let us, at least, not be deceived from indolence in the search; but let us first return to one of our statements concerning the Sophist; there was one thing which appeared to me especially characteristic of him.

Theaet. To what are you referring?

Str. We were saying of him, if I am not mistaken, that he was a disputer?

Theaet. We were.

Str. And does he not also teach others the art of disputation?

Theaet. Certainly he does.

Str. And about what does he profess that he teaches men to dispute? To begin at the beginning—Does he make them able
c to dispute about divine things, which are invisible to men in general?

Theaet. At any rate, he is said to do so.

Str. And what do you say of the visible things in heaven and earth, and the like?

Theaet. Certainly he disputes, and teaches to dispute about them.

Str. Then, again, in private conversation, when any universal assertion is made about generation and essence, we know that such persons are tremendous argufiers, and are able to impart their own skill to others.

Theaet. Undoubtedly.

Str. And do they not profess to make men able to dispute about d law and about politics in general?

Theaet. Why, no one would have anything to say to them, if they did not make these professions.

Str. In all and every art, what one should say if one wishes to contradict the craftsman himself is written down in a popular form, and he who likes may learn.

Theaet. I suppose that you are referring to the precepts of e Protagoras about wrestling and the other arts?

Str. Yes, my friend, and about a good many other things. In a word, does not the art of disputation seem to be an acquaintance, sufficient for controversy, with every subject in the world?

Theaet. Certainly; there does not seem to be much which is beyond its range.

Str. But oh! my dear youth, do you suppose this possible? for perhaps your young eyes may see things which to our duller sight do not appear.

Theaet. To what are you alluding? I do not think that I under- 233 stand your present question.

Str. I ask whether any human being can understand all things.

Theaet. Happy would mankind be if such a thing were possible!

Str. How, then, can any one who is ignorant have any sound argument to bring against him who knows?

Theaet. He cannot.

Str. Then why has the sophistical art such a mysterious power?

Theaet. To what do you refer?

Str. How do the Sophists make young men believe in their b supreme and universal wisdom? For if they neither disputed nor were thought to dispute rightly, or being thought to do so were deemed no wiser for their controversial skill, then, to quote your own observation, no one would give them money or be willing to learn their art.

Theaet. They certainly would not.

Str. But they are willing.

Theaet. Yes, they are.

c   *Str.* Yes, and the reason, as I should imagine, is that they are supposed to have knowledge of those things about which they dispute?

Theaet. Certainly.

Str. And they dispute, we have said, about all things?

Theaet. True.

Str. And therefore, to their disciples, they appear to be all-wise?

Theaet. Certainly.

Str. But they are not; for that was shown to be impossible.

Theaet. Impossible, of course.

Str. Then the Sophist has been shown to have a sort of conjectural or apparent knowledge only of all things, which is not the truth?

d   *Theaet.* Exactly; no better description of him could be given.

Str. Let us now take an illustration, which will still more clearly explain his nature.

Theaet. What is it?

Str. I will tell you, and you shall answer me, giving your very closest attention. Suppose that a person were to profess, not that he could speak or dispute, but that he knew how to make and do all things, by a single art.

e   *Theaet.* All things?

Str. I see that you do not understand the first word that I utter, for you do not understand the meaning of 'all'.

Theaet. No, I do not.

Str. Under all things, I include you and me, and also animals and trees.

Theaet. What do you mean?

Str. Suppose a person to say that he will make you and me, and all creatures.

234   *Theaet.* What would he mean by 'making'? He cannot be a husbandman;—for you said that he is a maker of animals.

Str. Yes; and I say that he is also the maker of the sea, and the earth, and the heavens, and the gods, and of all other things; and, further, that he can make them in no time, and sell them for a few pence.

Theaet. That must be a jest.

Str. And when a man says that he knows all things, and can teach them to another at a small cost, and in a short time, must one not think it a jest?

Theaet. Certainly.

Str. Do you know of any more artistic or graceful form of jest b than imitation?

Theaet. Certainly not; for imitation is a very comprehensive term, which includes under one class the most diverse sorts of things.

Str. We know, of course, that he who professes by one art to make all things is really a painter, and by the painter's art makes resemblances of real things which have the same name with them; and he can deceive the less intelligent sort of young children, to whom he shows his picutres at a distance, into the belief that he has the absolute power of making whatever he likes.

Theaet. Certainly.

Str. And may there not be supposed to be an imitative art of reasoning? Is it not possible to enchant the hearts of young men by words poured through their ears, when they are still at a distance from the truth of facts, by exhibiting to them fictitious arguments, and making them think that they are true, and that the speaker is the wisest of men in all things?

Theaet. Yes; why should there not be another such art? d

Str. But as time goes on, and their hearers advance in years, and come into closer contact with realities, and have learnt by sad experience to see and feel the truth of things, are not the greater part of them compelled to change many opinions which they formerly entertained, so that the great appears small to them, and the easy difficult, and all their dreamy speculations are overturned by the facts of life?

Theaet. That is my view, as far as I can judge, although, at my age, I may be one of those who see things at a distance only.

Str. And the wish of all of us, who are your friends, is and always will be to bring you as near to the truth as we can without painful experience. And now I should like you to tell me, whether the Sophist is not visibly a magician and imitator of true being; 235 or are we still disposed to think that he may have a true knowledge of the various matters about which he seems to have the power of contradiction?

Theaet. But how can he, Stranger? Is there any doubt, after what has been said, that he is some kind of a player [or jester¹].

Str. Then we must place him in the class of magicians and mimics.

Theaet. Certainly we must.

Str. And now our business is not to let the animal out, for we b have got him in a sort of dialectical net, and there is one thing which he decidedly will not escape.

Theaet. What is that?

Str. The inference that he is a juggler.

Theaet. Precisely my own opinion of him.

Str. Then, clearly, we ought as soon as possible to divide the image-making art, and go down to the net,² and, if the Sophist does not run away from us, to seize him according to the royal c command of Reason, to whom he should be delivered over with a report of the capture; and if he creeps into the recesses of the imitative art, and secretes himself in one of them, to divide again and follow him up until in some subsection of imitation he is caught. For our method of tackling each and all is one which neither he nor any other creature will ever escape in triumph.

Theaet. Well said; and let us do as you propose.

Str. Well, then, pursuing the same analytic method as before, d I think that I can discern two divisions of the imitative art, but I am not as yet able to see in which of them the desired form is to be found.

Theaet. Will you tell me first what are the two divisions of which you are speaking?

Str. One is the art of likeness-making;—generally a likeness of anything is made by producing a copy which is executed according to the proportions of the original, similar in length and e breadth and depth, each thing receiving also its appropriate colour.

Theaet. Is not this always the aim of imitation?

Str. Not always; in works either of sculpture or of painting, which are of any magnitude, there is a certain degree of deception;

---

¹ [See 234 a, where παιδία was translated 'jest'.]

² [The reference is probably not to hunting, but to the Persian method of rounding up the population of a district by means of a line of soldiers joining hands and marching across it; this was termed 'netting'. See Cornford, *P.T.K.*, p. 196.]

for if artists were to give the true proportions of their fair models, 236 the upper part, which is farther off, would appear to be out of proportion in comparison with the lower, which is nearer; and so they give up the truth in their images and make only the proportions which appear to be beautiful, disregarding the real ones.

Theaet. Quite true.

Str. And that which being other is also like, may we not fairly call a likeness or image?

Theaet. Yes.

Str. And may we not, as I did just now, call that part of the b imitative art which is concerned with making such images the art of likeness-making?

Theaet. Let that be the name.

Str. And what shall we call those resemblances of the beautiful, which appear such owing to the unfavourable position of the spectator, whereas if a person had the power of getting a correct view of works of such magnitude, they would appear not even like that to which they profess to be like? May we not call these 'appearances', since they appear only and are not really like?

Theaet. Certainly.

Str. There is a great deal of this kind of thing in painting, and c in all imitation.

Theaet. Of course.

Str. And may we not fairly call the sort of art, which produces an appearance and not an image, phantastic art?

Theaet. Most fairly.

Str. These then are the two kinds of image-making—the art of making likenesses, and phantastic or the art of making appearances?

Theaet. True.

Str. I was doubtful before in which of them I should place the Sophist, nor am I even now able to see clearly; verily he is a d wonderful and inscrutable creature. And now in the cleverest manner he has taken refuge in a class, which it is a hopeless task to examine.

Theaet. Yes, he has.

Str. Do you speak advisedly, or are you carried away at the moment by the habit of assenting into giving a hasty answer?

Theaet. May I ask to what you are referring?

Str. My dear friend, we are engaged in a very difficult specula-
e tion—there can be no doubt of that; for how a thing can appear
and seem, and not be, or how a man can say a thing which is not
true, has always been and still remains a very perplexing ques-
237 tion. How one ought to express the fact that it is truly possible to
say or think what is false—how one can say this without becoming involved in contradiction is indeed, Theaetetus, a perplexing
problem.[1]

Theaet. Why?

Str. He who says that falsehood exists has the audacity to
assert the being of not-being; for this is implied in the possibility
of falsehood. But, my boy, in the days when I was a boy, the
great Parmenides protested against this doctrine, and to the end
of his life he continued to inculcate the same lesson—always
repeating both in verse and out of verse:

> Keep your mind from this way of inquiry, for never will this
> be proved, that things which are not, are.

b Such is his testimony, which is confirmed by the very expression
which he incriminates, if it be briefly examined. Would you object
to begin with the consideration of the words themselves?

Theaet. Never mind about me; I am only desirous that you
should carry on the argument in the best way, and that you
should take me with you.

Str. Very good; and now say, do we venture to utter the forbidden word 'not-being'?

Theaet. Certainly we do.

Str. Let us be serious then, and consider the question neither
c in strife nor play: suppose that one of the hearers of Parmenides
was asked, 'To what is the term "not-being" to be applied?'—
do you know what sort of object he would single out in reply, and
what answer he would make to the inquirer?

Theaet. That is a difficult question, and one not to be answered
at all by a person like myself.

Str. There is at any rate no difficulty in seeing that the predicate 'not-being' is not applicable to any being.

Theaet. None, certainly.

Str. And if not to being, then not to something.

---

[1] [Cf. *Theaet.* 189 c.]

Theaet. Of course not.

Str. It is also plain, that in speaking of something we speak of d being, for to speak of an abstract something naked and isolated from all being is impossible.

Theaet. Impossible.

Str. You mean by assenting to imply that he who says something must say some one thing?

Theaet. Yes.

Str. Some in the singular (τί) you would say is the sign of one, some in the dual (τινέ) of two, some in the plural (τινές) of many?

Theaet. Exactly.

Str. Then he who says 'not something' must say absolutely e nothing.

Theaet. Most assuredly.

Str. Neither can we admit, I presume, that such a person speaks, but speaks of nothing. We cannot allow that one, who would fain express *that which is not*, ever speaks at all.

Theaet. The difficulty of the argument can no farther go.

Str. Not yet, my friend, is the time for such a word; for there 238 still remains of all perplexities the first and greatest, touching the very foundation of the matter.

Theaet. What do you mean? Do not be afraid to speak.

Str. To that which is, may be attributed [or added] some other thing which is?

Theaet. Certainly.

Str. But shall we say that it is possible to add something which is to that which is not?

Theaet. Impossible.

Str. And all number is to be reckoned among things which are?

Theaet. Yes, surely number, if anything, has a real existence. b

Str. Then we must not attempt to attribute to not-being number either in the singular or plural?

Theaet. The argument implies that we should be wrong in doing so.

Str. But how can a man either express in words or even conceive in thought things which are not or a thing which is not without number?

Theaet. How indeed?

Str. When we speak of things which are not, do we not endeavour to attribute plurality to not-being?

Theaet. Certainly.

Str. But, on the other hand, when we say 'what is not', do we not attribute unity?

Theaet. Manifestly.

Str. Nevertheless, we maintain that you may not and ought not to attribute being to not-being?

Theaet. Most true.

Str. Do you see, then, that not-being in itself can neither be spoken, uttered, or thought, but that it is unthinkable, unutterable, unspeakable, indescribable?

Theaet. Quite true.

d *Str.* But, if so, was I wrong in telling you just now that the difficulty which was coming is the greatest of all, and is there, in fact, a greater still behind?

Theaet. What is it?

Str. My dear friend, do not the very words show you that not-being can so effectively perplex anyone who endeavours to examine it, that he is bound to contradict himself as soon as he makes the attempt?

Theaet. What do you mean? Speak more clearly.

Str. Do not expect clearness from me. For I, who maintain
e that not-being has no part either in the one or many, just now spoke and am still speaking of not-being as one; for I say 'not-being'. Do you understand?

Theaet. Yes.

Str. But then, a little while ago I said that not-being *is* unutterable, unspeakable, indescribable: do you follow?

Theaet. I do after a fashion.[1]

Str. When I introduced the word 'is', did I not contradict what I said before?

239 *Theaet.* So it seems.

Str. And in using the singular verb, did I not speak of not-being as one?

Theaet. Yes.

Str. And when I spoke of not-being as indescribable and

---

[1] [Reading συνέπομαί πως.]

unspeakable and unutterable, in using each of these words in the singular, did I not refer to not-being as one?

Theaet. Certainly.

Str. And yet we say that, strictly speaking, it should not be defined either as one or many, and should not even be called 'it', for the use of that expression also would imply a form of unity.

Theaet. Quite true.

Str. How, then, can any one put any faith in me? For now, b as always, I am unequal to the examination of not-being. And therefore, as I was saying, do not look to me for the right way of speaking about not-being; but come, let us try the experiment with you.

Theaet. What do you mean?

Str. Make a noble effort, as becomes youth, and endeavour with all your might to speak of not-being in a right manner, without introducing into it either existence or unity or plurality.

Theaet. It would be a strange boldness in me which would c attempt the task when I see you thus discomfited.

Str. Say no more of ourselves; but until we find someone or other who can speak of not-being without number, we must acknowledge that the Sophist is a clever rogue who will not be got out of his hole.

Theaet. Most true.

Str. And if we say to him that he professes an art of making appearances, he will seize the opportunity which this expression d affords, and grappling with us, retort our argument upon ourselves; and when we call him an image-maker he will say, 'Pray what do you mean at all by an image?'—and I should like to know, Theaetetus, how we can possibly answer the younker's question?

Theaet. We shall doubtless tell him of the images which are reflected in water or in mirrors; also of sculptures, pictures, and other duplicates.

Str. I see, Theaetetus, that you have never made the acquaintance of the Sophist.

Theaet. Why do you think so?

Str. He will make believe to have his eyes shut, or to have none.

Theaet. What do you mean?

Str. When in your answer you tell him of something existing

240 in a mirror, or in sculpture, and address him as though he had eyes, he will laugh you to scorn, and will pretend that he knows nothing of mirrors and streams, or of sight at all; he will say that he is asking about an idea.

Theaet. What can he mean?

Str. The common notion pervading all these objects, which you speak of as many, and yet call by the single name of image, as though it were the unity under which they were all included. How will you maintain your ground against him?

Theaet. How, Stranger, can I describe an image except as something fashioned in the likeness of the true?

b *Str.* And do you mean this something to be some other true thing, or what do you mean?

Theaet. Certainly not another true thing, but only a resemblance.

Str. And you mean by true that which really is?

Theaet. Yes.

Str. And the not true is that which is the opposite of the true?

Theaet. Exactly.

Str. A resemblance, then, is not really real, if, as you say, not true?

Theaet. Nay, but it is in a certain sense.

Str. You mean to say, not in a true sense?

Theaet. Yes; it is in reality only an image.

Str. Then what we call an image is in reality really unreal.

c *Theaet.* Yes, it appears that not-being is, in this way, strangely complicated with being.

Str. Strangely! I should think so. See how, by his reciprocation of opposites, the many-headed Sophist has compelled us, quite against our will, to admit the existence of not-being.

Theaet. Yes, indeed, I see.

Str. The difficulty is how to define his art without falling into a contradiction.

Theaet. How do you mean? And where does the danger lie?

d *Str.* When we say that he deceives us with an illusion, and that his art is illusory, do we mean that our soul is led by his art to think falsely, or what do we mean?

Theaet. There is nothing else to be said.

Str. Again, false opinion is that form of opinion which thinks the opposite of the truth:—you would assent?

Theaet. Certainly.

Str. You mean to say that false opinion thinks what is not?

Theaet. Of course.

Str. Does false opinion think that things which are not are not, e or that in a certain sense they are?

Theaet. Things that are not must be imagined to exist in a certain sense, if any degree of falsehood is to be possible.

Str. And does not false opinion also think that things which most certainly exist do not exist at all?

Theaet. Yes.

Str. And here, again, is falsehood?

Theaet. Falsehood—yes.

Str. And in like manner, a false proposition will be deemed to be one which asserts the non-existence of things which are, and the existence of things which are not.

Theaet. There is no other way in which a false proposition can arise.

Str. There is not; but the Sophist will deny these statements. 241 And indeed how can any rational man assent to them, when they are added to the admissions already made? Do you see his point, Theaetetus?

Theaet. Of course he will say that we are contradicting our- selves when we hazard the assertion, that falsehood exists in b opinion and in words; for in maintaining this, we are compelled over and over again to assert being of not-being, which we admitted just now to be an utter impossibility.

Str. How well you remember! And now it is high time[1] to hold a consultation as to what we ought to do about the Sophist; for if we persist in looking for him in the class of false workers and magicians, you see that the handles for objection and the diffi- culties which will arise are very numerous and obvious.

Theaet. They are indeed.

Str. We have gone through but a very small portion of them, c and they are really infinite.

Theaet. If that is the case, we cannot possibly catch the Sophist.

Str. Shall we then be so faint-hearted as to give him up?

---

[1] [Retaining ὥρα δὴ βουλεύεσθαι, the manuscript reading.]

Theaet. Certainly not, I should say, if we can get the slightest hold upon him.

Str. Will you then forgive me, and, as your words imply, not be altogether displeased if I flinch a little from the grasp of such a sturdy argument?[1]

Theaet. To be sure I will.

d *Str.* I have a yet more urgent request to make.

Theaet. Which is——?

Str. That you will promise not to regard me as a parricide.

Theaet. And why?

Str. Because, in self-defence, I must test the philosophy of my father Parmenides, and try to prove by main force that in a certain sense not-being is, and that being, on the other hand, is not.

Theaet. Some attempt of the kind is clearly needed.

Str. Yes, a blind man, as they say, might see that, and, unless these questions are decided in one way or another, no one when he speaks of false words, or false opinion, or idols, or images, or

e imitations, or appearances, or about the arts which are concerned with them, can avoid falling into ridiculous contradictions.

Theaet. Most true.

242 *Str.* And therefore I must venture to lay hands on my father's argument; for if I am to be over-scrupulous, I shall have to give the matter up.

Theaet. Nothing in the world should ever induce us to do so.

Str. I have a third little request which I wish to make.

Theaet. What is it?

Str. You heard me say what I have always felt and still feel— that I have no heart for this argument?

Theaet. I did.

Str. I tremble at the thought of what I have said, and expect that you will deem me mad, when you hear of my sudden changes

b and shiftings; let me therefore observe, that I am examining the question entirely out of regard for you.

Theaet. There is no reason for you to fear that I shall impute any impropriety to you, if you attempt this refutation and proof; take heart, therefore, and proceed.

[1] [Or: 'as your words imply, be satisfied if we can squirm aside from so strong an argument, even to a slight extent'.]

Str. And where shall I begin the perilous enterprise? I think
that the road which I must take is——

Theaet. Which?—Let me hear.

Str. I think that we had better, first of all, consider the points
which at present are regarded as self-evident, lest we may have
fallen into some confusion, and be too ready to assent to one c
another, fancying that we are quite clear about them.

Theaet. Say more distinctly what you mean.

Str. I think that Parmenides, and all who ever yet undertook
to determine the number and nature of existences, talked to us in
rather a light and easy strain.

Theaet. How?

Str. As if we had been children, to whom they repeated each
his own mythus or story;—one said that there were three principles, and that at one time there was war between certain of
them; and then again there was peace, and they were married
and begat children, and brought them up; and another spoke of
two principles,—a moist and a dry, or a hot and a cold, and made
them marry and cohabit. The Eleatics, however, in our part of d
the world, say that all things are many in name, but in nature
one; this is their mythus, which goes back to Xenophanes, and is
even older. Then there are Ionian, and in more recent times
Sicilian, Muses who have arrived at the conclusion that to unite
the two principles is safer, and to say that being is one and many, e
and that these are held together by enmity and friendship, ever
parting, ever meeting, as the severer Muses assert, while the
gentler ones do not insist on the perpetual strife and peace, but 243
admit a relaxation and alternation of them; peace and unity
sometimes prevailing under the sway of Aphrodite, and then
again plurality and war, by reason of a principle of strife.
Whether any of them spoke the truth in all this is hard to determine; besides, antiquity and famous men should have reverence,
and not be liable to accusations so serious. Yet one thing may be
said of them without offence——

Theaet. What thing?

Str. That they went on their several ways disdaining to notice
people like ourselves; they did not care whether they took us with b
them, or left us behind them.

Theaet. How do you mean?

Str. I mean to say, that when they talk of one, two, or more elements, which are or have become or are becoming, or again of heat mingling with cold, assuming in some other part of their works[1] separations and mixtures,—tell me, Theaetetus, do you understand what they mean by these expressions? When I was a younger man, I used to fancy that I understood quite well what was meant by the term 'not-being', which is our present subject of dispute; and now you see in what a fix we are about it.

c   *Theaet.* I see.

Str. And yet it is possible that our perplexity of mind in regard to being is not less grave. We may fancy that it causes us no embarrassment, and that we understand when we hear the word spoken; we may contrast this with our ignorance of not-being, when in truth we are equally ignorant of both.

Theaet. I dare say.

Str. And the same may be said of all the terms just mentioned.

Theaet. True.

Str. The consideration of most of them may be deferred;
d but we had better now discuss the chief captain and leader of them.

Theaet. Of what are you speaking? You clearly think that we must first investigate what people mean by the word 'being'.

Str. You follow close at my heels, Theaetetus. For the right method, I conceive, will be to call into our presence the dualistic philosophers and to interrogate them. 'Come,' we will say, 'you, who affirm that hot and cold or any other two principles are the
e universe, what is this term which you apply to both of them, and what do you mean when you say that both and each of them "are"? How are we to understand the word "are"? Upon your view, are we to suppose that there is a third principle over and above the other two,—three in all, and not two? For clearly you cannot say that one of the two principles is being, and yet attribute being equally to both of them; for, if you did, whichever of the two is identified with being, will comprehend the other; and so they will be one and not two.'

Theaet. Very true.

---

[1] [This phrase has a strange sound, and recent editors adopt Radermacher's emendation ἄλλος εἴπῃ for ἄλλοθί πῃ. 'Or when another speaks of separations and mixtures,' &c.]

Str. 'But perhaps you mean to give the name of "being" to both of them together?'

Theaet. Quite likely.

Str. 'Then, friends,' we shall reply to them, 'the answer is 244 plainly that the two will still be resolved into one.'

Theaet. Most true.

Str. 'Since, then, we are puzzled, please make clear to us what you mean, when you speak of being; for there can be no doubt that you always from the first understood your own meaning, whereas we once thought that we understood you, but now we are in a great strait. Please to begin by explaining this matter to us, and let us no longer fancy that we understand you, when we entirely misunderstand you.' There will be no impropriety in our b demanding an answer to this question, either of the dualists or of the pluralists?

Theaet. Certainly not.

Str. And what about the assertors of the oneness of the all— must we not endeavour to ascertain from them what they mean by 'being'?

Theaet. By all means.

Str. Then let them answer this question: One, you say, alone is? 'Yes,' they will reply.

Theaet. True.

Str. And there is something which you call 'being'?[1]

Theaet. 'Yes.'

Str. And is being the same as one, and do you apply two names c to the same thing?

Theaet. What will be their answer, Stranger?

Str. It is clear, Theaetetus, that he who asserts as his hypothesis the unity of being will not be wholly at his ease in answering this or any other question.

Theaet. Why so?

Str. To admit of two names, and to affirm that there is nothing but unity, is surely ridiculous?

Theaet. Certainly.

Str. Moreover, such a thinker cannot be permitted to say that d there is any name at all; he could give no account of its nature.

---

[1] [Or, 'the real'. This second sense should be borne in mind throughout the following argument.]

Theaet. How so?

Str. To distinguish the name from the thing, implies duality.

Theaet. Yes.

Str. And yet he who identifies the name with the thing will be compelled to say that it is the name of nothing, or if he says that it is the name of something, even then it will follow that the name is the name of a name, and of nothing else.

Theaet. True.

Str. And 'the one'[1] can refer only to one thing—that is to say, to a name.

Theaet. Certainly.

Str. And would they say that the whole is other than the one that is, or the same with it?

e *Theaet.* To be sure they would, and they actually say so.

Str. If being is a whole, as Parmenides sings,—

> Every way like unto the fullness of a well-rounded sphere,
> Evenly balanced from the centre on every side,
> And must needs be neither greater nor less in any way,
> Neither on this side nor on that—

then being has a centre and extremes, and, having these, must also have parts.

Theaet. True.

245 *Str.* Yet there is no reason why that which has parts may not have the attribute of unity in the sum of all the parts, and in this way being all and a whole, may be one?

Theaet. Certainly.

Str. But that of which this is the condition cannot be absolute unity?

Theaet. Why not?

Str. Because, according to right reason, that which is truly one must be affirmed to be absolutely indivisible.

Theaet. Certainly.

b *Str.* But this indivisible, if made up of many parts, will contradict reason.

Theaet. I understand.

Str. Shall we say that being is one and a whole, because it has

---

[1] [This seems to be the sense, but the Greek text is corrupt and has not been successfully restored.]

the attribute of unity? Or shall we say that being is not a whole at all?

Theaet. That is a hard alternative to offer.

Str. Most true; for being, having in a certain sense the attribute of one, is yet proved not to be the same as one, and the all is therefore more than one.

Theaet. Yes.

Str. And yet if being be not a whole, through having the c attribute of unity, and there be such a thing as an absolute whole, being lacks something of its own nature?

Theaet. Certainly.

Str. Upon this view, again, being, having a defect of being, will become not-being?

Theaet. True.

Str. Further, the all once more becomes more than one, for being and the whole will each have their separate nature.

Theaet. Yes.

Str. But if the whole does not exist at all, all the previous difficulties remain the same, and there will be the further difficulty, that besides having no being, being can never have come d into being.

Theaet. Why so?

Str. Because that which comes into being always comes into being as a whole, so that he who does not give 'whole' a place among beings, cannot speak either of essence or generation as existing.

Theaet. Yes, that certainly appears to be true.

Str. Again; how can that which is not a whole have any quantity or number? For that which is of a definite number must necessarily be the whole of that number.

Theaet. Exactly.

Str. And there will be innumerable other points, each of them causing infinite trouble to him who says that being is either one e or two.

Theaet. The difficulties which are dawning upon us prove this; for one objection connects with another, and they are always involving what has preceded in a greater and worse perplexity.

Str. We are far from having exhausted the more exact thinkers who treat of being and not-being. But let us be content to leave

246 them, and proceed to view those who speak less precisely; and we shall find as the result of all, that the nature of being is quite as difficult to comprehend as that of not-being.

Theaet. Then now we will go to the others.

Str. There appears to be a sort of war of Giants and Gods going on amongst them; they are fighting with one another about the nature of reality.

Theaet. How is that?

Str. Some of them are dragging down all things from heaven and from the unseen to earth, and they literally grasp in their hands rocks and oaks; of all such things they lay hold, and obstinately maintain, that only the things which can be touched or handled have being, because they define being [reality] and

b body as one, and if anyone else says that what is not a body exists they altogether despise him, and will hear of no other view.

Theaet. I have often met with such men, and terrible fellows they are.

Str. And that is the reason why their opponents cautiously defend themselves from above, out of an unseen world, mightily contending that true reality consists of certain intelligible and incorporeal Ideas; the bodies of the Materialists, which by them are maintained to be the very truth, they break up into little bits

c by their arguments, and affirm them to be, not being, but generation and motion. Between the two armies, Theaetetus, there is always an endless conflict raging concerning these matters.

Theaet. True.

Str. Let us ask each party in turn, to give an account of that which they call reality.

Theaet. How shall we get it out of them?

Str. With those who make being to consist in ideas, there will be less difficulty, for they are civil people enough; but there will be very great difficulty, or perhaps even absolute impossibility, in getting an opinion out of those who drag everything down to

d matter. Shall I tell you what we must do?

Theaet. What?

Str. Let us, if we can; really improve them; but if this is not possible, let us imagine them to be better than they are, and more willing to answer in accordance with the rules of argument, and then their opinion will be more worth having; for that which better men acknowledge has more weight than that which is acknowledged by inferior men. Moreover we are no respecters of persons, but seekers after truth.

Theaet. Very good.   e

Str. Then now, on the supposition that they are improved, let us ask them to state their views, and do you interpret them.

Theaet. Agreed.

Str. Let them say whether they would admit that there is such a thing as a mortal animal.

Theaet. Of course they would.

Str. And do they not acknowledge this to be a body having a soul?

Theaet. Certainly they do.

Str. Meaning to say that the soul is something which exists?

Theaet. True.   247

Str. And do they not say that one soul is just, and another unjust, and that one soul is wise, and another foolish?

Theaet. Certainly.

Str. And that the just and wise soul becomes just and wise by the possession of justice and wisdom,[1] and the opposite under opposite circumstances?

Theaet. Yes, they do.

Str. But surely that which may be present or may be absent will be admitted by them to exist?

Theaet. Certainly.

Str. And, allowing that justice, wisdom, the other virtues, and b their opposites exist, as well as a soul in which they inhere, do they affirm any of them to be visible and tangible, or are they all invisible?

Theaet. They would hardly say that any of them are visible.

Str. And would they say that, being such, they are corporeal?

Theaet. They would distinguish: the soul would be said by them to have a body; but as to the other qualities of justice, wisdom, and the like, about which you asked, they would not venture either to deny their existence, or to maintain that they c were all corporeal.

Str. Verily, Theaetetus, I perceive a great improvement in them; the real aborigines, children of the dragon's teeth, would

---

[1] Reading with Professor Campbell δικαιοσύνης ἕξει καὶ φρονήσεως.

have been deterred by no shame at all, but would have obstinately asserted that nothing is which they are not able to squeeze in their hands.

Theaet. That is pretty much their notion.

Str. Let us push the question; for if they will admit that any,
d even the smallest particle of being, is incorporeal, it is enough; they must then say what that nature is which is common to both the corporeal and incorporeal, and which they have in their mind's eye when they say of both of them that they 'are'. Perhaps they may be puzzled; and if this is the case, there is a possibility that they may accept a notion of ours respecting the nature of being, having nothing of their own to offer.

Theaet. What is the notion? Tell me, and we shall soon see.

Str. My notion would be, that anything which possesses any
e sort of power to affect another, or to be affected by another, if only for a single moment, however trifling the cause and however slight the effect, has real existence; and I hold that the definition of being is simply power.

Theaet. They accept your suggestion, having nothing better of their own to offer.

Str. Very good; perhaps we, as well as they, may one day
248 change our minds; but, for the present, this may be regarded as the understanding which is established with them.

Theaet. Agreed.

Str. Let us now go to the friends of Ideas; of their opinions, too, you shall be the interpreter.

Theaet. I will.

Str. To them we say—You would distinguish being [reality] from generation?

Theaet. 'Yes,' they reply.

Str. And you would allow that we have contact with generation by the body, and through perception, but with true reality through thought, and by the soul; and such reality you would affirm to be always the same and immutable, whereas generation or becoming varies?

b *Theaet.* 'Yes; that is what we should affirm.'

Str. Well, fair sirs, we say to them, what is this contact which you assert of both? Do you agree with our recent definition?

Theaet. What definition?

Str. We said that being was an action or affection, arising out of a certain power in elements which meet with one another. Perhaps your ears, Theaetetus, may fail to catch their answer, which I recognize because I have been accustomed to hear it.

Theaet. And what is their answer?

Str. They deny the truth of what we were just now saying to c the aborigines about existence [reality].

Theaet. What was that?

Str. Any power of doing or suffering in a degree however slight was held by us to be a sufficient definition of being?

Theaet. True.

Str. They deny this, and say that the power of doing or suffering has some application to becoming, but that neither power is appropriate to being.

Theaet. And is there not some truth in what they say?

Str. Yes; but our reply will be, that we want to ascertain from them more distinctly, whether they further admit that the soul d knows, and that being or essence is known.

Theaet. There can be no doubt that they say so.

Str. And is knowing and being known doing or suffering, or both, or is the one doing and the other suffering, or has neither any share in either?

Theaet. Clearly, neither has any share in either; for if they say anything else, they will contradict themselves.

Str. I understand; they will reason thus—If knowing is a kind of action, it necessarily follows that being known is an affection. And on this view reality, in so far as it is known, is acted upon by e knowledge, and is therefore in motion; for that which is in a state of rest cannot be acted upon, as we affirm.

Theaet. True.

Str. And, O heavens, can we ever be made to believe that 249 motion and life and soul and mind are not present with perfect being?[1] Can we imagine that being is devoid of life and mind, and exists in solemn unmeaningness an everlasting fixture?

Theaet. That would be a dreadful thing to admit, Stranger.

Str. But shall we say that being has mind and not life?

Theaet. How is that possible?

---

[1] [This expression may refer to that which is real in the highest sense, or to the total of reality. See note on p. 323.]

Str. Or shall we say that both inhere in perfect being, but that it has no soul which contains them?

Theaet. And in what other way can it contain them?

Str. Or that being has mind and life and soul, but although endowed with soul remains absolutely unmoved?

b   *Theaet.* All three suppositions appear to me to be irrational.

Str. Under being, then, we must include motion, and that which is moved.

Theaet. Certainly.

Str. Then, Theaetetus, our inference is, that if there is no motion,[1] neither is there any mind anywhere, or about anything or belonging to anyone.

Theaet. Quite true.

Str. And yet this equally follows, if we grant that all things are in motion—upon this view too mind has no existence.

Theaet. How so?

c   *Str.* Do you think that sameness of condition and mode and subject could ever exist without a principle of rest?

Theaet. Certainly not.

Str. Can you see how without them mind could exist, or come into existence anywhere?

Theaet. No.

Str. And surely we must contend in every possible way against him who would annihilate knowledge and reason and mind, and yet ventures to speak confidently about anything.

Theaet. Yes, with all our might.

Str. Then the philosopher, who has the truest reverence for these qualities, cannot possibly accept the notion of those who say

d   that the whole is at rest, either as unity or in many forms: and he will be utterly deaf to those who assert universal motion. As children say entreatingly 'Give us both', so he will include both the moveable and immoveable in his definition of being and all.

Theaet. Most true.

Str. And now, do we not seem to have gained a fair notion of being?

Theaet. Yes truly.

Str. Alas, Theaetetus, methinks that we are now only beginning to see the real difficulty of the inquiry into the nature of it.

---

[1] [Reading ὄντων ⟨πάντων⟩, as proposed by Badham.]

Theaet. What do you mean?　　　　　　　　　　　　　　　　e

Str. O my friend, do you not see that nothing can exceed our ignorance, and yet we fancy that we are saying something good?

Theaet. I fancy so, at least; and I still do not quite understand in what respect we fail to realize our ignorance.

Str. Reflect: after having made these admissions, may we not　250 be justly asked the same questions which we ourselves were asking of those who said that all was hot and cold?

Theaet. What were they? Will you recall them to my mind?

Str. To be sure I will, and I will try to do so by putting questions to you as I did to them, and then we shall make progress.

Theaet. True.

Str. Would you not say that rest and motion are in the most entire opposition to one another?

Theaet. Of course.

Str. And yet you would say that both and either of them equally are?

Theaet. I should.　　　　　　　　　　　　　　　　　　　b

Str. And when you admit that both or either of them are, do you mean to say that both or either of them are in motion?

Theaet. Certainly not.

Str. Or do you wish to imply that they are both at rest, when you say that they are?

Theaet. Of course not.

Str. Then you conceive of being as some third and distinct nature, under which rest and motion are alike included;[1] and, observing that they both participate in being, you declare that they are.

Theaet. Truly we seem to have an intimation that being is　c some third thing, when we say that rest and motion are.

Str. Then being is not the combination of rest and motion, but something different from them.

Theaet. So it would appear.

Str. Being, then, according to its own nature, is neither in motion nor at rest.

Theaet. That is very much the truth.

　[1] [Punctuating the sentence after συλλαβών, as proposed by Campbell.]

Str. Where, then, is a man to look for help who would have any clear or fixed notion of being in his mind?

Theaet. Where, indeed?

Str. I scarcely think that he can look anywhere; for that which
d is not in motion must surely be at rest, and again, that which is not at rest must be in motion; but being, as has now been proved, is placed outside of both these classes. Is this possible?

Theaet. Utterly impossible.

Str. Here, then, is another thing which we ought to bear in mind.

Theaet. What?

Str. When we were asked to what we were to assign the appellation of not-being, we were in the greatest difficulty:—do you remember?

Theaet. To be sure.

e   *Str.* And are we not now in as great a difficulty about being?

Theaet. I should say, Stranger, that we are in one which is, if possible, even greater.

Str. The problem has been stated, and we must at present leave it there; and as being and not-being are involved in the same perplexity, there is hope that when the one appears more or
251 less distinctly, the other will equally appear; and if we are able to see neither, there may still be a chance of forcing a way for our argument in between them, without any great discredit.

Theaet. Very good.

Str. Let us inquire, then, how we come to predicate many names of the same thing.

Theaet. Give an example.

Str. I mean that we speak of man, for example, under many names—that we attribute to him colours and forms and magnitudes and virtues and vices, in all of which instances and in ten
b thousand others we not only speak of him as a man, but also as good, and having numberless other attributes; and in the same way anything else which we originally supposed to be one is described by us as many, and under many names.

Theaet. That is true.

Str. And thus we provide a rich feast for tyros, whether young or old; for there is nothing easier than to argue that the one cannot be many, or the many one; and great is their delight in

forbidding us to say that a man is good; for man, they insist, is
man and good is good. I dare say that you have met with persons c
who take an interest in such matters—they are often elderly
men, whose meagre sense is thrown into amazement by these
discoveries of theirs, which they believe to be the height of
wisdom.

Theaet. Certainly, I have.

Str. Then, not to exclude anyone who has ever speculated at
all upon the nature of being, let us put our questions to them as
well as to our former friends.

Theaet. What questions?

Str. Shall we refuse to attribute being to motion and rest, or
anything to anything, and assume that since they do not mingle, d
and are incapable of participating in one another, we must
represent them accordingly in our discourse? Or shall we gather
all into one class of things communicable with one another? Or
are some things communicable and others not?—Which of these
alternatives, Theaetetus, will they prefer?   e

Theaet. I have nothing to answer on their behalf.

Str. Suppose that you take all these hypotheses in turn, and
see what are the consequences which follow from each of them?

Theaet. Very good.

Str. First let us assume them to say that nothing is capable of
participating in anything else in any respect; in that case rest 252
and motion cannot participate in being at all.

Theaet. They cannot.

Str. But would either of them be if not participating in being?

Theaet. No.

Str. Then by this admission everything is instantly overturned,
as well the doctrine of universal motion as of universal rest, and
also the doctrine of those who distribute being into immutable
and everlasting kinds; for all these add on a notion of being, some
affirming that things 'are' truly in motion, and others that they
'are' truly at rest.

Theaet. Just so.

Str. Again, those who would at one time compound, and at b
another resolve all things, whether making them into one and out
of one creating infinity, or dividing them into finite elements,
and forming compounds out of these; whether they suppose the

processes of creation to be successive or continuous, would be talking nonsense in all this if there were no admixture.

Theaet. True.

Str. Most ridiculous of all will the men themselves be who want to carry out the argument and yet forbid us to call anything, because participating in some affection from another, by the name of that other.

c   *Theaet.* Why so?

Str. Why, because they are compelled to use the words 'to be', 'apart', 'from others', 'in itself', and ten thousand more, which they cannot give up, but must make the connecting links of discourse; and therefore they do not require to be refuted by others, but their enemy, as the saying is, inhabits the same house with them; they are always carrying about with them an adversary, like the wonderful ventriloquist, Eurycles, who out of their own bellies audibly contradicts them.

d   *Theaet.* Precisely so; a very true and exact illustration.

Str. And now, if we suppose that all things have the power of communion with one another—what will follow?

Theaet. Even I can solve that riddle.

Str. How?

Theaet. Why, because motion itself would be at rest, and rest again in motion, if they could be attributed to one another.

Str. But this is utterly impossible.

Theaet. Of course.

Str. Then only the third hypothesis remains.

Theaet. True.

Str. For, surely, either all things have communion with all; or
e nothing with any other thing; or some things communicate with some things and others not.

Theaet. Certainly.

Str. And two out of these three suppositions have been found to be impossible.

Theaet. Yes.

Str. Everyone then, who desires to answer truly, will adopt the third and remaining hypothesis of the communion of some with some.

Theaet. Quite true.

253   *Str.* This communion of some with some may be illustrated by

the case of letters; for some letters do not fit each other, while others do.

Theaet. Of course.

Str. And the vowels, especially, are a sort of bond which pervades all the other letters, so that without a vowel one consonant cannot be joined to another.

Theaet. True.

Str. But does everyone know what letters will unite with what? Or is art required to make a man a reliable judge of this?

Theaet. Art is required.

Str. What art?

Theaet. The art of grammar.

Str. And is not this also true of sounds high and low?—Is not b he who has the art to know what sounds mingle, a musician, and he who is ignorant, not a musician?

Theaet. Yes.

Str. And we shall find this to be generally true of art or the absence of art.

Theaet. Of course.

Str. And as classes are admitted by us in like manner to be some of them capable and others incapable of intermixture, must not he who would rightly show which kinds will unite, and which of them repel each other, proceed by science in the path of argument? By science, too, he must know whether there are some all-pervading connecting terms, which enable the other kinds to c blend; and, conversely, in divisions, whether there are not others which cause whole classes to become separate?

Theaet. To be sure he will require science, and, if I am not mistaken, the very greatest of all sciences.

Str. How are we to call it? By Zeus, have we not lighted unwittingly upon our free and noble science, and in looking for the Sophist have we not entertained the Philosopher unawares?

Theaet. What do you mean?

Str. Should we not say that the division according to classes, d which neither makes the same other, nor makes other the same, is the business of the dialectical science?

Theaet. That is what we should say.

Str. Then, surely, he who can divide rightly is able to see clearly one form pervading a scattered multitude, and many different forms contained under one higher form; and again, one form knit together into a single whole and pervading many such wholes; and many forms existing only in separation and isolation. This is the knowledge of classes which determines where

e they can have communion with one another and where not.

Theaet. Quite true.

Str. And the art of dialectic would be attributed by you only to the Philosopher pure and true?

Theaet. Who but he can be worthy?

Str. In this region, then, we shall discover the Philosopher, either now, or at any later time,[1] if we look for him; like the

254 Sophist, he is not easily discovered, but for a different reason.

Theaet. For what reason?

Str. Because the Sophist runs away into the darkness of not-being, in which he has learned by habit to feel about, and cannot be discovered because of the darkness of the place. Is not that true?

Theaet. It seems to be so.

Str. And the Philosopher, always holding converse through reason with the idea of being, is also dark from excess of light;

b for the souls of the many have no eye which can endure the vision of the divine.

Theaet. Yes; that seems to be quite as true as the other.

Str. Well, the Philosopher may hereafter be more fully considered by us, if we are disposed; but the Sophist must clearly not be allowed to escape until we have had a good look at him.

Theaet. Very good.

Str. Since, then, we are agreed that some classes have a communion with one another, and others not, and some have communion with a few and others with many, and that there is no

c reason why some should not have universal communion with all, let us now pursue the inquiry, as the argument suggests, not in relation to all Ideas, lest the multitude of them should confuse us, but let us select a few of those which are reckoned to be the principal ones, and consider their several natures and their capacity of communion with one another, in order that if we are not able to apprehend with perfect clearness the notions of being

[1] [Probably with allusion to the projected dialogue *The Philosopher*.]

and not-being, we may at least not fall short in the consideration of them, so far as they come within the scope of the present inquiry, if peradventure we may be allowed to assert that there is something which really is not, and yet escape unscathed. d

Theaet. We must do so.

Str. The most important of those genera which we have recently discussed are being itself and rest and motion.

Theaet. Yes, by far.

Str. And two of these are, as we affirm, incapable of communion with one another.

Theaet. Quite incapable.

Str. Whereas being surely has communion with both of them, for both of them are?

Theaet. Of course.

Str. That makes up three of them.

Theaet. To be sure.

Str. And each of them is other than the remaining two, but the same with itself.

Theaet. True. e

Str. But then, what is the meaning of these two words, 'same' and 'other'? Are they two new kinds other than the three, and yet always of necessity intermingling with them, so that we must inquire into five kinds instead of three; or when we speak of the same and other, are we unconsciously speaking of one of the three first kinds? 255

Theaet. Very likely we are.

Str. But, surely, motion and rest are neither the other nor the same.

Theaet. How is that?

Str. Whatever we attribute to motion and rest in common, cannot be either of them.

Theaet. Why not?

Str. Because motion would be at rest and rest in motion, for either of them, being predicated of both, will compel the other to change into the opposite of its own nature, because partaking of its opposite. b

Theaet. Quite true.

Str. Yet they surely both partake of the same and of the other?

Theaet. Yes.

Str. Then we must not assert that motion, any more than rest, is either the same or the other.

Theaet. No; we must not.

Str. But are we to conceive that being and the same are identical?

Theaet. Possibly.

Str. But if 'being' and 'the same' in no way differ in meaning, c then again in saying that motion and rest have being, we should also be saying that they are the same.

Theaet. Which surely cannot be.

Str. Then being and the same cannot be one.

Theaet. Scarcely.

Str. Then we may suppose the same to be a fourth class, which is now to be added to the three others.

Theaet. Quite true.

Str. And shall we call the other a fifth class? Or should we consider being and other to be two names of the same class?

Theaet. Very likely.

Str. But you would agree, if I am not mistaken, that there are two classes of things, some which exist in their own right, and others which are only said to *be* in relation to something else.

Theaet. Certainly.

d *Str.* And other is one of those terms which are always relative to an other?

Theaet. True.

Str. But this would not be the case unless there were a vast difference between being and the other; for, if the other, like being, belonged to both classes, then there would have been a kind of other which was not other than other. As it is, we find simply that whatever is other must of necessity be what it is in relation to some other.

Theaet. That is the true state of the case.

Str. Then we must admit the other as the fifth of our selected e classes.

Theaet. Yes.

Str. And we shall say that this is one which has penetrated all the remainder. For each severally is *other* than the rest, not by reason of its own nature, but because it has some share in the form of otherness.

Theaet. Quite true.

Str. Then let us now put the case with reference to each of the five.

Theaet. How?

Str. First there is motion, which we affirm to be absolutely 'other' than rest: what else can we say?

Theaet. It is so.

Str. And therefore is not rest.

Theaet. Certainly not.

Str. And yet is, because partaking of being.

Theaet. True. 256

Str. Again, motion is other than the same?

Theaet. Just so.

Str. And is therefore not the same.

Theaet. It is not.

Str. Yet, surely, motion was declared to be the same, because all things partake of sameness.

Theaet. Very true.

Str. Then we must admit, without grumbling, the statement that motion is the same and yet not the same; for when we apply these expressions to it, our point of view is different. We call it the same in relation to itself, because it partakes of b sameness; whereas we call it not the same because, having communion with otherness, it is thereby severed from the same, and has become not that but other; so that it is with equal justice spoken of as 'not the same'.

Theaet. To be sure.

Str. Likewise if movement *per se* in any point of view partook of rest, there would be no absurdity in calling motion stationary.

Theaet. Quite right,—that is, on the supposition that some classes mingle with one another, and others not.

Str. That such a communion of kinds is according to nature, c we had already proved[1] before we arrived at this part of our discussion.

Theaet. Certainly.

Str. Let us proceed, then. May we not say that motion is other than the other, having been also proved by us to be other than the same and other than rest?

[1] Cf. *supra,* 252.

Theaet. That is certain.

Str. Then, according to this view, motion is other and also not other?

Theaet. True.

Str. What is the next step? Shall we say that motion is other than the three and not other than the fourth,—for we agreed
d that there are five classes about and in the sphere of which we proposed to make inquiry?

Theaet. Surely we cannot admit that the number is less than it appeared to be just now.

Str. Then we may without fear contend that motion is other than being?

Theaet. Without the least fear.

Str. The plain result is that motion, since it partakes of being, really is and also is not?

Theaet. Nothing can be plainer.

Str. Then not-being necessarily exists in the case of motion and of every class; for the nature of the other entering into them
e all makes each of them other than being, and so non-existent; and therefore of all of them, in like manner, we may truly say that they are not; and again, inasmuch as they partake of being, that they are and are existent.

Theaet. So we may assume.

Str. Every class, then, has plurality of being and infinity of not-being.

257   *Theaet.* So we must infer.

Str. And being itself may be said to be other than the other kinds.

Theaet. Certainly.

Str. Then we may infer that being is not, in respect of as many other things as there are; for not being these it is itself one, and is not the other things, which are infinite in number.

Theaet. That is not far from the truth.

Str. And we must not quarrel with this result, since it is of the nature of classes to have communion with one another; and if anyone denies our present statement [viz. that being is not, &c.], let him first argue with our former conclusion [i.e. respecting the communion of Ideas], and then he may proceed to argue with what follows.

Theaet. Nothing can be fairer.

Str. Let me ask you to consider a further question. b

Theaet. What question?

Str. When we speak of not-being, we speak, I suppose, not of something opposed to being, but only different.

Theaet. What do you mean?

Str. When we speak of something as not great, does the expression seem to you to imply what is little any more than what is equal?

Theaet. Certainly not.

Str. If, therefore, it is said that negation implies contrariety, we shall refuse to admit this. The negative particles, οὐ and μή, when prefixed to words, imply merely a *difference* from the words, or more correctly from the things represented by the words, which c follow them.

Theaet. Quite true.

Str. There is another point to be considered, if you do not object.

Theaet. What is it?

Str. The nature of the other appears to me to be divided into fractions like knowledge.

Theaet. How so?

Str. Knowledge, like the other, is one; and yet every part of it which has a special province has some name peculiar to itself. To judge from names, there are many arts, and many branches of d knowledge.

Theaet. Quite true.

Str. And is not the case the same with the parts of the nature of otherness, which is also one?

Theaet. Very likely; but will you tell me how?

Str. There is some part of the other which is opposed to the beautiful?

Theaet. There is.

Str. Shall we say that this has or has not a name?

Theaet. It has; for whatever we call not-beautiful is other than the beautiful, not than something else.

Str. And now tell me another thing.

Theaet. What? e

Str. Is the not-beautiful anything but this—an existence parted off from a certain kind of existence, and again from another point of view opposed to an existing something?

Theaet. True.

Str. Then the not-beautiful turns out to be an instance of the opposition of being to being?

Theaet. Very true.

Str. But upon this view, is the beautiful a more real and the not-beautiful a less real existence?

Theaet. Not at all.

258   *Str.* And the not-great may be said to exist equally with the great?

Theaet. Equally.

Str. And, in the same way, the just must be placed in the same rank as the not-just—the one cannot be said to have any more existence than the other.

Theaet. True.

Str. The same may be said of other things; seeing that the nature of the other has a real existence, the parts of this nature must equally be supposed to exist.

Theaet. Of course.

Str. Then, as would appear, the opposition of a part of the
b other, and of a part of being, to one another, is, if I may venture to say so, as truly a reality as being itself, and implies not the opposite of being, but only what is other than being.

Theaet. Beyond question.

Str. What then shall we call it?

Theaet. Clearly, not-being; and this is the very nature for which the Sophist compelled us to search.

Str. And has not this, as you were saying, as real an existence as any other class? May I not say with confidence that not-being has an assured existence, and a nature of its own? Just as the
c great was found to be great and the beautiful beautiful, and the not-great not-great, and the not-beautiful not-beautiful, in the same manner not-being has been found to be and is not-being, and is to be reckoned one among the many classes of being. Do you, Theaetetus, still feel any doubt of this?

Theaet. None whatever.

Str. Do you observe that our scepticism has carried us beyond the range of Parmenides' prohibition?

Theaet. In what?

Str. We have advanced to a further point, and shown him more than he forbade us to investigate.

Theaet. How is that?

Str. Why, because he says—   d

> Never shall it be proved that not-being is, and do thou keep thy thoughts from this way of inquiry.

Theaet. Yes, he says so.

Str. Whereas, we have not only proved that things which are not are, but we have shown what form of being not-being is; for we have shown that the nature of the other exists, and is distributed over all things in their relations to one another; and whatever part of the other is opposed to being, this is e precisely what we have ventured to call not-being.

Theaet. And surely, Stranger, we were quite right.

Str. Let not anyone say, then, that the not-being, of which we venture to affirm the real existence, is the contrary of being. For as to whether there is an opposite of being, to that inquiry we have long said good-bye—it may or may not be, and may or may not be capable of definition. But as touching our present account 259 of not-being, let a man either convince us of error, or, so long as he cannot, he too must say, as we are saying, that there is a communion of classes, and that being, and difference or other, traverse all things and mutually interpenetrate, so that the other partakes of being, and by reason of this participation *is*, and yet is not that of which it partakes, but other, and if it is other than being, it is clearly a necessity that it should be not-being. And b again, being, through partaking of the other, becomes a class other than the remaining classes, and being other than all of them, is not each one of them, and is not all the rest, so that undoubtedly there are thousands upon thousands of cases in which being is not, and all other things, whether regarded individually or collectively, in many respects are, and in many respects are not.

Theaet. True.

Str. And if a man is sceptical of this contradiction, he must think how he can find something better to say; or if, like the inventor of a difficult trick, he delights in twisting an argument c

first in one direction and then in another, he is not making a
worthy use of his faculties, so we shall tell him; for the trick is
neither very ingenious nor very difficult to discover; but we can
tell him of something else the pursuit of which is noble and also
difficult.

Theaet. What is it?

Str. A thing of which I have already spoken;—letting alone
these puzzles as involving no difficulty, he should be able to
follow and criticize in detail every argument, and when a man
says that the same is in a manner other, or that other is the same,
d to understand and refute him from his own point of view, and in
the same respect in which he asserts either of these affections.
But to show that somehow and in some sense the same is other,
or the other same, or the great small, or the like unlike; and to
delight in always bringing forward such contradictions, is no
real refutation, but is clearly the new-born babe of someone who
is only beginning to approach the problem of being.

Theaet. To be sure.

Str. For certainly, my friend, the attempt to separate all
e existences from one another is a barbarism and utterly unworthy
of an educated or philosophical mind.

Theaet. Why so?

Str. The attempt at universal separation is the final annihila-
260 tion of all reasoning; for only by the union of conceptions with
one another do we attain to discourse of reason.

Theaet. True.

Str. And, observe that we were only just in time in making a
resistance to such separatists, and compelling them to admit that
one thing mingles with another.

Theaet. Why so?

Str. Why, that we might be able to assert discourse to be a
kind of being; for if we could not, the worst of all consequences
would follow; we should have no philosophy. Moreover, the
necessity for determining the nature of discourse presses upon us
at this moment; if utterly deprived of it, we could no more hold
b discourse; and deprived of it we should be if we admitted that
there was no admixture of natures at all.

Theaet. Very true. But I do not understand why at this moment
we must determine the nature of discourse.

Str. Perhaps you will see more clearly by the help of the following explanation.

Theaet. What explanation?

Str. Not-being has been acknowledged by us to be one among many classes diffused over all being.

Theaet. True.

Str. And thence arises the question, whether not-being mingles with opinion and language.

Theaet. How so?

Str. If not-being has no part in the proposition, then all things c must be true; but if not-being has a part, then false opinion and false speech are possible, for to think or to say what is not—is falsehood, which thus arises in the region of thought and in speech.

Theaet. That is quite true.

Str. And where there is falsehood surely there must be deceit.

Theaet. Yes.

Str. And if there is deceit, then all things must be full of idols and images and fancies.

Theaet. To be sure.

Str. Into that region the Sophist, as we said, made his escape, d and, when he had got there, denied the very possibility of falsehood; no one, he argued, either conceived or uttered falsehood, inasmuch as not-being did not in any way partake of being.

Theaet. True.

Str. And now, not-being has been shown to partake of being, and therefore he can scarcely continue fighting in this direction, but he will probably say that some forms partake of not-being, and some not, and that language and opinion are of the non-partaking class; and he will still fight to the death against the existence of the image-making and phantastic art, in which we e have placed him, because, as he will say, opinion and language do not partake of not-being, and unless this association can be formed, there can be no such thing as falsehood. And, with the view of meeting this evasion, we must begin by inquiring into the nature of language, opinion, and imagination, in order that when we find them we may observe their communion with not-being, and, having done so, may thus prove that falsehood exists; and 261 therein we will imprison the Sophist, if he deserves it, or, if not, we will let him go again and look for him in another class.

Theaet. Certainly, Stranger, there appears to be truth in what was said about the Sophist at first, that he was of a class not easily caught, for he seems to have abundance of defences, which he throws up, and which must every one of them be stormed before we can reach the man himself. And even now, we have with difficulty got through his first defence, which is the not-being of

b not-being, and lo! here is another; for we have still to show that falsehood exists in the sphere of language and opinion, and there will be another and another line of defence without end.

Str. Anyone, Theaetetus, who is able to advance even a little ought to be of good cheer, for what would he who is dispirited at a little progress do, if he were making none at all, or even under-

c going a repulse? Such a faint heart, as the proverb says, will never take a city: but now that we have succeeded in the point which you mention, the most formidable outwork has been taken, and those that remain will be lower and easier.

Theaet. Very true.

Str. Then, as I was saying, let us first of all obtain a conception of language and opinion, in order that we may have clearer grounds for determining whether not-being has any concern with them, or whether they are both always true, and neither of them ever false.

Theaet. Certainly.

d *Str.* Then, now, let us speak of names, as before we were speaking of forms and letters; for that is the direction in which the answer may be expected.

Theaet. And what is the question at issue about names?

Str. The question at issue is whether all names may be connected with one another, or none, or only some of them.

Theaet. Clearly the last is true.

Str. I understand you to say that words which have a meaning when in sequence may be connected, but that words which have

e no meaning when in sequence cannot be connected?

Theaet. What are you saying?

Str. What I thought that you intended when you gave your assent; for there are two sorts of intimation of being which are given by the voice.

Theaet. What are they?

Str. One of them is called nouns, and the other verbs.

Theaet. Describe them.

Str. That which denotes action we call a verb. 262

Theaet. True.

Str. And the other, which is an articulate mark set on those who do the actions, we call a noun.

Theaet. Quite true.

Str. Now a succession of nouns only can never form a sentence; neither can a succession of verbs without nouns.

Theaet. I do not understand you.

Str. I see that when you gave your assent you had something b else in your mind. But what I intended to say was, that a mere succession of nouns or of verbs is not discourse.

Theaet. What do you mean?

Str. I mean that words like 'walks', 'runs', 'sleeps', or any other words which denote action, however many of them you string together, do not make discourse.

Theaet. How can they?

Str. Or, again, when you say 'lion', 'stag', 'horse', or any other words which denote agents—neither in this way of stringing words together do you attain to discourse; for the sounds convey c no expression of action or inaction, or of the being of anything which is or is not, until verbs are mingled with nouns; then the words fit, and the smallest combination of them forms a sentence, and is the simplest and least form of discourse.

Theaet. Again I ask, What do you mean?

Str. When anyone says 'A man learns', would you not call this the simplest and least of sentences?

Theaet. Yes. d

Str. Yes, for he now arrives at the point of giving an intimation about something which is, or is becoming, or has become, or will be. And he not only names, but he achieves something, by connecting verbs with nouns; and therefore we say that he discourses, and to this connexion of words we give the name of discourse [or sentence].

Theaet. True.

Str. In conclusion, then, just as there appeared to be some things which fit one another, and other things which do not fit, so e there are some vocal signs which do, and others which do not, combine and form discourse.

Theaet. Quite true.

Str. There is another small matter.

Theaet. What is it?

Str. Every sentence must have and cannot help having a subject.[1]

Theaet. True.

Str. And must, in that case, be of a certain quality?

Theaet. Certainly.

Str. And now let us mind what we are about.

Theaet. We must do so.

Str. I will repeat a sentence to you in which a thing and an action are combined, by the help of a noun and a verb; and you shall tell me of whom the sentence speaks.

Theaet. I will, to the best of my power.

263 *Str.* 'Theaetetus sits'—not a very long sentence.

Theaet. Not very.

Str. Of whom does the sentence speak, and who is the subject? that is what you have to tell.

Theaet. Of me; I am the subject.

Str. Or this sentence, again——

Theaet. What sentence?

Str. 'Theaetetus, with whom I am now speaking, is flying.'

Theaet. That also is a sentence which will be admitted by everyone to speak of me, and to apply to me.

b *Str.* We agreed that every sentence must necessarily have a certain quality.

Theaet. Yes.

Str. And what is the quality of each of these two sentences?

Theaet. The one, as I imagine, is false, and the other true.

Str. The true says about you that which is, and as it is?

Theaet. Yes.

Str. And the false says what is other than real?

Theaet. Yes.

Str. And therefore speaks of things which are not, as if they were?

Theaet. Exactly.

Str. And says that things are real of you which are not; for, as

[1 Literally,' must belong to someone or something'. No technical term for 'subject' occurs here.]

we were saying, in regard to each thing or person, there is much that is and much that is not.

Theaet. Quite true.

Str. The second of the two sentences which related to you was c first of all an example of the shortest form consistent with our definition.

Theaet. Yes, this was implied in our recent admission.

Str. And, in the second place, it related to a subject?

Theaet. Yes.

Str. Who must be you, and can be nobody else?

Theaet. Unquestionably.

Str. And it would be no sentence at all if there were no subject, for, as we proved, a sentence which has no subject is impossible.

Theaet. Quite true.

Str. So that when, in some statement concerning you, the d different is affirmed as the same, and not-being as being, it seems to be precisely such a combination of nouns and verbs that is really and truly false discourse.

Theaet. Most true.

Str. And therefore thought, opinion, and imagination, all these are now proved to exist in our minds both as true and false?

Theaet. How so ?

Str. You will know better if you first gain a knowledge of what they are, and in what they severally differ from one another.   e

Theaet. Give me the knowledge which you would wish me to gain.

Str. Are not thought and speech the same, with this exception, that what is called thought is the unuttered conversation of the soul with herself ?

Theaet. Quite true.

Str. But the stream of thought which flows through the lips and is audible is called speech?

Theaet. True.

Str. And we know that there exists in speech——

Theaet. What exists ?

Str. Affirmation and denial.

Theaet. Yes, we know it.   264

Str. When this takes place in silence and in the mind only, have you any other name by which to call it but opinion?

Theaet. There can be no other name.

Str. And when opinion is presented, not simply, but with the help of sense-perception, can one rightly call this by any other name than imagination?

Theaet. No.

Str. Then, seeing that language is true and false, and that thought has been shown to be the conversation of the soul with b herself, and opinion to be the end of thinking, and imagination or phantasy to be the union of sense and opinion, the inference is that some of them, since they are akin to language, should have an element of falsehood as well as of truth?

Theaet. Certainly.

Str. Do you perceive then, that false opinion and speech have been discovered sooner than we expected?—For just now we seemed to be undertaking a task which would never be accomplished.

Theaet. I perceive.

Str. Then let us not be discouraged about the future; but now c having made this discovery, let us go back to our previous classification.

Theaet. What classification?

Str. We divided image-making into two sorts; the one likeness-making, the other imaginative or phantastic.

Theaet. True.

Str. And we said that we were uncertain in which we should place the Sophist.

Theaet. We did say so.

Str. And our heads began to go round more and more when it was asserted that there is no such thing as an image or idol or appearance, because in no manner or time or place can there d ever be such a thing as falsehood.

Theaet. True.

Str. But now, since there has been shown to be false speech and false opinion, there may be imitations of real existences, and out of this condition of the mind an art of deception may arise.

Theaet. Quite possible.

Str. And we have already admitted, in what preceded, that the Sophist was lurking in one of the divisions of the likeness-making art?

Theaet. Yes.

Str. Let us, then, renew the attempt, and in dividing any class, always take the part to the right, holding fast to that which holds e the Sophist, until we have stripped him of all his common properties, and reached his differentia or characteristic. Then we 265 may exhibit him in his true nature, first to ourselves and then to kindred dialectical spirits.

Theaet. Very good.

Str. You may remember that all art was originally divided by us into creative and acquisitve.

Theaet. Yes.

Str. And the Sophist was flitting before us in the acquisitive class, in the subdivisions of hunting, contests, merchandise, and the like.

Theaet. Very true.

Str. But now that the imitative art has enclosed him, it is clear that we must begin by dividing the art of creation; for imitation is a kind of creation—of images, however, as we affirm, and not b of real things.

Theaet. Quite true.

Str. In the first place, there are two kinds of creation.

Theaet. What are they?

Str. One of them is human and the other divine.

Theaet. I do not follow.

Str. Every power, as you may remember our saying originally, which causes things to exist, not previously existing, was defined by us as creative.

Theaet. I remember.

Str. Looking, now, at the world and all the animals and plants, c at things which grow upon the earth from seeds and roots, as well as at inanimate substances which are formed within the earth, fusile or non-fusile, shall we say that they come into existence—not having existed previously—by the creation of God, or shall we agree with vulgar opinion about them?

Theaet. What is it?

Str. The opinion that nature brings them into being from some spontaneous and unintelligent cause. Or shall we say that they are created by a divine reason and a knowledge which comes from God?

d   *Theaet.* I myself, perhaps owing to my youth, often waver in my view, but now when I look at you and see that you incline to refer them to God, I defer to your authority.

Str. Nobly said, Theaetetus, and if I thought that you were one of those who would hereafter change your mind, I would have gently argued with you, and forced you to assent; but as I perceive that you will come of yourself and without any argu-

e ment of mine, to that belief which, as you say, attracts you, I will not forestall the work of time. Let me suppose, then, that things which are said to be made by nature are the work of divine art, and that things which are composed by man out of these are works of human art. And so there are two kinds of making and production, the one human and the other divine.

Theaet. True.

Str. Then, now, subdivide each of the two sections which we have already.

Theaet. How do you mean?

266   *Str.* I mean to say that you should make a vertical division of production or invention, as you have already made a lateral one.

Theaet. I have done so.

Str. Then, now, there are in all four parts or segments—two of them have reference to us and are human, and two of them have reference to the gods and are divine.

Theaet. True.

Str. And, again, in the division which was supposed to be made in the other way, one part in each subdivision is the making of the things themselves, but the two remaining parts may most properly be called the making of images; and so the productive art is again divided into two parts.

b   *Theaet.* Tell me the divisions once more.

Str. I suppose that we, and the other animals, and the elements out of which things are made—fire, water, and the like —are known by us to be each and all the creation and work of God.

Theaet. True.

Str. And there are images of them, which are not them, but which correspond to them; and these are also the creation of a wonderful skill.

Theaet. What are they?

Str. The appearances which spring up of themselves in sleep or by day, such as a shadow when darkness arises in a fire, or the reflection which is produced when the light in bright and smooth c objects meets on their surface with an external light, and creates a perception the opposite of our ordinary sight.

Theaet. Yes; it is true that there are these two products of divine art, the object and the corresponding image.

Str. And what shall we say of human art? Do we not make one house by the art of building, and another by the art of drawing, which is a sort of dream created by man for those who are awake?

Theaet. Quite true.   d

Str. And other products of human creation are also twofold and go in pairs; there is the thing [with which the art of making the thing is concerned],[1] and the image [with which imitation is concerned.][1]

Theaet. Now I begin to understand, and am ready to acknowledge that there are two kinds of production, and each of them twofold; in the lateral division there is both a divine and a human production; in the vertical there are realities and a creation of a kind of similitudes.

Str. And let us recall to mind that of the image-making class the one part was to have been likeness-making, and the other phantastic, if it could be shown that falsehood is a reality and e belongs to the class of real being.

Theaet. Yes.

Str. And this appeared to be the case; and therefore now, without hesitation, we shall number the different kinds as two.

Theaet. True.

Str. Then, now, let us proceed to divide the phantastic art 267 into two.

Theaet. Where shall we make the division?

Str. There is one kind which is produced by an instrument, and another in which the creator of the appearance is himself the instrument.

Theaet. What do you mean?

Str. When anyone, by the use of his own body, makes his figure or his voice appear to resemble yours, imitation is the usual name for this part of the phantastic art.

[1] [The words bracketed are perhaps an interpolation.]

Theaet. Yes.

Str. Let this, then, be named the art of mimicry, and this the province assigned to it; as for the other division, we are weary

b and will give that up, leaving to someone else the duty of making the class and giving it a suitable name.

Theaet. Let us do as you say—assign a sphere to the one and leave the other.

Str. There is a further distinction, Theaetetus, which is worthy of our consideration, and for a reason which I will tell you.

Theaet. Let me hear.

Str. There are some who imitate, knowing what they imitate, and some who do not know. And what line of distinction can there possibly be greater than that which divides ignorance from knowledge?

Theaet. There can be no greater.

Str. Was not the sort of imitation of which we spoke just now the imitation of those who know? For he who would imitate you would surely know you and your figure?

c *Theaet.* Naturally.

Str. And what would you say of the figure or form of justice or of virtue in general? Are we not well aware that many, having no knowledge of either, but only a sort of opinion, try hard to make it seem that they *have* the thing about which they hold this opinion, and zealously express it, as far as they can, in word and deed?

Theaet. Yes, that is very common.

Str. And do they always fail in their attempt to be thought just, when they are not? Or is not the very opposite true?

Theaet. The very opposite.

d *Str.* Such a one, then, should be described as an imitator—to be distinguished from the other, as he who is ignorant is distinguished from him who knows?

Theaet. True.

Str. Can we find a suitable name for each of them? This is clearly not an easy task; for among the ancients, it would seem, there was some laziness and confusion of ideas, which prevented them from even making the attempt to divide genera into species; wherefore there is no great abundance of names. Yet, for the sake of distinctness, I will make bold to call the imitation which

is accompanied by opinion, the imitation of appearance—that e
which is accompanied by knowledge, an 'historical'[1] sort of
imitation.

Theaet. Granted.

Str. The former is our present concern, for the Sophist was
classed with imitators indeed, but not among those who have
knowledge.

Theaet. Very true.

Str. Let us, then, examine our imitator of appearance, and
see whether he is sound, like a piece of iron, or whether there is
still some crack in him.

Theaet. Let us examine him.

Str. Indeed there is a very considerable crack; for if you look,
you find that one of the two classes of imitators is a simple creature, who thinks that he knows that which he only fancies; the 268
other sort has knocked about among arguments, until he suspects
and fears that he is ignorant of that which to others he pretends
to know.

Theaet. There are certainly the two kinds which you describe.

Str. Shall we regard one as the simple imitator—the other as
the dissembling or ironical imitator?

Theaet. Very suitable.

Str. And shall we further speak of this latter class as having
one or two divisions?

Theaet. Answer yourself.

Str. Upon consideration, then, there appear to me to be two; b
there is the dissembler who harangues a multitude in public in
a long speech, and the dissembler who in private and in short
speeches compels the person who is conversing with him to
contradict himself.

Theaet. What you say is most true.

Str. And what place shall we assign to the maker of the longer
speeches? Is he the statesman or the popular orator?

Theaet. The latter.

Str. And what shall we call the other? Is he the philosopher
or the Sophist?

Theaet. The philosopher he cannot be, for upon our view he is

[1 Plato connects the noun ἱστορία, inquiry, with the adjective ἵστωρ, learned
or knowing.]

ignorant; but since he is an imitator of the wise he will have a
c name which is formed by an adaptation of the word σοφός.
What shall we name him? I am pretty sure that I cannot be
mistaken in terming him the true and very Sophist.

Str. Shall we bind up his name as we did before, making a
chain from one end of his genealogy to the other?

Theaet. By all means.

Str. He, then,[1] who traces the pedigree of his art as follows—
who, belonging to the conscious or dissembling section of the art
of causing self-contradiction, is an imitator of appearance, and
is separated from the class of phantastic which is a branch of
d image-making into that further division of creation, the juggling
of words, a creation human, and not divine—anyone who affirms
the real Sophist to be of this blood and lineage will say the very
truth.

Theaet. Undoubtedly.

---

[1] Reading τὸν δή.

STATESMAN

INTRODUCTION AND ANALYSIS

IN the *Phaedrus*, the *Republic*, the *Philebus*, the *Parmenides*, and the *Sophist*, we may observe the tendency of Plato to combine two or more subjects or different aspects of the same subject in a single dialogue. In the *Sophist* and *Statesman* especially we note that the discussion is partly regarded as an illustration of method, and that analogies are brought from afar which throw light on the main subject. And in his later writings generally we further remark a decline of style, and of dramatic power; the characters excite little or no interest, and the digressions are apt to overlay the main thesis; there is not the *callida junctura* of an artistic whole. Both the serious discussions and the jests are sometimes out of place. The invincible Socrates is withdrawn from view; and new foes begin to appear under old names. Plato is now chiefly concerned, not with the original Sophist, but with the sophistry of the schools of philosophy, which are making reasoning impossible; and is driven by them out of the regions of transcendental speculation back into the path of common sense. A logical or psychological phase takes the place of the doctrine of Ideas in his mind. He is constantly dwelling on the importance of regular classification, and of not putting words in the place of things. He has banished the poets, and is beginning to use a technical language. He is bitter and satirical, and seems to be sadly conscious of the realities of human life. Yet the ideal glory of the Platonic philosophy is not extinguished. He is still looking for a city in which kings are either philosophers or gods (cf. *Laws* iv. 713).

The *Statesman* has lost the grace and beauty of the earlier dialogues. The mind of the writer seems to be so overpowered in the effort of thought as to impair his style; at least his gift of expression does not keep up with the increasing difficulty of his theme. The idea of the king or statesman and the illustration of method are connected, not like the love and rhetoric of the *Phaedrus*, by 'little invisible pegs', but in a confused and inartistic manner, which fails to produce any impression of a whole on the mind of the reader. Plato apologizes for his tediousness, and acknowledges that the improvement of his audience has been his only aim in some of his digressions. His own image may be used as a motto of his style: like an inexpert statuary he has made the figure or outline too large (277 a), and is unable to give the proper colours or proportions to his work. He makes mistakes only to correct them—this seems to be his way of drawing attention to common dialectical errors. The Eleatic Stranger, here, as in the *Sophist*, has no appropriate character, and appears only as the expositor of a political ideal, in the delineation of which he is frequently interrupted by purely logical illustrations. The younger Socrates resembles his namesake in nothing but a name. The dramatic character is so completely forgotten, that a special reference is twice made to discussions in the *Sophist*; and this, perhaps, is the strongest ground which can be urged for doubting the genuineness of the work. But, when we remember that a similar allusion is made in the *Laws* (v. 739) to the *Republic*, we see that the entire disregard of dramatic propriety is not always a sufficient reason for doubting the genuineness of a Platonic writing (see *infra*).

The search after the Statesman, which is carried on, like that for the Sophist, by the method of dichotomy, gives an opportunity for many humorous and satirical remarks. Several of the jests are mannered and laboured: for example, the turn of words with which the dialogue opens; or the clumsy joke about man being an animal, who has a power of two-feet—which are both suggested by the presence of Theodorus, the geometrician. There is political as well as logical insight in refusing to admit the division of mankind into Hellenes and Barbarians: 'if a crane could speak, he would in like manner oppose men and all other animals to cranes'. The pride of the Hellene is further humbled, by being compared to a Phrygian or Lydian. Plato glories in this impartiality of the dialectical method, which places birds in juxtaposition with men, and the king side by side with the bird-catcher; king or vermin-destroyer are objects of equal interest to science (cf. *Parmen.* 130 d, e). There are other passages which show that the irony of Socrates was a lesson which Plato was not slow in learning—as, for example, the passing remark, that 'the kings and statesmen of our day are in their breeding and education very like their subjects'; or the anticipation that the rivals of the king will be found in the class of servants; or the imposing attitude of the priests, who are the established interpreters of the will of heaven, authorized by law. Nothing is more bitter in all his writings than his comparison of the contemporary politicians to lions, centaurs, satyrs, and other animals of a feebler sort, who are ever changing their forms and natures. But, as in the later dialogues generally, the play of humour and the charm of poetry have departed, never to return.

Still the *Politicus* contains a higher and more ideal conception of politics than any other of Plato's writings. The city of which there is a

pattern in heaven (*Rep.* ix) is here described as a Paradisiacal state
of human society. In the truest sense of all, the ruler is not man but
God; and such a government existed in a former cycle of human
history, and may again exist when the gods resume their care of
mankind. In a secondary sense, the true form of government is that
which has scientific rulers, who are irresponsible to their subjects. Not
power but knowledge is the characteristic of a king or royal person.
And the rule of a man is better and higher than law, because he is more
able to deal with the infinite complexity of human affairs. But mankind, in despair of finding a true ruler, are willing to acquiesce in any
law or custom which will save them from the caprice of individuals.
They are ready to accept any of the six forms of government which
prevail in the world. To the Greek, *nomos* was a sacred word, but the
political idealism of Plato soars into a region beyond; for the laws he
would substitute the intelligent will of the legislator. Education is
originally to implant in men's minds a sense of truth and justice, which
is the divine bond of states, and the legislator is to contrive human
bonds, by which dissimilar natures may be united in marriage and
supply the deficiencies of one another. As in the *Republic*, the government of philosophers, the causes of the perversion of states, the regulation of marriages, are still the political problems with which Plato's
mind is occupied. He treats them more slightly, partly because the
dialogue is shorter, and also because the discussion of them is perpetually crossed by the other interest of dialectic, which has begun to
absorb him.

The plan of the *Politicus* or *Statesman* may be briefly sketched as
follows: (1) By a process of division and subdivision we discover the
true herdsman or king of men. But before we can rightly distinguish
him from his rivals, we must view him, (2) as he is presented to us in
a famous ancient tale: the tale will also enable us to distinguish the
divine from the human herdsman or shepherd: (3) and besides our
fable, we must have an example; for our example we will select the
art of weaving, which will have to be distinguished from the kindred
arts; and then, following this pattern, we will separate the king from
his subordinates or competitors. (4) But are we not exceeding all due
limits; and is there not a measure of all arts and sciences, to which the
art of discourse must conform? There is; but before we can apply this
measure, we must know what is the aim of discourse: and our discourse only aims at the dialectical improvement of ourselves and
others.—Having made our apology, we return once more to the king
or statesman, and proceed to contrast him with pretenders in the same
line with him, under their various forms of government. (5) His

characteristic is, that he alone has science, which is superior to law and written enactments; these do but spring out of the necessities of mankind, when they are in despair of finding the true king. (6) The sciences which are most akin to the royal are the sciences of the general, the judge, the orator, which minister to him, but even these are subordinate to him. (7) Fixed principles are implanted by education, and the king or statesman completes the political web by marrying together dissimilar natures, the courageous and the temperate, the bold and the gentle, who are the warp and the woof of society.

The outline may be filled up as follows:

ANALYSIS

257 *Soc.* I have reason to thank you, Theodorus, for the acquaintance of Theaetetus and the Stranger. *Theod.* And you will have three times as much reason to thank me when they have delineated the Statesman and Philosopher, as well as the Sophist. *Soc.* Does the great geometrician apply the same measure to all three? Are they not divided by an interval which no geometrical ratio can express? *Theod.* By the god Ammon, Socrates, you are right; and I am glad to see that you have not forgotten your geometry. But before I retaliate on you, I must request the Stranger to finish the argument. . . . The Stranger suggests that Theaetetus shall be allowed to rest, and that Socrates[1] the younger shall respond in
258 his place; Theodorus agrees to the suggestion, and Socrates remarks that the name of the one and the face of the other give him a right to claim relationship with both of them. They propose to take the Statesman after the Sophist; his path they must determine, and part off all other ways, stamping upon them a single negative form (cf. *Soph.* 257).

The Stranger begins the inquiry by making a division of the arts and sciences into theoretical and practical—the one kind concerned with knowledge exclusively, and the other with action; arithmetic and the mathematical sciences are examples of the former, and carpentering and handicraft arts of the latter (cf. *Phil.* 55 foll.). Under which of the two shall we place the Statesman? Or rather, shall we not first ask, whether the king, statesman,
259 master, householder, practise one art or many? As the adviser of a physician may be said to have medical science and to be a

[1] [See the Introduction to the *Theaetetus*, p. 194, note 1.]

physician, so the adviser of a king has royal science and is a king. And the master of a large household may be compared to the ruler of a small state. Hence we conclude that the science of the king, statesman, and householder is one and the same. And this science is akin to knowledge rather than to action. For a king rules with his mind, and not with his hands.

But theoretical science may be a science either of judging, like arithmetic, or of ruling and superintending, like that of the architect or master-builder. And the science of the king is of the latter nature; but the power which he exercises is underived and uncontrolled,—a characteristic which distinguishes him from heralds, prophets, and other inferior officers. He is the wholesale dealer in command, and the herald, or other officer, retails his commands to others. Again, a ruler is concerned with the production of some object, and objects may be divided into living and lifeless, and rulers into the rulers of living and lifeless objects. And the king is not like the master-builder, concerned with lifeless matter, but has the task of managing living animals. And the tending of living animals may be either a tending of individuals, or a managing of herds. And the Statesman is not a groom, but a herdsman, and his art may be called either the art of managing a herd, or the art of collective management:—Which do you prefer? 'No matter.' Very good, Socrates, and if you are not too particular about words you will be all the richer some day in true wisdom. But how would you subdivide the herdsman's art? 'I should say, that there is one management of men, and another of beasts.' Very good, but you are in too great a hurry to get to man. All divisions which are rightly made should cut through the middle; if you attend to this rule, you will be more likely to arrive at classes. 'I do not understand the nature of my mistake.' Your division was like a division of the human race into Hellenes and Barbarians, or into Lydians or Phrygians and all other nations, instead of into male and female; or like a division of number into ten thousand and all other numbers, instead of into odd and even. And I should like you to observe further, that though I maintain a class to be a part, there is no similar necessity for a part to be a class. But to return to your division, you spoke of men and other animals as two classes—the second of which you comprehend under the general name of beasts. This is the

260

261

262

263

sort of division which an intelligent crane would make: he would put cranes into a class by themselves for their special glory, and jumble together all others, including man, in the class of beasts. An error of this kind can only be avoided by a more regular 264 subdivision. Just now we divided the whole class of animals into gregarious and non-gregarious, omitting the previous division into tame and wild. We forgot this in our hurry to arrive at man, and found by experience, as the proverb says, that 'the more haste the worse speed'.

And now let us begin again at the art of managing herds. You have probably heard of the fish-preserves in the Nile and in the ponds of the Great King, and of the nurseries of geese and cranes in Thessaly. These suggest a new division into the rearing or management of land-herds and of water-herds:—I need not say with which the king is concerned. And land-herds may be divided into walking and flying; and every idiot knows that the 265 political animal is a pedestrian. At this point we may take a longer or a shorter road, and as we are already near the end, I see no harm in taking the longer, which is the way of mesotomy, and accords with the principle which we were laying down. The tame, walking, herding animal, may be divided into two classes— the horned and the hornless, and the king is concerned with the hornless; and these again may be subdivided into animals having or not having cloven feet, or mixing or not mixing the breed; and the king or statesman has the care of animals which have not 266 cloven feet, and which do not mix the breed. And now, if we omit dogs, who can hardly be said to herd, I think that we have only two species left which remain undivided: and how are we to distinguish them? To geometricians, like you and Theaetetus, I can have no difficulty in explaining that man is a diameter, having a power of two feet; and the power of four-legged creatures, being the double of two feet, is the diameter of our diameter. There is another excellent jest which I spy in the two remaining species. Men and birds are both bipeds, and human beings are running a race with the airiest and freest of creation, in which they are far behind their competitors;—this is a great joke, and there is a still better in the juxtaposition of the bird-taker and the king, who may be seen scampering after them. For, as we remarked in discussing the Sophist, the dialectical method is no

respecter of persons. But we might have proceeded, as I was
saying, by another and a shorter road. In that case we should
have begun by dividing land animals into bipeds and quadrupeds, and bipeds into winged and wingless; we should then
have taken the Statesman and set him over the *bipes implume*, and
put the reins of government into his hands.

Here let us sum up:—The science of pure knowledge had a 267
part which was the science of command, and this had a part
which was a science of wholesale command; and this was divided
into the management of animals, and was again parted off into
the management of herds of animals, and again of land animals,
and these into hornless, and these into bipeds; and so at last we
arrived at man, and found the political and royal science. And
yet we have not clearly distinguished the political shepherd from
his rivals. No one would think of usurping the prerogatives of the 268
ordinary shepherd, who on all hands is admitted to be the trainer,
matchmaker, doctor, musician of his flock. But the royal shepherd
has numberless competitors, from whom he must be distinguished;
there are merchants, husbandmen, physicians, who will all dispute his right to manage the flock. I think that we can best
distinguish him by having recourse to a famous old tradition,
which may amuse as well as instruct us; the narrative is perfectly
true, although the scepticism of mankind is prone to doubt the
tales of old. You have heard what happened in the quarrel of
Atreus and Thyestes? 'You mean about the golden lamb?' No, 269
not that; but another part of the story, which tells how the sun
and stars once arose in the west and set in the east, and that the
god reversed their motion, as a witness to the right of Atreus.
'There is such a story.' And no doubt you have heard of the
empire of Cronos, and of the earthborn men? The origin of these
and the like stories is to be found in the tale which I am about to
narrate.

There was a time when God directed the revolutions of the
world, but at the completion of a certain cycle he let go; and the
world, by a necessity of its nature, turned back, and went round
the other way. For divine things alone are unchangeable; but
the earth and heavens, although endowed with many glories,
have a body, and are therefore liable to perturbation. In the case
of the world, the perturbation is very slight, and amounts only

to a reversal of motion. For the lord of moving things is alone
self-moved; neither can piety allow that he goes at one time in
one direction and at another time in another; or that God has
given the universe opposite motions; or that there are two gods,
270 one turning it in one direction, another in another. But the truth
is, that there are two cycles of the world, and in one of them it
is governed by an immediate Providence, and receives life and
immortality, and in the other is let go again, and has a reverse
action during infinite ages. This new action is spontaneous, and
is due to exquisite perfection of balance, to the vast size of the
universe, and to the smallness of the pivot upon which it turns.
All changes in the heaven affect the animal world, and this being
the greatest of them, is most destructive to men and animals. At
the beginning of the cycle before our own very few of them had
survived; and on these a mighty change passed. For their life
was reversed like the motion of the world, and first of all coming
to a stand then quickly returned to youth and beauty. The white
locks of the aged became black; the cheeks of the bearded man
were restored to their youth and fineness; the young men grew
softer and smaller, and, being reduced to the condition of children
in mind as well as body, began to vanish away; and the bodies of
those who had died by violence, in a few moments underwent a
271 parallel change and disappeared. In that cycle of existence there
was no such thing as the procreation of animals from one another,
but they were born of the earth, and of this our ancestors, who
came into being immediately after the end of the last cycle and
at the beginning of this, have preserved the recollection. Such
traditions are often now unduly discredited, and yet they may be
proved by internal evidence. For observe how consistent the
narrative is; as the old returned to youth, so the dead returned to
life; the wheel of their existence having been reversed, they rose
again from the earth : a few only were reserved by God for another
destiny. Such was the origin of the earthborn men.

'And is this cycle, of which you are speaking, the reign of
Cronos, or our present state of existence?' No, Socrates, that
blessed and spontaneous life belongs not to this, but to the previous state, in which God was the governor of the whole world,
and other gods subject to him ruled over parts of the world, as is
still the case in certain places. They were shepherds of men and

animals, each of them sufficing for those of whom he had the care. And there was no violence among them, or war, or devouring of one another. Their life was spontaneous, because in those days God ruled over man; and he was to man what man is now to the animals. Under his government there were no estates, or private possessions, or families; but the earth produced a sufficiency of all 272 things, and men were born out of the earth, having no traditions of the past; and as the temperature of the seasons was mild, they took no thought for raiment, and had no beds, but lived and dwelt in the open air.

Such was the age of Cronos, and the age of Zeus is our own. Tell me, which is the happier of the two? Or rather, shall I tell you that the happiness of these children of Cronos must have depended on how they used their time? If having boundless leisure, and the power of discoursing not only with one another but with the animals, they had employed these advantages with a view to philosophy, gathering from every nature some addition to their store of knowledge;—or again, if they had merely eaten and drunk, and told stories to one another, and to the beasts;— in either case, I say, there would be no difficulty in answering the question. But as nobody knows which they did, the question must remain unanswered. And here is the point of my tale. In the fulness of time, when the earthborn men had all passed away, the ruler of the universe let go the helm, and became a spectator; and destiny and natural impulse swayed the world. At the same instant all the inferior deities gave up their hold; the whole 273 universe rebounded, and there was a great earthquake, and utter ruin of all manner of animals. After a while the tumult ceased, and the universal creature settled down in his accustomed course, having authority over all other creatures, and following the instructions of his God and Father, at first more precisely, after-wards with less exactness. The reason of the falling off was the disengagement of a former chaos; 'a muddy vesture of decay' was a part of his original nature, out of which he was brought by his Creator, under whose immediate guidance, while he remained in that former cycle, the evil was minimized and the good increased to the utmost. And in the beginning of the new cycle all was well enough, but as time went on, discord entered in; at length the good was minimized and the evil everywhere diffused, and there was a danger of universal ruin. Then the Creator, seeing the world in great straits, and fearing that chaos and infinity would come again, in his tender care again placed himself at the helm and restored order, and made the world immortal and imperishable. Once more the cycle of life and generation was reversed; the infants grew into young men, and the young men 274 became greyheaded; no longer did the animals spring out of the earth; as the whole world was now lord of its own progress, so the parts were to be self-created and self-nourished. At first the case of men was very helpless and pitiable; for they were alone among the wild beasts, and had to carry on the struggle for existence without arts or knowledge, and had no food, and did not know how to get any. That was the time when Prometheus brought them fire, Hephaestus and Athene taught them arts, and other gods gave them seeds and plants. Out of these human life was framed; for mankind were left to themselves, and ordered their own ways, living, like the universe, in one cycle after one manner, and in another cycle after another manner.

Enough of the myth, which may show us two errors of which 275 we were guilty in our account of the king. The first and grand error was in choosing for our king a god, who belongs to the other cycle, instead of a man from our own; there was a lesser error also in our failure to define the nature of the royal functions. The myth gave us only the image of a divine shepherd, whereas the statesmen and kings of our own day very much resemble their subjects in education and breeding. On retracing our steps we find that we gave too narrow a designation to the art which was concerned with command-for-self over living creatures, when we called it the 'feeding' of animals in flocks. This would apply to all shepherds, with the exception of the Statesman; but if we say 'managing' or 'tending' animals, the term would include him 276 as well. Having remodelled the name, we may subdivide as before, first separating the human from the divine shepherd or manager. Then we may subdivide the human art of governing into the government of willing and unwilling subjects—royalty and tyranny—which are the extreme opposites of one another, 277 although we in our simplicity have hitherto confounded them.

And yet the figure of the king is still defective. We have taken up a lump of a fable, and have used more than we needed. Like statuaries, we have made some of the features out of proportion, and shall lose time in reducing them. Or our mythus may be compared to a picture, which is well drawn in outline, but is not yet enlivened by colour. And to intelligent persons language is, or ought to be, a better instrument of description than any picture. 'But what, Stranger, is the deficiency of which you speak?' No higher truth can be made clear without an example; every man seems to know all things in a dream, and to know nothing when he is awake. And the nature of example can only be illustrated by an example. Children are taught to read by 278 being made to compare cases in which they do not know a certain letter with cases in which they know it, until they learn to recognize it in all its combinations. Example comes into use when we identify something unknown with that which is known, and form a common notion of both of them. Like the child who is learning his letters, the soul recognizes some of the first elements of things; and then again is at fault and unable to recognize them when they are translated into the difficult language of facts. Let us, then, 279 take an example, which will illustrate the nature of example, and will also assist us in characterizing the political science, and in separating the true king from his rivals.

I will select the example of weaving, or, more precisely, weaving of wool. In the first place, all possessions are either productive or preventive; of the preventive sort are spells and antidotes, divine and human, and also defences, and defences are either arms or screens, and screens are veils and also shields against heat and cold, and shields against heat and cold are shelters and coverings, and coverings are blankets or garments, and garments are in one piece or have many parts; and of these latter, some are stitched and others are fastened, and of these again some are made of fibres of plants and some of hair, and of these some are cemented with water and earth, and some are fastened with their own material; the latter are called clothes, and are made by the art of clothing, from which the art of weaving differs only in name, as 280 the political differs from the royal science. Thus we have drawn several distinctions, but as yet have not distinguished the weaving of garments from the kindred and co-operative arts. For the first 281 process to which the material is subjected is the opposite of weaving—I mean carding. And the art of carding, and the whole

art of the fuller and the mender, are concerned with the treatment and production of clothes, as well as the art of weaving.
Again, there are the arts which make the weaver's tools. And if
we say that the weaver's art is the greatest and noblest of those
which have to do with woollen garments,—this, although true,
is not sufficiently distinct; because these other arts require to be
first cleared away. Let us proceed, then, by regular steps:—
There are causal or principal, and co-operative or subordinate
282 arts. To the causal class belong the arts of washing and mending,
of carding and spinning the threads, and the other arts of working
in wool; these are chiefly of two kinds, falling under the two great
categories of composition and division. Carding is of the latter
sort. But our concern is chiefly with that part of the art of wool-
working which composes, and of which one kind twists and the
other interlaces the threads, whether the firmer texture of the
283 warp or the looser texture of the woof. These are adapted to each
other, and the orderly composition of them forms a woollen
garment. And the art which presides over these operations is the
art of weaving.

But why did we go through this circuitous process, instead of
saying at once that weaving is the art of entwining the warp and
the woof? In order that our labour may not seem to be lost, I
must explain the whole nature of excess and defect. There are
two arts of measuring—one is concerned with relative size, and
the other has reference to a mean or standard of what is meet.
The difference between good and evil is the difference between a
mean or measure and excess or defect. All things require to be
compared, not only with one another, but with the mean, without
284 which there would be no beauty and no art, whether the art of
the statesman or the art of weaving or any other; for all the arts
guard against excess or defect, which are real evils. This we must
endeavour to show, if the arts are to exist; and the proof of this
will be a harder piece of work than the demonstration of the
existence of not-being which we proved in our discussion about
the Sophist. At present I am content with the indirect proof that
the existence of such a standard is necessary to the existence
of the arts. The standard or measure, which we are now only
applying to the arts, may be some day required with a view to
the demonstration of absolute truth.

We may now divide this art of measurement into two parts; placing in the one part all the arts which measure the relative size or number of objects, and in the other all those which depend upon a mean or standard. Many accomplished men say that the 285 art of measurement has to do with all things, but these persons, although in this notion of theirs they may very likely be right, are apt to fail in seeing the differences of classes—they jumble together in one the 'more' and the 'too much', which are very different things. Whereas the right way is to find the differences of classes, and to comprehend the things which have any affinity under the same class.

I will make one more observation by the way. When a pupil at a school is asked the letters which make up a particular word, is he not asked with a view to his knowing the same letters in all words? And our inquiry about the Statesman in like manner is intended not only to improve our knowledge of politics, but our reasoning powers generally. Still less would anyone analyse the nature of weaving for its own sake. There is no difficulty in exhibiting sensible images, but the greatest and noblest truths have no outward form adapted to the eye of sense, and are only revealed in thought. And all that we are now saying is said for the 286 sake of them. I make these remarks, because I want you to get rid of any impression that our discussion about weaving and about the reversal of the universe, and the other discussion about the Sophist and not-being, were tedious and irrelevant. Please to observe that they can only be fairly judged when compared with what is meet; and yet not with what is meet for producing pleasure, nor even meet for making discoveries, but for the great end of developing the dialectical method and sharpening the wits of the auditors. He who censures us, should prove that, if our words had been fewer, they would have been better calculated 287 to make men dialecticians.

And now let us return to our king or statesman, and transfer to him the example of weaving. The royal art has been separated from that of other herdsmen, but not from the causal and co-operative arts which exist in states; these do not admit of dichotomy, and therefore they must be carved neatly, like the limbs of a victim, not into more parts than are necessary. And first (1) we have the large class of instruments, which includes almost

everything in the world; from these may be parted off (2) vessels
which are framed for the preservation of things, moist or dry,
288 prepared in the fire or out of the fire. The royal or political art has
nothing to do with either of these, any more than with the arts of
making (3) vehicles, or (4) defences, whether dresses, or arms, or
walls, or (5) with the art of making ornaments, whether pictures
or other playthings, as they may be fitly called, for they have no
serious use. Then (6) there are the arts which furnish gold, silver,
wood, bark, and other materials, which should have been put
first; these, again, have no concern with the kingly science; any
289 more than the arts (7) which provide food and nourishment for
the human body, and which furnish occupation to the husbandman, huntsman, doctor, cook, and the like, but not to the king
or statesman. Further, there are small things, such as coins, seals,
stamps, which may with a little violence be comprehended in one
of the above-mentioned classes. Thus they will embrace every
species of property with the exception of animals,—but these have
been already included in the art of tending herds. There remains
only the class of slaves or ministers, among whom I expect that
the real rivals of the king will be discovered. I am not speaking
of the veritable slave bought with money, nor of the hireling who
290 lets himself out for service, nor of the trader or merchant, who at
best can only lay claim to economical and not to royal science.
Nor am I referring to government officials, such as heralds and
scribes, for these are only the servants of the rulers, and not the
rulers themselves. I admit that there may be something strange
in any servants pretending to be masters, but I hardly think that
I could have been wrong in supposing that the principal claimants
to the throne will be of this class. Let us try once more: There are
diviners and priests, who are full of pride and prerogative; these,
as the law declares, know how to give acceptable gifts to the gods,
and in many parts of Hellas the duty of performing solemn
sacrifices is assigned to the chief magistrate, as at Athens to the
King Archon. At last, then, we have found a trace of those whom
we were seeking. But still they are only servants and ministers.
291   And who are these who next come into view in various forms
of men and animals and other monsters appearing—lions and
centaurs and satyrs—who are these? I did not know them at first,
for everyone looks strange when he is unexpected. But now I

recognize the politician and his troop, the chief of Sophists, the prince of charlatans, the most accomplished of wizards, who must be carefully distinguished from the true king or statesman. And here I will interpose a question: What are the true forms of government? Are they not three—monarchy, oligarchy, and democracy? and the distinctions of freedom and compulsion, law and no law, poverty and riches expand these three into six. Monarchy may be divided into royalty and tyranny; oligarchy into aristocracy and plutocracy; and democracy may observe 292 the law or may not observe it. But are any of these governments worthy of the name? Is not government a science, and are we to suppose that scientific government is secured by the rulers being many or few, rich or poor, or by the rule being compulsory or voluntary? Can the many attain to science? In no Hellenic city are there fifty good draughts players, and certainly there are not as many kings, for by kings we mean all those who are possessed of the political science. A true government must therefore be the 293 government of one, or of a few. And they may govern us either with or without law, and whether they are poor or rich, and however they govern, provided they govern on some scientific principle,—it makes no difference. And as the physician may cure us with our will, or against our will, and by any mode of treatment, burning, bleeding, lowering, fattening, if he only proceeds scientifically: so the true governor may reduce or fatten or bleed the body corporate, while he acts according to the rules of his art, and with a view to the good of the state, whether according to law or without law.

'I do not like the notion that there can be good government without law.'

I must explain: Law-making certainly is the business of a king; 294 and yet the best thing of all is, not that the law should rule, but that the king should rule, for the varieties of circumstances are endless, and no simple or universal rule can suit them all, or last for ever. The law is just an ignorant brute of a tyrant, who insists always on his commands being fulfilled under all circumstances. 'Then why have we laws at all?' I will answer that question by asking you whether the training master gives a different discipline to each of his pupils, or whether he has a general rule of diet and exercise which is suited to the constitutions of the majority.

295 'The latter.' The legislator, too, is obliged to lay down general laws, and cannot enact what is precisely suitable to each particular case. He cannot be sitting at every man's side all his life, and prescribe for him the minute particulars of his duty, and therefore he is compelled to impose on himself and others the restriction of a written law. Let me suppose now, that a physician or trainer, having left directions for his patients or pupils, goes into a far country, and comes back sooner than he intended; owing to some unexpected change in the weather, the patient or pupil seems to require a different mode of treatment: Would he persist in his old commands, under the idea that all others are noxious and heterodox? Viewed in the light of science, would not the continuance of such regulations be ridiculous? And if the legislator,

296 or another like him, comes back from a far country, is he to be prohibited from altering his own laws? The common people say: Let a man persuade the city first, and then let him impose new laws. But is a physician only to cure his patients by persuasion, and not by force? Is he a worse physician who uses a little gentle violence in effecting the cure? Or shall we say, that the violence is just, if exercised by a rich man, and unjust, if by a poor man? May not any man, rich or poor, with or without law, and

297 whether the citizens like or not, do what is for their good? The pilot saves the lives of the crew, not by laying down rules, but by making his art a law, and, like him, the true governor has a strength of art which is superior to the law. This is scientific government, and all others are imitations only. Yet no great number of persons can attain to this science. And hence follows an important result. The true political principle is to assert the inviolability of the law, which, though not the best thing possible, is best for the imperfect condition of man.

298 I will explain my meaning by an illustration:—Suppose that mankind, indignant at the rogueries and caprices of physicians and pilots, call together an assembly, in which all who like may speak, the skilled as well as the unskilled, and that in their assembly they make decrees for regulating the practice of navigation and medicine which are to be binding on these professions for all time. Suppose that they elect annually by vote or lot those to whom authority in either department is to be delegated. And let

299 us further imagine, that when the term of their magistracy has

expired, the magistrates appointed by them are summoned before
an ignorant and unprofessional court, and may be condemned
and punished for breaking the regulations. They even go a step
farther, and enact, that he who is found inquiring into the truth
of navigation and medicine, and is seeking to be wise above what
is written, shall be called not an artist, but a dreamer, a prating
Sophist and a corrupter of youth; and if he try to persuade others
to investigate those sciences in a manner contrary to the law, he
shall be punished with the utmost severity. And like rules might
be extended to any art or science. But what would be the consequence?

'The arts would utterly perish, and human life, which is bad
enough already, would become intolerable.'

But suppose, once more, that we were to appoint someone as 300
the guardian of the law, who was both ignorant and interested,
and who perverted the law: would not this be a still worse evil
than the other? 'Certainly.' For the laws are based on some
experience and wisdom. Hence the wiser course is, that they
should be observed, although this is not the best thing of all, but
only the second best. And whoever, having skill, should try to
improve them, would act in the spirit of the lawgiver. But then,
as we have seen, no great number of men, whether poor or rich,
can be makers of laws. And so, the nearest approach to true
government is, when men do nothing contrary to their own 301
written laws and national customs. When the rich preserve their
customs and maintain the law, this is called aristocracy, or if they
neglect the law, oligarchy. When an individual rules according
to law, whether by the help of science or opinion, this is called
monarchy; and when he has royal science he is a king, whether
he be so in fact or not; but when he rules in spite of law, and is
blind with ignorance and passion, he is called a tyrant. These
forms of government exist, because men despair of the true king
ever appearing among them; if he were to appear, they would
joyfully hand over to him the reins of government. But, as there
is no natural ruler of the hive, they meet together and make laws.
And do we wonder, when the foundation of politics is in the letter
only, at the miseries of states? Ought we not rather to admire the 302
strength of the political bond? For cities have endured the worst
of evils time out of mind; many cities have been shipwrecked,

and some are like ships foundering, because their pilots are absolutely ignorant of the science which they profess.

Let us next ask, which of these untrue forms of government is the least bad, and which of them is the worst? I said at the beginning, that each of the three forms of government, royalty, aristocracy, and democracy, might be divided into two, so that the whole number of them, including the best, will be seven. Under monarchy we have already distinguished royalty and tyranny; of oligarchy there were two kinds, aristocracy and plutocracy; and democracy may also be divided, for there is a democracy which observes, and a democracy which neglects, the

303 laws. The government of one is the best and the worst—the government of a few is less bad and less good—the government of the many is the least bad and least good of them all, being the best of all lawless governments, and the worst of all lawful ones. But the rulers of all these states, unless they have knowledge, are maintainers of idols, and themselves idols—wizards, and also Sophists; for, after many windings, the term 'Sophist' comes home to them.

And now enough of centaurs and satyrs: the play is ended, and they may quit the political stage. Still there remain some other and better elements, which adhere to the royal science, and must be drawn off in the refiner's fire before the gold can become quite

304 pure. The arts of the general, the judge, and the orator, will have to be separated from the royal art; when the separation has been made, the nature of the king will be unalloyed. Now there are inferior sciences, such as music and others; and there is a superior science, which determines whether music is to be learnt or not, and this is different from them, and the governor of them. The science which determines whether we are to use persuasion, or not, is higher than the art of persuasion; the science which

305 determines whether we are to go to war, is higher than the art of the general. The science which makes the laws, is higher than that which only administers them. And the science which has this authority over the rest, is the science of the king or statesman.

Once more we will endeavour to view this royal science by the

306 light of our example. We may compare the state to a web, and I will show you how the different threads are drawn into one. You would admit—would you not?—that there are parts of virtue

(although this position is sometimes assailed by Eristics), and one part of virtue is temperance, and another courage. These are two principles which are in a manner antagonistic to one another; and they pervade all nature; the whole class of the good and beautiful is included under them. The beautiful may be sub-divided into two lesser classes: one of these is described by us in terms expressive of motion or energy, and the other in terms 307 expressive of rest and quietness. We say, how manly! how vigorous! how ready! and we say also, how calm! how temperate! how dignified! This opposition of terms is extended by us to all actions, to the tones of the voice, the notes of music, the workings of the mind, the characters of men. The two classes both have their exaggerations; and the exaggerations of the one are termed 'hardness', 'violence', 'madness'; of the other 'cowardliness', or 'sluggishness'. And if we pursue the inquiry, we find that these opposite characters are naturally at variance, and can hardly be reconciled. In lesser matters the antagonism between them is ludicrous, but in the State may be the occasion of grave disorders, and may disturb the whole course of human life. For the orderly class are always wanting to be at peace, and hence they pass imperceptibly into the condition of slaves; and the courageous 308 sort are always wanting to go to war, even when the odds are against them, and are soon destroyed by their enemies. But the true art of government, first preparing the material by education, weaves the two elements into one, maintaining authority over the carders of the wool, and selecting the proper subsidiary arts which are necessary for making the web. The royal science is queen of educators, and begins by choosing the natures which she is to train, punishing with death and exterminating those who are violently carried away to atheism and injustice, and enslaving 309 those who are wallowing in the mire of ignorance. The rest of the citizens she blends into one, combining the stronger element of courage, which we may call the warp, with the softer element of temperance, which we may imagine to be the woof. These she binds together, first taking the eternal elements of the honourable, the good, and the just, and fastening them with a divine cord in a heaven-born nature, and then fastening the animal elements with a human cord. The good legislator can implant by education the higher principles; and where they exist there is no difficulty in 310 inserting the lesser human bonds, by which the State is held together; these are the laws of intermarriage, and of union for the sake of offspring. Most persons in their marriages seek after wealth or power; or they are clannish, and choose those who are like themselves,—the temperate marrying the temperate, and the courageous the courageous. The two classes thrive and flourish at first, but they soon degenerate; the one becomes mad, and the other feeble and useless. This would not have been the case, if they had both originally held the same notions about the honourable and the good; for then they never would have allowed the temperate natures to be separated from the courageous, but they

311 would have bound them together by common honours and reputations, by intermarriages, and by the choice of rulers who combine both qualities. The temperate are careful and just, but are wanting in the power of action; the courageous fall short of them in justice, but in action are superior to them: and no State can prosper in which either of these qualities is wanting. The noblest and best of all webs or states is that which the royal science weaves, combining the two sorts of natures in a single texture, and in this enfolding freeman and slave and every other social element, and presiding over them all.

'Your picture, Stranger, of the king and statesman, no less than of the Sophist, is quite perfect.'

INTRODUCTION

The principal subjects[1] in the *Statesman* may be conveniently embraced

---

[1] [In regard to all these subjects the edition by A. Diès in the *Collection G. Budé* (1935) is invaluable. In the myth, several traits borrowed from the old mythology are found side by side with ideas suggested by earlier philosophical speculation, e.g. that of Empedocles. The assumption of two alternating world-periods, in one of which disorder is gradually increasing, is of course peculiar to this dialogue and cannot be reconciled with the system assumed in the *Timaeus*. It is probable that in reading this passage we should have in mind some physical model of the rotating heaven, as was suggested in an important paper by P. M. Schuhl (*Revue de Méta-physique et de Morale*, xxxix (1932)). The notion of recurring cycles of human civilization *within* these vaster world-periods also became prominent at this time: see Jaeger, *Aristotle*, chap. vi.

As to the second subject in Jowett's list, this dialogue completes the account of logical division given in the *Sophist*, *Philebus*, and *Phaedrus*, adding some new examples and also general observations on its right and wrong use.

With regard to the third and fifth subjects, the special contribution of this

under six or seven heads:—(1) the myth; (2) the dialectical interest; (3) the political aspects of the dialogue; (4) the satirical and paradoxical vein; (5) the necessary imperfection of law; (6) the relation of the work to the other writings of Plato; lastly (7), we may briefly consider the genuineness of the *Sophist* and *Statesman*, which can hardly be assumed without proof, since the two dialogues have been questioned by three such eminent Platonic scholars as Socher, Schaarschmidt, and Ueberweg. [This discussion is omitted in the fourth edition.]

I. The hand of the master is clearly visible in the myth. First in the connexion with mythology;—he wins a kind of verisimilitude for this as for his other myths, by adopting received traditions, of which he pretends to find an explanation in his own larger conception (cf. Introduction to *Critias*). The young Socrates has heard of the sun rising in the west and setting in the east, and of the earth-born men; but he has never heard the origin of these remarkable phenomena. Nor is Plato, here or elsewhere, wanting in denunciations of the incredulity of 'this latter age', on which the lovers of the marvellous have always delighted to enlarge. And he is not without express testimony to the truth of his narrative;—such testimony as, in the *Timaeus* (40 d), the first men gave of the names of the gods ('They must surely have known their own ancestors'). For the first generation of the new cycle, who lived near the time, are supposed to have preserved a recollection of a previous one. He also appeals to internal evidence, viz. the perfect coherence of the tale, though he is very well aware, as he says in the *Cratylus* (436 c, d), that there may be consistency in error as well as in truth. The gravity and minuteness with

dialogue has perhaps not been fully explained either by Jowett or by his successors. Knowledge of true general principles is here unfavourably contrasted with judgement of the particular person or situation. Plato rightly regards this judgement as the greatest test and manifestation of practical skill in any form. He supposes that it consists, not exactly in an intelligent application of a general principle to the given case, but in a judgement of this case by the same standards which would have been kept in view in any attempt to lay down general principles. In this argument, therefore, Plato attempts to apply in the sphere of politics and government what had been said in the *Phaedrus* with reference to education and rhetorical persuasion. Both dialogues alike seem to rest on the theory of knowledge secured in the *Sophist*; and one should not seek to minimize the difference, in political theory, between the *Statesman* and the *Republic*. It is true that there is some hint, in *Rep.* iv. 424–6, that the frantic attempt to regulate every detail of life by written law is a sign of political degeneracy, but this was said from a different point of view, and it is certainly not true that the guardian class in the *Republic* is to be trained in the kind of judgement which is now ascribed to the Statesman. The validity of Plato's argument no doubt depends, like that of the older Socratic arguments, on the appropriateness of the comparison between legislation or government and the arts.]

which some particulars are related also lend an artful aid. The profound interest and ready assent of the young Socrates, who is not too old to be amused 'with a tale which a child would love to hear', are a further assistance. To those who were naturally inclined to believe that the fortunes of mankind are influenced by the stars, or who maintained that some one principle, like the principle of the Same and the Other in the *Timaeus*, pervades all things in the world, the reversal of the motion of the heavens seemed necessarily to produce a reversal of the order of human life. The spheres of knowledge, which to us appear wide asunder as the poles, astronomy and medicine, were naturally connected in the minds of early thinkers, because there was little or nothing in the space between them. Thus there is a basis of philosophy, on which the improbabilities of the tale may be said to rest. These are some of the devices by which Plato, like a modern novelist, seeks to familiarize the marvellous.

The myth, like that of the *Timaeus* and *Critias*, is rather historical than poetical, in this respect corresponding to the general change in the later writings of Plato, when compared with the earlier ones. It is hardly a myth in the sense in which the term might be applied to the myth of the *Phaedrus*, the *Republic*, the *Phaedo*, or the *Gorgias*, but may be more aptly compared with the didactic tale in which Protagoras describes the fortunes of primitive man, or with the description of the gradual rise of a new society in the third book of the *Laws*. Some discrepancies may be observed between the mythology of the *Statesman* and the *Timaeus*, and between the *Timaeus* and the *Republic*. But there is no reason to expect that all Plato's visions of a former, any more than of a future, state of existence, should conform exactly to the same pattern. We do not find perfect consistency in his philosophy; and still less have we any right to demand this of him in his use of mythology and figures of speech. And we observe that while employing all the resources of a writer of fiction to give credibility to his tales, he is not disposed to insist upon their literal truth. Rather, as in the *Phaedo* (114 d), he says, 'Something of the kind is true'; or, as in the *Gorgias* (527 a), 'This you will think to be an old wive's tale, but you can think of nothing truer'; or, as in the *Statesman* (277 b), he describes his work as a 'mass of mythology', which was introduced in order to teach certain lessons; or, as in the *Phaedrus* (230 a), he secretly laughs at such stories while refusing to disturb the popular belief in them.

The greater interest of the myth consists in the philosophical lessons which Plato presents to us in this veiled form. Here, as in the tale of Er, the son of Armenius, he touches upon the question of freedom and necessity, both in relation to God and nature. For at first the universe is governed by the immediate providence of God,—this is the golden age,—but after a while the wheel is reversed, and man is left to himself. Like other theologians and philosophers, Plato relegates his explanation of the problem to a transcendental world; he speaks of what in modern language might be termed 'impossibilities in the nature of things', hindering God from continuing immanent in the world. But there is some inconsistency; for the 'letting go' is spoken of as a divine act, and is at the same time attributed to the necessary imperfection of matter; there is also a numerical necessity for the successive births of souls. At first, man and the world retain their divine instincts, but gradually degenerate. As in the Book of Genesis, the first fall of man is succeeded by a second; the misery and wickedness of the world increase continually. The reason of this further decline is supposed to be the disorganization of matter: the latent seeds of a former chaos are disengaged, and envelop all things. The condition of man becomes more and more miserable; he is perpetually waging an unequal warfare with the beasts. At length he obtains such a measure of education and help as is necessary for his existence. Though deprived of God's help, he is not left wholly destitute; he has received from Athene and Hephaestus a knowledge of the arts; other gods give him seeds and plants; and out of these human life is reconstructed. He now eats bread in the sweat of his brow, and has dominion over the animals, subjected to the conditions of his nature, and yet able to cope with them by divine help. Thus Plato may be said to represent in a figure—(1) the state of innocence; (2) the fall of man; (3) the still deeper decline into barbarism; (4) the restoration of man by the partial interference of God, and the natural growth of the arts and of civilized society. Two lesser features of this description should not pass unnoticed:—(*a*) the primitive men are supposed to be created out of the earth, and not after the ordinary manner of human generation—half the causes of moral evil are in this way removed; (*b*) the arts are attributed to a divine revelation: and so the greatest difficulty in the history of prehistoric man is solved. Though no one knew better than Plato that the introduction of the gods is not a reason, but an excuse for not giving a reason (*Crat.* 426), yet, considering that more than two thousand years later mankind are still discussing these problems, we may be satisfied to find in Plato a statement of the difficulties which arise in conceiving the relation of man to God and nature, without expecting to obtain from him a solution of them. In such a tale, as in the *Phaedrus*, various aspects of the Ideas were doubtless indicated to Plato's own mind, as the corresponding theological problems are to us.

The immanence of things in the Ideas, or the partial separation of them, and the self-motion of the supreme Idea, are probably the forms in which he would have interpreted his own parable.

He touches upon another question of great interest—the consciousness of evil—what in the Jewish Scriptures is called 'eating of the tree of the knowledge of good and evil'. At the end of the narrative (272 b), the Eleatic asks his companion whether this life of innocence, or that which men live at present, is the better of the two. He wants to distinguish between the mere animal life of innocence, the 'city of pigs', as it is comically termed by Glaucon in the *Republic*, and the higher life of reason and philosophy. But as no one can determine the state of man in the world before the Fall, 'the question must remain unanswered'. Similar questions have occupied the minds of theologians in later ages; but they can hardly be said to have found an answer. Professor Campbell well observes, that the general spirit of the myth may be summed up in the words of the *Lysis* (221): 'If evil were to perish, should we hunger any more, or thirst any more, or have any similar sensations? Yet perhaps the question what will or will not be is a foolish one, for who can tell?' As in the *Theaetetus*, evil is supposed to continue,—here, as the consequence of a former state of the world, a sort of mephitic vapour exhaling from some ancient chaos,—there, as involved in the possibility of good, and incident to the mixed state of man.

Once more—and this is the point of connexion with the rest of the dialogue—the myth is intended to bring out the difference between the ideal and the actual state of man. In all ages of the world men have dreamed of a state of perfection, which has been, and is to be, but never is, and seems to disappear under the necessary conditions of human society. The uselessness, the danger, the true value of such political ideals have often been discussed; youth is too ready to believe in them; age to disparage them. Plato's *prudens quaestio* respecting the comparative happiness of men in this and in a former cycle of existence is intended to elicit this contrast between the golden age and 'the life under Zeus' which is our own. To confuse the divine and human, or hastily apply one to the other, is a 'tremendous error'. Of the ideal or divine government of the world we can form no true or adequate conception; and this our mixed state of life, in which we are partly left to ourselves, but not wholly deserted by the gods, may contain some higher elements of good and knowledge than could have existed in the days of innocence under the rule of Cronos. So we may venture slightly to enlarge a Platonic thought which admits of a further application to Christian theology. Here are suggested also the distinctions between God causing and permitting evil, and between his more and less immediate government of the world.

II. The dialectical interest of the *Statesman* seems to contend in Plato's mind with the political; the dialogue might have been designated by two equally descriptive titles—either the 'Statesman', or 'Concerning method'. Dialectic, which in the earlier writings of Plato is a revival of the Socratic question and answer applied to definition, is now occupied with classification; there is nothing in which he takes greater delight than in processes of division (cf. *Phaedr.* 266 b); he pursues them to a length out of proportion to his main subject, and appears to value them as a dialectical exercise, and for their own sake. A poetical vision of some order or hierarchy of ideas or sciences has already been floating before us in the *Symposium* and the *Republic*. And in the *Phaedrus* this aspect of dialectic is further sketched out, and the art of rhetoric is based on the division of the characters of mankind into their several classes. The same love of divisions is apparent in the *Gorgias*. But in a well-known passage of the *Philebus* occurs the first criticism on the nature of classification. There we are exhorted not to fall into the common error of passing from unity to infinity, but to find the intermediate classes; and we are reminded that in any process of generalization, there may be more than one class to which individuals may be referred, and that we must carry on the process of division until we have arrived at the *infima species*.

These precepts are not forgotten, either in the *Sophist* or in the *Statesman*. The *Sophist* contains four examples of division, carried on by regular steps, until in four different lines of descent we detect the Sophist. In the *Statesman* the king or statesman is discovered by a similar process; and we have a summary, probably made for the first time, of possessions appropriated by the labour of man, which are distributed into seven classes. We are warned against preferring the shorter to the longer method;—if we divide in the middle, we are most likely to light upon species; at the same time, the important remark is made, that 'a part is not to be confounded with a class'. Having discovered the genus under which the king falls, we proceed to distinguish him from the collateral species. To assist our imagination in making this separation, we require an example. The higher ideas, of which we have a dreamy knowledge, can only be represented by images taken from the external world. But, first of all, the nature of example is explained by an example. The child is taught to read by comparing the letters in words which he knows with the same letters in unknown combinations; and this is the sort of process which we are about to attempt. As a parallel to the king we select the worker in wool, and compare the art of weaving with the royal science, trying to separate either of them from the inferior classes to which they are akin. This has the incidental advantage, that weaving and the web furnish us with a figure of speech, which we can afterwards transfer to the State.

There are two uses of examples or images—in the first place, they suggest thoughts—secondly, they give them a distinct form. In the infancy of philosophy, as in childhood, the language of pictures is natural to man: truth in the abstract is hardly won, and only by use familiarized to the mind. Examples are akin to analogies, and have a reflex influence on thought; they people the vacant mind, and may often originate new directions of inquiry. Plato seems to be conscious of the suggestiveness of imagery; the general analogy of the arts is constantly employed by him as well as the comparison of particular arts—weaving, the refining of gold, the learning to read, music, statuary, painting, medicine, the art of the pilot—all of which occur in this dialogue alone: though he is also aware that 'comparisons are slippery things', and may often give a false clearness to ideas. We shall find, in the *Philebus*, a division of sciences into practical and speculative, and into more or less speculative: here we have the idea of master-arts, or sciences which control inferior ones. Besides the supreme science of dialectic, 'which will forget us, if we forget her', another master-science for the first time appears in view—the science of government, which fixes the limits of all the rest. This conception of the political or royal science as, from another point of view, the science of sciences, which holds sway over the rest, is not originally found in Aristotle, but in Plato.

The doctrine that virtue and art are in a mean, which is familiarized to us by the study of the *Nicomachean Ethics*, is also first distinctly asserted in the *Statesman* of Plato. The too much and the too little are in restless motion: they must be fixed by a mean, which is also a standard external to them. The art of measuring or finding a mean between excess and defect, like the principle of division in the *Phaedrus*, receives a particular application to the art of discourse. The excessive length of a discourse may be blamed; but who can say what is excess, unless he is furnished with a measure or standard? Measure is the life of the arts, and may some day be discovered to be the single ultimate principle in which all the sciences are contained. Other forms of thought may be noted—the distinction between causal and co-operative arts, which may be compared with the distinction between primary and co-operative causes in the *Timaeus* (46 d); or between cause and condition in the *Phaedo* (99); the passing mention of economical science; the opposition of rest and motion, which is found in all nature; the general conception of two great arts of composition and division, in which are contained weaving, politics, dialectic; and in connexion with the conception of a mean, the two arts of measuring.

In the *Theaetetus*, Plato remarks that precision in the use of terms, though sometimes pedantic, is sometimes necessary. Here he makes the opposite reflection, that there may be a philosophical disregard of words. The evil of mere verbal oppositions, the requirement of an impossible accuracy in the use of terms, the error of supposing that philosophy was to be found in language, the danger of word-catching, have frequently been discussed by him in the previous dialogues, but nowhere has the spirit of modern inductive philosophy been more happily indicated than in the words of the *Statesman*:—'If you think more about things, and less about words, you will be richer in wisdom as you grow older' (261 e). A similar spirit is discernible in the remarkable expressions, 'the long and difficult language of facts' (278 d); and 'the interrogation of every nature, in order to obtain the particular contribution of each to the store of knowledge' (272 c). Who has described 'the feeble intelligence of all things' given by metaphysics better than the Eleatic Stranger in the words—'The higher ideas can hardly be set forth except through the medium of examples; every man seems to know all things in a kind of dream, and then again nothing when he is awake' (277 d)? Or where is the value of metaphysical pursuits more truly expressed than in the words,—'The greatest and noblest things have no outward image of themselves visible to man: therefore we should learn to give a rational account of them' (286 a)?

III. The political aspects of the dialogue are closely connected with the dialectical. As in the *Cratylus*, the legislator has 'the dialectician standing on his right hand'; so in the *Statesman*, the king or statesman is the dialectician, who, although he may be in a private station, is still a king. Whether he has the power or not, is a mere accident; or rather he has the power, for what ought to be is ('Was ist vernünftig, das ist wirklich'); and he ought to be and is the true governor of mankind. There is a reflection in this idealism of the Socratic 'Virtue is knowledge'; and, without idealism, we may remark that knowledge is a great part of power. Plato does not trouble himself to construct a machinery by which 'philosophers shall be made kings', as in the *Republic*: he merely holds up the ideal, and affirms that in some sense science is really supreme over human life.

He is struck by the observation 'quam parva sapientia regitur mundus', and is touched with a feeling of the ills which afflict states. The condition of Megara before and during the Peloponnesian War, of Athens under the Thirty and afterwards, of Syracuse and the other Sicilian cities in their alternations of democratic excess and tyranny, might naturally suggest such reflections. Some states he sees already shipwrecked, others foundering for want of a pilot; and he wonders not at their destruction, but at their endurance. For they ought to have perished long ago, if they had depended on the wisdom of their rulers. The mingled pathos and satire of this remark is characteristic of Plato's later style.

The king is the personification of political science. And yet he is something more than this,—the perfectly good and wise tyrant of the *Laws* (iv. 710), whose will is better than any law. He is the special providence who is always interfering with and regulating all things. Such a conception has sometimes been entertained by modern theologians, and by Plato himself, of the Supreme Being. But whether applied to Divine or to human governors the conception is faulty for two reasons, neither of which is noticed by Plato:—first, because all good government supposes a degree of co-operation in the ruler and his subjects,—an 'education in politics' as well as in moral virtue; secondly, because government, whether Divine or human, implies that the subject has a previous knowledge of the rules under which he is living. There is a fallacy, too, in comparing unchangeable laws with a personal governor. For the law need not necessarily be an 'ignorant and brutal tyrant', but gentle and humane, capable of being altered in the spirit of the legislator, and of being administered so as to meet the cases of individuals. Not only in fact, but in idea, both elements must remain—the fixed law and the living will; the written word and the spirit; the principles of obligation and of freedom; and their applications whether made by law or equity in particular cases.

There are two sides from which positive laws may be attacked:— either from the side of nature, which rises up and rebels against them in the spirit of Callicles in the *Gorgias*; or from the side of idealism, which attempts to soar above them,—and this is the spirit of Plato in the *Statesman*. But he soon falls, like Icarus, and is content to walk instead of flying; that is, to accommodate himself to the actual state of human things. Mankind have long been in despair of finding the true ruler; and therefore are ready to acquiesce in any of the five or six received forms of government as better than none. And the best thing which they can do (though only the second best in reality) is to reduce the ideal state to the conditions of actual life. Thus in the *Statesman*, as in the *Laws*, we have three forms of government, which we may venture to term, (1) the ideal, (2) the practical, (3) the sophistical—what ought to be, what might be, what is. And thus Plato seems to stumble, almost by accident, on the notion of a constitutional monarchy, or of a monarchy ruling by laws.

The divine foundations of a State are to be laid deep in education (*Rep.* iv. 423), and at the same time some little violence may be used in exterminating natures which are incapable of education (cf. *Laws*, x). Plato is strongly of opinion that the legislator, like the physician, may do men good against their will (cf. *Gorgias*, 522 foll.). The human bonds of states are formed by the intermarriage of dispositions adapted to supply the defects of each other. As in the *Republic*, Plato has observed that there are opposite natures in the world, the strong and the gentle, the courageous and the temperate, which, borrowing an expression derived from the image of weaving, he calls the warp and the woof of human society. To interlace these is the crowning achievement of political science. In the *Protagoras*, Socrates was maintaining that there was only one virtue, and not many: now Plato is inclined to think that there are not only parallel, but opposite virtues, and seems to see a similar opposition pervading all art and nature. But he is satisfied with laying down the principle, and does not inform us by what further steps the union of opposites is to be effected.

In the loose framework of a single dialogue Plato has thus combined two distinct subjects—politics and method. Yet they are not so far apart as they appear: in his own mind there was a secret link of connexion between them. For the philosopher or dialectician is also the only true king or statesman. In the execution of his plan Plato has invented or distinguished several important forms of thought, and made incidentally many valuable remarks. Questions of interest both in ancient and modern politics also arise in the course of the dialogue, which may with advantage be further considered by us:—

a. The imaginary ruler, whether God or man, is above the law, and is a law to himself and to others. Among the Greeks as among the Jews, law was a sacred name, the gift of God, the bond of states. But in the *Statesman* of Plato, as in the New Testament, the word has also become the symbol of an imperfect good, which is almost an evil. The law sacrifices the individual to the universal, and is the tyranny of the many over the few (cf. *Rep.* i. 359). It has fixed rules which are the props of order, and will not swerve or bend in extreme cases. It is the beginning of political society, but there is something higher—an intelligent ruler, whether God or man, who is able to adapt himself to the endless varieties of circumstances. Plato is fond of picturing the advantages which would result from the union of the tyrant who has power with the legislator who has wisdom: he regards this as the best and speediest way of reforming mankind. But institutions cannot thus be artificially created, nor can the external authority of a ruler impose laws for which a nation is unprepared. The greatest power, the highest wisdom, can only proceed one or two steps in advance of public opinion. In all stages of civilization human nature, after all our efforts, remains intractable,—not like clay in the hands of the potter, or marble under the chisel of the sculptor. Great changes occur in the history of nations, but they are brought about slowly, like the changes in the frame of nature, upon which the puny arm of man hardly makes an impression. And, speaking generally, the slowest growths, both in nature and in politics, are the most permanent.

b. Whether the best form of the ideal is a person or a law may fairly be doubted. The former is more akin to us: it clothes itself in poetry and art, and appeals to reason more in the form of feeling: in the latter there is less danger of allowing ourselves to be deluded by a figure of speech. The ideal of the Greek state found an expression in the deification of law: the ancient Stoic spoke of a wise man perfect in virtue, who was fancifully said to be a king; but neither they nor Plato had arrived at the conception of a person who was also a law. Nor is it easy for the Christian to think of God as wisdom, truth, holiness, and also as the wise, true, and holy one. He is always wanting to break through the abstraction and interrupt the law, in order that he may present to himself the more familiar image of a divine friend. While the impersonal has too slender a hold upon the affections to be made the basis of religion, the conception of a person on the other hand tends to degenerate into a new kind of idolatry. Neither criticism nor experience allows us to suppose that there are interferences with the laws of nature; the idea is inconceivable to us and at variance with facts. The philosopher or theologian who could realize to mankind that a person is a law, that the higher rule has no exception, that goodness, like knowledge, is also power, would breathe a new religious life into the world.

c. Besides the imaginary rule of a philosopher or a God, the actual forms of government have to be considered. In the infancy of political science, men naturally ask whether the rule of the many or of the few is to be preferred. If by 'the few' we mean 'the good' and by 'the many' 'the bad', there can be but one reply: 'The rule of one good man is better than the rule of all the rest, if they are bad.' For, as Heracleitus says, 'One is ten thousand if he be the best'. If, however, we mean by the rule of the few the rule of a class neither better nor worse than other classes, not devoid of a feeling of right, but guided mostly by a sense of their own interests, and by the rule of the many the rule of all classes, similarly under the influence of mixed motives, no one would hesitate to answer—'The rule of all rather than one, because all classes are more likely to take care of all than one of another; and the government has greater power and stability when resting on a wider basis.' Both in ancient and modern times the best-balanced form of government has been held to be the best; and yet it should not be so nicely balanced as to make action and movement impossible.

The statesman who builds his hope upon the aristocracy, upon the middle classes, upon the people, will probably, if he have sufficient experience of them, conclude that all classes are much alike, and that one is as good as another, and that the liberties of no class are safe in the hands of the rest. The higher ranks have the advantage in education and manners, the middle and lower in industry and self-denial; in every class, to a certain extent, a natural sense of right prevails, sometimes communicated from the lower to the higher, sometimes from the higher to the lower, which is too strong for class interests. There have been crises in the history of nations, as at the time of the Crusades or the Reformation, or the French Revolution, when the same inspiration has taken hold of whole peoples, and permanently raised the sense of freedom and justice among mankind.

But even supposing the different classes of a nation, when viewed impartially, to be on a level with each other in moral virtue, there remain two considerations of opposite kinds which enter into the problem of government. Admitting of course that the upper and lower classes are equal in the eye of God and of the law, yet the one may be by nature fitted to govern and the other to be governed. A ruling caste does not soon altogether lose the governing qualities, nor a subject class easily acquire them. Hence the phenomenon so often observed in the old Greek revolutions, and not without parallel in modern times, that the leaders of the democracy have been themselves of aristocratic origin. The people are expecting to be governed by representatives of their own, but the true man of the people either never appears, or is quickly altered by circumstances. Their real wishes hardly make themselves felt, although their lower interests and prejudices may sometimes be flattered and yielded to for the sake of ulterior objects by those who have political power. They will often learn by experience that the democracy has become a plutocracy. The influence of wealth, though not the enjoyment of it, has become diffused among the poor as well as among the rich; and society, instead of being safer, is more at the mercy of the tyrant, who, when things are at the worst, obtains a guard—that is, an army, and announces himself as the saviour.

The other consideration is of an opposite kind. Admitting that a few wise men are likely to be better governors than the unwise many, yet it is not in their power to fashion an entire people according to their behest. When with the best intentions the benevolent despot begins his régime, he finds the world hard to move. A succession of good kings has at the end of a century left the people an inert and unchanged mass. The Roman world was not permanently improved by the hundred years of Hadrian and the Antonines. The kings of Spain during the last century were at least equal to any contemporary sovereigns in virtue and ability. In certain states of the world the means are wanting to render a benevolent power effectual. These means are not a mere external organization of posts or telegraphs, hardly the introduction of new laws or modes of industry. A change must be made in the spirit of a people as well as in their externals. The ancient legislator did not really take a blank tablet and inscribe upon it the rules which reflection and experience had taught him to be for a nation's interest; no one would have obeyed him if he had. But he took the customs which he found already existing in a half-civilized state of society: these he reduced to form and inscribed on pillars; he defined what had before been undefined, and gave certainty to what was uncertain. No legislation ever sprang, like Athene, in full power out of the head either of God or man.

Plato and Aristotle are sensible of the difficulty of combining the wisdom of the few with the power of the many. According to Plato, he is a physician who has the knowledge of a physician, and he is a king who has the knowledge of a king. But how the king, one or more, is to obtain the required power, is hardly at all considered by him. He presents the idea of a perfect government, but except the regulation for mixing different tempers in marriage, he never makes any provision for the attainment of it. Aristotle, casting aside ideals, would place the government in a middle class of citizens, sufficiently numerous for stability, without admitting the populace; and such appears to have been the constitution which actually prevailed for a short time at Athens—the rule of the Five Thousand—characterized by Thucydides as the best government of Athens which he had known. It may however be doubted how far, either in a Greek or modern state, such a limitation is practicable or desirable; for those who are left outside the pale will always be dangerous to those who are within, while on the other hand the leaven of the mob can hardly affect the representation of a great country. There is reason for the argument in favour of a property qualification; there is reason also in the arguments of those who would include all and so exhaust the political situation.

The true answer to the question is relative to the circumstances of nations. How can we get the greatest intelligence combined with the greatest power? The ancient legislator would have found this question more easy than we do. For he would have required that all persons who had a share of government should have received their education from the State and have borne her burdens, and should have served in her fleets and armies. But though we sometimes hear the cry that we must 'educate the masses, for they are our masters', who would listen to a proposal that the franchise should be confined to the educated or to those who fulfil political duties? Then again, we know that the masses are not our masters, and that they are more likely to become so if we educate them. In modern politics so many interests have to be consulted that we are compelled to do, not what is best, but what is possible.

d. Law is the first principle of society, but it cannot supply all the wants of society, and may easily cause more evils than it cures. Plato is aware of the imperfection of law in failing to meet the varieties of circumstances: he is also aware that human life would be intolerable if every detail of it were placed under legal regulation. It may be a great evil that physicians should kill their patients or captains cast away their ships, but it would be a far greater evil if each particular in the practice of medicine or seamanship were regulated by law. Much has been said in modern times about the duty of leaving men to themselves, which is supposed to be the best way of taking care of them. The question is often asked, What are the limits of legislation in relation to morals? And the answer is to the same effect, that morals must take care of themselves. There is a one-sided truth in these answers, if they are regarded as condemnations of the interference with commerce in the last century or of clerical persecution in the Middle Ages. But *laissez-faire* is not the best but only the second best. What the best is, Plato does not attempt to determine; he only contrasts the imperfection of law with the wisdom of the perfect ruler.

Laws should be just, but they must also be certain, and we are obliged to sacrifice something of their justice to their certainty. Suppose a wise and good judge, who paying little or no regard to the law, attempted to decide with perfect justice the cases that were brought before him. To the uneducated person he would appear to be the ideal of a judge. Such justice has been often exercised in primitive times, or at the present day among eastern rulers. But in the first place it depends entirely on the personal character of the judge. He may be honest, but there is no check upon his dishonesty, and his opinion can only be overruled, not by any principle of law, but by the opinion of another judging like himself without law. In the second place, even if he be ever so honest, his mode of deciding questions would introduce an element of uncertainty into human life; no one would know beforehand what would happen to him, or would seek to conform in his conduct to any rule of law. For the compact which the law makes with men, that they shall be protected if they observe the law in their dealings with one another, would have to be substituted another principle of a more general character, that they shall be protected by the law if they act rightly in their dealings with one another. The complexity of human actions and also the uncertainty of their effects would be increased tenfold. For one of the principal advantages of law is not merely that it enforces honesty, but that it makes men act in the same way, and requires them to produce the same evidence of their acts. Too many laws may be the sign of a corrupt and overcivilized state of society, too few are the sign of an uncivilized one; as soon as commerce begins to grow, men make themselves customs which have the validity of laws. Even equity, which is the exception to the law, conforms to fixed rules and lies for the most part within the limits of previous decisions.

IV. The bitterness of the *Statesman* is characteristic of Plato's later style, in which the thoughts of youth and love have fled away, and we are no longer attended by the Muses or the Graces. We do not venture to say that Plato was soured by old age, but certainly the kindliness and courtesy of the earlier dialogues have disappeared. He sees the world under a harder and grimmer aspect: he is dealing with the reality of things, not with visions or pictures of them: he is seeking by the aid of dialectic only to arrive at truth. He is deeply impressed with the importance of classification: in this alone he finds the true measure of human things; and very often in the process of division curious results are obtained. For the dialectical art is no respecter of persons: king and vermin-taker are all alike to the philosopher. There may have been a time when the king was a god, but he now is pretty much on a level with his subjects in breeding and education. Man should be well advised that he is only one of the animals, and the Hellene in particular should be aware that he himself was the author of the distinction between Hellene and Barbarian, and that the Phrygian would equally divide mankind into Phrygians and Barbarians, and that some intelligent animal, like a crane, might go a step farther, and divide the animal world into cranes and all other animals. Plato cannot help laughing (cf. *Theaet.* 174) when he thinks of the king running after his subjects, like the pig-driver or the bird-taker. He would seriously have him consider how many competitors there are to his throne, chiefly among the class of serving-men. A good deal of meaning is lurking in the expression—'There is no art of feeding mankind worthy the name.' There is a similar depth in the remark,—'The wonder about states is not that they are short-lived, but that they last so long in spite of the badness of their rulers.'

V. There is also a paradoxical element in the *Statesman* which delights in reversing the accustomed use of words. The law which to the Greek was the highest object of reverence is an ignorant and brutal tyrant—the tyrant is converted into a beneficent king. The Sophist too is no longer, as in the earlier dialogues, the rival of the statesman, but assumes his form. Plato sees that the ideal of the State in his own day is more and more severed from the actual. From such ideals as he had once formed, he turns away to contemplate the decline of the Greek cities which were far worse now in his old age than they had been in his youth, and were to become worse and worse in the ages which followed. He cannot contain his disgust at the contemporary statesmen, sophists who had turned politicians, in various forms of men and animals, appearing, some like lions and centaurs, others like satyrs and monkeys. In this new disguise the Sophists make their last appearance on the scene : in the *Laws* Plato appears to have forgotten them, or at any rate makes only a slight allusion to them in a single passage (*Laws* x, 908 d).

VI. The *Statesman* is naturally connected with the *Sophist*. At first sight we are surprised to find that the Eleatic Stranger discourses to us, not only concerning the nature of Being and Not-being, but concerning the king and statesman. We perceive, however, that there is no inappropriateness in his maintaining the character of chief speaker, when we remember the close connexion which is assumed by Plato to exist between politics and dialectic. In both dialogues the Proteus Sophist is exhibited, first, in the disguise of an Eristic, secondly, of a false statesman. There are several lesser features which the two dialogues have in common. The styles and the situations of the speakers are very similar; there is the same love of division, and in both of them the mind of the writer is greatly occupied about method, to which he had probably intended to return in the projected 'Philosopher'.

The *Statesman* stands midway between the *Republic* and the *Laws*, and is also related to the *Timaeus*. The mythical or cosmical element reminds us of the *Timaeus*, the ideal of the *Republic*. A previous chaos in which the elements as yet were not is hinted at both in the *Timaeus* and *Statesman.* The same ingenious arts of giving verisimilitude to a fiction are practised in both dialogues, and in both, as well as in the myth at the end of the *Republic,* Plato touches on the subject of necessity and free will. The words in which he describes the miseries of states seem to be an amplification of the 'Cities will never cease from ill' of the *Republic.* The point of view in both is the same; and the differences not really important, e.g. in the myth, or in the account of the different kinds of states. But the treatment of the subject in the *Statesman* is fragmentary, and the shorter and later work, as might be expected, is less finished, and less worked out in detail. The idea of measure and the arrangement of the sciences supply connecting links both with the *Republic* and the *Philebus.*

More than any of the preceding dialogues, the *Statesman* seems to approximate in thought and language to the *Laws.* There is the same decline and tendency to monotony in style, the same self-consciousness, awkwardness, and over-civility (cf. 257 a, 263 b, 265 b, 277 a, b, 283 c, 286 b, 293 a); and in the *Laws* is contained the pattern of that second best form of government, which, after all, is admitted to be the only attainable one in this world. The 'gentle violence', the marriage of dissimilar natures, the figure of the warp and the woof, are also found in the *Laws.* Both expressly recognize the conception of a first or ideal state, which has receded into an invisible heaven. Nor does the account of the origin and growth of society really differ in them, if we make allowance for the mythic character of the narrative in the *Statesman.* The virtuous tyrant is common to both of them; and the Eleatic Stranger takes up a position similar to that of the Athenian Stranger in the *Laws.*

STATESMAN

Persons of the Dialogue

THEODORUS   THE ELEATIC STRANGER

SOCRATES   THE YOUNGER SOCRATES

Socrates. I owe you many thanks, indeed, Theodorus, for the 257 acquaintance both of Theaetetus and of the Stranger.

Theodorus. And in a little while, Socrates, you will owe me three times as many, when they have completed for you the delineation of the Statesman and of the Philosopher, as well as of the Sophist.

Soc. Sophist, statesman, philosopher! O my dear Theodorus, do my ears truly witness that this is the estimate formed of them by the great calculator and geometrician?

Theod. What do you mean, Socrates?   b

Soc. I mean that you rate them all at the same value, whereas they are really separated by an interval, which no geometrical ratio can express.

Theod. By Ammon, the god of Cyrene, Socrates, that is a very fair hit; and shows that you have not forgotten your geometry. I will retaliate on you at some other time, but I must now ask the Stranger, who will not, I hope, tire of his goodness to us, to proceed either with the Statesman or with the Philosopher, whichever he prefers.

Stranger. That is my duty, Theodorus; having begun I must c go on, and not leave the work unfinished. But what shall be done with Theaetetus?

Theod. In what respect?

Str. Shall we relieve him, and take his companion, the Young Socrates, instead of him? What do you advise?

Theod. Yes, give the other a turn, as you propose. The young always do better when they have intervals of rest.

Soc. I think, Stranger, that both of them may be said to be in d some way related to me; for the one, as you affirm, has the cut of my ugly face,[1] the other is called by my name. And we should 258

---

[1] Cf. *Theaet.* 143 e.

always be on the look-out to recognize a kinsman by the style of his conversation. I myself was discoursing with Theaetetus yesterday, and I have just been listening to his answers; my namesake I have not yet examined, but I must. Another time will do for me; today let him answer you.

Str. Very good. Young Socrates, do you hear what the elder Socrates is proposing?

Young Socrates. I do.

Str. And do you agree to his proposal?

Y. Soc. Certainly.

b   *Str.* As you do not object, still less can I. After the Sophist, then, I think that the Statesman naturally follows next in the order of inquiry. And please to say, whether he, too, should be ranked among those who have science.

Y. Soc. Yes.

Str. Then the sciences must be divided as before?

Y. Soc. I dare say.

Str. But yet the division will not be the same?

Y. Soc. How then?

c   *Str.* They will be divided at some other point.

Y. Soc. Yes.

Str. Where shall we discover the path of the Statesman? We must find this, and when we have separated it from others, mark it with a single sign, while we set the mark of another class upon all diverging paths. Thus our minds will be led to conceive of all kinds of knowledge under two classes.

Y. Soc. To find the path is your business, Stranger, and not mine.

d   *Str.* Yes, Socrates, but the discovery, when once made, must be yours as well as mine.

Y. Soc. Very good.

Str. Well, and are not arithmetic and certain other kindred arts, merely theoretical knowledge, wholly separated from action?

Y. Soc. True.

Str. But in the art of carpentering and all other handicrafts, the knowledge of the workman is, as it were, embodied in his

e operations, and plays a part in making material things which previously did not exist.

Y. Soc. Certainly.

Str. Then let us divide sciences in general into those which are practical and those which are purely intellectual.

Y. Soc. Let us assume these two divisions of science, which is one whole.

Str. Next, are 'statesman', 'king', 'master', or 'house-holder', one and the same; or is there a science or art answering to each of these names? Or rather, allow me to put the matter in another way.

Y. Soc. Let me hear.   259

Str. If any one who is in a private station has the skill to advise one of the public physicians, must not he also bear the professional name of the man whom he advises?

Y. Soc. Yes.

Str. And if any one who is in a private station is able to advise the ruler of a country, may not he be said to have the knowledge which the ruler himself ought to have?

Y. Soc. True.

Str. But surely the science of a true king is royal science?   b

Y. Soc. Yes.

Str. And will not he who possesses this knowledge, whether he happens to be a ruler or a private man, when regarded only in reference to his art, be truly called 'royal'?

Y. Soc. He certainly ought to be.

Str. Moreover, the householder and master are the same?

Y. Soc. Of course.

Str. Again, a large household may be compared to a small state:—will they differ at all, as far as government is concerned?

Y. Soc. They will not.

Str. Then, returning to the point which we were just now dis-   c cussing, do we not clearly see that there is one science of all of them; and this science may be called either royal or political or economical; we will not quarrel with any one about the name.

Y. Soc. Certainly not.

Str. This, too, is evident, that the king cannot do much with his hands, or with his whole body, towards the maintenance of his empire, compared with what he does by the intelligence and strength of his mind.

Y. Soc. Clearly not.

Str. Then, shall we say that the king has a greater affin-
d ity to knowledge than to manual arts and to practical life in
general?

Y. Soc. Certainly he has.

Str. Then we may put all together as one and the same—
statesmanship and the statesman—the kingly science and the king.

Y. Soc. Clearly.

Str. And now we shall only be proceeding in due order if we
go on to divide the sphere of cognitive science?

Y. Soc. Very good.

Str. Think whether you can find any joint or parting in it.

Y. Soc. Tell me of what sort.

e   *Str.* Such as this: You may remember that we made an art of
calculation?

Y. Soc. Yes.

Str. Which was, unmistakeably, one of the cognitive sciences?

Y. Soc. Certainly.

Str. And to this art of calculation which discerns the differences of numbers shall we assign any other function except to
pass judgement on their differences?

Y. Soc. How could we?

Str. You know that the master-builder does not work himself,
but is the ruler of workmen?

Y. Soc. Yes.

Str. He contributes science, not manual labour?

Y. Soc. True.

260   *Str.* And may therefore be justly said to share in theoretical
science?

Y. Soc. Quite true.

Str. But he ought not, like the calculator, to regard his functions as at an end when he has formed a judgement;—he must
assign to the individual workmen their appropriate task until
they have completed the work.

Y. Soc. True.

Str. Are not all such sciences cognitive, no less than arithmetic
and the like; and is not the difference between the two classes,
b that the one sort has the power of judging only, and the other of
command as well?

Y. Soc. So it would seem.

Str. May we not very properly say, that of all cognitive science, there are two divisions—one which commands, and the other which judges?

Y. Soc. For my own part, I should think so.

Str. And when men have anything to do in common, that they should be of one mind is surely a desirable thing?

Y. Soc. Very true.

Str. Then while you and I are at unity among ourselves, we need not mind about the fancies of others?

Y. Soc. Certainly not.

Str. And now, in which of these divisions shall we place the c king?—Is he a judge and a kind of spectator? Or, since he is clearly a master, shall we assign to him the art of command?

Y. Soc. The latter, clearly.

Str. Then we must see whether there is any mark of division in the art of command too. I am inclined to think that there is a distinction similar to that of manufacturer[1] and retail dealer, which parts off the king from the herald. d

Y. Soc. How is this?

Str. Why, does not the retailer receive and sell over again the productions of others, which have been sold before?

Y. Soc. Certainly he does.

Str. Are not heralds a class of men who receive instructions framed by their superiors, and pass them on as commands to others?

Y. Soc. Very true.

Str. Then shall we mingle the kingly art in the same class with the art of the interpreter, the boatswain, the prophet, the herald, e and the numerous kindred arts which exercise command; or, as in the preceding comparison we distinguished manufacturers from retailers,—shall we make a word following the same analogy, and refer kings to a supreme or 'ruling-for-self' division of science? There is no suitable existing name. We can neglect the rest, and leave it to receive a name from some one else. For we have set out to seek the ruler; and are not concerned with him who is not a ruler.

Y. Soc. Very good.

[1] [That is, in this context, one who is both the producer and the vendor of goods.]

261   *Str.* Thus a very fair distinction has been attained between this class and the rest, according as the commands are, or are not, original. And now we have to divide this class in turn, if we find that it invites any further division.

Y. Soc. By all means.

Str. Yes, I think that it does; please follow, and aid me in the division.

Y. Soc. At what point?

Str. We shall find, I believe, that every sort of ruler whom we
b can call to mind, issues his instructions with a view to producing something.

Y. Soc. Certainly.

Str. Nor is it particularly difficult to divide the things produced into two classes.

Y. Soc. How would you divide them?

Str. Of the whole class, some have life and some are without life.

Y. Soc. True.

Str. And by the help of this distinction we may make, if we please, a subdivision of the section of cognitive science which commands.

Y. Soc. At what point?

Str. One part may be set over the production of lifeless, the
c other of living objects; and in this way the whole will be bisected.

Y. Soc. Certainly.

Str. Of these two halves, let us leave one and take up the other; which may also be divided into two.

Y. Soc. Which of the two halves do you mean?

Str. Of course that which exercises command about animals. For, surely, the royal science does not sometimes have to preside, like that of a master-workman, over lifeless objects. His science is of a nobler kind, which exists among living beings, and is per-
d petually concerned with their control.

Y. Soc. True.

Str. And the breeding and tending of living beings may be observed to be sometimes a tending of the individual; in other cases, a common care of creatures in flocks?

Y. Soc. True.

Str. But the statesman is not a tender of individuals—not like the driver or groom of a single ox or horse; he is rather to be compared with the keeper of a drove of horses or oxen.

Y. Soc. That seems, at first, a probable view.

Str. Shall we call this art of tending many animals together, e the art of managing a herd, or the art of collective management?

Y. Soc. No matter;—whichever suggests itself to us in the course of conversation.

Str. Very good, Socrates; and, if you continue to be not too particular about names, you will be all the richer in wisdom when you are an old man. And now, as you say, leaving the discussion of the name,—can you see a way in which a person, by showing 262 the art of herding to be of two kinds, may cause that which is now sought amongst twice the number of things, to be then sought amongst half that number?

Y. Soc. I will try;—there appears to me to be one management of men and another of beasts.

Str. You have certainly divided them in a most straightforward and manly style; but you have fallen into an error which hereafter I think that we had better avoid.

Y. Soc. What is the error?

Str. I think that we had better not cut off a single small portion which is not a species, from many larger portions; the b part should be a species. To separate off at once the subject of investigation, is a most excellent plan, if only the separation be rightly made. Just now, you were under the impression that you knew the division, and you hastened the argument, because you saw that it would come to man. But you should not chip off too small a piece, my friend; the safer way is to cut through the middle; which is also the more likely way of finding classes. Attention to this principle makes all the difference in a process of c inquiry.

Y. Soc. What do you mean, Stranger?

Str. I will endeavour to speak more plainly out of love to your good parts, Socrates; and, although I cannot at present entirely explain the subject, I must try at least to make some progress, for the sake of clearness.

Y. Soc. What was the error of which, as you say, we were guilty in our recent division?

Str. The error was just as if someone who wanted to divide the d human race into two parts were to divide them after the fashion which prevails in this part of the world; here they cut off the Hellenes as one species, and all the other species of mankind, which are innumerable, and have no ties or common language, they include under the single name of 'barbarians', and because they have one name they are supposed to be of one species also. Or suppose that someone, intending to divide number into two parts, were to cut off ten thousand from all the rest, and make of it one species, comprehending the rest under another separate

e name, and should say that here too was a single class, because he had given it a single name. Whereas he would plainly make a much better and more equal and logical classification of numbers, if he divided them into odd and even; or of the human species, if he divided them into male and female; and only separated off Lydians or Phrygians, or any other tribe, and arrayed them against the rest of the world, when he could no longer make a

263 division into parts which were also classes.

Y. Soc. Very true; but I wish that this distinction between a part and a class could still be made somewhat plainer.

Str. O Socrates, best of men, you are imposing upon me a very difficult task. We have already digressed farther from our original intention than we ought, and you would have us wander still farther away. But we must now return to our subject; and here-

b after, when there is a leisure hour, we will follow up the other track; at the same time, I wish you to guard against imagining that you ever heard me declare—

Y. Soc. What?

Str. That a class and a part are distinct.

Y. Soc. What did I hear, then?

Str. That a class is necessarily a part of that of which it is termed a class, but there is no similar necessity that a part should be a class; that is the view which I should always wish you to attribute to me, Socrates.

Y. Soc. So be it.

c *Str.* There is another thing which I should like to know.

Y. Soc. What is it?

Str. The point at which we digressed; for, if I am not mistaken, the exact place was at the question, where you would divide the management of herds. To this you appeared rather too ready to answer that there were two species of animals; man being one, and all brutes making up the other.

Y. Soc. True.

Str. I thought that in taking away a part, you imagined that the remainder formed a class, because you were able to call them by the common name of brutes.   d

Y. Soc. That again is true.

Str. Suppose, now, O most courageous of dialecticians, that some wise and understanding creature, such as a crane is reputed to be, were to assign names on the same principle as you have done, and set up cranes against all other animals to their own special glorification, at the same time jumbling together all the others, including man, under a single name, which might well be 'brutes',—here would be the sort of error which we must try to e avoid.

Y. Soc. How can we be safe?

Str. If we do not divide the whole class of animals, we shall be less likely to fall into that error.

Y. Soc. We had better not take the whole?

Str. Yes, there lay the source of error in our former division.

Y. Soc. How?

Str. You remember how that part of cognitive science which was concerned with command, had to do with the rearing of living creatures,—I mean, with animals in herds?

Y. Soc. Yes.

Str. In that case, there was already implied a division of all 264 animals into tame and wild; those whose nature can be tamed are called tame, and those which cannot be tamed are called wild.

Y. Soc. True.

Str. And the political science of which we are in search, is and ever was concerned with tame animals, and must be sought amongst the gregarious animals.

Y. Soc. Yes.

Str. But then we ought not to divide, as we did, taking the whole class at once. Neither let us be in too great haste to arrive quickly at the political science; for this mistake has already b brought upon us the misfortune of which the proverb speaks.

Y. Soc. What is that?

Str. More haste, less speed. We should have taken time to make a sound division.

Y. Soc. And all the better, Stranger; we got what we deserved.

Str. Very well: Let us then begin again, and endeavour to divide the collective rearing of animals; for probably the completion of the argument will best show what you are so anxious to know. Tell me, then——

Y. Soc. What?

Str. Have you ever heard, as you very likely may—for I do not

c suppose that you ever actually visited them—of the preserves of fishes in the Nile, and in the ponds of the Great King; or you may have seen similar preserves in wells at home?

Y. Soc. Yes, to be sure, I have seen them, and I have often heard the others described.

Str. And you may have heard also, and may have been assured by report, although you have not travelled in those regions, of nurseries of geese and cranes in the plains of Thessaly?

Y. Soc. Certainly.

d *Str.* I asked you, because here is a new division of the management of herds, into the management of land and of water herds.

Y. Soc. There is.

Str. And do you agree that we ought to divide the collective rearing of herds into two corresponding parts, the one the rearing of water, and the other the rearing of land herds?

Y. Soc. Yes.

Str. There is surely no need to ask which of these two contains

e the royal art, for it is evident to everybody.

Y. Soc. Certainly.

Str. Any one can divide the herds which feed on dry land?

Y. Soc. How would you divide them?

Str. I should distinguish between those which fly and those which walk.

Y. Soc. Most true.

Str. And where shall we look for the political animal? Might not an idiot, so to speak, know that he is a pedestrian?

Y. Soc. Certainly.

Str. The art of managing the walking animal has to be proved capable of subdivision, just as you might halve an even number.[1]

[1] [Or, accepting Ast's conjecture ἄρτι τόν, 'just as you recently divided number'.]

Y. Soc. Clearly.

Str. Let me note that here appear in view two ways to that 265
part or class which the argument aims at reaching,—the one a
speedier way, which cuts off a small portion and leaves a large;
the other agrees better with the principle which we were laying
down, that as far as we can we should divide in the middle; but
it is longer. We can take either of them, whichever we please.

Y. Soc. Cannot we have both ways?

Str. Together? What a thing to ask! but, if you take them in
turn, you clearly may.

Y. Soc. Then I should like to have them in turn. b

Str. There will be no difficulty, as we are near the end; if
we had been at the beginning, or in the middle, I should have
demurred to your request; but now, in accordance with your
desire, let us begin with the longer way; while we are fresh, we
shall get on better. And now attend to the division.

Y. Soc. Let me hear.

Str. The tame walking herding animals are distributed by
nature into two classes.

Y. Soc. Upon what principle?

Str. The one grows horns; and the other is without horns.

Y. Soc. Apparently. c

Str. Suppose that you divide the science which manages
pedestrian animals into two corresponding parts, and define
them; for if you try to invent names for them, you will find the
intricacy too great.

Y. Soc. How must I speak of them, then?

Str. In this way: let the science of managing pedestrian animals
be divided into two parts, and one part assigned to the horned
herd, and the other to the herd that has no horns.

Y. Soc. All that you say has been abundantly proved, and may d
therefore be assumed.

Str. The king is clearly the shepherd of a polled herd, who have
no horns.

Y. Soc. That is evident.

Str. Shall we break up this hornless herd into sections, and
endeavour to assign to him what is his?

Y. Soc. By all means.

Str. Shall we distinguish them by their having or not having cloven feet, or by their mixing or not mixing the breed? You know what I mean.

Υ. Soc. What?

e   *Str.* I mean that horses and asses naturally breed from one another.

Υ. Soc. Yes.

Str. But the remainder of the hornless herd of tame animals will not mix the breed.

Υ. Soc. Very true.

Str. And of which kind of animal has the Statesman charge,— of a pure-bred race, or one which mixes with others?

Υ. Soc. Clearly of the unmixed.

Str. I suppose that we must divide this again as before.

Υ. Soc. We must.

266   *Str.* Every tame and herding animal has now been split up, with the exception of two species; for I hardly think that dogs should be reckoned among gregarious animals.

Υ. Soc. Certainly not; but how shall we divide the two remaining species?

Str. There is a measure of difference which may be appropriately employed by you and Theaetetus, who are students of geometry.

Υ. Soc. What is that?

Str. The diameter; and, again, the diameter of a diameter.[1]

Υ. Soc. What do you mean?

b   *Str.* Consider the power of progression with which the human race is naturally endowed,—does it not resemble a diameter whose power is two feet?

Υ. Soc. Just so.

Str. And the power of the remaining kind, being the power of twice two feet, may be said to be the diameter of our diameter.

Υ. Soc. Certainly; and now I think that I pretty nearly understand you.

c   *Str.* In these divisions, Socrates, I descry what would earn a name for us as jesters.

Υ. Soc. What is it?

---

[1] Cf. *Meno* 82 ff. [The 'diameter' (i.e. diagonal) of a square which has sides one foot in length is $\sqrt{2}$, or, in Greek terms, 'the power of two feet'. If a new square is erected on this diagonal, its diagonal will be $\sqrt{4}$.]

Str. Human beings have come out in the same class with the freest and airiest of creation, and have been running a race with them.

Y. Soc. I remark that very singular coincidence.

Str. And would you not expect the slowest to arrive last?

Y. Soc. Indeed I should.

Str. And there is a still more ridiculous consequence, that the king is found running about with the herd, and in close competition with the person who of all mankind is most of an adept at the airy life.[1]

Y. Soc. Certainly.

Str. Then here, Socrates, is still clearer evidence of the truth of what was said in the inquiry about the Sophist.[2]

Y. Soc. What?

Str. That the dialectical method is no respecter of persons, and does not set the great above the small, but always arrives in her own way at the truest result.

Y. Soc. Clearly.

Str. And now, I will not wait for you to ask me, but will of my own accord take you by the shorter road to the definition of a king.

Y. Soc. By all means.

Str. I say that we should have begun at first by dividing land animals into biped and quadruped; and since the winged herd, and that alone, comes out in the same class with man, we should divide bipeds into those which have feathers and those which have not, and when they have been divided, and the art of the management of mankind is brought to light, the time will have come to produce our Statesman and ruler, and set him like a charioteer in his place, and hand over to him the reins of state, for that too is a vocation which belongs to him.

Y. Soc. Very good; you have paid me the debt,—I mean, that you have completed the argument, and I suppose that you added the digression by way of interest.[3]

---

[1] i.e. the bird-catcher. Plato is here introducing a subdivision of bipeds into men and birds. Others, however, refer the passage to the division into quadrupeds and bipeds, making pigs compete with human beings and the pig-driver with the king. According to this explanation we must translate the words above, 'freest and airiest of creation', 'worthiest and laziest of creation'.

[2] Cf. *Soph.* 227 b.   [3] Cf. *Rep.* vi. 507 a.

Str. Then now, let us go back to the beginning, and join the links, which together make the definition of the name of the Statesman's art.

Y. Soc. By all means.

Str. The science of pure knowledge had, as we said originally, a part which was the science of rule or command, and from this was derived another part, which was called ruling-for-self, on the
b analogy of selling-for-self; an important section of this was the management of living animals, and this again was further limited to the management of them in herds, and again in herds of pedestrian animals. The chief division of the latter was the art of managing pedestrian animals which are without horns; this again has a part which can only be comprehended under one term by joining together three names,—shepherding pure-bred animals.
c The only further subdivision is the art of man-herding,—this has to do with bipeds, and is what we were seeking after, and have now found, being at once the royal and political.

Y. Soc. To be sure.

Str. And do you think, Socrates, that we really have done as you say?

Y. Soc. What?

Str. Do you think, I mean, that we have really fulfilled our intention?—There has been a sort of discussion, and yet the
d investigation seems to me not to be perfectly worked out: this is where the inquiry fails.

Y. Soc. I do not understand.

Str. I will try to make the thought, which is at this moment present in my mind, clearer to us both.

Y. Soc. Let me hear.

Str. There were many arts of shepherding, and one of them was the political, which had the charge of one particular herd?

Y. Soc. Yes.

Str. And this the argument defined to be the art of rearing, not horses or other brutes, but the art of rearing man collectively?

Y. Soc. True.

e *Str.* Note, however, a difference which distinguishes the king from all other shepherds.

Y. Soc. To what do you refer?

Str. I want to ask, whether any one of the others has a rival, called by the name of a different art, who professes and claims to share with him in the management of the herd?

Y. Soc. What do you mean?

Str. I mean to say that merchants, husbandmen, providers of food, and also training-masters and physicians, will all contend with the herdsmen of humanity, whom we call Statesmen, declaring that they themselves have the care of rearing or managing mankind, and that they rear not only the common 268 herd, but also the rulers themselves.

Y. Soc. Are they not right in saying so?

Str. Very likely they may be, and we will consider their claim. But we are certain of this,—that no one will raise a similar claim as against the herdsman, who is allowed on all hands to be the sole and only feeder and physician of his herd; he is also their match-maker and accoucheur; no one else knows that depart- b ment of science. And he is their merry-maker and musician, as far as their nature is susceptible of such influences, and no one can console and soothe his own herd better than he can, either with the natural tones of his voice or with instruments. And the same may be said of tenders of animals in general.

Y. Soc. Very true.

Str. But if this is as you say, can our argument about the king be true and unimpeachable? Were we right in selecting him out c of ten thousand other claimants to be the shepherd and rearer of the human flock?

Y. Soc. Surely not.

Str. Had we not reason just now[1] to apprehend, that although we may have described a sort of royal form, we have not as yet accurately worked out the true image of the Statesman? and that we cannot reveal him as he truly is in his own nature, until we have disengaged and separated him from those who hang about him and claim to share in his prerogatives?

Y. Soc. Very true. d

Str. And that, Socrates, is what we must do, if we do not mean to bring disgrace upon the argument at its close.

Y. Soc. We must certainly avoid that.

Str. Then let us make a new beginning, and travel by a different road.

[1] Cf. *supra,* 267 c, d.

Y. Soc. What road?

Str. I think that we may have a little amusement; there is a famous tale, of which a good portion may with advantage be interwoven, and then we may resume our series of divisions, and proceed in the old path until we arrive at the desired summit. Shall we do as I say?

Y. Soc. By all means.

Str. Listen, then, to a tale which a child would love to hear; and you are not too old for childish amusement.

Y. Soc. Let me hear.

Str. There did really happen, and will again happen, like many other events of which ancient tradition has preserved the record, the portent which is traditionally said to have occurred in the quarrel of Atreus and Thyestes. You have heard, no doubt, and remember what they say happened at that time?

Y. Soc. I suppose you to mean the token of the birth of the golden lamb.

Str. No, not that; but another part of the story, which tells how the sun and the stars once rose in the west, and set in the east, and that the god reversed their motion, and gave them that which they now have as a testimony to the right of Atreus.

Y. Soc. Yes; there is that legend also.

Str. Again, we have been often told of the reign of Cronos.

Y. Soc. Yes, very often.

Str. Did you ever hear that the men of former times were earth-born, and not begotten of one another?

Y. Soc. Yes, that is another old tradition.

Str. All these stories, and ten thousand others which are still more wonderful, have a common origin; many of them have been lost in the lapse of ages, or are repeated only in a disconnected form; but the origin of them is what no one has told, and may as well be told now; for the tale is suited to throw light on the nature of the king.

Y. Soc. Very good; and I hope that you will give the whole story, and leave out nothing.

Str. Listen, then. There is a time when God himself guides and helps to roll the world in its course; and there is a time, on the completion of a certain cycle, when he lets go, and the world being a living creature, and having originally received intelligence

from its author and creator, turns about and by an inherent d
necessity revolves in the opposite direction.

Y. Soc. Why is that?

Str. Why, because it is the property of the most divine things
of all to remain ever unchanged and the same, and body is not
included in this class. That which we term heaven or the universe,
although it has been endowed by the Creator with many glories,
partakes of a bodily nature, and therefore cannot be entirely
free from perturbation. But its motion is, as far as possible, single e
and in the same place, and of the same kind; and is therefore
only subject to a reversal, which is the least alteration possible.
Again, the leader[1] of all moving things is alone able to revolve
perpetually of himself; and to think that he moves them at
one time in one direction and at another time in the opposite
direction, is blasphemy. Considering all this, we must neither
say that the world turns itself for ever, nor again that God causes
it to turn, as a whole and for ever, in two opposite courses; nor
lastly that two Gods, having contrary purposes, make it move 270
round. But as I have already said (and this is the only remaining alternative) the world is guided at one time by an external divine power, and receives fresh life and immortality
from the renewing hand of the Creator, and again, when let go,
moves spontaneously, being set free at such a time as to have,
during millions of revolutions, a reverse movement: this is due
to its perfect balance, to its vast size, and to the fact that it turns
on the smallest pivot.

Y. Soc. Your account of the world seems to be very reasonable b
indeed.

Str. Let us now reflect and try to gather from what has been
said the nature of the phenomenon which we affirmed to be the
cause of all these wonders. It is this.

Y. Soc. What?

Str. The reversal which takes place from time to time of the
motion of the universe.

Y. Soc. How is that the cause?

Str. Of all changes of the heavenly motions, we may consider c
this to be the greatest and most complete.

---

[1] [i.e. the outermost celestial sphere, in contrast to other spheres which convey the planets.]

Υ. Soc. I should imagine so.

Str. And it may be supposed to result in the greatest changes to the human beings who are the inhabitants of the world at the time.

Υ. Soc. Such changes would naturally occur.

Str. And animals, as we know, survive with difficulty great and serious changes of many different kinds when they come upon them at once.

Υ. Soc. Very true.

Str. Hence there necessarily occurs a great destruction of them, which extends also to the life of man; few survivors of the race

d are left, and those who remain become the subjects of several novel and remarkable phenomena, and of one in particular, which takes place at the time when the transition is made to the cycle opposite to that in which we are now living.

Υ. Soc. What is it?

Str. The life of all animals first came to a standstill, and the mortal nature ceased to be or look older, and was then reversed

e and grew young and delicate; the white locks of the aged darkened again, and the cheeks of the bearded man became smooth, and recovered their former bloom; the bodies of youths in their prime grew softer and smaller, continually by day and night returning and becoming assimilated to the nature of a newly born child in mind as well as body; in the succeeding stage they wasted away and wholly disappeared. And the bodies of those who died by violence at that time quickly passed through the like changes, and in a few days were no more seen.

271   *Υ. Soc.* Then how, Stranger, were the animals created in those days; and in what way were they begotten of one another?

Str. It is evident, Socrates, that there was no such thing in the then order of nature as the procreation of animals from one another; the earth-born race, of which we hear in story, was the one which existed in those days—they rose again from the ground; and of this tradition, which is nowadays often unduly discredited, our ancestors, who were nearest in point of time to the

b end of the last period and came into being at the beginning of this, are to us the heralds. And mark how consistent the sequel of the tale is; after the return of age to youth, follows the return of the dead, who are lying in the earth, to life; simultaneously with the reversal of the world the wheel of their generation has been turned back, and they are put together and rise and live in the opposite order, unless God has carried any of them away to some other lot. According to this tradition they of necessity sprang from c the earth and have the name of earth-born, and so the above legend clings to them.

Y. Soc. Certainly that is quite consistent with what has preceded; but tell me, was the life which you said existed in the reign of Cronos in that cycle of the world, or in this? For the change in the course of the stars and the sun must have occurred in both.

Str. I see that you enter into my meaning;—no, that blessed and spontaneous life does not belong to the present cycle of the d world, but to the previous one. For at that time God governed the rotation of the world, and superintended its whole course, as he does now;[1] and moreover, the several parts of the universe were distributed in like manner under the rule of certain inferior deities. There were demigods, who were the shepherds of the various species and herds of animals, and each one was in all respects sufficient for those of whom he was the shepherd; neither e was there any violence, or devouring of one another, or war or quarrel among them; and I might tell of ten thousand other blessings which belonged to that dispensation. The reason why the life of man was, as tradition says, spontaneous, is as follows: In those days God himself was their shepherd, and ruled over them, just as man, who is by comparison a divine being, still rules over the lower animals. Under him there were no forms of government or separate possession of women and children; for all 272 men rose again from the earth, having no memory of the past. And although they had nothing of this sort, the earth gave them fruits in abundance, which grew on trees and shrubs unbidden, and were not planted by the hand of man. And they dwelt naked, and mostly in the open air, for the temperature of their seasons was mild; and they had no beds, but lay on soft couches of grass, which grew plentifully out of the earth. Such was the life of man b in the days of Cronos, Socrates; the character of our present life, which is said to be under Zeus, you know from your own

---

[1] [Compare *Laws* x. 903 b. The text is uncertain, but Hermann's insertion of καί after ὡς νῦν gives a satisfactory sense. The contrast is not between a state in which the world is left wholly to itself, and one in which every detail is supervised by the Gods; and Plato does not wish to give the impression that God is wholly absent from the world during its present phase.]

experience. Can you, and will you, determine which of them you deem the happier?

Y. Soc. Impossible.

Str. Then shall I determine for you as well as I can?

Y. Soc. By all means.

Str. Suppose that the nurslings of Cronos, having this bound-less leisure, and the power of holding intercourse, not only with men, but with the brute creation, had used all these advantages
c with a view to philosophy, conversing with the brutes as well as with one another, and learning of every nature which was gifted with any special power, and was able to contribute some special experience to the store of wisdom, there would be no difficulty in deciding that they would be a thousand times happier than the men of our own day. But if, while eating and drinking until they were full, they told stories to one another and to the animals— such stories as are now attributed to them—in this case also, as
d I should imagine, the answer would be easy. But until some satisfactory witness can be found of the love of that age for knowledge and discussion, we had better let the matter drop, and give the reason why we have unearthed this tale, and then we shall be able to get on. In the fullness of time, when the change was to take place, and the earth-born race had been exhausted,
e since every soul had completed its proper cycle of births and been sown in the earth her appointed number of times, the pilot of the universe let the helm go, and retired to his place of view; and then Fate and innate desire reversed the motion of the world. Then also all the inferior deities who share the rule of the supreme power, being informed of what was happening, let go the parts of
273 the world which were under their control. And the world turning round with a sudden shock, being impelled in an opposite direc-tion from beginning to end, was shaken by a mighty earthquake, which wrought a new destruction of all manner of animals. Afterwards, when sufficient time had elapsed, the tumult and confusion and earthquake ceased, and the universal creature, once more at peace, attained to a calm, and settled down into his own orderly and accustomed course, having the charge and rule
b of himself and of all the creatures which are contained in him, and executing, as far as he remembered them, the instructions of his Father and Creator, more precisely at first, but afterwards

with less exactness. The reason of the falling off was the admixture of matter in him; this was inherent in the primal nature, which was full of disorder, until attaining to the present order. From God, the constructor, the world has received nothing that is not good, but from the previous state come elements of evil and un- c righteousness, which, thence derived, first of all pass into the world, and are then transmitted to the animals. While the world was aided by the pilot in nurturing the animals, small was the evil, and great the good which he produced; and after the separation the world always fares best in every way while it is nearest to the time when he gave up the helm. But in the progress of time, the memory fades away, and the old discord again holds sway and bursts forth in full glory; and at last small is the good, d and great the admixture of evil which the world infuses, bringing itself and all things contained in it into danger of ruin. And therefore at that moment God, who set the world in order, seeing that it is in great straits, and fearing that all may be dissolved in the storm and disappear in infinite chaos, again seats himself at the helm; and bringing back the elements which have fallen into dissolution e and disorder during the previous time of independence, he sets them in order and restores them, and makes the world imperishable and immortal. And this is the whole tale, of which the first part will suffice to illustrate the nature of the king. For when the world turned towards the present cycle of generation, the age of man again stood still, and a change opposite to the previous one was the result. The small creatures which had almost disappeared grew in stature, and the newly born children of the earth became grey[1] and died and sank into the earth again. All things changed, 274 imitating and following the condition of the universe, and of necessity agreeing with that in their mode of conception and generation and nurture; for no animal was any longer allowed to come into being in the earth through composition by other agencies, but as the world was ordained to be the lord of his own progress, in like manner the parts were ordained to grow and generate and give nourishment, as far as they could, of themselves, impelled by a similar movement. And so we have arrived

[1] [Others translate 'born with hoary hair', but it is doubtful whether this is a true interpretation of the story. It seems rather to be supposed that the earth-born race spring up in the prime of life.]

b at the real end of this discourse; for although there might be much to tell of the lower animals, and of the condition out of which they changed and of the causes of the change, about men there is not much, and that little is more to the purpose. Deprived of the care of God, who had possessed and tended them, they were left helpless and defenceless, and were torn in pieces by the beasts, who were naturally fierce and had now grown wild. And

c in the first ages they were still without skill or resource; the food which once grew spontaneously had failed, and as yet they knew not how to procure it, because they had never felt the pressure of necessity. For all these reasons they were in a great strait; wherefore also the gifts spoken of in the old tradition were imparted to man by the gods, together with so much teaching and education as was indispensable; fire was given to them by Prometheus, the

d arts by Hephaestus and his fellow worker, Athene, seeds and plants by others. From these is derived all that has helped to frame human life; since the care of the Gods, as I was saying, had now failed men, and they had to order their course of life and make provision for themselves, as does the universal creature whom we men must imitate and follow, ever living and growing, at one time in the first manner, and at another time in the other.

e Enough of the story, which may be of use in showing us how greatly we erred in the delineation of the king and the statesman in our previous discourse.

Y. Soc. What was this great error of which you speak?

Str. There were two; the first a lesser one, the other was an error on a much larger and grander scale.

Y. Soc. What do you mean?

275 *Str.* I mean to say that when we were asked about a king and statesman of the present cycle and generation, we told of a shepherd of a human flock who belonged to the other cycle, and of one who was a god when he ought to have been a man; and this was a most serious error. Again, we declared him to be the ruler of the entire State, without explaining how: this was not the whole truth, nor very intelligible; but still it was true, and therefore the second error was not so great as the first.

Y. Soc. Very good.

Str. Before we can expect to have a perfect description of the statesman we must define the nature of his office.

Y. Soc. Certainly.

Str. And the myth was introduced in order to show, not only b that all others are rivals of the true shepherd who is the object of our search, but in order that we might have a clearer view of him who is alone worthy to receive this appellation, because he alone of shepherds and herdsmen, according to the image which we have employed, has the care of human beings.

Y. Soc. Very true.

Str. And I cannot help thinking, Socrates, that the form of the divine shepherd is even higher than that of a king; whereas the c statesmen who are now on earth seem to be much more like their subjects in character, and much more nearly to partake of their breeding and education.

Y. Soc. Certainly.

Str. Still they must be investigated all the same, to see whether, like the divine shepherd, they are above their subjects or on a level with them.

Y. Soc. Of course.

Str. To resume:—Do you remember that we spoke of a command-for-self exercised over animals, not singly but col- d lectively, which we called the art of rearing a herd?

Y. Soc. Yes, I remember.

Str. There, somewhere, lay our error; for we never included or mentioned the Statesman; and we did not observe that he had no place in our nomenclature.

Y. Soc. How was that?

Str. All other herdsmen 'rear' their herds, but this is not a suitable term to apply to the Statesman; we should have used a name which is common to them all.   e

Y. Soc. True, if there be such a name.

Str. Why, is not 'care' of herds applicable to all? For this implies no feeding, or any special duty; if we had said either 'tending' the herds, or 'managing' the herds, or 'having the care' of them, any such general term would have comprehended the Statesman with the rest, as the argument seems to require.

Y. Soc. Quite right; but what should have been the next step 276 in the division?

Str. As before we divided the art of 'rearing' herds accordingly as they were land or water herds, winged and wingless, mixing or not mixing the breed, horned and hornless, so we might divide by these same differences the 'tending' of herds, comprehending in our definition the kingship of today and that which exists under the reign of Cronos.

Y. Soc. That is clear; but I still ask, what is to follow.

Str. If the word had been 'managing' herds, instead of feeding
b or rearing them, no one would have argued that there was no care of men in the case of the politician, although it was justly contended that there was no human art of feeding them which was worthy of the name, or at least, if there were, many a man had a prior and greater right to share in such an art than any king.

Y. Soc. True.

Str. But no other art or science will have a prior or better right
c than the royal science to care for human society and to rule over men in general.

Y. Soc. Quite true.

Str. In the next place, Socrates, we must surely notice that a great error was committed in the last stage of our analysis.

Y. Soc. What was it?

Str. Why, supposing we were ever so sure that there is such an art as the art of rearing or feeding bipeds, there was no reason why we should call this the royal or political art, as though there were no more to be said.

Y. Soc. Certainly not.

Str. Our first duty, as we were saying, was to remodel the
d name, so as to have the notion of care rather than of feeding, and then to divide, for there may be still considerable divisions.

Y. Soc. How can they be made?

Str. First, by separating the divine shepherd from the human guardian or manager.

Y. Soc. True.

Str. And the art of management which is assigned to man would again have to be subdivided.

Y. Soc. On what principle?

Str. On the principle of voluntary and compulsory.

Y. Soc. Why?

e *Str.* Because, if I am not mistaken, there has been an error here; for our simplicity led us to rank king and tyrant together, whereas they are utterly distinct, like their modes of government.

Y. Soc. True.

Str. Then, now, as I said, let us make the correction and divide human care into two parts, on the principle of voluntary and compulsory.

Y. Soc. Certainly.

Str. And if we call the management of violent rulers tyranny, and the voluntary management of herds of voluntary bipeds politics, may we not further assert that he who has this latter art of management is the true king and statesman?

Y. Soc. I think, Stranger, that we have now completed the 277 account of the Statesman.

Str. Would that we had, Socrates, but I have to satisfy myself as well as you; and in my judgement the figure of the king is not yet perfected; like statuaries who, in their too great haste, having overdone the several parts of their work, lose time in cutting them down, so too we, partly out of haste, partly out of a magnanimous b desire to expose our former error, and also because we imagined that a king required grand illustrations, have taken up a marvellous lump of fable, and have been obliged to use more of it than was suitable. This made us discourse at large, and, nevertheless, the story never came to an end. And our discussion might be compared to a picture of some living being which had been fairly drawn in outline, but had not yet attained the life and clearness c which is given by the blending of colours. Now to intelligent persons a living being had better be delineated by language and discourse than by any painting or work of art: to the duller sort by works of art.

Y. Soc. Very true; but what is the imperfection which still remains? I wish that you would tell me.

Str. The higher ideas, my dear friend, can hardly be set forth d except through the medium of examples; every man seems to know all things in a dreamy sort of way, and then again to wake up and to know nothing.

Y. Soc. What do you mean?

Str. I fear that I have been unfortunate in raising a question about our experience of knowledge.

Y. Soc. Why so?

Str. Why, because my 'example' requires the assistance of another example.

e *Υ. Soc.* Proceed; you need not fear that I shall tire.

Str. I will proceed, finding, as I do, such a ready listener in you: when children are beginning to know their letters——

Υ. Soc. What are you going to say?

Str. That they distinguish the several letters well enough in
278 very short and easy syllables, and are able to tell them correctly.

Υ. Soc. Certainly.

Str. Whereas in other syllables they do not recognize the same letters, and think and speak falsely of them.

Υ. Soc. Very true.

Str. Will not the best and easiest way of bringing them to a knowledge of what they do not as yet know be——

Υ. Soc. Be what?

Str. To refer them first of all to cases in which they judged
b correctly about the letters in question, and then to compare these with the cases in which they do not as yet know, and to show them that the letters are the same, and have the same character in both combinations, until all cases in which they are right have been placed side by side with all cases in which they are wrong. In this way they have examples, and are made to learn how each letter in every syllable is called both different and the same—different, because it differs from all others, and
c the same, because it remains the same as itself.

Υ. Soc. Certainly.

Str. Are not examples formed in this manner? We take a thing and compare it with another distinct instance of the same thing, of which we have a right conception, and out of the comparison there arises one true notion, which includes both of them.

Υ. Soc. Apparently.

Str. Can we wonder, then, if the human mind naturally has
d the same uncertainty about the alphabet of things, and sometimes and in some cases is firmly fixed by the truth in each particular, and then, again, in other cases is altogether at sea; having somehow or other a correct notion of combinations, but when the same elements are transferred into the long and difficult language (syllables) of facts, being unable to recognize them?

Υ. Soc. There is nothing wonderful in that.

Str. Could any one, my friend, who began with false opinion ever expect to arrive even at a small portion of truth and to attain wisdom? e

Y. Soc. Hardly.

Str. Then you and I will not be far wrong if, now that we have seen the nature of example in general in a small and particular instance, we endeavour to *use* this method of example; that is to say, to derive the form of the royal art from lesser instances in the same class, and so discover by rules of art what the management of cities is; and then the dream will become a reality to us.

Y. Soc. Very true.

Str. Then, once more, let us resume the previous argument, 279 and as there were innumerable rivals of the royal race who claim to have the care of states, let us part them all off, and leave him alone; and, as I was saying, a model or example of this process has first to be framed.

Y. Soc. Exactly.

Str. What model is there which, on the smallest scale, can provide a sufficient analogy to the political occupation? Suppose, Socrates, that if we have no other example at hand, we choose b weaving, or, more precisely, weaving of wool—this will be quite enough, without taking the whole of weaving, to serve as evidence of what we hope to discover?

Y. Soc. Certainly.

Str. Why should we not apply to weaving the same processes of division and subdivision which we have already applied to other classes, and having passed as rapidly as we can through all c the steps, come to the point which is needed for our purpose?

Y. Soc. How do you mean?

Str. I shall reply by actually performing the process.

Y. Soc. Very good.

Str. All things which we make or acquire are either creative or preventive; of the preventive class are antidotes, divine and human, and also defences; and defences are either military weapons or protections; and protections are veils, and also shields against heat and cold, and shields against heat and cold d are shelters and coverings; and coverings are blankets and garments; and garments are some of them in one piece, and others of them are made in several parts; and of these latter some are stitched, others are fastened and not stitched; and of the not e stitched, some are made of the sinews of plants, and some of hair; and of these, again, some are cemented with water and earth, and others are fastened together by themselves. And these last defences and coverings which are fastened together by themselves are called cloaks, and the art which superintends them we may call, from the nature of the operation, the art of clothing, just as

280 before the name of statesmanship was derived from the State; and may we not say that the art of weaving, at least that largest portion of it which was concerned with the making of woollen cloaks (cf. 279 b), differs only in name from this art of clothing, in the same way that, in the previous case, the royal science differed from the political?

Y. Soc. Most true.

Str. In the next place, let us make the reflection, that the art of

b weaving cloaks, which an incompetent person might fancy to have been sufficiently described, has been separated off from several others which are of the same family, but not from those arts which collaborate closely with it.

Y. Soc. And which are the kindred arts?

Str. I see that I have not taken you with me. So I think that we had better go backwards, starting from the end. We just now parted off from the weaving of cloaks, the making of blankets, which differ from each other in that one is put under and the other is put around: and these are what I termed kindred arts.

Y. Soc. I understand.

c *Str.* And we have subtracted the manufacture of all articles made of flax and cords, and all that we just now metaphorically termed the sinews of plants, and we have also separated off the process of felting and the putting together of materials by stitching and sewing, of which the most important part is the cobbler's art.

Y. Soc. Precisely.

Str. Then we separated off the currier's art, which prepared coverings in entire pieces, and the art of sheltering, and subtracted the various arts of making water-tight which are employed

d in building, and in general in carpentering, and in other crafts, and all such arts as furnish impediments to thieving and acts of violence, and are concerned with making the lids of boxes and the fixing of doors, being divisions of the art of joining; and we also cut off the manufacture of arms, which is a section of the great and manifold art of making defences; and we originally began by parting off the whole of the magic art which is concerned with e antidotes, and have left, as would appear, the very art of which we were in search, the art of protection against winter cold, which fabricates woollen defences, and has the name of weaving.

Y. Soc. Very true.

Str. Yes, my boy, but that is not all; for the first process to 281 which the material is subjected is the opposite of weaving.

Y. Soc. How so?

Str. Weaving is a sort of uniting?

Y. Soc. Yes.

Str. But the first process is a separation of the clotted and matted fibres?

Y. Soc. What do you mean?

Str. I mean the work of the carder's art; for we cannot say that carding is weaving, or that the carder is a weaver.

Y. Soc. Certainly not.

Str. Again, if a person were to say that the art of making the warp and the woof was the art of weaving, he would say what b was paradoxical and false.

Y. Soc. To be sure.

Str. Shall we say that the whole art of the fuller or of the mender has nothing to do with the care and treatment of clothes, or are we to regard all these as arts of weaving?

Y. Soc. Certainly not.

Str. And yet surely all these arts will maintain that they are concerned with the treatment and production of clothes; they will dispute the exclusive prerogative of weaving, and though assigning a larger sphere to that, will still reserve a considerable field for themselves.

Y. Soc. Very true.   c

Str. Besides these, there are the arts which make tools and instruments of weaving, and which may be expected to claim at least to be co-operative causes in every work of the weaver.

Y. Soc. Most true.

Str. Well, then, suppose that we define weaving, or rather that part of it which has been selected by us, to be the greatest and noblest of arts which are concerned with woollen garments— d shall we be right? Is not the definition, although true, wanting in clearness and completeness; for do not all those other arts require to be first cleared away?

Y. Soc. True.

Str. Then the next thing will be to separate them, in order that the argument may proceed in a regular manner?

Y. Soc. By all means.

Str. Let us consider, in the first place, that there are two kinds of arts entering into everything which we do.

Y. Soc. What are they?

Str. The one kind is the [conditional or] co-operative, the other the principal cause of production.

Y. Soc. What do you mean?

e *Str.* The arts which do not manufacture the actual thing, but which furnish the necessary tools for the manufacture, without which the several arts could not fulfil their appointed work, are co-operative; but those which make the things themselves are causal.

Y. Soc. A very reasonable distinction.

Str. Thus the arts which make spindles, combs, and other instruments which play some part in the production of clothes, may be called co-operative, and those which treat and fabricate the things themselves, causal.

Y. Soc. Very true.

282 *Str.* The arts of washing and mending, and the other preparatory arts which belong to the causal class, may be supposed to come under one division of the great art of adornment; a division which may, as a whole, be named the fuller's art.

Y. Soc. Very good.

Str. Next, carding and spinning threads and all the parts of the process which are concerned with the actual manufacture of a woollen garment form a single art, which is one of those universally acknowledged,—the art of working in wool.

Y. Soc. To be sure.

b *Str.* Of working in wool, again, there are two divisions, and both these are parts of two arts at once.

Y. Soc. How is that?

Str. Carding and one half of the use of the comb, and the other processes of wool-working which separate the composite, may be classed together as belonging both to the art of wool-working, and also to one of the two great arts which are of universal application—the art of composition and the art of division.

Y. Soc. Yes.

Str. To the latter belong carding and the other processes of which I was just now speaking; the art of discernment or division c in wool and yarn, which is effected in one manner with the comb and in another with the hands, is variously described under all the names which I just now mentioned.

Y. Soc. Very true.

Str. Again, let us take some process of wool-working which is also a portion of the art of composition, and, dismissing the elements of division which we found there, make two halves, one on the principle of composition, and the other on the principle of division.

Y. Soc. Let that be done.

Str. And once more, Socrates, we must divide the part which belongs at once both to wool-working and composition, if we are d ever to discover satisfactorily the aforesaid art of weaving.

Y. Soc. We must.

Str. Yes, certainly, and let us call one part of the art the art of twisting threads, the other the art of combining them.

Y. Soc. Do I understand you, in speaking of twisting, to be referring to manufacture of the warp?

Str. Yes, and of the woof too; how, if not by twisting, is the woof made?

Y. Soc. There is no other way.

Str. Then suppose that you define the warp and the woof, for e I think that the definition will be of use to you.

Y. Soc. How shall I define them?

Str. As thus: A piece of carded wool which is drawn out lengthwise and breadthwise is said to be pulled out.

Y. Soc. Yes.

Str. And the wool thus prepared, when twisted by the spindle, and made into a firm thread, is called the warp, and the art which regulates these operations the art of spinning the warp.

Y. Soc. True.

Str. And the threads which are more loosely spun, having a softness proportioned to the intertexture of the warp and to the

283 degree of force used in dressing the cloth,—the threads which are thus spun are called the woof, and the art which is set over them may be called the art of spinning the woof.

Y. Soc. Very true.

Str. And, now, there can be no mistake about the nature of the part of weaving which we have undertaken to define. For when that part of the art of composition which is employed in the working of wool forms a web by the regular intertexture of warp and woof, the entire woven substance is called by us a woollen garment, and the art which presides over this is the art of weaving.

Y. Soc. Very true.

b 　*Str.* But why did we not say at once that weaving is the art of entwining warp and woof, instead of making a long and useless circuit?

Y. Soc. I thought, Stranger, that there was nothing useless in what was said.

Str. Very likely, but you may not always think so, my sweet friend; and in case any feeling of dissatisfaction should hereafter arise in your mind, as it very well may, let me lay down a prin-
c ciple which will apply to arguments in general.

Y. Soc. Proceed.

Str. Let us begin by considering the whole nature of excess and defect, and then we shall have a rational ground on which we may praise or blame too much length or too much shortness in discussions of this kind.

Y. Soc. Let us do so.

Str. The points on which I think that we ought to dwell are the following——

Y. Soc. What?

d 　*Str.* Length and shortness, excess and defect; with all of these the art of measurement is conversant.

Y. Soc. Yes.

Str. And the art of measurement has to be divided into two parts, with a view to our present purpose.

Y. Soc. Where would you make the division?

Str. As thus: I would make two parts, one having regard to the relativity of greatness and smallness to each other; and there is another, without which the existence of production would be impossible.

Υ. Soc. What do you mean?

Str. Do you not think that it is only natural for the greater to be called greater with reference to the less alone, and the less less with reference to the greater alone?   e

Υ. Soc. Yes.

Str. Well, but is there not also something exceeding and exceeded by the principle of the mean, both in speech and action, and is not this a reality, and the chief mark of difference between good and bad men?

Υ. Soc. So it seems.

Str. Then we must suppose that the great and small exist and are discerned in both these ways, and not, as we were saying before, only relatively to one another, but there must also be another comparison of them with the mean or ideal standard; would you like to hear the reason why?

Υ. Soc. Certainly.

Str. If we assume the greater to exist only in relation to the   284
less, there will never be any comparison of either with the mean.

Υ. Soc. True.

Str. And would not this doctrine be the ruin of all the arts and their creations; would not the art of the Statesman and the aforesaid art of weaving disappear? For all these arts are on the watch against excess and defect, not as unrealities, but as real evils, which occasion a difficulty in action; and the excellence or beauty of every work of art is due to this observance of measure.   b

Υ. Soc. Certainly.

Str. But if the science of the Statesman disappears, the search for the royal science will be impossible.

Υ. Soc. Very true.

Str. Well, then, as in the case of the Sophist[1] we extorted the inference that not-being had an existence, because here was the point at which the argument eluded our grasp, so in this we must compel the greater and less to be measurable, not only against one another, but also with regard to the production of the mean; for if this is not admitted, neither a statesman nor any   c
other man of action can be an undisputed master of his science.

Υ. Soc. Yes, we must certainly do again what we did then.

Str. But this, Socrates, is a greater work than the other, of

[1 241 d.]

which we only too well remember the length. I think, however, that we may fairly assume something of this sort——

Y. Soc. What?

d   *Str.* That we shall some day require this notion of a mean with a view to the demonstration of exact truth;[1] meanwhile, the argument that the very existence of the arts must be held to depend on the possibility of measuring more or less, not only with one another, but also with a view to the attainment of the mean, seems to afford a grand support and satisfactory proof of the doctrine which we are maintaining;[2] for if there are arts, there is a standard of measure, and if there is a standard of measure, there are arts; but if either is wanting, there is neither.

e   *Y. Soc.* True; and what is the next step?

Str. The next step clearly is to divide the art of measurement into two parts, as we have said already, and to place in the one part all the arts which measure number, length, depth, breadth, swiftness with their opposites; and to have another part in which they are measured with the mean, and the fit, and the opportune, and the due, and with all those words, in short, which denote a mean or standard removed from the extremes.

Y. Soc. Here are two vast divisions, embracing two very different spheres.

285   *Str.* There are many accomplished men, Socrates, who say, believing themselves to speak wisely, that the art of measurement is universal, and has to do with all things which come to be. And this means what we are now saying; for all things which come within the province of art do certainly in some sense partake of measure. But these persons, because they are not accustomed to distinguish classes according to real forms, jumble together two widely different things, relation to one another, and to a standard, under the idea that they are the same, and also fall into the converse error of dividing other things not according to their real

b   parts. Whereas the right way is, if a man has first seen the common nature of several things, to go on with the inquiry and not desist until he has found all the differences contained in it which

---

[1] [Perhaps a reference to the projected dialogue, *The Philosopher.*]

[2] [Or: 'meanwhile, to dwell only on what has been proved sufficiently for our present purpose, it seems to me that we have a grand support in the argument that the very existence of all the arts stands or falls with the possibility', &c.]

form distinct classes; nor again should he be able to rest contented with the manifold diversities which are seen in a multitude of things until he has comprehended all of them that have any affinity within the bounds of one similarity and embraced them within the reality of a single kind. But we have said enough on this head, and also of excess and defect; we have only to bear in mind that two divisions of the art of measurement have been discovered which are concerned with them, and not forget what they are.

Y. Soc. We will not forget.

Str. And now that this discussion is completed, let us go on to consider another question, which concerns not this argument only but the conduct of such arguments in general.

Y. Soc. What is this new question?

Str. Take the case of a child who is engaged in learning his letters: when he is asked what letters make up a word, should we say that the question is intended to improve his grammatical d knowledge of that particular word, or of all words?

Y. Soc. Clearly, in order that he may have a better knowledge of all words.

Str. And what is our purpose in this inquiry about the Statesman? Is it intended only to improve our knowledge of politics, or our power of reasoning generally?

Y. Soc. Clearly, as in the former example, the purpose is general.

Str. Still less would any rational man seek to analyse the notion of weaving for its own sake. But people seem to forget that some e things have by nature sensible images, which are readily known, and can be easily pointed out when anyone desires to answer an inquiry concerning them without any trouble or argument; whereas the greatest and most precious things that exist have no 286 outward image obviously designed for man's instruction, which one can make plain to sight or some other sense, and thus give thorough satisfaction to the mind of an inquirer. And therefore we ought to train ourselves to give and accept a rational account of each thing; for immaterial things, which are the noblest and greatest, are shown only in thought, and in no other way, and all that we are now saying is said for the sake of them. Moreover, there is always less difficulty if one begins with prac- b tice on a smaller scale.

Y. Soc. Very good.

Str. Let us call to mind the bearing of all this.

Y. Soc. What is it?

Str. I wanted to get rid of any impression of tediousness which we may have experienced in the lengthy examination of weaving, and the story of the reversal of the universe, and in the discussion concerning the Sophist and the being of not-being. I know that they were felt to be too long, and I reproached myself with this,

c fearing that they might be not only tedious but irrelevant; and all that I have now said is only designed to prevent the recurrence of any such disagreeables for the future.

Y. Soc. Very good. Will you proceed?

Str. Then I should like to observe that you and I, remembering what has been said, should praise or blame the length or shortness of discussions, not by comparing them with one another, but with what is fitting, having regard to that part of the art of measuring,

d which, as we said, was to be borne in mind.

Y. Soc. Very true.

Str. And yet, not everything is to be judged even with a view to what is fitting; for we should only want such a length as is suited to give pleasure, if at all, as a secondary matter; and reason tells us, that we should be contented to make the ease or rapidity of an inquiry, not our first, but our second object; the first and highest of all being to assert the great method of division according to species. No offence should be taken at the great length of a

e discourse, if it is calculated to sharpen the wits of the auditors. If it does this, it should be approved, and a shorter discourse should be similarly judged. Reason would also say to him who censures the length of discourses on such occasions as this, and cannot bear with their circumlocution, that he should not be in such a

287 hurry to drop the subject when he has complained that they are tedious, but should do his best to prove that if they had been shorter they would have made those who took part in them better dialecticians, and more capable of expressing the truth of things; about any other praise and blame by another standard, he need not trouble himself—he should pretend not to hear them. But we have had enough of this, as you will probably agree with me

b in thinking. Let us return to our Statesman, and apply to his case the aforesaid example of weaving.

Y. Soc. Very good;—let us do as you say.

Str. The art of the king has been separated from most of its companion arts, and, indeed, from all those which have to do with herds at all. There still remain, however, of the causal and co-operative arts those which are exercised within the city, and which must first be distinguished from one another.

Y. Soc. Very good.

Str. Do you know that these arts cannot easily be divided into two halves? The reason will, I think, be very evident as we pro- c ceed.

Y. Soc. Then we had better do so.

Str. We must carve them like a victim into members or limbs, since we cannot bisect them.[1] For we certainly should divide everything into as few parts as possible.

Y. Soc. What is to be done in this case?

Str. What we did in the example of weaving—all those arts which furnished the tools were regarded by us as co-operative.

Y. Soc. Yes.

Str. So now, and with still more reason, all arts which make any implement in a State, whether great or small, may be d regarded by us as co-operative, for without them neither State nor Statesmanship would be possible; and yet we are not inclined to say that any of them is a product of the kingly art.

Y. Soc. No, indeed.

Str. The task, which we have undertaken, of separating this class from others, is not an easy one; for there is plausibility in saying that anything in the world is the instrument of doing at least one thing. But there is another class of possessions in a e city, of which I have a word to say.

Y. Soc. What class do you mean?

Str. A class which may be described as not having this power;[2] that is to say, not like an instrument, framed to be a cause of production, but designed for the preservation of that which is produced.

Y. Soc. To what do you refer?

Str. To the class of vessels, as they are comprehensively termed,

---

[1] Cf. *Phaedr.* 265 e, *Phil.* 16 d.

[2] Or, taking the words in a different context, 'as not having political power—I say another class, because not like an instrument', &c.

which are constructed for the preservation of things moist and dry, of things prepared in the fire or out of the fire; this is a very large class, and has, if I am not mistaken, literally nothing to do

288 with the royal art of which we are in search.

T. Soc. Certainly not.

Str. There is also a third class of possessions to be noted, different from these and very extensive, moving or resting on land or water, honourable and also dishonourable. The whole of this class has one name, because it is intended to be sat upon, being always a seat for something.

T. Soc. What is it?

Str. A vehicle, which is not exactly the work of the Statesman, but of the carpenter, potter, and coppersmith.

T. Soc. I understand.

b *Str.* And is there not a fourth class which is again different, and in which most of the things formerly mentioned are contained, —every kind of dress, most sorts of arms, walls and enclosures, whether of earth or stone, and ten thousand other things? all of which being made for the sake of defence, the whole class may be truly called defences, and are for the most part to be regarded as the work of the builder or of the weaver, rather than of the Statesman.

T. Soc. Certainly.

c *Str.* Shall we add a fifth class, of ornamentation and drawing, and of the imitations produced by drawing and music, which are designed for amusement only, and may be fairly comprehended under one name?

T. Soc. What is it?

Str. Plaything is the name.

T. Soc. Certainly.

Str. That one name may be fitly predicated of all of them, for none of these things has a serious purpose—amusement is their sole aim.

d *T. Soc.* That again I understand.

Str. Then there is a class which provides materials for all these, out of which and in which the arts already mentioned fabricate their works;—this manifold class, I say, which is the creation and offspring of many other arts, may I not rank sixth?

T. Soc. What do you mean?

Str. I am referring to gold, silver, and other metals which are mined, and all that wood-cutting and shearing of every sort provides for the arts of carpentry and plaiting; and there is the process of barking and stripping the cuticle of plants, and the currier's art, which strips off the skins of animals, and other similar arts e which manufacture corks and papyri and cords, and provide for the manufacture of composite species out of simple kinds—the whole class may be termed the primitive and simple possession [or acquisition] of man, and with this the kingly science has no concern at all.

Υ. Soc. True.

Str. The provision of food, that is to say of all things which, by mixing their particles with the particles of the human body, have power to supply its wants, will form a seventh class, which 289 may be called by the general term of nourishment, unless you have any better name to offer. This, however, appertains rather to the husbandman, huntsman, trainer, doctor, cook, and is not to be assigned to the Statesman's art.

Υ. Soc. Certainly not.

Str. These seven classes include nearly every description of property, with the exception of tame animals. Consider;—there was the original material, which might fairly have been placed first; next come instruments, vessels, vehicles, defences, play- b things, nourishment; small things, which may be included under one of these—as for example, coins, seals and stamps—are omitted, for they have not in them the character of any larger kind which includes them; but some of them may, with a little forcing, be placed among ornaments, and others may be made to harmonize with the class of implements. The art of herding, which has been already divided into parts, will be found to have included all c property in tame animals, except slaves.

Υ. Soc. Very true.

Str. The class of slaves and ministers only remains, and I suspect that in this the real aspirants for the throne, who are the rivals of the king in the formation of the political web, will be discovered; just as spinners, carders, and the rest of them were the rivals of the weaver. All the others, who were termed co-operators, have been got rid of among the occupations already mentioned, and separated from the royal and political activity. d

Y. Soc. I agree.

Str. Let us go a little nearer, in order that we may be more certain of the complexion of this remaining class.

Y. Soc. Let us do so.

Str. We shall find from our present point of view that the humblest servants are in a condition, and engaged in a pursuit, the reverse of what we anticipated.

Y. Soc. Who are they?

Str. Those who have been purchased, and have so become e possessions; these are unmistakably to be called slaves, and certainly do not claim royal science.

Y. Soc. Certainly not.

Str. Again, freemen who of their own accord become the servants of the other classes in a State, and who exchange and equalize the products of husbandry and the other arts, some sitting in the market-place, others going from city to city by land or sea, and giving money in exchange for money or for other productions 290 —the money-changer, the merchant, the ship-owner, the retailer, will not put in any claim to statecraft or politics?

Y. Soc. No; unless, indeed, to the politics of commerce.

Str. But surely men whom we see acting as hirelings and serfs, and very happy to turn their hand to anything, will not profess to share in royal science?

Y. Soc. Certainly not.

Str. But what would you say of some other serviceable officials?

Y. Soc. Who are they, and what services do they perform?

b *Str.* There are heralds, and scribes perfected by practice, and divers others who have great skill in various sorts of business connected with the government of states—what shall we call them?

Y. Soc. They are the officials, and servants of the rulers, as you just now called them, but not themselves rulers.

Str. There may be something strange in any servant pretending to be a ruler, and yet I do not think that I could have been dreaming when I imagined that the principal claimants to political c science would be found somewhere in this neighbourhood.

Y. Soc. Very true.

Str. Well, let us draw nearer, and try the claims of some who have not yet been tested: in the first place, there are diviners, who have a portion of servile or ministerial science, since they are thought to be the interpreters of the gods to men.

Y. Soc. True.

Str. There is also the priestly class, who, as the law declares, know how to give the gods gifts from men in the form of sacrifices which are acceptable to them, and to ask on our behalf blessings d in return from them. Now both these are branches of the servile or ministerial art.

Y. Soc. Yes, clearly.

Str. And here I think that we seem to be getting on the right track; for the priest and the diviner are swollen with pride and prerogative, and they create an awful impression of themselves by the magnitude of their enterprises; in Egypt, the king himself is not allowed to reign, unless he have priestly powers, and if he should be of another class and has thrust himself in, he must get e enrolled in the priesthood. In many parts of Hellas, the duty of offering the most solemn propitiatory sacrifices is assigned to the highest magistracies, and you have a striking example here, at Athens, for the most solemn and national of the ancient sacrifices are said to be celebrated by him who has been chosen by lot to be the King Archon.

Y. Soc. Precisely.

Str. But who are these other kings and priests elected by lot 291 who now come into view followed by their retainers and a vast throng, as the former class disappears and the scene changes?

Y. Soc. Whom can you mean?

Str. They are a strange crew.

Y. Soc. Why strange?

Str. A minute ago I thought that they were animals of every tribe; for many of them are like lions and centaurs, and many b more like satyrs and such weak and shifty creatures;—protean shapes quickly changing into one another's forms and natures; and now, Socrates, I begin to see who they are.

Y. Soc. Who are they? You seem to be gazing on some strange vision.

Str. Yes; everyone looks strange when you do not know him; and just now I myself fell into this mistake—at first sight, coming suddenly upon him, I did not recognize the politician and his c troop.

Y. Soc. Who is he?

Str. The chief of Sophists and most accomplished of wizards, who must be separated from the true king or Statesman, however difficult that may be, if we are ever to see daylight in the present inquiry.

Y. Soc. That is a hope not lightly to be renounced.

Str. Never, if I can help it; and, first, let me ask you a question.

Y. Soc. What?

d   *Str.* Is not monarchy a recognized form of government?

Y. Soc. Yes.

Str. And, after monarchy, one would place next in order the government of the few?

Y. Soc. Of course.

Str. Is not the third form of government the rule of the multitude, which is called by the name of democracy?

Y. Soc. Certainly.

Str. And do not these three expand in a manner into five, producing out of themselves two other names?

Y. Soc. What are they?

e   *Str.* There is a criterion of voluntary and involuntary, poverty and riches, law and the absence of law, which men nowadays apply to them; the two first they subdivide accordingly, and ascribe to monarchy two forms and two corresponding names, royalty and tyranny.

Y. Soc. Very true.

Str. And any city which has passed into the control of the few is ranked as aristocracy or as oligarchy.

Y. Soc. Certainly.

292   *Str.* Democracy alone, whether rigidly observing the laws or not, and whether the multitude rule over the men of property with their consent or against their consent, always in ordinary language has the same name.

Y. Soc. True.

Str. But do you suppose that any form of government which is defined by these characteristics of the one, the few, or the many, of poverty or wealth, of voluntary or compulsory submission, of written law or the absence of law, can be a right one?

Y. Soc. Indeed, what is there to prevent it?

Str. Reflect; and follow me.   b

Y. Soc. In what direction?

Str. Shall we abide by what we said at first, or shall we retract our words?

Y. Soc. To what do you refer?

Str. If I am not mistaken, we said that royal power was a science?

Y. Soc. Yes.

Str. And a science of a peculiar kind, which was selected out of the rest as having a character which is at once judicial and authoritative?

Y. Soc. Yes.

Str. And of such authoritative science, one kind was concerned with lifeless things and another with living animals; and so we   c
proceeded in the division step by step up to this point, not losing the idea of science, but unable as yet to determine the nature of the particular science?

Y. Soc. True.

Str. Hence we are led to observe that the distinguishing principle of the State cannot be the few or many, the voluntary or involuntary, poverty or riches; but some notion of science must enter into it, if we are to be consistent with what has preceded.

Y. Soc. And we must be consistent.   d

Str. Well, then, our next question must necessarily be, In which of these various forms of States may the science of human government, which is among the greatest of all sciences and most difficult to acquire, be supposed to reside? That we must discover, and then we shall see who are the false politicians who pretend to be politicians but are not, although they persuade many, and shall separate them from the wise king.

Y. Soc. That, as the argument has already intimated, will be our duty.

Str. Do you think that the multitude in a State can attain   e
political science?

Y. Soc. Impossible.

Str. But, perhaps, in a city of a thousand men, there would be a hundred, or say fifty, who could?

Y. Soc. In that case political science would certainly be the easiest of all sciences; we know that there could not be found in a city of that number as many really first-rate draughts-players, if judged by the standard of the rest of Hellas, and there would certainly not be as many kings. For kings we may truly call those who possess royal science, whether they rule or not, as was shown in the previous argument.[1]

293   *Str.* Thank you for reminding me; and the consequence is that any true form of government can only be supposed to be the government of one, two, or, at any rate, of a few.

Y. Soc. Certainly.

Str. And these, whether they rule with the will, or against the will, of their subjects, with written laws or without written laws, and whether they are poor or rich, and whatever be the nature of their rule, must be supposed, according to our present view, to
b   rule on some scientific principle; just as the physician, whether he cures us against our will or with our will, and whatever be his mode of treatment,—incision, burning, or the infliction of some other pain,—whether he practises out of a book or not out of a book, and whether he be rich or poor, whether he purges or reduces in some other way, or even fattens his patients, if that is necessary for the welfare of their bodies, is a physician all the same, so long as he exercises authority over them according to rules of art, and does in fact heal and save those who undergo
c   his treatment. And this we lay down to be the only proper test of the art of medicine, or of any other art of command.

Y. Soc. Quite true.

Str. Then of governments likewise, that alone must be true, and worthy of the name, in which the governors are really found to possess science, and are not mere pretenders, whether they rule according to law or without law, over willing or unwilling
d   subjects, and are rich or poor themselves—none of these things can with any propriety be included in the notion of the ruler.

Y. Soc. True.

Str. And whether with a view to the public good they purge the city by killing some, or exiling some; whether they reduce the size of the body corporate by sending out from the hive swarms of citizens, or, by introducing persons from without, increase it; while they act according to the rules of wisdom and justice, and strive to improve the city, and maintain its health as far as they

---

[1] Cf. *supra*, 259 a.

have the power, the city over which they rule may on account of these characteristics be described as the only true State. All other e governments, so called, are not genuine or real, but only imitations of this, and some of them are better and some of them are worse; the better are said to be well governed, but they are mere imitations like the others.

Y. Soc. I agree, Stranger, in the greater part of what you say; but as to their ruling without laws—the expression has a harsh sound.

Str. You have been too quick for me, Socrates; I was just 294 going to ask you whether you objected to any of my statements. And now I see that we shall have to consider this notion of there being good government without laws.

Y. Soc. Certainly.

Str. There can be no doubt that legislation is in a manner the business of a king, and yet the best thing of all is not that the law should rule, but that a man should rule supposing him to have royal power accompanied by wisdom. Do you see why this is?

Y. Soc. Why?

Str. Because the law does not perfectly comprehend what is noblest and most just for all and therefore cannot enforce what is b best. The differences of men and actions, and the endless irregular movements of human things, do not admit of any universal and simple rule. And no art whatsoever can lay down a rule which will last for all time. Do you agree so far?

Y. Soc. I do.

Str. But the law, it is plain, is always striving to secure this object;—like an obstinate and ignorant tyrant, who will not c allow anything to be done contrary to his appointment, or any question to be asked—not even in sudden changes of circumstances, when something happens to be better than what he commanded for someone.

Y. Soc. Certainly; the law treats us all precisely in the manner which you describe.

Str. A perfectly simple principle can never be applied to a state of things which is the reverse of simple.

Y. Soc. True.

Str. Then if the law is not the perfection of right, why are we d compelled to make laws at all? The reason of this has next to be investigated.

Y. Soc. Certainly.

Str. Let me ask, whether you have not in your city, as there are in other cities, mass exercises with a view to competition in running, wrestling, and the like?

Y. Soc. Yes; they are very common among us.

Str. And what are the rules which are enforced on their pupils by professional trainers or by others having similar authority? Can you remember?

Y. Soc. To what do you refer?

Str. The training-masters do not think it possible to issue minute rules for individuals, or give everyone what is exactly suited to his constitution; they think that they ought to go more

e roughly to work, and to prescribe generally the regimen which will benefit the majority.

Y. Soc. Very true.

Str. And therefore they assign equal amounts of exercise to the whole squad; they send them forth together, and let them rest together from their running, wrestling, or whatever the form of bodily exercise may be.

Y. Soc. True.

295 *Str.* And now observe that the legislator who has to preside over the herd, and to enforce justice in their dealings with one another, will surely not be able, in enacting for the general good, to provide exactly what is suitable for each particular case.

Y. Soc. He cannot be expected to do so.

Str. He will, I suppose, rather lay down laws in a general form for the majority, roughly meeting the needs of individuals, alike in the case of laws which he delivers in writing, and of those unwritten laws which he forms from traditional customs of the country.

Y. Soc. He will be right.

Str. Yes, quite right; for how can he sit at every man's side all

b through his life, prescribing for him the exact particulars of his duty? Who, Socrates, would be equal to such a task? No one who really had the royal science, if he had been able to do this, would have imposed a restriction upon himself by these compositions which are entitled 'laws'.

Y. Soc. So I should infer from what has now been said.

Str. Or rather, my good friend, from what is going to be said.

Y. Soc. And what is that?

Str. Let us put to ourselves the case of a physician, or trainer, who is about to go into a far country, and is expecting to be a long c time away from his patients—thinking that his instructions will not be remembered unless they are written down, he will leave notes of them for the use of his pupils or patients.

Y. Soc. True.

Str. But what would you say, if he came back sooner than he had intended, and, owing to an unexpected change of the winds or other celestial influences, something else happened to be d better for them,—would he not venture to suggest this new remedy, although not contemplated in his former prescription? Would he persist in scrupulous observance of the original law, neither himself giving any new commandments, nor the patient daring to do otherwise than was prescribed, under the idea that this course only was healthy and medicinal, all others noxious and heterodox? If they were proposed in the sphere of science and true art, would not all such enactments be thought utterly e ridiculous?

Y. Soc. Utterly.

Str. And if he who gave laws, written or unwritten, determining what was good or bad, honourable or dishonourable, just or unjust, to the tribes of men who flock together in their several cities, and are governed in accordance with them; if, I say, this expert author of laws were suddenly to come again, or another like to him, is he to be prohibited from changing them?—would 296 not this prohibition be in reality quite as ridiculous as the other?

Y. Soc. Certainly.

Str. Do you know a plausible saying of the common people which is in point?

Y. Soc. I do not recall what you mean at the moment.

Str. They say that if anyone knows how the ancient laws may be improved, he must first persuade his own State of the improvement, and then he may legislate, but not otherwise.

Y. Soc. And are they not right?

Str. I dare say. But supposing that, on failing to persuade them, b he does use some violence for their good, what is this violence to be called? Or rather, before you answer, let me ask the same question in reference to our previous instances.

Y. Soc. What do you mean?

Str. Suppose that a physician, properly qualified in his art, has a patient, of whatever sex or age, whom he compels, when persuasion has failed, to do something for his good which is contrary to the written rules; what is this compulsion to be called? Would you ever dream of calling it by the name specially reserved for an error in the art, namely 'morbific'? Nothing could be more unjust than for the patient to whom such violence c is applied, to charge the physicians who practised the violence, with unskilful conduct, liable to produce disease?

Y. Soc. Most true.

Str. What name do we give to a similar error in the political art? Do we not call it evil, or disgrace, or injustice?

Y. Soc. Quite true.

Str. And so when the citizen, contrary to law and custom, is compelled to do what is juster and better and nobler than he did d before, the last and most absurd thing which he could say in objection to such violence, is that he has incurred disgrace or evil or injustice at the hands of those who compelled him.

Y. Soc. Very true.

Str. And shall we say that the violence, if exercised by a rich man, is just, and if by a poor man, unjust? May not any man, rich or poor, with or without a written code, with the will of the e citizens or against the will of the citizens, do what is for their interest? Is not this the true principle of government, according to which the wise and good man will order the affairs of his 297 subjects? As the pilot, by watching continually over the interests of the ship and of the crew,—not by laying down rules, but by making his art a law,—preserves the lives of his fellow sailors, even so, and in the selfsame way, may there not be a true form of polity created by those who are able to govern in a similar spirit, and who show a strength of art which is superior to the law? Nor can wise rulers ever err, in any action they perform, while they observe the one great rule of distributing perfect justice to b the citizens with intelligence and skill, and are able to preserve them, and, as far as may be, to make them better from being worse.

Y. Soc. No one can deny what has been now said.

Str. Neither, if you consider, can anyone deny the other statement.

Y. Soc. What was it?

Str. We said[1] that no large assembly of persons, whoever they may be, can attain political knowledge, enabling them to order a State wisely, but that our one true form of government is to be found in a small body, or in an individual, and that other c States are to be deemed imitations of this, as we said a little while ago, some for the better and some for the worse.

Y. Soc. What do you mean? I cannot have understood your previous remark about imitations.

Str. And yet it would be most unfortunate if, after making this suggestion, we abandon it and do not seek by the discussion of it to expose the error which prevails in this matter. d

Y. Soc. What do you mean?

Str. The idea which has to be grasped by us is not easy or familiar; but we may attempt to express it thus:—Supposing the government of which I have been speaking to be the only true model, then the others must use the written laws of this—in no other way can they be saved; they will have to do what is now generally approved, although not the best thing in the world.

Y. Soc. What is this?

Str. That no citizen should do anything contrary to the laws, e and that any infringement of them should be punished with death and the most extreme penalties; and this is very right and good when regarded as the second-best thing, if you set aside the first, of which I was just now speaking. Shall I explain the origin of what I call the second-best procedure?

Y. Soc. By all means.

Str. I must again have recourse to my favourite images; through them, and them alone, can I describe kings and rulers.

Y. Soc. What images?

Str. The noble pilot and the wise physician, who 'is worth many another man'[2]—in the similitude of these let us endeavour to discover some image of the king.

Y. Soc. What sort of an image?

Str. Well, such as this:—Suppose us all to reflect that we 298

---

[1] [293 a.] [2] [*Il.* xi. 514.]

suffer hideous treatment at the hands of both of them; the physician saves any whom he wishes to save, and any whom he wishes to maltreat he maltreats—cutting or burning them, and at the same time requiring them to bring him payments, which are a sort of tribute, of which little or nothing is spent upon the sick man, and the greater part is consumed by him and his domestics; and the finale is that he receives money from the
b relations of the sick man or from some enemy of his, and puts him out of the way. And the pilots of ships are guilty of numberless evil deeds of the same kind; they intentionally play false and leave you ashore when the hour of sailing arrives; or they cause mishaps at sea and cast away their freight; and are guilty of other rogueries. Now suppose that we, bearing all this in mind, were to determine, after consideration, that neither of these arts shall any
c longer be allowed to exercise absolute control either over freemen or over slaves, but that we will summon an assembly either of all the people, or of the rich only, and that anybody who likes, whatever may be his calling, or even if he have no calling, may offer an opinion either about seamanship or about diseases—whether as to the manner in which physic or surgical intruments are to be applied to the patient, or again about the vessels and the nautical
d implements which are required in navigation, and how to meet the dangers of winds and waves which are incidental to the voyage, how to behave when encountering pirates, and what is to be done with the old-fashioned galleys, if they have to fight with others of a similar build—and that, whatever shall be decreed by the multitude on these points, whether the advisers are doctors and pilots, or unskilled persons, shall be written down on triangular tablets and columns, or enacted although un-
e written to be national customs; and that in all future time vessels shall be navigated and remedies administered to the patient after this fashion.

Y. Soc. What a strange notion!

Str. Suppose further, that the people are to be governed by men appointed annually, either out of the rich, or out of the whole people, and that they are elected by lot; and that after their election they navigate vessels and heal the sick according to the written rules.

Y. Soc. Worse and worse.

Str. But hear what follows:—When the year of office has expired, all who have governed are to come before a court of review, in which the judges are either selected from the wealthy 299 classes or chosen by lot out of the whole people; and anybody who pleases may be their accuser, and may lay to their charge, that during the past year they have not navigated their vessels or healed their patients according to the letter of the law and the ancient customs of their ancestors; and if either of them is condemned, some of the judges must fix what he is to suffer or pay.

Y. Soc. He who is willing to take a command under such conditions, deserves to suffer any penalty, or pay any amount. b

Str. Yet once more, we shall have to enact that if anyone is detected inquiring into piloting and navigation, or into health and the true nature of medicine, or about the winds, or other conditions of the atmosphere, contrary to the written rules, and has any ingenious notions about such matters, he is not to be called a pilot or physician, but a cloudy prating sophist;— further, on the ground that he is a corrupter of the young, who would persuade them to follow the art of medicine or piloting in c an unlawful manner, and to exercise an arbitrary rule over their patients or ships, anyone who is qualified by law may inform against him, and indict him in some court, and then if he is found to be persuading any, whether young or old, to act contrary to the written law, he is to be punished with the utmost rigour; for no one should presume to be wiser than the laws; and as touching healing and health and piloting and navigation, the nature of them is known to all, for anybody may learn the written laws and d the national customs. If such were the mode of procedure, Socrates, about these sciences and about generalship, and any branch of hunting, or about painting or imitation in general, or carpentry, or any sort of handicraft, or husbandry and the whole art of the culture of plants, or if we were to see an art of rearing horses, or tending herds, or divination, or any ministerial service, or draughts-playing, or any science conversant with number, e whether simple or square or cube, or comprising motion,—I say, if all these things were done in this way according to written regulations, and not according to art, what would be the result?

Y. Soc. It is plain that all the arts would utterly perish, and could never be recovered, because inquiry would be unlawful.

And human life, which is bad enough already, would then become utterly unendurable.

300 *Str.* But what if, while compelling all these operations to be regulated by written law, we were to appoint as the guardian of the laws someone elected by a show of hands or by lot, and he, caring nothing about the written text, should proceed to act contrary to it from motives of interest or favour, and without any claim to knowledge,—would not this be a still worse evil than the former?

Y. Soc. Very true.

b *Str.* To go against the laws, which are based upon long experience, and upon the wisdom of counsellors who have graciously recommended them and persuaded the multitude to pass them, —to venture to do so would, I think, be a far greater error, more ruinous to every kind of action than any adherence to written law?

Y. Soc. Certainly.

c *Str.* Therefore, as there is a danger of this, the next best thing for those who frame a written law on any subject is not to allow either the individual or the multitude to break that law in any respect whatever.

Y. Soc. True.

Str. The laws would be copies of the true particulars of action as far as they admit of being written down from the lips of those who have knowledge?

Y. Soc. Certainly they would.

Str. And, as we were saying, he who has knowledge and is a true Statesman, will do many things within his own sphere of action by his art without regard to the laws, when he is of opinion d that something other than that which he has written down and enjoined to be observed during his absence would be better.

Y. Soc. Yes, we said so.

Str. And any individual or any number of men, having fixed laws, in acting contrary to them with a view to something better, would only be acting, as far as they are able, like the true Statesman?

Y. Soc. Certainly.

Str. If men who had no knowledge did such a thing, they would try to imitate the truth, but they would imitate it very ill; but if

they had knowledge, the imitation would be the perfect truth, e
and an imitation no longer.

Y. Soc. Quite true.

Str. Now, the principle that no great number of men are able
to acquire a knowledge of any art has been already admitted
by us.

Y. Soc. Yes, it has.

Str. Then the royal or political art, if there be such an art,
will never be attained either by most of the wealthy or by the
mass of the people.

Y. Soc. Impossible.

Str. Then the nearest approach which these lower forms of
government can ever make to the true government of the one 301
scientific ruler, is to do nothing contrary to their own written laws
and national customs.

Y. Soc. Very good.

Str. When the rich imitate the true form, such a government
is called aristocracy; and when they are regardless of the laws,
oligarchy.

Y. Soc. True.

Str. Or again, when an individual rules according to law in
imitation of him who knows, we call him a king; as long as the b
monarch rules according to law, we have no separate name to
show whether he rules with opinion or with knowledge.

Y. Soc. To be sure.

Str. Therefore, even when an individual truly possessing
knowledge rules, his name at least will surely be the same—he
will be called a king; and thus the five names of governments,
as they are now reckoned, become one.

Y. Soc. It seems so.

Str. And when an individual ruler governs neither by law nor
by custom, but following in the steps of the true man of science c
pretends that he can only act for the best by violating the written
code,[1] while in reality appetite and ignorance are the motives of
the imitation, may not such a one be called a tyrant?

Y. Soc. Certainly.

Str. And this we believe to be the origin of the tyrant and the

[1] [Or: 'that it is right to violate the written code if thereby one can achieve the
best'.]

king, of oligarchies, and aristocracies, and democracies,—because men are offended at the one monarch, and can never be made to believe that anyone can be worthy of such authority, or is able
d and willing to rule in the spirit of virtue and knowledge, and to dispense what is due to all, justly and holily; they fancy that he will be a despot who will wrong and harm and slay whom he pleases of us; for if there could be such a despot as we describe, they would acknowledge that we ought to be glad to have him, and that he alone would be the happy ruler of a true and perfect State.

Y. Soc. To be sure.

Str. But then, as the State is not like a beehive, and has no
e natural head who is at once recognized to be the superior both in body and in mind, mankind are obliged to meet and compose written laws, endeavouring, as it seems, to approach as nearly as they can to the true form of government.

Y. Soc. True.

Str. And when the foundation upon which States are built is in the letter only and in custom, and their action is not inspired by knowledge, can we wonder, Socrates, at the miseries which there are, and always will be, in them? Any other art, built on
302 such a foundation and thus conducted, would evidently ruin all that it touched. Ought we not rather to wonder at the natural strength of the political bond? For States have endured all this, time out of mind, and yet some of them still remain and are not overthrown, though many of them, like ships at sea, founder from time to time, and perish and have perished and will hereafter perish, through the badness of their pilots and crews, who have the worst sort of ignorance of the highest truths—I mean to say,
b that they are wholly unacquainted with politics, of which, above all other sciences, they believe themselves to have acquired the most perfect knowledge.

Y. Soc. Very true.

Str. Then the question arises:—Which of these untrue forms of government is the least oppressive to its subjects, though they are all oppressive; and which is the worst of them? Here is a consideration which is beside our present purpose, and yet having regard to the whole it seems to influence all our actions: we must **examine** it.

Υ. Soc. Yes, we must.

Str. You may say that of the three forms, the same is at once c the hardest and the easiest.

Υ. Soc. What do you mean?

Str. I am speaking of the three forms of government, which I mentioned at the beginning of this episode in our discussion— monarchy, the rule of the few, and the rule of the many.

Υ. Soc. True.

Str. If we divide each of these we shall have six, from which the true one may be distinguished as a seventh.

Υ. Soc. How would you make the division?

Str. Monarchy, as we said, can be divided into royalty and d tyranny; the rule of the few into aristocracy, which has an auspicious name, and oligarchy; and the rule of the many, which before we treated as single, and named democracy, must now be divided.

Υ. Soc. On what principle of division?

Str. On the same principle as before, although the name is now discovered to have a twofold meaning. For the distinction of e ruling with law or without law applies to this as well as to the rest.

Υ. Soc. Yes.

Str. The division served no useful purpose when we were looking for the perfect State, as we showed before. But now that this has been separated off, and, as we said, the others alone are left for us, the principle of law and the absence of law will bisect them all.

Υ. Soc. That would seem to follow, from the explanation you now give.

Str. Then monarchy, when bound by good prescriptions or laws, is the best of all the six, but when lawless is the most bitter and oppressive to the subject.

Υ. Soc. True.

Str. Whereas the government of the few, like the term 'few' 303 itself, which is intermediate between one and many, must be deemed intermediate in good and evil; but the government of the many is in every respect weak and unable to do either any great good or any great evil, when compared with the others, because the offices are too minutely subdivided and too many

hold them. And this therefore is the worst of all lawful governments, and the best of all lawless ones. If they are all without the
b restraints of law, democracy is the form in which to live is best;
if they are well ordered, then this is the last which you should
choose, as royalty, the first form, is by far the best, with the
exception of the seventh, for that must be ranked apart from
them all, as being among States what God is among men.

Y. Soc. You are quite right, and we should choose that
above all.

Str. The members of all these States, with the exception of the
c one which has knowledge, may be set aside as being not Statesmen but partisans,—upholders of the most monstrous idols, and
themselves idols; and, being the greatest imitators and magicians,
they are also the greatest of Sophists.

Y. Soc. The name of Sophist after many windings in the argument appears to have been most justly fixed upon the politicians,
as they are termed.

Str. And so our satyric drama has been played out; and the
troop of Centaurs and Satyrs, however unwilling to leave the
d stage, have at last been separated from the political science.

Y. Soc. So I perceive.

Str. There remain, however, natures still more troublesome,
because they are more nearly akin to the royal race, and more
difficult to discern; the examination of them may be compared
to the process of refining gold.

Y. Soc. What is your meaning?

Str. The workmen begin by sifting away the earth and stones
e and the like; there remain in a confused mass the valuable
elements akin to gold, which can only be separated by fire,—
copper, silver, and other precious metal;[1] these are at last refined
away with the help of the touchstone, until the gold is left quite
pure.

Y. Soc. Yes, that is the way in which these things are said to
be done.

Str. In like manner, all alien and uncongenial matter has been
separated from political science, and what is precious and of a

---

[1] [Literally: 'and sometimes also *adamant*'. For this metal, which may be haema-
tite or platinum, compare *Tim.* 59 b, and the notes of Rivaud and Bury on that
passage.]

kindred nature has been left; there remain the nobler arts of the general and the judge, and the higher sort of oratory which is an ally of the royal art, and persuades men to do justice, and assists 304 in guiding the helm of States:—How can we best clear away all these, leaving him whom we seek alone and unalloyed?

Y. Soc. That is obviously what has in some way to be attempted.

Str. If the attempt is all that is wanting, he shall certainly be brought to light; and I think that the illustration of music may assist in exhibiting him. Please to answer me a question.

Y. Soc. What question?

Str. There is such a thing as learning music or handicraft arts b in general?

Y. Soc. There is.

Str. And is there any higher art or science, having power to decide which of these arts are and are not to be learned;—what do you say?

Y. Soc. I should answer that there is.

Str. And do we acknowledge this science to be different from the others?

Y. Soc. Yes.

Str. And ought the other sciences to be superior to this, or no single science to any other? Or ought this science to be the over- c seer and governor of all the others?

Y. Soc. The latter.

Str. You mean to say that the science which judges whether we ought to learn or not must be superior to the science which is learned or which teaches?

Y. Soc. Far superior.

Str. And the science which determines whether we ought to persuade or not, must be superior to the science which is able to persuade?

Y. Soc. Of course.

Str. Very good; and to what science do we assign the power of persuading a multitude by a pleasing tale and not by teaching? d

Y. Soc. That power also, I think, must clearly be assigned to rhetoric.

Str. And to what science do we give the power of determining whether we are to employ persuasion or force towards anyone, or to refrain altogether?

Y. Soc. To that science which governs the arts of speech and persuasion.

Str. Which, if I am not mistaken, will be politics?

Y. Soc. Very good.

Str. Rhetoric seems to be quickly distinguished from politics, e being a different species, yet ministering to it.

Y. Soc. Yes.

Str. But what would you think of another sort of power [or science]?

Y. Soc. What is it?

Str. That which decides how military operations against our enemies ought to be conducted—is that to be regarded as a science or not?

Y. Soc. How can generalship and military tactics be regarded as other than a science?

Str. And is the art which is able and knows how to advise whether we are to go to war, or to make peace, the same as this or different?

Y. Soc. If we are to be consistent, we must say different.

305 *Str.* And we must also suppose that this rules the other, if we are not to give up our former notion?

Y. Soc. True.

Str. But, considering how great and terrible the whole art of war is, which other can we venture to designate as its superior but the truly royal art?

Y. Soc. No other.

Str. The art of the general is only ministerial, and therefore we cannot rank it as political?

Y. Soc. Hardly.

b *Str.* Once more, let us consider the power of the righteous judge.

Y. Soc. Very good.

Str. Is it not limited to deciding the dealings of men with one another to be just or unjust in accordance with the standard which he receives from the king and legislator,—showing his own peculiar virtue only in this, that he will refuse to be perverted by gifts, or fears, or pity, or by any sort of favour or enmity, into c deciding the suits of men with one another contrary to the appointment of the legislator?

Y. Soc. Yes; his office is such as you describe.

Str. Then the inference is that the power of the judge, again, is not royal, but only the power of a guardian of the laws which ministers to the royal power?

Y. Soc. So it appears.

Str. The review of all these sciences, then, shows that none of them is political or royal. For the truly royal ought not itself to d act, but to rule over those who are able to act; the king ought to know what is and what is not a fitting opportunity for taking the initiative in matters of the greatest importance within the State, whilst others should execute his orders.

Y. Soc. True.

Str. And, therefore, the arts which we have described, as they have no authority over themselves or one another, but are each of them concerned with some special action of their own, have, as they ought to have, special names corresponding to their several actions.

Y. Soc. I agree.   e

Str. But the science which is over them all, and has charge of the laws, and of all matters affecting the State, and truly weaves them all into one, if we would describe it under a name characteristic of their common nature,[1] most deservedly we may call 'politics'.

Y. Soc. Exactly so.

Str. Then, now that we have discovered the various classes in a State,[2] shall I analyse politics after the pattern which weaving supplied?

Y. Soc. I greatly wish that you would.   306

Str. Then I must describe the nature of the royal art of weaving, and show the manner of its operation, and the kind of texture which it produces.

Y. Soc. Clearly.

Str. A task has to be accomplished, which, although difficult, appears to be necessary.

Y. Soc. Certainly the attempt must be made.

Str. To assume that one part of virtue differs in kind from

[1] [Others translate: 'if we would describe its power by the name reserved for the commonwealth, we may most deservedly call it "politics"'.]
[2] Cf. *supra*, 287-90, 303-5.

another, is a position easily assailable by contentious disputants, who appeal to popular opinion.

b   *Y. Soc.* I do not understand.

Str. Let me put the matter in another way: I suppose that you would consider courage to be a part of virtue?

Y. Soc. Certainly I should.

Str. And you would think temperance to be different from courage; and likewise to be a part of virtue?

Y. Soc. True.

Str. I shall venture to put forward a strange theory about them.

Y. Soc. What is it?

Str. That they are two principles which, in a certain sense,
c thoroughly hate one another and are antagonistic throughout a great part of nature.

Y. Soc. How do you mean?

Str. I am stating a most unusual view—for all the parts of virtue are, I think, commonly said to be friendly to one another.

Y. Soc. Yes.

Str. Then let us carefully investigate whether this is universally true, or whether there are not parts of virtue which are at war with their kindred in some respect.

Y. Soc. Tell me how we shall consider that question.

Str. We must extend our inquiry to all those things which we consider beautiful and at the same time place in two opposite classes.

Y. Soc. Explain; what are they?

Str. Acuteness and quickness, whether in body or soul or in the
d movement of sound, and the imitations of them which painting and music supply, you must have praised yourself before now, or been present when others praised them.

Y. Soc. Certainly.

Str. And do you remember the terms in which, in such instances, they are praised?

Y. Soc. I do not.

Str. I wonder whether I can explain to you in words the thought which is passing in my mind.

e   *Y. Soc.* Why not?

Str. You fancy that this is all so easy: well, let us consider

these notions with reference to the opposite classes under which
they fall. When we admire quickness and energy and acuteness,
whether of thought or body or sound, as we do in numerous
instances of action, we express our praise of the quality which we
admire by one word, and that one word is manliness or courage.

Υ. Soc. How?

Str. We speak of an action as energetic and brave, quick and
manly, and vigorous too; and when we apply the name of which
I speak as the common attribute of all these natures, we certainly
praise them.

Υ. Soc. True.   307

Str. And on the contrary, do we not often praise the quiet
strain of action also?

Υ. Soc. Yes, vehemently.[1]

Str. And do we not then say the opposite of what we said of
the other?

Υ. Soc. How do you mean?

Str. We exclaim, How calm! How temperate! in admiration of
the slow and quiet working of the intellect, and of steadiness and
gentleness in action, of smoothness and depth of voice, and of all
rhythmical movement and of music in general, when these have b
a proper solemnity. Of all such actions we predicate not courage,
but a name indicative of order.

Υ. Soc. Very true.

Str. But when, on the other hand, either of these is out of place,
the names of either are changed into terms of censure.

Υ. Soc. How so?

Str. Too great sharpness or quickness or hardness is termed
violence or madness; too great slowness or weight or gentleness is
called cowardice or sluggishness; and we may observe, that for c
the most part these qualities, and the temperance and manliness
of the opposite characters, are arrayed as enemies on opposite
sides, and do not mingle with one another in their respective
actions; and if we pursue the inquiry, we shall find that men who
have these different qualities of mind differ from one another.

Υ. Soc. In what respect?

Str. In all those instances which I just now mentioned, and

---

[1] [Apparently a witticism of the same kind as is found at *Phil.* 24 b, where
Protarchus has used the same words, καὶ σφόδρα γε.]

d very likely in many others. According to their respective affinities to either class of actions they distribute praise and blame,— praise to the actions which are akin to their own, blame to those of the opposite party—and out of this many quarrels and occasions of quarrel arise among them.

Y. Soc. True.

Str. The difference between the two classes is, so far, a trivial concern; but in a State, and when affecting really important matters, becomes of all disorders the most hateful.

Y. Soc. To what do you refer?

e *Str.* To nothing short of the whole regulation of human life. For the orderly class are always ready to lead a peaceful life, quietly doing their own business; this is their manner of behaving with all men at home, and they are equally ready to find some way of keeping the peace with foreign States. And on account of this fondness of theirs for peace, which is often out of season where their influence prevails, they become by degrees unwarlike, and bring up their young men to be like themselves; they are at the mercy of their enemies; whence in a few years they and their children and the whole city often pass imperceptibly from the condition of freemen into that of slaves.

308 *Y. Soc.* What a cruel fate!

Str. And now think of what happens with those who tend rather towards courage. By perpetually inciting their country to go to war, owing to their excessive love of the military life, do they not raise up enemies against themselves many and mighty, and either utterly ruin their native land or enslave and subject it to its foes?

b *Y. Soc.* That, again, is true.

Str. Must we not admit, then, that where these two classes exist, they always feel the greatest antipathy and antagonism towards one another?

Y. Soc. We cannot deny it.

Str. And returning to the inquiry with which we began, have we not found that two considerable portions of virtue are naturally at variance with one another, and give rise to a similar opposition in the characters who are endowed with them?

Y. Soc. True.

Str. Let us consider a further point.

Y. Soc. What is it?

Str. I want to know, whether any constructive art will make c any thing within its own range, even the most trivial, out of an assortment of bad and good materials, if this can be helped? does not all art rather reject the bad as far as possible, and accept the good and fit materials, and from these elements, which will in part be like, in part unlike, gathering them all into one, produce a thing which is single in its power and its form?

Y. Soc. To be sure.

Str. Then the true and natural art of statesmanship will never d allow any State to be formed by a combination of good and bad men, if this can be avoided; but will evidently begin by testing human natures in play, and after testing them, will entrust them to proper teachers who are the ministers of her purposes—she will herself give orders, and maintain authority; just as the art of weaving maintains care and authority over the carders and all the others who prepare the material for weaving, commanding the subsidiary arts to execute such works as she deems necessary e for the weaving, which she herself must perform.

Y. Soc. Quite true.

Str. In like manner, the royal science appears to me to be the mistress of all lawful educators and instructors, and having this queenly power, will not permit them to train men in pursuits which will not produce some trait of character suited to her own work of synthesis, but will urge them to confine their education to these. Those who can have no share of manliness and temperance, or any other virtuous inclination, and, from the necessity of an evil nature, are violently carried away to godlessness and insolence and injustice, she gets rid of by death and exile, and punishes them with the greatest of disgraces.

Y. Soc. That is commonly said.

Str. But those who are wallowing in ignorance and baseness 309 she bows under the yoke of slavery.

Y. Soc. Quite right.

Str. The rest of the citizens, out of whom, with the help of education, something noble may be made, and who are capable of being combined by an expert hand, the kingly art blends and b weaves together; taking on the one hand those whose natures tend rather to courage, and viewing their firm character as the warp, and on the other hand those which incline to order and gentleness, and in the same image can be represented as spun thick and soft, after the manner of the woof—these, which are naturally opposed, she seeks to bind and weave together in the following manner——

Y. Soc. In what manner?

c   *Str.* First of all, she takes the eternal element of the soul and binds it with a divine cord, to which it is akin, and then the animal nature, and binds that with human cords.

Y. Soc. I do not understand what you mean.

Str. The meaning is, that the opinion about the honourable and the just and good and their opposites, which is true and confirmed by reason, is a divine principle, and when implanted in the soul, is implanted, as I maintain, in a nature of heavenly birth.

Y. Soc. Yes; what else should it be?

d   *Str.* Only the Statesman and the good legislator, having the inspiration of the royal muse, can implant this opinion, and he, only in the rightly educated, whom we were just now describing.

Y. Soc. Likely enough.

Str. But him who has no such power, we will not designate by any of the names which are the subject of the present inquiry.

Y. Soc. Very right.

Str. The courageous soul when attaining this truth becomes e civilized, and can thus be most surely rendered capable of partaking of justice; but should she not attain it, will be inclined to brutality. Is not that true?

Y. Soc. Certainly.

Str. And again, the peaceful and orderly nature, if sharing in these opinions, becomes truly temperate and wise, as far as this may be in a State, but if deprived of them, deservedly obtains the ignominious repute of silliness.

Y. Soc. Quite true.

Str. Can we say that such a connexion as this will lastingly unite the evil with one another or with the good, or that any science would seriously think of using a bond of this kind to join such materials?

Y. Soc. Impossible.

310   *Str.* But in those who were originally of a noble nature, and who have been nurtured in noble ways, and in those only, may we not say that union is implanted by law, and that it is for them

that art has this medicine to prescribe, and that this union of dissimilar and contrary parts of virtue is, as I have said, a bond of a diviner sort?

Y. Soc. Very true.

Str. Where this divine bond exists there is no difficulty in imagining, or when you have imagined, in creating, the other bonds, which are human only.

Y. Soc. How is that, and what bonds do you mean? b

Str. Rights of intermarriage, and ties which are formed between States by giving and taking children in marriage, or between individuals by private betrothals and espousals. For most persons form marriage connexions without due regard to what is best for the procreation of children.

Y. Soc. In what way?

Str. They seek after wealth and power, which in matrimony are objects not worthy even of a serious censure.

Y. Soc. There is no need to consider them at all.

Str. More reason is there to consider the practice of those who make family their chief aim, and to indicate their error. c

Y. Soc. Quite true.

Str. They act on no true principle at all, since they seek momentary ease and receive with open arms those who are like themselves, and hate those who are unlike them, being principally influenced by feelings of dislike.

Y. Soc. How so?

Str. The quiet orderly class seek for natures like their own, and as far as they can they marry and give in marriage exclusively in this class, and the courageous do the same; they seek natures like d their own, whereas they should both do precisely the opposite.

Y. Soc. How and why is that?

Str. Because courage, when untempered by the gentler nature during many generations, may at first bloom and strengthen, but at last bursts forth into downright madness.

Y. Soc. Like enough.

Str. And then, again, the soul which is overfull of modesty and has no element of courageous energy, and is thus transmitted e for many successive generations, is apt to grow too indolent, and at last to become utterly paralysed and useless.

Y. Soc. That, again, is quite likely.

M m

Str. It was of these bonds I said that there would be no difficulty in creating them, if only both classes originally held the same opinion about the honourable and good;—indeed, in this single work, the whole process of royal weaving is comprised—never to allow temperate natures to be separated from the brave, but to weave them together, like the warp and the woof, by common sentiments and honours and reputation, and by the giving of pledges to one another; and out of them forming one smooth and even web, always to entrust to them jointly the offices of State.

Y. Soc. How do you mean?

Str. Where one officer only is needed, you must choose a ruler who has both these qualities—when many, you must mingle some of each; for the temperate ruler is very careful and just and safe, but is wanting in vigour, and in that ruthless energy which achieves its object.

Y. Soc. Certainly, that is very true.

Str. The character of the courageous, on the other hand, falls short of the former in justice and caution, but has the power of action in a remarkable degree; and where either of these two qualities is wanting, there cities cannot altogether prosper either in their public or private life.

Y. Soc. Certainly they cannot.

Str. This then we declare to be the completion of the web of political action, which is created by a direct intertexture of the brave and temperate natures, whenever the royal science has drawn the two minds into communion with one another by unanimity and friendship, and having perfected the noblest and best of all the webs which political life admits, and enfolding therein all other inhabitants of cities, whether slaves or freemen, binds them in one fabric and governs and presides over them, and in so far as to be happy is vouchsafed to a city, in no particular fails to secure their happiness.

Y. Soc. Your picture, Stranger, of the king and statesman, no less than of the Sophist, is quite perfect.[1]

---

[1] [Several German scholars, following Schleiermacher, propose to assign this remark to the *elder* Socrates. Campbell and Burnet object that he would not be likely to interpose without giving young Socrates time to assent to the last proposition.]

PHILEBUS

INTRODUCTION AND ANALYSIS

THE *Philebus* appears to be one of the later writings of Plato, in which the style has begun to alter, and the dramatic and poetical element has become subordinate to the speculative and philosophical. In the development of abstract thought great advances have been made on the *Protagoras* or the *Phaedrus*, and even on the *Republic*. But there is a corresponding diminution of artistic skill, a want of character in the persons, a laboured march in the dialogue, and a degree of confusion and incompleteness in the general design. As in the speeches of Thucydides, the multiplication of ideas seems to interfere with the power of expression. Instead of the equally diffused grace and ease of the earlier dialogues there occur two or three highly wrought passages (pp. 15, 16, 63); instead of the ever-flowing play of humour, now appearing, now concealed, but always present, are inserted a good many bad jests, as we may venture to term them (cf. 17 e, 23 b, d, 28 c, 29 b, 30 e, 34 d, 36 b, 43 a, 46 a, 62 b). We may observe an attempt at artificial ornament (43 e, 53 d, e), and far-fetched modes of expression (48 d, 65 a); also clamorous demands on the part of his companions that Socrates shall answer his own questions (54 b, 57 a), as well as other defects of style, which remind us of the *Laws*. The connexion is often abrupt and inharmonious (24 c, &c.), and, at 42 d, e, 43 a, 48 a, b, 49, 50, far from clear. Many points require further explanation; e.g. the reference of pleasure to the indefinite class (31 a), compared with the assertion which almost immediately follows, that pleasure and pain naturally have their seat in the third or mixed class:[1] these two statements are unreconciled. In like manner, the table of goods does not distinguish between the two heads of measure and symmetry (66 a, b); and though a hint is given that the divine mind has the first place (22 c), nothing is said of this in the final summing-up. The relation of the goods to the sciences does not appear; though dialectic may be thought to correspond to the highest good, the sciences and arts and true opinions are enumerated in the fourth class. At 50 d, 67 b, we seem to have an intimation of a further discussion, in which some topics lightly passed over were to receive a fuller consideration. The various uses of the word 'mixed',

---

[1] [This may simply mean that the body, in which pleasure and pain arise, belongs to this class.]

for the mixed life, the mixed class of elements, the mixture of pleasures, or of pleasure and pain, are a further source of perplexity. Our ignorance of the opinions which Plato is attacking is also an element of obscurity. Many things in a controversy might seem relevant, if we knew to what they were intended to refer. But no conjecture will enable us to supply what Plato has not told us; or to explain, from our fragmentary knowledge of them, the relation in which his doctrine stood to the Eleatic being or the Megarian good, or to the theories of Aristippus or Antisthenes respecting pleasure. Nor are we able to say how far Plato in the *Philebus* conceives the finite and infinite (which occur both in the fragments of Philolaus and in the Pythagorean table of opposites) in the same manner as contemporary Pythagoreans.

There is little in the characters which is worthy of remark. The Socrates of the *Philebus* is devoid of any touch of Socratic irony, though here, as in the *Phaedrus* (235 c), he twice attributes the flow of his ideas to a sudden inspiration (20 b, 25 b, c). The interlocutor Protarchus, the son of Callias, who has been a hearer of Gorgias (58 a), is supposed to begin as a disciple of the partisans of pleasure, but is drawn over to the opposite side by the arguments of Socrates. The instincts of ingenuous youth are easily induced to take the better part. Philebus, who has withdrawn from the argument, is several times brought back again (18, 19, 22, 28), that he may support pleasure, of which he remains to the end the uncompromising advocate. On the other hand, the youthful group of listeners by whom he is surrounded, 'Philebus' boys' as they are termed, whose presence is several times intimated (16 a, b, 19 d, 67 b), are described as all of them at last convinced by the arguments of Socrates. They bear a very faded resemblance to the interested audiences of the *Charmides*, *Lysis*, or *Protagoras*. Other signs of relation to external life in the dialogue, or references to contemporary things and persons, with the single exception of the allusions to the anonymous enemies of pleasure (44 b, c), and the teachers of the flux (43 a), there are none.[1]

---

[1] [The subjects with which Plato is here concerned, namely, the relation between pleasure and the good life, and the psychology of pleasure, pain, and desire, are of a kind which may well have interested him at any period; and it is clear from the studied vagueness of his allusions that he proposes rather to examine general tendencies than to criticize individuals. Nevertheless, it is clear that there are frequent allusions to the contemporary situation, the meaning of which would have been clear to the first readers. It is no longer assumed that Plato was here concerned with the hedonism of Aristippus and the opposing views of the Cynics. It is clear from various passages in Aristotle's *Nicomachean Ethics*, Books vii and x, that Plato wrote with reference to a debate which had arisen in the Academy towards the end of his life. The names Protarchus and Philebus, which are uncommon, may be

The omission of the doctrine of recollection, derived from a previous state of existence, is a note of progress in the philosophy of Plato. The transcendental theory of pre-existent Ideas, which is chiefly discussed by him in the *Meno*, the *Phaedo*, and the *Phaedrus*, has given way to a psychological one. The omission is rendered more significant by his having occasion to speak of memory as the basis of desire. Of the Ideas he treats in the same sceptical spirit (15 a, b) which appears in his criticism of them in the *Parmenides* (131 ff.). He touches on the same difficulties and he gives no answer to them. His mode of speaking of the analytical and synthetical processes (16 b ff.) may be compared with his discussion of the same subject in the *Phaedrus* (265, 266); here he dwells on the importance of dividing the genera into all the species, while in the *Phaedrus* he conveys the same truth in a figure, when he speaks of carving the whole, which is described under the image of a victim, into parts or members, 'according to their natural articulation, without breaking any of them'. There is also a difference, which may be noted, between the two dialogues. For whereas in the *Phaedrus*, and also in the *Symposium*, the dialectician is described as a sort of enthusiast or lover, in the *Philebus*, as in all the later writings of Plato, the element of love is wanting; the topic is only introduced, as in the *Republic*, by

pseudonyms covering people who were still alive at the time of writing. Philebus' habit of addressing his companions as 'boys' (16 a, b) seems to mark him as an associate of the Pythagoreans.

Eudoxus of Cnidos, as we know from Aristotle, maintained that pleasure is the highest good not only for man, but for all sentient beings, arguing from the universal pursuit of pleasure and avoidance of pain. Speusippus denied the validity of such an argument, held that both pleasure and pain might be ranked as evils, and brought various formal arguments to show that pleasure cannot be a good. It was probably he who maintained that, if pleasure is by definition a process or a movement, it cannot be the highest good (cf. *Phil.* 53 d ff.) There are several references in the *Philebus* to the argument from the pursuit of pleasure by animals, which Aristotle attributes to Eudoxus (11 b, 60 a, 67 b).

However, it need not be assumed that the dialogue was written exclusively with reference to this debate. Plato had, of course, been familiar with hedonistic views, and with the principal objections to them, since the time of his earliest dialogues; moreover, the account of pleasure and pain which he gives in the *Philebus* and *Timaeus* is not unlike that which he had outlined long before, in less exact terms, in the *Gorgias* and *Republic*. The dialogue is also an important part of his *personal* endeavour to reach a satisfactory solution of metaphysical problems by dialectic, and is intelligible only in the light of the *Sophist* and *Timaeus*.

The persons to whom allusion is made at 44 b–c and 53 c cannot therefore be identified with certainty; but the background to the dialogue has been made much clearer by Burnet and other commentators on the *Ethics*, and by the latest editors of the *Philebus*, A. Diès (1940, in the *Collection G. Budé*) and R. Hackforth, *Plato's Examination of Pleasure* (1945). Other references will be given below in notes appended to this Introduction.]

way of illustration (cf. 53 d, *Rep.* v. 474 d, e). On other subjects of which they treat in common, such as the nature and kinds of pleasure, true and false opinion, the nature of the good, the order and relation of the sciences, the *Republic* is less advanced than the *Philebus*, which contains, perhaps, more metaphysical truth more obscurely expressed than any other Platonic dialogue. Here, as Plato expressly tells us, he is 'forging weapons of another make' (23 b), i.e. new categories and modes of conception, though 'some of the old ones might do again'.

But if superior in thought and dialectical power, the *Philebus* falls very far short of the *Republic* in fancy and feeling. The development of the reason undisturbed by the emotions seems to be the ideal at which Plato aims in his later dialogues. There is no mystic enthusiasm or rapturous contemplation of Ideas. Whether we attribute this change to the greater feebleness of age, or to the development of the quarrel between philosophy and poetry in Plato's own mind, or perhaps, in some degree, to a carelessness about artistic effect, when he was absorbed in abstract ideas, we can hardly be wrong in assuming, amid such a variety of indications, derived from style as well as subject, that the *Philebus* belongs to the later period of his life and authorship. But in this, as in all the later writings of Plato, there are not wanting thoughts and expressions in which he rises to his highest level (15, 16, 17, 63, 67).

The plan is complicated, or rather, perhaps, the want of plan renders the progress of the dialogue difficult to follow. A few leading ideas seem to emerge: the relation of the one and many, the four original elements, the kinds of pleasure, the kinds of knowledge, the scale of goods. These are only partially connected with one another. The dialogue is not rightly entitled 'Concerning pleasure' or 'Concerning good', but should rather be described as treating of the relations of pleasure and knowledge, after they have been duly analysed, to the good. (1) The question is asked, whether pleasure or wisdom is the chief good, or some nature higher than either; and if the latter, how pleasure and wisdom are related to this higher good. (2) Before we can reply with exactness, we must know the kinds of pleasure and the kinds of knowledge. (3) But still we may affirm generally, that the combined life of pleasure and wisdom or knowledge has more of the character of the good than either of them when isolated. (4) To determine which of them partakes most of the higher nature, we must know under which of the four unities or elements they respectively fall. These are, first, the infinite; secondly, the finite; thirdly, the union of the two; fourthly, the cause of the union. Pleasure is of the first, wisdom or knowledge of the third class, while reason or mind is akin to the fourth or highest.

(5) Pleasures are of two kinds, the mixed and unmixed. Of mixed pleasures there are three classes—(*a*) those in which both the pleasures and pains are corporeal, as in eating and hunger; (*β*) those in which there is a pain of the body and pleasure of the mind, as when you are hungry and are looking forward to a feast; (*γ*) those in which the pleasure and pain are both mental. Of unmixed pleasures there are four kinds: those of sight, hearing, smell, knowledge.

(6) The sciences are likewise divided into two classes, theoretical and productive: of the latter, one part is pure, the other impure. The pure part consists of arithmetic, mensuration, and weighing. Arts like carpentering, which have an exact measure, are to be regarded as higher than music, which for the most part is mere guess-work. But there is also a higher arithmetic, and a higher mensuration, which is exclusively theoretical; and a dialectical science, which is higher still and the truest and purest knowledge.

(7) We are now able to determine the composition of the perfect life. First, we admit the pure pleasures and the pure sciences; secondly, the impure sciences, but not the impure pleasures. We have next to discover what element of goodness is contained in this mixture. There are three criteria of goodness—beauty, symmetry, truth. These are clearly more akin to reason than to pleasure, and will enable us to fix the places of both of them in the scale of good. First in the scale is measure; the second place is assigned to symmetry; the third, to reason and wisdom; the fourth, to knowledge and true opinion; the fifth, to pure pleasures; and here the Muse says 'Enough'.

'Bidding farewell to Philebus and Socrates', we may now consider the metaphysical conceptions which are presented to us. These are (I) the paradox of unity and plurality; (II) the table of categories or elements; (III) the kinds of pleasure; (IV) the kinds of knowledge; (V) the conception of the good. We may then proceed to examine (VI) the relation of the *Philebus* to the *Republic*, and to other dialogues.

I. The paradox of the one and many originated in the restless dialectic of Zeno, who sought to prove the absolute existence of the one by showing the contradictions that are involved in admitting the existence of the many (cf. *Parm.* 128 ff.). Zeno illustrated the contradiction by well-known examples taken from outward objects. But Socrates seems to intimate that the time had arrived for discarding these hackneyed illustrations; such difficulties had long been solved by common sense (*solvitur ambulando*); the fact of the co-existence of opposites was a sufficient answer to them. He will leave them to Cynics and Eristics; the youth of Athens may discourse of them to their parents. To no rational man could the circumstance that the body is one, but has many members, be any longer a stumbling-block.

Plato's difficulty seems to begin in the region of ideas. He cannot understand how an absolute unity, such as the Eleatic being, can be broken up into a number of individuals, or be in and out of them at once. Philosophy had so deepened or intensified the nature of one or Being, by the thoughts of successive generations, that the mind could no longer imagine 'Being' as in a state of change or division. To say that the verb of existence is the copula, or that unity is a mere unit, is to us easy; but to the Greek in a particular stage of thought such an analysis involved the same kind of difficulty as the conception of God existing both in and out of the world would to ourselves. Nor was he assisted by the analogy of sensible objects. The sphere of mind was dark and mysterious to him; but instead of being illustrated by sense, the greatest light appeared to be thrown on the nature of ideas when they were contrasted with sense.

Both here and in the *Parmenides* (129 ff.), where similar difficulties are raised, Plato seems prepared to desert his ancient ground. He cannot tell the relation in which abstract ideas stand to one another, and therefore he transfers the one and many out of his transcendental world, and proceeds to lay down practical rules for their application to different branches of knowledge. As in the *Republic* he supposes the philosopher to proceed by regular steps, until he arrives at the Idea of good; as in the *Sophist* and *Politicus* he insists that in dividing the whole into its parts we should bisect in the middle in the hope of finding species; as in the *Phaedrus* (see above) he would have 'no limb broken' of the organism of knowledge;—so in the *Philebus* he urges the necessity of filling up all the intermediate links which occur (compare Bacon's *media axiomata*) in the passage from unity to infinity. With him the idea of science may be said to anticipate science; at a time when the sciences were not yet divided, he wants to impress upon us the importance of classification; neither neglecting the many individuals, nor attempting to count them all, but finding the genera and species under which they naturally fall. Here, then, and in the parallel passages of the *Phaedrus* and of the *Sophist*, is found the germ of the most fruitful notion of modern science.

At p. 15 Plato describes with ludicrous exaggeration the influence exerted by the one and many on the minds of young men in their first fervour of metaphysical enthusiasm (cf. *Rep.* vii. 539). But they are none the less an everlasting quality of reason or reasoning which never grows old in us. At first we have but a confused conception of them, analogous to the eyes blinking at the light in the *Republic*. To this Plato opposes the revelation from Heaven of the real relations of them, which some Prometheus, who gave the true fire from heaven, is supposed to have imparted to us. Plato is speaking at 15, 16 of two things—(1) the crude notion of the one and many, which powerfully affects the ordinary mind when first beginning to think (15 d–16 a); (2) the same notion when cleared up by the help of dialectic (16 c–e).

To us the problem of the one and many has lost its chief interest and perplexity. We readily acknowledge that a whole has many parts, that the continuous is also the divisible, that in all objects of sense there is a one and many, and that a like principle may be applied by analogy to purely intellectual conceptions. If we attend to the meaning of the words, we are compelled to admit that two contradictory statements are true. But the antinomy is so familiar as to be scarcely observed by us. Our sense of the contradiction, like Plato's, only begins in a higher sphere, when we speak of necessity and free-will, of mind and body, of Three Persons and One Substance, and the like. The world of knowledge is always dividing more and more; every truth is at first the enemy of every other truth. Yet without this division there can be no truth; nor any complete truth without the reunion of the parts into a whole. And hence the coexistence of opposites in the unity of the idea is regarded by Hegel as the supreme principle of philosophy; and the law of contradiction, which is affirmed by logicians to be an ultimate principle of the human mind, is displaced by another law, which asserts the coexistence of contradictories as imperfect and divided elements of the truth. Without entering further into the depths of Hegelianism, we may remark that this and all similar attempts to reconcile antinomies have their origin in the old Platonic problem of the 'one and many'.

II. 1. The first of Plato's categories or elements is the infinite. This is the negative of measure or limit; the unthinkable, the unknowable; of which nothing can be affirmed; the mixture or chaos which preceded distinct kinds in the creation of the world; the first vague impression of sense; the more or less which refuses to be reduced to rule, having certain affinities with evil, with pleasure, with ignorance, and which in the scale of being is farthest removed from the beautiful and good. To a Greek of the age of Plato, the idea of an infinite mind would have been an absurdity. He would have insisted that 'the good is of the nature of the finite', and that the infinite is a mere negative, which is on the level of sensation, and not of thought. He was aware that there was a distinction between the infinitely great and the infinitely small, but he would have equally denied the claim of either to true existence. Of that positive infinity, or infinite reality, which we attribute to God, he had no conception.

The Greek conception of the infinite would be more truly described, in our way of speaking, as the indefinite. To us, the notion of infinity is subsequent rather than prior to the finite, expressing not absolute vacancy or negation, but only the removal of limit or restraint, which we suppose to exist not before but after we have already set bounds to thought and matter, and divided them after their kinds. From different points of view, either the finite or infinite may be looked upon respectively both as positive and negative (cf. *Omnis determinatio est negatio*); and the conception of the one determines that of the other. The Greeks and the moderns seem to be nearly at the opposite poles in their manner of regarding them. And both are surprised when they make the discovery, as Plato has done in the *Sophist*, how large an element negation forms in the framework of their thoughts.

2, 3. The finite element which mingles with and regulates the infinite is best expressed to us by the word 'law'. It is that which measures all things and assigns to them their limit; which preserves them in their natural state, and brings them within the sphere of human cognition. This is described by the terms harmony, health, order, perfection, and the like. All things, in as far as they are good, even pleasures, which are for the most part indefinite, partake of this element. We should be wrong in attributing to Plato the conception of laws of nature derived from observation and experiment. And yet he has as intense a conviction as any modern philosopher that nature does not proceed by chance. But observing that the wonderful construction of number and figure, which he had within himself, and which seemed to be prior to himself, explained a part of the phenomena of the external world, he extended their principles to the whole, finding in them the true type both of human life and of the order of nature.

Two other points may be noticed respecting the third class. First, that Plato seems to be unconscious of any interval or chasm which separates the finite from the infinite. The one is in various ways and degrees working in the other. Hence he has implicitly answered the difficulty with which he started, of how the one could remain one and yet be divided among many individuals, or 'how ideas could be in and out of themselves', and the like. Secondly, that in this mixed class we find the idea of beauty. Good, when exhibited under the aspect of measure or symmetry, becomes beauty (64 e). And if we translate his language into corresponding modern terms, we shall not be far wrong in saying that here, as well as in the *Republic*, Plato conceives beauty under the idea of proportion.[1]

4. Last and highest in the list of principles or elements is the cause of the union of the finite and infinite, to which Plato ascribes the order of the world. Reasoning from man to the universe, he argues that as there is a mind in the one, there must be a mind in the other, which he identifies with the royal mind of Zeus.[2] This is the first cause of which 'our ancestors spoke', as he says, appealing to tradition, in the *Philebus* as well as in the *Timaeus*. The 'one and many' is also supposed to have been revealed by tradition. For the mythical element has not altogether disappeared.

Some characteristic differences may here be noted, which distinguish the ancient from the modern mode of conceiving God.

a. To Plato, the idea of God or mind is both personal and impersonal. Nor in ascribing, as appears to us, both these attributes to him, and in speaking of God both in the masculine and neuter gender, did he seem to himself inconsistent. For the difference between the personal and impersonal was not marked to him as to ourselves. We make a fundamental distinction between a thing and a person, while to Plato, by the help of various intermediate abstractions, such as end, good, cause, they appear almost to meet in one, or to be two aspects of the same. Hence, without any reconciliation or even remark, in the *Republic* he speaks at one time of God or Gods, and at another time of the Good. So in the *Phaedrus* he seems to pass unconsciously from the concrete to the abstract conception of the Ideas in the same dialogue. Nor in the *Philebus* is he careful to show in what relation the idea of the divine mind stands to the supreme principle of measure.

β. Again, to us there is a strongly marked distinction between a first cause and a final cause. And we should commonly identify a first cause with God, and the final cause with the world, which is His work. But Plato, though not a Pantheist, and very far from confounding God with the world, tends to identify the first with the final cause. The cause of the union of the finite and infinite might be described as a higher law; the final measure which is the highest expression of the good may also be described as the supreme law. Both these conceptions are realized chiefly by the help of the material world; and

[1] [Holding that the belief in objective Ideas has long before this been abandoned, Jowett does not need to ask what place Plato intends them to occupy in the present division. Various views on this subject are examined by R. G. Bury, Appendix D, and by Grube, *Plato's Thought*, 301 ff.]

[2] [The form of the argument here may owe something to Diogenes of Apollonia, who certainly influenced Socrates and other Athenian thinkers of the fifth century. See Jaeger, *Theology of the Early Greek Philosophers* (1947), p. 246.]

therefore when we pass into the sphere of ideas can hardly be distinguished.

The four principles are required for the determination of the relative places of pleasure and wisdom. Plato has been saying that we should proceed by regular steps from the one to the many. Accordingly, before assigning the precedence either to good or pleasure, he must first find out and arrange in order the general principles of things. Mind is ascertained to be akin to the nature of the cause, while pleasure is found in the infinite or indefinite class. We may now proceed to divide pleasure and knowledge after their kinds.

III. 1. Plato speaks of pleasure as indefinite, as relative, as a generation, and in all these points of view as in a category distinct from good. For again we must repeat, that to the Greek 'the good is of the nature of the finite', and, like virtue, either is, or is nearly allied to, knowledge. The modern philosopher would remark that the indefinite is equally real with the definite. Health and mental qualities are in the concrete undefined; they are nevertheless real goods, and Plato rightly regards them as falling under the finite class. Again, we are able to define objects or ideas, not in so far as they are in the mind, but in so far as they are manifested externally, and can therefore be reduced to rule and measure. And if we adopt the test of definiteness, the pleasures of the body are more capable of being defined than any other pleasures. As in art and knowledge generally, we proceed from without inwards, beginning with facts of sense, and passing to the more ideal conceptions of mental pleasure, happiness, and the like.

2. Pleasure is depreciated as relative, while good is exalted as absolute. But this distinction seems to arise from an unfair mode of regarding them; the abstract idea of the one is compared with the concrete experience of the other. For all pleasure and all knowledge may be viewed either abstracted from the mind, or in relation to the mind (cf. Arist. *Nic. Eth.* x. 3, 4). The first is an idea only, which may be conceived as absolute and unchangeable, and then the abstract idea of pleasure will be equally unchangeable with that of knowledge. But when we come to view either as phenomena of consciousness, the same defects are for the most part incident to both of them. Our hold upon them is equally transient and uncertain; the mind cannot be always in a state of intellectual tension, any more than capable of feeling pleasure always. The knowledge which is at one time clear and distinct, at another seems to fade away, just as the pleasure of health after sickness, or of eating after hunger, soon passes into a neutral state of unconsciousness and indifference. Change and alternation are necessary for the mind as well as for the body; and in this is to be

acknowledged, not an element of evil, but rather a law of nature. The chief difference between subjective pleasure and subjective knowledge in respect of permanence is that the latter, when our feeble faculties are able to grasp it, still conveys to us an idea of unchangeableness which cannot be got rid of.

3. In the language of ancient philosophy, the relative character of pleasure is described as becoming or generation. This is relative to being or essence, and from one point of view may be regarded as the Heraclitean flux in contrast with the Eleatic being; from another, as the transient enjoyment of eating and drinking compared with the supposed permanence of intellectual pleasures. But to us the distinction is unmeaning, and belongs to a stage of philosophy which has passed away. Plato himself seems to have suspected that the continuance or life of things is quite as much to be attributed to a principle of rest as of motion (cf. *Charm.* 159, 160; *Cratyl.* 437). A later view of pleasure is found in Aristotle, who agrees with Plato in many points, e.g. in his view of pleasure as a restoration to nature, in his distinction between bodily and mental, between necessary and non-necessary pleasures.[1] But he is also in advance of Plato; for he affirms that pleasure is not in the body at all; and hence not even the bodily pleasures are to be spoken of as generations, but only as accompanied by generation (*Nic. Eth.* x. 3, 6; i. 8, 10).

4. Plato attempts to identify vicious pleasures with some form of error, and insists that the term 'false' may be applied to them: in this he appears to be carrying out in a confused manner the Socratic doctrine, that virtue is knowledge, vice ignorance. He will allow of no distinction between the pleasures and the erroneous opinions on which they are founded, whether arising out of the illusion of distance or not. But to this we naturally reply with Protarchus, that the pleasure is what it is, although the calculation may be false, or the after-effects painful. It is difficult to acquit Plato, to use his own language, of being a 'tiro in dialectics', when he overlooks such a distinction. Yet, on the other hand, we are hardly fair judges of confusions of thought in those who view things differently from ourselves.

5. There appears also to be an incorrectness in the notion which occurs both here and in the *Gorgias*, of the simultaneousness of merely bodily pleasures and pains. We may, perhaps, admit, though even

---

[1] [This seems to be a mistake. While Aristotle agrees that a 'restoration to nature' is *incidentally* pleasant, he argues against the view that pleasure is a process or movement of any kind, using the distinction between movement and activity, ἐνέργεια. An excellent comparison of the views of Plato and Aristotle is given by A. E. Taylor, *Commentary on the Timaeus*, pp. 447–62.]

this is not free from doubt, that the feeling of pleasurable hope or recollection is, or rather may be, simultaneous with acute bodily suffering. But there is no such coexistence of the pain of thirst with the pleasures of drinking; they are not really simultaneous, for the one expels the other. Nor does Plato seem to have considered that the bodily pleasures, except in certain extreme cases, are unattended with pain. Few philosophers will deny that a degree of pleasure attends eating and drinking; and yet surely we might as well speak of the pains of digestion which follow, as of the pains of hunger and thirst which precede them. Plato's conception is derived partly from the extreme case of a man suffering pain from hunger or thirst, partly from the image of a full and empty vessel. But the truth is rather, that while the gratification of our bodily desires constantly affords some degree of pleasure, the antecedent pains are scarcely perceived by us, being almost done away with by use and regularity.

6. The desire to classify pleasures as accompanied or not accompanied by antecedent pains, has led Plato to place under one head the pleasures of smell and sight, as well as those derived from sounds of music and from knowledge. He would have done better to make a separate class of the pleasures of smell, having no association of mind, or perhaps to have divided them into natural and artificial. The pleasures of sight and sound might then have been regarded as being the expression of ideas. But this higher and truer point of view never appears to have occurred to Plato. Nor has he any distinction between the fine arts and the mechanical; and, neither here nor anywhere, an adequate conception of the beautiful in external things.

7. Plato agrees partially with certain 'surly or fastidious' philosophers, as he terms them, who defined pleasure to be the absence of pain. They are also described as eminent in physics. There is unfortunately no school of Greek philosophy known to us which combined these two characteristics. Antisthenes, who was an enemy of pleasure, was not a physical philosopher; the atomists, who were physical philosophers, were not enemies of pleasure. Yet such a combination of opinions is far from being impossible. Plato's omission to mention them by name has created the same uncertainty respecting them which also occurs respecting the 'friends of Ideas' and the 'materialists' in the *Sophist*.

On the whole, this discussion is one of the least satisfactory in the dialogues of Plato. While the ethical nature of pleasure is scarcely considered, and the merely physical phenomenon imperfectly analysed, too much weight is given to ideas of measure and number, as the sole principle of good. The comparison of pleasure and knowledge is really a comparison of two elements, which have no common measure, and which cannot be excluded from each other. Feeling is not opposed to knowledge, and in all consciousness there is an element of both. The most abstract kinds of knowledge are inseparable from some pleasure or pain, which accompanies the acquisition or possession of them: the student is liable to grow weary of them, and soon discovers that continuous mental energy is not granted to men. The most sensual pleasure, on the other hand, is inseparable from the consciousness of pleasure; no man can be happy who, to borrow Plato's illustration, is leading the life of an oyster. Hence (by his own confession) the main thesis is not worth determining; the real interest lies in the incidental discussion. We can no more separate pleasure from knowledge in the *Philebus* than we can separate justice from happiness in the *Republic*.

IV. An interesting account is given in the *Philebus* of the rank and order of the sciences or arts, which agrees generally with the scheme of knowledge in the sixth book of the *Republic*. The chief difference is, that the position of the arts is more exactly defined. They are divided into an empirical part and a scientific part, of which the first is mere guess-work, the second is determined by rule and measure. Of the more empirical arts, music is given as an example; this, although affirmed to be necessary to human life (62 b), is depreciated. Music is regarded from a point of view entirely opposite to that of the *Republic*, not as a sublime science, co-ordinate with astronomy, but as full of doubt and conjecture. According to the standard of accuracy which is here adopted, it is rightly placed lower in the scale than carpentering, because the latter is more capable of being reduced to measure.

The theoretical element of the arts may also become a purely abstract science, when separated from matter, and is then said to be pure and unmixed. The distinction which Plato here makes seems to be the same as that between pure and applied mathematics, and may be expressed in the modern formula—science is art theoretical, art is science practical. In the reason which he gives for the superiority of the pure science of number over the mixed or applied, we can only agree with him in part. He says that the numbers which the philosopher employs are always the same, whereas the numbers which are used in practice represent different sizes or quantities. He does not see that this power of expressing different quantities by the same symbol is the characteristic and not the defect of numbers, and is due to their abstract nature;—although we admit of course what Plato seems to feel in his distinctions between pure and impure knowledge, that the imperfection of matter enters into the applications of them.

Above the other sciences, as in the *Republic*, towers dialectic, which is the science of eternal being, apprehended by the purest mind and reason. The lower sciences, including the mathematical, are akin to opinion rather than to reason, and are placed together in the fourth class of goods. The relation in which they stand to dialectic is obscure in the *Republic*, and is not cleared up in the *Philebus*.

V. Thus far we have only attained to the vestibule or antechamber of the good; for there is a good exceeding knowledge, exceeding essence, which, like Glaucon in the *Republic* (vi. 509), we find a difficulty in apprehending. This good is now to be exhibited to us under various aspects and gradations. The relative dignity of pleasure and knowledge has been determined; but they have not yet received their exact position in the scale of goods. Some difficulties occur to us in the enumeration: First, how are we to distinguish the first from the second class of goods, or the second from the third? Secondly, why is there no mention of the supreme mind? Thirdly, the nature of the fourth class. Fourthly, the meaning of the allusion to a sixth class, which is not further investigated.

(1) Plato seems to proceed in his table of goods, from the more abstract to the less abstract; from the subjective to the objective; until at the lower end of the scale we fairly descend into the region of human action and feeling. To him, the greater the abstraction the greater the truth, and he is always tending to see abstractions within abstractions; which, like the Ideas in the *Parmenides*, are always appearing one behind another. Hence we find a difficulty in following him into the sphere of thought which he is seeking to attain. First in his scale of goods he places measure, in which he finds the eternal nature: this would be more naturally expressed in modern language as eternal law, and seems to be akin both to the finite and to the mind or cause, which were two of the elements in the former table. Like the supreme nature in the *Timaeus*, like the ideal beauty in the *Symposium* or the *Phaedrus*, or like the ideal good in the *Republic*, this is the absolute and unapproachable being. But this being is manifested in symmetry and beauty everywhere, in the order of nature and of mind, in the relations of men to one another. For the word 'measure' he now substitutes the word 'symmetry', as if intending to express measure conceived as relation. He then proceeds to regard the good no longer in an objective form, but as the human reason seeking to attain truth by the aid of dialectic; such at least we naturally infer to be his meaning, when we consider that both here and in the *Republic* the sphere of νοῦς or mind is assigned to dialectic. (2) It is remarkable (see above) that this personal conception of mind is confined to the human mind, and not, as at 22 c, extended to the divine. (3) If we may be allowed to

interpret one dialogue of Plato by another, the sciences of figure and number are probably classed with the arts and true opinions, because they proceed from hypotheses (cf. *Rep.* vi. 511). (4) The sixth class, if a sixth class is to be added, is playfully set aside by a quotation from Orpheus: Plato means to say that a sixth class, if there is such a class, is not worth considering, because pleasure, having only gained the fifth place in the scale of goods, is already out of the running.

VI. We may now endeavour to ascertain the relation of the *Philebus* to the other dialogues.[1] Here Plato shows the same indifference to his own doctrine of Ideas which he has already manifested in the *Parmenides* and the *Sophist*. The principle of the one and many of which he here speaks, is illustrated by examples in the *Sophist* and *Statesman*. Notwithstanding the differences of style, many resemblances may be noticed between the *Philebus* and *Gorgias*. The theory of the simultaneousness of pleasure and pain is common to both of them (*Phil.* 36 b, *Gorgias* 496 e); there is also a common tendency in them to take up arms against pleasure, although the view of the *Philebus*, which is probably the later of the two dialogues, is the more moderate. At 46 a, b, there seems to be an allusion to the passage in the *Gorgias* (494), in which Socrates dilates on the pleasures of itching and scratching. Nor is there any real discrepancy in the manner in which Gorgias and his art are spoken of in the two dialogues. For Socrates, at p. 58, is far from implying that the art of rhetoric has a real sphere of practical usefulness: he only means that the refutation of the claims of Gorgias is not necessary for his present purpose. He is saying in effect: 'Admit, if you please, that rhetoric is the greatest and usefullest of sciences:—this does not prove that dialectic is not the purest and most exact.' From the *Sophist* and *Statesman* we know that his hostility towards the sophists and rhetoricians was not mitigated in later life; although both in the *Statesman* and *Laws* he admits of a higher use of rhetoric.

Reasons have been already given for assigning a late date to the *Philebus*. That the date is probably later than that of the *Republic*, may be further argued on the following grounds:—1. The general resemblance to the later dialogues and to the *Laws*: 2. The more complete account of the nature of good and pleasure: 3. The distinction between perception, memory, recollection, and opinion (34–38) which indicates a great progress in psychology; also between understanding and imagination, which is described under the figure of the scribe and the painter (39). A superficial notion may arise that Plato

---

[1] [Nothing is said here of the relationship between the *Philebus* and *Timaeus*. See Hackforth, *Plato's Examination of Pleasure*, pp. 37–39.]

probably wrote shorter dialogues, such as the *Philebus*, the *Sophist*, and the *Statesman*, as studies or preparations for longer ones. This view may be natural; but on further reflection is seen to be fallacious, because these three dialogues are found to make an advance upon the metaphysical conceptions of the *Republic*. And we can more easily suppose that Plato composed shorter writings after longer ones, than suppose that he lost hold of further points of view which he had once attained.

It is more easy to find traces of the Pythagoreans, Eleatics, Megarians, Cynics, Cyrenaics, and of the ideas of Anaxagoras, in the *Philebus*, than to say how much is due to each of them. Had we fuller records of those old philosophers, we should probably find Plato in the midst of the fray attempting to combine Eleatic and Pythagorean doctrines, and seeking to find a truth beyond either being or number; setting up his own concrete conception of good against the abstract practical good of the Cynics, or the abstract intellectual good of the Megarians, and his own idea of classification against the denial of plurality in unity which is also attributed to them; warring against the Eristics as destructive of truth, as he had formerly fought against the sophists; taking up a middle position between the Cynics and Cyrenaics in his doctrine of pleasure; asserting with more consistency than Anaxagoras the existence of an intelligent mind and cause. Of the Heracliteans, whom he is said by Aristotle to have cultivated in his youth, he speaks in the *Philebus*, as in the *Theaetetus* and *Cratylus*, with irony and contempt. But we have not the knowledge which would enable us to pursue further the line of reflection here indicated; nor can we expect to find perfect clearness or order in the first efforts of mankind to understand the working of their own minds. The ideas which they are attempting to analyse, they are also in process of creating; the abstract universals of which they are seeking to adjust the relations have been already excluded by them from the category of relation.

ANALYSIS

The *Philebus*, like the *Cratylus*, is supposed to be the continuation of a previous discussion. An argument respecting the comparative claims of pleasure and wisdom to rank as the chief good has been already carried on between Philebus and Socrates. The argument is now transferred to Protarchus, the son of Callias (19 b), a noble Athenian youth, sprung from a family which had spent 'a world of money' on the Sophists (cf. *Apol.* 20 a, b; *Crat.* 391 c; *Protag.* 337 d). Philebus, who appears to be the teacher (16 b, 36 d), or

elder friend, and perhaps the lover (53 d), of Protarchus, takes
no further part in the discussion beyond asserting in the strongest
manner his adherence, under all circumstances, to the cause of
pleasure.

Socrates suggests that they shall have a first and second palm
of victory. For there may be a good higher than either pleasure
or wisdom, and then neither of them will gain the first prize, but
whichever of the two is more akin to this higher good will have a
right to the second. They agree, and Socrates opens the game by
enlarging on the diversity and opposition which exists among
pleasures. For there are pleasures of all kinds, good and bad,
wise and foolish—pleasures of the temperate as well as of the
intemperate. Protarchus replies that although pleasures may
be opposed in so far as they spring from opposite sources,
nevertheless as pleasures they are alike. Yes, retorts Socrates,
pleasure is like pleasure, as figure is like figure and colour like
colour; yet we all know that there is great variety among figures
and colours. Protarchus does not see the drift of this remark; and
Socrates proceeds to ask how he can have a right to attribute a
new predicate (i.e. 'good') to pleasures in general, when he
cannot deny that they are different. What common property in
all of them does he mean to indicate by the term 'good'? If he
continues to assert that there is some trivial sense in which
pleasure is one, Socrates may retort by saying that knowledge is
one, but the result will be that such merely verbal and trivial
conceptions, whether of knowledge or pleasure, will spoil the
discussion, and will prove the incapacity of the two disputants.
In order to avoid this danger, he proposes that they shall beat a
retreat, and, before they proceed, come to an understanding about
the 'high argument' of the one and the many.

Protarchus agrees to the proposal, but he is under the impression that Socrates means to discuss the common question—how
a sensible object can be one, and yet have opposite attributes,
such as 'great' and 'small', 'light' and 'heavy', or how there can
be many members in one body, and the like wonders. Socrates
has long ceased to see any wonder in these phenomena; his difficulties begin with the application of number to abstract unities
(e.g. 'man', 'good') and with the attempt to divide them. For have
these unities of idea any real existence? How, if imperishable,

can they enter into the world of generation? How, as units, can they be divided and dispersed among different objects? Or do they exist in their entirety in each object? These difficulties are but imperfectly answered by Socrates in what follows.

We speak of a one and many, which is ever flowing in and out of all things, concerning which a young man often runs wild in his first metaphysical enthusiasm, talking about analysis and
16 synthesis to his father and mother and the neighbours, hardly sparing even his dog. This 'one in many' is a revelation of the order of the world, which some Prometheus first made known to our ancestors; and they, who were better men and nearer the gods than we are, have handed it down to us. To know how to
17 proceed by regular steps from one to many, and from many to one, is just what makes the difference between eristic and dialectic. And the right way of proceeding is to look for one idea or class in all things, and when you have found one to look for more than one, and for all that there are, and when you have found them all and regularly divided a particular field of knowledge into classes, you may leave the further consideration of individuals. But you must not pass at once either from unity to infinity, or from infinity to unity. In music, for example, you may begin with the most general notion, but this alone will not make you a musician: you must know also the number and nature of the intervals, and the systems which are framed out of them, and the rhythms of the dance which correspond to them. And when you have a similar knowledge of any other subject,
18 you may be said to know that subject. In speech again there are infinite varieties of sound, and someone who was a wise man, or more than man, comprehended them all in the classes of mutes, vowels, and semivowels, and gave to each of them a name, and assigned them to the art of grammar.

'But whither, Socrates, are you going? And what has this to do with the comparative eligibility of pleasure and wisdom?' Socrates replies, that before we can adjust their respective claims,
19 we want to know the number and kinds of both of them. What
20 are they? He is requested to answer the question himself. That he will, if he may be allowed to make one or two preliminary remarks. In the first place he has a dreamy recollection of hearing that neither pleasure nor knowledge is the highest good, for the

good should be perfect and sufficient. But is the life of pleasure 21
perfect and sufficient, when deprived of memory, consciousness,
anticipation? Is not this the life of an oyster? Or is the life of
mind sufficient, if devoid of any particle of pleasure? Must not 22
the union of the two be higher and more eligible than either
separately? And is not the element which makes this mixed life
eligible more akin to mind than to pleasure? Thus pleasure is
rejected and mind is rejected. And yet there may be a life of mind,
not human but divine, which conquers still.

But, if we are to pursue this argument farther, we shall require 23
some new weapons; and by this, I mean a new classification of
existence. (1) There is a finite element of existence, and (2) an
infinite, and (3) the union of the two, and (4) the cause of the
union. More may be added if they are wanted, but at present we
can do without them. And first of the infinite or indefinite:— 24
that is the class which is denoted by the terms more and less, and
is always in a state of comparison. All words or ideas to which the
words 'slightly', 'extremely', and other comparative expressions
are applied, fall under this class. The infinite would be no longer 25
infinite, if limited or reduced to measure by number and quantity.
The opposite class is the limited or finite, and includes all things
which have number and quantity. And there is a third class of
generation into essence by the union of the finite and infinite, in
which the finite gives law to the infinite;—under this are comprehended health, strength, temperate seasons, harmony, beauty, 26
and the like. The goddess of beauty saw the universal wantonness
of all things, and gave law and order to be the salvation of the
soul. But no effect can be generated without a cause, and therefore
there must be a fourth class, which is the cause of generation; for 27
the cause or agent is not the same as the patient or effect.

And now, having obtained our classes, we may determine in
which our conqueror life is to be placed: clearly in the third or
mixed class, in which the finite gives law to the infinite. And in
which is pleasure to find a place? As clearly in the infinite or indefinite, which alone, as Protarchus thinks (who seems to confuse
the infinite with the superlative), gives to pleasure the character
of the absolute good. Yes, retorts Socrates, and also to pain the 28
character of absolute evil. And therefore the infinite cannot be
that which imparts to pleasure the nature of the good. But where

shall we place mind? That is a very serious and awful question, which may be prefaced by another. Is mind or chance the lord of the universe? All philosophers will say the first, and yet, perhaps, they may be only magnifying themselves. And for this

29 reason I should like to consider the matter a little more deeply, even though some lovers of disorder in the world should ridicule my attempt.

Now the elements—earth, air, fire, water—exist in us, and they exist in the cosmos; but they are purer and fairer in the cosmos

30 than they are in us, and they come to us from thence. And as we have a soul as well as a body, in like manner the elements of the finite, the infinite, the union of the two, and the cause, are found to exist in us. And if they, like the elements, exist in us, and the three first exist in the world, must not the fourth or cause which is the noblest of them, exist in the world? And this cause is wisdom or mind, the royal mind of Zeus, who is the king of all, as there are other gods who have other noble attributes. Observe how well this agrees with the testimony of men of old, who affirmed mind to be the ruler of the universe. And remember that mind

31 belongs to the class which we term the cause, and pleasure to the infinite or indefinite class. We will examine the place and origin of both.

What is the origin of pleasure? Her natural seat is the mixed class, in which health and harmony were placed. Pain is the violation, and pleasure the restoration of limit. There is a natural

32 union of finite and infinite, which in hunger, thirst, heat, cold, is impaired—this is painful, but the return to nature, in which the elements are restored to their normal proportions, is pleasant. Here is our first class of pleasures. And another class of pleasures and pains are hopes and fears; these are in the mind only. And inasmuch as the pleasures are unalloyed by pains and the pains by pleasures, the examination of them may show us whether all pleasure is to be desired, or whether this entire desirableness is not rather the attribute of another class. But if pleasures and pains consist in the violation and restoration of limit, may there

33 not be a neutral state, in which there is neither dissolution nor restoration? That is a further question, and admitting, as we must, the possibility of such a state, there seems to be no reason why the life of wisdom should not exist in this neutral state,

which is, moreover, the state of the gods, who cannot, without indecency, be supposed to feel either joy or sorrow.

The second class of pleasures involves memory. There are affections which are extinguished before they reach the soul, and of these there is no consciousness, and therefore no memory. And there are affections which the body and soul feel together, 34 and this feeling is termed consciousness. And memory is the preservation of consciousness, and reminiscence is the recovery of consciousness. Now the memory of pleasure, when a man is in 35 pain, is the memory of the opposite of his actual bodily state, and is therefore not in the body, but in the mind. And there may be an intermediate state, in which a person is balanced between pleasure and pain; in his body there is want which is a cause of 36 pain, but in his mind a sure hope of replenishment, which is pleasant. (But if the hope be converted into despair, he has two pains and not a balance of pain and pleasure.) Another question is raised: May not pleasures, like opinions, be true and false? 37 In the sense of being real, both must be admitted to be true: nor can we deny that to both of them qualities may be attributed; for pleasures as well as opinions may be described as good or bad. 38 And though we do not all of us allow that there are true and false pleasures, we all acknowledge that there are some pleasures associated with right opinion, and others with falsehood and ignorance. Let us endeavour to analyse the nature of this association.

Opinion is based on perception, which may be correct or mistaken. You may see a figure at a distance, and say first of all, 'This is a man', and then say, 'No, this is an image made by the shepherds'. And you may affirm this in a proposition to your companion, or make the remark mentally to yourself. Whether 39 the words are actually spoken or not, on such occasions there is a scribe within who registers them, and a painter who paints the images of the things which the scribe has written down in the soul, —at least that is my own notion of the process; and the words and images which are inscribed by them may be either true or false; and they may represent either past, present, or future. And, representing the future, they must also represent the pleasures and pains of anticipation—the visions of gold and other fancies which 40 are never wanting in the mind of man. Now these hopes, as they are termed, are propositions, which are sometimes true, and sometimes false; for the good, who are the friends of the gods, see true pictures of the future, and the bad false ones. And as there may be opinion about things which are not, were not, and will not be, which is opinion still, so there may be pleasure about things which are not, were not, and will not be, which is pleasure still,—that is to say, false pleasure; and only when false, can 41 pleasure, like opinion, be vicious. Against this conclusion Protarchus protests.

Leaving his denial for the present, Socrates proceeds to show that some pleasures are false from another point of view. In desire, as we admitted, the body is divided from the soul, and hence pleasures and pains are often simultaneous. And we further admitted that both of them belonged to the infinite class. How, then, 42 can we compare them? Are we not liable, or rather certain, as in the case of sight, to be deceived by distance and relation? In this case the pleasures and pains are not false because based upon false opinion, but are themselves false. And there is another illusion: pain has often been said by us to arise out of the derangement—pleasure out of the restoration—of our nature. But in passing from one to the other, do we not experience neutral states, which although they appear pleasurable or painful are 43 really neither? For even if we admit, with the wise man whom Protarchus loves (and only a wise man could have ever entertained such a notion), that all things are in a perpetual flux, still these changes are often unconscious, and devoid either of pleasure or pain. We assume, then, that there are three states—pleasurable, painful, neutral; we may embellish a little by calling them gold, silver, and that which is neither.

44   But there are certain natural philosophers who will not admit a third state. Their instinctive dislike of pleasure leads them to affirm that pleasure is only the absence of pain. They are noble fellows, and, although we do not agree with them, we may use them as diviners who will indicate to us the right track. They will say, that the nature of anything is best known from the examination of extreme cases, e.g. the nature of hardness from the examination of the hardest things; and that the nature of pleasure will be best understood from an examination of the most intense 45 pleasures. Now these are the pleasures of the body, not of the mind; the pleasures of disease and not of health, the pleasures of

the intemperate and not of the temperate. I am speaking, not of the frequency or continuance, but only of the intensity of such pleasures, and this is given them by contrast with the pain or sickness of body which precedes them. Their morbid nature is illus- 46 trated by the lesser instances of itching and scratching, respecting which I swear that I cannot tell whether they are a pleasure or a pain. (1) Some of these arise out of a transition from one state of the body to another, as from cold to hot; (2) others are caused by the contrast of an internal pain and an external pleasure in the body: sometimes the feeling of pain predominates, as in itching and tingling, when they are relieved by scratching; sometimes the feeling of pleasure: or the pleasure which they give may be 47 quite overpowering, and is then accompanied by all sorts of unutterable feelings which have a death of delights in them. But there are also mixed pleasures which are in the mind only. For are not love and sorrow as well as anger 'sweeter than honey', and 48 also full of pain? Is there not a mixture of feelings in the spectator of tragedy? and of comedy also? 'I do not understand that last.' Well, then, with the view of lighting up the obscurity of these mixed feelings, let me ask whether envy is painful. 'Yes.' And yet the envious man finds something pleasing in the misfortunes of others? 'True.' And ignorance is a misfortune? 'Certainly.' And one form of ignorance is self-conceit—a man may fancy himself richer, fairer, better, wiser than he is? 'Yes.' And he who thus 49 deceives himself may be strong or weak? 'He may.' And if he is strong we fear him, and if he is weak we laugh at him, which is a pleasure, and yet we envy him, which is a pain? These mixed 50 feelings are the rationale of tragedy and comedy, and equally the rationale of the greater drama of human life.[1] Having shown how sorrow, anger, envy are feelings of a mixed nature, I will reserve the consideration of the remainder for another occasion.

Next follow the unmixed pleasures; which, unlike the 51

[1] There appears to be some confusion in this passage. There is no difficulty in seeing that in comedy, as in tragedy, the spectator may view the performance with mixed feelings of pain as well as of pleasure; nor is there any difficulty in understanding that envy is a mixed feeling, which rejoices not without pain at the misfortunes of others, and laughs at their ignorance of themselves. But Plato seems to think further that he has explained the feeling of the spectator in comedy sufficiently by a theory which only applies to comedy in so far as in comedy we laugh at the conceit or weakness of others. He has certainly given a very partial explanation of the ridiculous.

philosophers of whom I was speaking, I believe to be real. These unmixed pleasures are: (1) the pleasures derived from beauty of form, colour, sound, smell, which are absolutely pure; and in
52 general those which are unalloyed with pain: (2) the pleasures derived from the acquisition of knowledge, which in themselves are pure, but may be attended by an accidental pain of forgetting; this, however, arises from a subsequent act of reflection, of which we need take no account. At the same time, we admit that the latter pleasures are the property of a very few. To these pure and unmixed pleasures we ascribe measure, whereas all others belong to the class of the infinite, and are liable to every species of excess. And here several questions arise for consideration:—What is the meaning of pure and impure, of moderate and immoderate? We
53 may answer the question by an illustration: purity of white paint consists in the clearness or quality of the white, and this is distinct from the quantity or amount of white paint; a little pure white is fairer than a great deal which is impure. But there is another question:—pleasure is affirmed by ingenious philosophers to be a generation; they say that there are two natures—one self-existent, the other dependent; the one noble and majestic, the other failing in both these qualities. 'I do not understand.' There are lovers and there are loves. 'Yes, I know, but what is the application?' The argument is in play, and desires to intimate that there are relatives and there are absolutes, and that the
54 relative is for the sake of the absolute; and generation is for the sake of essence. Under relatives I class all things done with a view to generation; and essence is of the class of good. But if essence is of the class of good, generation must be of some other class; and our friends, who affirm that pleasure is a generation, would laugh at the notion that pleasure is a good; and at that other notion,
55 that pleasure is produced by generation, which is only the alternative of destruction. Who would prefer such an alternation to the equable life of pure thought? Here is one absurdity, and not the only one, to which the friends of pleasure are reduced. For is there not also an absurdity in affirming that good is of the soul only; or in declaring that the best of men, if he be in pain, is bad?

And now, from the consideration of pleasure, we pass to that of knowledge. Let us reflect that there are two kinds of knowledge —the one creative or productive, and the other educational and philosophical. Of the creative arts, there is one part purer or more akin to knowledge than the other. There is an element of guess-work and an element of number and measure in them. In 56 music, for example, especially in flute-playing, the conjectural element prevails; while in carpentering there is more application of rule and measure. Of the creative arts, then, we may make two classes—the less exact and the more exact. And the exacter part of all of them is really arithmetic and mensuration. But arithmetic and mensuration again may be subdivided with reference either to their use in the concrete, or to their nature in the abstract —as they are regarded popularly in building and binding, or theoretically by philosophers. And, borrowing the analogy of 57 pleasure, we may say that the philosophical use of them is purer than the other. Thus we have two arts of arithmetic, and two of mensuration. And truest of all in the estimation of every rational man is dialectic, or the science of being, which will forget and disown us, if we forget and disown her.

'But, Socrates, I have heard Gorgias say that rhetoric is the 58 greatest and usefullest of arts; and I should not like to quarrel either with him or you.' Neither is there any inconsistency, Protarchus, with his statement in what I am now saying; for I am not maintaining that dialectic is the greatest or usefullest, but only that she is the truest of arts; my remark is not quantitative but qualitative, and refers not to the advantage or reputation of either, but to the degree of truth which they attain—here Gorgias will not care to compete; this is what we affirm to be possessed in the highest degree by dialectic. And do not let us appeal to 59 Gorgias or Philebus or Socrates, but ask, on behalf of the argument, what are the highest truths which the soul has the power of attaining. And is not this the science which has a firmer grasp of them than any other? For the arts generally are only occupied with matters of opinion, and with the production and action and passion of this sensible world. But the highest truth is that which is eternal and unchangeable. And reason and wisdom are concerned with the eternal; and these are the very claimants, if not for the first, at least for the second place, whom I propose as rivals to pleasure.

And now, having the materials, we may proceed to mix them— first recapitulating the question at issue. 60

Philebus affirmed pleasure to be the good, and assumed them to be one nature; I affirmed that they were two natures, and declared that knowledge was more akin to the good than pleasure. I said that the two together were more eligible than either taken singly;

61 and to this we adhere. Reason intimates, as at first, that we should seek the good not in the unmixed life, but in the mixed.

The cup is ready, waiting to be mingled, and here are two fountains, one of honey, the other of pure water, out of which to make the fairest possible mixture. There are pure and impure pleasures, pure and impure sciences. Let us consider the sections of each which have the most of purity and truth; to admit them all

62 indiscriminately would be dangerous. First we will take the pure sciences; but shall we mingle the impure—the art which uses the false rule and the false measure? That we must, if we are any of us to find our way home; man cannot live upon pure mathematics alone. And must I include music, which is admitted to be guess-work? 'Yes, you must, if human life is to have any humanity.' Well, then, I will open the door and let them all in; they shall mingle in an Homeric 'meeting of the waters'. And now we turn to the pleasures; shall I admit them? 'Admit first of all the pure

63 pleasures; secondly, the necessary.' And what shall we say about the rest? First, ask the pleasures—they will be very happy to dwell with wisdom. Secondly, ask the arts and sciences—they reply that the excesses of intemperance are the ruin of them; and that they would rather only have the pleasures of health and tem-

64 perance, which are the handmaidens of virtue. But still we want truth? That is now added; and so the argument is complete, and may be compared to an incorporeal law, which is to hold fair rule over a living body. And now we are at the vestibule of the good, in which there are three chief elements—truth, symmetry,

65 and beauty. These will be the criterion of the comparative claims of pleasure and wisdom.

Which has the greater share of truth? Surely wisdom; for pleasure is the veriest impostor in the world, and the perjuries of lovers have passed into a proverb.

Which of symmetry? Wisdom again; for nothing is more immoderate than pleasure.

66 Which of beauty? Once more, wisdom; for pleasure is often unseemly, and the greatest pleasures are put out of sight.

Not pleasure, then, ranks first in the scale of good, but measure, and eternal harmony.

Second comes the symmetrical and beautiful and perfect.

Third, mind and wisdom.

Fourth, sciences and arts and true opinions.

Fifth, painless pleasures.

Of a sixth class, I have no more to say. Thus, pleasure and mind may both renounce the claim to the first place. But mind 67 is ten thousand times nearer to the chief good than pleasure. Pleasure ranks fifth and not first, even though all the animals in the world assert the contrary.

INTRODUCTION

The *Philebus* is probably the latest in time of the writings of Plato with the exception of the *Laws*. We have in it therefore the last development of his philosophy. The extreme and one-sided doctrines of the Cynics and Cyrenaics are included in a larger whole (20, 21, 44, &c.); the relations of pleasure and knowledge to each other and to the good are authoritatively determined (63 ff.); the Eleatic being and the Heraclitean flux no longer divide the empire of thought (25 ff.); the Mind of Anaxagoras has become the Mind of God and of the World. The great distinction between pure and applied science for the first time has a place in philosophy; the natural claim of dialectic to be the queen of the Sciences is once more affirmed. This latter is the bond of union which pervades the whole or nearly the whole of the Platonic writings. And here as in several other dialogues (*Phaedr.* 265, *Rep.* 534 ff., *Symp.* 210 ff., &c.) it is presented to us in a manner playful yet also serious, and sometimes as if the thought of it were too great for human utterance and came down from heaven direct (16 c, 25 b). It is the organization of knowledge wonderful to think of at a time when knowledge itself could hardly be said to exist. It is this more than any other element which distinguishes Plato, not only from the pre-Socratic philosophers, but from Socrates himself.

We have not yet reached the confines of Aristotle, but we make a somewhat nearer approach to him in the *Philebus* than in the earlier Platonic writings. The germs of logic are beginning to appear, but they are not collected into a whole, or made a separate science or system. Many thinkers of many different schools have to be interposed between the *Parmenides* or *Philebus* of Plato, and the *Physics* or *Metaphysics* of Aristotle. It is this interval upon which we have to fix our minds if we would rightly understand the character of the transition from one to the other. Plato and Aristotle do not dovetail into one another; nor does the one begin where the other ends; there is a gulf between them not to be measured by time, which in the fragmentary state of our knowledge it is impossible to bridge over. It follows that the one cannot be interpreted by the other. At any rate, it is not Plato who is to be interpreted by Aristotle, but Aristotle by Plato. Of all philosophy and of all art the true understanding is to be sought not in the afterthoughts of posterity, but in the elements out of which they have arisen. For the previous stage is a tendency towards the ideal at which they are aiming; the later is a declination or deviation from them, or even a perversion of them. No man's thoughts were ever so well expressed by his disciples as by himself.

But although Plato in the *Philebus* does not come into any close connexion with Aristotle, he is now a long way from himself and from the beginnings of his own philosophy. At the time of his death he left his system still incomplete; or he may be more truly said to have had no system, but to have lived in the successive stages or moments of metaphysical thought which presented themselves from time to time. The earlier discussions about universal ideas and definitions seem to have died away; the correlation of ideas has taken their place. The flowers of rhetoric and poetry have lost their freshness and charm; and a technical language has begun to supersede and overgrow them. But the power of thinking tends to increase with age, and the experience of life to widen and deepen. The good is summed up under categories which are not *summa genera*, but heads or gradations of thought. The question of pleasure and the relation of bodily pleasures to mental, which is hardly treated of elsewhere in Plato, is here analysed with great subtlety. The mean or measure is now made the first principle of good. Some of these questions reappear in Aristotle, as does also the distinction between metaphysics and mathematics. But there are many things in Plato which have been lost in Aristotle; and many things in Aristotle not to be found in Plato. The most remarkable deficiency in Aristotle is the disappearance of the Platonic dialectic, which in the Aristotelian school is only used in a comparatively unimportant and trivial sense. The most remarkable additions are the invention of the syllogism, the conception of happiness as the foundation of morals, the reference of human actions to the standard of the better mind of the world, or of the one 'sensible man' or 'superior person'. His conception of οὐσία, or essence, is not an advance upon Plato, but a return to the poor and meagre abstractions of the Eleatic philosophy. The dry attempt to reduce the pre-Socratic philosophy by

his own rather arbitrary standard of the four causes contrasts unfavourably with Plato's general discussion of the same subject (*Soph.*
242–3). To attempt further to sum up the differences between the
two great philosophers would be out of place here. Any real discussion
of their relation to one another must be preceded by an examination
into the nature and character of the Aristotelian writings and the form
in which they have come down to us. This inquiry is not really
separable from an investigation of Theophrastus as well as Aristotle
and of the remains of other schools of philosophy as well as of the
Peripatetics. But, without entering on this wide field, even a superficial consideration of the logical and metaphysical works which pass
under the name of Aristotle, whether we suppose them to have come
directly from his hand or to be the tradition of his school, is sufficient
to show how great was the mental activity which prevailed in the
latter half of the fourth century B.C.; what eddies and whirlpools of
controversies were surging in the chaos of thought, what transformations of the old philosophies were taking place everywhere, what
eclecticisms and syncretisms and realisms and nominalisms were
affecting the mind of Hellas. The decline of philosophy during this
period is no less remarkable than the loss of freedom; and the two are
not unconnected with each other. But of the multitudinous sea of
opinions which were current in the age of Aristotle we have no exact
account. We know of them from allusions only. And we cannot with
advantage fill up the void of our knowledge by conjecture: we can
only make allowance for our ignorance.

There are several passages in the *Philebus* which are very characteristic of Plato, and which we shall do well to consider not only in
their connexion, but apart from their connexion as inspired sayings or
oracles which receive their full interpretation only from the history of
philosophy in later ages. The more serious attacks on traditional
beliefs which are often veiled under an unusual simplicity or irony are
of this kind. Such, for example, is the excessive and more than human
awe which Socrates expresses about the names of the gods (12 c),
which may be not unaptly compared with the importance attached by
mankind to theological terms in other ages; for this also may be
comprehended under the satire of Socrates. Let us observe the religious
and intellectual enthusiasm which shines forth in the following, 'The
power and faculty of loving the truth, and of doing all things for the
sake of the truth' (58 d): or, again, the singular acknowledgement in
23 b, which may be regarded as the anticipation of a new logic, that
'In going to war for mind I must have weapons of a different make

from those which I used before, although some of the old ones may do again'. Let us pause awhile to reflect on a sentence (29 a) which is full of meaning to reformers of religion or to the original thinker of all ages: 'Shall we then agree with them of old time, and merely reassert the notions of others without risk to ourselves; or shall we venture also to share in the risk and bear the reproach which will await us'? i.e. if we assert mind to be the author of nature. Let us note the remarkable words (30 d), 'That in the divine nature of Zeus there is the soul and mind of a King, because there is in him the power of the cause', a saying in which theology and philosophy are blended and reconciled; not omitting to observe the deep insight into human nature which is shown by the repetition of the same thought (28 c) 'All philosophers are agreed that mind is the king of heaven and earth' with the ironical addition, 'in this way truly they magnify themselves'. Nor let us pass unheeded the indignation felt by the generous youth (29 a) at the 'blasphemy' of those who say that chaos and chance medley created the world; or the significance of the words 'Those who said *of old time* that mind rules the universe' (30 d); or the pregnant observation (43 c) that 'We are not always conscious of what we are doing or of what happens to us', a chance expression to which if philosophers had attended they would have escaped many errors in psychology. We may contrast the contempt which is poured upon the verbal difficulty of the one and many, and the seriousness with which the unity of opposites is regarded from the higher point of view of abstract ideas (14 c, 15): or compare the simple manner in which the question of cause and effect (27) and their mutual dependence is regarded by Plato (to which modern science has returned in Mill and Bacon), and the cumbrous fourfold division of causes in the *Physics* and *Metaphysics* of Aristotle, for which it has puzzled the world to find a use in so many centuries. When we consider the backwardness of knowledge in the age of Plato, the boldness with which he looks forward into the distance, the many questions of modern philosophy which are anticipated in his writings, may we not truly describe him in his own words as a 'spectator of all time and of all existence'?

PHILEBUS

Persons of the Dialogue

SOCRATES   PROTARCHUS   PHILEBUS

Socrates. Observe, Protarchus, the nature of the position which 11
you are now going to take from Philebus, and what the other
position is which I maintain, and which, if you do not approve of
it, is to be controverted by you. Shall you and I sum up the two b
sides?

Protarchus. By all means.

Soc. Philebus was saying that enjoyment and pleasure and
delight, and the class of feelings akin to them, are a good to every
living being, whereas I contend, that not these, but wisdom and
intelligence and memory, and their kindred, right opinion and
true reasoning, are better and more desirable than pleasure for
all who are able to partake of them, and that to all such who are c
or ever will be, the possession of them is the most advantageous
thing in the world. Have I not given, Philebus, a fair statement
of the two sides of the argument?

Philebus. Nothing could be fairer, Socrates.

Soc. And do you, Protarchus, accept the position which is
assigned to you?

Pro. I cannot do otherwise, since our fair Philebus has left the
field.

Soc. Surely the truth about these matters ought, by all means,
to be ascertained.

Pro. Certainly.   d

Soc. Shall we further agree——

Pro. To what?

Soc. That you and I must now try to indicate some state and
disposition of the soul which has the property of making all men
happy.

Pro. Yes, by all means.

Soc. And you say that pleasure, and I say that wisdom, is such
a state?

Pro. True.

Soc. And what if there be a third state, which is better than
e either? Then both of us are vanquished—are we not? But if this
life, which can be relied upon to make men happy, turns out to be
more akin to pleasure than to wisdom, the life of pleasure may
12 still have the advantage over the life of wisdom.

Pro. True.

Soc. Or suppose that the better life is more nearly allied to
wisdom, then wisdom conquers, and pleasure is defeated;—do
you agree?

Pro. Certainly.

Soc. And what do you say, Philebus?

Phi. I say, and shall always say, that pleasure is easily the
conqueror; but you must decide for yourself, Protarchus.

Pro. You, Philebus, have handed over the argument to me,
and have no longer the right to make or not to make an agreement
with Socrates.

b *Phi.* True enough. I hereby declare myself free from the discussion, and call the goddess of Pleasure to witness.

Pro. You may appeal to us; we too will be the witnesses of
your words. And now, Socrates, whether Philebus is pleased or
displeased, we will proceed with the argument.

Soc. Then let us begin with the goddess herself, of whom
Philebus says that she is called Aphrodite, but that her real name
is Pleasure.

Pro. Very good.

c *Soc.* The awe which I always feel, Protarchus, about the names
of the gods is more than human—it exceeds all other fears. And
now I would not sin against Aphrodite by naming her amiss; let
her be called what she pleases. But Pleasure I know to be manifold, and with her, as I was just now saying, we must begin, and
consider what her nature is. She has one name, and therefore you
would imagine that she is one; and yet surely she takes the most
varied and even unlike forms. For do we not say that the intem-
d perate has pleasure, and that the temperate has pleasure in his
very temperance,—that the fool is pleased when he is full of
foolish fancies and hopes, and that the wise man has pleasure in
his wisdom? and how foolish would anyone be who affirmed
that all these opposite pleasures are severally alike!

Pro. Why, Socrates, they are opposed in so far as they spring from opposite sources, but they are not in themselves opposite. For must not pleasure be of all things most absolutely like e pleasure,—that is, like itself?

Soc. Yes, my good friend, just as colour is like colour;—in so far as colours are colours, there is no difference between them; and yet we all know that black is not only unlike, but even absolutely opposed to white: or again, as figure is like figure, for all figures are comprehended under one class; and yet of particular figures some are absolutely opposed to one another, and the rest show an infinite diversity. And we might find similar examples 13 in many other things; therefore do not rely upon this argument, which would go to prove the unity of the most extreme opposites. And I suspect that we shall find a similar opposition among pleasures.

Pro. Very likely; but how will this invalidate the argument?

Soc. Why, I shall reply, that dissimilar as they are, you apply to them a new predicate, for you say that all pleasant things are good; now there can be no argument to show that the pleasant is not pleasant; but whereas we say that most pleasures are bad, b though there are some good ones as well, you call them all alike good, and at the same time are compelled, if you are pressed, to acknowledge that they are unlike. And so you must tell us what is the identical quality existing alike in good and bad pleasures, which makes you designate all of them as good.

Pro. What do you mean, Socrates? Do you think that anyone who asserts pleasure to be the good, will tolerate the notion that some pleasures are good and others bad? c

Soc. But perhaps you will acknowledge that they are different from one another, and sometimes opposed?

Pro. Not in so far as they are pleasures.

Soc. That is a return to the old position, Protarchus, and so we are to say (are we?) that there is no difference in pleasures, but that they are all alike; and the examples which have just been cited do not pierce our dull minds, but we fall into the state of the d weakest and most inexperienced reasoners, and speak as they do.

Pro. What do you mean?

Soc. Why, I mean to say, that in self-defence I may, if I like, follow your example, and assert boldly that the two things most unlike are most absolutely alike; and the result will be that you and I will prove ourselves to be very tiros in the art of disputing; and the argument will be blown away and lost. Suppose that we put back, and like wrestlers return to the old position; then perhaps we may come to an understanding with one another.

e   *Pro.* How do you mean?

Soc. Shall I, Protarchus, have my own question asked of me by you?

Pro. What question?

Soc. Ask me whether wisdom and science and mind, and those other qualities which I, when asked by you at first what is the nature of the good, affirmed to be good, are not in the same case with the pleasures of which you spoke.

Pro. What do you mean?

Soc. The sciences are a numerous class, and will be found to present great differences. But even admitting that, like the plea-

14   sures, they are opposite as well as different, should I be worthy of the name of dialectician if, in order to avoid this difficulty, I were to say (as you are saying of pleasure) that there is no difference between one science and another;—would not the argument founder and disappear like a forgotten legend, although we might ourselves escape drowning by clinging to a fallacy?

Pro. May none of this befall us, except the deliverance! Yet I like the even-handed justice which is applied to both our arguments. Let us assume, then, that there are many and diverse pleasures, and many and different sciences.

b   *Soc.* And let us have no concealment, Protarchus, of the differences between my argument and yours; but let us bring them to the light in the hope that, in the process of testing them, they may show whether pleasure is to be called the good, or wisdom, or some third quality; for surely we are not now simply contending in order that my view or that yours may prevail, but I presume that we ought both of us to be fighting for the truth.

Pro. Certainly we ought.

c   *Soc.* Then let us have a more definite understanding and establish the principle on which the argument rests.

Pro. What principle?

Soc. A principle about which all men are always in a difficulty, and some men sometimes against their will.

Pro. Speak plainer.

Soc. The principle which has just turned up, which is a marvel of nature; for that one should be many or many one, are wonderful propositions; and he who affirms either is very open to attack.

Pro. Do you mean, when a person says that I, Protarchus, am by nature one and also many, dividing the single 'me' into many d 'me's', and even opposing them as great and small, light and heavy, and in ten thousand other ways?

Soc. Those, Protarchus, are the common and acknowledged paradoxes about the one and many, which I may say that everybody has by this time agreed to dismiss as childish and obvious and detrimental to the true course of thought; and no more favour is shown to that other puzzle, in which a person arguing that a thing is divisible into limbs or parts, and making his opponent c admit that they together form the original one, then heaps ridicule upon him as one who has admitted something monstrous, that the one is many and infinite, and the many are only one.

Pro. But what, Socrates, are those other marvels connected with this subject which, as you imply, have not yet become common and acknowledged? 15

Soc. When, my boy, the one does not belong to the class of things that are born and perish, as in the instance just given, for in those cases, and when unity is of this concrete nature, there is, as I was saying, a universal consent that there is no need to test it by argument; but when the assertion is made that man is one, or ox is one, or beauty one, or the good one, then the interest which attaches to these and similar unities and the attempt which is made to divide them give birth to a controversy.

Pro. Of what nature?

Soc. In the first place, whether we must suppose that any such b unities *are*, and have real existence; and then how each individual unity, being always the same, and incapable either of generation or of destruction, nevertheless undoubtedly *is*, or shares in being;[1] and then there remains the question of its presence in the infinity of the world of generation, whether we must think that it is dispersed and has become many, or that it is still entire and yet divided from itself, which latter would seem to be the greatest

---

[1] [Compare *Parmen.* 151 e–2 a. The problem is how entities which are eternal and timeless can be said to *be*, if that word is understood to denote existence at the present time.]

impossibility of all, for how can one and the same thing be at the same time in one and in many things? These, Protarchus, are the
c real difficulties, and this is the one and many to which they relate; just as they are the source of the greatest perplexity if ill decided, so the right determination of them is the greatest possible gain.

Pro. Then, Socrates, let us begin by clearing up these questions.

Soc. That is what I should wish.

Pro. And I am sure that all my other friends will be glad to hear them discussed; Philebus, fortunately for us, is not disposed to move, and we had better not stir him up with questions.

d *Soc.* Good; and where shall we begin this great and multifarious battle, in which such various points are at issue? Shall we begin thus?

Pro. How?

Soc. We say that the one and many become identified in our propositions, and that now, as in time past, they run about together, in every sentence which is uttered, and that this union of them will never cease, and is not now beginning, but is, as I believe, an everlasting quality of propositions themselves which never grows old. But any young man, when he first tastes these subtleties, is delighted, and fancies that he has found a treasure
e of wisdom; in the first enthusiasm of his joy he leaves no stone, or rather no thought unturned, now rolling up the many into the one, and kneading them together, now unfolding and dividing them; he puzzles himself first and above all, and then he proceeds to puzzle his neighbours, whether they are older or younger, or of his own age—that makes no difference; neither father nor
16 mother does he spare; no human being who has ears is safe from him, hardly even his dog, and a barbarian would have no chance of escaping him, if an interpreter could only be found.

Pro. Considering, Socrates, how many we are, and that all of us are young men, is there not a danger that we and Philebus may all set upon you, if you abuse us? We understand what you mean; but is there no charm by which we may dispel all this confusion,
b no more excellent way of arriving at the truth? If there is, we hope that you will guide us into that way, and we will do our best to follow, for the inquiry in which we are engaged, Socrates, is not unimportant.

Soc. The reverse of unimportant, my boys, as Philebus calls you, and there neither is nor ever will be a better than my own favourite way, which has nevertheless already often deserted me and left me helpless in the hour of need.

Pro. Tell us what that is.

Soc. One which may be easily pointed out, but is by no means c easy of application; it is the parent of all the discoveries in the arts.

Pro. Tell us what it is.

Soc. A gift of heaven, which, as I conceive, the gods tossed among men by the hands of a new Prometheus, and therewith a blaze of light; and the ancients, who were our betters and nearer the gods than we are, handed down the tradition, that whatever things are said to be are composed of one and many, and have the finite[1] and infinite implanted in them: seeing, then, that d such is the order of the world, we too ought in every inquiry to begin by laying down one idea of that which is the subject of inquiry; this unity we shall find in everything. Having found it, we may next proceed to look for two, if there be two, or, if not, then for three or some other number, subdividing each of these units, until at last the unity with which we began is seen not only to be one and many and infinite, but also a definite number; the infinite must not be suffered to approach the many until the entire number of the species intermediate between unity and infinity has been discovered,—then, and not till then, we may e rest from division, and without further troubling ourselves about the endless individuals may allow them to drop into infinity. This, as I was saying, is the way of considering and learning and teaching one another, which the gods have handed down to us. But the wise men of our time are either too quick or too slow in 17 conceiving plurality in unity. Having no method, they make their one and many anyhow, and from unity pass at once to infinity; the intermediate steps never occur to them. And this, I repeat, is what makes the difference between the mere art of disputation and true dialectic.

Pro. In part I think that I understand you, Socrates, but in part also I must ask you to explain your meaning more clearly.

Soc. I may illustrate my meaning by the letters of the alphabet, Protarchus, which you were made to learn as a child. b

Pro. How do they afford an illustration?

[1] ['the finite': see p. 575 n.]

Soc. The sound which passes through the lips whether of an individual or of all men is one and yet infinite.

Pro. Very true.

Soc. And yet not by knowing either that sound is one or that sound is infinite are we perfect in the art of speech, but the knowledge of the number and nature of sounds is what makes a man a grammarian.

Pro. Very true.

Soc. And the knowledge which makes a man a musician is of the same kind.

Pro. How so?

c   *Soc.* Sound is one in music as well as in grammar?

Pro. Certainly.

Soc. And there is a higher note and a lower note, and a note of equal pitch:—may we affirm so much?

Pro. Yes.

Soc. But you would not be a real musician if this was all that you knew; though if you did not know this you would know almost nothing of music.

Pro. Nothing.

Soc. But when you have learned what sounds are high and d what low, and the number and nature of the intervals and their limits or proportions, and the systems compounded out of them, which our fathers discovered, and have handed down to us who are their descendants under the name of harmonies; when you have learned also how similar affections appear and come to be in the movements of bodies, which when measured by numbers ought, as they say, to be called rhythms and measures; and they tell us that the same principle should be applied to every one and many; when, I say, you have learned all this, then, my dear e friend, you have technical skill; and you may be said to understand any other subject, when you have a similar grasp of it. But the infinity of kinds and the infinity of individuals which there is in each of them, when not classified, creates in every one of us a state of infinite ignorance; and he who never looks for number in anything, will not himself be looked for in the number of famous men.

18   *Pro.* I think that what Socrates is now saying is excellent, Philebus.

Phi. I think so too, but how do his words bear upon us and upon the argument?

Soc. Philebus is right in asking that question of us, Protarchus.

Pro. Indeed he is, and you must answer him.

Soc. I will; but you must let me make one little remark first about these matters; I was saying, that he who begins with any individual unity, should proceed from that, not to infinity, but to a definite number, and now I say conversely, that he who has to begin with infinity should not jump to unity, but he should look b about for some number representing a certain quantity, and thus out of all end in one. And now let us return for an illustration of our principle to the case of letters.

Pro. What do you mean?

Soc. Some god or divine man, who in the Egyptian legend is said to have been Theuth, observing that the human voice was infinite, first distinguished in this infinity a certain number of vowels, and then other letters which had sound, but were not c pure vowels (i.e. the semivowels); these too exist in a definite number; and lastly, he distinguished a third class of letters which we now call mutes, without voice and without sound, and divided these, and likewise the two other classes of vowels and semivowels, into the individual sounds, and told the number of them, and gave to each and all of them the name of letters; and observing that none of us could learn any one of them individually and not learn them all, and in consideration of this common bond which in a manner united them, he assigned to them all d a single art, and this he called the art of grammar or letters.

Phi. The illustration, Protarchus, has assisted me in understanding the original statement, but I still feel the defect of which I just now complained.

Soc. Are you going to ask, Philebus, what this has to do with the argument?

Phi. Yes, that is a question which Protarchus and I have long been asking.

Soc. Assuredly you have already arrived at the answer to the question which, as you say, you have been so long asking.

Phi. How so? e

Soc. Did we not begin by inquiring into the comparative eligibility of pleasure and wisdom?

Phi. Certainly.

Soc. And we maintain that they are each of them one?

Phi. True.

Soc. And the precise question to which the previous discussion desires an answer is, how they are one and also many [i.e. how they have one genus and many species], and are not at once infinite, and what number of species is to be assigned to either of them before they pass into infinity.[1]

19   *Pro.* That is a very serious question, Philebus, to which Socrates has ingeniously brought us round, and please to consider which of us shall answer him; there may be something ridiculous in my being unable to answer, and therefore imposing the task upon you, when I have undertaken the whole charge of the argument, but if neither of us were able to answer, the result methinks would

b   be still more ridiculous. Let us consider, then, what we are to do:—Socrates, if I understood him rightly, is asking whether there are or are not kinds of pleasure, and what is the number and nature of them, and the same of wisdom.

Soc. Most true, O son of Callias; and the previous argument showed that if we are not able to tell the kinds of everything that has unity, likeness, sameness, or their opposites, none of us will ever be of the smallest use in any inquiry.

c   *Pro.* That seems to be very near the truth, Socrates. Happy would the wise man be if he knew all things, and the next best thing for him is that he should know himself. Why do I say so at this moment? I will tell you. You, Socrates, have granted us this opportunity of conversing with you, and are ready to assist us in determining what is the best of human possessions. For when Philebus said that pleasure and delight and enjoyment and the like were the chief good, you answered—No, not those, but

d   another class of goods; and we are constantly reminding ourselves of what you said, and very properly, in order that we may not forget to examine and compare the two. And these goods, which in your opinion are to be designated as superior to pleasure, and are the true objects of pursuit, are mind, knowledge, understanding, art, and all that is akin to them. These were the two opposing views, and we playfully threatened that you should

e   not be allowed to go home until the question was settled; and you

---

[1] i.e. into the infinite number of individuals.

agreed, and placed yourself at our disposal. And now, as children say, what has been fairly given cannot be taken back; cease then to fight against us in this way.

Soc. In what way?

Phi. Do not perplex us, and keep asking questions of us to 20 which we have not as yet any sufficient answer to give; let us not imagine that a general puzzling of us all is to be the end of our discussion, but if we are unable to answer, do you answer, as you have promised. Consider, then, whether you will divide pleasure and knowledge according to their kinds; or you may let the matter drop, if you are able and willing to find some other mode of clearing up our controversy.

Soc. If you say that, I have nothing to apprehend, for the b words 'if you are willing' dispel all my fear; and, moreover, a god seems to have recalled something to my mind.

Phi. What is that?

Soc. I remember hearing long ago certain discussions about pleasure and wisdom, whether awake or in a dream I cannot tell; they were to the effect that neither the one nor the other of them was the good, but some third thing, which was different from them, and better than either. If this can at once be clearly established, then pleasure will lose the victory, for the good will c cease to be identified with her:—am I not right?

Pro. Yes.

Soc. And there will cease to be any need of distinguishing the kinds of pleasures, as I am inclined to think, but this will appear more clearly as we proceed.

Pro. Capital, Socrates; pray go on as you propose.

Soc. But, let us first agree on some little points.

Pro. What are they?

Soc. Is the good to be ranked as perfect or imperfect? d

Pro. The most perfect, Socrates, of all things.

Soc. And is the good sufficient?

Pro. Yes, certainly, and in a degree surpassing all other things.

Soc. And no one can deny that all beings who have apprehension of the good hunt after it, and are eager to catch it and wear it about them, and care not for the attainment of anything which is not accompanied by good.

Pro. That is undeniable.

e   *Soc.* Now let us part off the life of pleasure from the life of wisdom, and pass them in review.

Pro. How do you mean?

Soc. Let there be no wisdom in the life of pleasure, nor any pleasure in the life of wisdom, for if either of them is the chief good, it cannot be supposed to want anything, but if either is

21 shown to want anything, then it cannot really be the chief good.

Pro. It cannot indeed.

Soc. And will you yourself be our test of these two lives?

Pro. Certainly.

Soc. Then answer.

Pro. Ask.

Soc. Would you choose, Protarchus, to live all your life long in the enjoyment of the greatest pleasures?

Pro. Certainly I should.

Soc. Would you consider that there was still anything wanting to you if you had perfect pleasure?

Pro. Certainly not.

Soc. Reflect; would you not feel the want of wisdom and

b intelligence and forethought, and similar qualities?[1]

Pro. Why should I? Having pleasure I should have all things.

Soc. Living thus, you would always throughout your life enjoy the greatest pleasures?

Pro. I should.

Soc. But if you had neither mind, nor memory, nor knowledge, nor true opinion, you would in the first place be utterly ignorant of whether you were pleased or not, because you would be entirely devoid of intelligence.

Pro. Certainly.

Soc. And similarly, if you had no memory you would not recollect that you had ever been pleased, nor would the slightest

c recollection of the pleasure which you feel at any moment remain with you; and if you had no true opinion you would not think that you were pleased when you were; and if you had no power of calculation you would not be able to calculate on future

---

[1] [μὴ δέοι ἄν Klitsch, Burnet: μηδὲ ὁρᾶν MSS. With the latter reading translate, as in previous editions: 'Would you not at any rate want sight?']

pleasure, and your life would not be the life of a man, but of a mollusc, or any creature of the sea which 'lives' enclosed in a shell. Could this be otherwise?

Pro. No.   d

Soc. But is such a life to be chosen?

Pro. I cannot answer you, Socrates; the argument has taken away from me the power of speech.

Soc. We must not weaken;—let us now take the life of mind and examine it in turn.

Pro. And what is this life of mind?

Soc. I want to know whether anyone of us would consent to live, having wisdom and mind and knowledge and memory of all things, but having no sense of pleasure or pain, either more or e less, and wholly unaffected by these and the like feelings?

Pro. Neither life, Socrates, appears eligible to me, nor is likely, as I should imagine, to be chosen by anyone else.

Soc. What would you say, Protarchus, to both of these in one, 22 or to one that was made out of the union of the two?

Pro. Out of the union, that is, of pleasure with mind and wisdom?

Soc. Yes, that is the life which I mean.

Pro. There can be no difference of opinion; not some but all would surely choose this third rather than either of the other two, and in addition to them.

Soc. But do you see the consequence?

Pro. To be sure I do. The consequence is, that two out of the three lives which have been proposed are neither sufficient nor b eligible for man or for animal.

Soc. Then now there can be no doubt that neither of them has the good, for the one which had would certainly have been sufficient and perfect and eligible for all plants and animals, if they were able to spend their whole lives in the activity selected; and if any of us had chosen any other, he would have chosen contrary to the nature of the truly eligible, and not of his own free will, but either through ignorance or from some unhappy necessity.

Pro. Certainly that seems to be true.

Soc. And now have I not sufficiently shown that Philebus' c goddess is not to be regarded as identical with the good?

Phi. Neither is your 'mind' the good, Socrates, for that will be open to the same objections.

Soc. Perhaps, Philebus, you may be right in saying so of my 'mind'; but of the true, which is also the divine mind, far otherwise. However, I shall not at present claim the first place for mind as against the mixed life; but we must come to some under-

d standing about the second place. For you might affirm pleasure and I mind to be the cause of the mixed life; and in that case although neither of them would be the good, one of them might be imagined to be the cause of the good. And I might proceed further to argue in opposition to Philebus, that the element which makes this mixed life eligible and good, is more akin and more similar to mind than to pleasure. And if this is true, pleasure cannot be truly said to share either in the first or second place,

e and does not, if I may trust my own mind, attain even to the third.

Pro. Truly, Socrates, pleasure appears to me to have had a fall;

23 in fighting for the palm, she has been smitten by the argument, and is laid low. I must say that mind would have fallen too, and may therefore be thought to show discretion in not putting forward a similar claim. And if pleasure were deprived not only of the first but of the second place, she would be terribly damaged in the eyes of her admirers, for not even to them would she still appear as fair as before.

Soc. Well, but had we not better leave her now, and not pain her by applying the crucial test, and finally detecting her?

Pro. Nonsense, Socrates.

b   *Soc.* Why? because I said that we had better not pain pleasure, which is an impossibility?

Pro. Yes, and more than that, because you do not seem to be aware that none of us will let you go home until you have finished the argument.

Soc. Heavens! Protarchus, that will be a tedious business, and just at present not at all an easy one. For in going to war in the cause of mind, who is aspiring to the second prize, I ought to have weapons of another make from those which I used before; some, however, of the old ones may do again. And must I then finish the argument?

Pro. Of course you must.

Soc. Let us be very careful in laying the foundation.   c

Pro. What do you mean?

Soc. Let us divide all existing things into two, or rather, if you do not object, into three classes.

Pro. Upon what principle would you make the division?

Soc. Let us take some of our newly-found notions.

Pro. Which of them?

Soc. Were we not saying that God revealed a finite element of existence, and also an infinite?[1]

Pro. Certainly.

Soc. Let us assume these two principles, and also a third class, which is compounded out of them; but I fear that I am ridiculously   d clumsy at these processes of division and enumeration.

Pro. What do you mean, my good friend?

Soc. I say that a fourth class is still wanted.

Pro. What will that be?

Soc. Find the cause whereby the two principles are mixed, and add this as a fourth class to the three others.

Pro. And would you like to have a fifth class or cause of resolution as well as a cause of composition?

Soc. Not, I think, at present; but if I want a fifth at some future   e time you shall allow me to have it.

Pro. Certainly.

Soc. Firstly, then, let us set apart three of the four classes for examination, and among these choose two. Let each first be viewed as many, in a state of division and dispersal; then let us endeavour to reunite them, and think how each of them came to be both one and many.

Pro. If you would explain to me a little more about them,   24 perhaps I might be able to follow you.

Soc. Well, the two classes are the same which I mentioned before, one the finite, and the other the infinite; I will first show that the infinite is in a certain sense many, and the finite may be hereafter discussed.

Pro. I agree.

---

[1] [As the ensuing argument shows, *finite* and *infinite* do not exactly represent the Greek πέρας and ἄπειρον; but we retain them as being preferable to the unusual terms *limit* and *unlimited*. πέρας is not so much *the finite* as *finitude*; a finite *thing*, as later examples show, belongs to the third class.]

Soc. And now consider well; for the question to which I invite your attention is difficult and controverted. When you speak of hotter and colder, can you conceive any limit in those qualities? Does not the more and less, which dwells in their very nature, b prevent their having any end? for if they had an end, the more and less would themselves have an end.

Pro. That is most true.

Soc. Ever, as we say, into the hotter and the colder there enters a more and a less.

Pro. Yes.

Soc. Then, says the argument, there is never any end of them, and being endless they must also be infinite.

Pro. Yes, Socrates, that is exceedingly true.

Soc. Yes, my dear Protarchus, and your answer reminds me c that such an expression as 'exceedingly', which you have just uttered, and also the term 'slightly', have the same significance as more or less; for whenever they occur they do not allow of the existence of quantity—they are always introducing degrees into actions, instituting a comparison of a more or a less excessive or a more or a less slight, and at each creation of more or less, quantity disappears. For, as I was just now saying, if quantity and measure did not disappear, but were allowed to intrude in d the sphere of more and less and the other comparatives, these last would be driven out of their own domain. When definite quantity is once admitted, there can be no longer a 'hotter' or a 'colder' (for these are always progressing, and are never in one stay); but definite quantity is at rest, and has ceased to progress. Which proves that comparatives, such as the hotter and the colder, are to be ranked in the class of the infinite.

Pro. Your remark certainly has the look of truth, Socrates; but these subjects, as you were saying, are difficult to follow at first. I think, however, that if I could hear the argument repeated by e you once or twice, there would be a substantial agreement between us.

Soc. Yes, and I will try to meet your wish; but, as I would rather not waste time in the enumeration of endless particulars, let me know whether I may not assume as a note of the infinite——

Pro. What?

Soc. I want to know whether such things as appear to us to admit of more or less, or are denoted by the words 'exceedingly', 'slightly', 'extremely', and the like, may not be referred to the 25 class of the infinite, which is their unity, for, as was asserted in the previous argument, all things that were divided and dispersed should be brought together, and have the mark or seal of some one nature, if possible, set upon them—do you remember?

Pro. Yes.

Soc. And all things which do not admit of more or less, but admit their opposites, that is to say, first of all, equality and the equal, or again, the double, or any other ratio of number to number and measure to measure—all these may, I think, be b rightly reckoned by us in the class of the limited or finite; what do you say?

Pro. Excellent, Socrates.

Soc. And now what nature shall we ascribe to the third or compound kind?

Pro. You, I think, will have to tell me that.

Soc. Rather God will tell you, if there be any god who will listen to my prayers.

Pro. Offer up a prayer, then, and think.

Soc. I am thinking, Protarchus, and I believe that some god has befriended us.

Pro. What do you mean, and what proof have you to offer of c what you are saying?

Soc. I will tell you, and do you listen to my words.

Pro. Proceed.

Soc. Were we not speaking just now of hotter and colder?

Pro. True.

Soc. Add to them drier, wetter, more, less, swifter, slower, greater, smaller, and all that in the preceding argument we considered as a single nature, admitting more and less.

Pro. In the class of the infinite, you mean? d

Soc. Yes; and now mingle this with the other.

Pro. What is the other?

Soc. The class of the finite which we ought to have brought together as we did the infinite; but, perhaps,[1] it will come to the

---

[1] [25 d 7, ἀλλ' ἴσως κτλ. The sense of this passage, though it has usually been missed, is clear, and there is no need for alteration in the text. At 25 d 2 the process of blending the two simple classes was begun. Socrates immediately remembers that

same thing if we do so now;—for in the process of bringing both
the elements together for mixture, the nature of the second element will be revealed.

Pro. How so, and what do you mean by this element?

Soc. The class of the equal and the double, and any class which
makes a reconciliation between opposites and by introducing
e number creates harmony and proportion among the different
elements.

Pro. I understand; you seem to me to mean that the various
opposites, when you mingle with them the class of the finite, each
give birth to something new.

Soc. Yes, that is my meaning.

Pro. Proceed.

Soc. Does not the right participation in the finite give health—
in disease, for instance?

26　*Pro.* Certainly.

Soc. And whereas the high and low, the swift and the slow are
infinite or unlimited, does not the addition of the principles
aforesaid introduce a limit, and perfect the whole frame of music?[1]

Pro. Yes, certainly.

Soc. Or, again, when cold and heat prevail, does not the introduction of them take away excess and indefiniteness, and infuse
moderation and harmony?

Pro. Certainly.

b　*Soc.* And from a like admixture of the finite and infinite come
the seasons, and all the delights of life?

Pro. Most true.

Soc. I omit ten thousand other things, such as beauty and health
and strength, and the many beauties and high perfections of the
soul: O my beautiful Philebus, methinks the goddess of Harmony,
seeing the universal wantonness and wickedness of all things,

---

he has not yet given instances of πέρας, which is the second element in the mixture.
But no harm is done, for its nature will appear whilst the mixture itself is being
formed. In τούτων ἀμφοτέρων συναγομένων the reference is to the third class, the
mixed; in κἀκείνη to the second class, the finite. There is no need to transpose
ἀλλ᾽ . . . γενήσεται to 25 e 2, with Jackson. The point is that τὸ μεικτόν is already
under review, and τὸ πέρας is to be reviewed at the same time.]

[1] [26 a 3 ἆρ᾽ οὐ ταὐτὰ ἐγγιγνόμενα, κτλ. ἐγγιγνόμενα is bracketed by Burnet. He
also reads, in 26 a 6 below, ἐγγενομένη, so that the subject of the verbs throughout the
passage is the τούτων ὀρθὴ κοινωνία mentioned in 25 e 7. We prefer, however, to
retain the traditional text.]

and that there was in them no limit to pleasures and self-indulgence, devised the limit of law and order, whereby, as you say, Philebus, she extinguished, or as I maintain, delivered them. c —What think you, Protarchus?

Pro. Her ways are much to my mind, Socrates.

Soc. You will observe that I have spoken of three classes?

Pro. Yes, I think that I understand you: you mean to say that the infinite is one class, and that the finite is a second class of existences; but what you would make the third I am not so certain.

Soc. That is because the amazing variety of the third class is too much for you, my dear friend; but there was not this difficulty with the infinite, which also comprehended many classes, for all of them were marked with the seal of more and less, and therefore d appeared one.

Pro. True.

Soc. And the finite or limit had not many divisions, and we readily acknowledged it to be by nature one?

Pro. Yes.

Soc. Yes, indeed; and when I speak of the third class, understand me to include under one name any offspring of these, being a birth into true being, effected by the measure which the limit introduces.

Pro. I understand.

Soc. Still there was, as we said, a fourth class to be investigated, e and you must assist in the investigation; for does not everything which comes into being, of necessity come into being through a cause?

Pro. Yes, certainly; for how can there be anything which has no cause?

Soc. And is not the agent the same as the cause in all except name? the agent and the cause may be rightly called one?

Pro. Very true.   27

Soc. And the same may be said of the patient and the effect; we shall find that they too differ, as I have just said, only in name —shall we not?

Pro. We shall.

Soc. The agent or cause always naturally leads, and the patient or effect naturally follows it?

Pro. Certainly.

Soc. Then the cause and what is subordinate to it in generation are not the same, but different?

Pro. True.

Soc. Did not the things which were generated, and the things out of which they were generated, furnish all the three classes?

Pro. Yes.

Soc. And the creator or cause of them has been satisfactorily
b proven to be distinct from them,—and may therefore be called a fourth principle?

Pro. So let us call it.

Soc. Quite right; but now, having distinguished the four, I think that we had better refresh our memories by recapitulating each of them in order.

Pro. By all means.

Soc. Then the first I call the infinite or unlimited, and the second the finite or limited; then follows the third, a being which came into being by a mixture of these elements; and I do not think that I shall be far wrong in speaking of the cause of mixture
c and generation as the fourth.

Pro. Certainly not.

Soc. And now what is the next question, and how came we hither? Were we not inquiring whether the second place belonged to pleasure or wisdom?

Pro. We were.

Soc. And now, having determined these points, shall we not be better able to decide about the first and second place, which was the original subject of dispute?

Pro. I dare say.

Soc. We said, if you remember, that the mixed life of pleasure
d and wisdom was the conqueror—did we not?

Pro. True.

Soc. And we see, I think, what is the nature of this life and to what class it is to be assigned?

Pro. Beyond a doubt.

Soc. This is evidently comprehended in the third or mixed class; which is not composed of any two particular ingredients, but of all the elements of infinity, bound down by the finite, and may therefore be truly said to comprehend the conqueror life.

Pro. Most true.

Soc. And what shall we say, Philebus, of your life which is all e sweetness; and in which of the aforesaid classes is that to be placed? Perhaps you will allow me to ask you a question before you answer?

Phi. Let me hear.

Soc. Have pleasure and pain a limit, or do they belong to the class which admits of more and less?

Phi. They belong to the class which admits of more, Socrates; for pleasure would not be perfectly good[1] if she were not infinite in quantity and degree.

Soc. Nor would pain, Philebus, be perfectly evil.[1] And there- 28 fore the infinite cannot be that element which imparts to pleasure some degree of good. But now—admitting, if you like, that pain and pleasure are of the nature of the infinite—in which of the aforesaid classes, O Protarchus and Philebus, can we without irreverence place wisdom and knowledge and mind? And let us be careful, for I think that the danger will be very serious if we err on this point.

Phi. You magnify, Socrates, the importance of your favourite b god.

Soc. And you, my friend, are also magnifying your favourite goddess; but still I must beg you to answer the question.

Pro. Socrates is quite right, Philebus, and we must submit to him.

Phi. And did not you, Protarchus, propose to answer in my place?

Pro. Certainly I did; but I am now in a great strait, and I must entreat you, Socrates, to be our spokesman, and then we shall not say anything wrong or disrespectful of your favourite.

Soc. I must obey you, Protarchus; nor is the task which you c impose a difficult one; but did I really, as Philebus implies, disconcert you with my playful solemnity, when I asked the question to what class mind and knowledge belong?

Pro. You did, indeed, Socrates.

Soc. Yet the answer is easy, since all philosophers assert with one voice that mind is the king of heaven and earth—in reality they are magnifying themselves. And perhaps they are right. But still I should like to consider the class of mind, if you do not object, a little more fully.

---

[1] [Reading πανάγαθον and πάγκακον with Bekker and Bury.]

d   *Phi.* Take your own course, Socrates, and never mind length; we shall not tire of you.

Soc. Very good; let us begin then, Protarchus, by asking a question.

Pro. What question?

Soc. Whether all this which they call the universe is left to the guidance of unreason and chance medley, or, on the contrary, as others before us have declared, ordered and governed by a marvellous intelligence and wisdom.

e   *Pro.* Wide asunder are the two assertions, illustrious Socrates, for that which you were just now saying to me appears to be blasphemy; but the other assertion, that mind orders all things, is worthy of the aspect of the world, and of the sun, and of the moon, and of the stars and of the whole circle of the heavens; and never will I say or think otherwise.

Soc. Shall we then [1]agree with our predecessors in maintaining[1] this doctrine,—not merely reasserting the notions of others,

29   without risk to ourselves,—but shall we share in the danger, and take our part of the reproach which will await us, when an advanced thinker declares that all is disorder?

Pro. That would certainly be my wish.

Soc. Then now please to consider the next stage of the argument.

Pro. Let me hear.

Soc. We see that the elements which enter into the nature of the bodies of all animals are fire, water, air, and 'there is land' as the storm-tossed sailor cries,[2] present in the mixture.

b   *Pro.* An apt comparison; for truly the storm gathers over us, and we are at our wit's end.

Soc. There is something to be remarked about each of these elements.

Pro. What is it?

Soc. Only a small fraction of each of them exists in us, and that of a mean sort, and not in any way pure, or having any power worthy of its nature. One instance will prove this of all of them; there is fire within us, and in the universe.

Pro. True.

---

[1] Or, 'maintain in accordance with our previous statements': but cf. *supra* 28 d, and *infra* 30 d.

[2] [The comma after χειμαζόμενοι in Burnet's text should be omitted.]

Soc. And is not our fire small and weak and mean? But the c fire in the universe is wonderful in quantity and beauty, and in every power that fire has.

Pro. Most true.

Soc. And is the fire in the universe nourished and generated and increased by the fire in us, or is the fire in you and me, and in other animals, dependent on the universal fire?

Pro. That is a question which does not deserve an answer.

Soc. Right; and you would say the same, if I am not mistaken, d of the earth which is in animals and the earth which is in the universe, and you would give a similar reply about all the other elements?

Pro. Why, how could any man who gave any other be deemed in his senses?

Soc. I do not think that he could—but now go on to the next step. When we saw those elements of which we have been speaking gathered up in one, did we not call them a body?

Pro. We did.

Soc. And the same may be said of the cosmos, which for the e same reason may be considered to be a body, because made up of the same elements.

Pro. Very true.

Soc. But is our body nourished wholly by this body, or is this body nourished by our body, thence deriving and having those effects of which we were just now[1] speaking?

Pro. That again, Socrates, is a question which does not deserve to be asked.

Soc. Well, tell me, is this question worth asking? 30

Pro. What question?

Soc. May not our body be said to have a soul?

Pro. Clearly.

Soc. And whence comes that soul, my dear Protarchus, unless the body of the universe, which contains elements like those in our bodies but in every way fairer, had also a soul? Can there be another source?

Pro. Clearly, Socrates, that is the only source.

Soc. Why, yes, Protarchus; for surely we cannot imagine that of the four classes present in all things, the finite, the infinite, the

---

[1] [At 29 c 5.]

b composition of the two, and the cause, the fourth is responsible for the greatest benefits among mankind, giving to our bodies souls, and the art of self-management, and of healing disease, and operating in other ways to heal and organize, so that it is acclaimed as wisdom in every sphere—we cannot, I say, imagine that whereas the selfsame elements exist, both in the entire heaven and in great provinces of the heaven, only fairer and purer, the same cause should not also in that higher sphere have designed the noblest and fairest things?

c *Pro.* Such a supposition is quite unreasonable.

Soc. Then if this be denied, should we not be wise in adopting the other view and maintaining that there is in the universe a mighty infinite and an adequate limit, of which we have often spoken, as well as a presiding cause of no mean power, which orders and arranges years and seasons and months, and may be justly called wisdom and mind?

Pro. Most justly.

Soc. And wisdom and mind cannot exist without soul?

Pro. Certainly not.

d *Soc.* And in the divine nature of Zeus would you not say that there is the soul and mind of a king, because there is in him the power of the cause? And other gods have other attributes, by which they are pleased to be called.

Pro. Very true.

Soc. Do not then suppose that these words are rashly spoken by us, O Protarchus, for they are in harmony with the testimony of those who said of old time that mind rules the universe.

Pro. True.

Soc. And they furnish an answer to my inquiry;[1] for they

e imply that mind is the parent[2] of that class in which we included the causes of all things; and I think that you now have my answer.

Pro. I have indeed, and yet I did not observe that you had answered.

Soc. A jest is sometimes refreshing, Protarchus, when it interrupts hard work.

31 *Pro.* Very true.

Soc. I think, friend, that we have now pretty clearly set

[1] [Cf. 28 a.]   [2] [Reading γενούστης.]

forth the class to which mind belongs and what is the power of mind.

Pro. True.

Soc. And the class to which pleasure belongs has also been long ago discovered?

Pro. Yes.

Soc. And let us remember, too, of both of them, (1) that mind was akin to the cause and of this family; and (2) that pleasure is infinite and belongs to the class which neither has, nor ever will have in itself, a beginning, middle, or end of its own.

Pro. I shall be sure to remember. b

Soc. We must next examine in what subject they occur and under what conditions they are generated. And we will begin with pleasure, since her class was first examined; and yet pleasure cannot be rightly tested apart from pain.

Pro. If this is the road, let us take it.

Soc. I wonder whether you would agree with me about the origin of pleasure and pain.

Pro. What do you mean? c

Soc. I mean to say that their natural seat is in the mixed class.

Pro. And would you tell me again, my dear Socrates, which of the aforesaid classes is the mixed one?

Soc. I will, my fine fellow, to the best of my ability.

Pro. Very good.

Soc. Let us then understand the mixed class to be that which we placed third in the list of four.

Pro. That which followed the infinite and the finite; and in which you ranked health, and, if I am not mistaken, harmony.

Soc. Capital; and now will you please to give me your best d attention?

Pro. Proceed; I am attending.

Soc. I say that when the harmony in animals is dissolved, during such time there is both a dissolution of their natural state and a generation of pain.

Pro. That is very probable.

Soc. And the restoration of harmony and return to nature is the source of pleasure, if I may be allowed to speak in the fewest and shortest words about matters of the greatest moment.

Pro. I believe that you are right, Socrates; but will you try to be a little plainer?

Soc. Do not obvious and everyday phenomena furnish the simplest illustration?

Pro. What phenomena do you mean?

Soc. Hunger, for example, is a dissolution and a pain.

Pro. True.

Soc. Whereas eating is a replenishment and a pleasure?

Pro. Yes.

Soc. Thirst again is a destruction and a pain, but the effect of moisture replenishing the dry place is a pleasure: once more, the unnatural separation and dissolution caused by heat is painful, and the natural restoration and refrigeration is pleasant.

Pro. Very true.

Soc. And the unnatural freezing of the moisture in an animal is pain, and the natural process of resolution and return of the elements to their original state is pleasure. And would not the general proposition seem to you to hold, that when the natural union of the finite and infinite in a sentient being is destroyed, this destruction, as I was observing before, is pain, and that the process of return of all things to their own nature is pleasure?

Pro. Granted; what you say has a general truth.

Soc. Here then is one kind of pleasures and pains originating severally in the two processes which we have described?

Pro. Good.

Soc. Let us next assume that in the soul herself there is an antecedent hope of pleasure which is sweet and refreshing, and an expectation of pain, fearful and anxious.

Pro. Yes; this is another kind of pleasures and pains, which is of the soul only, apart from the body, and is produced by expectation.

Soc. Right; for in the analysis of these kinds, if they are pure, as I suppose them to be, the pleasures being unalloyed with pain and the pains with pleasure, methinks that we shall see clearly whether the whole class of pleasure is to be desired, or whether this quality of entire desirableness is not rather to be attributed to another of the classes which have been mentioned; and whether pleasure and pain, like heat and cold, and other things of the same kind, are not sometimes to be desired and sometimes not to be desired, as being not in themselves good, but only sometimes and in some instances admitting of the nature of good.

Pro. You say most truly that this is the track which the investigation should pursue.

Soc. Well, then, assuming that pain ensues on the dissolution, and pleasure on the restoration of the harmony, let us now ask e what will be the condition of animated beings who are neither in process of restoration nor of dissolution. And mind what you say: I ask whether any animal who is in that condition can possibly have any feeling of pleasure or pain, great or small?

Pro. Certainly not.

Soc. Then here we have a third state, over and above that of 33 pleasure and of pain?

Pro. Very true.

Soc. And do not forget that there is such a state; it will make a great difference in our judgement of pleasure, whether we remember this or not. And I should like to say a few words about it.

Pro. What have you to say?

Soc. Why, you know that if a man chooses the life of wisdom, there is no reason why he should not live in this neutral state.

Pro. You mean that he may live neither rejoicing nor sor- b rowing?

Soc. Yes; and if I remember rightly, when the lives were compared, no degree of pleasure, whether great or small, was thought to be necessary to him who chose the life of thought and wisdom.

Pro. Yes, certainly, we said so.

Soc. Then he will live without pleasure; and who knows whether this may not be the most divine of all lives?

Pro. Indeed, the gods surely cannot be supposed to have either joy or sorrow.

Soc. Certainly not—there would be a great impropriety in the assumption of either alternative. But this is a point which may be considered hereafter if in any way relevant to the argument, c and we will place it to the account of mind in her contest for the second place, should she have to resign the first.

Pro. Just so.

Soc. The other class of pleasures, which as we were saying is purely mental, is entirely derived from memory.

Pro. What do you mean?

Soc. I must first of all analyse memory, or rather perception which is prior to memory, if the subject of our discussion is ever to be properly cleared up.

d   *Pro.* How will you proceed?

Soc. Let us imagine affections of the body which are extinguished before they reach the soul, and leave her unaffected; and again, other affections which vibrate through both soul and body, and impart a shock to both and to each of them.

Pro. Granted.

Soc. And the soul may be truly said to be oblivious of the first but not of the second?

e   *Pro.* Quite true.

Soc. When I say oblivious, do not suppose that I here mean forgetfulness in a literal sense; for forgetfulness is the exit of memory, which in this case has not yet entered; and to speak of the loss of that which is not yet in existence, and never has been, is a contradiction; do you see?

Pro. Yes.

Soc. Then just be so good as to change the terms.

Pro. How shall I change them?

34   *Soc.* Instead of the oblivion of the soul, when you are describing the state in which she is unaffected by the shocks of the body, say unconsciousness or insensibility.

Pro. I see.

Soc. And the union or communion of soul and body in one feeling and motion would be properly called consciousness or sensation?

Pro. Most true.

Soc. Then now we know the meaning of the word sensation?

Pro. Yes.

Soc. Hence memory may, I think, be rightly described as the preservation of sensation?

b   *Pro.* Right.

Soc. But do we not distinguish recollection from memory?

Pro. I think so.

Soc. And when the soul recovers by her own unaided power

some feeling which she previously experienced in company with the body, is not this what we call recollecting?

Pro. Certainly.

Soc. And again when she revives by herself alone the lost memory of some sensation or knowledge, the recovery in all such cases is termed recollection?

Pro. Very true.

Soc. There is a reason why I say all this.

Pro. What is it?

Soc. I want to attain the plainest possible notion of pleasure and desire, as they exist in the mind only, apart from the body; and the previous analysis helps to show the nature of both.

Pro. Then now, Socrates, let us proceed to the next point.

Soc. There are certainly many things to be considered in discussing the generation and whole complexion[1] of pleasure. Indeed, before any advance can be made we must determine the nature and seat of desire.

Pro. Aye; let us inquire into that, for we shall lose nothing.

Soc. Nay, Protarchus, we shall surely lose the puzzle if we find the answer.

Pro. A fair retort; but let us proceed.

Soc. Did we not place hunger, thirst, and the like, in the class of desires?

Pro. Certainly.

Soc. And yet they are very different; what common nature have we in view when we call them by a single name?

Pro. By heavens, Socrates, that is a question which is not easily answered; but it must be answered.

Soc. Then let us go back to our examples.

Pro. Where shall we begin?

Soc. Do we mean anything when we say 'a man thirsts'?

Pro. Yes.

Soc. We mean to say that he 'is empty'?

Pro. Of course.

Soc. And is not thirst desire?

Pro. Yes, of drink.

Soc. Would you say of drink, or of replenishment with drink?

Pro. I should say, of replenishment with drink.

---

[1] [Retaining τήν in 34 c 10.]

Soc. Then he who is empty desires, as would appear, the opposite of what he experiences; for he is empty and desires to be full?

Pro. Clearly so.

Soc. But how can a man who is empty for the first time, attain either by perception or memory to any apprehension of replenishment, of which he has no present or past experience?

Pro. Impossible.

b   *Soc.* And yet he who desires, surely desires something?

Pro. Of course.

Soc. He does not desire that which he experiences, for he experiences thirst, and thirst is emptiness; but he desires replenishment?

Pro. True.

Soc. Then there must be something in the thirsty man which in some way apprehends replenishment?

Pro. There must.

Soc. And that cannot be the body, for the body is supposed to be emptied?

Pro. Yes.

Soc. The only remaining alternative is that the soul apprehends the replenishment by the help of memory; as is obvious, c for what other way can there be?

Pro. I cannot imagine any other.

Soc. But do you see the consequence?

Pro. What is it?

Soc. That there is no such thing as desire of the body.

Pro. Why so?

Soc. Why, because the argument shows that the endeavour of every animal is to the reverse of his bodily state.

Pro. Yes.

Soc. And the impulse which leads him to the opposite of what he is experiencing proves that he has a memory of the opposite state.

Pro. True.

d   *Soc.* And the argument, having proved that memory is the power by which we are attracted towards the objects of desire, proves also that the impulses and the desires and the moving principle of the whole animal have their origin in the soul.

Pro. Most true.

Soc. The argument will not allow that our body either hungers or thirsts or has any similar experience.

Pro. Quite right.

Soc. Let me make a further observation; the argument appears to me to imply that there is a kind of life which consists in these affections.

Pro. Of what affections, and of what kind of life, are you e speaking?

Soc. I am speaking of being emptied and replenished, and of all that relates to the preservation and destruction of living beings, as well as of the pain which is felt in one of these states and of the pleasure which succeeds to it.

Pro. True.

Soc. And what would you say of the intermediate state?

Pro. What do you mean by 'intermediate'?

Soc. I mean when a person is in actual suffering and yet remembers past pleasures which, if they would only return, would relieve him; but as yet he has them not. May we not say of him, that he is in an intermediate state?   36

Pro. Certainly.

Soc. Would you say that he was wholly pained or wholly pleased?

Pro. Nay, I should say that he has two pains; in his body there is the actual experience of pain, and in his soul longing and expectation.

Soc. What do you mean, Protarchus, by the two pains? May not a man who is empty have at one time a manifest hope of being filled, and at other times be quite in despair?   b

Pro. Very true.

Soc. And has he not the pleasure of memory when he is hoping to be filled, and yet in that he is empty is he not at the same time in pain?

Pro. Certainly.

Soc. Then man and the other animals have at the same time both pleasure and pain?

Pro. I suppose so.

Soc. But when a man is empty and has no hope of being filled, there will be the double experience of pain. You observed

c this and inferred that the double experience was the single case
possible.

Pro. Quite true, Socrates.

Soc. Shall the inquiry into these states of feeling be made the
occasion of raising a question?

Pro. What question?

Soc. Whether we ought to say that the pleasures and pains of
which we are speaking are true or false, or some true and some false.

Pro. But how, Socrates, can there be false pleasures and pains?

Soc. And how, Protarchus, can there be true and false fears,
or true and false expectations, or true and false opinions?

d   *Pro.* I grant that opinions may be true or false, but not these
other things.

Soc. What do you mean? I am afraid that we are raising a very
serious inquiry.

Pro. There I agree.

Soc. And yet, my boy, for you are one of Philebus' boys,[1]
the point to be considered is whether the inquiry is relevant
to the previous argument.

Pro. Surely.

Soc. No tedious and irrelevant discussion can be allowed;
what is said should be pertinent.

Pro. Right.

e   *Soc.* I am always wondering at the question which has now
been raised. What is your position? Do you deny that some
pleasures are false, and others true?

Pro. To be sure I do.

Soc. Would you say that no one ever seemed to rejoice and yet
did not rejoice, or seemed to feel pain and yet did not feel pain,
sleeping or waking, mad or lunatic?

Pro. So we have all been accustomed to hold, Socrates.

37   *Soc.* But were you right? Shall we inquire into the truth of
your opinion?

Pro. I think that we should.

Soc. Let us then put into more precise terms the question
which has arisen about pleasure and opinion. Is there such a
thing as opinion?

Pro. Yes.

[1] [Cf. 16 a.]

Soc. And such a thing as pleasure?

Pro. Yes.

Soc. And such a thing as an object of opinion?

Pro. True.

Soc. And an object in which that which is pleased takes pleasure?

Pro. Quite correct.

Soc. And whether the opinion be right or wrong, makes no difference; it will still be an opinion?

Pro. Certainly. b

Soc. And he who is pleased, whether he is rightly pleased or not, will always have a real feeling of pleasure?

Pro. Yes; that is also quite true.

Soc. Then, how can opinion be both true and false, and pleasure true only, although pleasure and opinion are both equally real?

Pro. Yes; that is the question.

Soc. You mean that opinion admits of truth and falsehood, and hence becomes not merely opinion, but opinion of a certain c quality; and this is what you think should be examined?

Pro. Yes.

Soc. And further, even if we admit the existence of qualities in other objects, but think pleasure and pain to be simple and devoid of quality, we must agree upon the reasons for this.

Pro. Clearly.

Soc. But there is no difficulty in seeing that pleasure and pain as well as opinion have qualities, for they are great or small, and have various degrees of intensity; as was indeed said long ago by us.

Pro. Quite true. d

Soc. And if badness attaches to any of them, Protarchus, then we should speak of a bad opinion or of a bad pleasure?

Pro. Quite true, Socrates.

Soc. And if rightness attaches to any of them, should we not speak of a right opinion or right pleasure; and in like manner of the reverse of rightness?

Pro. Certainly.

Soc. And if what is opined be erroneous, might we not say that e the opinion, being erroneous, is not right or rightly opined?

Pro. Certainly.

Soc. And if we see a pleasure or pain which errs in respect of its object, shall we call that right or good, or by any honourable name?

Pro. Not if the pleasure is mistaken; how could we?

Soc. And surely pleasure often appears to accompany an opinion which is not true, but false?

38 *Pro.* Certainly it does; and in that case, Socrates, as we were saying, the opinion is false, but no one could call the actual pleasure false.

Soc. How eagerly, Protarchus, do you rush to the defence of pleasure!

Pro. Nay, Socrates, I only repeat what I hear.

Soc. And is there no difference, my friend, between that pleasure which is associated with right opinion and knowledge, and that which is often found in all of us associated with falsehood and ignorance?

b *Pro.* There must be a very great difference between them.

Soc. Then, now let us proceed to contemplate this difference.

Pro. Lead, and I will follow.

Soc. Well, then, my view is——

Pro. What is it?

Soc. We agree—do we not?—that there is such a thing as false, and also such a thing as true opinion?

Pro. Yes.

Soc. And pleasure and pain, as I was just now saying, are often consequent upon these—upon true and false opinion, I mean.

Pro. Very true.

Soc. And do not opinion and the endeavour to form an opinion always spring from memory and perception?

c *Pro.* Certainly.

Soc. Might we imagine the process to be something of this nature?

Pro. Of what nature?

Soc. An object may be often seen at a distance not very clearly, and the seer may want to determine what it is which he sees.

Pro. Very likely.

Soc. Soon he begins to interrogate himself.

Pro. In what manner?

Soc. He asks himself—'What is that which appears to be standing by the rock under the tree?' This is the question which he may d be supposed to put to himself when he sees such an appearance.

Pro. True.

Soc. To which he may guess the right answer, saying as if in a whisper to himself—'It is a man.'

Pro. Very good.

Soc. Or again, he may be misled, thinking that it is a figure made by some shepherds, and call it an image.

Pro. Yes.

Soc. And if he has a companion, he repeats his thought to him e in articulate sounds, and what was before an opinion, has now become a proposition.

Pro. Certainly.

Soc. But if he be walking alone when these thoughts occur to him, he may not unfrequently keep them in his mind for a considerable time.

Pro. Very true.

Soc. Well, now, I wonder whether you would agree in my explanation of this phenomenon.

Pro. What is your explanation?

Soc. I think that the soul at such times is like a book.

Pro. How so?

Soc. Memory and perception meet, and they and their atten- 39 dant feelings seem to me almost to write down words in the soul. When the inscribing feeling[1] writes truly, then true opinion and true propositions are formed within us in consequence of its work— but when the scribe within us writes falsely, the result is false.

Pro. I quite assent and agree to your statement.

Soc. I must bespeak your favour also for another artist, who is b busy at the same time in the chambers of the soul.

Pro. Who is he?

Soc. The painter, who, after the scribe has done his work, draws images in the soul of the things which he has described.

Pro. But when and how does he do this?

Soc. When a man, besides receiving from sight or some other sense certain opinions or statements, sees in his mind the images

---

[1] [Retaining τοῦτο τὸ πάθημα in 39 a 4. The composite feeling formed of memory, perception, and their attendant feelings is now spoken of in the singular.]

c of the subjects of them;—is not this a very common mental phenomenon?

Pro. Certainly.

Soc. And the images answering to true opinions and words are true, and to false opinions and words false; are they not?

Pro. They are.

Soc. If we are right so far, there arises a further question.

Pro. What is it?

Soc. Whether we experience the feeling of which I am speaking only in relation to the present and the past, or in relation to the future also?

Pro. I should say in relation to all times alike.

d *Soc.* Have not purely mental pleasures and pains been described already as in some cases anticipations of the bodily ones; from which we may infer that anticipatory pleasures and pains are a passing experience having to do with the future?

Pro. Most true.

Soc. And do all those writings and paintings which, as we were saying a little while ago, are produced in us, relate to the past

e and present only, and not to the future?

Pro. To the future, very much.

Soc. When you say 'Very much', you mean to imply that all these representations are hopes[1] about the future, and that mankind are filled with hopes in every stage of existence?

Pro. Exactly.

Soc. Answer me another question.

Pro. What question?

Soc. A just and pious and good man is the friend of the gods; is he not?

Pro. Certainly he is.

Soc. And the unjust and utterly bad man is the reverse?

40 *Pro.* True.

Soc. And all men, as we were saying just now, are always filled with hopes?

Pro. Certainly.

Soc. And these hopes, as they are termed, are propositions which exist in the minds of each of us?

---

[1] [The word ἐλπίς, translated 'hope', has also in Greek the neutral meaning 'expectation'.]

Pro. Yes.

Soc. And besides there are also the images pictured in us; a man may often have a vision of a heap of gold, and pleasures ensuing, and in the picture there may be a likeness of himself mightily rejoicing over his good fortune.

Pro. True. b

Soc. And may we not say that the good, being friends of the gods, have generally true pictures presented to them, and the bad false pictures?

Pro. Certainly.

Soc. The bad, too, have pleasures painted in their fancy as well as the good; but I presume that they are false pleasures.

Pro. They are.

Soc. The bad then commonly delight in false pleasures, and c the good in true pleasures?

Pro. Undoubtedly.

Soc. Then upon this view there are false pleasures in the souls of men which are a ludicrous imitation of the true, and there are pains of a similar character?

Pro. There are.

Soc. And did we not allow that a man who had an opinion at all had a real opinion, but often about things which had no existence either in the past, present, or future?

Pro. Quite true.

Soc. And this was the source of false opinion and opining; am d I not right?

Pro. Yes.

Soc. And must we not attribute to pleasure and pain a similar real but illusory character?

Pro. How do you mean?

Soc. I mean to say that a man must be admitted to have real pleasure who is pleased with anything or anyhow; but that he may be pleased about things which neither have nor have ever had any real existence; often indeed, and perhaps most often, they are never likely to exist.

Pro. Yes, Socrates, that again is undeniable. e

Soc. And may not the same be said about fear and anger and the like; are they not often false?

Pro. Quite so.

Soc. And can opinions be good or bad except in as far as they are true or false?

Pro. In no other way.

41 *Soc.* Nor can pleasures be conceived to be bad except in so far as they are false.

Pro. Nay, Socrates, that is the very opposite of the truth; for no one would call pleasures and pains bad because they are false, but by reason of some other great corruption to which they are liable.

Soc. Well, of pleasures which are corrupt and caused by corruption we will hereafter speak, if we care to continue the inquiry; for the present I would rather show by another argu-

b ment that there are many false pleasures existing or coming into existence in us, because this may assist our final decision.

Pro. Very true; that is to say, if there are such pleasures.

Soc. I think that there are, Protarchus; but this is an opinion which should be well assured, and not rest upon a mere assertion.

Pro. Very good.

Soc. Then now, like wrestlers, let us approach and grasp this new argument.

Pro. Proceed.

Soc. We were maintaining a little while since, that when

c desires, as they are termed, exist in us, then the body is separately affected apart from the soul—do you remember?

Pro. Yes, I remember that you said so.

Soc. And the soul was supposed to desire the opposite of the bodily state, while the body was the source of any pleasure or pain which was experienced.

Pro. True.

Soc. Then now you may infer what happens in such cases.

Pro. What am I to infer?

d *Soc.* That in such cases pleasures and pains are present simultaneously; and the perceptions of them are found side by side, as has been already shown, though they are opposites.

Pro. Clearly.

Soc. And there is another point to which we have agreed.

Pro. What is it?

Soc. That pleasure and pain both admit of more and less, and that they are of the class of infinites.

Pro. Certainly, we said so.

Soc. But how can we rightly judge of them?

Pro. In what respect? Explain. e

Soc. If it is our intention to judge of their comparative importance and intensity, measuring pleasure against pain, and pain against pain, and pleasure against pleasure——

Pro. Yes, such is our intention, and this is how we wish to judge.

Soc. Well, take the case of sight. If the nearness or distance of 42 magnitudes obscures their true proportions, and makes us opine falsely, shall we not find the same illusion happening in the case of pleasures and pains?

Pro. Yes, Socrates, and in a degree far greater.

Soc. Then what we are now saying is the opposite of what we were saying shortly before.

Pro. What was that?

Soc. Then the opinions were true and false, and infected the pleasures and pains with their own falsity. b

Pro. Very true.

Soc. But now it is the pleasures which are said to be true and false because they are seen at various distances, and subjected to comparison; the pleasures appear to be greater and more vehement when placed side by side with the pains, and the pains when placed side by side with the pleasures.

Pro. Certainly, and for the reason which you mention.

Soc. And suppose you part off from pleasures and pains the element which makes them appear to be greater or less than they really are: you will acknowledge that this element is illusory, and c you will never say that the corresponding excess or defect of pleasure or pain is real or true.

Pro. Certainly not.

Soc. Next let us see whether in another direction we may not find pleasures and pains existing and appearing in living beings, which are still more false than these.

Pro. What are they, and how shall we find them?

Soc. If I am not mistaken, I have often repeated that pains and aches and suffering and uneasiness of all sorts arise out of a corruption of nature caused by concretions, and dissolutions, and d repletions, and evacuations, and also by growth and decay.

Pro. Yes, that has been often said.

Soc. And we have also agreed that the restoration of the natural state is pleasure?

Pro. Right.

Soc. But now let us suppose an interval of time at which the body experiences none of these changes.

Pro. When can that be, Socrates?

e *Soc.* Your question, Protarchus, does not help the argument.

Pro. Why not, Socrates?

Soc. Because it does not prevent me from repeating mine.

Pro. And what was that?

Soc. Why, Protarchus, admitting that there is no such interval, I may ask what would be the necessary consequence if there were.

Pro. You mean, what would happen if the body were not changed either for good or bad?

Soc. Yes.

Pro. Why then, Socrates, I should suppose that there would be neither pleasure nor pain.

43 *Soc.* Very good; but if I am not mistaken, you would probably assert that we must always be experiencing one of them; that is what the wise tell us; for, say they, all things are ever flowing up and down.

Pro. Yes, and their words are of no mean authority.

Soc. Of course, for they are no mean authorities themselves; and I should like to avoid the brunt of their argument. Shall I tell you how I mean to escape from them? And you shall be the partner of my flight.

Pro. How?

Soc. To them we will say: 'Good; but are we, or living things b in general, always conscious of what happens to us—for example, of our growth, or the like? Are we not, on the contrary, almost wholly unconscious of this and similar phenomena?' You must answer for them.

Pro. The latter alternative is the true one.

Soc. Then we were not right in saying, just now, that motions going up and down cause pleasures and pains?

Pro. True.

c *Soc.* A better and more unexceptionable way of speaking will be——

Pro. What?

Soc. If we say that the great changes produce pleasures and pains, but that the moderate and lesser ones do neither.

Pro. That, Socrates, is the more correct mode of speaking.

Soc. But if this be true, the life to which I was just now referring again appears.

Pro. What life?

Soc. The life which we affirmed to be devoid both of pain and of joy.

Pro. Very true.

Soc. We may assume then that there are three lives, one pleasant, one painful, and the third which is neither; what d say you?

Pro. I should say as you do that there are three of them.

Soc. But if so, the negation of pain will not be the same with pleasure.

Pro. Certainly not.

Soc. Then when you hear a person saying, that always to live without pain is the pleasantest of all things, what would you understand him to mean by that statement?

Pro. I think that by pleasure he must mean the negative of pain.

Soc. Let us take any three things; or suppose that we embellish e a little and call the first gold, the second silver, and there shall be a third which is neither.

Pro. Very good.

Soc. Now, can that which is neither be either gold or silver?

Pro. Impossible.

Soc. No more can that neutral or middle life be rightly or reasonably spoken or thought of as pleasant or painful.

Pro. Certainly not.

Soc. And yet, my friend, there are, as we know, persons who 44 say and think so.

Pro. Certainly.

Soc. And do they think that they have pleasure when they are free from pain?

Pro. They say so.

Soc. And they must think or they would not say that they have pleasure.

Pro. I suppose not.

Soc. And yet if pleasure and the negation of pain are of distinct natures, they are wrong.

Pro. But they are undoubtedly of distinct natures.

Soc. Then shall we take the view that they are three, as we were just now saying, or that they are two only—the one being b a state of pain, which is an evil, and the other a cessation of pain, which is of itself a good, and is called pleasant?

Pro. But why, Socrates, do we ask the question at all? I do not see the reason.

Soc. Can it be that you, Protarchus, have never heard of certain enemies of our friend Philebus?

Pro. And who may they be?

Soc. Certain persons who are reputed to be masters in natural philosophy, who deny the very existence of pleasure.

Pro. Indeed!

c *Soc.* They say that what the school of Philebus calls pleasures are all of them only avoidances of pain.

Pro. And would you, Socrates, have us agree with them?

Soc. Why, no, I would rather use them as a sort of diviners, who divine the truth, not by rules of art, but by an instinctive repugnance and extreme detestation which a noble nature has of the power of pleasure, in which they think that there is nothing sound, and her seductive influence is declared by them to be d witchcraft, and not pleasure. This is the use which you may make of them. And when you have considered the various grounds of their dislike, you shall hear from me what I deem to be true pleasures. Having thus examined the nature of pleasure from both points of view, we will bring her up for judgement.

Pro. Well said.

Soc. Then let us enter into an alliance with these philosophers and follow in the track of their dislike. I imagine that they would say something of this sort; they would begin at the beginning, and ask whether, if we wanted to know the nature of any quality, e such as hardness, we should be more likely to discover it by looking at the hardest things, rather than at the least hard. You, Protarchus, shall answer these severe gentlemen as you answer me.

Pro. By all means, and I reply to them, that you should look at the greatest instances.

Soc. Then if we want to see the true nature of pleasures as a

class, we should not look at the most diluted pleasures, but at the 45
most extreme and most vehement?

Pro. In that every one will agree.

Soc. And the obvious instances of the greatest pleasures, as we
have often said, are the pleasures of the body?

Pro. Certainly.

Soc. And are they felt by us to be or become greater, when we
are sick or when we are in health? And here we must be careful
in our answer, or we shall come to grief. For perhaps we might
be tempted to answer, 'When we are in health.'   b

Pro. Yes, that is the natural answer.

Soc. Well, but are not those pleasures the most intense which
are preceded by the most intense desires?

Pro. True.

Soc. And do not people who are in a fever, or any similar
illness, feel cold or thirst or other bodily affections more intensely?
Am I not right in saying that they know deeper want and enjoy
greater pleasure in the satisfaction of their want?

Pro. That is obvious as soon as it is said.

Soc. Well, then, shall we not be right in saying, that if a person c
would wish to see the greatest pleasures he ought to go and look,
not at health, but at disease? And here you must distinguish:—
do not imagine that I mean to ask whether those who are very ill
have more pleasures than those who are well, but understand
that I am speaking of the magnitude of pleasure; I want to know
where pleasures are found to be most intense. For, as I say, we
have to discover what is pleasure, and what they mean by
pleasure who deny her very existence.

Pro. I think I follow you.   d

Soc. You will soon have a better opportunity of showing
whether you do or not, Protarchus. Answer now, and tell me
whether you see, I will not say more, but more intense and
excessive pleasures in wantonness than in temperance? Reflect
before you speak.

Pro. I understand you, and see that there is a great difference
between them; the temperate are restrained by the wise man's
aphorism of 'Never too much', which is their rule, but excess of e
pleasure possessing the minds of fools and wantons becomes
madness and makes them shout with delight.

Soc. Very good, and if this be true, then the greatest pleasures will clearly be found in some vicious state of soul and body and not in a virtuous state, and the greatest pains too.

46　*Pro.* Certainly.

Soc. And ought we not to select some of these for examination, and see what makes them the greatest?

Pro. To be sure we ought.

Soc. Take the case of the pleasures which arise out of certain disorders.

Pro. What disorders?

Soc. The pleasures of unseemly disorders, which our severe friends utterly detest.

Pro. What pleasures?

Soc. Such, for example, as the relief of itching and other ailments by scratching, which is the only remedy required. For what in Heaven's name is the feeling to be called which is thus produced in us?—Pleasure or pain?

Pro. A villainous mixture of some kind, Socrates, I should say.

b　*Soc.* I did not introduce the argument, O Protarchus, with any personal reference to Philebus, but because, without the observation of these and similar pleasures, we shall never be able to determine the point at issue.

Pro. Then we had better proceed to analyse this family of pleasures.

Soc. You mean the pleasures which are mingled with pain?

Pro. Exactly.

Soc. There are some mixtures which are of the body, and only
c　in the body, and others which are of the soul, and only in the soul; while there are other mixtures of pleasures with pains, common both to soul and body, which in their composite state are called sometimes pleasures and sometimes pains.

Pro. How is that?

Soc. Whenever, in the restoration or in the derangement of nature, a man experiences two opposite feelings; for example, when he is cold and is growing warm, or again, when he is hot and is becoming cool, and he wants to have the one and be rid of the other;—the sweet has a bitter, as the common saying is, and
d　both together fasten upon him and create irritation and in time drive him to distraction.

Pro. That description is very true to nature.

Soc. And in these sorts of mixtures the pleasures and pains are sometimes equal, and sometimes one or other of them predominates?

Pro. True.

Soc. Of cases in which the pain exceeds the pleasure, an example is afforded by itching, of which we were just now speaking, and tingling. When the boiling and inflamed element is in the parts within, and the rubbing and motion[1] only relieves the surface, and does not reach the parts affected, men put them to the fire, and then in their despair change to a contrary e temperature; by which means they sometimes obtain immense pleasure, sometimes contrary sensations of pain and pleasure in the inner and outer parts: now whichever sensation prevails, the effect is due to the forcible separation of what is united, or to the union of what is separated, and to the juxtaposition of pleasure 47 and pain.[2]

Pro. Quite so.

Soc. Sometimes the element of pleasure prevails in a man, and whereas the slight undercurrent of pain makes him tingle, and causes a gentle irritation, the much greater infusion of pleasure creates an excitement in him,—he even leaps for joy, he assumes all sorts of attitudes, he changes all manner of colours, he gasps for breath, and is quite amazed, and utters the most irrational exclamations.

Pro. Yes, indeed.   b

Soc. He will say of himself, and others will say of him, that he is dying with these delights; and the more dissipated and unintelligent he is, the more vehemently he pursues them at all times and in every way; of all pleasures he declares them to be the greatest; and he reckons him who lives in the most constant enjoyment of them to be the happiest of mankind.

Pro. That, Socrates, is a very true description of the opinions of the majority about pleasures.

Soc. Yes, Protarchus, quite true of such mixed pleasures as c

---

[1] Reading with the MSS. κινήσει.

[2] [Two emendations are needed in Burnet's text: (1) his correction of ἀπορίαις, 'despair', to πυρίαις, 'vapour-baths', seems too ingenious to be true; (2) in 46 e 6 καί should be retained. The last phrase says more simply what had before been said with technicality; and καί is explanatory.]

arise out of the communion of external and internal sensations in the body; there are also cases in which the mind contributes an opposite element to the body, whether of pleasure or pain, and the two unite and form one mixture. Concerning these I have already remarked, that when a man is empty he desires to be full, and that his hope for the future is pleasant, his emptiness painful. But now I must further add what I omitted before, that in all

d these and similar emotions in which body and mind are opposed (and they are innumerable), pleasure and pain coalesce in one.

Pro. I believe that to be quite true.

Soc. There still remains one other sort of admixture of pleasures and pains.

Pro. What is that?

Soc. The union which, as we were saying, the mind often experiences of purely mental feelings.

Pro. What do you mean?

e *Soc.* Why, do we not speak of anger, fear, desire, sorrow, love, emulation, envy, and the like, as pains which belong to the soul only?

Pro. Yes.

Soc. And shall we not find them also full of the most wonderful pleasures? need I remind you of the anger

'Which stirs even a wise man to violence,
And is sweeter than honey and the honeycomb?'

And you remember how pleasures mingle with pains in lamentation and bereavement?

Pro. Yes, there is a natural connexion between them.

48 *Soc.* And you remember also how at the sight of tragedies the spectators smile through their tears?

Pro. Certainly I do.

Soc. And are you aware that even at a comedy the soul experiences a mixed feeling of pain and pleasure?

Pro. I do not quite understand you.

b *Soc.* I admit, Protarchus, that there is some difficulty in recognizing this mixture of feelings at a comedy.

Pro. There is, I think.

Soc. And the greater the obscurity of the case the more desirable is the examination of it, because the difficulty in detecting other cases of mixed pleasures and pains will be less.

Pro. Proceed.

Soc. I have just mentioned envy; would you not call that a pain of the soul?

Pro. Yes.

Soc. And yet the envious man evidently finds something in the misfortunes of his neighbours at which he is pleased?

Pro. Certainly.   c

Soc. And ignorance, and what is termed clownishness, are surely an evil?

Pro. To be sure.

Soc. From these considerations learn to know the nature of the ridiculous.

Pro. Explain.

Soc. The ridiculous is in short[1] the specific name which is used to describe the vicious form of a certain habit; and of vice in general it is that kind which is most at variance with the inscription at Delphi.

Pro. You mean, Socrates, 'Know thyself.'

Soc. I do; and the opposite would be, 'Know not thyself.'   d

Pro. Certainly.

Soc. And now, O Protarchus, try to divide this into three.

Pro. Indeed I am afraid that I cannot.

Soc. Do you mean to say that I must make the division for you?

Pro. Yes, and what is more, I beg that you will.

Soc. Are there not three ways in which ignorance of self may be shown?

Pro. What are they?

Soc. In the first place, about money; the ignorant may fancy   e
himself richer than he is.

Pro. Yes, that is a very common error.

Soc. And still more often he will fancy that he is taller or fairer than he is, or that he has some other advantage of person which he really has not.

Pro. Of course.

Soc. And yet surely by far the greatest number err about the third class of goods, those of the soul; they imagine themselves to be much better men than they are.   49

---

[1] [Omitting the comma at κεφάλαιον, 48 c 6.]

Pro. Yes, that is by far the commonest delusion.

Soc. And of all the virtues, is not wisdom the one which the mass of mankind are always claiming, and which most arouses in them a spirit of contention and lying conceit of wisdom?

Pro. Certainly.

Soc. And may not all this be truly called an evil condition?

Pro. Very evil.

Soc. But we must make a further twofold division, Protarchus, if we would see in envy of the childish sort a singular mixture of
b pleasure and pain. What, then, is our next step? All who are silly enough to entertain this lying conceit of themselves may of course be divided, like the rest of mankind, into two classes—one having power and might; and the other the reverse.

Pro. Certainly.

Soc. Let this, then, be the principle of division; those of them who are weak and unable to revenge themselves, when they are laughed at, may be truly called ridiculous, but those who are powerful and can defend themselves may be more truly described
c as formidable and hateful; for ignorance in the powerful is hateful and horrible, because hurtful to others both in reality and in fiction, but powerless ignorance may be reckoned, and in truth is, ridiculous.

Pro. That is very true, but I do not as yet see where is the admixture of pleasures and pains.

Soc. Well, then, let us examine the nature of envy.

Pro. Proceed.

Soc. Is not envy an unrighteous pleasure, and also an un-
d righteous pain?

Pro. Most true.

Soc. There is nothing envious or wrong in rejoicing at the misfortunes of enemies?

Pro. Certainly not.

Soc. But to feel joy instead of sorrow at the sight of our friends' misfortunes—is not that wrong?

Pro. Undoubtedly.

Soc. Did we not say that ignorance was always an evil?

Pro. True.

Soc. And the three kinds of vain conceit in our friends which
e we enumerated—the vain conceit of beauty, of wisdom, and of

wealth, are ridiculous if they are weak, and detestable when they are powerful: may we not say, as I was saying before, that our friends who are in this state of mind, when harmless to others, are simply ridiculous?

Pro. They are ridiculous.

Soc. And do we not acknowledge this state of mind, like all ignorance, to be a misfortune?

Pro. Certainly.

Soc. And do we feel pain or pleasure in laughing at it?

Pro. Clearly we feel pleasure. 50

Soc. And we agreed that the source of this pleasure which we feel at the misfortunes of friends was envy?

Pro. Certainly.

Soc. Then the argument shows that when we laugh at the folly of our friends, pleasure, in mingling with envy, mingles with pain, for envy has been acknowledged by us to be mental pain, and laughter is pleasant; and on such occasions we envy and laugh at the same instant.

Pro. True.

Soc. And the argument implies that there are combinations of b pleasure and pain in lamentations, and in tragedy and comedy, not only on the stage, but on the greater stage of human life; and so in endless other cases.

Pro. I do not see how any one can deny what you say, Socrates, however eager he may be to assert the opposite opinion.

Soc. I mentioned anger, desire, sorrow, fear, love, emulation, envy, and similar emotions, as examples in which we should find c a mixture of the two elements so often named; did I not?

Pro. Yes.

Soc. We may observe that our conclusions hitherto have had reference only to sorrow and envy and anger.

Pro. I see.

Soc. Then many other cases still remain?

Pro. Certainly.

Soc. And why do you suppose me to have pointed out to you the admixture which takes place in comedy? Why but to convince you that there was no difficulty in showing the mixed d nature of fear and love and similar affections; and I thought that when I had given you the illustration, you would have let me off, and have acknowledged as a general truth that the body without the soul, and the soul without the body, as well as the two united, are susceptible of all sorts of admixtures of pleasures and pains; and so further discussion would have been unnecessary. And now I want to know whether I may depart; or will you keep me here until midnight? I fancy that I may obtain my release without many words;—if I promise that tomorrow I will give you an account of all these cases. But at present I would rather sail in another direction, and go to other matters which remain to be settled, before the judgement can be given which Philebus demands.

Pro. Very good, Socrates; in what remains take your own course.

Soc. Then after the mixed pleasures the unmixed should have their turn; this is the natural and necessary order.

51 *Pro.* Excellent.

Soc. These, in turn, then, I will now endeavour to indicate; for with the maintainers of the opinion that all pleasures are a cessation of pain, I do not agree, but, as I was saying, I use them as witnesses, that there are pleasures which seem only and are not, and there are others again which have great power and appear in many forms, yet are intermingled with pains, and are partly alleviations of agony and distress, both of body and mind.

b *Pro.* Then what pleasures, Socrates, should we be right in conceiving to be true?

Soc. True pleasures are those which are given by beauty of colour and form, and most of those which arise from smells; those of sound, again, and in general those of which the want is painless and unconscious, and of which the fruition is palpable to sense and pleasant and unalloyed with pain.[1]

Pro. Once more, Socrates, I must ask what you mean.

Soc. My meaning is certainly not obvious, and I will endeavour c to be plainer. I do not mean by beauty of form such beauty as that of animals or pictures, which the many would suppose to be my meaning; but, says the argument, understand me to mean straight lines and circles, and the plane or solid figures which are formed out of them by turning-lathes and rulers and measurers of angles; for these I affirm to be not only relatively beautiful, like other

---

[1] [Retaining the words καθαρὰς λυπῶν in 51 b 7.]

things, but they are eternally and absolutely beautiful, and they
have peculiar pleasures, quite unlike the pleasures of scratching.
And there are colours which are of the same character, and have d
similar pleasures; now do you understand my meaning?

Pro. I am trying to understand, Socrates, and I hope that you
will try to make your meaning clearer.

Soc. When sounds are smooth and clear, and have a single
pure tone, then I mean to say that they are not relatively but
absolutely beautiful, and have natural pleasures of the same
character.

Pro. Yes, there are such pleasures.

Soc. The pleasures of smell are of a less ethereal sort, but in e
having no necessary admixture of pain, in the manner in which
the enjoyment is felt, and the subject which feels it, in all this I
deem them analogous to the others. Here then are two kinds of
our unmixed pleasures.

Pro. I understand.

Soc. To these may be added the pleasures of knowledge, if no 52
hunger of knowledge and no pain caused by such hunger precede
them.

Pro. And this is the case.

Soc. Well, but if a man has become replete with knowledge
and later loses his knowledge through oblivion, does the loss seem
to you to entail any pain?

Pro. Not by nature, but there may be times of reflection,
when he feels grief at the loss of his knowledge.   b

Soc. Yes, my friend, but at present we are enumerating only
the natural perceptions, and have nothing to do with reflection.

Pro. In that case you are right in saying that the loss of knowledge is not attended with pain.

Soc. These pleasures of knowledge, then, are unmixed with
pain; and they are not the pleasures of the many but of a very few.

Pro. Quite true.

Soc. And now, having fairly separated the pure pleasures and c
those which may be rightly termed impure, let us further add to
our description of them, that the pleasures which are in excess
have no measure, but that those which are not in excess have
measure; the great, the excessive, whether more or less frequent,
we shall be right in referring to the class of the infinite, and of the

more and less, which pours through body and soul alike; and the
d others we shall refer to the class which has measure.

Pro. Quite right, Socrates.

Soc. Still there is something more to be considered about
pleasures.

Pro. What is it?

Soc. When you speak of purity and simplicity, or of excess,
abundance, greatness and sufficiency, in what relation do these
terms stand to truth?[1]

Pro. Why do you ask, Socrates?

Soc. Because, Protarchus, I should wish to test pleasure and
knowledge in every possible way, in order that if there be a pure
e and impure element in either of them, I may present the pure
element for judgement, and then they will be more easily judged
of by you and by me and by all of us.

Pro. Most true.

Soc. Let us investigate all the pure kinds; first selecting for
consideration a single instance.

Pro. What instance shall we select?

53 *Soc.* Suppose that we first of all take whiteness.

Pro. Very good.

Soc. How can there be purity in whiteness, and what purity?
Is that purest which is greatest or most in quantity, or that which
is most unadulterated and freest from any admixture of other
colours?

Pro. Clearly that which is most unadulterated.

Soc. True, Protarchus; and so the purest white, and not the
b greatest or largest in quantity, is to be deemed truest and most
beautiful?

Pro. Right.

Soc. And we shall be quite right in saying that a little pure
white is whiter and fairer and truer than a great deal that is
mixed.

Pro. Perfectly right.

Soc. There is no need of adducing many similar examples in
illustration of the argument about pleasure; one such is sufficient
to prove to us that a small pleasure or a small amount of pleasure,

---

[1] [Omitting the question-mark at εἶναι, and keeping the manuscript reading
ἱκανόν in 52 d 8.]

if pure or unalloyed with pain, is always pleasanter and truer and fairer than a great pleasure or a great amount of pleasure of c another kind.

Pro. Assuredly; and the instance you have given is quite sufficient.

Soc. But what do you say of another question:—have we not heard that pleasure is always a generation, and has no true being? Do not certain ingenious philosophers teach this doctrine, and ought not we to be grateful to them?

Pro. What do they mean?

Soc. I will explain to you, my dear Protarchus, what they d mean, by putting a question.

Pro. Ask, and I will answer.

Soc. I assume that there are two natures, one self-existent, and the other ever in want of something.

Pro. What manner of natures are they?

Soc. The one majestic ever, the other inferior.

Pro. You speak riddles.

Soc. You have seen loves good and fair, and also brave lovers of them.

Pro. I should think so.

Soc. Search the universe for two terms which are like these two e and are present everywhere.

Pro. Yet a third time I must say, Be a little plainer, Socrates.

Soc. There is no difficulty, Protarchus; the argument is only in play, and insinuates that some things are for the sake of something else (relatives), and that other things are the ends which the former class subserve (absolutes).

Pro. Your many repetitions have slowly made me understand.

Soc. As the argument proceeds, my boy, I dare say that the 54 meaning will become clearer.

Pro. Very likely.

Soc. Here are two new principles.

Pro. What are they?

Soc. One is the generation of all things, and the other is being.

Pro. I readily accept from you both generation and being.

Soc. Very right; and would you say that generation is for the sake of being, or being for the sake of generation?

Pro. You want to know whether that which is called being is, in its essence, subservient to generation.

Soc. Yes.

b *Pro.* Tell me, I beseech you, if this is the question you are asking: Do you believe, Protarchus, that ship-building is for the sake of ships, or ships for the sake of ship-building, and likewise in all other such cases?

Soc. That is precisely my question.

Pro. Why do you not answer yourself, Socrates?

Soc. I have no objection, but you must take your part.

Pro. Certainly.

c *Soc.* My answer is, that all things instrumental, remedial, material, are given to us with a view to generation; and that each generation is relative to, or for the sake of, some particular being or essence; and that the whole of generation is relative to the whole of being.

Pro. Assuredly.

Soc. Then pleasure, being a generation, must surely be for the sake of some being?

Pro. True.

Soc. And that for the sake of which something else is done must be placed in the class of good, and that which is done for the sake of something else, in some other class, my good friend.

Pro. Most certainly.

d *Soc.* Then pleasure, being a generation, will be rightly placed in some other class than that of good?

Pro. Quite right.

Soc. Then, as I said at first, we ought to be very grateful to him who first pointed out that pleasure was a generation only, and had no true being at all; for he is clearly one who laughs at the notion of pleasure being a good.

Pro. Assuredly.

Soc. And he would surely laugh also at those who make
e generation their highest end.

Pro. Of whom are you speaking, and what do they mean?

Soc. I am speaking of those who when they are cured of hunger or thirst or any other defect by some process of generation are delighted at the process because it is a pleasure; and they say that they would not wish to live without these and other feelings of a like kind which might be mentioned.

Pro. That is certainly what they appear to think. 55

Soc. And is not destruction universally admitted to be the opposite of generation?

Pro. Certainly.

Soc. Then he who chooses thus, would choose generation and destruction rather than that third sort of life, in which, as we were saying, was neither pleasure nor pain, but only the purest possible thought.

Pro. He who would make us believe pleasure to be a good is involved in great absurdities, Socrates.

Soc. Great, indeed; and there is yet another of them.

Pro. What is it?

Soc. Is there not an absurdity in arguing that there is nothing b good or noble in the body, or in anything else, but that good is in the soul only, and that the only good of the soul is pleasure; and that courage or temperance or understanding, or any other good of the soul, is not really a good?—and is there not yet a further absurdity in our being compelled to say that he who has a feeling of pain and not of pleasure is bad at the time when he is suffering pain, even though he be the best of men; and again, that he who has a feeling of pleasure, in so far as he is pleased at the time when he is pleased, in that degree excels in virtue? c

Pro. Nothing, Socrates, can be more irrational than all this.

Soc. And now, having subjected pleasure to every sort of test, let us not appear to be too sparing of mind and knowledge: let us ring their metal bravely, and see if there be unsoundness in any part, until we have found out what in them is of the purest nature; and then the truest elements both of pleasure and knowledge may be brought up for judgement.

Pro. Right.

Soc. Knowledge has two parts,—the one productive, and the d other educational?

Pro. True.

Soc. And in the productive or handicraft arts, is not one part more akin to knowledge, and the other less; and may not the one part be regarded as the purest, and the other as the more impure?

Pro. Certainly.

Soc. Let us separate the superior or dominant elements in each of them.

Pro. What are they, and how do you separate them?

e *Soc.* I mean to say, that if arithmetic, mensuration, and weighing be taken away from any art, that which remains will not be much.

Pro. Not much, certainly.

Soc. The rest will be only conjecture, and the better use of the senses which is given by experience and practice, with the help of a certain power of guessing, which is commonly called art, and 56 is perfected by attention and pains.

Pro. Nothing more, assuredly.

Soc. Music, for instance, is full of this empiricism; for sounds are harmonized, not by measure, but by skilful conjecture; the music of the flute is always trying to guess the pitch of each vibrating note, and is therefore mixed up with much that is doubtful and has little which is certain.

Pro. Most true.

b *Soc.* And the same will be found to hold good of medicine and husbandry and piloting and generalship.

Pro. Very true.

Soc. The art of the builder, on the other hand, which uses a number of measures and instruments, attains by their help to a greater degree of accuracy than the other arts.

Pro. How is that?

Soc. In ship-building and house-building, and in other branches of the art of carpentering, the builder has his rule, lathe, com-c pass, line, and a most ingenious machine for straightening wood.

Pro. Very true, Socrates.

Soc. Then now let us divide the arts of which we were speaking into two kinds,—the arts which, like music, are less exact in their results, and those which, like carpentering, are more exact.

Pro. Let us make that division.

Soc. Of the latter class, the most exact of all are those which we just now spoke of as primary.

Pro. I see that you mean arithmetic, and the kindred arts of weighing and measuring.

Soc. Certainly, Protarchus; but are not these also distinguish- d able into two kinds?

Pro. What are the two kinds?

Soc. In the first place, arithmetic is of two kinds, one of which is popular, and the other philosophical.

Pro. How would you distinguish them?

Soc. There is a wide difference between them, Protarchus; some arithmeticians reckon unequal units; as for example, two armies, two oxen, two very large things or two very small things. The party who are opposed to them insist that every unit in ten e thousand must be the same as every other unit.

Pro. Undoubtedly there is, as you say, a great difference among the votaries of the science; and there may be reasonably supposed to be two sorts of arithmetic.

Soc. And when we compare the art of mensuration which is used in building with philosophical geometry, or the art of com- 57 putation which is used in trading with exact calculation, shall we say of either of the pairs that it is one or two?

Pro. On the analogy of what has preceded, I should be of opinion that they were severally two.

Soc. Right; but do you understand why I have discussed the subject?

Pro. I think so, but I should like to be told by you.

Soc. The argument has all along been seeking a parallel to pleasure, and true to that original design, has gone on[1] to ask whether one sort of knowledge is purer than another, as one b pleasure is purer than another.

Pro. Clearly that was the intention.

Soc. And has not the argument in what has preceded already shown[2] that the arts have different provinces, and vary in their degrees of certainty?

Pro. Very true.

Soc. And just now did not the argument first designate a particular art by a common term, thus making us believe in the unity of that art; and then again, as if speaking of two different things, proceed to inquire whether the art as pursued by philosophers, c

---

[1] [Accepting the emendation προβεβηκέναι in 57 a 11.]

[2] [Retaining the manuscript reading ἀνευρίσκειν. The infinitive is dependent on δοκεῖ in 57 a 9, and represents an imperfect indicative.]

or as pursued by non-philosophers, has more of certainty and purity?

Pro. That is the very question which the argument is asking.

Soc. And how, Protarchus, shall we answer the inquiry?

Pro. O Socrates, we have reached a point at which the difference of clearness in different kinds of knowledge is enormous.

Soc. Then the answer will be the easier.

Pro. Certainly; and let us say in reply, that the mathematical and geometrical sciences far surpass all others; and that those
d branches of them which are animated by the pure philosophic impulse are infinitely superior in the accuracy and truth of their measures and numbers.

Soc. Then this is your judgement; and this is the answer which, upon your authority, we will give to all masters of the art of misinterpretation?

Pro. What answer?

Soc. That there are two arts of arithmetic, and two of mensuration; and also several other arts which in like manner have this double nature, and yet only one name.

e   *Pro.* Let us boldly return this answer to the masters of whom you speak, Socrates, and hope for good luck.

Soc. We have explained what we term the most exact arts or sciences.

Pro. Very good.

Soc. And yet, Protarchus, dialectic will refuse to acknowledge us, if we do not award to her the first place.

58   *Pro.* And pray, what is dialectic?

Soc. Clearly everyone would recognize what we here call by that name; for I am sure that all men who have a grain of intelligence will admit that the knowledge which has to do with being and reality, and sameness and unchangeableness, is by far the truest of all. But how would you decide this question, Protarchus?

Pro. I have often heard Gorgias maintain, Socrates, that the art of persuasion far surpassed every other; this, as he says, is by
b far the best of them all, for to it all things submit, not by compulsion, but of their own free will. Now, I should not like to be found on the opposite side either to you or to him.

Soc. I think you would have said 'in the opposite camp', if you were not ashamed?

Pro. As you please.

Soc. May I not have led you into a misapprehension?

Pro. How?

Soc. Dear Protarchus, I never asked which was the greatest or best or usefullest of arts or sciences, but which had clearness and c accuracy, and the greatest amount of truth, however humble and little useful an art. And as for Gorgias, if you do not deny that his art has the advantage in usefulness to mankind, he will not quarrel with you for saying that the study of which I am speaking is superior in this particular of essential truth; as in the comparison of white colours, a little whiteness, if that little be only pure, was said to be superior in truth to a great mass which is impure. d And now let us give our best attention and consider well, not the comparative use or reputation of the sciences, but the power or faculty, if there be such, which the soul has of loving the truth, and of doing all things for the sake of it; let us search into the pure element of mind and intelligence, and then we shall be able to say whether the science of which I have been speaking is most likely to possess the faculty, or whether there be some other which has higher claims.

Pro. Well, I have been considering, and I can hardly think e that any other science or art has a firmer grasp of the truth than this.

Soc. Do you say so because you observe that the arts in general 59 and those engaged in them make use of opinion, and are resolutely engaged in the investigation of matters of opinion? Even he who supposes himself to be occupied with nature is really occupied with the things of this world, how created, how acting or acted upon. Is not this the sort of inquiry in which his life is spent?

Pro. True.

Soc. He is labouring, not after eternal being, but about things which are becoming, or which will or have become.

Pro. Very true.

Soc. And can we say that any of these things which neither have been nor will be fixed, and are not fixed at the present b moment, when judged by the strict rule of truth ever become certain?

Pro. Impossible.

Soc. How can anything fixed be concerned with that which has no fixedness?

Pro. How indeed?

Soc. Then mind and science when employed about such changing things do not attain the highest truth?

Pro. I should imagine not.

Soc. And now let us bid farewell, a long farewell, to you or me or Philebus or Gorgias, and urge on behalf of the argument a single point.

c *Pro.* What point?

Soc. Let us say that the stable and pure and true and un-alloyed has to do with the things which are eternal and unchangeable and unmixed, or if not, at any rate with things which are most akin to them; and that all other things are to be placed in a second or inferior class.

Pro. Very true.

Soc. And of the names expressing cognition, ought not the fairest to be given to the fairest things?

Pro. That is natural.

d *Soc.* And are not mind and wisdom the names which are to be honoured most?

Pro. Yes.

Soc. These names may therefore be said to have their truest and most exact application when the mind is engaged in the contemplation of true being?

Pro Certainly.

Soc. And these were the names which I adduced of the rivals of pleasure?

Pro. Very true, Socrates.

Soc. In the next place, as to the mixture, here are the in-
e gredients, pleasure and wisdom, and we may be compared to artists who have their materials ready to their hands.

Pro. Yes.

Soc. And now we must begin to mix them?

Pro. By all means.

Soc. But had we not better have a preliminary word and refresh our memories?

Pro. Of what?

Soc. Of that which I have already mentioned. Well says the

proverb, that we ought to repeat twice and even thrice that which 60
is good.

Pro. Certainly.

Soc. Well then, by Zeus, let us proceed, and I will make what
I believe to be a fair summary of the argument.

Pro. Let me hear.

Soc. Philebus says that pleasure is the true end of all living
beings, at which all ought to aim, and moreover that it is the
chief good of all, and that the two names 'good' and 'pleasant'
are correctly given to one thing and one nature; Socrates, on the
other hand, begins by denying this, and further says, that in b
nature as in name they are two, and that wisdom partakes more
than pleasure of the good. Is not and was not this what we were
saying, Protarchus?

Pro. Certainly.

Soc. And is there not and was there not a further point which
was conceded between us?

Pro. What was it?

Soc. That the good differs from all other things.

Pro. In what respect?   c

Soc. In that the being who possesses good always everywhere
and in all things has the most perfect sufficiency, and is never in
need of anything else.

Pro. Exactly.

Soc. And did we not endeavour to make an imaginary separation of wisdom and pleasure, assigning to each a distinct life, so
that pleasure was wholly excluded from wisdom, and wisdom in
like manner had no part whatever in pleasure?

Pro. We did.

Soc. And did we think that either of them alone would be d
sufficient?

Pro. Certainly not.

Soc. And if we erred in any point, then let anyone who will,
take up the inquiry again and set us right; and assuming memory
and wisdom and knowledge and true opinion to belong to the
same class, let him consider whether he would desire to possess or
acquire,—I will not say pleasure, however abundant or intense,
if he has no real perception that he is pleased, nor any consciousness of what he feels, nor any recollection, however momentary,

of the feeling,—but would he desire to have anything at all, if
e these faculties were wanting to him? And about wisdom I ask
the same question; can you conceive that anyone would choose
to have all wisdom absolutely devoid of pleasure, rather than
with a certain degree of pleasure, or all pleasure devoid of wisdom, rather than with a certain degree of wisdom?

Pro. Certainly not, Socrates; but why repeat such questions
any more?

61 *Soc.* Then the perfect and universally preferred and entirely
good cannot possibly be either of them?

Pro. Impossible.

Soc. Then now we must ascertain the nature of the good more
or less accurately, in order, as we were saying, that the second
place may be duly assigned?

Pro. Right.

Soc. Have we not found a road which leads towards the good?

Pro. What road?

Soc. Supposing that a man had to be found, and you could
b discover in what house he lived, would not that be a great step
towards the discovery of the man himself?

Pro. Certainly.

Soc. And now reason intimates to us, as at our first beginning,
that we should seek the good, not in the unmixed life but in the
mixed.

Pro. True.

Soc. There is greater hope of finding that which we are seeking
in the life which is well mixed than in that which is not?

Pro. Far greater.

Soc. Then now let us mingle, Protarchus, at the same time
c offering up a prayer to Dionysus or Hephaestus, or whoever is the
god who presides over the ceremony of mingling.

Pro. By all means.

Soc. Are not we the cup-bearers? and here are two fountains
which are flowing at our side: one, which is pleasure, may be
likened to a fountain of honey; the other, wisdom, a sober
draught in which no wine mingles, is of water astringent but
healthful; out of these we must seek to make the fairest of all
possible mixtures.

Pro. Certainly.

Soc. Tell me first;—should we be most likely to succeed if we d mingled every sort of pleasure with every sort of wisdom?

Pro. Perhaps we might.

Soc. But I should be afraid of the risk, and I think that I can show a safer plan.

Pro. What is it?

Soc. One pleasure was supposed by us to be truer than another, and one art to be more exact than another.

Pro. Certainly.

Soc. There was also supposed to be a difference in sciences; some of them regarding only the transient and perishing, and e others the permanent and imperishable and everlasting and immutable; and when judged by the standard of truth, the latter, as we thought, were truer than the former.

Pro. Very good and right.

Soc. If, then, we were to begin by mingling the sections of each class which have the most of truth, will not the union suffice to give us the loveliest of lives, or shall we still want some elements of another kind?

Pro. I think that we ought to do what you suggest. 62

Soc. Let us suppose a man who has understanding of the true nature of justice, and a power of reasoning not inferior to his understanding; and, moreover, let him have the same grasp of all other things.

Pro. We will suppose such a man.

Soc. Will he have enough of knowledge if he is acquainted only with the divine circle and sphere, and knows nothing of our human spheres and circles, so that in building or some other b operation[1] he does not know whether he is handling a straight rule or a circle?

Pro. The knowledge which is only superhuman, Socrates, is ridiculous in man.

Soc. What do you mean? Do you mean that you are to throw into the cup and mingle the impure and uncertain art which uses the false measure and the false circle?

Pro. Yes, we must, if any of us is ever to find his way home.

---

[1] [The text here does not require emendation. καὶ τοῖς ἄλλοις may refer to operations similar to building, or it may, as often in Greek, be used of two mutually exclusive classes. In this case the words 'or some other operation' are not required.]

c   *Soc.* And am I to include music, which, as I was saying just now, is full of guesswork and imitation, and is wanting in purity?

Pro. Yes, I think that you must, if human life is to be a life at all.

Soc. Well, then, suppose that I give way, and, like a door-keeper who is pushed and overborne by the mob, I open the door wide, and let knowledge of every sort stream in, and the pure mingle with the impure?

d   *Pro.* I do not know, Socrates, that any great harm would come of having them all, if only you have the first sort.

Soc. Well, then, shall I let them all flow into what Homer poetically terms 'a meeting of the waters'?

Pro. By all means.

Soc. There—I have let them in, and now I must return to the fountain of pleasure. For we were not permitted to begin by mingling in a single stream the true portions of both according to our original intention; but the love of all knowledge constrained us to let all the sciences flow in together before the pleasures.

e   *Pro.* Quite true.

Soc. And now the time has come for us to consider about the pleasures also, whether we shall in like manner let them go all at once, or at first only the true ones.

Pro. It will be by far the safer course to let flow the true ones first.

Soc. Let them flow, then; and now, if there are any necessary pleasures, as there were arts and sciences necessary, must we not mingle them?

Pro. Yes; the necessary pleasures should certainly be allowed to mingle.

63   *Soc.* The knowledge of the arts has been admitted to be innocent and useful always; and if we say of pleasures in like manner that all of them are good and innocent for all of us at all times, we must let them all mingle?

Pro. What shall we say about them, and what course shall we take?

Soc. Do not ask me, Protarchus; but ask the daughters of pleasure and wisdom to answer for themselves.

b   *Pro.* How?

Soc. Tell us, O beloved—shall we call you pleasures or by some other name?—would you rather live with or without wisdom? I am of opinion that they would certainly answer as follows:

Pro. How?

Soc. They would answer, as we said before:—'For any single class to be left by itself pure and isolated is not good, nor altogether possible; and if we are to make comparisons of one class with another and choose, there is no better companion than c knowledge of things in general, and likewise the perfect knowledge, if that may be, of each of ourselves in every respect.'[1]

Pro. And our answer will be:—In that ye have spoken well.

Soc. Very true. And now let us go back and interrogate wisdom and mind:—Would you like to have any pleasures in the mixture? And they will reply:—'What pleasures do you mean?'

Pro. Likely enough.

Soc. And we shall take up our parable and say:—Do you wish d to have the greatest and most vehement pleasures for your companions in addition to the true ones? 'Why, Socrates,' they will say, 'how can we? seeing that they are the source of ten thousand hindrances to us; they trouble the souls of men, which are our habitation, with their madness; they prevent us from coming to the birth, and are commonly the ruin of the children which are born to us, causing them to be forgotten and unheeded; but the true e and pure pleasures, of which you spoke, you may deem to be of our family, and also those pleasures which accompany health and temperance, and which every virtue, like a goddess, has in her train to follow her about wherever she goes,—mingle these and not the others; there would be great want of sense in anyone who desires to see a fair mixture and a perfect harmony, and to find in it what is the highest good in man and in the universe, and to divine what is the true form of good—there would be great want 64 of sense in his allowing the pleasures, which are always in the company of folly and vice, to mingle with mind in the cup.'—Is not this a very rational and suitable reply, which mind has made, both on her own behalf, as well as on the behalf of memory and true opinion?

Pro. Most certainly.

[1] Reading αὐτῶν ἡμῶν.

Soc. And still there must be something more added, which is a necessary ingredient in every mixture.

b   *Pro.* What is that?

Soc. Unless truth enter into the composition, nothing can truly be created or subsist.

Pro. Impossible.

Soc. Quite impossible; and now you and Philebus must tell me whether anything is still wanting in the mixture, for to my way of thinking the argument is now completed, and may be compared to an incorporeal law, which is going to hold fair rule over a living body.

Pro. I agree with you, Socrates.

c   *Soc.* And may we not say with reason that we are now at the vestibule of the habitation of the good?

Pro. I think that we are.

Soc. What, then, is there in the mixture which is most precious, and which is the principal cause why such a state is universally beloved by all? When we have discovered it, we will proceed to ask whether this omnipresent nature is more akin to pleasure or to mind.

d   *Pro.* Quite right; in that way we shall be better able to judge.

Soc. And there is no difficulty in seeing the cause which renders any mixture either of the highest value or of none at all.

Pro. What do you mean?

Soc. Every man knows it.

Pro. What?

Soc. He knows that any want of measure and symmetry in any mixture whatever must always of necessity be fatal, both to the elements and to the mixture, which is then not a mixture, but

e   only a confused medley which brings unmixed confusion on the possessor of it.

Pro. Most true.

Soc. And now the power of the good has retired into the region of the beautiful; for measure and symmetry are beauty and virtue all the world over.

Pro. True.

Soc. Also we said that truth was to form an element in the mixture.

Pro. Certainly.

Soc. Then, if we are not able to hunt the good with one idea 65 only, with three we may catch our prey; beauty, symmetry, truth are the three, and these taken together we may regard as the single cause of the mixture, and the mixture as being good by reason of the infusion of them.

Pro. Quite right.

Soc. And now, Protarchus, any man could decide well enough whether pleasure or wisdom is more akin to the highest good, and more honourable among gods and men.   b

Pro. Clearly, and yet perhaps the argument had better be pursued to the end.

Soc. We must take each of them separately in their relation to pleasure and mind, and pronounce upon them; for we ought to see to which of the two they are severally most akin.

Pro. You are speaking of beauty, truth, and measure?

Soc. Yes, Protarchus, take truth first, and, after passing in review mind, truth, pleasure, pause awhile and make answer to c yourself,—whether pleasure or mind is more akin to truth.

Pro. There is no need to pause, for the difference between them is palpable; pleasure is the veriest impostor in the world; and it is said that in the pleasures of love, which appear to be the greatest, perjury is excused by the gods; for pleasures, like children, have d not the least particle of reason in them; whereas mind is either the same as truth, or the most like truth, and the truest.

Soc. Shall we next consider measure, in like manner, and ask whether pleasure has more of this than wisdom, or wisdom than pleasure?

Pro. Here is another question which may be easily answered; for I imagine that nothing can ever be more immoderate than the transports of pleasure, or more in conformity with measure than mind and knowledge.

Soc. Very good; but there still remains the third test: Has e mind a greater share of beauty than pleasure, and is mind or pleasure the fairer of the two?

Pro. No one, Socrates, either awake or dreaming, ever saw or imagined mind or wisdom to be in aught unseemly, at any time, past,[1] present, or future.

Soc. Right.

---

[1] [Reading γενόμενον.]

Pro. But when we see some one indulging in pleasures, perhaps in the greatest of pleasures, the ridiculous or disgraceful nature of the action makes us ashamed; and so we put them out of sight, and consign them to darkness, under the idea that they ought not to meet the eye of day.

Soc. Then, Protarchus, you will proclaim everywhere, by word of mouth to this company, and by messengers bearing the tidings far and wide, that pleasure is not the first of possessions, nor yet the second, but that in measure, and the mean, and the suitable, and the like, the eternal nature has been found.[1]

Pro. Yes, that seems to be the result of what has been now said.

Soc. In the second class is contained the symmetrical and beautiful and perfect or sufficient, and all which are of that family.

Pro. True.

Soc. And if you reckon in the third class mind and wisdom, you will not be far wrong, if I divine aright.

Pro. I dare say.

Soc. And would you not put in the fourth class the goods which we were affirming to appertain specially to the soul—sciences and arts and true opinions as we called them? These come after the third class, and form the fourth, as they are certainly more akin to good than pleasure is.

Pro. Surely.

Soc. The fifth class are the pleasures which were defined by us as painless, being the pure pleasures of the soul herself, as we termed them, which accompany, some the sciences, and some the senses.

Pro. Perhaps.

Soc. And now, as Orpheus says,

'With the sixth generation cease the glory of my song.'

Here, at the sixth award, let us make an end; all that remains is to set the crown on our discourse.

Pro. True.

Soc. Then let us sum up and reassert what has been said, thus offering the third libation to the saviour Zeus.

[1] [Reading ηὑρῆσθαι φύσιν. In ed. 1 Jowett read ᾑρῆσθαι and translated: 'or whatever similar attributes the eternal nature may be deemed to have attained'.]

Pro. How?

Soc. Philebus affirmed that pleasure was always and absolutely the good.

Pro. I understand; this third libation, Socrates, of which you spoke, meant a recapitulation.

Soc. Yes, but listen to the sequel; convinced of what I have e just been saying, and feeling indignant at the doctrine, which is maintained, not by Philebus only, but by thousands of others, I affirmed that mind was far better and far more excellent, as an element of human life, than pleasure.

Pro. True.

Soc. But, suspecting that there were other things which were also better, I went on to say that if there was anything better than either, then I would claim the second place for mind over pleasure, and pleasure would lose the second place as well as the first.

Pro. You did.

Soc. Nothing could be more satisfactorily shown than the 67 unsatisfactory nature of both of them.

Pro. Very true.

Soc. The claims both of pleasure and mind to be the absolute good have been entirely disproven in this argument, because they are both wanting in self-sufficiency and also in adequacy and perfection.

Pro. Most true.

Soc. But, though they must both resign in favour of another, mind is ten thousand times nearer and more akin to the nature of the conqueror than pleasure.

Pro. Certainly.

Soc. And, according to the judgement which has now been given, pleasure will rank fifth.

Pro. True.

Soc. But not first; no, not even if all the oxen and horses b and animals in the world by their pursuit of enjoyment proclaim her to be so;—although the many, trusting in them as diviners trust in birds, determine that pleasures make up the good of life, and deem the lusts of animals to be sounder evidence than a passion for the inspirations of the philosophical Muse.

Pro. And now, Socrates, we tell you that the truth of what you have been saying is approved by the judgement of all of us.

Soc. And will you let me go?

Pro. There is a little which yet remains, and I will remind you of it, for I am sure that you will not be the first to go away from an argument.

TIMAEUS

INTRODUCTION AND ANALYSIS

THE influence which the *Timaeus* has exercised upon posterity is due partly to a misunderstanding. In the supposed depths of this dialogue the Neo-Platonists found hidden meanings and connexions with the Jewish and Christian Scriptures, and out of them they elicited doctrines quite at variance with the spirit of Plato. Believing that he was inspired by the Holy Ghost, or had received his wisdom from Moses, they seemed to find in his writings the Christian Trinity, the Word, the Church, the creation of the world in a Jewish sense, as they really found the personality of God or of mind, and the immortality of the soul. All religions and philosophies met and mingled in the schools of Alexandria, and the Neo-Platonists had a method of interpretation which could elicit any meaning out of any words. They were really incapable of distinguishing between the opinions of one philosopher and another—between Aristotle and Plato, or between the serious thoughts of Plato and his passing fancies. They were absorbed in his theology and were under the dominion of his name, while that which was truly great and truly characteristic in him, his effort to realize and connect abstractions, was not understood by them at all. Yet the genius of Plato and Greek philosophy reacted upon the East, and a Greek element of thought and language overlaid and partly reduced to order the chaos of Orientalism. And kindred spirits, like St. Augustine, even though they were acquainted with his writings only through the medium of a Latin translation, were profoundly affected by them, seeming to find 'God and his word everywhere insinuated' in them (August. *Confess.* viii. 2).

There is no danger of the modern commentators on the *Timaeus* falling into the absurdities of the Neo-Platonists. In the present day we are well aware that an ancient philosopher is to be interpreted from himself and by the contemporary history of thought. We know that mysticism is not criticism. The fancies of the Neo-Platonists are only interesting to us because they exhibit a phase of the human mind which prevailed widely in the first centuries of the Christian era, and is not wholly extinct in our own day. But they have nothing to do with the interpretation of Plato, and in spirit they are opposed to him. They are the feeble expression of an age which has lost the power not only of creating great works, but of understanding them. They are the spurious birth of a marriage between philosophy and tradition, between Hellas and the East—εἰκὸς γεννᾶν νόθα καὶ φαῦλα (*Rep.* vi. 496 a). Whereas the so-called mysticism of Plato is purely Greek, arising out of his imperfect knowledge and high aspirations, and is the growth of an age in which philosophy is not wholly separated from poetry and mythology.

A greater danger with modern interpreters of Plato is the tendency to regard the *Timaeus* as the centre of his system. We do not know how Plato would have arranged his own dialogues, or whether the thought of arranging any of them, besides the two 'trilogies' which he has expressly connected, was ever present to his mind. But, if he had arranged them, there are many indications that this is not the place which he would have assigned to the *Timaeus*. We observe, first of all, that the dialogue is put into the mouth of a Pythagorean philosopher, and not of Socrates. And this is required by dramatic propriety; for the investigation of nature was expressly renounced by Socrates in the *Phaedo* (96 ff.). Nor does Plato himself attribute any importance to his guesses at science. He is not at all absorbed by them, as he is by the Idea of good. He is modest and hesitating, and confesses that his words partake of the uncertainty of the subject (*Tim.* 29 c). The dialogue is primarily concerned with the animal creation, including under this term the heavenly bodies, and with man only as one among the animals. But we can hardly suppose that Plato would have preferred the study of nature to man, or that he would have deemed the formation of the world and the human frame to have the same interest which he ascribes to the mystery of being and not-being, or to the great political problems which he discusses in the *Republic* and the *Laws*. There are no speculations on physics in the other dialogues of Plato, and he himself regards the consideration of them as a rational pastime only (cf. 59 d, &c.). He is beginning to feel the need of further divisions of knowledge; and is becoming aware that besides dialectic, mathematics, and the arts, there is another field which has been hitherto unexplored by him. But he has not as yet defined this intermediate territory which lies somewhere between medicine and mathematics, and he would have felt that there was as great an impiety in ranking theories of physics first in the order of knowledge as in placing the body before the soul.

It is true, however, that the *Timaeus* is by no means confined to speculations on physics. The deeper foundations of the Platonic philosophy, such as the nature of God, the distinction of the sensible and intellectual, the great original conceptions of time and space, also appear in it. They are found principally in the first half of the dialogue.

The construction of the heavens is for the most part ideal; the cyclic year serves as the connexion between the world of absolute being and of generation, just as the number of population in the *Republic* (viii. 546) is the expression or symbol of the transition from the ideal to the actual state. In some passages we are uncertain whether we are reading a description of astronomical facts or contemplating processes of the human mind (37 c), or of that divine mind (cf. *Phil.* 22 d) which in Plato is hardly separable from it. The characteristics of man are transferred to the world-animal, as for example when intelligence and knowledge are said to be perfected by the circle of the same, and true opinion by the circle of the other; and conversely the motions of the world-animal reappear in man; its amorphous state continues in the child (44), and in both, disorder and chaos are gradually succeeded by stability and order. It is not however to passages like these that Plato is referring when he speaks of the uncertainty of his subject, but rather to the composition of bodies, to the relations of colours, the nature of diseases, and the like, about which he truly feels the lamentable ignorance prevailing in his own age.

We are led by Plato himself to regard the *Timaeus*, not as the centre or inmost shrine of the edifice, but as a detached building in a different style, framed, not after the Socratic, but after some Pythagorean model. As in the *Cratylus* and *Parmenides*, we are uncertain whether Plato is expressing his own opinions, or appropriating and perhaps improving the philosophical speculations of others. In all three dialogues he is exerting his dramatic and imitative power; in the *Cratylus* mingling a satirical and humorous purpose with true principles of language; in the *Parmenides* overthrowing Megarianism by a sort of ultra-Megarianism, which discovers contradictions in the one as great as those which have been previously shown to exist in the Ideas. There is a similar uncertainty about the *Timaeus*; in the first part he scales the heights of transcendentalism, in the latter part he treats in a bald and superficial manner of the functions and diseases of the human frame. He uses the thoughts and almost the words of Parmenides when he discourses of being and of essence, adopting from old religion into philosophy the conception of God, and from the Megarians the Idea of good. He agrees with Empedocles and the Atomists in attributing the greater differences of kinds to the figures of the elements and their movements into and out of one another. With Heracleitus, he acknowledges the perpetual flux; like Anaxagoras, he asserts the predominance of mind, although admitting an element of necessity which reason is incapable of subduing; like the Pythagoreans he supposes the mystery of the world to be contained in number. Many, if not all the elements of the pre-Socratic philosophy are included in the *Timaeus*. It is a composite or eclectic work of imagination, in which Plato, without naming them, gathers up into a kind of system the various elements of philosophy which preceded him.

If we allow for the difference of subject, and for some growth in Plato's own mind, the discrepancy between the *Timaeus* and the other dialogues will not appear to be great. It is probable that the relation of the Ideas to God or of God to the world was differently conceived by him at different times of his life. In all his later dialogues we observe a tendency in him to personify mind or God, and he therefore naturally inclines to view creation as the work of design. The creator is like a human artist who frames in his mind a plan which he executes by the help of his servants. Thus the language of philosophy which speaks of first and second causes is crossed by another sort of phraseology: 'God made the world because he was good, and the daemons ministered to him.' The *Timaeus* is cast in a more theological and less philosophical mould than the other dialogues, but the same general spirit is apparent; there is the same dualism or opposition between the ideal and actual (51 b ff.)—the soul is prior to the body (34 c), the intelligible and unseen to the visible and corporeal (28). There is the same distinction between knowledge and opinion (37 c) which occurs in the *Theaetetus* and *Republic*, the same enmity to the poets (19 d), the same combination of music and gymnastics (88 c). The doctrine of transmigration is still held by him (90 e ff.), as in the *Phaedrus* and *Republic*; and the soul has a view of the heavens in a prior state of being (41 e). The Ideas also remain, but they have become types in nature, forms of men, animals, birds, fishes (39 e). And the attribution of evil to physical causes (86 d, e) accords with the doctrine which he maintains in the *Laws* (ix. 861) respecting the involuntariness of vice.

The style and plan of the *Timaeus* differ greatly from that of any other of the Platonic dialogues. The language is weighty, abrupt, and in some passages sublime. But Plato has not the same mastery over his instrument which he exhibits in the *Phaedrus* or *Symposium*. Nothing can exceed the beauty or art of the introduction, in which he is using words after his accustomed manner. But in the rest of the work the power of language seems to fail him, and the dramatic form is wholly given up. He could write in one style, but not in another, and the Greek language had not as yet been fashioned by any poet or philosopher to describe physical phenomena. The early physiologists had generally written in verse;[1] the prose writers, like Democritus and

[1] [This is an error. Prose was the usual medium, and Parmenides and Empedocles are exceptions to the general rule.]

Anaxagoras, as far as we can judge from their fragments, never attained to a periodic style. And hence we find the same sort of clumsiness in the *Timaeus* of Plato which characterizes the philosophical poem of Lucretius. There is a want of flow and often a defect of rhythm; the meaning is sometimes obscure, and there is a greater use of apposition and more of repetition than occurs in Plato's earlier writings. The sentences are less closely connected and also more involved; the antecedents of demonstrative and relative pronouns are in some cases remote and perplexing. The greater frequency of participles and of absolute constructions gives the effect of heaviness. The descriptive portion of the *Timaeus* retains traces of the first Greek prose composition; for the great master of language was speaking on a theme with which he was imperfectly acquainted, and had no words in which to express his meaning. The rugged grandeur of the opening discourse of Timaeus (28–31) may be compared with the more harmonious beauty of a similar passage in the *Phaedrus* (245).

To the same cause we may attribute the want of plan. Plato had not the command of his materials which would have enabled him to produce a perfect work of art. Hence there are several new beginnings and resumptions and formal or artificial connexions; we miss the *callida iunctura* of the earlier dialogues. His speculations about the Eternal, his theories of creation, his mathematical anticipations, are supplemented by desultory remarks on the one immortal and the two mortal souls of man, on the functions of the bodily organs in health and disease, on sight, hearing, smell, taste, and touch. He soars into the heavens, and then, as if his wings were suddenly clipped, he walks ungracefully and with difficulty upon the earth. The greatest things in the world, and the least things in man, are brought within the compass of a short treatise. But the intermediate links are missing, and we cannot be surprised that there should be a want of unity in a work which embraces astronomy, theology, physiology, and natural philosophy in a few pages.

It is not easy to determine how Plato's cosmos may be presented to the reader in a clearer and shorter form; or how we may supply a thread of connexion to his ideas without giving greater consistency to them than they possessed in his mind, or adding on consequences which would never have occurred to him. For he has glimpses of the truth, but no comprehensive or perfect vision. There are isolated expressions about the nature of God which have a wonderful depth and power (29 e ff., 37 ff.); but we are not justified in assuming that these had any greater significance to the mind of Plato than language of a neutral and impersonal character. . . . With a view to the illustration of the *Timaeus* I propose to divide this Introduction into sections, of which (1) the first will contain an outline of the Dialogue: (2) I shall consider the aspects of nature which presented themselves to Plato and his age, and the elements of philosophy which entered into the conception of them: (3) the theology and physics of the *Timaeus*, including the soul of the world, the conception of time and space, and the composition of the elements: (4) in the fourth section I shall consider the Platonic astronomy, and the position of the earth. There will remain, (5) the psychology, (6) the physiology of Plato, and (7) his analysis of the senses to be briefly commented upon: (8) lastly, we may examine in what points Plato approaches or anticipates the discoveries of modern science.

---

§ 1

ANALYSIS

17, 18 Socrates begins the *Timaeus* with a summary of the *Republic*.[1] He lightly touches upon a few points,—the division of labour and distribution of the citizens into classes, the double nature and training of the guardians, the community of property and of women and children. But he makes no mention of the second education, or of the government of philosophers.

19 And now he desires to see the ideal State set in motion; he would like to know how she behaved in some great struggle. But he is unable to invent such a narrative himself; and he is afraid that the poets are equally incapable; for, although he pretends to have nothing to say against them, he remarks that they are a tribe of imitators, who can only describe what they have seen. And he fears that the sophists, who are plentifully supplied with graces of speech, in their erratic way of life having never had a city or house of their own, may through want of experience err in their conception of philosophers and statesmen.

20 'And therefore to you I turn, Timaeus, citizen of Locris, who are at once a philosopher and a statesman, and to you, Critias, whom all Athenians know to be similarly accomplished, and to Hermocrates, who is also fitted by nature and education to share in our discourse.' *Her.* 'We will do our best, and have been already preparing; for on our way home, Critias told us of an ancient tradition, which I wish, Critias, that you would repeat to

---

[1] [Rather, 'of a conversation on the previous day'.]

Socrates.' 'I will, if Timaeus approves.' 'I approve.' Listen then, Socrates, to a tale of Solon's, who, being the friend of Dropidas my great-grandfather, told it to my grandfather Critias, and he told me. The narrative related to ancient famous actions of the Athenian people, and to one especially, which I will rehearse in 21 honour of you and of the goddess. Critias when he told this tale of the olden time, was ninety years old, I being not more than ten. The occasion of the rehearsal was the day of the Apaturia called the Registration of Youth, at which our parents gave prizes for recitation. Some poems of Solon were recited by the boys. They had not at that time gone out of fashion, and the recital of them led some one to say, perhaps in compliment to Critias, that Solon was not only the wisest of men but also the best of poets. The old man brightened up at hearing this, and said: Had Solon only had the leisure which was required to complete the famous legend which he brought with him from Egypt he would have been as distinguished as Homer and Hesiod. 'And what was the subject of the poem?' said the person who made the remark. The subject was a very noble one; he described the most famous action in which the Athenian people were ever engaged. But the memory of their exploits has passed away owing to the lapse of time and the extinction of the actors. 'Tell us', said the other, 'the whole story, and where Solon heard the story.' He replied—There is at the head of the Egyptian Delta, where the river Nile divides, a city and district called Sais; the city was the birthplace of King Amasis, and is under the protection of the goddess Neith or Athene. The citizens have a friendly feeling towards the Athenians, believing themselves to be related to them. Hither came Solon, and was received with honour; and here he 22 first learnt, by conversing with the Egyptian priests, how ignorant he and his countrymen were of antiquity. Perceiving this, and with the view of eliciting information from them, he told them the tales of Phoroneus and Niobe, and also of Deucalion and Pyrrha, and he endeavoured to count the generations which had since passed. Thereupon an aged priest said to him: 'O Solon, Solon, you Hellenes are ever young, and there is no old man who is a Hellene.' 'What do you mean?' he asked. 'In mind,' replied the priest, 'I mean to say that you are children; there is no opinion or tradition of knowledge among you which is white with

age; and I will tell you why. Like the rest of mankind you have suffered from convulsions of nature, which are chiefly brought about by the two great agencies of fire and water. The former is symbolized in the Hellenic tale of young Phaëthon who drove his father's horses the wrong way, and having burnt up the earth was himself burnt up by a thunderbolt. For there occurs at long intervals a derangement of the heavenly bodies, and then the earth is destroyed by fire. At such times, and when fire is the agent, those who dwell by rivers or on the seashore are safer than those who dwell upon high and dry places, who in their turn are safer when the danger is from water. Now the Nile is our saviour from fire, and as there is little rain in Egypt, we are not harmed by water; whereas in other countries, when a deluge comes, the inhabitants are swept by the rivers into the sea. The memorials which your own and other nations have once had of the famous actions of mankind perish in the waters at certain periods; and the rude survivors in the mountains begin again, knowing nothing of the
23 world before the flood. But in Egypt the traditions of our own and other lands are by us registered for ever in our temples. The genealogies which you have recited to us out of your own annals, Solon, are a mere children's story. For in the first place, you remember one deluge only and there were many of them, and you know nothing of that fairest and noblest race of which you are a seed or remnant. The memory of them was lost, because there was no written voice among you. For in the times before the great flood Athens was the greatest and best of cities and did the noblest deeds and had the best constitution of any under the face of heaven.' Solon marvelled, and desired to be informed of the particulars. 'You are welcome to hear them', said the priest, 'both for your own sake and for that of the city, and above all for the sake of the goddess who is the common foundress of both our cities. Nine thousand years have elapsed since she founded yours, and eight thousand since she founded ours, as our annals record. Many laws exist among us which are the counterpart of yours as
24 they were in the olden time. I will briefly describe them to you, and you shall read the account of them at your leisure in the sacred registers. In the first place, there was a caste of priests among the ancient Athenians, and another of artisans; also castes of shepherds, hunters, and husbandmen, and lastly of

warriors, who, like the warriors of Egypt, were separated from the rest, and carried shields and spears, a custom which the goddess first taught you, and then the Asiatics, and we among Asiatics first received from her. Observe again, what care the law took in the pursuit of wisdom, searching out the deep things of the world, and applying them to the use of man. The spot of earth which the goddess chose had the best of climates, and produced the wisest men; in no other was she herself, the philosopher and warrior goddess, so likely to have votaries. And there you dwelt as became the children of the gods, excelling all men in virtue, and many famous actions are recorded of you. The most famous of them all was the overthrow of the island of Atlantis. This great island lay over against the Pillars of Heracles, in extent greater than Libya and Asia put together, and was the passage to other islands and to a great ocean of which the 25 Mediterranean sea was only the harbour; and within the Pillars the empire of Atlantis reached in Europe to Tyrrhenia and in Libya to Egypt. This mighty power was arrayed against Egypt and Hellas and all the countries bordering on the Mediterranean. Then your city did bravely, and won renown over the whole earth. For at the peril of her own existence, and when the other Hellenes had deserted her, she repelled the invader, and of her own accord gave liberty to all the nations within the Pillars. A little while afterwards there were great earthquakes and floods and your warrior race all sank into the earth; and the great island of Atlantis also disappeared in the sea. This is the explanation of the shallows which are found in that part of the Atlantic ocean.'

Such was the tale, Socrates, which Critias heard from Solon; and I noticed when listening to you yesterday, how close the resemblance was between your city and citizens and the ancient Athenian State. But I would not speak at the time, because I 26 wanted to refresh my memory. I had heard the old man when I was a child, and though I could not remember the whole of our yesterday's discourse, I was able to recall every word of this, which is branded into my mind; and I am prepared, Socrates, to rehearse to you the entire narrative. The imaginary State which you were describing may be identified with the reality of Solon, and our antediluvian ancestors may be your citizens. 'That is

excellent, Critias, and very appropriate to a Panathenaic festival;
27 the truth of the story is a great advantage.' Then now let me
explain to you the order of our entertainment; first, Timaeus,
who is a natural philosopher, will speak of the origin of the world,
going down to the creation of man, and then I shall receive the
men whom he has created, and some of whom will have been
educated by you, and introduce them to you as the lost Athenian
citizens of whom the Egyptian record spoke. As the law of Solon
prescribes, we will bring them into court and acknowledge their
claims to citizenship. 'I see', replied Socrates, 'that I shall be well
entertained; and do you, Timaeus, offer up a prayer and begin.'

Tim. All men who have any right feeling, at the beginning of
any enterprise, call upon the Gods; and he who is about to speak
of the origin of the universe has a special need of their aid. May
my words be acceptable to them, and may I speak in the manner
which will be most intelligible to you and will best express my
own meaning!

First, I must distinguish between that which always is and
never becomes and which is apprehended by reason and reflec-
28 tion, and that which always becomes and never is and is conceived by opinion with the help of sense. All that becomes and is
created is the work of a cause, and that is fair which the artificer
makes after an eternal pattern, but whatever is fashioned after a
created pattern is not fair. Is the world created or uncreated?—
that is the first question. Created, I reply, being visible and
tangible and having a body, and therefore sensible; and if
sensible, then created; and if created, made by a cause, and the
29 cause is the ineffable father of all things, who had before him an
eternal archetype. For to imagine that the archetype was created
would be blasphemy, seeing that the world is the noblest of
creations, and God is the best of causes. And the world being
thus created according to the eternal pattern is the copy of something; and we may assume that words are akin to the matter of
which they speak. What is spoken of the unchanging or intelligible
must be certain and true; but what is spoken of the created
image can only be probable; being is to becoming what truth is
to belief. And amid the variety of opinions which have arisen
about God and the nature of the world we must be content to
take probability for our rule, considering that I, who am the

speaker, and you, who are the judges, are only men; to probability we may attain but no further.

Soc. Excellent, Timaeus; I like your manner of approaching
the subject—proceed.

Tim. Why did the Creator make the world? . . . He was good,
and therefore not jealous, and being free from jealousy he desired
that all things should be like himself. Wherefore he set in order 30
the visible world, which he found in disorder. Now he who is
the best could only create the fairest; and reflecting that of visible
things the intelligent is superior to the unintelligent, he put intelligence in soul and soul in body, and framed the universe to
be the best and fairest work in the order of nature, and the world
became a living soul through the providence of God.

In the likeness of what animal was the world made?—that is
the third question. . . . The form of the perfect animal was a
whole, and contained all intelligible beings, and the visible
animal, made after the pattern of this, included all visible
creatures.

Are there many worlds or one only?—that is the fourth ques- 31
tion. . . . One only. For if in the original there had been more than
one they would have been the parts of a third, which would have
been the true pattern of the world; and therefore there is, and
will ever be, but one created world. Now that which is created is
of necessity corporeal and visible and tangible,—visible and
therefore made of fire,—tangible and therefore solid and made of
earth. But two terms must be united by a third, which is a mean 32
between them; and had the earth been a surface only, one mean
would have sufficed, but two means are required to unite solid
bodies. And as the world was composed of solids, between the
elements of fire and earth God placed two other elements of air
and water, and arranged them in a continuous proportion—

fire:air::air:water, and air:water::water:earth,

and so put together a visible and palpable heaven, having harmony and friendship in the union of the four elements; and
being at unity with itself it was indissoluble except by the hand
of the framer. Each of the elements was taken into the universe
whole and entire; for he considered that the animal should be
perfect and one, leaving no remnants out of which another animal 33

could be created, and should also be free from old age and disease, which are produced by the action of external forces. And as he was to contain all things, he was made in the all-containing form of a sphere, round as from a lathe and every way equidistant from the centre, as was natural and suitable to him. He was finished and smooth, having neither eyes nor ears, for there was nothing without him which he could see or hear; and he had no need to carry food to his mouth, nor was there air for him to breathe; and he did not require hands, for there was nothing of which he 34 could take hold, nor feet, with which to walk. All that he did was done rationally in and by himself, and he moved in a circle turning within himself, which is the most intellectual of motions; but the other six motions were wanting to him; wherefore the universe had no feet or legs.

And so the thought of God made a God in the image of a perfect body, having intercourse with himself and needing no other, but in every part harmonious and self-contained and truly blessed. The soul was first made by him—the elder to rule the younger; not in the order in which our wayward fancy has led us to describe them, but the soul first and afterwards the body. 35 God took of the unchangeable and indivisible and also of the divisible and corporeal, and out of the two he made a third nature, which was in a mean between them, and partook of the same and the other, the intractable nature of the other being compressed into the same. Having made a compound of all the three, he proceeded to divide the entire mass into portions 36 related to one another in the ratios of 1, 2, 3, 4, 9, 8, 27, and proceeded to fill up the double and triple intervals thus—

$$\overline{1}, \tfrac{4}{3}, \tfrac{3}{2}, \overline{2}, \tfrac{8}{3}, 3, \overline{4}, \tfrac{16}{3}, 6, \overline{8}:$$
$$\overline{1}, \tfrac{3}{2}, 2, \overline{3}, \tfrac{9}{2}, 6, \overline{9}, \tfrac{27}{2}, 18, \overline{27};$$

in which double series of numbers are two kinds of means; the one exceeds and is exceeded by equal parts of the extremes, e.g. 1, $\tfrac{4}{3}$, 2; the other kind of mean is one which is equidistant from the extremes, e.g. 2, 4, 6. In this manner there were formed intervals of thirds, 3:2, of fourths, 4:3, and of ninths, 9:8. And next he filled up the intervals of a fourth with ninths, leaving a remnant which is in the ratio of 256:243. The entire compound was divided by him lengthways into two parts, which he united at the centre like the letter X, and bent them into an inner and outer circle or sphere, cutting one another again at a point over against the point at which they cross. The outer circle or sphere was named the sphere of the same—the inner, the sphere of the other or diverse; and the one revolved horizontally to the right, the other diagonally to the left. To the sphere of the same which was undivided he gave dominion, but the sphere of the other or diverse was distributed into seven unequal orbits, having intervals in ratios of twos and threes, three of either sort, and he bade the orbits move in opposite directions to one another—three of them, the Sun, Mercury, Venus, with equal swiftness, and the remaining four—the Moon, Saturn, Mars, Jupiter, with unequal swiftness to the three and to one another, but all in due proportion.

When the Creator had made the soul he made the body within her; and the soul interfused everywhere from the centre to the circumference of heaven, herself turning in herself, began a divine life of rational and everlasting motion. The body of heaven is 37 visible, but the soul is invisible, and partakes of reason and harmony, and is the best of creations, being the work of the best. And being composed of the same, the other, and the essence, these three, and also divided and bound in harmonical proportion, and revolving within herself—the soul when touching anything which has essence, whether divided or undivided, is stirred to utter the sameness or diversity of that and some other thing, and to tell how and when and where individuals are affected or related, whether in the world of change or of essence. When reason is in the neighbourhood of sense, and the circle of the other or diverse is moving truly, then arise true opinions and beliefs; when reason is in the sphere of thought, and the circle of the same runs smoothly, then intelligence is perfected.

When the Father who begat the world saw the image which he had made of the eternal Gods moving and living, he rejoiced; and in his joy resolved, since the archetype was eternal, to make the creature eternal as far as this was possible. Wherefore he made an image of eternity which is time, having an uniform motion according to number, parted into months and days and years, and also having greater divisions of past, present, and future. These all apply to becoming in time, and have no meaning in relation to the eternal nature, which ever is and never was

or will be; for the unchangeable is never older or younger, and
38 when we say that he 'was' or 'will be', we are mistaken, for these
words are applicable only to becoming, and not to true being;
and equally wrong are we in saying that what has become *is*
become and that what becomes *is* becoming, and that the non-
existent *is* non-existent. . . . These are the forms of time which
imitate eternity and move in a circle measured by number.

Thus was time made in the image of the eternal nature; and it
was created together with the heavens, in order that if they were
dissolved, it might perish with them. And God made the sun and
moon and five other wanderers, as they are called, seven in all,
and to each of them he gave a body moving in an orbit, being
one of the seven orbits into which the circle of the other was
divided. He put the moon in the orbit which was nearest to the
earth, the sun in that next, the morning star and Mercury in the
orbits which move opposite to the sun but with equal swiftness—
this being the reason why they overtake and are overtaken by one
another. All these bodies became living creatures, and learnt
their appointed tasks, and began to move, the nearer more
39 swiftly, the remoter more slowly, according to the diagonal movement of the other. And since this was controlled by the movement
of the same, the seven planets in their courses appeared to describe
spirals; and that appeared fastest which was slowest, and that
which overtook others appeared to be overtaken by them. And
God lighted a fire in the second orbit from the earth which is
called the sun, to give light over the whole heaven, and to teach
intelligent beings that knowledge of number which is derived
from the revolution of the same. Thus arose day and night, which
are the periods of the most intelligent nature; a month is created
by the revolution of the moon, a year by that of the sun. Other
periods of wonderful length and complexity are not observed by
men in general; there is moreover a cycle or perfect year at the
completion of which they all meet and coincide. . . . To this end
the stars came into being, that the created heaven might imitate
the eternal nature.

Thus far the universal animal was made in the divine image,
but the other animals were not as yet included in him. And God
created them according to the patterns or species of them which
40 existed in the divine original. There are four of them: one of

gods, another of birds, a third of fishes, and a fourth of beasts. The gods were made in the form of a circle, which is the most perfect figure and the figure of the universe. They were created chiefly of fire, that they might be bright, and were made to know and follow the best, and to be scattered over the heavens, of which they were to be the glory. Two kinds of motion were assigned to them—first, the revolution in the same and around the same, in peaceful unchanging thought of the same; and to this was added a forward motion which was under the control of the same. Thus then the fixed stars were created, being divine and eternal animals, revolving on the same spot, and the wandering stars, in their courses, were created in the manner already described. The earth, which is our nurse, clinging around the pole extended through the universe, he made to be the guardian and artificer of night and day, first and eldest of gods that are in the interior of heaven. Vain would be the labour of telling all the figures of them, moving as in dance, and their juxtapositions and approximations, and when and where and behind what other stars they appear or disappear—to tell of all this without looking at a plan of them would be labour in vain.

The knowledge of the other gods is beyond us, and we can only accept the traditions of the ancients, who were the children of the gods, as they said; for surely they must have known their own ancestors. Although they give no proof, we must believe them as is customary. They tell us that Oceanus and Tethys were the children of Earth and Heaven; that Phorcys, Cronos, and Rhea came in the next generation, and were followed by Zeus and 41 Hera, whose brothers and children are known to everybody.

When all of them, both those who show themselves in the sky, and those who retire from view, had come into being, the Creator addressed them thus:—'Gods, sons of gods, my works, if I will, are indissoluble. That which is bound may be dissolved, but only an evil being would dissolve that which is harmonious and happy. And although you are not immortal you shall not die, for I will hold you together. Hear me, then:—Three tribes of mortal beings have still to be created, but if created by me they would be like gods. Do ye therefore make them; I will implant in them the seed of immortality, and you shall weave together the mortal and immortal, and provide food for them, and receive them

again in death.' Thus he spake, and poured the remains of the elements into the cup in which he had mingled the soul of the universe. They were no longer pure as before, but diluted; and the mixture he distributed into souls equal in number to the stars, and assigned each to a star—then having mounted them, as in a chariot, he showed them the nature of the universe, and told them of their future birth and human lot. They were to be sown in the planets, and out of them was to come forth the most
42 religious of animals, which would hereafter be called man. The souls were to be implanted in bodies, which were in a perpetual flux, whence, he said, would arise, first, sensation; secondly, love, which is a mixture of pleasure and pain; thirdly, fear and anger, and the opposite affections: and if they conquered these, they would live righteously, but if they were conquered by them, unrighteously. He who lived well would return to his native star, and would there have a blessed existence; but, if he lived ill, he would pass into the nature of a woman, and if he did not then alter his evil ways, into the likeness of some animal, until the reason which was in him reasserted her sway over the elements of fire, air, earth, water, which had engrossed her, and he regained his first and better nature. Having given this law to his creatures, that he might be guiltless of their future evil, he sowed them, some in the earth, some in the moon, and some in the other planets; and he ordered the younger gods to frame human bodies for them and to make the necessary additions to them, and to avert from them all but self-inflicted evil.

Having given these commands, the Creator remained in his own nature. And his children, receiving from him the immortal principle, borrowed from the world portions of earth, air, fire,
43 water, hereafter to be returned, which they fastened together, not with the adamantine bonds which bound themselves, but by little invisible pegs, making each separate body out of all the elements, subject to influx and efflux, and containing the courses of the soul. These swelling and surging as in a river moved irregularly and irrationally in all the six possible ways, forwards, backwards, right, left, up, and down. But violent as were the internal and alimentary fluids, the tide became still more violent when the body came into contact with flaming fire, or the solid earth, or gliding waters, or the stormy wind; the motions pro-

duced by these impulses pass through the body to the soul and have the name of sensations. Uniting with the ever-flowing current, they shake the courses of the soul, stopping the revolution of the same and twisting in all sorts of ways the nature of the other, and the harmonical ratios of twos and threes and the mean terms which connect them, until the circles are bent and disordered and their motion becomes irregular. You may imagine a position of the body in which the head is resting upon the ground, and the legs are in the air, and the top is bottom and the left right. And something similar happens when the disordered motions of the soul come into contact with any external thing; they say the same or the other in a manner which is the very 44 opposite of the truth, and they are false and foolish, and have no guiding principle in them. And when external impressions enter in, they are really conquered, though they seem to conquer.

By reason of these affections the soul is at first without intelligence, but as time goes on the stream of nutriment abates, and the courses of the soul regain their proper motion, and apprehend the same and the other rightly, and become rational. The soul of him who has education is whole and perfect and escapes the worst disease, but, if a man's education be neglected, he walks lamely through life and returns good for nothing to the world below. This, however, is an after-stage—at present, we are only concerned with the creation of the body and soul.

The two divine courses were encased by the gods in a sphere which is called the head, and is the god and lord of us. And to this they gave the body to be a vehicle, and the members to be instruments, having the power of flexion and extension. Such was 45 the origin of legs and arms. In the next place, the gods gave a forward motion to the human body, because the front part of man was the more honourable and had authority. And they put in a face in which they inserted organs to minister in all things to the providence of the soul. They first contrived the eyes, into which they conveyed a light akin to the light of day, making it to flow through the pupils. When the light of the eye is surrounded by the light of day, then like falls upon like, and they unite and form one body which conveys to the soul the motions of visible objects. But when the visual ray goes forth into the darkness, then unlike falls upon unlike—the eye no longer sees, and we go to sleep. The fire or light, when kept in by the eyelids, equalizes the inward motions, and there is rest accompanied by few dreams; 46 only when the greater motions remain they engender in us corresponding visions of the night. And now we shall be able to understand the nature of reflections in mirrors. The fires from within and from without meet about the smooth and bright surface of the mirror; and because they meet in a manner contrary to the usual mode, the right and left sides of the object are transposed. In a concave mirror the top and bottom are inverted, but this is no transposition.

These are the second causes which God used as his ministers in fashioning the world. They are thought by many to be the prime causes, but they are not so; for they are destitute of mind and reason, and the lover of mind will not allow that there are any prime causes other than the rational and invisible ones— these he investigates first, and afterwards the causes of things which are moved by others, and which work by chance and without order. Of the second or concurrent causes of sight I have already spoken, and I will now speak of the higher purpose of 47 God in giving us eyes. Sight is the source of the greatest benefits to us; for if our eyes had never seen the sun, stars, and heavens, the words which we have spoken would not have been uttered. The sight of them and their revolutions has given us the knowledge of number and time, the power of inquiry, and philosophy, which is the great blessing of human life; not to speak of the lesser benefits which even the vulgar can appreciate. God gave us the faculty of sight that we might behold the order of the heavens and create a corresponding order in our own erring minds. To the like end the gifts of speech and hearing were bestowed upon us; not for the sake of irrational pleasure, but in order that we might harmonize the courses of the soul by sympathy with the harmony of sound, and cure ourselves of our irregular and graceless ways.

Thus far we have spoken of the works of mind; and there are other works done from necessity, which we must now place beside 48 them; for the creation is made up of both, mind persuading necessity as far as possible to work out good. Before the heavens there existed fire, air, water, earth, which we suppose men to know, though no one has explained their nature, and we erroneously maintain them to be the letters or elements of the whole, although they cannot reasonably be compared even to syllables or first compounds. I am not now speaking of the first principles of things, because I cannot discover them by our present mode of inquiry. But as I observed the rule of probability at first, I will begin anew, seeking by the grace of God to observe it still.

In our former discussion I distinguished two kinds of being— the unchanging or invisible, and the visible or changing. But now 49 a third kind is required, which I shall call the receptacle or nurse of generation. There is a difficulty in arriving at an exact notion of this third kind, because the four elements themselves are of inexact natures and easily pass into one another, and are too transient to be detained by any one name; wherefore we are compelled to speak of water or fire, not as substances, but as qualities. They may be compared to images made of gold, which 50 are continually assuming new forms. Somebody asks what they are; if you do not know, the safest answer is to reply that they are gold. In like manner there is a universal nature out of which all things are made, and which is like none of them; but they enter into and pass out of her, and are made after patterns of the true in a wonderful and inexplicable manner. The containing principle may be likened to a mother, the source or spring to a father, the intermediate nature to a child; and we may also remark that the matter which receives every variety of form must be formless, like the inodorous liquids which are prepared to receive scents, or the smooth and soft materials on which figures are impressed. In the same way space or matter is neither earth nor fire nor air 51 nor water, but an invisible and formless being which receives all things, and in an incomprehensible manner partakes of the intelligible. But we may say, speaking generally, that fire is that part of this nature which is inflamed, water that which is moistened, and the like.

Let me ask a question in which a great principle is involved: Is there an essence of fire and the other elements, or are there only fires visible to sense? I answer in a word: If mind is one thing and true opinion another, then there are self-existent essences; but if mind is the same with opinion, then the visible and corporeal is most real. But they are not the same, and they have a different

origin and nature. The one comes to us by instruction, the other
by persuasion; the one is rational, the other is irrational; the one
is immovable, the other movable, by persuasion; the one is
possessed by every man, the other by the gods and by very few
men. And we must acknowledge that as there are two kinds of
knowledge, so there are two kinds of being corresponding to
52 them; the one uncreated, indestructible, immovable, which is
seen by intelligence only; the other created, which is always
becoming in place and vanishing out of place, and is apprehended by opinion and sense. There is also a third nature—that
of space, which is indestructible, and is perceived by a kind of
spurious reason without the help of sense. This is presented to us
in a dreamy manner, and yet is said to be necessary, for we say
that all things must be somewhere in space. For they are the
images of other things and must therefore have a separate
existence and exist in something (i.e. in space). But true reason
assures us that while two things (i.e. the idea and the image)
are different they cannot inhere in one another, so as to be one
and two at the same time.

To sum up: Being and generation and space, these three,
existed before the heavens, and the nurse or vessel of generation,
moistened by water and inflamed by fire, and taking the forms of
air and earth, assumed various shapes. By the motion of the
vessel, the elements were divided, and like grain winnowed by
fans, the close and heavy particles settled in one place, the light
53 and airy ones in another. At first they were without reason or
measure, and had only certain faint traces of themselves, until
God fashioned them by figure and number. In this, as in every
other part of creation, I suppose God to have made things, as
far as was possible, fair and good, out of things not fair and good.

And now I will explain to you the generation of the world by
a method with which your scientific training will have made you
familiar. Fire, air, earth, and water are bodies and therefore
solids, and solids are contained in planes, and plane rectilinear
figures are made up of two kinds of right-angled triangles;
one having the opposite sides equal (isosceles), the other with
unequal sides (scalene). These we may fairly assume to be the
original elements of fire and the other bodies; what principles are
prior to these God only knows, and he of men whom God loves.

Next, we must determine what are the four most beautiful figures which are unlike one another and yet sometimes capable of resolution into one another. . . . Of the two kinds of triangles the 54 equal-sided has but one form, the unequal-sided has an infinite variety of forms; and there is none more beautiful than that which forms the half of an equilateral triangle. Let us then choose two triangles; one, the isosceles, the other, that form of scalene which has the square of the longer side [forming the right-angle] three times as great as the square of the lesser side; and affirm that, out of these, fire and the other elements have been constructed.

I was wrong in imagining that all the four elements could be generated into and out of one another. For as they are formed, three of them from the triangle which has the sides unequal, the fourth from the triangle which has equal sides, three can be resolved into one another, but the fourth cannot be resolved into them nor they into it. So much for their passage into one another: I must now speak of their construction. From the triangle of which the hypotenuse is twice the lesser side the three first regular solids are formed—first, the equilateral pyramid or 55 tetrahedron; secondly, the octahedron; thirdly, the icosahedron; and from the isosceles triangle is formed the cube. And there is a fifth figure [which is made out of twelve pentagons], the dodeca-hedron—this God used as a model for the twelvefold division of the Zodiac.

Let us now assign the geometrical forms to their respective elements. The cube is the most stable of them because resting on a quadrangular plane surface, and composed of isosceles triangles. To earth then, which is the most stable of bodies and the most easily modelled of them, may be assigned the form of a 56 cube; and the remaining forms to the other elements,—to fire the pyramid, to air the octahedron, and to water the icosahedron, —according to their degrees of lightness or heaviness or power, or want of power, of penetration. The single particles of any of the elements are not seen by reason of their smallness; they only become visible when collected. The ratios of their motions, numbers, and other properties, are ordered by the God, who harmonized them as far as necessity permitted.

The probable conclusion is as follows:—Earth, when dissolved by the more penetrating element of fire, whether acting immediately or through the medium of air or water, is decomposed but not transformed. Water, when divided by fire or air, becomes one part fire, and two parts air. A volume of air divided becomes two of fire. On the other hand, when condensed, two volumes of fire make a volume of air; and two and half parts of air condense into

57 one of water. Any element which is fastened upon by fire is cut by the sharpness of the triangles, until at length, coalescing with the fire, it is at rest; for similars are not affected by similars. When two kinds of bodies quarrel with one another, then the tendency to decomposition continues until the smaller either escapes to its kindred element or becomes one with its conqueror. And this tendency in bodies to condense or escape is a source of motion. . . . Where there is motion there must be a mover, and where there is a mover there must be something to move. These cannot exist in what is uniform, and therefore motion is due to want of

58 uniformity. But then why, when things are divided after their kinds, do they not cease from motion? The answer is, that the circular motion of all things compresses them, and the finer and more subtle particles of the lighter elements, such as fire and air, are thrust into the interstices of the larger, each of them penetrating according to their rarity, and thus all the elements are on their way up and down everywhere and always into their own places. Hence there is a principle of inequality, and therefore of motion, in all time.

In the next place, we may observe that there are different kinds of fire—(1) flame, (2) light that burns not, (3) the red heat of the embers of fire. And there are varieties of air, as for example, the pure aether, the opaque mist, and other nameless forms. Water, again is of two kinds, liquid and fusile. The liquid is composed of small and unequal particles, the fusile of large and uniform particles and is more solid, but nevertheless melts at the

59 approach of fire, and then spreads upon the earth. When the substance cools, the fire passes into the air, which is displaced, and forces together and condenses the liquid mass. This process is called cooling and congealment. Of the fusile kinds the fairest and heaviest is gold; this is hardened by filtration through rock, and is of a bright yellow colour. An offshoot of gold which is darker and denser than the rest is called adamant. Another kind is called copper, which is harder and yet lighter because the interstices

are larger than in gold. There is mingled with it a fine and small portion of earth which comes out in the form of rust [verdigris]. These are a few of the conjectures which philosophy forms, when, leaving the eternal nature, she turns for innocent recreation to consider the truths of generation.

Water which is mingled with fire is called liquid because it rolls upon the earth, and soft because its bases give way. This becomes more equable when separated from fire and air, and then congeals into hail or ice, or the looser forms of hoar frost or snow. There are other waters which are called juices and are .60 distilled through plants. Of these we may mention, first, wine, which warms the soul as well as the body; secondly, oily substances, as for example, oil or pitch; thirdly, honey, which relaxes the contracted parts of the mouth and so produces sweetness; fourthly, vegetable acid, which is frothy and has a burning quality and dissolves the flesh. Of the kinds of earth, that which is filtered through water passes into stone, the water is broken up by the earth and escapes in the form of air—this in turn presses upon the mass of earth, and the earth, compressed into an indissoluble union with the remaining water, becomes rock. Rock, when it is made up of equal particles, is fair and transparent, but the reverse when of unequal. Earth is converted into pottery when the watery part is suddenly drawn away; or if moisture remains, the earth, when fused by fire, becomes, on cooling, a stone of a black colour. When the earth is finer and of a briny nature then two half-solid bodies are formed by separating the water,—soda and salt. The strong compounds of earth and water are not soluble by water, but only by fire. Earth itself, when not con- 61 solidated, is dissolved by water; when consolidated, by fire only. The cohesion of water, when strong, is dissolved by fire only; when weak, either by air or fire, the former entering the interstices, the latter penetrating even the triangles. Air when strongly condensed is indissoluble by any power which does not reach the triangles, and even when not strongly condensed is only resolved by fire. Compounds of earth and water are unaffected by water while the water occupies the interstices in them, but begin to liquefy when fire enters into the interstices of the water. They are of two kinds, some of them, like glass, having more earth, others, like wax, having more water in them.

Having considered objects of sense, we now pass on to sensation. But we cannot explain sensation without explaining the nature of flesh and of the mortal soul; and as we cannot treat of both together, in order that we may proceed at once to the sensations we must assume the existence of body and soul.

What makes fire burn? The fineness of the sides, the sharpness of the angles, the smallness of the particles, the quickness of the
62 motion. Moreover, the pyramid, which is the figure of fire, is more cutting than any other. The feeling of cold is produced by the larger particles of moisture outside the body trying to eject the smaller ones in the body which they compress. The struggle which arises between elements thus unnaturally brought together causes shivering. That is hard to which the flesh yields, and soft which yields to the flesh, and these two terms are also relative to one another. The yielding matter is that which has the slenderest base, whereas that which has a rectangular base is compact and repellent. Light and heavy are wrongly explained with reference to a lower and higher in place. For in the universe, which is a sphere, there is no opposition of above or below, and that which
63 is to us above would be below to a man standing at the antipodes. The greater or less difficulty in detaching any element from its like is the real cause of heaviness or of lightness. If you draw the earth into the dissimilar air, the particles of earth cling to their native element, and you more easily detach a small portion than a large. There would be the same difficulty in moving any of the upper elements towards the lower. The smooth and the rough are severally produced by the union of evenness with compactness,
64 and of hardness with inequality.

Pleasure and pain are the most important of the affections common to the whole body. According to our general doctrine of sensation, parts of the body which are easily moved readily transmit the motion to the mind; but parts which are not easily moved have no effect upon the patient. The bones and hair are of the latter kind, sight and hearing of the former. Ordinary affections are neither pleasant nor painful. The impressions of sight afford an example of these, and are neither violent nor
65 sudden. But sudden replenishments of the body cause pleasure, and sudden disturbances, as for example cuttings and burnings, have the opposite effect.

From sensations common to the whole body, we proceed to those of particular parts. The affections of the tongue appear to be caused, by contraction and dilation, but they have more of roughness or smoothness than is found in other affections. Earthy particles, entering into the small veins of the tongue which reach to the heart, when they melt into and dry up the little veins, are astringent if they are rough; or if not so rough, they are only harsh, and if excessively abstergent, like potash and soda, bitter. Purgatives of a weaker sort are called salt and, having no bitterness, are rather agreeable. Inflammatory bodies, which by their lightness are carried up into the head, cutting all that comes in 66 their way, are termed pungent. But when these are refined by putrefaction, and enter the narrow veins of the tongue, and meet there particles of earth and air, two kinds of globules are formed —one of earthy and impure liquid, which boils and ferments, the other of pure and transparent water, which are called bubbles; of all these affections the cause is termed acid. When, on the other hand, the composition of the deliquescent particles is congenial to the tongue, and disposes the parts according to their nature, this remedial power in them is called sweet.

Smells are not divided into kinds; all of them are transitional, and arise out of the decomposition of one element into another, for the simple air or water is without smell. They are vapours or mists, thinner than water and thicker than air: and hence in drawing in the breath, when there is an obstruction, the air passes, but there is no smell. They have no names, but are dis- 67 tinguished as pleasant and unpleasant, and their influence extends over the whole region from the head to the navel.

Hearing is the effect of a stroke which is transmitted through the ears by means of the air, brain, and blood to the soul, beginning at the head and extending to the liver. The sound which moves swiftly is acute; that which moves slowly is grave; that which is uniform is smooth, and the opposite is harsh. Loudness depends on the quantity of the sound. Of the harmony of sounds I will hereafter speak (80).

Colours are flames which emanate from all bodies, having particles corresponding to the sense of sight. Some of the particles are less and some larger, and some are equal to the parts of the sight. The equal particles appear transparent; the large contract, and the lesser dilate the sight. White is produced by the dilation, black by the contraction, of the particles of sight. There is also a swifter motion of another sort of fire which forces a way through 68 the passages of the eyes, and elicits from them a union of fire and water which we call tears. The inner fire flashes forth, and the outer finds a way in and is extinguished in the moisture, and all sorts of colours are generated by the mixture. This affection is termed by us dazzling, and the object which produces it is called bright. There is yet another sort of fire which mingles with the moisture of the eye without flashing, and produces a colour like blood—to this we give the name of red. A bright element mingling with red and white produces a colour which we call auburn. The law of proportion, however, according to which compound colours are formed, cannot be determined scientifically or even probably. Red, when mingled with black and white, gives a purple hue, which becomes umber when the colours are burnt and there is a larger admixture of black. Flame-colour is a mixture of auburn and dun; dun of white and black; yellow of white and auburn. White and bright meeting, and falling upon a full black, become dark blue; dark blue mingling with white becomes a light blue; the union of flame-colour and black makes leek-green. There is no difficulty in seeing how other colours are probably composed. But he who should attempt to test the truth of this by experiment, would forget the difference of the human and divine nature. God only is able to compound and resolve substances; such experiments are impossible to man.

These are the elements of necessity which the Creator received in the world of generation when he made the all-sufficient and perfect creature, using the secondary causes as his ministers, but himself fashioning the good in all things. For there are two sorts of causes, the one divine, the other necessary; and we should 69 seek to discover the divine above all, and, for their sake, the necessary, because without them the higher cannot be attained by us.

Having now before us the causes out of which the rest of our discourse is to be framed, let us go back to the point at which we began, and add a fair ending to our tale. As I said at first, all things were originally a chaos in which there was no order or proportion. The elements of this chaos were arranged by the

Creator, and out of them he made the world. Of the divine he himself was the author, but he committed to his offspring the creation of the mortal. From him they received the immortal soul, but themselves made the body to be its vehicle, and constructed within another soul which was mortal, and subject to terrible affections—pleasure, the inciter of evil; pain, which deters from good; rashness and fear, foolish counsellors; anger hard to be appeased; hope easily led astray. These they mingled with irrational sense and all-daring love according to necessary laws, and so framed man. And, fearing to pollute the divine element, they gave the mortal soul a separate habitation in the breast, parted off from the head by a narrow isthmus. And as in 70 a house the women's apartments are divided from the men's, the cavity of the thorax was divided into two parts, a higher and a lower. The higher of the two, which is the seat of courage and anger, lies nearer to the head, between the midriff and the neck, and assists reason in restraining the desires. The heart is the house of guard in which all the veins meet, and through them reason sends her commands to the extremity of her kingdom. When the passions are in revolt, or danger approaches from without, then the heart beats and swells; and the creating powers, knowing this, implanted in the body the soft and bloodless substance of the lung, having a porous and springy nature like a sponge, and being kept cool by drink and air which enters through the trachea.

The part of the soul which desires meat and drink was placed between the midriff and navel, where they made a sort of manger; and here they bound it down, like a wild animal, away from the council-chamber, and leaving the better principle undisturbed to advise quietly for the good of the whole. For the Creator knew 71 that the belly would not listen to reason, and was under the power of idols and fancies. Wherefore he framed the liver to connect with the lower nature, contriving that it should be compact, and bright, and sweet, and also bitter and smooth, in order that the power of thought which originates in the mind might there be reflected, terrifying the belly with the elements of bitterness and gall, and a suffusion of bilious colours when the liver is contracted, and causing pain and misery by twisting out of its place the lobe and closing up the vessels and gates. And the converse happens when some gentle inspiration coming from intelligence mirrors the opposite fancies, giving rest and sweetness and freedom, and at night, moderation and peace accompanied with prophetic insight, when reason and sense are asleep. For the authors of our being, in obedience to their Father's will and in order to make men as good as they could, gave to the liver the power of divination, which is never active when men are awake or in health; but when they are under the influence of 72 some disorder or enthusiasm then they receive intimations, which have to be interpreted by others who are called prophets, but should rather be called interpreters of prophecy; after death these intimations become unintelligible. The spleen which is situated in the neighbourhood, on the left side, keeps the liver bright and clean, as a napkin does a mirror, and the evacuations of the liver are received into it; and being a hollow tissue it is for a time swollen with these impurities, but when the body is purged it returns to its natural size.

The truth concerning the soul can only be established by the word of God. Still, we may venture to assert what is probable both concerning soul and body.

73 The creative powers were aware of our tendency to excess. And so when they made the belly to be a receptacle for food, in order that men might not perish by insatiable gluttony, they formed the convolutions of the intestines, in this way retarding the passage of food through the body, lest mankind should be absorbed in eating and drinking, and the whole race become impervious to divine philosophy.

The creation of bones and flesh was on this wise. The foundation of these is the marrow which binds together body and soul, and the marrow is made out of such of the primary triangles as are adapted by their perfection to produce all the four elements. These God took and mingled them in due proportion, making as many kinds of marrow as there were hereafter to be kinds of souls. The receptacle of the divine soul he made round, and called that portion of the marrow brain, intending that the vessel containing this substance should be the head. The remaining part he divided into long and round figures, and to these as to anchors fastening the mortal soul, he proceeded to make the rest of the body, first forming for both parts a covering of bone. The bone was formed by sifting pure smooth earth and wetting it with marrow. It was then thrust alternately into fire and water, and thus rendered insoluble by either. Of bone he made a globe 74 which he placed around the brain, leaving a narrow opening, and around the marrow of the neck and spine he formed the vertebrae, like hinges, which extended from the head through the whole of the trunk. And as the bone was brittle and liable to mortify and destroy the marrow by too great rigidity and susceptibility to heat and cold, he contrived sinews and flesh—the first to give flexibility, the second to guard against heat and cold, and to be a protection against falls, containing a warm moisture, which in summer exudes and cools the body, and in winter is a defence against cold. Having this in view, the Creator mingled earth with fire and water and mixed with them a ferment of acid and salt, so as to form pulpy flesh. But the sinews he made of a mixture of bone and unfermented flesh, giving them a mean nature between the two, and a yellow colour. Hence they were more glutinous than flesh, but softer than bone. The bones which have most of the living soul within them he covered with the thinnest film of flesh, those which have least of it, he lodged deeper. At the joints he diminished the flesh in order not to impede the flexure of the limbs, and also to avoid clogging the perceptions of the mind. About the thighs and arms, which have no sense because there is 75 little soul in the marrow, and about the inner bones, he laid the flesh thicker. For where the flesh is thicker there is less feeling, except in certain parts which the Creator has made solely of flesh, as for example, the tongue. Had the combination of solid bone and thick flesh been consistent with acute perceptions, the Creator would have given man a sinewy and fleshy head, and then he would have lived twice as long. But our creators were of opinion that a shorter life which was better was preferable to a longer which was worse, and therefore they covered the head with thin bone, and placed the sinews at the extremity of the head round the neck, and fastened the jawbones to them below the face. And they framed the mouth, having teeth and tongue and lips, with a view to the necessary and the good; for food is a necessity, and the river of speech is the best of rivers. Still, the head could not be left a bare globe of bone on account of the extremes of heat and cold, nor be allowed to become dull and

senseless by an overgrowth of flesh. Wherefore it was covered by
76 a peel or skin which met and grew by the help of the cerebral
humour. The diversity of the sutures was caused by the struggle
of food against the course of the soul. The skin of the head was
pierced by fire, and out of the punctures came forth a moisture,
part liquid, and part of a skinny nature, which was hardened by
the pressure of the external cold and became hair. And God gave
hair to the head of man to be a light covering, so that it might
not interfere with his perceptions. Nails were formed by combining sinew, skin, and bone, and were made by the creators with
a view to the future when, as they knew, women and other
animals who would require them would be framed out of man.

77 The gods also mingled natures akin to that of man with other
forms and perceptions. Thus trees and plants were created, which
were originally wild and have been adapted by cultivation to our
use. They partake of that third kind of life which is seated between
the midriff and the navel, and is altogether passive and incapable
of reflection.

When the creators had furnished all these natures for our sustenance, they cut channels through our bodies as in a garden,
watering them with a perennial stream. Two were cut down the
back, along the back bone, where the skin and flesh meet, one on
the right and the other on the left, having the marrow of generation between them. In the next place, they divided the veins about
the head and interlaced them with each other in order that they
might form an additional link between the head and the body,
and that the sensations from both sides might be diffused throughout the body. In the third place, they contrived the passage of
78 liquids, which may be explained in this way:—Finer bodies
retain coarser, but not the coarser the finer, and the belly is
capable of retaining food, but not fire and air. God therefore
formed a network of fire and air to irrigate the veins, having
within it two lesser nets, and stretched cords reaching from both
the lesser nets to the extremity of the outer net. The inner parts
of the net were made by him of fire, the lesser nets and their
cavities of air. The two latter he made to pass into the mouth; the
one ascending by the air-pipes from the lungs, the other by the
side of the air-pipes from the belly. The entrance to the first he
divided into two parts, both of which he made to meet at the

channels of the nose, that when the mouth was closed the passage connected with it might still be fed with air. The cavity of the network he spread around the hollows of the body, making the entire receptacle to flow into and out of the lesser nets and the lesser nets into and out of it, while the outer net found a way into and out of the pores of the body, and the internal heat followed the air to and fro. These, as we affirm, are the phenomena of respiration. And all this process takes place in order that the body may be watered and cooled and nourished, and the meat and drink digested and liquefied and carried into the veins.   79

The causes of respiration have now to be considered. The exhalation of the breath through the mouth and nostrils displaces the external air, and at the same time leaves a vacuum into which through the pores the air which is displaced enters. Also the vacuum which is made when the air is exhaled through the pores is filled up by the inhalation of breath through the mouth and nostrils. The explanation of this double phenomenon is as follows:—Elements move towards their natural places. Now as every animal has within him a fountain of fire, the air which is inhaled through the mouth and nostrils, on coming into contact with this, is heated; and when heated, in accordance with the law of attraction, it escapes by the way it entered toward the place of fire. On leaving the body it is cooled and drives round the air which it displaces through the pores into the empty lungs. This again is in turn heated by the internal fire and escapes, as it entered, through the pores.

The phenomena of medical cupping-glasses, of swallowing, and   80 of the hurling of bodies, are to be explained on a similar principle; as also sounds, which are sometimes discordant on account of the inequality of them, and again harmonious by reason of equality. The slower sounds reaching the swifter, when they begin to pause, by degrees assimilate with them: whence arises a pleasure which even the unwise feel, and which to the wise becomes a higher sense of delight, being an imitation of divine harmony in mortal motions. Streams flow, lightnings play, amber and the magnet attract, not by reason of attraction, but because 'nature abhors a vacuum', and because things, when compounded or dissolved, move different ways, each to its own place.

I will now return to the phenomena of respiration. The fire, entering the belly, minces the food, and as it escapes, fills the veins by drawing after it the divided portions, and thus the streams of nutriment are diffused through the body. The fruits or herbs which are our daily sustenance take all sorts of colours when intermixed, but the colour of red or fire predominates, and hence the liquid which we call blood is red, being the nurturing principle

81 of the body, whence all parts are watered and empty places filled.

The process of repletion and depletion is produced by the attraction of like to like, after the manner of the universal motion. The external elements by their attraction are always diminishing the substance of the body: the particles of blood, too, formed out of the newly digested food, are attracted towards kindred elements within the body and so fill up the void. When more is taken away than flows in, then we decay; and when less, we grow and increase.

The young of every animal has the triangles new and closely locked together, and yet the entire frame is soft and delicate, being newly made of marrow and nurtured on milk. These triangles are sharper than those which enter the body from without in the shape of food, and therefore they cut them up. But as life advances, the triangles wear out and are no longer able to assimilate food; and at length, when the bonds which unite the triangles of the marrow become undone, they in turn unloose the bonds of the soul; and if the release be according to nature, she then flies away with joy. For the death which is natural is pleasant, but that which is caused by violence is painful.

Everyone may understand the origin of diseases. They may

82 be occasioned by the disarrangement or disproportion of the elements out of which the body is framed. This is the origin of many of them, but the worst of all owe their severity to the following causes: There is a natural order in the human frame according to which the flesh and sinews are made of blood, the sinews out of the fibres, and the flesh out of the congealed substance which is formed by separation from the fibres. The glutinous matter which comes away from the sinews and the flesh, not only binds the flesh to the bones, but nourishes the bones and waters the marrow. When these processes take place in regular order the body is in health.

But when the flesh wastes and returns into the veins there is discoloured blood as well as air in the veins, having acid and salt qualities, from which is generated every sort of phlegm and bile. All things go the wrong way and cease to give nourishment to the body, no longer preserving their natural courses, but at war 83 with themselves and destructive to the constitution of the body. The oldest part of the flesh which is hard to decompose blackens from long burning, and from being corroded grows bitter, and as the bitter element refines away, becomes acid. When tinged with blood the bitter substance has a red colour, and this when mixed with black takes the hue of grass; or again, the bitter substance has an auburn colour, when new flesh is decomposed by the internal flame. To all which phenomena some physician or philosopher who was able to see the one in many has given the name of bile. The various kinds of bile have names answering to their colours. Lymph or serum is of two kinds: first, the whey of blood, which is gentle; secondly, the secretion of dark and bitter bile, which, when mingled under the influence of heat with salt, is malignant and is called acid phlegm. There is also white phlegm, formed by the decomposition of young and tender flesh, and covered with little bubbles, separately invisible, but becoming visible when collected. The water of tears and perspiration and similar substances is also the watery part of fresh phlegm. All these humours become sources of disease when the blood is replenished in irregular ways and not by food or drink. The danger, however, is not so great when the foundation remains, for then there is a possibility of recovery. But when the substance which unites the flesh and bones is diseased, and is no longer renewed from the muscles and sinews, and instead of being oily 84 and smooth and glutinous becomes rough and salt and dry, then the fleshy parts fall away and leave the sinews bare and full of brine, and the flesh gets back again into the circulation of the blood, and makes the previously mentioned disorders still greater. There are other and worse diseases which are prior to these; as when the bone through the density of the flesh does not receive sufficient air, and becomes stagnant and gangrened, and crumbling away passes into the food, and the food into the flesh, and the flesh returns again into the blood. Worst of all and most fatal is the disease of the marrow, by which the whole course of the body is reversed.

There is a third class of diseases which are produced, some by wind and some by phlegm and some by bile. When the lung, which is the steward of the air, is obstructed by rheums, and in one part no air, and in another too much, enters in, then the parts which are unrefreshed by air corrode, and other parts are distorted by the excess of air; and in this manner painful diseases are produced. The most painful are caused by wind generated within the body, which gets about the great sinews of the shoulders—these are termed tetanus. The cure of them is difficult, and in most cases they are relieved only by
85 fever. White phlegm, which is dangerous if kept in, by reason of the air bubbles, is not equally dangerous if able to escape through the pores, although it variegates the body, generating divers kinds of leprosies. If, when mingled with black bile, it disturbs the courses of the head in sleep, there is not so much danger; but if it assails those who are awake, then the attack is far more dangerous, and is called epilepsy or the sacred disease. Acid and salt phlegm is the source of catarrh.

Inflammations originate in bile, which is sometimes relieved by boils and swellings, but when detained, and above all when mingled with pure blood, generates many inflammatory disorders, disturbing the position of the fibres which are scattered about in the blood in order to maintain the balance of rare and dense which is necessary to its regular circulation. If the bile, which is only stale blood, or liquefied flesh, comes in little by little, it is congealed by the fibres and produces internal cold and shuddering. But when it enters with more of a flood it overcomes the fibres by its heat and reaches the spinal marrow, and burning up the cables of the soul sets her free from the body. When on the other hand the body, though wasted, still holds out, then the bile
86 is expelled, like an exile from a factious state, causing diarrhœas and dysenteries and similar disorders. The body which is diseased from the effects of fire is in a continual fever; when air is the agent, the fever is quotidian; when water, the fever intermits a day; when earth, which is the most sluggish element, the fever intermits three days and is with difficulty shaken off.

Of mental disorders there are two sorts, one madness, the other ignorance, and they may be justly attributed to disease. Excessive pleasures or pains are among the greatest diseases, and deprive men of their senses. When the seed about the spinal marrow is too abundant, the body has too great pleasures and pains; and during a great part of his life he who is the subject of them is more or less mad. He is often thought bad, but this is a mistake; for the truth is that the intemperance of lust is due to the fluidity of the marrow produced by the loose consistency of the bones. And this is true of vice in general, which is commonly regarded as disgraceful, whereas it is really involuntary and arises from a bad habit of the body and evil education. In like manner the soul is often made vicious by the influence of bodily pain; the briny phlegm and other bitter and bilious humours wander over the body and find no exit, but are compressed within, and mingle their own vapours with the motions of the soul, and are carried 87 to the three places of the soul, creating infinite varieties of trouble and melancholy, of rashness and cowardice, of forgetfulness and stupidity. When men are in this evil plight of body, and evil forms of government and evil discourses are superadded, and there is no education to save them, they are corrupted through two causes; but of neither of them are they really the authors. For the planters are to blame rather than the plants, the educators and not the educated. Still, we should endeavour to attain virtue and avoid vice; but this is part of another subject.

Enough of disease—I have now to speak of the means by which the mind and body are to be preserved, a higher theme than the other. The good is the beautiful, and the beautiful is the symmetrical, and there is no greater or fairer symmetry than that of body and soul, as the contrary is the greatest of deformities. A leg or an arm too long or too short is at once ugly and unserviceable, and the same is true if body and soul are disproportionate. For a strong and impassioned soul may 'fret the pigmy body to 88 decay', and so produce convulsions and other evils. The violence of controversy, or the earnestness of inquiry, will often generate inflammations and rheums which are not understood, or assigned to their true cause by the professors of medicine. And in like manner the body may be too much for the soul, darkening the reason, and quickening the animal desires. The only security is to preserve the balance of the two, and to this end the mathematician or philosopher must practise gymnastics, and the gymnast must cultivate music. The parts of the body too must be treated in the same way—they should receive their appropriate exercise. For the body is set in motion when it is heated and cooled by the elements which enter in, or is dried up and moistened by external things; and, if given up to these processes when at rest, it is liable to destruction. But the natural motion, as in the world, so also in the human frame, produces harmony and divides hostile powers.

89 The best exercise is the spontaneous motion of the body, as in gymnastics, because most akin to the motion of mind; not so good is the motion of which the source is in another, as in sailing or riding; least good when the body is at rest and the motion is in parts only, which is a species of motion imparted by physic. This should only be resorted to by men of sense in extreme cases; lesser diseases are not to be irritated by medicine. For every disease is akin to the living being and has an appointed term, just as life has, which depends on the form of the triangles, and cannot be protracted when they are worn out. And he who, instead of accepting his destiny, endeavours to prolong his life by medicine, is likely to multiply and magnify his diseases. Regimen and not medicine is the true cure, when a man has time at his disposal.

Enough of the nature of man and of the body, and of training and education. The subject is a great one and cannot be adequately treated as an appendage to another. To sum up all in a word: there are three kinds of soul located within us, and any one of them, if remaining inactive, becomes very weak; if exer-

90 cised, very strong. Wherefore we should duly train and exercise all three kinds.

The divine soul God lodged in the head, to raise us, like plants which are not of earthly origin, to our kindred; for the head is nearest to heaven. He who is intent upon the gratification of his desires and cherishes the mortal soul, has all his ideas mortal, and is himself mortal in the truest sense. But he who seeks after knowledge and exercises the divine part of himself in godly and immortal thoughts, attains to truth and immortality, as far as is possible to man, and also to happiness, while he is training up within him the divine principle and indwelling power of order. There is only one way in which one person can benefit another; and that is by assigning to him his proper nurture and motion. To the motions of the soul answer the motions of the universe, and by the study of these the individual is restored to his original nature.

Thus we have finished the discussion of the universe, which, according to our original intention, has now been brought down to the creation of man. Completeness seems to require that something should be briefly said about other animals: first of women, who are probably degenerate and cowardly men. And when they degenerated, the gods implanted in men the desire of union with 91 them, creating in man one animate substance and in woman another in the following manner:—The outlet for liquids they connected with the living principle of the spinal marrow, which the man has the desire to emit into the fruitful womb of the woman; this is like a fertile field in which the seed is quickened and matured, and at last brought to light. When this desire is unsatisfied the man is over-mastered by the power of the generative organs, and the woman is subjected to disorders from the obstruction of the passages of the breath, until the two meet and pluck the fruit of the tree.

The race of birds was created out of innocent, light-minded men, who thought to pursue the study of the heavens by sight; these were transformed into birds, and grew feathers instead of hair. The race of wild animals were men who had no philosophy, and never looked up to heaven or used the courses of the head, but followed only the influences of passion. Naturally they turned to their kindred earth, and put their forelegs to the ground, and their heads were crushed into strange oblong forms. Some 92 of them have four feet, and some of them more than four,—the latter, who are the more senseless, drawing closer to their native element; the most senseless of all have no limbs and trail their whole body on the ground. The fourth kind are the inhabitants of the waters; these are made out of the most senseless and ignorant and impure of men, whom God placed in the uttermost parts of the world in return for their utter ignorance, and caused them to respire water instead of the pure element of air. Such are the laws by which animals pass into one another.

And so the world received animals, mortal and immortal, and was fulfilled with them, and became a visible God, comprehending the visible, made in the image of the Intellectual, being the one perfect only-begotten heaven.

INTRODUCTION

§ 2

[1] THE charge of premature generalization which is often urged against ancient philosophers is really an anachronism. For they can hardly be said to have generalized at all. They may be said more truly to have cleared up and defined by the help of experience ideas which they already possessed. The beginnings of thought about nature must always have this character. A true method is the result of many ages of experiment and observation, and is ever going on and enlarging with the progress of science and knowledge. At first men personify nature, then they form impressions of nature, at last they conceive 'measure' or laws of nature. They pass out of mythology into philosophy. Early science is not a process of discovery in the modern sense; but rather a process of correcting by observation, and to a certain extent only, the first impressions of nature, which mankind, when they began to think, had received from poetry or language or unintelligent sense. Of all scientific truths the greatest and simplest is the uniformity of nature; this was expressed by the ancients in many ways, as fate, or necessity, or measure, or limit. Unexpected events, of which the cause was unknown to them, they attributed to chance (cf. Thucyd. i. 140). But their conception of nature was never that of law interrupted by exceptions,—a somewhat unfortunate metaphysical invention of modern times, which is at variance with facts and has failed to satisfy the requirements of thought.

§ 3

[2] Plato's account of the soul is partly mythical or figurative, and

---

[1] [The concluding paragraph of a passage dealing in general with the characteristics of ancient science.]

[2] [Jowett here gives a useful survey of the theological and scientific doctrine of the *Timaeus*, but our knowledge of its background has naturally been extended in many ways. Some indication of this will be given in notes appended to these sections. The principal points of interest are these. (*a*) Diogenes of Apollonia, a philosopher of the fifth century, had deeply influenced the Athenians of his day, among them Socrates, as we know from Aristophanes' caricature in the *Clouds* and from Xenophon. It is now thought that he was the first to insist on a teleological interpretation of the physical world. He appealed both to the intricate structure of the bodies of animals and to the regularity of the cosmic movements. Plato had always been impressed by the need for such an explanation of nature, but at the time of writing the *Phaedo* evidently felt himself unable to furnish it. Here he takes up the task and employs arguments similar to those of Diogenes, with reference to fourth-century science. The parallel between the human individual and the universe is also the foundation of his argument in *Philebus* 28 c-31 a.

(*b*) With regard to astronomy, Plato was probably acquainted with two systems, in both of which the apparent movement of the planets was derived from regular

partly literal. Not that either he or we can draw a line between them, or say, 'This is poetry, this is philosophy'; for the transition from the one to the other is imperceptible. Neither must we expect to find in him absolute consistency. He is apt to pass from one level or stage of thought to another without always making it apparent that he is changing his ground. In such passages we have to interpret his meaning by the general spirit of his writings. To reconcile his inconsistencies would be contrary to the first principles of criticism and fatal to any true understanding of him.

There is a further difficulty in explaining this part of the *Timaeus*— the natural order of thought is inverted. We begin with the most

spherical movements. According to the first, which is said to have been propounded by Eudoxus in answer to a problem formulated by Plato himself, the Earth is viewed as the centre of a system of concentric spheres. According to the other system, that of the Italian Pythagoreans, the Earth, together with the planets, revolves about a central Fire. The former is evidently assumed in the *Timaeus* but it has been thought that there is some hint of the latter system at the end of the *Critias* (121 c); and Plutarch reports on the authority of Theophrastus that Plato in old age repented of having assigned the central position to the Earth.

(*c*) Many discoveries in mathematics which were at one time assigned to the early Pythagoreans are now supposed to represent work done under Plato's own auspices in the Academy or, at least, to be the work of *fourth*-century Pythagoreans with whom he was acquainted. Plato's account of the mutual transformation of the elements is based upon the theory of regular solid figures which, as has been seen (vol. 3, p. 194), is said to have been completed by Theaetetus. In brief, many factors which to Jowett were a sign of Pythagorean influence may rather reflect Plato's natural interest in the work of his own Academy.

(*d*) It is well known that Plato nowhere mentions Democritus, and it was long supposed that he was not acquainted with his work. Most authorities would now agree that the *Timaeus* is in part directed against Democritus. Whereas his atoms were of indefinite shape and size and he held that the world could be fully explained without reference to intelligent design, Plato's corpuscles are regular solids built up from two kinds of triangle. In the dialectical dialogues also there seems to be some rivalry with Democritus. The 'atomic' species attained by Plato's logical division, separated from other species by logical otherness, takes the place of the physical atom separated from other atoms by the void.

(*e*) In the passage describing the composition of the world-soul, modern editors formerly bracketed the words αὖ πέρι, but Grube (*Class. Philol.* xxvii (1932)) and Cornford have shown that these words are necessary and that the sentence was correctly construed by Proclus. In this sentence also the word οὐσία has its usual Platonic sense, true being or existence, and does not denote a mysterious 'essence' intermediate between the intelligible and the sensible.

Commentaries on the *Timaeus* have been published by A. Rivaud in the *Collection G. Budé* (Paris, 1925), by A. E. Taylor (Oxford, 1928), and F. M. Cornford, *Plato's Cosmology* (London, Kegan Paul, 1937). The first and third of these include a translation. Translations of the *Timaeus* and *Critias* have been published by A. E. Taylor (London, Methuen, 1929), and by R. G. Bury in the Loeb Classical Library, 1929.]

abstract, and proceed from the abstract to the concrete. We are searching into things which are upon the utmost limit of human intelligence, and then of a sudden we fall rather heavily to the earth. There are no intermediate steps which lead from one to the other. But the abstract is a vacant form to us until brought into relation with man and nature. God and the world are mere names, like the Being of the Eleatics, unless some human qualities are added on to them. Yet the negation has a kind of unknown meaning to us. The priority of God and of the world which he is imagined to have created to all other existences, gives a solemn awe to them. And as in other systems of theology and philosophy, that of which we know least has the greatest interest to us.

There is no use in attempting to define or explain the first God in the Platonic system, who has sometimes been thought to answer to God the Father; or the world, in whom the Fathers of the Church seemed to recognize 'the firstborn of every creature'. Nor need we discuss at length how far Plato agrees in the later Jewish idea of creation, according to which God made the world out of nothing. For his original conception of matter as something which has no qualities is really a negation. Moreover in the Hebrew Scriptures the creation of the world is described, even more explicitly than in the *Timaeus*, not as a single act, but as a work or process which occupied six days. There is a chaos in both, and it would be untrue to say that the Greek, any more than the Hebrew, had any definite belief in the eternal existence of matter. The beginning of things vanished into the distance. The real creation began, not with matter, but with Ideas. According to Plato in the *Timaeus*, God took of the same and the other, of the divided and undivided, of the finite and infinite, and made essence,[1] and out of the three combined created the soul of the world. To the soul he added a body formed out of the four elements. The general meaning of these words is that God imparted determinations of thought, or, as we might say, gave law and variety to the material universe. The elements are moving in a disorderly manner before the work of creation begins (30 a); and there is an eternal pattern of the world, which, like the 'Idea of good', is not the Creator himself, but not separable from him. The pattern too, though eternal, is a creation, a world of thought prior to the world of sense, which may be compared to the wisdom of God in the book of Ecclesiasticus, or to the 'God in the form of a globe' of the old Eleatic philosophers. The visible, which already exists, is fashioned in the likeness of this eternal pattern. On the other hand, there is no truth of which Plato is more firmly convinced than

[1] [This account of his procedure is superseded by the translation now given.]

of the priority of the soul to the body, both in the universe and in man. So inconsistent are the forms in which he describes the works which no tongue can utter—his language, as he himself says (29 c), partaking of his own uncertainty about the things of which he is speaking.

We may remark in passing, that the Platonic compared with the Jewish description of the process of creation has less of freedom or spontaneity. The Creator in Plato is still subject to a remnant of necessity which he cannot wholly overcome (cf. 35 a). When his work is accomplished he remains in his own nature. Plato is more sensible than the Hebrew prophet of the existence of evil, which he seeks to put as far as possible out of the way of God (cf. 42 d). And he can only suppose this to be accomplished by God retiring into himself and committing the lesser works of creation to inferior powers. (Compare, however, *Laws* x. 903 for another solution of the difficulty.)

Nor can we attach any intelligible meaning to his words when he speaks of the visible being in the image of the invisible (28). For how can that which is divided be like that which is undivided? or that which is changing be the copy of that which is unchanging? All the old difficulties about the Ideas come back upon us in an altered form. We can imagine two worlds, one of which is the mere double of the other, or one of which is an imperfect copy of the other, or one of which is the vanishing ideal of the other; but we cannot imagine an intellectual world which has no qualities—'a thing in itself'—a point which has no parts or magnitude, which is nowhere, and nothing. This cannot be the archetype according to which God made the world, and is in reality, whether in Plato or in Kant, a mere negative residuum of human thought.

There is another aspect of the same difficulty which appears to have no satisfactory solution. In what relation does the archetype stand to the Creator himself? For the Idea or pattern of the world is not the thought of God, but a separate, self-existent nature, of which creation is the copy. We can only reply, (1) that to the mind of Plato subject and object were not yet distinguished; (2) that he supposes the process of creation to take place in accordance with his own theory of Ideas; and as we cannot give a consistent account of the one, neither can we of the other. He means (3) to say that the creation of the world is not a material process of working with legs and arms, but ideal and intellectual; according to his own fine expression, 'the thought of God made the God that was to be' (34 a). He means (4) to draw an absolute distinction between the invisible or unchangeable which is, or is the place of, mind or being, and the world of sense or becoming which is visible and changing. He means (5) that the Idea of the world is prior to the world, just as the other Ideas are prior to sensible objects; and like them may be regarded as eternal and self-existent, and also, like the Idea of good, may be viewed apart from the divine mind.

There are several other questions which we might ask and which can receive no answer, or at least only an answer of the same kind as the preceding. How can matter be conceived to exist without form? Or, how can the essences or forms of things be distinguished from the eternal ideas, or essence itself from the soul? Or, how could there have been motion in the chaos when as yet time was not? Or, how did chaos come into existence, if not by the will of the Creator? Or, how could there have been a time when the world was not, if time was not? Or, how could the Creator have taken portions of an indivisible same? Or, how could space or anything else have been eternal when time is only created? Or, how could the surfaces of geometrical figures have formed solids? We must reply again that we cannot follow Plato in all his inconsistencies, but that the gaps of thought are probably more apparent to us than to him. He would, perhaps, have said that 'the first things are known only to God and to him of men whom God loves'. How often have the gaps in Theology been concealed from the eye of faith! And we may say that only by an effort of metaphysical imagination can we hope to understand Plato from his own point of view; we must not ask for consistency. Everywhere we find traces of the Platonic theory of knowledge expressed in an objective form, which by us has to be translated into the subjective, before we can attach any meaning to it. And this theory is exhibited in so many different points of view, that we cannot with any certainty interpret one dialogue by another; e.g. the *Timaeus* by the *Parmenides* or *Phaedrus* or *Philebus*.

The soul of the world may also be conceived as the personification of the numbers and figures in which the heavenly bodies move. Imagine these as in a Pythagorean dream, stripped of qualitative difference and reduced to mathematical abstractions. They too conform to the principle of the same, and may be compared with the modern conception of laws of nature. They are in space, but not in time, and they are the makers of time. They are represented as constantly thinking of the same; for thought in the view of Plato is equivalent to truth or law, and need not imply a human consciousness, a conception which is familiar enough to us, but has no place, hardly even a name, in ancient Greek philosophy. To this principle of the same is opposed the principle of the other—the principle of irregularity and disorder, of necessity and chance, which is only partially impressed by mathematical laws and figures. (We may observe by the way, that the principle of the other, which is the principle of plurality and variation in the *Timaeus*, has nothing in common with the 'other' of the *Sophist*, which is the principle of determination.) The element of the same dominates to a certain extent over the other—the fixed stars keep the 'wanderers' of the inner circle in their courses (36 c), and a similar principle of fixedness or order appears to regulate the bodily constitution of man (89 a, 90 d). But there still remains a rebellious seed of evil derived from the original chaos, which is the source of disorder in the world, and of vice and disease in man.

But what did Plato mean by essence, οὐσία, which is the intermediate nature compounded of the same and the other, and out of which, together with these two, the soul of the world is created? It is difficult to explain a process of thought so strange and unaccustomed to us, in which modern distinctions run into one another and are lost sight of. First, let us consider once more the meaning of the same and the other. The same is the unchanging and indivisible, the heaven of the fixed stars, partaking of the divine nature, which, having law in itself, gives law to all besides and is the element of order and permanence in man and on the earth. It is the rational principle, mind regarded as a work, as creation—not as the creator. The old tradition of Parmenides and of the Eleatic being, the foundation of so much in the philosophy of Greece and of the world, was lingering in Plato's mind. The other is the variable or changing element, the residuum of disorder or chaos, which cannot be reduced to order, nor altogether banished, the source of evil, seen in the errors of man and also in the wanderings of the planets, a necessity which protrudes through nature. Of this, too, there was a shadow in the Eleatic philosophy in the realm of Opinion, which, like a mist, seemed to darken the purity of truth in itself.—So far the words of Plato may perhaps find an intelligible meaning. But when he goes on to speak of the essence which is compounded out of both, the track becomes fainter and we can only follow him with hesitating steps. But still we find a trace reappearing of the teaching of Anaxagoras: 'All was confusion, and then mind came and arranged things.' We have already remarked that Plato was not acquainted with the modern distinction of subject and object, and therefore he sometimes confuses mind and the things of mind—νοῦς and νοητά. By οὐσία he clearly means some conception of the intelligible and the intelligent; it belongs to the class of νοητά. Matter, being, the same, the eternal,— for any of these terms, being almost vacant of meaning, is equally suitable to express indefinite existence,—are compared or united with the other or diverse, and out of the union or comparison is elicited the Idea of intelligence, the 'One in many', brighter than any Promethean fire (cf. *Phil.* 16 c), which co-existing with them and so forming a new existence is or becomes the intelligible world. . . . So we may perhaps venture to paraphrase or interpret or put into other words the parable in which Plato has wrapped up his conception of the creation of the world. The explanation may help to fill up with figures of speech the void of knowledge.

The entire compound was divided by the Creator in certain proportions and reunited; it was then cut into two strips, which were bent into an inner circle and an outer, both moving with a uniform motion around a centre, the outer circle containing the fixed, the inner the wandering stars. The soul of the world was diffused everywhere from the centre to the circumference. To this God gave a body, consisting at first of fire and earth, and afterwards receiving an addition of air and water; because solid bodies, like the world, are always connected by two middle terms and not by one. The world was made in the form of a globe, and all the material elements were exhausted in the work of creation.

The proportions in which the soul of the world as well as the human soul is divided answer to a series of numbers 1, 2, 3, 4, 9, 8, 27, composed of the two Pythagorean progressions 1, 2, 4, 8 and 1, 3, 9, 27, of which the number 1 represents a point, 2 and 3 lines, 4 and 8, 9 and 27 the squares and cubes respectively of 2 and 3. This series, of which the intervals are afterwards filled up, probably represents (1) the diatonic scale according to the Pythagoreans and Plato; (2) the order and distances of the heavenly bodies; and (3) may possibly contain an allusion to the music of the spheres, which is referred to in the myth at the end of the *Republic*. The meaning of the words that 'solid bodies are always connected by two middle terms' or mean proportionals has been much disputed. The most received explanation is that of Martin, who supposes that Plato is only speaking of surfaces and solids compounded of prime numbers (i.e. of numbers not made up of two factors, or, in other words, only measurable by unity). The square of any such number represents a surface, the cube a solid. The squares of any two such numbers (e.g. 2^2, $3^2 = 4$, 9) have always a single mean proportional (e.g. 4 and 9 have the single mean 6), whereas the cubes of primes (e.g. 3^3 and 5^3) have always two mean proportionals (e.g. 27 : 45 : 75 : 125). But to this explanation of Martin's it may be objected (1) that Plato nowhere says that his proportion is to be limited to prime numbers; (2) that the limitation of surfaces to squares is also not to be found in his words; nor (3) is there any evidence to show that the distinction of prime from other numbers was known to him. What Plato chiefly intends to express is that a solid requires a stronger bond than a surface; and that the double bond which is given by two means is stronger than the single bond given by one. Having reflected on the singular numerical phenomenon of the existence of one mean proportional between two square numbers or rather perhaps only between the two lowest squares; and of two mean proportionals between two cubes, perhaps again confining his attention to the two lowest cubes, he finds in the latter symbol an expression of the relation of the elements, as in the former an image of the combination of two surfaces. Between fire and earth, the two extremes, he remarks that there are introduced, not one, but two elements, air and water, which are compared to the two mean proportionals between two cube numbers. The vagueness of his language does not allow us to determine whether anything more than this was intended by him.

Leaving the further explanation of details, which the reader will find discussed at length in Boeckh and Martin, we may now return to the main argument: Why did God make the world? Like man, he must have a purpose; and his purpose is the diffusion of that goodness or good which he himself is. The term 'goodness' is not to be understood in this passage as meaning benevolence or love, in the Christian sense of the term, but rather law, order, harmony, like the Idea of good in the *Republic*. The ancient mythologers, and even the Hebrew prophets, had spoken of the jealousy of God; and the Greek had imagined that there was a Nemesis always attending the prosperity of mortals. But Plato delights to think of God as the author of order in his works, who, like a father, lives over again in his children, and can never have too much of good or friendship among his creatures. Only, as there is a certain remnant of evil inherent in matter which he cannot get rid of, he detaches himself from them and leaves them to themselves, that he may be guiltless of their faults and sufferings.

Between the ideal and the sensible Plato interposes the two natures of time and space. Time is conceived by him to be only the shadow or image of eternity which ever is and never has been or will be, but is described in a figure only as past or future. This is one of the great thoughts of early philosophy, which are still as difficult to our minds as they were to the early thinkers; or perhaps more difficult, because we more distinctly see the consequences which are involved in such an hypothesis. All the objections which may be urged against Kant's doctrine of the ideality of space and time at once press upon us. If time is unreal, then all which is contained in time is unreal—the succession of human thoughts as well as the flux of sensations; there is no connecting link between φαινόμενα and ὄντα. Yet, on the other hand, we are conscious that knowledge is independent of time, that truth is not a thing of yesterday or tomorrow, but an 'eternal now'. To the 'spectator of all time and all existence' the universe remains at rest. The truths of geometry and arithmetic in all their combinations are always the same. The generations of men, like the leaves of the forest, come and go, but the mathematical laws by which the world is governed remain, and seem as if they could never change. The ever-present image of space is transferred to time—succession is conceived as extension. (We remark that Plato does away with the above and below in space, as he has done away with the absolute existence of past and future.) The course of time, unless regularly marked by divisions of number, partakes of the indefiniteness of the Heraclitean flux. By such reflections we may conceive the Greek to have attained the metaphysical conception of eternity, which to the Hebrew was gained by meditation on the Divine Being. No one saw that this objective was really a subjective, and involved the subjectivity of all knowledge. 'Non in tempore sed cum tempore finxit Deus mundum', says St. Augustine, repeating a thought derived from the *Timaeus*, but apparently unconscious of the results to which his doctrine would have led.

The contradictions involved in the conception of time or motion, like the infinitesimal in space, were a source of perplexity to the mind of the Greek, who was driven to find a point of view above or beyond them. They had sprung up in the decline of the Eleatic philosophy and were very familiar to Plato, as we gather from the *Parmenides*. The consciousness of them had led the great Eleatic philosopher to describe the nature of God or Being under negatives. He sings of 'Being unbegotten and imperishable, unmoved and never-ending, which never was nor will be, but always is, one and continuous, which cannot spring from any other; for it cannot be said or imagined not to be.' The idea of eternity was for a great part a negation. There are regions of speculation in which the negative is hardly separable from the positive, and even seems to pass into it. Not only Buddhism, but Greek as well as Christian philosophy, show that it is quite possible that the human mind should retain an enthusiasm for mere negations. In different ages and countries there have been forms of light in which nothing could be discerned and which have nevertheless exercised a life-giving and illumining power. For the higher intelligence of man seems to require, not only something above sense, but above knowledge, which can only be described as Mind or Being or Truth or God or the unchangeable and eternal element, in the expression of which all predicates fail and fall short. Eternity or the eternal is not merely the unlimited in time but the truest of all Being, the most real of all realities, the most certain of all knowledge, which we nevertheless only see through a glass darkly. The passionate earnestness of Parmenides contrasts with the vacuity of the thought which he is revolving in his mind.

Space is said by Plato to be the 'containing vessel or nurse of generation'. Reflecting on the simplest kinds of external objects, which to the ancients were the four elements, he was led to a more general notion of a substance, more or less like themselves, out of which they were fashioned. He would not have them too precisely distinguished. Thus seems to have arisen the first dim perception of ὕλη or matter, which has played so great a part in the metaphysical philosophy of Aristotle and his followers. But besides the material out of which the elements are made, there is also a space in which they are contained. There arises thus a second nature which the senses are incapable of discerning and which can hardly be referred to the intelligible class. For it is and it is not, it is nowhere when filled, it is nothing when empty. Hence it is said to be discerned by a kind of spurious or analogous reason, partaking so feebly of existence as to be hardly perceivable, yet always reappearing as the containing mother or nurse of all things. It had not that sort of consistency to Plato which has been given to it in modern times by geometry and metaphysics. Neither of the Greek words by which it is described are so purely abstract as the English word 'space' or the Latin *spatium*. Neither Plato nor any other Greek would have spoken of χρόνος καὶ τόπος or χώρα in the same manner as we speak of 'time' and 'space'.

Yet space is also of a very permanent or even eternal nature; and Plato seems more willing to admit of the unreality of time than of the unreality of space; because, as he says, all things must necessarily exist in space. We, on the other hand, are disposed to fancy that even if space were annihilated time might still survive. He admits indeed that our knowledge of space is of a dreamy kind, and is given by a spurious reason without the help of sense. (Cf. the hypotheses and images of *Rep.* vi. 511.) It is true that it does not attain to the clearness of Ideas. But like them it seems to remain, even if all the objects contained in it are supposed to have vanished away. Hence it was natural for Plato to conceive of it as eternal. We must remember further that in his attempt to realize either space or matter the two abstract ideas of weight and extension, which are familiar to us, had never passed before his mind.

Thus far God, working according to an eternal pattern, out of his goodness has created the same, the other, and the essence (compare the three principles of the *Philebus*—the finite, the infinite, and the union of the two), and out of them has formed the outer circle of the fixed stars and the inner circle of the planets, divided according to certain musical intervals; he has also created time, the moving image of eternity, and space, existing by a sort of necessity and hardly distinguishable from matter. The matter out of which the world is formed is not absolutely void, but retains in the chaos certain germs or traces of the elements. These Plato, like Empedocles, supposed to be four in number—fire, air, earth, and water. They were at first mixed together; but already in the chaos, before God fashioned them by form and number, the greater masses of the elements had an appointed place. Into the confusion ($\mu\hat{\iota}\gamma\mu\alpha$) which preceded Plato does not attempt further to penetrate. They are called elements, but they are so far from being elements ($\sigma\tauo\iota\chi\epsilon\hat{\iota}\alpha$) or letters in the higher sense that they are not even syllables or first compounds. The real elements are two triangles, the rectangular isosceles which has but one form, and the most beautiful of the many forms of rectangular scalene, which is half of an equilateral triangle. By the combination of these triangles which exist in an infinite variety of sizes, the surfaces of the four elements are constructed.

That there were only five regular solids was already known to the ancients; and out of the surfaces which he has formed Plato proceeds to generate the four first of the five. He perhaps forgets that he is only putting together surfaces and has not provided for their transformation into solids. The first solid is a regular pyramid, of which the base and sides are formed by four equilateral or twenty-four rectangular scalene triangles. Each of the four solid angles in this figure is a little larger than the largest of obtuse angles. The second solid is composed of the same triangles, which unite as eight equilateral triangles, and make one solid angle out of four plane angles—six of these angles form a regular octahedron. The third solid is a regular icosahedron, having twenty triangular equilateral bases, and therefore 120 rectangular scalene triangles. The fourth regular solid, or cube, is formed by the combination of four isosceles triangles into one square and of six squares into a cube. The fifth regular solid, or dodecahedron, cannot be formed by a combination of either of these triangles, but each of its faces may be regarded as composed of thirty triangles of another kind. Probably Plato notices this as the only remaining regular polyhedron, which from its approximation to a globe, and possibly because, as Plutarch remarks, it is composed of $12 \times 30 = 360$ scalene triangles

(*Platon. Quaest.* 5), representing thus the signs and degrees of the Zodiac, as well as the months and days of the year, God may be said to have 'used in the delineation of the universe'. According to Plato earth was composed of cubes, fire of regular pyramids, air of regular octahedrons, water of regular icosahedrons. The stability of the last three increases with the number of their sides.

The elements are supposed to pass into one another, but we must remember that these transformations are not the transformations of real solids, but of imaginary geometrical figures; in other words, we are composing and decomposing the faces of substances and not the substances themselves—it is a house of cards which we are pulling to pieces and putting together again (cf. however *Laws* x. 894 a). Yet perhaps Plato may regard these sides or faces as only the forms which are impressed on pre-existent matter. It is remarkable that he should speak of each of these solids as a possible world in itself, though upon the whole he inclines to the opinion that they form one world and not five. To suppose that there is an infinite number of worlds, as Democritus (Hippolyt. *Ref. Haer.* i. 13) had said, would be, as he satirically observes, 'the characteristic of a very indefinite and ignorant mind' (55 c, d).

The twenty triangular faces of an icosahedron form the faces or sides of two regular octahedrons and of a regular pyramid ($20 = 8 \times 2 + 4$); and therefore, according to Plato, a particle of water when decomposed is supposed to give two particles of air and one of fire. So because an octahedron gives the sides of two pyramids ($8 = 4 \times 2$), a particle of air is resolved into two particles of fire.

The transformation is effected by the superior power or number of the conquering elements. The manner of the change is (1) a separation of portions of the elements from the masses in which they are collected; (2) a resolution of them into their original triangles; and (3) a reunion of them in new forms. Plato himself proposes the question, Why does motion continue at all when the elements are settled in their places? He answers that although the force of attraction is continually drawing similar elements to the same spot, still the revolution of the universe exercises a condensing power, and thrusts them again out of their natural places. Thus want of uniformity, the condition of motion, is produced (57 d ff.). In all such disturbances of matter there is an alternative for the weaker element: it may escape to its kindred, or take the form of the stronger—becoming denser, if it be denser, or rarer, if rarer. This is true of fire, air, and water, which, being composed of similar triangles, are interchangeable; earth, however, which has triangles peculiar to itself, is capable of dissolution, but not of change (56 d ff.). Of the interchangeable elements, fire, the rarest, can only become a denser, and water, the densest, only a rarer: but air may become a denser or a rarer. No single particle of the elements is visible, but only the aggregates of them are seen. The subordinate species depend, not upon differences of form in the original triangles, but upon differences of size. The obvious physical phenomena from which Plato has gathered his views of the relations of the elements seem to be the effect of fire upon air, water, and earth, and the effect of water upon earth. The particles are supposed by him to be in a perpetual process of circulation caused by inequality. This process of circulation does not admit of a vacuum, as he tells us in his strange account of respiration (79 b).

Of the phenomena of light and heavy he speaks afterwards, when treating of sensation, but they may be more conveniently considered by us in this place. They are not, he says, to be explained by 'above' and 'below', which in the universal globe have no existence (62 d), but by the attraction of similars towards the great masses of similar substances; fire to fire, air to air, water to water, earth to earth. Plato's doctrine of attraction implies not only (1) the attraction of similar elements to one another, but also (2) of smaller bodies to larger ones. Had he confined himself to the latter he would have arrived, though, perhaps, without any further result or any sense of the greatness of the discovery, at the modern doctrine of gravitation. He does not observe that water has an equal tendency towards both water and earth. So easily did the most obvious facts which were inconsistent with his theories escape him.

The general physical doctrines of the *Timaeus* may be summed up as follows: (1) Plato supposes the greater masses of the elements to have been already settled in their places at the creation: (2) they are four in number, and are formed of rectangular triangles variously combined into regular solid figures: (3) three of them, fire, air, and water, admit of transformation into one another; the fourth, earth, cannot be similarly transformed: (4) different sizes of the same triangles form the lesser species of each element: (5) there is an attraction of like to like—smaller masses of the same kind being drawn towards greater: (6) there is no void, but the particles of matter are ever pushing one another round and round (περίωσις). Like the atomists, Plato attributes the differences between the elements to differences in geometrical figures. But he does not explain the process by which surfaces become solids; and he characteristically ridicules Democritus for not seeing that the worlds are finite and not infinite.

§ 4

[1] The astronomy of Plato is based on the two principles of the same and the other, which God combined in the creation of the world. The soul, which is compounded of the same, the other, and the essence, is diffused from the centre to the circumference of the heavens. We speak of a soul of the universe; but more truly regarded, the universe of the *Timaeus* is a soul, governed by mind, and holding in solution a residuum of matter or evil, which the author of the world is unable to expel, and of which Plato cannot tell us the origin. The creation, in Plato's sense, is really the creation of order; and the first step in giving order is the division of the heavens into an inner and outer circle of the other and the same, of the divisible and the indivisible, answering to the two spheres, of the planets and of the world beyond them, all together moving around the earth, which is their centre. To us there is a difficulty in apprehending how that which is at rest can also be in motion, or that which is indivisible exist in space. But the whole description is so ideal and imaginative that we can hardly venture to attribute to many of Plato's words in the *Timaeus* any more meaning than to his mythical account of the heavens in the *Republic* and in the *Phaedrus*. (Cf. his denial of the 'blasphemous opinion' that there are planets or wandering stars; all alike move in circles—*Laws* vii. 821–2.) The stars are the habitations of the souls of men, from which they come and to which they return. In attributing to the fixed stars only the most perfect motion—that which is on the same spot or circling around the same—he might perhaps have said that to 'the spectator of all time and all existence', to borrow once more his own grand expression, or viewed, in the language of Spinoza, *sub specie aeternitatis*, they were still at rest, but appeared to move in order to teach men the periods of time. Although absolutely in motion, they are relatively at rest; or we may conceive of them as resting, while the space in which they are contained, or the whole *anima mundi*, revolves.

The universe revolves around a centre once in twenty-four hours, but the orbits of the fixed stars take a different direction from those of the planets. The outer and the inner sphere cross one another and meet again at a point opposite to that of their first contact; the first moving in a circle from left to right along the side of a parallelogram which is supposed to be inscribed in it, the second also moving in a

---

[1] [The astronomical passages of the *Timaeus* are examined in Sir Thomas Heath's *Aristarchus of Samos*, chap. xv. With regard to the rotation of the Earth, see Taylor, *Commentary*, pp. 226 ff., and Cornford, *P. C.*, pp. 120 ff. Jowett's treatment of this topic has been abbreviated.]

circle along the diagonal of the same parallelogram from right to left; or, in other words, the first describing the path of the equator, the second the path of the ecliptic. The motion of the second is controlled by the first, and hence the oblique line in which the planets are supposed to move becomes a spiral. The motion of the same is said to be undivided, whereas the inner motion is split into seven unequal orbits —the intervals between them being in the ratio of two and three, three of either:—the Sun, moving in the opposite direction to Mercury and Venus, but with equal swiftness; the remaining four, Moon, Saturn, Mars, Jupiter, with unequal swiftness to the former three and to one another. Thus arises the following progression:—Moon 1, Sun 2, Venus 3, Mercury 4, Mars 8, Jupiter 9, Saturn 27. This series of numbers is the compound of the two Pythagorean ratios, having the same intervals, though not in the same order, as the mixture which was originally divided in forming the soul of the world.

Plato was struck by the phenomenon of Mercury, Venus, and the Sun appearing to overtake and be overtaken by one another. The true reason of this, namely, that they lie within the circle of the earth's orbit, was unknown to him, and the reason which he gives—that the two former move in an opposite direction to the latter—is far from explaining the appearance of them in the heavens. All the planets, including the sun, are carried round in the daily motion of the circle of the fixed stars, and they have a second or oblique motion which gives the explanation of the different lengths of the sun's course in different parts of the earth. The fixed stars have also two movements —a forward movement in their orbit which is common to the whole circle; and a movement on the same spot around an axis, which Plato calls the movement of thought about the same. In this latter respect they are more perfect than the wandering stars, as Plato himself terms them in the *Timaeus*, although in the *Laws* (loc. cit.) he condemns the appellation as blasphemous.

The revolution of the world around the earth, which is accomplished in a single day and night, is described as being the most perfect or intelligent. Yet Plato also speaks of an *annus magnus* or cyclical year, in which periods wonderful for their complexity are found to coincide in a perfect number, i.e. a number which equals the sum of its factors, as $6 = 1+2+3$. This, although not literally contradictory, is in spirit irreconcilable with the perfect revolution of twenty-four hours. The same remark may be applied to the complexity of the appearances and occultations of the stars, which, if the outer heaven is supposed to be moving around the centre once in twenty-four hours, must be confined to the effects produced by the seven planets. Plato seems to confuse the actual observation of the heavens with his desire to find in them mathematical perfection. The same spirit is carried yet further by him in the passage already quoted from the *Laws*, in which he affirms their wanderings to be an appearance only, which a little knowledge of mathematics would enable men to correct.

We have now to consider the much discussed question of the rotation or immobility of the earth. Plato's doctrine on this subject is contained in the following words:—'The earth, which is our nurse, compacted [*or* revolving] around the pole which is extended through the universe, he made to be the guardian and artificer of night and day, first and eldest of gods that are in the interior of heaven' (40 b, c). There is an unfortunate doubt in this passage (1) about the meaning of the word ἰλλομένην, which is translated either 'compacted' or 'revolving', and is equally capable of both explanations. A doubt (2) may also be raised as to whether the words 'artificer of day and night' are consistent with the mere passive causation of them, produced by the immobility of the earth in the midst of the circling universe. We must admit, further, (3) that Aristotle attributed to Plato the doctrine of the rotation of the earth on its axis. On the other hand it has been urged that if the earth goes round with the outer heaven and sun in twenty-four hours, there is no way of accounting for the alternation of day and night; since the equal motion of the earth and sun would have the effect of absolute immobility. To which it may be replied that Plato never says that the earth goes round with the outer heaven and sun; although the whole question depends on the relation of earth and sun, their movements are nowhere precisely described. But if we suppose, with Mr. Grote, that the diurnal rotation of the earth on its axis and the revolution of the sun and outer heaven precisely coincide, it would be difficult to imagine that Plato was unaware of the consequence. . . .

The final conclusion at which we arrive is that there is nearly as much to be said on the one side of the question as on the other, and that we are not perfectly certain, whether, as Boeckh and the majority of commentators, ancient as well as modern, are inclined to believe, Plato thought that the earth was at rest in the centre of the universe, or, as Aristotle and Mr. Grote suppose, that it revolved on its axis. Whether we assume the earth to be stationary in the centre of the universe, or to revolve with the heavens, no explanation is given of the variation in the length of days and nights at different times of the year. The relations of the earth and heavens are so indistinct in the *Timaeus* and so figurative in the *Phaedo*, *Phaedrus*, and *Republic*, that we must give up the hope of ascertaining how they were imagined by Plato, if he had any fixed or scientific conception of them at all.

§ 5

The soul of the world is framed on the analogy of the soul of man, and many traces of anthropomorphism blend with Plato's highest flights of idealism. The heavenly bodies are endowed with thought; the principles of the same and other exist in the universe as well as in the human mind. The soul of man is made out of the remains of the elements which had been used in creating the soul of the world; these remains, however, are diluted to the third degree; by this Plato expresses the measure of the difference between the soul human and divine. The human soul, like the cosmical, is framed before the body, as the mind is before the soul of either (30 b)—this is the order of the divine work—and the finer parts of the body, which are more akin to the soul, such as the spinal marrow, are prior to the bones and flesh. The brain, the containing vessel of the divine part of the soul, is (nearly) in the form of a globe, which is the image of the gods, who are the stars, and of the universe.

There is, however, an inconsistency in Plato's manner of conceiving the soul of man; he cannot get rid of the element of necessity which is allowed to enter. He does not, like Kant, attempt to vindicate for men a freedom out of space and time; but he acknowledges him to be subject to the influence of external causes, and leaves hardly any place for freedom of the will. The lusts of men are caused by their bodily constitution (86 c), though they may be increased by bad education and bad laws, which implies that they may be decreased by good education and good laws. He appears to have an inkling of the truth that to the higher nature of man evil is involuntary. This is mixed up with the view which, while apparently agreeing with it, is in reality the opposite of it, that vice is due to physical causes (86 d). In the *Timaeus*, as well as in the *Laws*, he also regards vices and crimes as simply involuntary; they are diseases analogous to the diseases of the body, and arising out of the same causes. If we draw together the opposite poles of Plato's system, we find that, like Spinoza, he combines idealism with fatalism (see *infra*, p. 699).

The soul of man is divided by him into three parts, answering roughly to the charioteer and steeds of the *Phaedrus*, and to the λόγος, θυμός, and ἐπιθυμία of the *Republic* and *Nicomachean Ethics*. First, there is the immortal nature of which the brain is the seat, and which is akin to the soul of the universe. This alone thinks and knows and is the ruler of the whole. Secondly, there is the higher mortal soul which, though liable to perturbations of her own, takes the side of reason against the lower appetites. The seat of this is the heart, in which courage, anger, and all the nobler affections are supposed to reside. There the veins all meet; it is their centre or house of guard whence they carry the orders of the thinking being to the extremities of his kingdom. There is also a third or appetitive soul, which receives the commands of the immortal part, not immediately but mediately, through the liver, which reflects on its surface the admonitions and threats of the reason.

The liver is imagined by Plato to be a smooth and bright substance, having a store of sweetness and also of bitterness, which reason freely uses in the execution of her mandates. In this region, as ancient superstition told, were to be found intimations of the future. But Plato is careful to observe that although such knowledge is given to the inferior parts of man, it requires to be interpreted by the superior. Reason, and not enthusiasm, is the true guide of man; he is only inspired when he is demented by some distemper or possession. The ancient saying, that 'only a man in his senses can judge of his own actions', is approved by modern philosophy too. The same irony which appears in Plato's remark, that 'the men of old time must surely have known the gods who were their ancestors, and we should believe them as custom requires', is also manifest in his account of divination.

The appetitive soul is seated in the belly, and there imprisoned like a wild beast, far away from the council-chamber, as Plato graphically calls the head, in order that the animal passions may not interfere with the deliberations of reason. Though the soul is said by him to be prior to the body, yet we cannot help seeing that it is constructed on the model of the body—the threefold division into the rational, passionate, and appetitive corresponding to the head, heart, and belly. The human soul differs from the soul of the world in this respect, that it is enveloped and finds its expression in matter, whereas the soul of the world is not only enveloped or diffused in matter, but is the element in which matter moves. The breath of man is within him, but the air or aether of heaven is the element which surrounds him and all things.

[1] Pleasure and pain are attributed in the *Timaeus* to the suddenness of our sensations—the first being a sudden restoration, the second a sudden violation, of nature (cf. *Phil.* 31 d). The sensations become conscious to us when they are exceptional. Sight is not attended either

---

[1] [An excellent note on this subject will be found in A. E. Taylor's *Commentary*, pp. 447–62. The views of Plato and Aristotle are here stated and compared with each other and with those of modern psychologists.]

by pleasure or pain, but hunger and the appeasing of hunger are pleasant and painful because they are extraordinary.

<h2 style="text-align:center">§ 6</h2>

I shall not attempt to connect the physiological speculations of Plato either with ancient or modern medicine. What light I can throw upon them will be derived from the comparison of them with his general system.

There is no principle so apparent in the physics of the *Timaeus*, or in ancient physics generally, as that of continuity. The world is conceived of as a whole, and the elements are formed into and out of one another; the varieties of substances and processes are hardly known or noticed. And in a similar manner the human body is conceived of as a whole, and the different substances of which, to a superficial observer, it appears to be composed—the blood, flesh, sinews—like the elements out of which they are formed, are supposed to pass into one another in regular order, while the infinite complexity of the human frame remains unobserved. And diseases arise from the opposite process— when the natural proportions of the four elements are disturbed, and the secondary substances which are formed out of them, namely, blood, flesh, sinews, are generated in an inverse order.

Plato found heat and air within the human frame, and the blood circulating in every part. He assumes in language almost unintelligible to us that a network of fire and air envelops the greater part of the body. This outer net contains two lesser nets, one corresponding to the stomach, the other to the lungs; and the entrance to the latter is forked or divided into two passages which lead to the nostrils and to the mouth. In the process of respiration the external net is said to find a way in and out of the pores of the skin: while the interior of it and the lesser nets move alternately into each other. The whole description is figurative, as Plato himself implies (79 d) when he speaks of 'a fountain of fire *which we compare* to the network of a creel'. He really means by this what we should describe as a state of heat or temperature in the interior of the body. The 'fountain of fire' or heat is also in a figure the circulation of the blood. The passage is partly imagination, partly fact.

He has a singular theory of respiration for which he accounts solely by the movement of the air in and out of the body; he does not attribute any part of the process to the action of the body itself. The air has a double ingress and a double exit, through the mouth or nostrils, and through the skin. When exhaled through the mouth or nostrils, it leaves a vacuum which is filled up by other air finding a way in through the pores, this air being thrust out of its place by the exhalation from the mouth and nostrils. There is also a corresponding process of inhalation through the mouth or nostrils, and of exhalation through the pores. The inhalation through the pores appears to take place nearly at the same time as the exhalation through the mouth; and conversely. The internal fire is in either case the propelling cause outwards—the inhaled air, when heated by it, having a natural tendency to move out of the body to the place of fire; while the impossibility of a vacuum is the propelling cause inwards.

Thus we see that this singular theory is dependent on two principles largely employed by Plato in explaining the operations of nature, the impossibility of a vacuum and the attraction of like to like. To these there has to be added a third principle, which is the condition of the action of the other two,—the interpenetration of particles in proportion to their density or rarity. It is this which enables fire and air to permeate the flesh.

Plato's account of digestion and the circulation of the blood is closely connected with his theory of respiration. Digestion is supposed to be effected by the action of the internal fire, which in the process of respiration moves into the stomach and minces the food. As the fire returns to its place, it takes with it the minced food or blood; and in this way the veins are replenished. Plato does not inquire how the blood is separated from the faeces.

Of the anatomy and functions of the body he knew very little,—e.g. of the uses of the nerves in conveying motion and sensation, which he supposed to be communicated by the bones and veins; he was also ignorant of the distinction between veins and arteries;—the latter term he applies to the vessels which conduct air from the mouth to the lungs;—he supposes the lung to be hollow and bloodless; the spinal marrow he conceives to be the seed of generation; he confuses the parts of the body with the states of the body—the network of fire and air is spoken of as a bodily organ; he has absolutely no idea of the phenomena of respiration, which he attributes to a law of equalization in nature, the air which is breathed out displacing other air which finds a way in; he is wholly unacquainted with the process of digestion. Except the general divisions into the spleen, the liver, the belly, and the lungs, and the obvious distinctions of flesh, bones, and the limbs of the body, we find nothing that reminds us of anatomical facts. But we find much which is derived from his theory of the universe, and transferred to man, as there is much also in his theory of the universe which is suggested by man. The microcosm of the human body is the lesser image of the macrocosm. The courses of the same and the other affect both; they are made of the same elements and therefore in the same proportions. Both are intelligent natures endued with the power of self-motion, and the same equipoise is maintained in both. The animal is a sort of 'world' to the particles of the blood which circulate in it. All the four elements entered into the original composition of the human frame; the bone was formed out of smooth earth; liquids of various kinds pass to and fro; the network of fire and air irrigates the veins. Infancy and childhood is the chaos or first turbid flux of sense prior to the establishment of order; the intervals of time which may be observed in some intermittent fevers correspond to the density of the elements. The spinal marrow, including the brain, is formed out of the finest sorts of triangles, and is the connecting link between body and mind. Health is only to be preserved by imitating the motions of the world in space, which is the mother and nurse of generation. The work of digestion is carried on by the superior sharpness of the triangles forming the substances of the human body to those which are introduced into it in the shape of food. The freshest and acutest forms of triangles are those that are found in children, but they become more obtuse with advancing years; and when they finally wear out and fall to pieces, old age and death supervene.

As in the *Republic*, Plato is still the enemy of the purgative treatment of physicians, which, except in extreme cases, no man of sense will ever adopt. For, as he adds, with an insight into the truth, 'every disease is akin to the nature of the living being and is only irritated by stimulants'. He is of opinion that nature should be left to herself, and is inclined to think that physicians are in vain (cf. *Laws* vi. 761 c—where he says that warm baths would be more beneficial to the limbs of the aged rustic than the prescriptions of a not over-wise doctor). If he seems to be extreme in his condemnation of medicine and to rely too much on diet and exercise, he might appeal to nearly all the best physicians of our own age in support of his opinions, who often speak to their patients of the worthlessness of drugs. For we ourselves are sceptical about medicine, and very unwilling to submit to the purgative treatment of physicians. May we not claim for Plato an anticipation of modern ideas as about some questions of astronomy and physics, so also about medicine? As in the *Charmides* (156–7) he tells us that the body cannot be cured without the soul, so in the *Timaeus* he strongly asserts the sympathy of soul and body; any defect of either is the occasion of the greatest discord and disproportion in the other. Here too may be a presentiment that in the medicine of the future the interdependence of mind and body will be more fully recognized, and that the influence of the one over the other may be exerted in a manner which is not now thought possible.

§ 7

In Plato's explanation of sensation we are struck by the fact that he has not the same distinct conception of organs of sense which is familiar to ourselves. The senses are not instruments, but rather passages, through which external objects strike upon the mind. The eye is the aperture through which the stream of vision passes, the ear is the aperture through which the vibrations of sound pass. But that the complex structure of the eye or the ear is in any sense the cause of sight and hearing he seems hardly to be aware.

The process of sight is the most complicated (cf. *Rep.* vi. 507–8), and consists of three elements—the light which is supposed to reside within the eye, the light of the sun, and the light emitted from external objects. When the light of the eye meets the light of the sun, and both together meet the light issuing from an external object, this is the simple act of sight. When the particles of light which proceed from the object are exactly equal to the particles of the visual ray which meet them from within, then the body is transparent. If they are larger and contract the visual ray, a black colour is produced; if they are smaller and dilate it, a white. Other phenomena are produced by the variety and motion of light. A sudden flash of fire at once elicits light and moisture from the eye, and causes a bright colour. A more subdued light, on mingling with the moisture of the eye, produces a red colour. Out of these elements all other colours are derived. All of them are combinations of bright and red with white and black. Plato himself tells us that he does not know in what proportions they combine, and he is of opinion that such knowledge is granted to the gods only. To have seen the affinity of them to each other and their connexion with light is not a bad basis for a theory of colours. We must remember that they were not distinctly defined to his, as they are to our eyes; he saw them, not as they are divided in the prism, or artificially manufactured for the painter's use, but as they exist in nature, blended and confused with one another.

We can hardly agree with him when he tells us that smells do not admit of kinds. He seems to think that no definite qualities can attach to bodies which are in a state of transition or evaporation; he also makes the subtle observation that smells must be denser than air, though thinner than water, because when there is an obstruction to the breathing, air can penetrate, but not smell.

The affections peculiar to the tongue are of various kinds, and, like many other affections, are caused by contraction and dilation. Some of them are produced by rough, others by abstergent, others by inflammatory substances,—these act upon the testing instruments of the tongue, and produce a more or less disagreeable sensation, while other particles congenial to the tongue soften and harmonize them. The instruments of taste reach from the tongue to the heart. Plato has a lively sense of the manner in which sensation and motion are communicated from one part of the body to the other, though he confuses the affections with the organs. Hearing is a blow which passes through the ear and ends in the region of the liver, being transmitted by means of the air, the brain, and the blood to the soul. The swifter sound is acute, the sound which moves slowly is grave. A great body of sound is loud, the opposite is low. Discord is produced by the swifter and slower motions of two sounds, and is converted into harmony when the swifter motions begin to pause and are overtaken by the slower.

The general phenomena of sensation are partly internal, but the more violent are caused by conflict with external objects. Proceeding by a method of superficial observation, Plato remarks that the more sensitive parts of the human frame are those which are least covered by flesh, as is the case with the head and the elbows. Man, if his head had been covered with a thicker pulp of flesh, might have been a longer-lived animal than he is, but could not have had as quick perceptions. On the other hand, the tongue is one of the most sensitive of organs; but then this is made, not to be a covering to the bones which contain the marrow or source of life, but with an express purpose, and in a separate mass (75 a).

§ 8

We have now to consider how far in any of these speculations Plato approximated to the discoveries of modern science. The modern physical philosopher is apt to dwell exclusively on the absurdities of ancient ideas about science, on the haphazard fancies and *a priori* assumptions of ancient teachers, on their confusion of facts and ideas, on their inconsistency and blindness to the most obvious phenomena. He measures them not by what preceded them, but by what has followed them. He does not consider that ancient physical philosophy was not a free inquiry, but a growth, in which the mind was passive rather than active, and was incapable of resisting the impressions which flowed in upon it. He hardly allows to the notions of the ancients the merit of being the stepping-stones by which he has himself risen to a higher knowledge. He never reflects how great a thing it was to have formed a conception, however imperfect, either of the human frame as a whole, or of the world as a whole. According to the view taken in these volumes the errors of ancient physicists were not separable from the intellectual conditions under which they lived. Their genius was their own; and they were not the rash and hasty generalizers which, since the days of Bacon, we have been apt to suppose them. The thoughts of men widened to receive experience; at first they seemed to know all things as in a dream: after a while they look at them closely and hold them in their hands. They begin to arrange them in classes and to connect causes with effects. General notions are necessary to the apprehension of particular facts, the meta-physical to the physical. Before men can observe the world, they must be able to conceive it.

To do justice to the subject, we should consider the physical philo-sophy of the ancients as a whole; we should remember, (1) that the nebular theory was the received belief of several of the early physicists; (2) that the development of animals out of fishes who came to land, and of man out of the animals, was held by Anaximander in the sixth century before Christ (cf. Plut. *Symp. Quaest.* viii. 8. 4; *Plac. Phil.* v. 19. 4); (3) that even by Philolaus and the early Pythagoreans, the earth was held to be a body like the other stars revolving in space around the sun or a central fire; (4) that the beginnings of chemistry are discernible in the 'similar particles' of Anaxagoras. Also they knew or thought (5) that there was a sex in plants as well as in animals; (6) they were aware that musical notes depended on the relative length or tension of the strings from which they were emitted, and were measured by ratios of number; (7) that mathematical laws pervaded the world; and even qualitative differences were supposed to have their origin in number and figure; (8) the annihilation of matter was denied by several of them, and the seeming disappearance of it held to be a transformation only. For, although one of these discoveries might have been supposed to be a happy guess, taken together they seem to imply a great advance and almost maturity of natural knowledge.

We should also remember, when we attribute to the ancients hasty generalizations and delusions of language, that physical philosophy and metaphysical too have been guilty of similar fallacies in quite recent times. We by no means distinguish clearly between mind and body, between ideas and facts. Have not many discussions arisen about the Atomic theory in which a point has been confused with a material atom? Have not the natures of things been explained by imaginary entities, such as life or phlogiston, which exist in the mind only? Has not disease been regarded, like sin, sometimes as a negative and necessary, sometimes as a positive or malignant principle? The 'idols' of Bacon are nearly as common now as ever; they are inherent in the human mind, and when they have the most complete dominion over us, we are least able to perceive them. We recognize them in the ancients, but we fail to see them in ourselves.

Such reflections, although this is not the place in which to dwell upon them at length, lead us to take a favourable view of the speculations of the *Timaeus*. We should consider not how much Plato actually knew, but how far he has contributed to the general ideas of physics, or supplied the notions which, whether true or false, have stimulated the minds of later generations in the path of discovery. Some of them may seem old-fashioned, but may nevertheless have had a great influence in promoting system and assisting inquiry, while in others we hear the latest word of physical or metaphysical philosophy. There is also an intermediate class, in which Plato falls short of the truths of modern science, though he is not wholly unacquainted with them. (1) To the first class belongs the teleological theory of creation. Whether all things in the world can be explained as the result of natural laws, or whether we must not admit of tendencies and marks of design also, has been a question much disputed of late years. Even if all phenomena are the result of natural forces, we must admit that there are many things in heaven and earth which are as well expressed under the image of mind or design as under any other. At any rate, the language of Plato has been the language of natural theology down to our own time, nor can any description of the world wholly dispense with it. The notion of first and second or co-operative causes, which originally appears in the *Timaeus*, has likewise survived to our own day, and has been a great peace-maker between theology and science. Plato also approaches very near to our doctrine of the primary and secondary qualities of matter (61 ff.). (2) Another popular notion which is found in the *Timaeus* is the feebleness of the human intellect—'God knows the original qualities of things; man can only hope to attain to probability.' We speak in almost the same words of human intelligence, but not in the same manner of the uncertainty of our knowledge of nature. The reason is that the latter is assured to us by experiment, and is not contrasted with the certainty of ideal or mathematical knowledge. But the ancient philosopher never experimented: in the *Timaeus* Plato seems to have thought that there would be impiety in making the attempt; he, for example, who tried experiments in colours would 'forget the difference of the human and divine natures' (68 d). Their indefiniteness is probably the reason why he singles them out, as especially incapable of being tested by experiment. (Compare the saying of Anaxagoras—Sext. *Pyrrh*. i. 33—that since snow is made out of water and water is black, snow ought to be black.)

The greatest 'divination' of the ancients was the supremacy which they assigned to mathematics in all the realms of nature; for in all of them there is a foundation of mechanics. Even physiology partakes of figure and number; and Plato is not wrong in attributing them to the human frame, but in the omission to observe how little could be explained by them. Thus we may remark in passing that the most fanciful of ancient philosophies is also the most nearly verified in fact. The fortunate guess that the world is a sum of numbers and figures has been the most fruitful of anticipations. The 'diatonic' scale of the Pythagoreans and Plato suggested to Kepler that the secret of the distances of the planets from one another was to be found in mathematical proportions. The doctrine that the heavenly bodies all move in a circle is known by us to be erroneous; but without such an error how could the human mind have comprehended the heavens? Astronomy, even in modern times, has made far greater progress by the high *a priori* road than could have been attained by any other. Yet, strictly speaking—and the remark applies to ancient physics generally—this high *a priori* road was based upon *a posteriori* grounds. For there were no facts of which the ancients were so well assured by experience as facts of number. Having observed that they held good in a few instances, they applied them everywhere; and in the complexity of which they were capable found the explanation of the equally complex phenomena of the universe. They seemed to see them in the least things as well as in the greatest; in atoms, as well as in suns and stars; in the human body as well as in external nature. And now a favourite speculation of modern chemistry is the explanation of qualitative difference by quantitative, which is at present verified to a certain extent and may hereafter be of far more universal application. What is this but the atoms of Democritus and the triangles of Plato? The ancients should not be wholly deprived of the credit of their guesses because they were unable to prove them. May they not have had, like the animals, an instinct of something more than they knew?

Besides general notions we seem to find in the *Timaeus* some more precise approximations to the discoveries of modern physical science. First, the doctrine of equipoise. Plato affirms, almost in so many words, that nature abhors a vacuum. Whenever a particle is displaced, the rest push and thrust one another until equality is restored. We must remember that these ideas were not derived from any definite experiment, but were the original reflections of man, fresh from the first observation of nature. The latest word of modern philosophy is continuity and development, but to Plato this is the beginning and foundation of science; there is nothing that he is so strongly persuaded of as that the world is one, and that all the various existences which are contained in it are only the transformations of the same soul of the world acting on the same matter. He would have readily admitted that out of the protoplasm all things were formed by the gradual process of creation; but he would have insisted that mind and intelligence—not meaning by this, however, a conscious mind or person—were prior to them, and could alone have created them. Into the workings of this eternal mind or intelligence he does not enter further; nor would there have been any use in attempting to investigate the things which no eye has seen nor any human language can express.

Lastly, there remain two points in which he seems to touch great discoveries of modern times—the law of gravitation, and the circulation of the blood.

(1) The law of gravitation, according to Plato, is a law, not only of the attraction of lesser bodies to larger ones, but of similar bodies to similar, having a magnetic power as well as a principle of gravitation. He observed that earth, water, and air had settled down to their places, and he imagined fire or the exterior aether to have a place beyond air. When air seemed to go upwards and fire to pierce through air—when water and earth fell downward, they were seeking their native elements. He did not remark that his own explanation did not suit all phenomena; and the simpler explanation, which assigns to bodies degrees of heaviness and lightness proportioned to the mass and distance of the bodies which attract them, never occurred to him. Yet the affinities of similar substances have some effect upon the composition of the world, and of this Plato may be thought to have had an anticipation. He may be described as confusing the attraction of gravitation with the attraction of cohesion. The influence of such affinities and the chemical action of one body upon another in long periods of time have become a recognized principle of geology.

(2) Plato is perfectly aware—and he could hardly be ignorant—that blood is a fluid in constant motion. He also knew that blood is partly a solid substance consisting of several elements, which, as he might have observed in the use of 'cupping-glasses' (79 e), decompose and die, when no longer in motion. But the specific discovery that the blood flows out on one side of the heart through the arteries and returns through the veins on the other, which is commonly called the circulation of the blood, was absolutely unknown to him.

A further study of the *Timaeus* suggests some afterthoughts which may be conveniently brought together in this place. The topics which I propose briefly to reconsider are (*a*) the relation of the *Timaeus* to the other dialogues of Plato and to the previous philosophy; (*b*) the nature of God and of creation; (*c*) the morality of the *Timaeus*:—

(*a*) The *Timaeus* is more imaginative and less scientific than any other of the Platonic dialogues. It is conjectural astronomy, conjectural natural philosophy, conjectural medicine. The writer himself is constantly repeating that he is speaking what is probable only. The dialogue is put into the mouth of Timaeus, a Pythagorean philosopher, and therefore here, as in the *Parmenides*, we are in doubt how far Plato is expressing his own sentiments. Hence the connexion with the other dialogues is comparatively slight. We may fill up the lacunae of the *Timaeus* by the help of the *Republic* or *Phaedrus*: we may identify the same and the other with the πέρας and ἄπειρον of the *Philebus*. We may find in the *Laws* or in the *Statesman* parallels with the account of creation and of the first origin of man. It would be possible to frame a scheme in which all these various elements might have a place. But such a mode of proceeding would be unsatisfactory, because we have no reason to suppose that Plato intended his scattered thoughts to be collected in a system. There is a common spirit in his writings, and there are certain general principles, such as the opposition of the sensible and intellectual, and the priority of mind, which run through all of them; but he has no definite forms of words in which he consistently expresses himself. While the determinations of human thought are in process of creation he is necessarily tentative and uncertain. And there is least of definiteness whenever, either in describing the beginning or the end of the world, he has recourse to myths. These are not the fixed modes in which spiritual truths are revealed to him, but the efforts of imagination, by which at different times and in various manners he seeks to embody his conceptions. The clouds of mythology are still resting upon him, and he has not yet pierced 'to the heaven of the fixed stars' which is beyond them. It is safer then to admit the inconsistencies of the *Timaeus*, or to endeavour to fill up what is wanting from our own imagination, inspired by a study of the dialogue, than to refer to other Platonic writings,—and still less should we refer to the successors of Plato,—for the elucidation of it.

More light is thrown upon the *Timaeus* by a comparison of the previous philosophies. For the physical science of the ancients was traditional, descending through many generations of Ionian and Pythagorean philosophers. Plato does not look out upon the heavens and describe what he sees in them, but he builds upon the foundations of others, adding something out of the 'depths of his own self-consciousness'. Socrates had already spoken of God the creator, who made all things for the best. While he ridiculed the superficial explanations of phenomena which were current in his age, he recognized the marks both of benevolence and of design in the frame of man and in the world. The apparatus of winds and waters is contemptuously rejected by him in the *Phaedo*, but he thinks that there is a power greater than that of any Atlas in the 'best' (*Phaedo* 97 ff.; cf. Arist. *Metaph.* i. 4–5). Plato, following his master, affirms this principle of the best, but he acknowledges that the best is limited by the conditions of matter. In the generation before Socrates, Anaxagoras had brought together 'Chaos' and 'Mind'; and these are connected by Plato in the *Timaeus*, but in accordance with his own mode of thinking he has interposed between them the idea or pattern according to which mind worked. The circular impulse (περίωσις) of the one philosopher answers to the circular movement (περιχώρησις) of the other. But unlike Anaxagoras, Plato made the sun and stars living beings and not masses of earth or metal. The Pythagoreans again had framed a world out of numbers, which they constructed into figures. Plato adopted their speculations and improved upon them by a more exact knowledge of geometry. The Atomists too made the world, if not out of geometrical figures, at least out of different forms of atoms, and these atoms resembled the triangles of Plato in being too small to be visible. But though the physiology of the *Timaeus* is partly borrowed from them, they are either ignored by Plato or referred to with a secret contempt and dislike. He looks with more favour on the Pythagoreans, whose intervals of number applied to the distances of the planets reappear in the *Timaeus*. It is probable that among the Pythagoreans living in the fourth century B.C., there were already some who, like Plato, made the earth their centre. Whether he obtained his circles of the same and other from any previous thinker is uncertain. The four elements are taken from Empedocles; the interstices of the *Timaeus* may also be compared with his πόροι. The passage of one element into another is common to Heracleitus and several of the Ionian philosophers. So much of a syncretist is Plato, though not after the manner of the neo-Platonists. For the elements which he borrows from others are fused and transformed by his own genius. On the other hand we find fewer traces in Plato of early Ionic or Eleatic speculation. He does not imagine the world of sense to be made up of opposites or to be in a perpetual flux, but to vary within certain limits which are controlled by what he calls the principle of the same. Unlike the Eleatics, who relegated the world to the sphere of not-being, he admits creation to have an existence which is real and even eternal, although dependent on the will of the creator (41 a, b). Instead of maintaining the doctrine that the void has a necessary place in the existence of the world, he rather affirms the modern thesis that nature abhors a vacuum, as in the *Sophist* he also denies the reality of not-being (cf. Aristot. *Metaph.* i. 4, § 9). But though in these respects he differs from them, he is deeply penetrated by the spirit of their philosophy; he differs from them with reluctance, and gladly recognizes the 'generous depth' of Parmenides (*Theaet.* 183 e).

There is a similarity between the *Timaeus* and the fragments of Philolaus, which by some has been thought to be so great as to create a suspicion that they are derived from it. Philolaus is known to us from the *Phaedo* of Plato as a Pythagorean philosopher residing at Thebes in the latter half of the fifth century B.C., after the dispersion of the original Pythagorean society. He was the teacher of Simmias and Cebes, who became disciples of Socrates. We have hardly any other information about him. The story that Plato had purchased three books of his writings from a relation is not worth repeating; it is only a fanciful way in which an ancient biographer dresses up the fact that there was supposed to be a resemblance between the two writers. Similar gossiping stories are told about the sources of the *Republic* and the *Phaedo*. That there really existed in antiquity a work passing under the name of Philolaus there can be no doubt. Fragments of this work are preserved to us, chiefly in Stobaeus, a few in Boethius and other writers. They remind us of the *Timaeus*, as well as of the *Phaedrus* and *Philebus*. When the writer says (Stob. *Eclog.* i. 22. 7) that all things are either finite (definite) or infinite (indefinite), or a union of the two, and that this antithesis and synthesis pervades all art and nature, we are reminded of the *Philebus* (23 ff.). When he calls the centre of the world ἑστία, we have a parallel to the *Phaedrus* (247 a). His distinction between the world of order, to which the sun and moon and the stars belong, and the world of disorder, which lies in the region between the moon and the earth, approximates to Plato's sphere of the same and of the other. Like Plato (*Tim.* 62 c ff.), he denied the above and below in space, and said that all things were the same in relation to a centre. He speaks also of the world as one and indestructible: 'for neither from within nor from without does it admit of destruction' (cf. *Tim.* 33). He mentions ten heavenly bodies, including the sun and moon, the earth and the counter-earth (ἀντίχθων), and in the midst of them all he places the central fire, around which they are moving— this is hidden from the earth by the counter-earth. Of neither is there any trace in Plato, who makes the earth the centre of his system. Philolaus magnifies the virtues of particular numbers, especially of the number ten (Stob. *Eclog.* i. 2. 3), and descants upon odd and even numbers, after the manner of the later Pythagoreans. It is worthy of

remark that these mystical fancies are nowhere to be found in the
writings of Plato, although the importance of number as a form and
also an instrument of thought is ever present to his mind. Both
Philolaus and Plato agree in making the world move in certain
numerical ratios according to a musical scale: though Böckh is of
opinion that the two scales, of Philolaus and of the *Timaeus*, do not
correspond. . . . We appear not to be sufficiently acquainted with the
early Pythagoreans to know how far the statements contained in these
fragments corresponded with their doctrines; and we therefore cannot pronounce, either in favour of the genuineness of the fragments,
with Böckh and Zeller, or, with Valentine Rose and Schaarschmidt,
against them. But it is clear that they throw but little light upon the
Timaeus, and that their resemblance to it has been exaggerated.[1]

That there is a degree of confusion and indistinctness in Plato's
account both of man and of the universe has been already acknowledged. We cannot tell (nor could Plato himself have told) where the
figure or myth ends and the philosophical truth begins; we cannot
explain (nor could Plato himself have explained to us) the relation of
the Ideas to appearance, of which one is the copy of the other, and yet
of all things in the world they are the most opposed and unlike. This
opposition is presented to us in many forms, as the antithesis of the
one and many, of the finite and infinite, of the intelligible and sensible,
of the unchangeable and the changing, of the indivisible and the
divisible, of the fixed stars and the planets, of the creative mind and
the primeval chaos. These pairs of opposites are so many aspects of the
great opposition between Ideas and phenomena—they easily pass into
one another; and sometimes the two members of the relation differ in
kind, sometimes only in degree. As in Aristotle's matter and form, the
connexion between them is really inseparable; for if we attempt to
separate them they become devoid of content and therefore indistinguishable; there is no difference between the Idea of which nothing
can be predicated, and the chaos or matter which has no perceptible
qualities—between being in the abstract and nothing. Yet we are
frequently told that the one class of them is the reality and the other
appearance; and one is often spoken of as the double or reflection of
the other. For Plato never clearly saw that both elements had an
equal place in mind and in nature; and hence, especially when we
argue from isolated passages in his writings, or attempt to draw what

[1] [Burnet, *E.Gr.Ph.*[4] 281 ff., and E. Frank, *Platon u. die sogenannten Pythagoreer*
(Halle, 1923), Appendix xx, pp. 263–335, give grounds for doubting the authenticity of these fragments, which has, however, been defended by R. Mondolfo in
vol. ii of the Italian edition of Zeller's *History of Greek Philosophy* (1939).]

appear to us to be the natural inferences from them, we are full of perplexity. There is a similar confusion about necessity and free will, and about the state of the soul after death. Also he sometimes supposes that God is immanent in the world, sometimes that he is transcendent. And having no distinction of objective and subjective, he passes imperceptibly from one to the other; from intelligence to soul, from eternity to time. These contradictions may be softened or concealed by a judicious use of language, but they cannot be wholly got rid of. That an age of intellectual transition must also be one of inconsistency; that the creative is opposed to the critical or defining habit of mind or time, has been often repeated by us. But, as Plato would say, 'there is no harm in repeating twice or thrice' (*Laws* vi. 754 c) what is important for the understanding of a great author.

It has not, however, been observed, that the confusion partly arises out of the elements of opposing philosophies which are preserved in him. He holds these in solution, he brings them into relation with one another, but he does not perfectly harmonize them. They are part of his own mind, and he is incapable of placing himself outside of them and criticizing them. They grow as he grows; they are a kind of composition with which his own philosophy is overlaid. In early life he fancies that he has mastered them : but he is also mastered by them ; and in language (cf. *Soph.* 243 b) which may be compared with the hesitating tone of the *Timaeus*, he confesses in his later years that they are full of obscurity to him. He attributes new meanings to the words of Parmenides and Heracleitus ; but at times the old Eleatic philosophy appears to go beyond him ; then the world of phenomena disappears, but the doctrine of Ideas is also reduced to nothingness. All of them are nearer to one another than they themselves supposed, and nearer to him than he supposed. All of them are antagonistic to sense and have an affinity to number and measure and a presentiment of Ideas. Even in Plato they still retain their contentious or controversial character, which was developed by the growth of dialectic. He is never able to reconcile the first causes of the pre-Socratic philosophers with the final causes of Socrates himself. There is no intelligible account of the relation of numbers to the universal Ideas, or of universals to the Idea of good. He found them all three, in the Pythagorean philosophy and in the teaching of Socrates and of the Megarians respectively ; and, because they all furnished modes of explaining and arranging phenomena, he is unwilling to give up any of them, though he is unable to unite them in a consistent whole.

Lastly, Plato, though an idealist philosopher, is Greek and not Oriental in spirit and feeling. He is no mystic or ascetic ; he is not seeking in vain to get rid of matter or to find absorption in the divine nature, or in the soul of the universe. And therefore we are not surprised to find that his philosophy in the *Timaeus* returns at last to a worship of the heavens, and that to him, as to other Greeks, nature, though containing a remnant of evil, is still glorious and divine. He takes away or drops the veil of mythology, and presents her to us in what appears to him to be the form—fairer and truer far—of mathematical figures. It is this element in the *Timaeus*, no less than its affinity to certain Pythagorean speculations, which gives it a character not wholly in accordance with the other dialogues of Plato.

(*b*) The *Timaeus* contains an assertion perhaps more distinct than is found in any of the other dialogues (cf. *Rep.* ii. 379 a; *Laws* x. 901–2) of the goodness of God. 'He was good himself, and he fashioned the good everywhere.' He was not 'a jealous God', and therefore he desired that all other things should be equally good. He is the *idea* of good who has now become a person, and speaks and is spoken of as God. Yet his personality seems to appear only in the act of creation. In so far as he works with his eye fixed upon an eternal pattern he is like the human artificer in the *Republic* (vi. 501 b; x. 597). Here the theory of Platonic Ideas intrudes upon us. God, like man, is supposed to have an ideal of which Plato is unable to tell us the origin. He may be said, in the language of modern philosophy, to resolve the divine mind into subject and object.

The first work of creation is perfected, the second begins under the direction of inferior ministers. The supreme God is withdrawn from the world and returns to his own accustomed nature (*Tim.* 42 e). As in the *Statesman* (272 e), he retires to his place of view. So early did the Epicurean doctrine take possession of the Greek mind, and so natural is it to the heart of man, when he has once passed out of the stage of mythology into that of rational religion. For he sees the marks of design in the world; but he no longer sees or fancies that he sees God walking in the garden or haunting stream or mountain. He feels also that he must put God as far as possible out of the way of evil, and therefore he banishes him from an evil world. Plato is sensible of the difficulty; and he often shows that he is desirous of justifying the ways of God to man. Yet on the other hand, in the tenth book of the *Laws* (899, 900 ff.) he passes a censure on those who say that the Gods have no care of human things.

The creation of the world is the impression of order on a previously existing chaos. The formula of Anaxagoras—'all things were in chaos or confusion, and then mind came and disposed them'—is a summary of the first part of the *Timaeus*. It is true that of a chaos without differ-

ences no idea could be formed. All was not mixed but one; and therefore it was not difficult for the later Platonists to draw inferences by
which they were enabled to reconcile the narrative of the *Timaeus* with
the Mosaic account of the creation. Neither, when we speak of mind or
intelligence, do we seem to get much farther in our conception than
circular motion, which was deemed to be the most perfect. Plato, like
Anaxagoras, while commencing his theory of the universe with ideas
of mind and of the best, is compelled in the execution of his design to
condescend to the crudest physics.

(*c*) The morality of the *Timaeus* is singular, and it is difficult to
adjust the balance between the two elements of it. The difficulty
which Plato feels is that which all of us feel, and which is increased
in our own day by the progress of physical science, how the responsibility of man is to be reconciled with his dependence on natural causes.
And sometimes, like other men, he is more impressed by one aspect
of human life, sometimes by the other. In the *Republic* he represents
man as freely choosing his own lot in a state prior to birth—a conception which, if taken literally, would still leave him subject to the dominion of necessity in his after life; in the *Statesman* he supposes the human
race to be preserved in the world only by a divine interposition; while
in the *Timaeus* the supreme God commissions the inferior deities to
avert from him all but self-inflicted evils—words which imply that all
the evils of men are really self-inflicted. And here, like Plato (54 b;—
the insertion of a note in the text of an ancient writer is a literary
curiosity worthy of remark), we may take occasion to correct an error
which occurred at p. 684. For there we too hastily said that Plato in
the *Timaeus* regarded all 'vices and crimes as involuntary'. But the
fact is that he is inconsistent with himself; in one and the same
passage (86) vice is attributed to the relaxation of the bodily frame,
and yet we are exhorted to avoid it and pursue virtue. It is also
admitted that good and evil conduct are to be attributed respectively
to good and evil laws and institutions. These cannot be given by
individuals to themselves; and therefore human actions, in so far as
they are dependent upon them, are regarded by Plato as involuntary
rather than voluntary. Like other writers on this subject, he is unable
to escape from some degree of self-contradiction. He had learned from
Socrates that vice is ignorance, and suddenly the doctrine seems to him
to be confirmed by observing how much of the good and bad in
human character depends on the bodily constitution. So in modern
times the speculative doctrine of necessity has often been supported
by physical facts.

The *Timaeus* also contains an anticipation of the stoical life according to nature. Man contemplating the heavens is to regulate his erring life according to them. He is to partake of the repose of nature and of the order of nature, to bring the variable principle in himself into harmony with the principle of the same. The ethics of the *Timaeus* may be summed up in the single idea of 'law'. To feel habitually that he is part of the order of the universe is one of the highest ethical motives of which man is capable. Something like this is what Plato means when he speaks of the soul 'moving about the same in unchanging thought of the same'. He does not explain how man is acted upon by the lesser influences of custom or of opinion; or how the commands of the soul watching in the citadel are conveyed to the bodily organs. But this perhaps, to use once more expressions of his own, 'is part of another subject' (87 b) or 'may be more suitably discussed on some other occasion' (38 b).

There is no difficulty, by the help of Aristotle and later writers, in criticizing the *Timaeus* of Plato, in pointing out the inconsistencies of the work, in dwelling on the ignorance of anatomy displayed by the author, in showing the fancifulness or unmeaningness of some of his reasons. But the *Timaeus* still remains the greatest effort of the human mind to conceive the world as a whole which the genius of antiquity has bequeathed to us.

One more aspect of the *Timaeus* remains to be considered—the mythological or geographical. Is it not a wonderful thing that a few pages of one of Plato's dialogues have grown into a great legend, not confined to Greece only, but spreading far and wide over the nation of Europe and reaching even to Egypt and Asia? Like the tale of Troy, or the legend of the Ten Tribes (cf. Ewald, *Hist. of Isr.*, vol. v), which perhaps originated in a few verses of 2 Esdras xiii, it has become famous, because it has coincided with a great historical fact. Like the romance of King Arthur, which has had so great a charm, it has found a way over the seas from one country and language to another. It inspired the navigators of the fifteenth and sixteenth centuries; it foreshadowed the discovery of America. It realized the fiction so natural to the human mind, because it answered the inquiry about the origin of the arts, that there had somewhere existed an ancient primitive civilization. It might find a place wherever men chose to look for it; in North, South, East, or West; in the Islands of the Blest; before the entrance of the Straits of Gibraltar, in Sweden or in Palestine. It mattered little whether the description in Plato agreed with the locality assigned to it or not. It was a legend so adapted to the human mind that it made a habitation for itself in any country. It was an island in the clouds, which might be seen anywhere by the eye of faith. It was a subject especially congenial to the ponderous industry of certain French and Swedish writers, who delighted in heaping up learning of all sorts but were incapable of using it.

M. Martin has written a valuable dissertation on the opinions entertained respecting the Island of Atlantis in ancient and modern times. It is a curious chapter in the history of the human mind. The tale of Atlantis is the fabric of a vision, but it has never ceased to interest mankind. It was variously regarded by the ancients themselves. The stronger heads among them, like Strabo and Longinus, were as little disposed to believe in the truth of it as the modern reader in Gulliver or Robinson Crusoe. On the other hand, there is no kind or degree of absurdity or fancy in which the more foolish writers, both of antiquity and of modern times, have not indulged respecting it. The neo-Platonists, loyal to their master, like some commentators on the Christian Scriptures, sought to give an allegorical meaning to what they also believed to be an historical fact. It was as if someone in our own day were to convert the poems of Homer into an allegory of the Christian religion, at the same time maintaining them to be an exact and veritable history. In the Middle Ages the legend seems to have been half-forgotten until revived by the discovery of America. It helped to form the Utopia of Sir Thomas More and the New Atlantis of Bacon, although probably neither of those great men were at all imposed upon by the fiction. It was most prolific in the seventeenth or in the early part of the eighteenth century, when the human mind, seeking for Utopias or inventing them, was glad to escape out of the dullness of the present into the romance of the past or some ideal of the future. The later forms of such narratives contained features taken from the Edda, as well as from the Old and New Testament; also from the tales of missionaries and the experiences of travellers and of colonists.

The various opinions respecting the Island of Atlantis have no interest for us except in so far as they illustrate the extravagances of which men are capable. But this is a real interest and a serious lesson, if we remember that now as formerly the human mind is liable to be imposed upon by the illusions of the past, which are ever assuming some new form.[1]

[1] [With reference to the legend of Atlantis, see Friedländer, *Platon*, vol. i, Appendix II; Taylor, translation of *Timaeus and Critias*, Appendix II, pp. 131-3; Bidez, *Eos*, Appendix II, pp. 19-40.]

TIMAEUS

Persons of the Dialogue

SOCRATES   CRITIAS

TIMAEUS   HERMOCRATES

Socrates. One, two, three; but where, my dear Timaeus, is the 17
fourth of those who were yesterday my guests and are to be my
entertainers today?

Timaeus. He has been taken ill, Socrates; for he would not
willingly have been absent from this gathering.

Soc. Then, if he is not coming, you and the two others must
supply his place.

Tim. Certainly, and we will do our utmost not to disappoint b
you; having been handsomely entertained by you yesterday,
those of us who remain should be only too glad to return your
hospitality.

Soc. Do you remember what were the points of which I
required you to speak?

Tim. We remember some of them, and you will be here to
remind us of anything which we have forgotten: or rather, if we
are not troubling you, will you briefly recapitulate the whole,
and then the particulars will be more firmly fixed in our memories?

Soc. To be sure I will: the chief theme of my yesterday's dis- c
course was the State—how constituted and of what citizens
composed it would seem likely to be most perfect.

Tim. Yes, Socrates; and what you said of it was very much to
our mind.

Soc. Did we not begin by separating the husbandmen and the
artisans from the class of defenders of the State?

Tim. Yes.

Soc. And when we had given to each one that single employment and particular art which was suited to his nature, we spoke d
of those who were intended to be our warriors, and said that they
were to be guardians of the city against attacks from within as
well as from without, and to have no other employment; they 18
were to be merciful in judging their subjects, of whom they were

by nature friends, but fierce to their enemies, when they came across them in battle.

Tim. Exactly.

Soc. We said, if I am not mistaken, that the guardians should be gifted with a temperament in a high degree both passionate and philosophical; and that then they would be as they ought to be, gentle to their friends and fierce with their enemies.

Tim. Certainly.

Soc. And what did we say of their education? Were they not to be trained in gymnastic, and music, and all other sorts of knowledge which were proper for them?[1]

Tim. Very true.

b *Soc.* And being thus trained they were not to consider gold or silver or anything else to be their own private property; they were to be like hired troops, receiving pay for keeping guard from those who were protected by them—the pay was to be no more than would suffice for men of simple life; and they were to spend in common, and to live together in the continual practice of virtue, which was to be their sole pursuit.

Tim. That was also said.

c *Soc.* Neither did we forget the women; of whom we declared, that their natures should be harmoniously developed by training, equally with those of the men, and that common pursuits should be assigned to them all both in time of war and in their ordinary life.

Tim. That, again, was as you say.

Soc. And what about the procreation of children? Or rather was not the proposal too singular to be forgotten? for all wives and children were to be in common, to the intent that no one should ever know his own child, but they were to imagine that

d they were all one family; those who were within a suitable limit of age were to be brothers and sisters, those who were of an elder generation parents and grandparents, and those of a younger, children and grandchildren.

Tim. Yes, and the proposal is easy to remember, as you say.

Soc. And do you also remember how, with a view of securing as far as we could the best breed, we said that the chief magis-

e trates, male and female, should contrive secretly, by the use of

---

[1] Or 'which are akin to these'; or τούτοις may be taken with ἐν ἅπασι.

certain lots, so to arrange the nuptial meeting, that the bad of either sex and the good of either sex might pair with their like; and there was to be no quarrelling on this account, for they would imagine that the union was a mere accident, and was to be attributed to the lot?

Tim. I remember.

Soc. And you remember how we said that the children of the good parents were to be educated, and the children of the bad 19 secretly dispersed among the inferior citizens; and while they were all growing up the rulers were to be on the look-out, and to bring up from below in their turn those who were worthy, and those among themselves who were unworthy were to take the places of those who came up?

Tim. True.

Soc. Then have I now given you all the heads of our yesterday's discussion? Or is there anything more, my dear Timaeus, which has been omitted?

Tim. Nothing, Socrates; the discussion was just as you have b said.

Soc. I should like, before proceeding farther, to tell you how I feel about the State which we have described. I might compare myself to a person who, on beholding beautiful animals either created by the painter's art, or, better still, alive but at rest, is seized with a desire of seeing them in motion or engaged in some struggle or conflict to which their forms appear suited; this is my c feeling about the State which we have been describing. There are conflicts which all cities undergo, and I should like to hear someone tell of our own city carrying on a struggle against her neighbours, and how she went out to war in a becoming manner, and when at war showed by the greatness of her actions and the magnanimity of her words in dealing with other cities a result worthy of her training and education. Now I, Critias and Hermocrates, am conscious that I myself should never be able to cele- d brate the city and her citizens in a befitting manner, and I am not surprised at my own incapacity; to me the wonder is rather that the poets present as well as past are no better—not that I mean to depreciate them; but everyone can see that they are a tribe of imitators, and will imitate best and most easily the life in which they have been brought up; while that which is beyond the

range of a man's education he finds hard to carry out in action,
e and still harder adequately to represent in language. I am aware
that the Sophists have plenty of brave words and fair conceits,
but I am afraid that being only wanderers from one city to
another, and having never had habitations of their own, they may
fail in their conception of philosophers and statesmen, and may
not know what they do and say in time of war, when they are
fighting or holding parley with their enemies. And thus people
of your class are the only ones remaining who are fitted by nature
and education to take part at once both in politics and philo-
20 sophy. Here is Timaeus, of Locris in Italy, a city which has
admirable laws, who is himself in wealth and rank the equal
of any of his fellow citizens; he has held the most important and
honourable offices in his own state, and, as I believe, has scaled
the heights of all philosophy; and here is Critias, whom every
Athenian knows to be no novice in the matters of which we are
speaking; and as to Hermocrates, I am assured by many witnesses that his genius and education qualify him to take part in
any speculation of the kind. And therefore yesterday when I saw
b that you wanted me to describe the formation of the State, I
readily assented, being very well aware, that, if you only would,
none were better qualified to carry the discussion farther, and that
when you had engaged our city in a suitable war, you of all men
living could best exhibit her playing a fitting part. When I had
completed my task, I in return imposed this other task upon you.
You conferred together and agreed to entertain me today, as I
c had entertained you, with a feast of discourse. Here am I in
festive array, and no man can be more ready for the promised
banquet.

Hermocrates. And we too, Socrates, as Timaeus says, will not be
wanting in enthusiasm; and there is no excuse for not complying
with your request. As soon as we arrived yesterday at the guest-
chamber of Critias, with whom we are staying, or rather on our
way thither, we talked the matter over, and he told us an ancient
d tradition, which I wish, Critias, that you would repeat to Socrates,
so that he may help us to judge whether it will satisfy his requirements or not.

Critias. I will, if Timaeus, who is our other partner, approves.

Tim. I quite approve.

Crit. Then listen, Socrates, to a tale which, though strange, is certainly true, having been attested by Solon, who was the wisest of the seven sages. He was a relative and a dear friend of my e great-grandfather, Dropides, as he himself says in many passages of his poems; and he told the story to Critias, my grandfather, who remembered and repeated it to us. There were of old, he said, great and marvellous actions of the Athenian city, which 21 have passed into oblivion through lapse of time and the destruction of mankind, and one in particular, greater than all the rest. This we will now rehearse. It will be a fitting monument of our gratitude to you, and a hymn of praise true and worthy of the goddess, on this her day of festival.

Soc. Very good. And what is this ancient famous action of the Athenians, ¹which Critias declared, on the authority of Solon, to be not a mere legend, but an actual fact?¹

Crit. I will tell an old-world story which I heard from an aged man; for Critias, at the time of telling it, was, as he said, nearly ninety years of age, and I was about ten. Now the day was that b day of the Apaturia which is called the Registration of Youth, at which, according to custom, our parents gave prizes for recitations, and the poems of several poets were recited by us boys, and many of us sang the poems of Solon, which at that time had not gone out of fashion. One of our tribe, either because he thought so or to please Critias, said that in his judgement Solon was not only the wisest of men, but also the noblest² of poets. The old c man, as I very well remember, brightened up at hearing this and said, smiling: Yes, Amynander, if Solon had only, like other poets, made poetry the business of his life, and had completed the tale which he brought with him from Egypt, and had not been compelled, by reason of the factions and troubles which he found stirring in his own country when he came home, to attend to other matters, in my opinion he would have been as famous as d Homer or Hesiod, or any poet.

And what was the tale about, Critias? said Amynander.

About the greatest action which the Athenians ever did, and which ought to have been the most famous, but, through the

---

¹ Or 'which, though unrecorded in history, Critias declared, on the authority of Solon, to be an actual fact?'

² [ἐλευθεριώτατον, most liberal or independent.]

lapse of time and the destruction of the actors, it has not come down to us.

Tell us, said the other, the whole story, and how and from whom Solon heard this veritable tradition.

e He replied:—In the Egyptian Delta, at the head of which the river Nile divides, there is a certain district which is called the district of Sais, and the great city of the district is also called Sais, and is the city from which King Amasis came. The citizens have a deity for their foundress; she is called in the Egyptian tongue Neith, and is asserted by them to be the same whom the Hellenes call Athene; they are great lovers of the Athenians, and say that they are in some way related to them. To this city came

22 Solon, and was received there with great honour; he asked the priests who were most skilful in such matters about antiquity, and made the discovery that neither he nor any other Hellene knew anything worth mentioning about the times of old. On one occasion, wishing to draw them on to speak of antiquity, he began to tell about the most ancient things in our part of the world— about Phoroneus, who is called 'the first man', and about Niobe; and after the Deluge, of the survival of Deucalion and Pyrrha;

b and he traced the genealogy of their descendants, and reckoning up the dates, tried to compute how many years ago the events of which he was speaking happened. Thereupon one of the priests, who was of a very great age, said: O Solon, Solon, you Hellenes are never anything but children, and there is not an old man among you. Solon in return asked him what he meant. I mean to say, he replied, that in mind you are all young; there is no old opinion handed down among you by ancient tradition, nor any

c science which is hoary with age. And I will tell you why. There have been, and will be again, many destructions of mankind arising out of many causes; the greatest have been brought about by the agencies of fire and water, and other lesser ones by innumerable other causes. There is a story, which even you have preserved, that once upon a time Phaëthon, the son of Helios, having yoked the steeds in his father's chariot, because he was not able to drive them in the path of his father, burnt up all that was upon the earth, and was himself destroyed by a thunderbolt. Now this has the form of a myth, but really signifies a declination

d of the bodies moving in the heavens around the earth, and a great conflagration of things upon the earth, which recurs after long intervals; at such times those who live upon the mountains and in dry and lofty places are more liable to destruction than those who dwell by rivers or on the sea-shore. And from this calamity we are preserved by the liberation of the Nile, who is our never-failing saviour.[1] When, on the other hand, the gods purge the earth with a deluge of water, the survivors in your country are herdsmen and shepherds who dwell on the mountains, but those who, like you, live in cities are carried by the rivers into the sea. Whereas in this land, neither then nor at any other time, e does the water come down from above on the fields, having always a tendency to come up from below; for which reason the traditions preserved here are the most ancient. The fact is, that wherever the extremity of winter frost or of summer sun does not prevent, mankind exist, sometimes in greater, sometimes in lesser numbers. And whatever happened either in your country or in 23 ours, or in any other region of which we are informed—if there were any actions noble or great or in any other way remarkable, they have all been written down by us of old, and are preserved in our temples. Whereas just when you and other nations are beginning to be provided with letters and the other requisites of civilized life, after the usual interval, the stream from heaven, like a pestilence, comes pouring down, and leaves only those of you who are destitute of letters and education; and so you have b to begin all over again like children, and know nothing of what happened in ancient times, either among us or among yourselves. As for those genealogies of yours which you just now recounted to us, Solon, they are no better than the tales of children. In the first place you remember a single deluge only, but there were many previous ones; in the next place, you do not know that there formerly dwelt in your land the fairest and noblest race of men which ever lived, and that you and your whole city are c descended from a small seed or remnant of them which survived. And this was unknown to you, because, for many generations, the survivors of that destruction died, leaving no written word. For there was a time, Solon, before the great deluge of all, when

---

[1] [Accepting the view of Professor Glanville that in λυόμενος there is a reference to an artificial irrigation system. See Cornford, *Plato's Cosmology*, Appendix I, p. 366.]

the city which now is Athens was first in war and in every way
the best governed of all cities, and is said to have performed the
noblest deeds and to have had the fairest constitution of any of
d which tradition tells, under the face of heaven. Solon marvelled
at his words, and earnestly requested the priests to inform him
exactly and in order about these former citizens. You are welcome
to hear about them, Solon, said the priest, both for your own sake
and for that of your city, and above all, for the sake of the goddess who is the common patron and parent and educator of both
our cities. She founded your city a thousand years before ours,[1]
e receiving from the Earth and Hephaestus the seed of your race,
and afterwards she founded ours, of which the constitution is
recorded in our sacred registers to be 8,000 years old. As touching
your citizens of 9,000 years ago, I will briefly inform you of their
24 laws and of their most famous action; the exact particulars of the
whole we will hereafter go through at our leisure in the sacred
registers themselves. If you compare these very laws with ours
you will find that many of ours are the counterpart of yours as
they were in the olden time. In the first place, there is the caste
of priests, which is separated from all the others; next, there are
the artificers, who ply their several crafts by themselves and do
not intermix; and also there is the class of shepherds and of
b hunters, as well as that of husbandmen; and you will observe,
too, that the warriors in Egypt are distinct from all the other
classes, and are commanded by the law to devote themselves
solely to military pursuits; moreover, the weapons which they
carry are shields and spears, a style of equipment which the
goddess taught of Asiatics first to us, as in your part of the world
first to you. Then as to wisdom, do you observe how our law
from the very first made a study of the whole order of things,
c extending even to prophecy and medicine which gives health;
out of these divine elements deriving what was needful for human
life, and adding every sort of knowledge which was akin to them.
All this order and arrangement the goddess first imparted to you
when establishing your city; and she chose the spot of earth in
which you were born, because she saw that the happy temperament of the seasons in that land would produce the wisest of men.

[1] Observe that Plato gives the same date (9,000 years ago) for the foundation of
Athens and for the repulse of the invasion from Atlantis. (*Crit.* 108 e.)

Wherefore the goddess, who was a lover both of war and of d wisdom, selected and first of all settled that spot which was the most likely to produce men most like herself. And there you dwelt, having such laws as these and still better ones, and excelled all mankind in all virtue, as became the children and disciples of the gods.

Many great and wonderful deeds are recorded of your state in our histories. But one of them exceeds all the rest in greatness and valour. For these histories tell of a mighty power which un- e provoked made an expedition against the whole of Europe and Asia, and to which your city put an end. This power came forth out of the Atlantic Ocean, for in those days the Atlantic was navigable; and there was an island situated in front of the straits which are by you called the pillars of Heracles; the island was larger than Libya and Asia put together, and was the way to other 25 islands, and from these you might pass to the whole of the oppo- site continent which surrounded the true ocean; for this sea which is within the Straits of Heracles is only a harbour, having a narrow entrance, but that other is a real sea, and the land surrounding it on every side may be most truly called a boundless continent. Now in this island of Atlantis there was a great and wonderful empire which had rule over the whole island and several others, and over parts of the continent, and, furthermore, the men of b Atlantis had subjected the parts of Libya within the columns of Heracles as far as Egypt, and of Europe as far as Tyrrhenia. This vast power, gathered into one, endeavoured to subdue at a blow our country and yours and the whole of the region within the straits; and then, Solon, your country shone forth, in the excel- lence of her virtue and strength, among all mankind. She was pre-eminent in courage and military skill, and was the leader of the Hellenes. And when the rest fell off from her, being com- c pelled to stand alone, after having undergone the very extremity of danger, she defeated and triumphed over the invaders, and preserved from slavery those who were not yet subjugated, and generously liberated all the rest of us who dwell within the pillars. But afterwards there occurred violent earthquakes and floods; and in a single day and night of misfortune all your warlike men d in a body sank into the earth, and the island of Atlantis in like manner disappeared in the depths of the sea. For which reason the sea in those parts is impassable and impenetrable, because there is a shoal of mud in the way; and this was caused by the subsidence of the island.

c I have told you briefly, Socrates, what the aged Critias heard from Solon and related to us. And when you were speaking yesterday about your city and citizens, the tale which I have just been repeating to you came into my mind, and I remarked with astonishment how, by some mysterious coincidence, you agreed in almost every particular with the narrative of Solon; but I did 26 not like to speak at the moment. For a long time had elapsed, and I had forgotten too much; I thought that I must first of all run over the narrative in my own mind, and then I would speak. And so I readily assented to your request yesterday, considering that in all such cases the chief difficulty is to find a tale suitable to our purpose, and that with such a tale we should be fairly well provided.

And therefore, as Hermocrates has told you, on my way home b yesterday I at once communicated the tale to my companions as I remembered it; and after I left them, during the night by thinking I recovered nearly the whole of it. Truly, as is often said, the lessons of our childhood make a wonderful impression on our memories; for I am not sure that I could remember all the discourse of yesterday, but I should be much surprised if I forgot any of these things which I have heard very long ago. I listened c at the time with childlike interest to the old man's narrative; he was very ready to teach me, and I asked him again and again to repeat his words, so that like an indelible picture they were branded into my mind. As soon as the day broke, I rehearsed them as he spoke them to my companions, that they, as well as myself, might have something to say. And now, Socrates, to make an end of my preface, I am ready to tell you the whole tale. I will give you not only the general heads, but the particulars, as they were told to me. The city and citizens, which you yesterday described to us in fiction, we will now transfer to the world of d reality. It shall be the ancient city of Athens, and we will suppose that the citizens whom you imagined, were our veritable ancestors, of whom the priest spoke; they will perfectly harmonize, and there will be no inconsistency in saying that the citizens of your republic are these ancient Athenians. Let us divide the subject among us, and all endeavour according to our ability gracefully to execute the task which you have imposed upon us. Consider then, Socrates, if this narrative is suited to the purpose, or whether we should seek for some other instead.　　　　　e

Soc. And what other, Critias, can we find that will be better than this, which is natural and suitable to the festival of the goddess, and has the very great advantage of being a fact and not a fiction? How or where shall we find another if we abandon this? We cannot, and therefore you must tell the tale, and good luck to you; and I in return for my yesterday's discourse will now rest　27 and be a listener.

Crit. Let me proceed to explain to you, Socrates, the order in which we have arranged our entertainment. Our intention is, that Timaeus, who is the most of an astronomer amongst us, and has made the nature of the universe his special study, should speak first, beginning with the generation of the world and going down to the creation of man; next, I am to receive the men whom he has created, and of whom some will have profited by the excellent education which you have given them; and then, in accordance　b with the tale of Solon, and equally with his law, we will bring them into court and make them citizens, as if they were those very Athenians whom the sacred Egyptian record has recovered from oblivion, and thenceforward we will speak of them as Athenians and fellow citizens.

Soc. I see that I shall receive in my turn a perfect and splendid feast of reason. And now, Timaeus, you, I suppose, should speak next, after duly calling upon the Gods.

Tim. All men, Socrates, who have any degree of right feeling,　c at the beginning of every enterprise, whether small or great, always call upon God. And we, too, who are going to discourse of the nature of the universe, how created or how existing without creation, if we be not altogether out of our wits, must invoke the aid of Gods and Goddesses and pray that our words may be above all acceptable to them and in consequence to ourselves. Let this, then, be our invocation of the Gods, to which I add an　d exhortation of myself to speak in such manner as will be most intelligible to you, and will most accord with my own intent.

First then, in my judgement, we must make a distinction and ask, What is that which always is and has no becoming; and what

is that which is always becoming and never is? That which is apprehended by intelligence and reason is always in the same
28 state; but that which is conceived by opinion with the help of sensation and without reason, is always in a process of becoming and perishing and never really is. Now everything that becomes or is created must of necessity be created by some cause, for without a cause nothing can be created. The work of the creator, whenever he looks to the unchangeable and fashions the form and nature of his work after an unchangeable pattern, must
b necessarily be made fair and perfect; but when he looks to the created only, and uses a created pattern, it is not fair or perfect. Was the heaven then or the world, whether called by this or by any other more appropriate name—assuming the name, I am asking a question which has to be asked at the beginning of an inquiry about anything—was the world, I say, always in existence and without beginning? or created, and had it a beginning? Created, I reply, being visible and tangible and having a body,
c and therefore sensible; and all sensible things are apprehended by opinion and sense and are in a process of creation and created. Now that which is created must, as we affirm, of necessity be created by a cause. But the father and maker of all this universe is past finding out; and even if we found him, to tell of him to all men would be impossible. This question, however, we must ask about the world: Which of the patterns had the artificer in view when he made it,—the pattern of the unchangeable, or of that
29 which is created? If the world be indeed fair and the artificer good, it is manifest that he must have looked to that which is eternal; but if what cannot be said without blasphemy is true, then to the created pattern. Everyone will see that he must have looked to the eternal; for the world is the fairest of creations and he is the best of causes. And having been created in this way, the world has been framed in the likeness of that which is apprehended by reason and mind and is unchangeable, and must therefore of necessity, if this is admitted, be a copy of something.
b Now it is all-important that the beginning of everything should be according to nature. And in speaking of the copy and the original we may assume that words are akin to the matter which they describe; when they relate to the lasting and permanent and intelligible, they ought to be lasting and unalterable, and, as far

as their nature allows, irrefutable and invincible—nothing less. But when they express only the copy or likeness and not the c eternal things themselves, they need only be likely and analogous to the former words: as being is to becoming, so is truth to belief. If then, Socrates, amid the many opinions about the gods and the generation of the universe, we are not able to give notions which are altogether and in every respect exact and consistent with one another, do not be surprised. Enough, if we adduce probabilities as likely as any others; for we must remember that I who am the speaker, and you who are the judges, are only d mortal men, and we ought to accept the tale which is probable and inquire no further.

Soc. Excellent, Timaeus; and we will do precisely as you bid us. The prelude is charming, and is already accepted by us— may we beg of you to proceed to the strain?

Tim. Let me tell you then why the creator made this world of generation. He was good, and the good can never have any e jealousy of anything. And being free from jealousy, he desired that all things should be as like himself as they could be. This is in 30 the truest sense the origin of creation and of the world, as we shall do well in believing on the testimony of wise men: God desired that all things should be good and nothing bad, so far as this was attainable. Wherefore also finding the whole visible sphere not at rest, but moving in an irregular and disorderly fashion, out of disorder he brought order, considering that this was in every way better than the other. Now the deeds of the best could never be or have been other than the fairest; and the creator, reflecting on the things which are by nature visible, found that no unintelli- b gent creature taken as a whole could ever be fairer than the intelligent taken as a whole; and again that intelligence could not be present in anything which was devoid of soul. For which reason, when he was framing the universe, he put intelligence in soul, and soul in body, that he might be the creator of a work which was by nature fairest and best. On this wise, using the language of probability, we may say that the world came into being—a living creature truly endowed with soul and intelligence by the providence of God.   c

This being supposed, let us proceed to the next stage: In the likeness of what animal did the Creator make the world? It

would be an unworthy thing to liken it to any nature which
exists as a part only; for nothing can be beautiful which is like
any imperfect thing; but let us suppose the world to be the very
image of that whole of which all other animals both individually
and in their tribes are portions. For the original of the universe
d contains in itself all intelligible beings, just as this world comprehends us and all other visible creatures. For the Deity, intending
to make this world like the fairest and most perfect of intelligible
beings, framed one visible animal comprehending within itself all
31 other animals of a kindred nature. Are we right in saying that
there is one world, or that they are many and infinite? There
must be one only, if the created copy is to accord with the original.
For that which includes all other intelligible creatures cannot
have a second or companion; in that case there would be need
of another living being which would include both, and of which
they would be parts, and the likeness would be more truly said
to resemble not them, but that other which included them. In
b order then that the world might be solitary, like the perfect
animal, the creator made not two worlds or an infinite number
of them; but there is and ever will be one only-begotten and
created heaven.

Now that which is created is of necessity corporeal, and also
visible and tangible. And nothing is visible where there is no fire,
or tangible which has no solidity, and nothing is solid without
earth. Wherefore also God in the beginning of creation made the
body of the universe to consist of fire and earth. But two things
c cannot be rightly put together without a third; there must be
some bond of union between them. And the fairest bond is that
which makes the most complete fusion of itself and the things
which it combines; and proportion is best adapted to effect such
a union. For whenever in any three numbers, whether cube or
square, there is a mean, which is to the last term what the first
32 term is to it; and again, when the mean is to the first term as the
last term is to the mean,—then the mean becoming first and last,
and the first and last both becoming means, they will all of them
of necessity come to be the same, and having become the same
with one another will be all one. If the universal frame had been
created a surface only and having no depth, a single mean would
b have sufficed to bind together itself and the other terms; but now,

as the world must be solid, and solid bodies are always compacted not by one mean but by two, God placed water and air in the mean between fire and earth, and made them to have the same proportion so far as was possible (as fire is to air so is air to water, and as air is to water so is water to earth); and thus he bound and put together a visible and tangible heaven. And for these reasons, and out of such elements which are in number four, c the body of the world was created, and it was harmonized by proportion, and therefore has the spirit of friendship; and having been reconciled to itself, it was indissoluble by the hand of any other than the framer.

Now the creation took up the whole of each of the four elements; for the Creator compounded the world out of all the fire and all the water and all the air and all the earth, leaving no part of any of them nor any power of them outside. His intention was, in the first place, that the animal should be as far as possible a perfect d whole and of perfect parts: secondly, that it should be one, 33 leaving no remnants out of which another such world might be created: and also that it should be free from old age and un-affected by disease. Considering that if heat and cold and other powerful forces surround composite bodies and attack them from without, they decompose them before their time, and by bringing diseases and old age upon them, make them waste away—for this cause and on these grounds he made the world one whole, having every part entire, and being therefore perfect and not liable to old age and disease. And he gave to the world the figure b which was suitable and also natural. Now to the animal which was to comprehend all animals, that figure would be suitable which comprehends within itself all other figures. Wherefore he made the world in the form of a globe, round as from a lathe, having its extremes in every direction equidistant from the centre, the most perfect and the most like itself of all figures; for he considered that the like is infinitely fairer than the unlike. This he finished off, making the surface smooth all round for many c reasons; in the first place, because the living being had no need of eyes when there was nothing remaining outside him to be seen; nor of ears when there was nothing to be heard; and there was no surrounding atmosphere to be breathed; nor would there have been any use of organs by the help of which he might receive his food or get rid of what he had already digested, since there was nothing which went from him or came into him: for there was nothing beside him. Of design he was created thus, his own waste providing his own food, and all that he did or suffered

d taking place in and by himself; for the Creator conceived that a being which was self-sufficient would be far more excellent than one which lacked anything. And, as he had no need to take anything or defend himself against anyone, the Creator did not think it necessary to bestow upon him hands: nor had he any

34 need of feet, nor of the whole apparatus of walking; but the movement suited to his spherical form was assigned to him, being of all the seven that which is most appropriate to mind and intelligence; and he was made to move in the same manner and on the same spot, within his own limits revolving in a circle. All the other six motions were taken away from him, and he was made not to partake of their deviations. And as this circular movement required no feet, the universe was created without legs and without feet.

Such was the whole plan of the eternal God about the god

b that was to be;[1] he made it smooth and even, having a surface in every direction equidistant from the centre, a body entire and perfect, and formed out of perfect bodies. And in the centre he put the soul, which he diffused throughout the body, making it also to be the exterior environment of it;[2] and he made the universe a circle moving in a circle, one and solitary, yet by reason of its excellence able to converse with itself, and needing no other friendship or acquaintance. Having these purposes in view he created the world a blessed god.

Now God did not make the soul after the body, although we

c are speaking of them in this order; for when he put them together he would never have allowed that the elder should be ruled by the younger; but this is a random manner of speaking which we have, because somehow we ourselves too are very much under the dominion of chance. Whereas he made the soul in origin and excellence prior to and older than the body, to be the ruler and mistress, of whom the body was to be the subject. And he made

---

[1] [There should probably be a colon in the Greek after λογισθείς.]

[2] [Better: 'which he diffused through the whole, and also spread over all the body round about'. (1st ed.)]

her out of the following elements and on this wise: From the 35
being which is indivisible and unchangeable, and from that kind
of being which is distributed among bodies, he compounded a
third and intermediate kind of being. He did likewise[1] with the
same and the different, blending together the indivisible kind
of each with that which is portioned out in bodies. Then, taking
the three new elements, he mingled them all into one form,
compressing by force the reluctant and unsociable nature of the
different into the same. When he had mingled them with [the b
intermediate kind of] being and out of three made one, he again
divided this whole into as many portions as was fitting, each
portion being a compound of the same, the different, and
being. And he proceeded to divide after this manner:—First of
all, he took away one part of the whole [1], and then he separated
a second part which was double the first [2], and then he took
away a third part which was half as much again as the second
and three times as much as the first [3], and then he took a
fourth part which was twice as much as the second [4], and a
fifth part which was three times the third [9], and a sixth part
which was eight times the first [8], and a seventh part which was c
twenty-seven times the first [27]. After this he filled up the double
intervals [i.e. between 1, 2, 4, 8] and the triple [i.e. between 1, 3, 36
9, 27], cutting off yet other portions from the mixture and
placing them in the intervals, so that in each interval there were
two kinds of means, the one exceeding and exceeded by equal
parts of its extremes [as for example 1, $\frac{4}{3}$, 2, in which the mean $\frac{4}{3}$
is one-third of 1 more than 1, and one-third of 2 less than 2], the
other being that kind of mean which exceeds and is exceeded by
an equal number.[2] Where there were intervals of $\frac{3}{2}$ and of $\frac{4}{3}$ and
of $\frac{9}{8}$, made by the connecting terms in the former intervals, he
filled up all the intervals of $\frac{4}{3}$ with the interval of $\frac{9}{8}$, leaving a b
fraction over; and the interval which this fraction expressed was
in the ratio of 256 to 243.[3] And thus the whole mixture out of
which he cut these portions was all exhausted by him. This entire

---

[1] [The words αὖ πέρι, which have been bracketed by some modern editors,
should be retained: see p. 669.]

[2] e.g. $\overline{1}, \frac{4}{3}, \frac{3}{2}, \overline{2}, \frac{8}{3}, 3, \overline{4}, \frac{16}{3}, 6, \overline{8}$; and
$\overline{1}, \frac{3}{2}, 2, \overline{3}, \frac{9}{2}, 6, \overline{9}, \frac{27}{2}, 18, \overline{27}$.

[3] e.g. $243 : 256 :: \frac{81}{64} : \frac{4}{3} :: \frac{243}{128} : 2 :: \frac{81}{32} : \frac{8}{3} :: \frac{243}{64} : 4 :: \frac{81}{16} : \frac{16}{3} :: \frac{243}{32} : 8$.
(MARTIN.)

compound he divided lengthways into two parts, which he joined
to one another at the centre like the letter **X**, and bent them into
c a circular form, connecting them with themselves and each other
at the point opposite to their original meeting-point; and, comprehending them in a uniform revolution upon the same axis, he
made the one the outer and the other the inner circle. Now the
motion of the outer circle he called the motion of the same, and
the motion of the inner circle the motion of the other or diverse.[1]
The motion of the same he carried round by the side[2] to the right,
and the motion of the diverse diagonally[3] to the left. And he gave
dominion to the motion of the same and like, for that he left
d single and undivided; but the inner motion he divided in six
places and made seven unequal circles having their intervals in
ratios of two and three, three of each, and bade the orbits proceed in a direction opposite to one another; and three [Sun,
Mercury, Venus] he made to move with equal swiftness, and the
remaining four [Moon, Saturn, Mars, Jupiter] to move with
unequal swiftness to the three and to one another, but in due
proportion.

Now when the Creator had framed the soul according to his
will, he formed within her the corporeal universe, and brought
e the two together, and united them centre to centre. The soul,
interfused everywhere from the centre to the circumference of
heaven, of which also she is the external envelopment, herself
turning in herself, began a divine beginning of never-ceasing and
37 rational life enduring throughout all time. The body of heaven
is visible, but the soul is invisible, and partakes of reason and
harmony, and being made by the best of intellectual and everlasting natures, is the best of things created. And because she is
composed of the same and of the different and of being, these
three, and is divided and united in due proportion, and in her
revolutions returns upon herself, the soul, when touching anything which has being, whether dispersed in parts or undivided,
is stirred through all her powers, to declare the sameness or

---

[1] [The same and the diverse, in this new contrast, represent respectively the
movements of the sphere of the fixed stars and of the various planetary spheres.
They must not be confused with the sameness and difference mentioned shortly
before as constituents of the World-soul (35 a).]

[2] i.e. of the rectangular figure supposed to be inscribed in the circle of the same.

[3] i.e. across the rectangular figure from corner to corner.

difference of that thing and some other; and to what individuals are related, and by what affected, and in what way and how and b when, both in the world of generation and in the world of immutable being.[1] And when reason, which works with equal truth, whether she be in the circle of the diverse or of the same— in voiceless silence holding her onward course in the sphere of the self-moved—when reason, I say, is hovering around the sensible world and when the circle of the diverse also moving truly imparts the intimations of sense to the whole soul, then arise opinions and beliefs sure and certain. But when reason is con- c cerned with the rational, and the circle of the same moving smoothly declares it, then intelligence and knowledge are neces- sarily achieved. And if anyone affirms that in which these two are found to be other than the soul, he will say the very opposite of the truth.

When the father and creator saw the creature which he had made moving and living, the created image of the eternal gods, he rejoiced, and in his joy determined to make the copy still more like the original; and as this was an eternal living being, he sought to make the universe eternal, so far as might be. Now the nature d of the ideal being was everlasting, but to bestow this attribute in its fullness upon a creature was impossible. Wherefore he resolved to have a moving image of eternity, and when he set in order the heaven, he made this image eternal but moving according to number, while eternity itself rests in unity; and this image we call time. For there were no days and nights and months and years before the heaven was created, but when he constructed the heaven he created them also. They are all parts of time, and the past and future are created species of time, which we unconsciously but wrongly transfer to eternal being; for we say that it 'was', or 'is', or 'will be', but the truth is that 'is' alone is properly attri- buted to it, and that 'was' and 'will be' are only to be spoken of becoming in time, for they are motions, but that which is im- movably the same for ever cannot become older or younger by time; nor can it be said that it came into being in the past, or has come into being now, or will come into being in the future; nor is it subject at all to any of those states which affect moving

[1] [Compare *Phaedr.* 271 d, where these acts of apprehension are illustrated in the special instance of rhetorical skill.]

and sensible things and of which generation is the cause. These are the forms of time, which imitates eternity and revolves according to a law of number. Moreover, when we say that what has b become *is* become and what becomes *is* becoming, and that what will become *is* about to become and that the non-existent *is* non-existent,—all these are inaccurate modes of expression.[1] But perhaps this whole subject will be more suitably discussed on some other occasion.

Time, then, and the heaven came into being at the same instant in order that, having been created together, if ever there was to be a dissolution of them, they might be dissolved together. It was framed after the pattern of the eternal nature, that it might resemble this as far as was possible; for the pattern exists from c eternity, and the created heaven has been, and is, and will be, in all time. Such was the mind and thought of God in the creation of time. The sun and moon and five other stars, which are called the planets, were created by him in order to distinguish and preserve the numbers of time; and when he had made their several bodies, he placed them in the orbits in which the circle of the d other was revolving [cf. 36 d],—in seven orbits seven stars. First, there was the moon in the orbit nearest the earth, and next the sun, in the second orbit above the earth; then came the morning star and the star said to be sacred to Hermes, moving in orbits which have an equal swiftness with the sun, but in an opposite direction;[2] and this is the reason why the sun and Hermes and Lucifer regularly overtake and are overtaken by each other. To enumerate the places which he assigned to the other stars, and to give all the reasons why he assigned them, although a secondary e matter, would give more trouble than the primary. These things at some future time, when we are at leisure, may have the consideration which they deserve, but not at present.

Now, when each of the stars which were necessary to the creation of time had come to its proper orbit, and they had become living creatures having bodies fastened by vital chains, and learnt their appointed task, moving in the motion of the 39 diverse, which is diagonal, and passes through and is governed by[3]

---

[1] Cf. *Parmen.* 141.
[2] [Literally 'but endowed with an opposite force'; the allusion is mysterious.]
[3] [Reading ἰοῦσάν τε καὶ κρατουμένην.]

the motion of the same, they revolved, some in a larger and some in a lesser orbit,—those which had the lesser orbit revolving faster, and those which had the larger more slowly. Now by reason of the motion of the same, those which revolved fastest appeared to be overtaken by those which moved slower although they really overtook them; for the motion of the same made them all turn in a spiral, and, because some went one way and some b another, that which receded most slowly from the sphere of the same, which was the swiftest, appeared to follow it most nearly. That there might be some visible measure of their relative swiftness and slowness as they proceeded in their eight courses, God lighted a fire, which we now call the sun, in the second from the earth of these orbits, that it might give light to the whole of heaven, and that the animals, as many as nature intended, might participate in number, learning arithmetic from the revolution of the same and the like. Thus, then, and for this reason the night c and the day were created, being the period of the one most intelligent revolution. And the month is accomplished when the moon has completed her orbit and overtaken the sun, and the year when the sun has completed his own orbit. Mankind, with hardly an exception, have not remarked the periods of the other stars, and they have no name for them, and do not measure them against one another by the help of number, and hence they can scarcely be said to know that their wanderings, being of vast d number and admirable for their variety, make up time. And yet there is no difficulty in seeing that the perfect number of time fulfils the perfect year when all the eight revolutions, having their relative degrees of swiftness, are accomplished together and attain their completion at the same time, measured by the rotation of the same and equally moving. After this manner, and for these reasons, came into being such of the stars as in their heavenly progress received reversals of motion, to the end that the created heaven might be as like as possible to the perfect and intelligible e animal, by imitation of its eternal nature.

Thus far and until the birth of time the created universe was made in the likeness of the original, but inasmuch as all animals were not yet comprehended therein, it was still unlike. Therefore the creator proceeded to fashion it after the nature of the pattern in this remaining point. Now as in the ideal animal the mind

perceives ideas or species of a certain nature and number, he
thought that this created animal ought to have species of a like
40 nature and number. There are four such; one of them is the
heavenly race of the gods; another, the race of birds whose way
is in the air; the third, the watery species; and the fourth, the
pedestrian and land creatures. Of the heavenly and divine, he
created the greater part out of fire, that they might be the
brightest of all things and fairest to behold, and he fashioned
them after the likeness of the universe in the figure of a circle, and
made them follow the intelligent motion of the supreme, distributing them over the whole circumference of heaven, which
was to be a true cosmos or glorious world spangled with them all
over. And he gave to each of them two movements: the first, a
b movement on the same spot after the same manner, whereby they
ever continue to think consistently the same thoughts about the
same things, in the same respect; the second, a forward movement, in which they are controlled by the revolution of the same
and the like; but by the other five motions they were unaffected
[cf. 43 b], in order that each of them might attain the highest
perfection. And for this reason the fixed stars were created, to be
divine and eternal animals, ever-abiding and revolving after the
same manner and on the same spot; and the other stars which
reverse their motion and are subject to deviations of this kind,
were created in the manner already described. The earth, which
is our nurse, clinging[1] around the pole which is extended through
the universe, he framed to be the guardian and artificer of night
c and day, first and eldest of gods that are in the interior of heaven.
Vain would be the attempt to tell all the figures of them circling
as in dance, and their juxtapositions, and the return of them in
their revolutions upon themselves, and their approximations, and
to say which of these deities in their conjunctions meet, and which
of them are in opposition, and in what order they get behind and
before one another, and when they are severally eclipsed to our
d sight and again reappear, sending terrors and intimations of the
future to those who cannot calculate their movements—to attempt
to tell of all this without a visible representation of the heavenly
system[2] would be labour in vain. Enough on this head; and now

---

[1] Or 'circling'.
[2] Reading τοῖς οὐ δυναμένοις and τούτων αὐτῶν.

let what we have said about the nature of the created and visible gods have an end.

To know or tell the origin of the other divinities is beyond us, and we must accept the traditions of the men of old time who affirm themselves to be the offspring of the gods—that is what they say—and they must surely have known their own ancestors. How c can we doubt the word of the children of the gods? Although they give no probable or certain proofs, still, as they declare that they are speaking of what took place in their own family, we must conform to custom and believe them. In this manner, then, according to them, the genealogy of these gods is to be received and set forth.

Oceanus and Tethys were the children of Earth and Heaven, and from these sprang Phorcys and Cronos and Rhea, and all that generation; and from Cronos and Rhea sprang Zeus and Hera, and all those who are said to be their brethren, and others 41 who were the children of these.

Now, when all of them, both those who visibly appear in their revolutions as well as those other gods who are of a more retiring nature, had come into being, the creator of the universe addressed them in these words: 'Gods, children of gods,[1] who are my works, and of whom I am the artificer and father, my creations are indissoluble, if so I will. All that is bound may be undone, but b only an evil being would wish to undo that which is harmonious and happy. Wherefore, since ye are but creatures, ye are not altogether immortal and indissoluble, but ye shall certainly not be dissolved, nor be liable to the fate of death, having in my will a greater and mightier bond than those with which ye were bound at the time of your birth. And now listen to my instructions:—Three tribes of mortal beings remain to be created— without them the universe will be incomplete, for it will not contain every kind of animal which it ought to contain, if it is to be c perfect. On the other hand, if they were created by me and received life at my hands, they would be on an equality with the gods. In order then that they may be mortal, and that this universe may be truly universal, do ye, according to your natures, betake yourselves to the formation of animals, imitating the power which was shown by me in creating you. The part of them worthy of the name immortal, which is called divine and is the guiding

[1] [Text uncertain. See Cornford, *P.C.*, Appendix 3, pp. 367–70.]

principle of those who are willing to follow justice and you—of that divine part I will myself sow the seed, and having made a beginning, I will hand the work over to you. And do ye then
d interweave the mortal with the immortal, and make and beget living creatures, and give them food, and make them to grow, and receive them again in death.'

Thus he spake, and once more into the cup in which he had previously mingled the soul of the universe he poured the remains of the elements, and mingled them in much the same manner; they were not, however, pure as before, but diluted to the second and third degree. And having made it he divided the whole mixture into souls equal in number to the stars, and assigned each soul to a star; and having there placed them as in a chariot,
e he showed them the nature of the universe, and declared to them the laws of destiny, according to which their first birth would be one and the same for all,—no one should suffer a disadvantage at his hands; they were to be sown in the instruments of time severally adapted to them, and to come forth the most religious
42 of animals; and as human nature was of two kinds, the superior race was of such-and-such a character, and would hereafter be called man. Now, when they should be implanted in bodies by necessity, and be always gaining or losing some part of their bodily substance, then in the first place it would be necessary that they should all have in them one and the same faculty of sensation, arising out of irresistible impressions; in the second place, they must have love, in which pleasure and pain mingle; also fear
b and anger, and the feelings which are akin or opposite to them; if they conquered these they would live righteously, and if they were conquered by them, unrighteously. He who lived well during his appointed time was to return and dwell in his native star, and there he would have a blessed and congenial existence. But if he failed in attaining this, at the second birth he would pass into a woman, and if, when in that state of being, he did not
c desist from evil, he would continually be changed into some brute who resembled him in the evil nature which he had acquired, and would not cease from his toils and transformations until he helped the revolution of the same and the like within him to draw in its train[1] the turbulent mob of later accretions, made up of

---

[1] [Reading συνεπισπώμενος.]

fire and air and water and earth, and by this victory of reason over the irrational returned to the form of his first and better state. Having given all these laws to his creatures, that he might d be guiltless of future evil in any of them, the creator sowed some of them in the earth, and some in the moon, and some in the other instruments of time; and when he had sown them he committed to the younger gods the fashioning of their mortal bodies, and desired them to furnish what was still lacking to the human soul, and having made all the suitable additions, to rule over e them, and to pilot the mortal animal in the best and wisest manner which they could, and avert from him all but self-inflicted evils.

When the creator had made all these ordinances he remained in his own accustomed nature, and his children heard and were obedient to their father's word, and receiving from him the immortal principle of a mortal creature, in imitation of their own creator they borrowed portions of fire, and earth, and water, and air from the world, which were hereafter to be restored—these 43 they took and welded them together, not with the indissoluble chains by which they were themselves bound, but with little pegs too small to be visible, making up out of all the four elements each separate body, and fastening the courses of the immortal soul in a body which was in a state of perpetual influx and efflux. Now these courses, detained as in a vast river, neither overcame nor b were overcome; but were hurrying and hurried to and fro, so that the whole animal was moved and progressed, irregularly however and irrationally and anyhow, in all the six directions of motion, wandering backwards and forwards, and right and left, and up and down, and in all the six directions. For great as was the advancing and retiring flood which provided nourishment, the affections produced by external contact caused still greater tumult—when the body of anyone met and came into collision c with some external fire, or with the solid earth or the gliding waters, or was caught in the tempest borne on the air, and the motions produced by any of these impulses were carried through the body to the soul. All such notions have consequently received the general name of 'sensations', which they still retain.[1] And they did in fact at that time create a very great and mighty

[1] [Αἴσθησις, sensation, is here probably derived from ἀίσσειν, rush.]

d movement; uniting with the ever-flowing stream in stirring up and violently shaking the courses of the soul, they completely stopped the revolution of the same by their opposing current, and hindered it from predominating and advancing; and they so disturbed the nature of the other or diverse, that the three double intervals [i.e. between 1, 2, 4, 8], and the three triple intervals [i.e. between 1, 3, 9, 27], together with the mean terms and connecting links which are expressed by the ratios of 3:2, and 4:3, and of 9:8,—these, although they cannot be wholly undone except by him who united them, were twisted by them in all sorts

e of ways, and the circles were broken and disordered in every possible manner, so that when they moved they were tumbling to pieces, and moved irrationally, at one time in a reverse direction, and then again obliquely, and then upside down, as you might imagine a person who is upside down and has his head leaning upon the ground and his feet up against something in the air; and when he is in such a position, both he and the spectator fancy that the right of either is his left, and the left right. If, when powerfully experiencing these and similar effects the revolutions

44 of the soul come in contact with some external thing, either of the class of the same or of the other, they speak of the same or of the other in a manner the very opposite of the truth;[1] and they become false and foolish, and there is no course or revolution in them which has a guiding or directing power; and if again any sensations enter in violently from without and drag after them the whole vessel of the soul, then the courses of the soul, though they seem to conquer, are really conquered.

And by reason of all these affections, the soul, when encased in

b a mortal body, now, as in the beginning, is at first without intelligence; but when the flood of growth and nutriment abates, and the courses of the soul, calming down, go their own way and become steadier as time goes on, then the several circles return to their natural form, and their revolutions are corrected, and they call the same and the other by their right names, and make the possessor of them to become a rational being. And if these combine in him with any true nurture or education, he attains the

c fullness and health of the perfect man, and escapes the worst

---

[1] [This is to be contrasted with the true reasoning and judgement of the World-soul, in which the circles are not disturbed, 37 a–b.]

disease of all; but if he neglects education he walks lame to the
end of his life, and returns imperfect and good for nothing to the
world below. This, however, is a later stage; at present we must
treat more exactly the subject before us, which involves a preliminary inquiry into the generation of the body and its members,
and how the soul was created,—for what reason and by what
providence of the gods; and holding fast to probability, we must d
pursue our way.

First, then, the gods, imitating the spherical shape of the
universe, enclosed the two divine courses in a spherical body,
that, namely, which we now term the head, being the most
divine part of us and the lord of all that is in us: to this the gods,
when they put together the body, gave all the other members
to be servants, considering that it must partake of every sort of
motion. In order then that it might not tumble about among the
high and deep places of the earth, but might be able to get over e
the one and out of the other, they provided the body to be its
vehicle and means of locomotion; which consequently had length
and was furnished with four limbs extended and flexible; these
God contrived to be instruments of locomotion with which it
might take hold and find support, and so be able to pass through 45
all places, carrying on high the dwelling-place of the most sacred
and divine part of us. Such was the origin of legs and hands,
which for this reason were attached to every man; and the gods,
deeming the front part of man to be more honourable and more
fit to command than the hinder part, made us to move mostly in
a forward direction. Wherefore man must needs have his front
part unlike and distinguished from the rest of his body. And so
in the vessel of the head, they first of all put a face in which they
inserted organs to minister in all things to the providence of the
soul, and they appointed this part, which has authority, to be the b
natural front. And of the organs they first contrived the eyes
to give light, and the principle according to which they were
inserted was as follows: So much of fire as would not burn, but
gave a gentle light, they formed into a substance akin to the light
of everyday life;[1] and the pure fire which is within us and related
thereto they made to flow through the eyes in a stream smooth
and dense, compressing the whole eye, and especially the centre

---

[1] [The word ἡμέρα, day, is here supposed to be akin to ἥμερον, gentle.]

c part, so that it kept out everything of a coarser nature, and allowed to pass only this pure element. When the light of day surrounds the stream of vision, then like falls upon like, and they coalesce, and one body is formed by natural affinity in the line of vision, wherever the light that falls from within meets with an external object. And the whole stream of vision, being similarly

d affected in virtue of similarity, diffuses the motions of what it touches or what touches it over the whole body, until they reach the soul, causing that perception which we call sight. But when night comes on and the external and kindred fire departs, then the stream of vision is cut off; for going forth to an unlike element it is changed and extinguished, being no longer of one nature with the surrounding atmosphere which is now deprived of fire:

e and so the eye no longer sees, and we feel disposed to sleep. For when the eyelids, which the gods invented for the preservation of sight, are closed, they keep in the internal fire; and the power of the fire diffuses and equalizes the inward motions; when they are equalized, there is rest, and when the rest is profound, sleep

46 comes over us scarce disturbed by dreams; but where any greater motions still remain, according to their nature and locality, they engender within us corresponding visions in dreams, which are remembered by us when we awaken to the external world. And now there is no longer any difficulty in understanding the creation of images in mirrors and all smooth and bright surfaces. For from the communion of the internal and external fires, and again from the union of them and their numerous transformations when they meet in the mirror, all these appearances of necessity arise,

b when the fire from the face coalesces with the fire from the eye on the bright and smooth surface. And right appears left and left right, because the visual rays come into contact with the rays emitted by the object in a manner contrary to the usual mode of meeting; but the right appears right, and the left left, when the position of one of the two concurring lights is reversed; and this happens when the mirror is concave and its smooth surface

c repels the right stream of vision to the left side, and the left to the right.[1] Or if the mirror be turned vertically, then the

---

[1] He is speaking of two kinds of mirrors, first the plane, secondly the concave; and the latter is supposed to be placed, first horizontally, and then vertically.

concavity makes the countenance appear to be all upside down, and the lower rays are driven upwards and the upper downwards.

All these are to be reckoned among the second and co-operative causes which God, carrying into execution the idea of the best as far as possible, uses as his ministers. They are thought by most men not to be the second, but the prime causes of all things, because they freeze and heat, and contract and dilate, and the like. But they are not so, for they are incapable of reason or intellect; the only being which can properly have mind is the invisible soul, whereas fire and water, and earth and air, are all of them visible bodies. The lover of intellect and knowledge ought to explore causes of intelligent nature first of all, and, secondly, of those things which, being moved by others, are compelled to move others. And this is what we too must do. Both kinds of causes should be acknowledged by us, but a distinction should be made between those which are endowed with mind and are the workers of things fair and good, and those which are deprived of intelligence and always produce chance effects without order or design. Of the second or co-operative causes of sight, which help to give to the eyes the power which they now possess, enough has been said. I will therefore now proceed to speak of the higher use and purpose for which God has given them to us. The sight in my opinion is the source of the greatest benefit to us, for had we never seen the stars, and the sun, and the heaven, none of the words which we have spoken about the universe would ever have been uttered. But now the sight of day and night, and the months and the revolutions of the years, have created number, and have given us a conception of time, and the power of inquiring about the nature of the universe; and from this source we have derived philosophy, than which no greater good ever was or will be given by the gods to mortal man. This is the greatest boon of sight: and of the lesser benefits why should I speak? even the ordinary man if he were deprived of them would bewail his loss, but in vain. Thus much let me say however: God invented and gave us sight to the end that we might behold the courses of intelligence in the heaven, and apply them to the courses of our own intelligence which are akin to them, the unperturbed to the perturbed; and that we, learning them and partaking of the natural truth of

reason, might imitate the absolutely unerring[1] courses of God
and regulate our own vagaries. The same may be affirmed of
speech and hearing: they have been given by the gods to the
same end and for a like reason. For this is the principal end of
speech, whereto it most contributes. Moreover, so much of music
as is adapted to the sound of the voice[2] and to the sense of hearing

d is granted to us for the sake of harmony; and harmony, which has
motions akin to the revolutions of our souls, is not regarded by
the intelligent votary of the Muses as given by them with a view
to irrational pleasure, which is deemed to be the purpose of it in
our day, but as meant to correct any discord which may have
arisen in the courses of the soul, and to be our ally in bringing her
into harmony and agreement with herself; and rhythm too was

e given by them for the same reason, on account of the irregular
and graceless ways which prevail among mankind generally, and
to help us against them.

Thus far in what we have been saying, with small exceptions,
the works of intelligence have been set forth; and now we must
place by the side of them in our discourse the things which come
into being through necessity—for the creation of this world is the

48 combined work of necessity and mind. Mind, the ruling power,
persuaded necessity to bring the greater part of created things to
perfection; and thus and after this manner in the beginning,
through necessity made subject to reason, this universe was
created. But if a person will truly tell of the way in which the
work was accomplished, he must include the variable cause as
well, and explain its influence. Wherefore, we must return again

b and find another suitable beginning, as about the former matters,
so also about these. To which end we must consider the nature of
fire, and water, and air, and earth, such as they were prior to the
creation of the heaven, and what was happening to them in this
previous state;[3] for no one has as yet explained the manner of
their generation, but we speak of fire and the rest of them, as
though men knew their natures, and we maintain them to be
the first principles and letters or elements of the whole, when they

---

[1] [With allusion to the name *planets*, 'wanderers', which men in their ignorance
have applied to some of the heavenly bodies. Cf. 39 c.]

[2] Reading φωνῇ and placing the comma after ἀκοήν.

[3] Cf. *infra*, 53 a.

cannot reasonably be compared by a man of any sense even to c
syllables or first compounds. And let me say thus much: I will
not now speak of the first principle or principles of all things, or
by whatever name they are to be called, for this reason,—because
it is difficult to set forth my opinion according to the method of
discussion which we are at present employing. Do not imagine,
any more than I can bring myself to imagine, that I should be
right in undertaking so great and difficult a task. Remembering
what I said at first about probability, I will do my best to give as d
probable an explanation as any other,—or rather, more probable;
and I will first go back to the beginning and try to speak of each
thing and of all.[1] Once more, then, at the commencement of my
discourse, I call upon God, and beg him to be our saviour out of
a strange and unwonted inquiry, and to bring us to the haven of
probability. So now let us begin again. e

This new beginning of our discussion of the universe requires
a fuller division than the former; for then we made two classes,
now a third must be revealed. The two sufficed for the former
discussion: one, which we assumed, was a pattern intelligible and
always the same; and the second was only the imitation of the
pattern, generated and visible. There is also a third kind which 49
we did not distinguish at the time, conceiving that the two would
be enough. But now the argument seems to require that we should
set forth in words another kind, which is difficult of explanation
and dimly seen. What nature are we to attribute to this new kind
of being? We reply, that it is the receptacle, and in a manner the
nurse, of all generation. I have spoken the truth; but I must b
express myself in clearer language, and this will be an arduous
task for many reasons, and in particular because I must first
raise questions concerning fire and the other elements, and determine what each of them is; for to say, with any probability or
certitude, which of them should be called water rather than fire,
and which should be called any of them rather than all or some
one of them, is a difficult matter. How, then, shall we settle this
point, and what questions about the elements may be fairly
raised?

---

[1] Putting the comma after μᾶλλον δέ; or, following Stallbaum and omitting the
comma, 'or rather, before entering on this probable discussion, we will begin
again, and try to speak of each thing and of all'.

In the first place, we see that what we just now called water,
c by condensation, I suppose, becomes stone and earth; and this
same element, when melted and dispersed, passes into vapour
and air. Air, again, when inflamed, becomes fire; and again fire,
when condensed and extinguished, passes once more into the
form of air; and once more, air, when collected and condensed,
produces cloud and mist; and from these, when still more compressed, comes flowing water, and from water comes earth and
stones once more; and thus generation appears to be transmitted
d from one to the other in a circle. Thus, then, as the several
elements never present themselves in the same form, how can anyone have the assurance to assert positively that any of them,
whatever it may be, is one thing rather than another? No one
can. But much the safest plan is to speak of them as follows:—
Anything which we see to be continually changing, as, for
example, fire, we must not call 'this' or 'that', but rather say
that it is 'of such a nature'; nor let us speak of water as 'this',
but always as 'such'; nor must we imply that there is any stability
in any of those things which we indicate by the use of the words
'this' and 'that', supposing ourselves to signify something thereby;
for they are too volatile to be detained in any such expressions as
'this', or 'that', or 'relative to this', or any other mode of speaking
which represents them as permanent. We ought not to apply
'this' to any of them, but rather the word 'such'; which expresses
the similar principle circulating in each and all of them; for
example, that should be called 'fire' which is of such a nature
always, and so of everything that has generation. That in which
the elements severally grow up, and appear, and decay, is alone
50 to be called by the name 'this' or 'that'; but that which is of a
certain nature, hot or white, or anything which admits of opposite
qualities, and all things that are compounded of them, ought not
to be so denominated. Let me make another attempt to explain
my meaning more clearly. Suppose a person to make all kinds
of figures of gold and to be always remodelling each form into all
the rest;—somebody points to one of them and asks what it is.
b By far the safest and truest answer is, That is gold; and not to call
the triangle or any other figures which are formed in the gold
'these', as though they had existence, since they are in process of
change while he is making the assertion; but if the questioner be

willing to take the safe and indefinite expression, 'such', we should be satisfied. And the same argument applies to the universal nature which receives all bodies—that must be always called the same; for, inasmuch as she always receives all things, she never departs at all from her own nature, and never in any way, or at any time, assumes a form like that of any of the things which enter into her; she is the natural recipient of all impres- c sions, and is stirred and informed by them, and appears different from time to time by reason of them. But the forms which enter into and go out of her are the likenesses of eternal realities modelled after their patterns in a wonderful and mysterious manner, which we will hereafter investigate. For the present we have only to conceive of three natures: first, that which is in process of generation; secondly, that in which the generation takes place; and thirdly, that of which the thing generated is a d resemblance naturally produced. And we may liken the receiving principle to a mother, and the source or spring to a father, and the intermediate nature to a child; and may remark further, that if the model is to take every variety of form, then the matter in which the model is fashioned will not be duly prepared, unless it is formless, and free from the impress of any of those shapes which it is hereafter to receive from without. For if the matter were like e any of the supervening forms, then whenever any opposite or entirely different nature was stamped upon its surface, it would take the impression badly, because it would intrude its own shape. Wherefore, that which is to receive all forms should have no form; as in making perfumes they first contrive that the liquid substance which is to receive the scent shall be as inodorous as possible; or as those who wish to impress figures on soft substances do not allow any previous impression to remain, but begin by making the surface as even and smooth as possible. In the same 51 way that which is to receive perpetually and through its whole extent the resemblances of all eternal beings ought to be devoid of any particular form. Wherefore, the mother and receptacle of all created and visible and in any way sensible things, is not to be termed earth, or air, or fire, or water, or any of their compounds, or any of the elements from which these are derived, but is an invisible and formless being which receives all things and in some mysterious way partakes of the intelligible, and is most b incomprehensible. In saying this we shall not be far wrong; as far, however, as we can attain to a knowledge of her from the previous considerations, we may truly say that fire is that part of her nature which from time to time is inflamed, and water that which is moistened, and that the mother substance becomes earth and air, in so far as she receives the impressions of them.

c   Let us consider this question more precisely. Is there any self-existent fire? and do all those things which we call self-existent exist? or are only those things which we see, or in some way perceive through the bodily organs, truly existent, and nothing whatever besides them? And are those intelligible forms, of which we are accustomed to speak, nothing at all, and only a name? Here is a question which we must not leave unexamined or undetermined, nor must we affirm too confidently that there can be no decision; neither must we interpolate in our present

d long discourse a digression equally long, but if it is possible to set forth a great principle in a few words, that is just what we want.

Thus I state my view:—If mind and true opinion are two distinct classes, then I say that there certainly are these self-existent ideas unperceived by sense, and apprehended only by the mind; if, however, as some say, true opinion differs in no respect from mind, then everything that we perceive through the

e body is to be regarded as most real and certain. But we must affirm them to be distinct, for they have a distinct origin and are of a different nature; the one is implanted in us by instruction, the other by persuasion; the one is always accompanied by true reason, the other is without reason; the one cannot be overcome by persuasion, but the other can: and lastly, every man may be said to share in true opinion, but mind is the attribute of the gods and of very few men. Wherefore also we must acknowledge that one kind of being is the form which is always the same, uncreated

52 and indestructible, never receiving anything into itself from without, nor itself going out to any other, but invisible and imperceptible by any sense, and of which the contemplation is granted to intelligence only. And there is another nature of the same name with it, and like to it, perceived by sense, created, always in motion, becoming in place and again vanishing out of place, which is apprehended by opinion jointly with sense. And there

b is a third nature, which is space, and is eternal, and admits not of destruction and provides a home for all created things, and is apprehended when all sense is absent, by a kind of spurious reason, and is hardly real; which we beholding as in a dream, say of all existence that it must of necessity be in some place and occupy a space, but that what is neither in heaven nor in earth has no existence. Of these and other things of the same kind, relating to the true and waking reality of nature, we have only this dreamlike sense, and we are unable to cast off sleep and deter- c mine the truth about them. For an image, since the reality, after which it is modelled, does not belong to it,[1] and it exists ever as the fleeting shadow of some other, must be inferred to be in another [i.e. in space], grasping existence in some way or other, or it could not be at all. But true and exact reason, vindicating the nature of true being, maintains that while two things [i.e. the image and space] are different they cannot exist one of them in the other and so be one and also two at the same time.

Thus have I concisely given the result of my thoughts; and my d verdict is that being and space and generation, these three, existed in their three ways before the heaven; and that the nurse of generation, moistened by water and inflamed by fire, and receiving the forms of earth and air, and experiencing all the affections which accompany these, presented a strange variety of appearances; and being full of powers which were neither similar nor equally balanced, was never in any part in a state of e equipoise, but swaying unevenly hither and thither, was shaken by them, and by its motion again shook them; and the elements when moved were separated and carried continually, some one way, some another; as, when grain is shaken and winnowed by fans and other instruments used in the threshing of corn, the close and heavy particles are borne away and settle in one direction, 53 and the loose and light particles in another. In this manner, the four kinds or elements were then shaken by the receiving vessel, which, moving like a winnowing machine, scattered far away from one another the elements most unlike, and forced the most similar elements into close contact. Wherefore the various elements had distinct places also before they were arranged so as to form the universe. At first, however, they were all without

---

[1] Or, 'since in its very intention it is not self-existent'—which, though obscure, avoids any inaccuracy of construction.

b reason and measure. But when the world began to get into order, fire and water and earth and air did indeed show faint traces of themselves, but were altogether in such a condition as one may expect to find wherever God is absent. Such, I say, being their nature, God now fashioned them by form and number. Let it be consistently maintained by us in all that we say that God made them as far as possible the fairest and best, out of things which were not fair and good. And now I will endeavour to show you the disposition and generation of them by an unaccustomed

c argument, which I am compelled to use; but I believe that you will be able to follow me, for your education has made you familiar with the methods of science.

In the first place, then, as is evident to all, fire and earth and water and air are bodies. And every sort of body possesses volume, and every volume must necessarily be bounded by surfaces; and every rectilinear surface is composed of triangles; and all triangles are originally of two kinds, both of which are made

d up of one right and two acute angles; one of them has at either end of the base the half of a divided right angle, having equal sides, while in the other the right angle is divided into unequal parts, having unequal sides. These, then, proceeding by a combination of probability with demonstration, we assume to be the original elements of fire and the other bodies; but the principles which are prior to these God only knows, and he of men who is the

e friend of God. And next we have to determine what are the four most beautiful bodies which could be formed, unlike one another, yet in some instances capable of resolution into one another; for having discovered thus much, we shall know the true origin of earth and fire and of the proportionate and intermediate elements. For we shall not be willing to allow that there are any distinct kinds of visible bodies fairer than these. Wherefore we must endeavour to construct the four forms of bodies which excel in beauty, and secure the right to say that we have sufficiently

54 apprehended their nature. Now of the two triangles, the isosceles has one form only; the scalene or unequal-sided has an infinite number. Of the infinite forms we must again select the most beautiful, if we are to proceed in due order, and anyone who can point out a more beautiful form than ours for the construction of these bodies shall carry off the palm, not as an enemy, but as a

friend. Now, the one which we maintain to be the most beautiful of all the many triangles (and we need not speak of the others) is that of which the double forms a third triangle which is equilateral; the reason of this would be long to tell; he who disproves b what we are saying, and shows that we are mistaken,[1] may claim a friendly victory. Then let us choose two triangles, out of which fire and the other elements have been constructed, one isosceles, the other having the square of the longer side equal to three times the square of the lesser side.

Now is the time to explain what was before obscurely said: there was an error in imagining that all the four elements might be generated by and into one another; this, I say, was an erro- c neous supposition, for there are generated from the triangles which we have selected four kinds—three from the one which has the sides unequal; the fourth alone is framed out of the isosceles triangle. Hence they cannot all be resolved into one another, a great number of small bodies being combined into a few large ones, or the converse. But three of them can be thus resolved and compounded, for they all spring from one, and when the greater bodies are broken up, many small bodies will spring up out of them and take their own proper figures; or, again, when many d small bodies are dissolved into their triangles, by their total number, they can form one large mass of another kind. So much for their passage into one another. I have now to speak of their several kinds, and show out of what combinations of numbers each of them was formed. The first will be the simplest and smallest construction, and its element is that triangle which has its hypotenuse twice the lesser side. When two such triangles are e joined at the diagonal, and this is repeated three times, and the triangles rest their diagonals and shorter sides on the same point as a centre, a single equilateral triangle is formed out of six triangles; and four equilateral triangles, if put together, make out of every three plane angles one solid angle, being that which is nearest to the most obtuse of plane angles; and out of the com- 55 bination of these four angles arises the first solid form which distributes into equal and similar parts the whole circle in which it is inscribed. The second species of solid is formed out of the same

---

[1] [Reading ἀνευρόντι μὴ οὕτως ἔχον (Hermann). With δή, the sense is: 'he who examines this and shows that it is so'.]

triangles, which unite as eight equilateral triangles and form one solid angle out of four plane angles, and out of six such angles the second body is completed. And the third body is made up of 120

b triangular elements, forming twelve solid angles, each of them included in five plane equilateral triangles, having altogether twenty bases, each of which is an equilateral triangle. The one element [that is, the triangle which has its hypotenuse twice the lesser side] having generated these figures, generated no more; but the isosceles triangle produced the fourth elementary figure, which is compounded of four such triangles, joining their right angles in a centre, and forming one equilateral quadrangle. Six of these united form eight solid angles, each of which is made by

c the combination of three plane right angles; the figure of the body thus composed is a cube, having six plane quadrangular equilateral bases. There was yet a fifth combination[1] which God used in the delineation of the universe with figures of animals.

Now, he who, duly reflecting on all this, inquires whether the worlds are to be regarded as indefinite or definite in number, will be of opinion that the notion of their indefiniteness is character-

d istic of a sadly indefinite and ignorant mind. He, however, who raises the question whether they are to be truly regarded as one or five, takes up a more reasonable position. Arguing from probabilities, I am of opinion that they are one; another, regarding the question from another point of view, will be of another mind. But, leaving this inquiry, let us proceed to distribute the elementary forms, which have now been created in idea, among the four elements.

To earth, then, let us assign the cubical form; for earth is the

e most immovable of the four and the most plastic of all bodies, and that which has the most stable bases must of necessity be of such a nature. Now, of the triangles which we assumed at first, that which has two equal sides is by nature more firmly based than that which has unequal sides; and of the compound figures

---

[1] [This is the regular dodecahedron. At *Phaedo*, 110 b, the earth was compared to a ball made by sewing together five pentagonal pieces of leather, variously coloured. The material, being flexible, will expand into a sphere. There is here some hint of a division of the sky, as seen from the earth, into twelve regions. There is still some uncertainty about the way in which the idea of the zodiac reached Greece, but it is natural to find here some trace of the information brought back from the East by Eudoxus. See Bidez, *Eos*, chap. iv.]

which are formed out of either, the plane equilateral quadrangle has necessarily a more stable basis than the equilateral triangle, both in the whole and in the parts. Wherefore, in assigning this 56 figure to earth, we adhere to probability; and to water we assign that one of the remaining forms which is the least movable; and the most movable of them to fire; and to air that which is intermediate. Also we assign the smallest body to fire, and the greatest to water, and the intermediate in size to air; and, again, the acutest body to fire, and the next in acuteness to air, and the third to water. Of all these elements, that which has the fewest bases must necessarily be the most movable, for it must be the b acutest and most penetrating in every way, and also the lightest as being composed of the smallest number of similar particles: and the second body has similar properties in a second degree, and the third body in the third degree. Let it be agreed, then, both according to strict reason and according to probability, that the pyramid is the solid which is the original element and seed of fire; and let us assign the element which was next in the order of generation to air, and the third to water. We must imagine all these to be so small that no single particle of any of the four kinds c is seen by us on account of their smallness: but when many of them are collected together their aggregates are seen. And the ratios of their numbers, motions, and other properties, every-where God, as far as necessity allowed or gave consent, has exactly perfected, and harmonized in due proportion.

From all that we have just been saying about the elements or kinds, the most probable conclusion is as follows:—earth, when d meeting with fire and dissolved by its sharpness, whether the dissolution take place in the fire itself or perhaps in some mass of air or water, is borne hither and thither, until its parts, meeting together and mutually harmonizing, again become earth; for they can never take any other form. But water, when divided by fire or by air, on re-forming, may become one part fire and two parts air; and a single volume of air divided becomes two of fire. e Again, when a small body of fire is contained in a larger body of air or water or earth, and both are moving, and the fire struggling is overcome and broken up, then two volumes of fire form one volume of air; and when air is overcome and cut up into small pieces, two and a half parts of air are condensed into one part of

water. Let us consider the matter in another way. When one of
57 the other elements is fastened upon by fire, and is cut by the
sharpness of its angles and sides, it coalesces with the fire, and
then ceases to be cut by them any longer. For no element which is
one and the same with itself can be changed by or change another
of the same kind and in the same state. But so long as in the process of transition the weaker is fighting against the stronger, the
dissolution continues. Again, when a few small particles, enclosed
b in many larger ones, are in process of decomposition and extinction, they only cease from their tendency to extinction when they
consent to pass into the conquering nature, and fire becomes air
and air water. But if bodies of another kind go and attack them[1]
[i.e. the small particles], the latter continue to be dissolved until,
being completely forced back and dispersed, they make their
escape to their own kindred, or else, being overcome and assimi-
c lated to the conquering power, they remain where they are and
dwell with their victors, and from being many become one. And
owing to these affections, all things are changing their place, for
by the motion of the receiving vessel the bulk of each class is
distributed into its proper place; but those things which become
unlike themselves and like other things, are hurried by the
shaking into the place of the things to which they grow like.

Now all unmixed and primary bodies are produced by such
causes as these. As to the subordinate species which are included
in the greater kinds, they are to be attributed to the varieties in
the structure of the two original triangles. For either structure
d did not originally produce the triangle of one size only, but some
larger and some smaller, and there are as many sizes as there are
species of the four elements. Hence when they are mingled with
themselves and with one another there is an endless variety of
them, which those who would arrive at the probable truth of
nature ought duly to consider.

Unless a person comes to an understanding about the nature
and conditions of rest and motion, he will meet with many
e difficulties in the discussion which follows. Something has been
said of this matter already, and something more remains to be

---

[1] [Reading εἰς αὐτά. Burnet's text εἰς ταὐτά gives no satisfactory sense. Cornford, reading εἰς ταῦτα, translates: 'If they (the smaller particles) are on their way to these (air or water),' *P.C.*, p. 227.]

said, which is, that motion never exists in what is uniform. For to conceive that anything can be moved without a mover is hard or indeed impossible, and equally impossible to conceive that there can be a mover unless there be something which can be moved;—motion cannot exist where either of these is wanting, and for these to be uniform is impossible; wherefore we must assign rest to uniformity and motion to the want of uniformity. 58 Now inequality is the cause of the nature which is wanting in uniformity; and of this we have already described the origin. But there still remains the further point—why things when divided after their kinds do not cease to pass through one another and to change their place—which we will now proceed to explain. In the revolution of the universe are comprehended all the four elements, and this being circular and having a tendency to come together, compresses everything and will not allow any place to be left void. Wherefore, also, fire above all things b penetrates everywhere, and air next, as being next in rarity of the elements; and the two other elements in like manner penetrate according to their degrees of rarity. For those things which are composed of the largest particles have the largest void left in their compositions, and those which are composed of the smallest particles have the least. And the contraction caused by the compression thrusts the smaller particles into the interstices of the larger. And thus, when the small parts are placed side by side with the larger, and the lesser divide the greater and the greater unite the lesser, all the elements are borne up and down c and hither and thither towards their own places; for the change in the size of each changes its position in space. And these causes generate an inequality which is always maintained, and is continually creating a perpetual motion of the elements in all time.

In the next place we have to consider, first, that there are divers kinds of fire. There are, for example, first, flame; and secondly, those emanations of flame which do not burn but only give light to the eyes; thirdly, the remains of fire, which are seen in red-hot embers after the flame has been extinguished. There d are similar differences in the air; of which the brightest part is called the aether, and the most turbid sort mist and darkness; and there are various other nameless kinds which arise from the inequality of the triangles. Water, again, admits in the first place of a division into two kinds; the one liquid and the other fusile. The liquid kind is composed of the small and unequal particles of water; and moves itself and is moved by other bodies owing to the want of uniformity and the shape of its particles; whereas the

e fusile kind, being formed of large and uniform particles, is more stable than the other, and is heavy and compact by reason of its uniformity. But when fire gets in and dissolves the particles and destroys the uniformity, it has greater mobility, and becoming fluid is thrust forth by the neighbouring air and spreads upon the earth; and this dissolution of the solid masses is called melting,

59 and their spreading out upon the earth flowing. Again, when the fire goes out of the fusile substance, it does not pass into a vacuum, but into the neighbouring air; and the air which is displaced forces together the liquid and still moveable mass into the place which was occupied by the fire, and unites it with itself. Thus compressed the mass resumes its equability, and is again at unity with itself, because the fire which was the author of the inequality has retreated; and this departure of the fire is called cooling, and the coming together which follows upon it is termed congealment.

b Of all the kinds termed fusile, that which is the densest and is formed out of the finest and most uniform parts is that most precious possession called gold, which is hardened by filtration through rock; this is unique in kind, and has both a glittering and a yellow colour. A shoot of gold, which is so dense as to be very hard, and takes a black colour, is termed adamant. There is also another kind which has parts nearly like gold, and of which there are several species; it is denser than gold, and it contains a

c small and fine portion of earth, and is therefore harder, yet also lighter because of the great interstices which it has within itself; and this substance, which is one of the bright and denser kinds of water, when solidified is called copper. There is an alloy of earth mingled with it, which, when the two parts grow old and are disunited, shows itself separately and is called rust. The remaining phenomena of the same kind there will be no difficulty in reasoning out by the method of probabilities. A man may sometimes set aside meditations about eternal things, and for recrea-

d tion turn to consider the truths of generation which are probable only; he will thus gain a pleasure not to be repented of, and secure for himself while he lives a wise and moderate pastime.

Let us grant ourselves this indulgence, and go through the probabilities relating to the same subjects which follow next in order.

Water which is mingled with fire, so much as is fine and liquid (being so called by reason of its motion and the way in which it rolls along the ground), and soft, because its bases give way and are less stable than those of earth, when separated from fire and air and isolated, becomes more uniform, and by their retirement is compressed into itself; and if the condensation be very great, e the water above the earth becomes hail, but on the earth, ice; and that which is congealed in a less degree and is only half solid, when above the earth is called snow, and when upon the earth, and condensed from dew, hoar-frost. Then, again, there are the numerous kinds of water which have been mingled with one another, and are distilled through plants which grow in the earth; and this whole class is called by the name of juices or saps. The unequal admixture of these fluids creates a variety of species; 6 most of them are nameless, but four which are of a fiery nature are clearly distinguished and have names. First, there is wine, which warms the soul as well as the body: secondly, there is the oily nature, which is smooth and divides the visual ray, and for this reason is bright and shining and of a glistening appearance, including pitch, the juice of the castor berry, oil itself, and other things of a like kind: thirdly, there is the class of substances which b expand the contracted parts[1] of the mouth, until they return to their natural state, and by reason of this property create sweetness;—these are included under the general name of honey: and, lastly, there is a frothy nature, which differs from all juices, having a burning quality which dissolves the flesh; it is called *opos* (a vegetable acid).

As to the kinds of earth, that which is filtered through water passes into stone in the following manner:—The water which mixes with the earth and is broken up in the process changes into air, and taking this form mounts into its own place. But as there c is no surrounding vacuum it thrusts away the neighbouring air, and this being rendered heavy, and, when it is displaced, having been poured around the mass of earth, forcibly compresses it and drives it into the vacant space whence the new air had come up;

[1] Cf. 65 c, 66 c.

and the earth when compressed by the air into an indissoluble union with water becomes rock. The fairer sort is that which is made up of equal and similar parts and is transparent; that which has the opposite qualities is inferior. But when all the watery part is suddenly drawn out by fire, a more brittle substance is formed, to which we give the name of pottery. Sometimes also moisture may remain, and the earth which has been fused by fire becomes, when cool, a certain stone of a black colour.[1] A like separation of the water which had been copiously mingled with them may occur in two substances composed of finer particles of earth and of a briny nature; out of either of them a half-solid body is then formed, soluble in water—the one, soda, which is used for purging away oil and earth, the other, salt, which harmonizes so well in combinations pleasing to the palate, and is, as the law testifies, a substance dear to the gods. The compounds of earth and water are not soluble by water, but by fire only, and for this reason:—Neither fire nor air melts masses of earth; for their particles, being smaller than the interstices in its structure, have plenty of room to move without forcing their way, and so they leave the earth unmelted and undissolved; but particles of water, which are larger, force a passage, and dissolve and melt the earth. Wherefore earth when not consolidated by force is dissolved by water only; when consolidated, by nothing but fire; for this is the only body which can find an entrance. The cohesion of water again, when very strong, is dissolved by fire only—when weaker, then either by air or fire—the former entering the interstices, and the latter penetrating even the triangles. But nothing can dissolve air, when strongly condensed, which does not reach the elements or triangles; or if not strongly condensed, then only fire can dissolve it. As to bodies composed of earth and water, while the water occupies the vacant interstices of the earth in them which are compressed by force, the particles of water which approach them from without, finding no entrance, flow around the entire mass and leave it undissolved; but the particles of fire enter into the interstices of the water and fire does to water what water does to earth.[2] Such particles are the sole causes of the compound body

---

[1] [Perhaps lava. See Cornford *P.C.*, p. 256, note 2, and compare Arist. *Meteor.* 383 b 9.]

[2] [Reading, with Cook Wilson, τοῦτο πῦρ ὕδωρ.]

of earth and water liquefying and becoming fluid. Now these bodies are of two kinds; some of them, such as glass and the fusible sort of stones, have less water than they have earth; on the other hand, substances of the nature of wax and incense have more of water entering into their composition. c

I have thus shown the various classes of bodies as they are diversified by their forms and combinations and changes into one another, and now I must endeavour to set forth their affections and the causes of them. In the first place, the bodies which I have been describing are necessarily objects of sense. But we have not yet considered the origin of flesh, or what belongs to flesh, or of that part of the soul which is mortal. And these things cannot be adequately explained without also explaining the affections which are concerned with sensation, nor the latter without the former: and yet to explain them together is hardly possible; for which reason we must assume first one or the other and afterwards examine the nature of our hypothesis.[1] In order, then, that the affections may follow regularly after the elements, let us presuppose the existence of body and soul. d

First, let us inquire what we mean by saying that fire is hot; and about this we may reason from the dividing or cutting power which it exercises on our bodies. We all of us feel that fire is sharp; and we may further consider the fineness of the sides, and the sharpness of the angles, and the smallness of the particles, and the swiftness of the motion;—all this makes the action of fire violent and sharp, so that it cuts whatever it meets. And we must not forget that the original figure of fire [i.e. the pyramid], more than any other form, has a dividing power which cuts our bodies into small pieces (κερματίζει), and thus naturally produces that affection which we call heat; and hence the origin of the name (θερμός, κέρμα). Now, the opposite of this is sufficiently manifest; nevertheless we will not fail to describe it. For the larger particles of moisture which surround the body, entering in and driving out the lesser, but not being able to take their places, compress the moist principle in us; and this from being unequal and disturbed, is forced by them into a state of rest, which is due to equability and compression. But things which are contracted contrary to nature are by nature at war, and force themselves e

62

b

[1] Omitting ὕστερα.

apart; and to this war and convulsion the name of shivering and trembling is given; and the whole affection and the cause of the affection are both termed cold. That is called hard to which our flesh yields, and soft which yields to our flesh; and things are also termed hard and soft relatively to one another. That which yields has a small base; but that which rests on quadrangular

c bases is firmly posed and belongs to the class which offers the greatest resistance; so too does that which is the most compact and therefore most repellent. The nature of the light and the heavy will be best understood when examined in connexion with our notions of above and below; for it is quite a mistake to suppose that the universe is parted into two regions, separate from and opposite to each other, the one a lower to which all things tend which have any bulk, and an upper to which things only ascend against their will. For as the universe is in the form of a

d sphere, all the extremities, being equidistant from the centre, are equally extremities, and the centre, which is equidistant from them, is equally to be regarded as the opposite of them all. Such being the nature of the world, when a person says that any of these points is above or below, may he not be justly charged with using an improper expression? For the centre of the world cannot be rightly called either above or below, but is the centre and nothing else; and the circumference is not the centre, and has in no one part of itself a different relation to the centre from what it has in any of the opposite parts. Indeed, when it is in every direction similar, how can one rightly give to it names which

63 imply opposition? For if there were any solid body in equipoise at the centre of the universe, there would be nothing to draw it to this extreme rather than to that, for they are all perfectly similar; and if a person were to go round the world in a circle, he would often, when standing at the antipodes of his former position, speak of the same point as above and below; for, as I was saying just now, to speak of the whole which is in the form of a globe as having one part above and another below is not like a sensible man. The reason why these names are used, and the circumstances under which they are ordinarily applied by us to the division of the heavens, may be elucidated by the following

b supposition:—If a person were to stand in that part of the universe which is the appointed place of fire, and where there is the great mass of fire to which fiery bodies gather—if, I say, he were to ascend thither, and, having the power to do this, were to abstract particles of fire and put them in scales and weigh them, and then, raising the balance, were to draw the fire by force towards the uncongenial element of the air, it would be very evident that he could compel the smaller mass more readily than c the larger; for when two things are simultaneously raised by one and the same power, the smaller body must necessarily yield to the superior power with less reluctance than the larger; and the larger body is called heavy and said to tend downwards, and the smaller body is called light and said to tend upwards. And we may detect ourselves who are upon the earth doing precisely the same thing. For we often separate earthy natures, and sometimes earth itself, and draw them into the uncongenial element of air by force and contrary to nature, both clinging to their kindred elements. But that which is smaller yields to the impulse given by d us towards the dissimilar element more easily than the larger; and so we call the former light, and the place towards which it is impelled we call above, and the contrary state and place we call heavy and below respectively. Now the relations of these must necessarily vary, because the principal masses of the different elements hold opposite positions; for that which is light, heavy, below or above in one place will be found to be and become contrary and transverse and every way diverse in relation to that e which is light, heavy, below or above in an opposite place. And about all of them this has to be considered:—that in some cases the tendency of each towards its kindred element makes the body which is moved heavy, and the place towards which the motion tends below, but things which have an opposite tendency we call by an opposite name. Such are the causes which we assign to these phenomena. As to the smooth and the rough, any one who sees them can explain the reason of them to another. For roughness is hardness mingled with irregularity, and smoothness 64 is produced by the joint effect of uniformity and density.

The most important of the affections which concern the whole body remains to be considered,—that is, the cause of pleasure and pain in the perceptions of which I have been speaking, and in all other things which are perceived by sense through the parts of the body, and have both pains and pleasures attendant on them.

Let us imagine the causes of every affection, whether of sense or not, to be of the following nature, remembering that we have

b already distinguished between the nature which is easy and which is hard to move; for this is the direction in which we must hunt the prey which we mean to take. A body which is of a nature to be easily moved, on receiving an impression however slight, spreads abroad the motion in a circle, the parts communicating with each other, until at last, reaching the principle of mind, they announce the quality of the agent. But a body of the opposite kind, being immobile, and not extending to the surrounding region, merely receives the impression, and does not stir any of

c the neighbouring parts; and since the parts do not distribute the original impression to other parts, it has no effect of motion on the whole animal, and therefore produces no effect on the patient. This is true of the bones and hair and other more earthy parts of the human body; whereas what was said above relates mainly to sight and hearing, because they have in them the greatest amount of fire and air. Now we must conceive of pleasure and pain in this way. An impression produced in us contrary to nature

d and violent, if sudden, is painful; and, again, the sudden return to nature is pleasant; but a gentle and gradual return is imperceptible and *vice versa*. On the other hand the impression of sense which is easily produced is most readily felt, but is not accompanied by pleasure or pain; such, for example, are the affections of the sight, which, as we said above, is a body naturally uniting with our body in the day-time [45]; for cuttings and burnings and other affections which happen to the sight do not

e give pain, nor is there pleasure when the sight returns to its natural state; yet very clear and strong sensations arise for every affection of sight, whether the eye is passive or is deliberately turned upon an object. The reason is that no violence at all is involved in the separation and reunion of the visual ray. But bodies formed of larger particles yield to the agent only with a struggle; and then they impart their motions to the whole and cause pleasure and pain—pain when alienated from their natural

65 conditions, and pleasure when restored to them. Things which experience gradual withdrawings and emptyings of their nature, and great and sudden replenishments, fail to perceive the emptying, but are sensible of the replenishment; and so they occasion

no pain, but the greatest pleasure, to the mortal part of the soul,
as is manifest in the case of perfumes. But things which are changed
all of a sudden, and only gradually and with difficulty return to
their own nature, have effects in every way opposite to the former, b
as is evident in the case of burnings and cuttings of the body.

Thus have we discussed the general affections of the whole
body, and the names of the agents which produce them. And
now I will endeavour to speak of the affections of particular parts,
and the causes and agents of them, as far as I am able. In the first
place let us set forth what was omitted when we were speaking of c
juices, concerning the affections peculiar to the tongue. These,
too, like most of the other affections, appear to be caused by certain contractions and dilations, but they have besides more of
roughness and smoothness than is found in other affections; for
whenever earthy particles enter into the small veins which are
the testing instruments of the tongue, reaching to the heart, and d
fall upon the moist, delicate portions of flesh—when, as they are
dissolved, they contract and dry up the little veins, they are
astringent if they are rougher, but if not so rough, then only
harsh. Those particles which act upon these veins as an abstergent, and purge the whole surface of the tongue, if they do it
in excess, and so encroach as to consume some part of the flesh itself, like potash and soda, are all termed bitter. But the particles e
which are deficient in the alkaline quality, and which cleanse only
moderately, are called salt, and having no bitterness or roughness, are regarded as rather agreeable than otherwise. Bodies which
share in and are made smooth by the heat of the mouth, and which
are inflamed, and again in turn inflame that which heats them,
and which are so light that they are carried upwards to the sensations of the head, and cut all that comes in their way, by reason of 66
these qualities in them are all termed pungent. There are other
particles which, previously refined by putrefaction, enter into
the narrow veins, and being duly proportioned to the particles of
earth and air which are there, set them whirling about one
another, and while they are in a whirl cause them to dash against
and enter into one another, and so form hollows surrounding the
particles that enter—which watery vessels of air (for a film of b
moisture, sometimes earthy, sometimes pure, is spread around
the air) are hollow spheres of water; and those of them which are

pure, are transparent, and are called bubbles, while those composed of the earthy liquid, which is in a state of general agitation
and effervescence, are said to boil or ferment;—of all these
affections the cause is termed acid. And there is the opposite

c affection arising from an opposite cause, when the mass of entering particles, immersed in the moisture of the mouth, is congenial
to the tongue, and smooths and oils over the roughness, and
relaxes the parts which are unnaturally contracted, and contracts
the parts which are relaxed, and disposes them all according to
their nature;—that sort of remedy of violent affections is pleasant
and agreeable to every man, and has the name sweet. But enough
of this.

d   The faculty of smell does not admit of differences of kind; for
all smells are of a half-formed nature, and no element is so proportioned as to have any smell. The veins about the nose are too
narrow to admit earth and water, and too wide to detain fire
and air; and for this reason no one ever perceives the smell of any
of them; but smells always proceed from bodies that are damp,
or putrefying, or liquefying, or evaporating, and are perceptible

e only in the intermediate state, when water is changing into air
and air into water; and all of them are either vapour or mist.
That which is passing out of air into water is mist, and that which
is passing from water into air is vapour; and hence all smells are
thinner than water and thicker than air. The proof of this is, that
when there is any obstruction to the respiration, and a man
draws in his breath by force, then no smell filters through, but the

67 air without the smell alone penetrates. Wherefore the varieties of
smell have no name, and they have not many, or definite and
simple kinds; but they are distinguished only as painful and
pleasant, the one sort irritating and disturbing the whole cavity
which is situated between the head and the navel, the other
having a soothing influence, and restoring this same region to an
agreeable and natural condition.

   In considering the third kind of sense, hearing, we must speak

b of the causes in which it originates. We may in general assume
sound to be a blow which passes through the ears, and is transmitted by means of the air, the brain, and the blood, to the soul,
and that hearing is the vibration of this blow, which begins in
the head and ends in the region of the liver. The sound which

moves swiftly is acute, and the sound which moves slowly is grave, and that which is regular is equable and smooth, and the reverse is harsh. A great body of sound is loud, and a small body c of sound the reverse. Respecting the harmonies of sound I must hereafter speak.

There is a fourth class of sensible things, having many intricate varieties, which must now be distinguished. They are called by the general name of colours, and are a flame which emanates from every sort of body, and has particles corresponding to the sense of sight. I have spoken already, in what has preceded, of the causes which generate sight, and in this place it will be natural d and suitable to give a rational theory of colours.

Of the particles coming from other bodies which fall upon the sight, some are smaller and some are larger, and some are equal to the parts of the sight itself. Those which are equal are imperceptible, and we call them transparent. The larger produce contraction, the smaller dilation, in the sight, exercising a power akin to that of hot and cold bodies on the flesh, or of astringent bodies on the tongue, or of those heating bodies which we termed pungent. White and black are similar effects of contraction and dilation in another sphere, and for this reason have a different appearance. Wherefore, we ought to term white that which dilates the visual ray, and the opposite of this black. There is also a swifter motion of a different sort of fire which strikes and dilates the ray of sight until it reaches the eyes, forcing a way through their passages and melting them, and eliciting from them a union 68 of fire and water which we call tears, being itself an opposite fire which comes to them from an opposite direction—the inner fire flashes forth like lightning, and the outer finds a way in and is extinguished in the moisture, and all sorts of colours are generated by the mixture. This affection is termed dazzling, and the object which produces it is called bright and flashing. There is another sort of fire which is intermediate, and which reaches and mingles b with the moisture of the eye without flashing; and in this, the fire mingling with the ray of the moisture, produces a colour like blood, to which we give the name of red. A bright hue mingled with red and white gives the colour called auburn (ξανθόν). The law of proportion, however, according to which the several colours are formed, even if a man knew he would be foolish in

telling, for he could not give any necessary reason, nor indeed
c any tolerable or probable explanation of them. Again, red, when
mingled with black and white, becomes purple, but it becomes
umber (ὄρφνινον) when the colours are burnt as well as mingled
and the black is more thoroughly mixed with them. Flame-
colour (πυρρόν) is produced by a union of auburn and dun
(φαιόν), and dun by an admixture of black and white; pale
yellow (ὠχρόν), by an admixture of white and auburn. White
and bright meeting, and falling upon a full black, become dark
blue (κυανοῦν), and when dark blue mingles with white, a light
blue (γλαυκόν) colour is formed, as flame-colour with black makes
d leek-green (πράσιον). There will be no difficulty in seeing how and
by what mixtures the colours derived from these are made according to the rules of probability. He, however, who should attempt
to verify all this by experiment, would forget the difference of the
human and divine nature. For God only has the knowledge and
also the power which are able to combine many things into one
and again resolve the one into many. But no man either is or ever
will be able to accomplish either the one or the other operation.
e   These are the elements, thus of necessity then subsisting, which
the creator of the fairest and best of created things associated with
himself, when he made the self-sufficing and most perfect God,
using the necessary causes as his ministers in the accomplishment
of his work, but himself contriving the good in all his creations.
Wherefore we may distinguish two sorts of causes, the one divine
and the other necessary, and may seek for the divine in all things,
69 as far as our nature admits, with a view to the blessed life; but the
necessary kind only for the sake of the divine, considering that
without them and when isolated from them, these higher things
for which we look cannot be apprehended or received or in any
way shared by us.

      Seeing, then, that we have now prepared for our use the various
classes of causes which are the material out of which the remainder
of our discourse must be woven, just as wood is the material of the
carpenter, let us revert in a few words to our beginning, and
hasten back to the point from which we set out on our road
hither. We may then endeavour to crown our tale with a suitable
b conclusion.

      As I said at first, when all things were in disorder God created in each thing in relation to itself, and in all things in relation to each other, all the measures and harmonies which they could possibly receive. For in those days nothing had any proportion except by accident; nor was there anything deserving to be called by the names which we now use—as, for example, fire, water, and the rest of the elements. All these the creator first set in order, and out of them he constructed the universe, which was c a single animal comprehending in itself all other animals, mortal and immortal. Now of the divine, he himself was the creator, but the creation of the mortal he committed to his offspring. And they, imitating him, received from him the immortal principle of the soul; and around this they proceeded to fashion a mortal body, and made it to be the vehicle of the soul, and constructed within the body a soul of another nature which was mortal, subject to terrible and irresistible affections,—first of all, pleasure, the d greatest incitement to evil; then, pain, which deters from good; also rashness and fear, two foolish counsellors; anger hard to be appeased, and hope easily led astray;—these they mingled with irrational sense and with all-daring love according to necessary laws, and so framed man. Wherefore, fearing to pollute the divine any more than was absolutely unavoidable, they gave to the mortal nature a separate habitation in another part of the e body, placing the neck between them to be the isthmus and boundary, which they constructed between the head and breast, to keep them apart. And in the breast, and in what is termed the thorax, they encased the mortal soul; and as the one part of this was superior and the other inferior they divided the cavity of the thorax into two parts, as the women's and men's apartments are 70 divided in houses, and placed the midriff to be a wall of partition between them. That part of the inferior soul which is endowed with courage and passion and loves contention they settled nearer the head, midway between the midriff and the neck, in order that being obedient to the rule of reason it might join with it in controlling and restraining the desires when they are no longer willing of their own accord to obey ¹the word of command¹ issuing from the citadel.

The heart, the knot of the veins and the fountain of the blood b which races through all the limbs, was set in the place of guard,

¹ [Edn. 1 better, 'the command of reason'.]

that when the might of passion was roused by reason making proclamation of any wrong assailing them from without or being perpetrated by the desires within, quickly the whole power of feeling in the body, perceiving these commands and threats, might obey and follow through every turn and alley, and thus allow the principle of the best to have the command in all of
c them. But the gods, foreknowing that the palpitation of the heart in the expectation of danger and excitement of passion must cause it to swell and become inflamed,[1] formed and implanted as a supporter to the heart the lung, which was, in the first place, soft and bloodless, and also had within hollows like the pores of a sponge, in order that by receiving the breath and the drink, it
d might give coolness and the power of respiration and alleviate the heat. Wherefore they cut the air-channels leading to the lung, and placed the lung about the heart as a soft spring, that, when passion was rife within, the heart, beating against a yielding body, might be cooled and suffer less, and might thus become more ready to join with passion in the service of reason.

The part of the soul which desires meats and drinks and the other things of which it has need by reason of the bodily nature,
e they placed between the midriff and the boundary of the navel, contriving in all this region a sort of manger for the food of the body; and there they bound it down like a wild animal which was chained up with man, and must be nourished if man was to exist. They appointed this lower creation his place here in order that he might be always feeding at the manger, and have his dwelling as far as might be from the council-chamber, making as
71 little noise and disturbance as possible, and permitting the best part to advise quietly for the good of the whole and the individual. And knowing that this lower principle in man would not comprehend reason, and even if attaining to some degree of perception would never naturally care for rational notions, but that it would be especially led by phantoms and visions night and day,— planning to make this very weakness serve a purpose, God com-
b bined with it the liver, and placed it in the house of the lower nature, contriving that it should be solid and smooth, and bright and sweet, and should also have a bitter quality, in order that the

---

[1] [Reading διάπυρος for διὰ πυρὸς in 70 c 3. This adjective is frequent in Plato: cf. *Tim.* 58 c, 74 b, 88 a.]

power of thought, which proceeds from the mind, might be reflected as in a mirror which receives likenesses of objects and gives back images of them to the sight; and so might strike terror into the desires, when, making use of the bitter part of the liver, to which it is akin, it comes threatening and invading, and diffusing this bitter element swiftly through the whole liver produces colours like bile, and contracting every part makes it wrinkled and rough; and twisting out of its right place and con- c torting the lobe and closing and shutting up the vessels and gates, causes pain and loathing. And the converse happens when some gentle inspiration of the understanding pictures images of an opposite character, and allays the bile and bitterness by refusing to stir or touch the nature opposed to itself, but by making use of the natural sweetness of the liver, corrects all things and makes them to be right and smooth and free, and renders the portion of d the soul which resides about the liver happy and joyful, enabling it to pass the night in peace, and to practise divination in sleep, inasmuch as it has no share in mind and reason. For the authors of our being, remembering the command of their father when he bade them create the human race as good as they could, that they might correct our inferior parts and make them to attain a measure of truth, placed in the liver the seat of divination. And e herein is a proof that God has given the art of divination not to the wisdom, but to the foolishness of man. No man, when in his wits, attains prophetic truth and inspiration; but when he receives the inspired word, either his intelligence is enthralled in sleep, or he is demented by some distemper or possession. And he who would understand what he remembers to have been said, whether in a dream or when he was awake, by the prophetic and 72 inspired nature, or would determine by reason the meaning of the apparitions which he has seen, and what indications they afford to this man or that, of past, present or future good and evil, must first recover his wits. But, while he continues demented, he cannot judge of the visions which he sees or the words which he utters; the ancient saying is very true, that 'only a man who has his wits can act or judge about himself and his own affairs'. And for this reason it is customary to appoint interpreters to be judges of the true inspiration. Some persons call them prophets, b being blind to the fact that they are only the expositors of dark

sayings and visions, and are not to be called prophets at all, but
only interpreters of prophecy.

Such is the nature of the liver, which is placed as we have
described in order that it may give prophetic intimations. During
the life of each individual these intimations are plainer, but after
his death the liver becomes blind, and delivers oracles too obscure
c to be intelligible. The neighbouring organ [the spleen] is situated
on the left-hand side, and is constructed with a view of keeping
the liver bright and pure,—like a napkin, always ready prepared
and at hand to clean the mirror. And hence, when any impurities
arise in the region of the liver by reason of disorders of the body,
the loose nature of the spleen, which is composed of a hollow and
bloodless tissue, receives them all and clears them away; and
d when filled with the unclean matter, it swells and festers, but,
again, when the body is purged, shrinks and settles down into
the same place as before.

Concerning the soul, as to which part is mortal and which divine,
and how and why they are separated, and in what company they
are placed, if God acknowledges that we have spoken the truth,
then, and then only, can we be confident; still, we may venture to
assert that what has been said by us is probable, and will be rendered more probable by investigation. Let us assume thus much.
e The creation of the rest of the body follows next in order, and
this we may investigate in a similar manner. And it appears to
be very meet that the body should be framed on the following
principles:—

The authors of our race were aware that we should be intemperate in eating and drinking, and take a good deal more than
was necessary or proper, by reason of gluttony. In order then that
disease might not quickly destroy us, and lest our mortal race
73 should perish without fulfilling its end—intending to provide
against this, the gods made what is called the lower belly, to be a
receptacle for the superfluous meat and drink, and formed the
convolution of the bowels, so that the food might be prevented
from passing quickly through and compelling the body to require
more food, thus producing insatiable gluttony, and making the
whole race an enemy to philosophy and culture, and rebellious
against the divinest element within us.
b The bones and flesh, and other similar parts of us, were made

as follows. The first principle of all of them was the generation of the marrow. For the bonds of life which unite the soul with the body are made fast there, and they are the root and foundation of the human race. The marrow itself is created out of other materials: God took such of the primary triangles as were straight and smooth, and were adapted to produce fire and water, and air and earth in the highest perfection—these, I say, he separated from their kinds, and mingling them in due proportions with c one another, made the marrow out of them to be a universal seed of every mortal kind; and in this seed he then planted and enclosed the souls, and in the original distribution gave to the marrow as many and various forms as the different kinds of souls were hereafter to receive. That which, like a field, was to receive the divine seed, he made round every way, and called that portion of the marrow, brain, intending that, when an animal was perfected, the vessel containing this substance should be the d head; but that which was intended to contain the remaining and mortal part of the soul he distributed into figures at once round and elongated, and he called them all by the name 'marrow'; and to these, as to anchors, fastening the bonds of the whole soul, he proceeded to fashion around them the entire framework of our body, constructing for the marrow, first of all, a complete covering of bone.

Bone was composed by him in the following manner. Having sifted pure and smooth earth he kneaded it and wetted it with e marrow, and after that he put it into fire and then into water, and once more into fire and again into water—in this way by frequent transfers from one to the other he made it insoluble by either. Out of this he fashioned, as in a lathe, a globe made of bone, which he placed around the brain, and in this he left a narrow 74 opening; and around the marrow of the neck and back he formed vertebrae which he placed under one another like pivots, beginning at the head and extending through the whole of the trunk. Thus wishing to preserve the entire seed, he enclosed it in a stone-like casing, inserting joints, and using in the formation of them the power of the other or diverse as an intermediate nature, that they might have motion and flexure. Then again, considering that the bone would be too brittle and inflexible, and when b heated and again cooled would soon mortify and destroy the seed

within—having this in view, he contrived the sinews and the
flesh, that so binding all the members together by the sinews,
which admitted of being stretched and relaxed about the vertebrae, he might thus make the body capable of flexion and extension, while the flesh would serve as a protection against the
summer heat and against the winter cold, and also against falls,
softly and easily yielding to external bodies, like articles made of
c felt; and containing in itself a warm moisture which in summer
exudes and makes the surface damp, would impart a natural
coolness to the whole body; and again in winter by the help of
this internal warmth would form a very tolerable defence against
the frost which surrounds it and attacks it from without. He who
modelled us, considering these things, mixed earth with fire and
water and blended them; and making a ferment of acid and salt,
d he mingled it with them and formed soft and succulent flesh. As
for the sinews, he made them of a mixture of bone and unfermented flesh, attempered so as to be in a mean, and gave them a
yellow colour; wherefore the sinews have a firmer and more
glutinous nature than flesh, but a softer and moister nature than
the bones. With these God covered the bones and marrow, binding them together by sinews, and then enshrouded them all in an
e upper covering of flesh. The more living and sensitive of the
bones he enclosed in the thinnest film of flesh, and those which
had the least life within them in the thickest and most solid flesh.
So again on the joints of the bones, where reason indicated that
no more was required, he placed only a thin covering of flesh,
that it might not interfere with the flexion of our bodies and
make them unwieldy because difficult to move; and also that it
might not, by being crowded and pressed and matted together,
destroy sensation by reason of its hardness, and impair the
75 memory and dull the edge of intelligence. Wherefore also the
thighs and the shanks and the hips, and the bones of the arms and
the forearms, and other parts which have no joints, and the inner
bones, which on account of the rarity of the soul in their marrow
are destitute of reason—all these are abundantly provided with
flesh; but such as have mind in them are in general less fleshy,
except where the creator has made some part solely of flesh in
order to give sensation,—as, for example, the tongue. But commonly this is not the case. For the nature which comes into being

and grows up in us by a law of necessity does not admit of the b
combination of solid bone and much flesh with acute perceptions.
More than any other part the framework of the head would have
had them, if they could have co-existed, and the human race,
having a strong and fleshy and sinewy head, would have had a
life twice or many times as long as it now has, and also more
healthy and free from pain. But our creators, considering whether
they should make a longer-lived race which was worse, or a c
shorter-lived race which was better, came to the conclusion that
every one ought to prefer a shorter span of life, which was better,
to a longer one which was worse; and therefore they covered the
head with thin bone, but not with flesh and sinews, since it had
no joints; and thus the head was added, having more wisdom
and sensation than the rest of the body, but also being in every
man far weaker. For these reasons and after this manner God d
placed the sinews at the extremity of the head, in a circle round
the neck, and glued them together by the principle of likeness
and fastened the extremities of the jawbones to them below the
face, and the other sinews he dispersed throughout the body,
fastening limb to limb. The framers of us framed the mouth, as
now arranged, having teeth and tongue and lips, with a view to
the necessary and the good, contriving the way in for necessary e
purposes, the way out for the best purposes; for that is necessary
which enters in and gives food to the body; but the river of
speech, which flows out of a man and ministers to the intelligence,
is the fairest and noblest of all streams. Still the head could
neither be left a bare frame of bones, on account of the extremes
of heat and cold in the different seasons, nor yet be allowed to be
wholly covered, and so become dull and senseless by reason of an
overgrowth of flesh. The fleshy nature was not therefore wholly
dried up, but a large sort of peel was parted off and remained 76
over, which is now called the skin. This met and grew by the
help of the cerebral moisture, and became the circular envelopment of the head. And the moisture, rising up under the sutures,
watered and closed in the skin upon the crown, forming a sort of
knot. The diversity of the sutures was caused by the power of the
courses within the soul and of the food; the sutures were more
numerous where these were strongly opposed to one another,
fewer if the struggle were less violent. This skin the divine power b

pierced all round with fire, and out of the punctures which were thus made the moisture issued forth, and the liquid and heat which was pure came away, and a mixed part which was composed of the same material as the skin, and had a fineness equal to the punctures, was borne up by its own impulse and extended far outside the head, but being too slow to escape, was thrust

c back by the external air, and rolled up underneath the skin, where it took root. Thus the hair sprang up in the skin, being akin to it because it is like threads of leather, but rendered harder and closer through the pressure of the cold, by which each hair, while in process of separation from the skin, is compressed and cooled. Wherefore the creator formed the head hairy, making use of the causes which I have mentioned, and reflecting also that instead

d of flesh the brain needed the hair to be a light covering or guard, which would give shade in summer and shelter in winter, and at the same time would not impede our quickness of perception. From the combination of sinew, skin, and bone, in the structure of the finger, there arises a triple compound, which, when dried up, takes the form of one hard skin partaking of all three natures, and was fabricated by these second causes, but designed by mind which is the principal cause with an eye to the future. For our

e creators well knew that women and other animals would some day be framed out of men, and they further knew that many animals would require the use of nails for many purposes; wherefore they fashioned in men at their first creation the rudiments of nails. For this purpose and for these reasons they caused skin, hair, and nails to grow at the extremities of the limbs.

And now that all the parts and members of the mortal animal

77 had come together, since its life of necessity consisted of fire and breath,[1] and it therefore wasted away by dissolution and depletion, the gods contrived the following remedy: They mingled a nature akin to that of man with other forms and perceptions, and thus created another kind of animal. These are the trees and plants and seeds which have been improved by cultivation and are now domesticated among us; anciently there were only the

b wild kinds, which are older than the cultivated. For everything that partakes of life may be truly called a living being, and the animal of which we are now speaking partakes of the third kind

[1] [Or 'had to be passed amid fire and air'.]

of soul, which is said to be seated between the midriff and the navel, having no part in opinion or reason or mind, but only in feelings of pleasure and pain and the desires which accompany them. For this nature is always in a passive state, and is not endowed by nature with the power of revolving in and about itself, repelling the motion from without and using its own, in such a way as to observe and reflect upon any of its own concerns. c Wherefore it lives and does not differ from a living being, but is fixed and rooted in the same spot, having no power of self-motion.

Now after the superior powers had created all these natures to be food for us who are of the inferior nature, they cut various channels through the body as through a garden, that it might be watered as from a running stream. In the first place, they cut two hidden channels or veins down the back where the skin and the d flesh join, which answered severally to the right and left side of the body. These they let down along the backbone, so as to have the marrow of generation between them, where it was most likely to flourish, and in order that the stream coming down from above might flow freely to the other parts, and equalize the irrigation. In the next place, they divided the veins about the head, and interlacing them, they sent them in opposite directions; those e coming from the right side they sent to the left of the body, and those from the left they diverted towards the right, so that they and the skin might together form a bond which should fasten the head to the body, since the crown of the head was not encircled by sinews; and also in order that the sensations from both sides might be distributed over the whole body. And next, they ordered the water-courses of the body in a manner which I will describe, and which will be more easily understood if we begin 78 by admitting that all things composed of lesser parts retain the greater, but those composed of greater parts cannot retain the lesser. Now of all natures fire has the smallest parts, and therefore penetrates through earth and water and air and their compounds, nor can anything hold it. And a similar principle applies to the human belly; for when meats and drinks enter it, it holds them, but it cannot hold air and fire, because the particles of b which they consist are smaller than its own structure.

These elements, therefore, God employed for the sake of distributing moisture from the belly into the veins, weaving together a network of fire and air like a creel, having at the entrance two lesser creels; further he constructed one of these with two openings, and from the lesser creels he extended cords reaching all round to c the extremities of the network. All the interior of the net he made of fire, but the lesser creels and their cavity, of air. The network he took and spread over the newly formed animal in the following manner:—He let the lesser creels pass into the mouth; there were two of them, and one he let down by the air-pipes into the lungs, the other by the side of the air-pipes into the belly. The former he divided into two branches, both of which he made to pass out at the channels of the nose, so that when the way through the mouth was not open, the streams of the mouth as well were replenished d through the nose. With the other cavity (i.e. of the greater creel) he enveloped the hollow parts of the body, and at one time he made all this to flow into the lesser creels, quite gently, for they are composed of air, and at another time he caused the lesser creels to flow back again; and the net he made to find a way in and out through the pores of the body, and the rays of fire which are bound fast within followed the passage of the air either way, e never at any time ceasing so long as the mortal being holds together. This process, as we affirm, the name-giver named inspiration and expiration. And all this movement, active as well as passive, takes place in order that the body, being watered and cooled, may receive nourishment and life; for when the respiration is going in and out, and the fire, which is fast bound within, follows it, and ever and anon moving to and fro, enters through 79 the belly and reaches the meat and drink, it dissolves them, and dividing them into small portions and guiding them through the passages where it goes, pumps them as from a fountain into the channels of the veins, and makes the stream of the veins flow through the body as through a conduit.

Let us once more consider the phenomena of respiration, and inquire into the causes which have made it what it is. They are b as follows:—Seeing that there is no such thing as a vacuum into which any of those things which are moved can enter, and the breath is carried from us into the external air, the next point is, as will be clear to every one, that it does not go into a vacant space, but pushes its neighbour out of its place, and that which is

thrust out in turn drives out its neighbour; and in this way everything of necessity at last comes round to that place from whence
the breath came forth, and enters in there, and following the
breath, fills up the vacant space; and this goes on like the rotation c
of a wheel, because there can be no such thing as a vacuum.
Wherefore also the breast and the lungs, when they emit the
breath, are replenished by the air which surrounds the body and
which enters in through the pores of the flesh and is driven round
in a circle; and again, the air which is sent away and passes out
through the body forces the breath inwards through the passage
of the mouth and the nostrils. Now the origin of this movement
may be supposed to be as follows. In the interior of every animal
the hottest part is that which is around the blood and veins; it is d
in a manner an internal fountain of fire, which we compared to
the network of a creel, being woven all of fire and extended
through the centre of the body, while the outer parts are composed of air. Now we must admit that heat naturally proceeds
outward to its own place and to its kindred element; and as there
are two exits for the heat, the one out through the body, and the
other through the mouth and nostrils, when it moves towards the e
one, it drives round the air at the other, and that which is driven
round falls into the fire and becomes warm, and that which goes
forth is cooled. But when the heat changes its place, and the
particles at the other exit grow warmer, the hotter air inclining in
that direction and carried towards its native element, fire, pushes
round the air at the other; and this being affected in the same
way and communicating the same impulse, a circular motion
swaying to and fro is produced by the double process, which we
call inspiration and expiration.

The phenomena of medical cupping-glasses and of the swallowing of drink and of the projection of bodies, whether discharged 80
in the air or bowled along the ground, are to be investigated on a
similar principle; and swift and slow sounds, which appear to be
high and low, and are sometimes discordant on account of their
inequality, and then again harmonical on account of the equality
of the motion which they excite in us. For when the motions of
the antecedent swifter sounds begin to pause and the two are
equalized, the slower sounds overtake the swifter and then propel b
them. When they overtake them they do not intrude a new and

discordant motion, but introduce the beginnings of a slower, which answers to the swifter as it dies away, thus producing a single mixed expression out of high and low, whence arises a pleasure which even the unwise feel, and which to the wise becomes a higher sort of delight, being an imitation of divine harmony in mortal motions. Moreover, as to the flowing of

c water, the fall of the thunderbolt, and the marvels that are observed about the attraction of amber and the Heraclean stones, —in none of these cases is there any attraction; but he who investigates rightly, will find that such wonderful phenomena are attributable to the combination of certain conditions,—the non-existence of a vacuum, the fact that objects push one another round, and that they change places, passing severally into their proper positions as they are divided or combined.

d   Such, as we have seen, is the nature and such are the causes of respiration,—the subject in which this discussion originated. For the fire cuts the food and following the breath surges up within, fire and breath rising together and filling the veins by drawing up out of the belly and pouring into them the cut portions of the food; and so the streams of food are kept flowing through the whole body in all animals. And fresh cuttings from kindred

e substances, whether the fruits of the earth or herb of the field, which God planted to be our daily food, acquire all sorts of colours by their intermixture; but red is the most pervading of them, a quality created by the cutting action of fire and by the impression which it makes on a moist substance; and hence the liquid which circulates in the body has a colour such as we have described. The liquid itself we call blood, which nourishes the

81 flesh and the whole body, whence all parts are watered and empty places filled.

Now the process of repletion and evacuation is effected after the manner of the universal motion by which all kindred substances are drawn towards one another. For the external elements which surround us are always causing us to consume away, and distributing and sending off like to like; the particles of blood, too, which are divided and contained within the frame of the animal

b as in a sort of heaven, are compelled to imitate the motion of the universe. Each, therefore, of the divided parts within us, being carried to its kindred nature, replenishes the void. When more is taken away than flows in, then we decay, and when less, we grow and increase.

The frame of the entire creature when young has the triangles of each kind new, and may be compared to the keel of a vessel which is just off the stocks; they are locked firmly together and yet the whole mass is soft and delicate, being freshly formed of marrow and nurtured on milk. Now when the triangles out of c which meats and drinks are composed come in from without, and are comprehended in the body, being older and weaker than the triangles already there, the frame of the body gets the better of them and its newer triangles cut them up, and so the animal grows great, being nourished by a multitude of similar particles. But when the roots of the triangles are loosened by having undergone many conflicts with many things in the course of time, they are no longer able to cut or assimilate the food which enters, but d are themselves easily divided by the bodies which come in from without. In this way every animal is overcome and decays, and this affection is called old age. And at last, when the bonds by which the triangles of the marrow are united no longer hold, and are parted by the strain of existence, they in turn loosen the bonds of the soul, and she, obtaining a natural release, flies away with joy. For that which takes place according to nature is pleasant, e but that which is contrary to nature is painful. And thus death, if caused by disease or produced by wounds, is painful and violent; but that sort of death which comes with old age and fulfils the debt of nature is the easiest of deaths, and is accompanied with pleasure rather than with pain.

Now every one can see whence diseases arise. There are four natures out of which the body is compacted, earth and fire and 82 water and air, and the unnatural excess or defect of these, or the change of any of them from its own natural place into another, or—since there are more kinds than one of fire and of the other elements—the assumption by any of these of a wrong kind, or any similar irregularity, produces disorders and diseases; for when any of them is produced or changed in a manner contrary to nature, the parts which were previously cool grow warm, and b those which were dry become moist, and the light become heavy, and the heavy light; all sorts of changes occur. For, as we affirm, a thing can only remain the same with itself, whole and sound, when the same is added to it, or subtracted from it, in the same respect and in the same manner and in due proportion; and whatever comes or goes away in violation of these laws causes all manner of changes and infinite diseases and corruptions. Now there is a second class of structures which are also natural, and

c this affords a second opportunity of observing diseases to him who would understand them. For whereas marrow and bone and flesh and sinews are composed of the four elements, and the blood, though after another manner, is likewise formed out of them, most diseases originate in the way which I have described; but the worst of all owe their severity to the fact that the generation of these substances proceeds in a wrong order; they are then destroyed. For the natural order is that the flesh and sinews should be made of blood, the sinews out of the fibres to which

d they are akin, and the flesh out of the clots which are formed when the fibres are separated. And the glutinous and rich matter which comes away from the sinews and the flesh, not only glues the flesh to the bones, but nourishes and imparts growth to the bone which surrounds the marrow; and there remains a part, consisting of the purest and smoothest and oiliest sort of triangles, which filters through the solid texture of the bones, from which it

e drops like dew and waters the marrow. Now when each process takes place in this order, health commonly results; when in the opposite order, disease. For when the flesh becomes decomposed and sends back the wasting substance into the veins, then an over-supply of blood of diverse kinds, mingling with air in the veins, having variegated colours and bitter properties, as well as acid and saline qualities, contains all sorts of bile and serum and phlegm. For all things go the wrong way, and having become

83 corrupted, first they taint the blood itself, and then ceasing to give nourishment to the body they are carried along the veins in all directions, no longer preserving the order of their natural courses, but at war with themselves, because they receive no good from one another, and are hostile to the abiding constitution of the body, which they corrupt and dissolve. The oldest part of the flesh which is corrupted, being hard to decompose, from long burning grows black, and from being everywhere corroded

b becomes bitter, and is injurious to every part of the body which is still uncorrupted. Sometimes, when the bitter element is refined away, the black part assumes an acidity which takes the place of the bitterness; at other times the bitterness being tinged with blood has a redder colour; and this, when mixed with black, takes the hue of grass; and again, an auburn colour mingles with the bitter matter when new flesh is decomposed by the fire which surrounds the internal flame;—to all which symptoms some c physician perhaps, or rather some philosopher, who had the power of seeing in many dissimilar things one nature deserving of a name, has assigned the common name of bile. But the other kinds of bile are variously distinguished by their colours. As for serum, that sort which is the watery part of blood is innocent, but that which is a secretion of black and acid bile is malignant when mingled by the power of heat with any salt substance, and is then called acid phlegm. Again, the substance which is formed by the liquefaction of new and tender flesh when air is present, if inflated and encased in liquid so as to form bubbles, which d separately are invisible owing to their small size, but when collected are of a bulk which is visible, and have a white colour arising out of the generation of foam—all this decomposition of tender flesh when intermingled with air is termed by us white phlegm. And the whey or sediment of newly formed phlegm is sweat and tears, and includes the various daily discharges by e which the body is purified. Now all these become causes of disease when the blood is not replenished in a natural manner by food and drink but gains bulk from opposite sources in violation of the laws of nature. When the several parts of the flesh are separated 84 by disease, if the foundation remains, the power of the disorder is only half as great, and there is still a prospect of an easy recovery; but when that which binds the flesh to the bones is diseased, and no longer being separated off from the muscles and sinews,[1] ceases to give nourishment to the bone and to unite flesh and bone, and from being oily and smooth and glutinous becomes rough and salt and dry, owing to bad regimen, then all the substance thus corrupted crumbles away under the flesh and the sinews, and separates from the bone, and the fleshy parts fall away from their foundation and leave the sinews bare and full b of brine, and the flesh again gets into the circulation of the blood and makes the previously mentioned disorders still greater. And

[1] Reading αὐτό for αὖ τό and ἅμα for αἷμα.

if these bodily affections be severe, still worse are the prior disorders; as when the bone itself, by reason of the density of the flesh, does not obtain sufficient air, but becomes mouldy and hot

c and gangrened and receives no nutriment, and the natural process is inverted, and the bone crumbling passes into the food, and the food into the flesh, and the flesh again falling into the blood makes all maladies that may occur more virulent than those already mentioned. But the worst case of all is when the marrow is diseased, either from excess or defect; and this is the cause of the very greatest and most fatal disorders, in which the whole course of the body is reversed.

There is a third class of diseases which may be conceived of as arising in three ways; for they are produced sometimes by wind,

d and sometimes by phlegm, and sometimes by bile. When the lung, which is the dispenser of the air to the body, is obstructed by rheums and its passages are not free, some of them not acting, while through others too much air enters, then the parts which are unrefreshed by air corrode, while in other parts the excess of air forcing its way through the veins distorts them and decomposing the body is enclosed in the midst of it and occupies the midriff; thus numberless painful diseases are produced, accom-

e panied by copious sweats. And oftentimes when the flesh is dissolved in the body, wind, generated within and unable to escape, is the source of quite as much pain as the air coming in from without; but the greatest pain is felt when the wind gets about the sinews and the veins of the shoulders, and swells them up, and so twists back the great tendons and the sinews which are connected with them. These disorders are called tetanus and opisthotonus, by reason of the tension which accompanies them. The cure of them is difficult; relief is in most cases given by fever

85 supervening. The white phlegm, though dangerous when detained within by reason of the air-bubbles, yet if it can communicate with the outside air, is less severe, and only discolours the body, generating leprous eruptions and similar diseases. When it is mingled with black bile and dispersed about the courses of the

b head, which are the divinest part of us, the attack if coming on in sleep, is not so severe; but when assailing those who are awake it is hard to be got rid of, and being an affection of a sacred part, is most justly called sacred. An acid and salt phlegm, again, is the source of all those diseases which take the form of catarrh, but they have many names because the places into which they flow are manifold.

Inflammations of the body come from burnings and inflamings, and all of them originate in bile. When bile finds a means of discharge, it boils up and sends forth all sorts of tumours; but when c imprisoned within, it generates many inflammatory diseases, above all when mingled with pure blood; since it then displaces the fibres which are scattered about in the blood and are designed to maintain the balance of rare and dense, in order that the blood may not be so liquefied by heat as to exude from the pores of the body, nor again become too dense and thus find a difficulty in d circulating through the veins. The fibres are so constituted as to maintain this balance; and if any one brings them all together when the blood is dead and in process of cooling, then the blood which remains becomes fluid, but if they are left alone, they soon congeal by reason of the surrounding cold. The fibres having this power over the blood, bile, which is only stale blood, and which from being flesh is dissolved again into blood, at the first influx coming in little by little, hot and liquid, is congealed by the power of the fibres; and so congealing and made to cool, it e produces internal cold and shuddering. When it enters with more of a flood and overcomes the fibres by its heat, and boiling up throws them into disorder, if it have power enough to maintain its supremacy, it penetrates the marrow and burns up what may be termed the cables of the soul, and sets her free; but when there is not so much of it, and the body though wasted still holds out, the bile is itself mastered, and is either exuded from the whole body, or is thrust through the veins into the lower or upper belly, and is driven out of the body like an exile from a state in which there has been civil war; whence arise diarrhoeas and dysenteries, 86 and all such disorders. When the constitution is disordered by excess of fire, continuous heat and fever are the result; when excess of air is the cause, then the fever is quotidian; when of water, which is a more sluggish element than either fire or air, then the fever is a tertian; when of earth, which is the most sluggish of the four, and is only purged away in a four-fold period, the result is a quartan fever, which can with difficulty be shaken off.

b   Such is the manner in which diseases of the body arise; the disorders of the soul, which depend upon the body, originate as follows. We must acknowledge disease of the mind to be a want of intelligence; and of this there are two kinds; to wit, madness and ignorance. In whatever state a man experiences either of them, that state may be called disease; and excessive pains and pleasures are justly to be regarded as the greatest diseases to which the soul is liable. For a man who is in great joy or in great

c   pain, in his unseasonable eagerness to attain the one and to avoid the other, is not able to see or to hear anything rightly; but he is mad, and is at the time utterly incapable of any participation in reason. He who has the seed about the spinal marrow too plentiful and overflowing, like a tree overladen with fruit, has many throes, and also obtains many pleasures in his desires and their offspring, and is for the most part of his life deranged,

d   because his pleasures and pains are so very great; his soul is rendered foolish and disordered by his body; yet he is regarded not as one diseased, but as one who is voluntarily bad, which is a mistake. The truth is that sexual intemperance is a disease of the soul due chiefly to the moisture and fluidity which is produced in one of the elements by the loose consistency of the bones. And in general, all that which is termed the incontinence of pleasure and is deemed a reproach under the idea that the wicked voluntarily do wrong is not justly a matter for reproach. For no man is

e   voluntarily bad; but the bad become bad by reason of an ill disposition of the body and bad education, things which are hateful to every man and happen to him against his will. And in the case of pain too in like manner the soul suffers much evil from the body. For where the acid and briny phlegm and other bitter and bilious humours wander about in the body, and find no exit or escape, but are pent up within and mingle their own

87   vapours with the motions of the soul, and are blended with them, they produce all sorts of diseases, more or fewer, and in every degree of intensity; and being carried to the three places of the soul, whichever they may severally assail, they create infinite varieties of ill-temper and melancholy, of rashness and cowardice, and also of forgetfulness and stupidity. Further, when to this evil

b   constitution of body evil forms of government are added and evil discourses are uttered in private as well as in public, and no sort of instruction is given in youth to cure these evils, then all of us who are bad become bad from two causes which are entirely beyond our control. In such cases the planters are to blame rather than the plants, the educators rather than the educated. But however that may be, we should endeavour as far as we can by education, and pursuits, and learning, to avoid vice and attain virtue; this, however, is part of another subject.

There is a corresponding inquiry concerning the mode of treat- c ment by which the mind and the body are to be preserved, about which it is meet and right that I should say a word in turn; for it is more our duty to speak of the good than of the evil. Everything that is good is fair, and the fair is not without proportion, and the animal which is to be fair must have due proportion. Now we perceive lesser symmetries or proportions and reason about them, but of the highest and greatest we take no heed; for there is no d proportion or disproportion more productive of health and disease, and virtue and vice, than that between soul and body themselves. This however we do not perceive, nor do we reflect that when a weak or small frame is the vehicle of a great and mighty soul, or conversely, when a little soul is encased in a large body, then the whole animal is not fair, for it lacks the most important of all symmetries; but the due proportion of mind and body is the fairest and loveliest of all sights to him who has the seeing eye. Just as a body which has a leg too long, or which is e unsymmetrical in some other respect, is an unpleasant sight, and also, when doing its share of work, is much distressed and makes convulsive efforts, and often stumbles through awkwardness, and is the cause of infinite evil to its own self—in like manner we should conceive of the double nature which we call the living being; and when in this compound there is an impassioned soul more powerful than the body, that soul, I say, convulses and fills 88 with disorders the whole inner nature of man; and when eager in the pursuit of some sort of learning or study, causes wasting; or again, when teaching or disputing in private or in public, and strifes and controversies arise, inflames and dissolves the composite frame of man and introduces rheums; and the nature of this phenomenon is not understood by most professors of medicine, who ascribe it to the opposite of the real cause. And once more, when a body large and too strong for the soul is united to a small b and weak intelligence, then inasmuch as there are two desires natural to man,—one of food for the sake of the body, and one of wisdom for the sake of the diviner part of us—then, I say, the motions of the stronger, getting the better and increasing their own power, but making the soul dull, and stupid, and forgetful, engender ignorance, which is the greatest of diseases. There is one protection against both kinds of disproportion:—that we should not move the body without the soul or the soul without the body, and thus they will be on their guard against each other, and be

c healthy and well balanced. And therefore the mathematician or any one else whose thoughts are much absorbed in some intellectual pursuit, must allow his body also to have due exercise, and practise gymnastic; and he who is careful to fashion the body, should in turn impart to the soul its proper motions, and should cultivate the arts and all philosophy, if he would deserve to be called truly fair and truly good. And the separate parts should be

d treated in the same manner, in imitation of the pattern of the universe; for as the body is heated and also cooled within by the elements which enter into it, and is again dried up and moistened by external things, and experiences these and the like affections from both kinds of motions, the result is that the body if given up to motion when in a state of quiescence is overmastered and perishes; but if any one, in imitation of that which we call the foster-mother and nurse of the universe, will not allow the body ever to be inactive, but is always producing motions and agita-

e tions through its whole extent, which form the natural defence against other motions both internal and external, and by moderate exercise reduces to order according to their affinities the particles and affections which are wandering about the body, as we have already said when speaking of the universe,[1] he will not allow enemy placed by the side of enemy to stir up wars and disorders in the body, but he will place friend by the side of friend, so as to create health. Now of all motions that is the best which is

89 produced in a thing by itself, for it is most akin to the motion of thought and of the universe; but that motion which is caused by others is not so good, and worst of all is that which moves the body, when at rest, in parts only and by some external agency. Wherefore of all modes of purifying and re-uniting the body the

[1] *Supra*, 33 a.

best is gymnastic; the next best is a surging motion, as in sailing
or any other mode of conveyance which is not fatiguing; the
third sort of motion may be of use in a case of extreme necessity, b
but in any other will be adopted by no man of sense: I mean the
purgative treatment of physicians; for diseases unless they are
very dangerous should not be irritated by medicines, since every
form of disease is in a manner akin to the living being, whose
complex frame has an appointed term of life. For not the whole
race only, but each individual—barring inevitable accidents— c
comes into the world having a fixed span, and the triangles in us
are originally framed with power to last for a certain time, beyond
which no man can prolong his life. And this holds also of the
constitution of diseases; if any one regardless of the appointed
time tries to subdue them by medicine, he only aggravates and
multiplies them. Wherefore we ought always to manage them by
regimen, as far as a man can spare the time, and not provoke a d
disagreeable enemy by medicines.

Enough of the composite animal, and of the body which is a
part of him, and of the manner in which a man may train and be
trained by himself so as to live most according to reason: and we
must above and before all provide that the element which is to
train him shall be the fairest and best adapted to that purpose.
A minute discussion of this subject would be a serious task;[1] but e
if, as before, I am to give only an outline, the subject may not
unfitly be summed up as follows.

I have often remarked that there are three kinds of soul located
within us, having each of them motions, and I must now repeat
in the fewest words possible, that one part, if remaining inactive
and ceasing from its natural motion, must necessarily become
very weak, but that which is trained and exercised, very strong.
Wherefore we should take care that the movements of the differ- 90
ent parts of the soul should be in due proportion.

And we should consider that God gave the sovereign part of
the human soul to be the divinity of each one, being that part
which, as we say, dwells at the top of the body, and inasmuch as
we are a plant not of an earthly but of a heavenly growth, raises
us from earth to our kindred who are in heaven. And in this we
say truly; for the divine power suspends the head and root of us

_____
[1] [Ed. 1 better 'a sufficiently long business of itself'.]

b　from that place where the generation of the soul first began, and thus makes the whole body upright. When a man is always occupied with the cravings of desire and ambition, and is eagerly striving to satisfy them, all his thoughts must be mortal, and, as far as it is possible altogether to become such, he must be mortal every whit, because he has cherished his mortal part. But he who has been earnest in the love of knowledge and of true wisdom, and has exercised his intellect more than any other part of him,

c　must have thoughts immortal and divine, if he attain truth, and in so far as human nature is capable of sharing in immortality, he must altogether be immortal; and since he is ever cherishing the divine power, and has the divinity within him in perfect order, he will be singularly happy. Now there is only one way of taking care of things, and this is to give to each the food and motion which are natural to it. And the motions which are naturally akin to the divine principle within us are the thoughts

d　and revolutions of the universe. These each man should follow, and by learning the harmonies and revolutions of the universe, should correct the courses of the head which were corrupted at our birth, and should assimilate the thinking being to the thought, renewing his original nature, so that having assimilated them he may attain to that best life which the gods have set before mankind, both for the present and the future.

e　　Thus our original design of discoursing about the universe down to the creation of man is nearly completed. A brief mention may be made of the generation of other animals, so far as the subject admits of brevity; in this manner our argument will best attain a due proportion. On the subject of animals, then, the following remarks may be offered. Of the men who came into the world, those who were cowards or led unrighteous lives may with reason be supposed to have changed into the nature of

91　women in the second generation. And this was the reason why at that time the gods created in us the desire of sexual intercourse, contriving in man one animated substance, and in woman another, which they formed respectively in the following manner. The outlet for drink by which liquids pass through the lung under the kidneys and into the bladder, which receives and then by the pressure of the air emits them, was so fashioned by them as to penetrate also into the body of the marrow, which passes

from the head along the neck and through the back, and which b
in the preceding discourse we have named the seed. And the
seed having life, and becoming endowed with respiration, produces in that part in which it respires a lively desire of emission,
and thus creates in us the love of procreation. Wherefore also in
men the organ of generation becoming rebellious and masterful,
like an animal disobedient to reason, and maddened with the
sting of lust, seeks to gain absolute sway; and the same is the case c
with the so-called womb or matrix of women; the animal within
them is desirous of procreating children, and when remaining
unfruitful long beyond its proper time, gets discontented and
angry, and wandering in every direction through the body, closes
up the passages of the breath, and, by obstructing respiration,
drives them to extremity, causing all varieties of disease, until at
length the desire and love of the man and the woman, bringing
them together[1] and as it were plucking the fruit from the tree, d
sow in the womb, as in a field, animals unseen by reason of their
smallness and without form; these again are separated and
matured within; they are then finally brought out into the light,
and thus the generation of animals is completed.

Thus were created women and the female sex in general. But
the race of birds was created out of innocent lightminded men,
who, although their minds were directed toward heaven, imagined, in their simplicity, that the clearest demonstration of the
things above was to be obtained by sight; these were remodelled
and transformed into birds, and they grew feathers instead of
hair. The race of wild pedestrian animals, again, came from those e
who had no philosophy in any of their thoughts, and never
considered at all about the nature of the heavens, because they
had ceased to use the courses of the head, but followed the
guidance of those parts of the soul which are in the breast. In
consequence of these habits of theirs they had their front legs and
their heads resting upon the earth to which they were drawn by
natural affinity; and the crowns of their heads were elongated
and of all sorts of shapes, into which the courses of the soul were
crushed by reason of disuse. And this was the reason why they
were created quadrupeds and polypods: God gave the more 92
senseless of them the more support that they might be more

---

[1] Reading ξυνδυάζοντες (conj. Hermann).

attracted to the earth. And the most foolish of them, who trail their bodies entirely upon the ground and have no longer any need of feet, he made without feet to crawl upon the earth. The

b fourth class were the inhabitants of the water: these were made out of the most entirely senseless and ignorant of all, whom the transformers did not think any longer worthy of pure respiration, because they possessed a soul which was made impure by all sorts of transgression; and instead of the subtle and pure medium of air, they gave them the deep and muddy sea to be their element of respiration; and hence arose the race of fishes and oysters, and other aquatic animals, which have received the most remote

c habitations as a punishment of their outlandish ignorance. These are the laws by which all animals pass into one another, now, as in the beginning, changing as they lose or gain wisdom and folly.

We may now say that our discourse about the nature of the universe has an end. The world has received animals, mortal and immortal, and is fulfilled with them, and has become a visible animal containing the visible—the sensible God who is the image of the intellectual,[1] the greatest, best, fairest, most perfect—the one only-begotten heaven.

[1] Or reading ποιητοῦ—'of his maker'.

CRITIAS

INTRODUCTION AND ANALYSIS

THE *Critias* is a fragment which breaks off in the middle of a sentence. It was designed to be the second part of a trilogy, which, like the other great Platonic trilogy of the *Sophist, Statesman, Philosopher*, was never completed. Timaeus had brought down the origin of the world to the creation of man, and the dawn of history was now to succeed the philosophy of nature. The *Critias* is also connected with the *Republic*. Plato, as he has already told us (*Tim.* 19, 20), intended to represent the ideal state engaged in a patriotic conflict. This mythical conflict is prophetic or symbolical of the struggle of Athens and Persia, perhaps in some degree also of the wars of the Greeks and Carthaginians, in the same way that the Persian is prefigured by the Trojan war to the mind of Herodotus, or as the narrative of the first part of the *Aeneid* is intended by Virgil to foreshadow the wars of Carthage and Rome. The small number of the primitive Athenian citizens (20,000), 'which is about their present number' (*Crit.* 112 d), is evidently designed to contrast with the myriads and barbaric array of the Atlantic hosts. The passing remark in the *Timaeus* (25 c) that Athens was left alone in the struggle, in which she conquered and became the liberator of Greece, is also an allusion to the later history. Hence we may safely conclude that the entire narrative is due to the imagination of Plato, who has used the name of Solon and introduced the Egyptian priests to give verisimilitude to his story. To the Greek such a tale, like that of the earth-born men, would have seemed perfectly accordant with the character of his mythology, and not more marvellous than the wonders of the East narrated by Herodotus and others: he might have been deceived into believing it. But it appears strange that later ages should have been imposed upon by the fiction. As many attempts have been made to find the great island of Atlantis, as to discover the country of the lost tribes. Without regard to the description of Plato, and without a suspicion that the whole narrative is a fabrication, interpreters have looked for the spot in every part of the globe, America, Arabia Felix, Ceylon, Palestine, Sardinia, Sweden.

ANALYSIS

106   Timaeus concludes with a prayer that his words may be acceptable to the God whom he has revealed, and Critias, whose turn
107 follows, begs that a larger measure of indulgence may be conceded to him, because he has to speak of men whom we know
108 and not of gods whom we do not know. Socrates readily grants
his request, and anticipating that Hermocrates will make a
similar petition, extends by anticipation a like indulgence to him.

   Critias returns to his story, professing only to repeat what
Solon was told by the priests. The war of which he was about to
speak had occurred 9,000 years ago.[1] One of the combatants was
the city of Athens, the other was the great island of Atlantis.
109 Critias proposes to speak of these rival powers first of all, giving
to Athens the precedence; the various tribes of Greeks and
barbarians who took part in the war will be dealt with as they
successively appear on the scene.

   In the beginning the gods agreed to divide the earth by lot in a
friendly manner, and when they had made the allotment they
settled their several countries, and were the shepherds or rather
the pilots of mankind, whom they guided by persuasion, and not
by force. Hephaestus and Athena, brother and sister deities, in
mind and art united, obtained as their lot the land of Attica, a
land suited to the growth of virtue and wisdom; and there they
settled a brave race of children of the soil, and taught them how
to order the state. Some of their names, such as Cecrops, Erechtheus, Erichthonius, and Erysichthon, were preserved and adopted in later times, but the memory of their deeds has passed
away; for there have since been many deluges, and the remnant
who survived in the mountains were ignorant of the art of writing,
and during many generations were wholly devoted to acquiring
110 the means of life. . . . And the armed image of the goddess which
was dedicated by the ancient Athenians is an evidence to other
ages that men and women had in those days, as they ought always
to have, common virtues and pursuits. There were various classes
of citizens, including handicraftsmen and husbandmen and a
superior class of warriors who dwelt apart, and were educated,
and had all things in common, like our guardians. Attica in those

---

[1] Cf. *supra*, p. 712, footnote.

days extended southwards to the Isthmus, and inland to the
heights of Parnes and Cithaeron, and between them and the sea 111
included the district of Oropus. The country was then, as what
remains of it still is, the most fertile in the world, and abounded
in rich plains and pastures. But in the course of ages much of the
soil was washed away and disappeared in the deep sea. And the
inhabitants of this fair land were endowed with intelligence and
the love of beauty.

The Acropolis of the ancient Athens extended to the Ilissus and 112
Eridanus, and included the Pnyx, and the Lycabettus on the
opposite side to the Pnyx, having a level surface and deep soil.
The side of the hill was inhabited by craftsmen and husbandmen;
and the warriors dwelt by themselves on the summit, around the
temples of Hephaestus and Athene, in an enclosure which was
like the garden of a single house. In winter they retired into
houses on the north of the hill, in which they held their syssitia.
These were modest dwellings, which they bequeathed unaltered
to their children's children. In summer time the south side was
inhabited by them, and then they left their gardens and dining-
halls. In the midst of the Acropolis was a fountain, which gave
an abundant supply of cool water in summer and warm in
winter; of this there are still some traces. They were careful to
preserve the number of fighting men and women at 20,000, which
is equal to that of the present military force. And so they passed
their lives as guardians of the citizens and leaders of the Hellenes.
They were a just and famous race, celebrated for their beauty
and virtue all over Europe and Asia.

And now I will speak to you of their adversaries, but first I 113
ought to explain that the Greek names were given to Solon in an
Egyptian form, and he inquired their meaning and translated
them. His manuscript was left with my grandfather Dropides,
and is now in my possession. . . . In the division of the earth
Poseidon obtained as his portion the island of Atlantis, and there
he begat children whose mother was a mortal. Towards the sea
and in the centre of the island there was a very fair and fertile
plain, and near the centre, about fifty stadia from the plain, there
was a low mountain in which dwelt a man named Evenor and
his wife Leucippe, and their daughter Cleito, of whom Poseidon
became enamoured. He to secure his love enclosed the mountain

with rings or zones varying in size, two of land and three of sea, which his divine power readily enabled him to excavate and fashion, and, as there was no shipping in those days, no man could get into the place. To the interior island he conveyed under the earth springs of water hot and cold, and supplied the land
114 with all things needed for the life of man. Here he begat a family consisting of five pairs of twin male children. The eldest was Atlas, and him he made king of the centre island, while to his twin brother, Eumelus, or Gadeirus, he assigned that part of the country which was nearest the Straits. The other brothers he made chiefs over the rest of the island. And their kingdom extended as far as Egypt and Tyrrhenia. Now Atlas had a fair posterity, and great treasures derived from mines—among them that precious metal orichalcum; and there was abundance of
115 wood, and herds of elephants, and pastures for animals of all kinds, and fragrant herbs, and grasses, and trees bearing fruit. These they used, and employed themselves in constructing their temples, and palaces, and harbours, and docks, in the following manner:—First, they bridged over the zones of sea, and made a way to and from the royal palace which they built in the centre island. This ancient palace was ornamented by successive generations; and they dug a canal which passed through the zones of
116 land from the island to the sea. The zones of earth were surrounded by walls made of stone of divers colours, black and white and red, which they sometimes intermingled for the sake of ornament; and as they quarried they hollowed out beneath the edges of the zones double docks having roofs of rock. The outermost of the walls was coated with brass, the second with tin, and the third, which was the wall of the citadel, flashed with the red light of orichalcum. In the interior of the citadel was a holy temple, dedicated to Cleito and Poseidon, and surrounded by an enclosure of gold, and there was Poseidon's own temple, which was covered with silver, and the pinnacles with gold. The roof was of ivory, adorned with gold and silver and orichalcum, and the rest of the interior was lined with orichalcum. Within was an image of the god standing in a chariot drawn by six winged horses, and touching the roof with his head; around him were a hundred Nereids, riding on dolphins. Outside the temple were placed golden statues of all who had held office as kings, and of their wives;

there was an altar too, and there were palaces, corresponding to 117 the greatness and glory both of the kingdom and of the temple.

Also there were fountains of hot and cold water, and suitable buildings surrounding them, and trees, and there were baths both of the kings and of private individuals, and separate baths for women, and also for cattle. The water from the baths was carried to the grove of Poseidon, and by aqueducts over the bridges to the outer circles. And there were temples in the zones, and in the larger of the two there was a racecourse for horses, which ran all round the island. The guards were distributed in the zones according to the trust reposed in them; the most trusted of them were stationed in the citadel. The docks were full of triremes and stores. The land between the harbour and the sea was surrounded by a wall, and was crowded with dwellings, and the harbour and canal resounded with the din of human voices.

The plain around the city was highly cultivated and sheltered 118 from the north by mountains; it was oblong, and where falling out of the straight line followed the circular ditch, which was of an incredible depth. This depth received the streams which came down from the mountains, as well as the canals of the interior, and found a way to the sea. The entire country was divided into 119 sixty thousand lots, each of which was a square of ten stadia; and the owner of a lot was bound to furnish the sixth part of a war-chariot, so as to make up ten thousand chariots, two horses and riders upon them, a pair of chariot-horses without a seat, and an attendant and charioteer, two hoplites, two archers, two slingers, three stone-shooters, three javelin-men, and four sailors to make up the complement of twelve hundred ships.

Each of the ten kings was absolute in his own city and kingdom. The relations of the different governments to one another were determined by the injunctions of Poseidon, which had been inscribed by the first kings on a column of orichalcum in the temple of Poseidon, at which the kings and princes gathered together and held a festival every fifth and every sixth year alternately. Around the temple ranged the bulls of Poseidon, one of which the ten kings caught and sacrificed, shedding the blood of the victim over the inscription, and vowing not to transgress the laws of their father Poseidon. When night came, they put on azure robes and 120 gave judgement against offenders. The most important of their laws related to their dealings with one another. They were not to take up arms against one another, and were to come to the rescue if any of their brethren were attacked. They were to deliberate in common about war, and the king was not to have the power of life and death over his kinsmen, unless he had the assent of the majority.

For many generations, as tradition tells, the people of Atlantis were obedient to the laws and to the gods, and practised gentleness and wisdom in their intercourse with one another. They knew that they could only have the true use of riches by not caring 121 about them. But gradually the divine portion of their souls became diluted with too much of the mortal admixture, and they began to degenerate, though to the outward eye they appeared glorious as ever at the very time when they were filled with all iniquity. The all-seeing Zeus, wanting to punish them, held a council of the gods, and when he had called them together, he spoke as follows:—

INTRODUCTION

No one knew better than Plato how to invent 'a noble lie'. Observe (1) the innocent declaration of Socrates, that the truth of the story is a great advantage: (2) the manner in which traditional names and indications of geography are intermingled ('Why, here be truths!'): (3) the extreme minuteness with which the numbers are given, as in the Old Epic poetry: (4) the ingenious reason assigned for the Greek names occurring in the Egyptian tale (113 a): (5) the remark that the armed statue of Athena indicated the common warrior life of men and women (110 b): (6) the particularity with which the third deluge before that of Deucalion is affirmed to have been the great destruction (112 a): (7) the happy guess that great geological changes have been effected by water: (8) the indulgence of the prejudice against sailing beyond the Columns, and the popular belief of the shallowness of the ocean in that part: (9) the confession that the depth of the ditch in the Island of Atlantis was not to be believed, and 'yet he could only repeat what he had heard' (118 c), compared with the statement made in an earlier passage that Poseidon, being a God, found no difficulty in contriving the water-supply of the centre island (113 e): (10) the mention of the old rivalry of Poseidon and Athene, and the creation of the first inhabitants out of the soil. Plato here, as elsewhere, ingeniously gives the impression that he is telling the truth which mythology had corrupted.

The world, like a child, has readily, and for the most part un-hesitatingly, accepted the tale of the Island of Atlantis. In modern times we hardly seek for traces of the submerged continent; but even Mr. Grote is inclined to believe in the Egyptian poem of Solon of which there is no evidence in antiquity; while others, like Martin, discuss the Egyptian origin of the legend, or like M. de Humboldt, whom he quotes, are disposed to find in it a vestige of a widely spread tradition. Others, adopting a different vein of reflection, regard the Island of Atlantis as the anticipation of a still greater island—the Continent of America. 'The tale', says M. Martin, 'rests upon the authority of the Egyptian priests; and the Egyptian priests took a pleasure in deceiving the Greeks.' He never appears to suspect that there is a greater deceiver or magician than the Egyptian priests, that is to say, Plato himself, from the dominion of whose genius the critic and natural philosopher of modern times are not wholly emancipated. Although worthless in respect of any result which can be attained by them, discussions like those of M. Martin (*Timée*, tome i, pp. 257–332) have an interest of their own, and may be compared to the similar discussions regarding the Lost Tribes (2 Esdras xiii. 40), as showing how the chance word of some poet or philosopher has given birth to endless religious or historical inquiries. (See Introduction to the *Timaeus*, pp. 702–3.)

In contrasting the small Greek city numbering about twenty thousand inhabitants with the barbaric greatness of the island of Atlantis, Plato probably intended to show that a state, such as the ideal Athens, was invincible, though matched against any number of opponents (cf. *Rep.* iv. 423 b). Even in a great empire there might be a degree of virtue and justice, such as the Greeks believed to have existed under the sway of the first Persian kings. But all such empires were liable to degenerate, and soon incurred the anger of the gods. Their Oriental wealth, and splendour of gold and silver, and variety of colours, seemed also to be at variance with the simplicity of Greek notions. In the island of Atlantis, Plato is describing a sort of Babylon-ian or Egyptian city, to which he opposes the frugal life of the true Hellenic citizen. It is remarkable that in his brief sketch of them, he idealizes the husbandmen 'who are lovers of honour and true husband-men' (111 e), as well as the warriors who are his sole concern in the *Republic*; and that though he speaks of the common pursuits of men and women, he says nothing of the community of wives and children.

It is singular that Plato should have prefixed the most detested of Athenian names to this dialogue, and even more singular that he should have put into the mouth of Socrates a panegyric on him (*Tim.*

20 a).[1] Yet we know that his character was accounted infamous by Xenophon, and that the mere acquaintance with him was made a subject of accusation against Socrates. We can only infer that in this, and perhaps in some other cases, Plato's characters have no reference to the actual facts. The desire to do honour to his own family, and the connexion with Solon, may have suggested the introduction of his name. Why the *Critias* was never completed, whether from accident, or from advancing age, or from a sense of the artistic difficulty of the design, cannot be determined.

[1] [As Burnet has shown (*Greek Philosophy from Thales to Plato*, p. 338) the Critias after whom this dialogue is named, and who is praised by Socrates, is not the detested oligarch Critias, but his grandfather.]

CRITIAS

Persons of the Dialogue

CRITIAS	TIMAEUS
HERMOCRATES	SOCRATES

Timaeus. How thankful I am, Socrates, that I have arrived at 106
last, and, like a weary traveller after a long journey, may be at
rest! And I pray the god who has existed from the beginning of
time,[1] and has now been by me revealed, to grant that my words
may endure in so far as they have been spoken truly and accept- b
ably to him; but if unintentionally I have said anything wrong, I
pray that he will impose upon me a just retribution, and the just
retribution of him who errs is that he should be set right. Wishing,
then, to speak truly in future concerning the generation of the
gods, I pray him to give me knowledge, which of all medicines is
the most perfect and best. And now having offered my prayer I
deliver up the argument to Critias, who is to speak next according
to our agreement.[2]

Critias. And I, Timaeus, accept the trust, and as you at first
said that you were going to speak of high matters, and begged c
that some forbearance might be shown to you, I too ask the same
or greater forbearance for what I am about to say. And although 107
I very well know that my request may appear to be somewhat
ambitious and discourteous, I must make it nevertheless. For will
any man of sense deny that you have spoken well? I can only
attempt to show that I ought to have more indulgence than you,
because my theme is more difficult; and I shall argue that to
seem to speak well of the gods to men is far easier than to speak b
well of men to men: for the inexperience and utter ignorance of
his hearers about any subject is a great assistance to him who has
to speak of it, and we know how ignorant we are concerning the
gods. But I should like to make my meaning clearer, if you will
follow me. All that is said by any of us can only be imitation and
representation. And if we consider the likenesses of bodies divine c

[1] [The world, which was shown in the previous discourse to be a divine being.]
[2] *Tim.* 27 a.

and human, and the different degrees of resemblance which the spectator requires from the painter according to the difficulty of his task, we shall see that we are satisfied with the artist who is able in any degree to imitate the earth and its mountains, and the rivers, and the woods, and the universe, and the things that are and move therein, and further, that knowing nothing precise

d about such matters, we do not examine or analyse the painting; all that is required is a sort of indistinct and deceptive mode of shadowing them forth. But when a person endeavours to paint the human form we are quick at finding out defects, and our familiar knowledge makes us severe judges of any one who does not render every point of similarity. And we may observe the same thing to happen in discourse; we are satisfied with a picture of divine and heavenly things which has very little likeness to them; but we are more precise in our criticism of mortal and human things. Wherefore if at the moment of speaking I cannot

e suitably express my meaning, you must excuse me, considering that to form approved likenesses of human things is the reverse

108 of easy. This is what I want to suggest to you, and at the same time to beg, Socrates, that I may have not less, but more indulgence conceded to me in what I am about to say. Which favour, if I am right in asking, I hope that you will be ready to grant.

Socrates. Certainly, Critias, we will grant your request, and we will grant the same by anticipation to Hermocrates, as well as to you and Timaeus; for I have no doubt that when his turn comes a little while hence, he will make the same request which you

b have made. In order, then, that he may provide himself with a fresh beginning, and not be compelled to say the same things over again, let him understand that the indulgence is already extended by anticipation to him. And now, friend Critias, I will announce to you the judgement of the theatre. They are of opinion that the last author was wonderfully successful, and that you will need a great deal of indulgence before you will be able to fill his place.

Hermocrates. The warning, Socrates, which you have addressed

c to him, I must also take to myself. But remember, Critias, that faint heart never yet raised a trophy; and therefore you must go and attack the argument like a man. First invoke Apollo and the

Muses, and then let us hear you sound the praises and show forth
the virtues of your ancient citizens.

Crit. Friend Hermocrates, you, who are stationed last and
have another in front of you, have not lost heart as yet; the gravity
of the situation will soon be revealed to you; meanwhile I accept
your exhortations and encouragements. But besides the gods and d
goddesses whom you have mentioned, I would specially invoke
Mnemosyne; for all the important part of my discourse is dependent on her favour, and if I can recollect and recite enough of what
was said by the priests and brought hither by Solon, I doubt not
that I shall satisfy the requirements of this theatre. And now,
making no more excuses, I will proceed.

Let me begin by observing first of all, that nine thousand was e
the sum of years which had elapsed since the war which was said
to have taken place between those who dwelt outside the pillars
of Heracles and all who dwelt within them; this war I am going
to describe. Of the combatants on the one side, the city of Athens
was reported to have been the leader and to have fought out the
war; the combatants on the other side were commanded by the
kings of Atlantis, which, as I have said, once existed, greater in
extent than Libya and Asia, and afterwards when sunk by an
earthquake, became an impassable barrier of mud to those voya-
gers from hence who attempt to cross the ocean which lies
beyond.[1] The progress of the history will unfold the various 109
nations of barbarians and families of Hellenes which then existed,
as they successively appear on the scene; but I must describe first
of all the Athenians of that day, and their enemies who fought
with them, and then the respective powers and governments of
the two kingdoms. Let us give the precedence to Athens.

In the days of old, the gods had the whole earth distributed b
among them by allotment.[2] There was no quarrelling; for you
cannot rightly suppose that the gods did not know what was
proper for each of them to have, or, knowing this, that they
would seek to procure for themselves by contention that which
more properly belonged to others. They all of them by just
apportionment obtained what they wanted, and peopled their

---

[1] [Plato does not say, as most translations suggest, that the barrier prevented
access to the ocean, but that it prevented a voyage across the ocean.]

[2] Cf. *Polit.* 271 ff.

own districts; and when they had peopled them they tended us, their nurslings and possessions, as shepherds tend their flocks, c excepting only that they did not use blows or bodily force, as shepherds do, but governed us like pilots from the stern of the vessel, which is an easy way of guiding animals, holding our souls by the rudder of persuasion according to their own pleasure;— thus did they guide all mortal creatures. Now different gods had their allotments in different places which they set in order. Hephaestus and Athene, who were brother and sister, and sprang from the same father, having a common nature, and being united also in the love of philosophy and art, both obtained as their common portion this land, which was naturally adapted for d wisdom and virtue; and there they implanted brave children of the soil, and put into their minds the order of government; their names are preserved, but their actions have disappeared by reason of the destruction of those who received the tradition, and the lapse of ages. For when there were any survivors, as I have already said, they were men who dwelt in the mountains; and they were ignorant of the art of writing, and had heard only the names of the chiefs of the land, but very little about their actions. The names they were willing enough to give to their children; but e the virtues and the laws of their predecessors they knew only by obscure traditions; and as they themselves and their children lacked for many generations the necessaries of life, they directed their attention to the supply of their wants, and of them they conversed, to the neglect of events that had happened in times 110 long past; for mythology and the inquiry into antiquity find their way into cities in company with leisure, when they see some of the citizens already provided with the necessaries of life, but not before. And this is the reason why the names of the ancients have been preserved to us and not their actions. This I infer because Solon said that the priests in their narrative of that war mentioned b most of the names which are recorded prior to the time of Theseus, such as Cecrops, and Erechtheus, and Erichthonius, and Erysich- thon, and the names of the women in like manner. Moreover, since military pursuits were then common to men and women, the men of those days in accordance with the custom of the time set up a figure and image of the goddess in full armour, to be a

¹ Cf. Arist. *Metaphys*. I. 1, § 16.

testimony that all animals which associate together, male as well c
as female, may, if they please, practise in common the excellence which is typical of their kind.

Now the country was inhabited in those days by various classes
of citizens;—there were artisans, and there were husbandmen,
and there was also a warrior class originally set apart by divine
men. The latter dwelt by themselves, and had all things suitable
for nurture and education; neither had any of them anything d
of their own, but they regarded all that they had as common
property; nor did they claim to receive of the other citizens anything more than their necessary food. And they practised all the
pursuits which we yesterday described as those of our imaginary
guardians. Concerning the country the Egyptian priests said
what is not only probable but manifestly true, that the boundaries
were in those days fixed by the Isthmus, and that in the direction
of the continent they extended as far as the heights of Cithaeron
and Parnes; the boundary line came down in the direction of the
sea, having the district of Oropus on the right, and with the river e
Asopus as the limit on the left. The land was the best in the world,
and was therefore able in those days to support a vast army,
exempt from the labours of the soil. Even the remnant of Attica
which now exists may compare with any region in the world for
the variety and excellence of its fruits and the suitableness of its III
pastures to every sort of animal, which proves what I am saying;
but in those days the country was fair as now and yielded far
more abundant produce. How shall I establish my words? and in
what respect can it be truly called a remnant of the land that
then was? The whole country is only a long promontory extending far into the sea away from the rest of the continent, while the
surrounding basin of the sea is everywhere deep in the neighbourhood of the shore. Many great deluges have taken place during
the nine thousand years, for that is the number of years which
have elapsed since the time of which I am speaking; and during b
all this time and through so many changes, there has never been
any considerable accumulation of the soil coming down from the
mountains, as in other places, but the earth has fallen away all
round and sunk out of sight.[1] The consequence is, that in com-

---

[1] [Ed. 1, 'it has always been carried round in a circle and disappeared in the
depths below'.]

parison of what then was, there are remaining only the bones of the wasted body, as they may be called, as in the case of small islands, all the richer and softer parts of the soil having fallen away, and the mere skeleton of the land being left. But in the

c primitive state of the country, its mountains were high hills covered with soil, and the plains, as they are termed by us, of Phelleus were full of rich earth, and there was abundance of wood in the mountains. Of this last the traces still remain, for although some of the mountains now only afford sustenance to bees, not so very long ago there were still to be seen roofs of timber cut from trees growing there, which were of a size sufficient to cover the largest houses; and there were many other high trees, cultivated

d by man and bearing abundance of food for cattle. Moreover, the land reaped the benefit of the annual rainfall, not as now losing the water which flows off the bare earth into the sea, but, having an abundant supply in all places, and receiving it into herself and treasuring it up in the close clay soil, it let off into the hollows the streams which it absorbed from the heights, providing everywhere abundant fountains and rivers, of which there may still be observed sacred memorials in places where fountains once existed; and this proves the truth of what I am saying.

e Such was the natural state of the country, which was cultivated, as we may well believe, by true husbandmen, who made husbandry their business, and were lovers of honour, and of a noble nature, and had a soil the best in the world, and abundance of water, and in the heaven above an excellently attempered climate. Now the city in those days was arranged on this wise. In

112 the first place the Acropolis was not as now. For the fact is that a single night of excessive rain washed away the earth and laid bare the rock; at the same time there were earthquakes, and then occurred the extraordinary inundation, which was the third before the great destruction of Deucalion. But in primitive times the hill of the Acropolis extended to the Eridanus and Ilissus, and included the Pnyx on one side, and the Lycabettus as a boundary on the opposite side to the Pnyx, and was all well covered with soil, and level at the top, except in one or two places. Outside the

b Acropolis and under the sides of the hill there dwelt artisans, and such of the husbandmen as were tilling the ground near; the warrior class dwelt by themselves around the temples of Athene and Hephaestus at the summit, which moreover they had enclosed with a single fence like the garden of a single house. On the north side they had dwellings in common and had erected halls for dining in winter, and had all the buildings which they needed for their common life, besides temples, but there was no adorning c of them with gold and silver, for they made no use of these for any purpose; they took a middle course between meanness and ostentation, and built modest houses in which they and their children's children grew old, and they handed them down to others who were like themselves, always the same. But in summertime they left their gardens and gymnasia and dining halls, and then the southern side of the hill was made use of by them for the same purpose. Where the Acropolis now is there was a fountain, which was choked by the earthquake, and has left only the few d small streams which still exist in the vicinity, but in those days the fountain gave an abundant supply of water for all and of suitable temperature in summer and in winter. This is how they dwelt, being the guardians of their own citizens and the leaders of the Hellenes, who were their willing followers. And they took care to preserve the same number of men and women through all time, being so many as could already perform, or could still perform, military service,—that is to say, about twenty thousand. e Such were the ancient Athenians, and after this manner they righteously administered their own land and the rest of Hellas; they were renowned all over Europe and Asia for the beauty of their persons and for the many virtues of their souls, and of all men who lived in those days they were the most illustrious. And next, if I have not forgotten what I heard when I was a child, I will impart to you the character and origin of their adversaries. For friends should not keep their stories to themselves, but have them in common.

Yet, before proceeding farther in the narrative, I ought to warn 113 you, that you must not be surprised if you should perhaps hear Hellenic names given to foreigners. I will tell you the reason of this: Solon, who was intending to use the tale for his poem, inquired into the meaning of the names, and found that the early Egyptians in writing them down had translated them into their own language, and he recovered the meaning of the several names and when copying them out again translated them into b our language. My grandfather[1] had the original writing, which is still in my possession, and was carefully studied by me when I was a child. Therefore if you hear names such as are used in this country, you must not be surprised, for I have told how they came to be introduced. The tale, which was of great length, began as follows:—

I have before remarked in speaking of the allotments of the gods, that they distributed the whole earth into portions differing c in extent, and made for themselves temples and instituted sacrifices. And Poseidon, receiving for his lot the island of Atlantis, begat children by a mortal woman, and settled them in a part of the island, which I will describe. Towards the sea, half-way down the length of the whole island, there was a plain which is said to have been the fairest of all plains and very fertile. Near the plain again, and also in the centre of the island at a distance of about fifty stadia, there was a mountain not very high on any side. In this mountain there dwelt one of the earth-born primeval men d of that country, whose name was Evenor, and he had a wife named Leucippe, and they had an only daughter who was called Cleito. The maiden had already reached womanhood, when her father and mother died; Poseidon fell in love with her and had intercourse with her, and breaking the ground, inclosed the hill in which she dwelt all round, making alternate zones of sea and land larger and smaller, encircling one another; there were two of land and three of water, which he turned as with a lathe, each having its circumference equidistant every way from the centre, e so that no man could get to the island, for ships and voyages were not as yet. He himself, being a god, found no difficulty in making special arrangements for the centre island, bringing up two springs of water from beneath the earth, one of warm water and the other of cold, and making every variety of food to spring up abundantly from the soil. He also begat and brought up five pairs of twin 114 male children; and dividing the island of Atlantis into ten portions, he gave to the first-born of the eldest pair his mother's dwelling and the surrounding allotment, which was the largest and best, and made him king over the rest; the others he made princes, and gave them rule over many men, and a large territory. And he named them all; the eldest, who was the first king,

---

[1] [See *Tim.* 20 e ff., where, however, no writing is mentioned.]

he named Atlas, and after him the whole island and the ocean were called Atlantic. To his twin brother, who was born after b him, and obtained as his lot the extremity of the island towards the pillars of Heracles, facing the country which is now called the region of Gades in that part of the world, he gave the name which in the Hellenic language is Eumelus, in the language of the country which is named after him, Gadeirus. Of the second pair of twins he called one Ampheres, and the other Evaemon. To the elder of the third pair of twins he gave the name Mneseus, and Autochthon to the one who followed him. Of the fourth pair of c twins he called the elder Elasippus, and the younger Mestor. And of the fifth pair he gave to the elder the name of Azaes, and to the younger that of Diaprepes. All these and their descendants for many generations were the inhabitants and rulers of divers islands in the open sea; and also, as has been already said, they held sway in our direction over the country within the pillars as far as Egypt and Tyrrhenia. Now Atlas had a numerous and honourable family, and they retained the kingdom, the eldest d son handing it on to his eldest for many generations; and they had such an amount of wealth as was never before possessed by kings and potentates, and is not likely ever to be again, and they were furnished with everything which they needed, both in the city and country. For because of the greatness of their empire many things were brought to them from foreign countries, and the island itself provided most of what was required by them for e the uses of life. In the first place, they dug out of the earth whatever was to be found there, solid as well as fusile, and that which is now only a name and was then something more than a name, orichalcum, was dug out of the earth in many parts of the island, being more precious in those days than anything except gold. There was an abundance of wood for carpenter's work, and sufficient maintenance for tame and wild animals. Moreover, there were a great number of elephants in the island; for as there was 115 provision for all other sorts of animals, both for those which live in lakes and marshes and rivers, and also for those which live in mountains and on plains, so there was for the animal which is the largest and most voracious of all. Also whatever fragrant things there now are in the earth, whether roots, or herbage, or woods, or essences which distil from fruit and flower, grew and thrived

in that land; also the fruit which admits of cultivation, both the
dry sort, which is given us for nourishment and any other which
we use for food—we call them all by the common name of pulse,
b and the fruits having a hard rind, affording drinks and meats and
ointments, and good store of chestnuts and the like, which furnish
pleasure and amusement, and are fruits which spoil with keeping,
and the pleasant kinds of dessert, with which we console ourselves
after dinner, when we are tired of eating—all these that sacred
island which then beheld the light of the sun, brought forth fair
and wondrous and in infinite abundance. With such blessings
the earth freely furnished them; meanwhile they went on con-
c structing their temples and palaces and harbours and docks. And
they arranged the whole country in the following manner:—

First of all they bridged over the zones of sea which surrounded
the ancient metropolis, making a road to and from the royal
palace. And at the very beginning they built the palace in the
habitation of the god and of their ancestors, which they continued to ornament in successive generations, every king sur-
d passing the one who went before him to the utmost of his power,
until they made the building a marvel to behold for size and for
beauty. And beginning from the sea they bored a canal of three
hundred feet in width and one hundred feet in depth and fifty
stadia in length, which they carried through to the outermost
zone, making a passage from the sea up to this, which became a
harbour, and leaving an opening sufficient to enable the largest
e vessels to find ingress. Moreover, they divided at the bridges the
zones of land which parted the zones of sea, leaving room for a
single trireme to pass out of one zone into another, and they
covered over the channels so as to leave a way underneath for the
ships; for the banks were raised considerably above the water.
Now the largest of the zones into which a passage was cut from
the sea was three stadia in breadth, and the zone of land which
came next of equal breadth; but the next two zones, the one of
water, the other of land, were two stadia, and the one which
116 surrounded the central island was a stadium only in width. The
island in which the palace was situated had a diameter of five
stadia. All this including the zones and the bridge, which was the
sixth part of a stadium in width, they surrounded by a stone wall
on every side, placing towers and gates on the bridges where the

sea passed in. The stone which was used in the work they quarried
from underneath the centre island, and from underneath the
zones, on the outer as well as the inner side. One kind was white,
another black, and a third red, and as they quarried, they at the b
same time hollowed out docks double within, having roofs formed
out of the native rock. Some of their buildings were simple, but
in others they put together different stones, varying the colour to
please the eye, and to be a natural source of delight. The entire
circuit of the wall, which went round the outermost zone, they
covered with a coating of brass, and the circuit of the next wall
they coated with tin, and the third, which encompassed the c
citadel, flashed with the red light of orichalcum. The palaces in
the interior of the citadel were constructed on this wise:—In the
centre was a holy temple dedicated to Cleito and Poseidon, which
remained inaccessible, and was surrounded by an enclosure of
gold; this was the spot where the family of the ten princes was
conceived and saw the light, and thither the people annually
brought the fruits of the earth in their season from all the ten
portions, to be an offering to each of the ten. Here was Poseidon's
own temple which was a stadium in length, and half a stadium in d
width, and of a proportionate height, having a strange barbaric
appearance. All the outside of the temple, with the exception of
the pinnacles, they covered with silver, and the pinnacles with
gold. In the interior of the temple the roof was of ivory, curiously
wrought everywhere with gold and silver and orichalcum; and
all the other parts, the walls and pillars and floor, they coated
with orichalcum. In the temple they placed statues of gold: there
was the god himself standing in a chariot—the charioteer of six e
winged horses—and of such a size that he touched the roof of
the building with his head; around him there were a hundred
Nereids riding on dolphins, for such was thought to be the number
of them by the men of those days. There were also in the interior
of the temple other images which had been dedicated by private
persons. And around the temple on the outside were placed
statues of gold of all who had been numbered among the ten
kings, both them and their wives, and there were many other
great offerings of kings and of private persons, coming both
from the city itself and from the foreign cities over which they
held sway. There was an altar too, which in size and workman-

ship corresponded to this magnificence, and the palaces, in like manner, answered to the greatness of the kingdom and the glory
117 of the temple.

In the next place, they had fountains, one of cold and another of hot water, in gracious plenty flowing; and they were wonderfully adapted for use by reason of the pleasantness and excellence of their waters.[1] They constructed buildings about them and planted suitable trees; also they made cisterns, some open to the
b heaven, others roofed over, to be used in winter as warm baths; there were the kings' baths, and the baths of private persons, which were kept apart; and there were separate baths for women, and for horses and cattle, and to each of them they gave as much adornment as was suitable. Of the water which ran off they carried some to the grove of Poseidon, where were growing all manner of trees of wonderful height and beauty, owing to the excellence of the soil, while the remainder was conveyed by aqueducts along the bridges to the outer circles; and there were
c many temples built and dedicated to many gods; also gardens and places of exercise, some for men, and others for horses in both of the two islands formed by the zones; and in the centre of the larger of the two there was set apart a race-course of a stadium in width, and in length allowed to extend all round the island, for horses to race in. Also there were guard-houses at intervals for the main body of guards, whilst the more trusted of them
d were appointed to keep watch in the lesser zone, which was nearer the Acropolis; while the most trusted of all had houses given them within the citadel, near the persons of the kings. The docks were full of triremes and naval stores, and all things were quite ready for use. Enough of the plan of the royal palace.

Leaving the palace and passing out across the three harbours,
e you came to a wall which began at the sea and went all round: this was everywhere distant fifty stadia from the largest zone or harbour, and enclosed the whole, the ends meeting at the mouth of the channel which led to the sea. The entire area was densely crowded with habitations; and the canal and the largest of the harbours were full of vessels and merchants coming from all parts, who, from their numbers, kept up a multitudinous

[1] Reading ἑκατέρου πρὸς τὴν χρῆσιν.

sound of human voices, and din and clatter of all sorts night and day.

I have described the city and the environs of the ancient palace nearly in the words of Solon, and now I must endeavour to represent to you the nature and arrangement of the rest of the 118 land. The whole country was said by him to be very lofty and precipitous on the side of the sea, but the country immediately about and surrounding the city was a level plain, itself surrounded by mountains which descended towards the sea; it was smooth and even, and of an oblong shape, extending in one direction three thousand stadia, but across the centre inland it was two thousand stadia. This part of the island looked towards the south, b and was sheltered from the north. The surrounding mountains were celebrated for their number and size and beauty, far beyond any which still exist, having in them also many wealthy villages of country folk, and rivers, and lakes, and meadows supplying food enough for every animal, wild or tame, and much wood of various sorts, abundant for each and every kind of work.

I will now describe the plain, as it was fashioned by nature and by the labours of many generations of kings through long ages. c It was naturally for the most part rectangular and oblong, and where falling out of the straight line had been made regular by the surrounding ditch. The depth, and width, and length of this ditch were incredible, and gave the impression that a work of such extent, in addition to so many others, could never have been artificial. Nevertheless I must say what I was told. It was excavated to the depth of a hundred feet, and its breadth was a stadium everywhere; it was carried round the whole of the plain, d and was ten thousand stadia in length. It received the streams which came down from the mountains, and winding round the plain and meeting at the city, was there let off into the sea. Farther inland, likewise, straight canals of a hundred feet in width were cut from it through the plain, and again let off into the ditch leading to the sea: these canals were at intervals of a hundred stadia, and by them they brought down the wood from e the mountains to the city, and conveyed the fruits of the earth in ships, cutting transverse passages from one canal into another, and to the city. Twice in the year they gathered the fruits of the earth—in winter having the benefit of the rains of heaven, and

in summer the water which the land supplied, when they introduced streams from the canals.

As to the population, each of the lots in the plain had to find a
119 leader for the men who were fit for military service, and the size
of a lot was a square of ten stadia each way, and the total number
of all the lots was sixty thousand. And of the inhabitants of the
mountains and of the rest of the country there was also a vast
multitude, which was distributed among the lots and had leaders
assigned to them according to their districts and villages. The
leader was required to furnish for the war the sixth portion of a
war-chariot, so as to make up a total of ten thousand chariots;
b also two horses and riders for them, and a pair of chariot-horses
without a car, accompanied by a horseman who could fight on
foot carrying a small shield, and having a charioteer who stood
behind the man-at-arms to guide the two horses; also, he was
bound to furnish two heavy-armed soldiers, two archers, two
slingers, three stone-shooters and three javelin-men, who were
light-armed, and four sailors to make up the complement of
twelve hundred ships. Such was the military order of the royal
city—the order of the other nine governments varied, and it
would be wearisome to recount their several differences.

c   As to offices and honours, the following was the arrangement
from the first. Each of the ten kings in his own division and in his
own city had the absolute control of the citizens, and, in most
cases, of the laws, punishing and slaying whomsoever he would.
Now the order of precedence among them and their mutual
relations were regulated by the commands of Poseidon which the
law had handed down. These were inscribed by the first kings on
d a pillar of orichalcum, which was situated in the middle of the
island, at the temple of Poseidon, whither the kings were gathered
together every fifth and every sixth year alternately, thus giving
equal honour to the odd and to the even number. And when
they were gathered together they consulted about their common
interests, and inquired if any one had transgressed in anything,
and passed judgement, and before they passed judgement they
gave their pledges to one another on this wise:—There were
bulls who had the range of the temple of Poseidon; and the ten
kings, being left alone in the temple, after they had offered
e prayers to the god that they might capture the victim which was

acceptable to him, hunted the bulls, without weapons, but with staves and nooses; and the bull which they caught they led up to the pillar and cut its throat over the top of it so that the blood fell upon the sacred inscription. Now on the pillar, besides the laws, there was inscribed an oath invoking mighty curses on the disobedient. When therefore, after slaying the bull in the accustomed manner, they proceeded to burn its limbs, they filled a bowl of wine and cast in a clot of blood for each of them; the rest of the victim they put in the fire, after having purified the column all round. Then they drew from the bowl in golden cups, and pouring a libation on the fire, they swore that they would judge according to the laws on the pillar, and would punish him who in any point had already transgressed them, and that for the future they would not, if they could help, offend against the writing on the pillar, and would neither command others, nor obey any ruler who commanded them, to act otherwise than according to the laws of their father Poseidon. This was the prayer which each of them offered up for himself and for his descendants, at the same time drinking and dedicating the cup out of which he drank in the temple of the god; and after they had supped and satisfied their needs, when darkness came on, and the fire about the sacrifice was cool, all of them put on most beautiful azure robes, and, sitting on the ground, at night, over the embers of the sacrifices by which they had sworn, and extinguishing all the fire about the temple, they received and gave judgement, if any of them had an accusation to bring against any one; and when they had given judgement, at daybreak they wrote down their sentences on a golden tablet, and dedicated it together with their robes to be a memorial.

There were many special laws affecting the several kings inscribed about the temples; but the most important was the following: They were not to take up arms against one another, and they were all to come to the rescue if any one in any of their cities attempted to overthrow the royal house; like their ancestors, they were to deliberate in common about war and other matters, giving the supremacy to the descendants of Atlas. And the king was not to have the power of life and death over any of his kinsmen unless he had the assent of the majority of the ten.

Such was the vast power which the god settled in the lost island of Atlantis; and this he afterwards directed against our land for the following reasons, as tradition tells: For many generations, as

e long as the divine nature lasted in them, they were obedient to the laws, and well-affectioned towards the god, whose seed they were; for they possessed true and in every way great spirits, uniting gentleness with wisdom in the various chances of life, and in their intercourse with one another. They despised everything but virtue, caring little for their present state of life, and thinking lightly of the possession of gold and other property, which seemed only a burden to them; neither were they intoxicated by luxury;

121 nor did wealth deprive them of their self-control; but they were sober, and saw clearly that all these goods are increased by virtue and friendship with one another, whereas by too great regard and respect for them they are lost, and virtue with them. By such reflections and by the continuance in them of a divine nature, the qualities which we have described grew and increased among them; but when the divine portion began to fade away, and became diluted too often and too much with the mortal ad-

b mixture, and the human nature got the upper hand, they then, being unable to bear their fortune, behaved unseemly, and to him who had an eye to see grew visibly debased, for they were losing the fairest of their precious gifts; but to those who had no eye to see the true happiness, they appeared glorious and blessed at the very time when they were becoming tainted with unrighteous ambition and power. Zeus, the god of gods, who rules according to law, and is able to see into such things, perceiving that an honourable race was in a woeful plight, and wanting to inflict punish-

c ment on them that they might be chastened and improve, collected all the gods into their most holy habitation, which, being placed in the centre of the world, beholds all created things. And when he had called them together, he spake as follows:—

PRINTED IN
GREAT BRITAIN
AT THE
UNIVERSITY PRESS
OXFORD
BY
CHARLES BATEY
PRINTER
TO THE
UNIVERSITY

The Dialogues of Plato
2339875

This book is due for return on or before the last date
shown above but it may be renewed by personal
application, post, or telephone, quoting this date and
the book number.

HERTFORDSHIRE COUNTY LIBRARY
COUNTY HALL, HERTFORD.

L.32